COLOUR IMAGE SCIENCE

COLOUR IMAGE SCIENCE

Exploiting Digital Media

Edited by

Lindsay W. MacDonald

and

M. Ronnier Luo

Colour & Imaging Institute
University of Derby, UK

JOHN WILEY & SONS, LTD

Telephone (+44) 1243 779777

Email (for orders and customer service enquiries): cs-books@wiley.co.uk
Visit our Home Page on www.wileyeurope.com or www.wiley.com

Other Wiley Editorial Offices

John Wiley & Sons Inc., 111 River Street, Hoboken, NJ 07030, USA

Jossey-Bass, 989 Market Street, San Francisco, CA 94103-1741, USA

Wiley-VCH Verlag GmbH, Boschstr. 12, D-69469 Weinheim, Germany

John Wiley & Sons Australia Ltd, 33 Park Road, Milton, Queensland 4064, Australia

John Wiley & Sons (Asia) Pte Ltd, 2 Clementi Loop #02-01, Jin Xing Distripark, Singapore 129809

John Wiley & Sons Canada Ltd, 22 Worcester Road, Etobicoke, Ontario, Canada M9W 1L1

Library of Congress Cataloging-in-Publication Data

Colour image science : exploiting digital media / edited by Lindsay W. MacDonald and M. Ronnier Luo.
p.cm.
Includes bibliographical references and index.
1. Image processing – Digital techniques. 2. Color. I. MacDonald, L. W. (Lindsay W.), 1950-II. Luo, M. Ronnier.

TA1637 .C645 2002
621.36′7 – dc21 2001057381

British Library Cataloguing in Publication Data

A catalogue record for this book is available from the British Library

ISBN 0-471-49927-7

Typeset in 10/12pt Times by Laserwords Private Limited, Chennai, India
Printed and bound in Great Britain by Biddles Ltd, Guildford and King's Lynn
This book is printed on acid-free paper responsibly manufactured from sustainable forestry in which at least two trees are planted for each one used for paper production.

Contents

PART 3 Image processing

Colour plates

Plate 1 (Top six images) (Chapter 2, Fig. 2.2, pg. 33) For colour memory cue 4, the uniform colour patch of the original colour O was displayed together with the image context, i.e. it was displayed as part of a photorealistic image. O is in a black frame. Top row, sky; middle row, Caucasian skin; bottom row, plant. (Bottom) (Chapter 2, Fig. 2.5, pg. 36) The choice figure. This example corresponds to a photo in Figure 2.2. The observer had to choose the colour patch corresponding best to the later memory colour M'

Plate 2 (Top) (Chapter 3, Fig. 3.6, pg. 60) The four original test images. Left to right: SCID Musicians, SHIPP Harbor, Fruit, Gaudi. Image and palette were pasted into a single sheet (Photos N7 and N7A of ISO Standard 12640:1997, Figure 1, are reproduced with the permission of the International Organization for Standardization, ISO. This standard can be obtained from any ISO member and from the website of the ISO Central Secretariat at the following address: http://www.iso.org. Copyright remains with ISO. SHIPP Harbour and Fruit images: taken from K. Sakamoto, H. Urabe, Standard High Precision Pictures. The Fifth Color Imaging Conference: Color Science, Systems, and Applications 1997. (Bottom) (Chapter 4, Fig. 4.9, pg. 87) Simulated polyp images under 18 kinds of illuminant.

Plate 3 (Top) (Chapter 8, Fig. 8.2, pg. 157) Determining the target spotting colour. (Bottom) (Chapter 9, Fig. 9.3, pg. 167) The higher an observer's visual attention, the higher his or her ability of spatial discrimination. One observer might discern only 12 regions on (a) but another might perceive tens of regions or even more. (a) Original image; (b) image segmented into 12 regions; (c) RAG of image (b); (d) image oversegmented into 150 regions; (e) RAG of image (d).

Plate 4 (Chapter 10, Fig. 10.2, pg. 189) (a) Original image, (b) image quantised using 2 bits per colour channel, (c) image quantised using 11 colour classes corresponding to basic colour names, (d) image quantised by partitioning the HSV colour space into 64 bins, (e) image quantised in 64 colours using colour space clustering, (f) image quantised in 64 colours using a segmentation algorithm.

Plate 5 (Chapter 10, Fig. 10.9, pg. 201) (a) Original image and (b) simulation of a warm illuminant: (a1) shows the retinex proposed by Marini *et al.* on image (a) and (b1) shows the same retinex on image (b); (a2) shows the retinex proposed by Funt *et al.* on image (a) and (b2) shows the same retinex on image (b).

Plate 6 (Top) (Chapter 11, Fig. 11.2, Pg. 217) Copy A was made so that each area in Copy A was lighter ($\Delta L^* = +10$) and less red ($\Delta a^* = -10$) and yellower ($\Delta b^* = +10$) than Original. The first important observation is that Copy A is a fairly good reproduction, considering that it has $\Delta E^* = 17$ for each area. Copy B was made so that $\Delta E^* = 17$ changes were made in many different directions. In this case the ΔE^* were chosen to change the appearance of the display. The outer corner patches moved closer in colour to each other. The other, mid-side patches moved closer in colour to the inner areas. The net effect is that Copy B does not look at all like Original. It looks like a different display. Nevertheless, if judged by the ΔE^* colour metric, Copy B is exactly as good a reproduction as Copy A. (Bottom) (Chapter 11, Fig. 11.9, Pg. 224) Original E is surrounded by eight reproductions. In all cases there are 10 pie-shaped colour patches. For all eight reproductions each individual patch differs from Original by one chip in the Munsell colour book. That means each individual chip is a constant distance from the original in Munsell uniform colour space. Thus, changes in lightness, chroma and hue are equal. Along the left to right axis (DEF), the original and reproductions vary only in lightness. All 10 patches in D are one Munsell chip lighter than the original. All 10 patches in F are one Munsell chip darker than the original. Along the top to bottom axis (BEH), the original and reproductions vary only in hue. All 10 patches in B are shifted counterclockwise by one Munsell chip from the original. All 10 patches in H are shifted clockwise by one Munsell chip from the original. Along the upper left to bottom right axis (AEI), the original and reproductions vary only in chroma. All 10 patches in A are one Munsell chip less saturated than the original. All 10 patches in I are one Munsell chip more saturated than the original. Reproductions A, B, D, F, H, I are still reasonable reproductions despite the one-chip colour shifts. Reproductions C and G are examples of individual colour shifts in hue, lightness and saturation. Unlike systematic shifts, individual shifts create unacceptable distortions of the original. An error of one Munsell chip is acceptable if it is global but not if it is local.

Plate 7 (Top) (Chapter 11, Fig. 11.12, pg. 229) Goalin, Bestin and NewProductOut. (a) The three colour images: NewProductOut looks much closer to Goalin than to Bestin; both Bestin and NewProductOut are within the limited gamut of the Toyo inks (uncoated). (b, c, d) Blue, green and red colour separation images. By comparing NewProductOut with Goalin, we can see that the gamut retinex product preserved the spatial relationships in each separation. The gamut Toyo profile that modified Goalin to make Bestin adjusted each pixel independent of all the others. NewProductOut used spatial comparisons and gamut information to calculate the value at each pixel. The improvement in matching appearances can be seen by studying the three sets of colour separations. In each image the 12-patch Jobo target shows the rendition of six grey areas in the top two rows and the colours blue, green and red above yellow, magenta and cyan in the bottom two rows. (Bottom) (Chapter 13, Fig. 13.7, pg. 269) Four test images: (a) IT8, (b) Ski, (c) Smile, (d) Orchid (IT8 is reproduced by permission from Eastman Kodak Company. Ski is reprinted by permission of Fujifilm Electronic Imaging Limited. Smile: photos N1 and N1A and N6 and N6A of ISO Standard 12640 : 1997, Figure 1, are reproduced with the permission of the International Organization for Standardization, ISO. This standard can be obtained from any ISO member and from the website of the ISO Central Secretariat at the following address: http//www.iso.org. Copyright remains with ISO).

Plate 8 The colours resulting from the gamut compression calculation for all combinations of J and C within the source colour gamut (see page 305). The dotted lines indicate the positions of the destination and core gamuts, within which the colours remain unchanged.

Plate 9 (Top) (Chapter 16, Fig. 16.8, pg. 351) Some mapping results for Window: (left) focal mapping F0, (right) RLC50; (top) clipping, (bottom) linear compression. (Bottom) (Chapter 17, Fig. 17.1, pg. 359) Conceptual representation of an interval scale of overall image quality based on metrics of perceived image differences. The extreme right image is the reference image and image quality decreases to the left.

Plate 10 (Top) (Chapter 17, Fig. 17.4, pg. 362) Predictions of the Pattanaik *et al.* model over a large absolute range of luminance ($cd\,m^{-2}$): (a) 0.1, (b) 1.0, (c) 10, (d) 100, (e) 1000, (f) 10 000. Note the changes in colourfulness and acuity with luminance level. (Bottom) (Chapter 17, Fig. 17.5, pg. 363) The top row shows raw radiance images (no adaptation model) for images simulating yellowish, neutral and bluish illumination. Compare them with images based on the chromatic adaptation model intrinsic to the Pattanaik *et al.* model (bottom row). Note the prediction of incomplete chromatic adaptation.

Plate 11 (Top) (Chapter 19, Fig. 19.4, pg. 403) (top) The set of natural images collected for the colour categorisation research; (middle) its randomised version; and (bottom) the sampling of 10 000 pixels used to compute colour categories. Reproduced by permission of Eastman Kodak Company. (Bottom) (Chapter 19, Fig. 19.10, pg. 412) Original Girls image (top) and quantised images with four levels of L^* (upper pair), four levels of H (middle pair) and four levels of C^* (lower pair). Images were quantised using four cluster centres derived from (left) the image with uniformly distributed RGB grey values and (right) the sampling of the natural images. Photos N7 and N7A of ISO Standard 12640:1997, Fig. 1, are reproduced with the permission of the International Organization for Standardization, ISO. This standard can be obtained from any ISO member and from the website of the ISO Central Secretariat at the following address: http://www.iso.org. Copyright remains with ISO.

Plate 12 (Top) (Chapter 19, Fig. 19.13, pg. 415) Illustration of the categorical colour quantisation: (a) original 'Street' image from the ISO standard colour image data; (b) the quantised image created using L^*, u^* and v^* coordinates of the 11 cluster centres found in this research. These images are N2 and N2A of ISO standard 12640: 1997, reproduced with permission of the International Organization for Standardization, ISO. (Bottom) (Chapter 19, Fig. 19.15, pg. 177) Example of colour contrast assessment: (a) original image, (b) colour contrast image, (c) colour edges superimposed on the colour contrast image, (d) colour edges superimposed on the original image.

Foreword

We are increasingly aware of the ways in which digital media affect our lives, our work, and our recreation. This dominant trend of modern life is pervasive and significant. The correct use of colour is a crucially important factor in the effectiveness of imagery presented through digital media, and many subtle issues arise. It therefore comes as no surprise to find the present state of research in colour image science exciting and vigorous. It is laden with abundant opportunities in the methods, applications, and optimal exploitation of digital media.

The organisers of the Colour Image Science 2000 meeting, held in Derby in April 2000, clearly understood the vigour, breadth and importance of these research trends. They arranged in their technical programme both to distil the essence of the present research agenda and to point toward the emergent directions of future thinking. This fascinating collection of papers is the result.

Colour is a fundamentally human phenomenon: colour only exists insofar as it can be perceived by a person, and it is heavily dependent on variations in viewing conditions. The presentation of satisfactory colour imagery therefore demands a detailed understanding of human colour vision, the use of models able to encapsulate the requisite subtleties, and the application of devices able to capture, represent and reproduce the necessary data. The reader will find the diversity of these topics addressed in the context of an increasingly digital world.

Because an understanding of human colour vision is fundamental to successful colour imaging technologies, new knowledge about human visual performance and the interaction of the human visual system with its environment is of great interest to the field. The chapters presented herein emphasise the need to consider properties of the visual system in the design of imaging systems and image processing algorithms. In the past it has been common to focus on human response to colour stimuli while excluding any consideration of spatial variables, as if the two existed independently in separate dimensions of human experience. The CIE system of colorimetry has frequently been misused in this respect, by applying it to all manner of targets, overlooking the fact that the colour matching functions of the CIE standard observer apply only to a field size of 2° when viewed under standard conditions. Separate bodies of literature and models have thus arisen in the colour science and vision science research communities, with little engagement between the two. An emergent trend, evident in this book, is the move beyond this limiting assumption, towards the integrative idea that understanding of spatial vision is important to colour image science.

The human visual system is trichromatic, and so it has long been accepted that three channels of colour information should be necessary (and sufficient) for good colour image reproduction. Furthermore, the technology used to capture, encode, transmit, and display colour images has until now typically instantiated this belief, primarily because any potential gain of using more than three channels has usually been outweighed by the technological costs. Now, however, the freedom and flexibility provided by digital systems has renewed interest worldwide in the potential for spectral image reproduction. The potential gains include accurate image information for archiving and data collection, more realistic simulation of colour appearance under a variety of viewing conditions, and quite simply, more accurate colour reproduction. It will be evident at once to the reader of the chapters on multispectral imaging that this is a research area with rich growth potential.

Several chapters present the latest research in colour difference modelling applied to imaging, and several combine aspects of colour appearance with spatial vision. These approaches hold great potential for future models of appearance and image quality, as does a novel approach to colour specification relying on higher level processes of colour categorisation. The exploration of how such information might be used to improve colour image reproduction is fascinating.

It is often the case that a desired colour cannot be produced on a given device because it falls outside the gamut of colours the device can represent. Gamut mapping is the process of adjusting the desired colours so that they all fall within the device's capability. The development and testing of gamut mapping algorithms has been a very hot research topic in colour image science for the past few years. Different gamut mapping algorithms are intended to satisfy different reproduction objectives, for example the accuracy of colours represented or the maintenance of important information within the image. Recent results are interspersed with a contemporary overview of the problem, and a novel technique to incorporate the properties of spatial vision into a gamut mapping process is proposed.

The final chapter brings together all the concepts discussed in earlier sections, placed in the context of real-world imaging technology required to produce pleasing, useful and profitable results. Current technological problems are highlighted. Important lessons may be learned from historical practice in colour photography and these are applicable to digital systems. This overview puts the pieces together at a systems level and describes a comprehensive basis for future research and development in the field.

The Colour Image Science 2000 meeting in Derby provided a vivid snapshot of a colourful world at the turn of the millennium. This book captures that same excitement, and is a valuable map into the future for both research and product development.

Ian Gatley
Director, Chester F. Carlson Center for Imaging Science
Rochester Institute of Technology, USA

Contributors

Dr Kobus Barnard
Computer Science Division
University of California
387 Soda Hall #1776
Berkeley
CA 94720-1776
USA
e-mail: kobus@cs.berkeley.edu

Dr Peter Bodrogi
University of Veszprem
Egyetem Street 10
PO Box 158
H-8200 Veszprem
Hungary
e-mail: bodrogi@almos.vein.hu

Dr Hans Brettel
Software Imaging Team
École Nationale Supérieure des Télécommunications
46, rue Berrault Redmond
F-75013 Paris
France
e-mail: brettel@tsi.enst.fr

Dipl.-Ing. Hendrik Büring
Technical Electronics Institute
Aachen University of Technology
Templergraben 55
D-52056 Aachen
Germany
e-mail: buering@ite.rwth-aachen.de

Dr Maeng-Sub Cho
CSTL/ETRI
161 Kajong-dong
Yusong-Gu
Taejon, 305-350
Korea
e-mail: choms@etri.re.kr

Mr Gianluigi Ciocca
ITIM
National Research Council
Via Ampere 56
I-20131 Milano
Italy

Dr Philippe Colantoni
Laboratoire LIGIV EA 3070
Université Jean Monnet
3, rue Javelin Pagnon-BP 505
F-42007 Saint-Etienne
Cedex 1
France
e-mail: colanton@vision.univ-st-etienne.fr

Prof. Mark Fairchild
Rochester Institute of Technology
54 Lomb Memorial Drive
Rochester
NY 14623
USA
e-mail: mdf@cis.rit.edu

Prof. Brian Funt
School of Computing Science
Simon Fraser University
Burnaby, BC, V5A 1S6
Canada
e-mail: funt@cs.sfu.ca

Prof. Ian Gatley
Rochester Institute of Technology
54 Lomb Memorial Drive
Rochester
NY 14623
USA
e-mail: ixgpci@rit.edu

Mr Phil Green
Colour Imaging Group
London College of Printing
Elephant & Castle
London
SE1 6SB
UK
e-mail: p_green@compuserve.com

Dr Jon Y. Hardeberg
Gjøvik University College
Postboks 191
N-2802 Gjøvik
Norway
e-mail: jon.hardeberg@hig.no

Dr Patrick Herzog
Technical Electronics Institute
Aachen University of Technology
Templergraben 55
D-52056 Aachen
Germany
e-mail: herzog@ite.rwth-aachen.de

Prof. Robert Hunt
Barrowpoint
18 Millennium Close
Odstock Road
Salisbury SP2 8TB
UK
e-mail: rwghunt@odstock.freeserve.co.uk

Prof. Ralph Jacobson
Imaging Technology Research Group
University of Westminster
Harrow Campus
Watford Road
Harrow
HA1 3TP
UK
e-mail: jacobsr@wmin.ac.uk

Dr Byoung-Ho Kang
CSTL/ETRI
161 Kajong-dong
Yusong-Gu
Taejon, 305-350
Korea
e-mail: bhkang@etri.re.kr

Dr Friedhelm König
Technical Electronics Institute
Aachen University of Technology
Templergraben 55
D-52056 Aachen
Germany
e-mail: friedhelm.koenig.fk@germany.agfa.com

Ms Georgina Kwei
Electronic Arts
4330 Sanderson Way
Burnaby, BC, V5G 4X
Canada
e-mail: gkwei@ea.com

Prof. Ronnier Luo
Colour & Imaging Institute
University of Derby
Kingsway House East
Derby
DE22 3HL
UK
e-mail: M.R.Luo@colour.derby.ac.uk

Prof. Lindsay MacDonald
Colour & Imaging Institute
University of Derby
Kingsway House East
Derby
DE22 3HL
UK
e-mail: L.W.MacDonald@derby.ac.uk

Dr John McCann
McCann Imaging
161 Claflin Street
Belmont MA, 02478
USA
e-mail: mccanns@tiac.net

Prof. Yoichi Miyake
Dept. of Information and Computer Sciences
Faculty of Engineering
Chiba University
1-33 Yayoi-cho
Inage-ku, Chiba-shi
Chiba 263
Japan
e-mail: miyake@ics.tj.chiba-u.ac.jp

Dr Kimiyoshi Miyata
Dept. of Information and Computer Sciences
Faculty of Engineering
Chiba University
1-33 Yayoi-cho
Inage-ku, Chiba-shi
Chiba 263
Japan
e-mail: miyata@icsd6.tj.chiba-u.ac.jp

Dr Jan Morovic
Colour & Imaging Institute
University of Derby
Kingsway House East
Derby
DE22 3HL
UK
e-mail: j.morovic@derby.ac.uk

Miss Caterina Ripamonti
Colour & Imaging Institute
University of Derby
Kingsway House East
Derby
DE22 3HL
UK
e-mail: C.Ripamonti@derby.ac.uk

Dr Raimondo Schettini
ITIM
National Research Council
Via Ampere 56
I-20131 Milano
Italy
e-mail: schettini@itim.mi.cnr.it

Dr Francis Schmitt
Software Imaging Team
École Nationale Supérieure des Télécommunications
46, rue Berrault Redmond
F-75013 Paris
France
e-mail: schmitt@ima.enst.fr

Mr Pei-Li Sun
Colour & Imaging Institute
University of Derby
Kingsway House East
Derby
DE22 3HL
UK
e-mail: P.Sun@derby.ac.uk

Dr Tünde Tarczali
University of Veszprem
Egyetem Street 10
PO Box 158
H-8200 Veszprem
Hungary
e-mail: jane@ond.vein.hu

Dr Mitch Thomson
Colour & Imaging Institute
University of Derby
Kingsway House East
Derby
DE22 3HL
UK
e-mail: m.g.a.thomson@derby.ac.uk

Prof. Alain Trémeau
Laboratoire LIGIV EA 3070
Université Jean Monnet
3, rue Javelin Pagnon-BP 505
F-42007 Saint-Etienne
Cedex 1
France
e-mail: tremeau@vision.univ-st-etienne.fr

Dr Sophie Triantaphillidou
School of Communication Design and Media
University of Westminster
Watford Road
Northwick Park
Harrow
HA1 3TP
UK
e-mail: triants@westminster.ac.uk

Mr Joan Uroz
Hewlett Packard
Av Graells 501
E-08190 S Cugat del Valles
Barcelona
Spain
e-mail: joan_uroz@hp.com

Dr Stephen Westland
Colour & Imaging Institute
University of Derby
Kingsway House East
Derby
DE22 3HL
UK
e-mail: s.westland@colour.derby.ac.uk

Mr Kaida Xiao
Colour & Imaging Institute
University of Derby
Kingsway House East
Derby
DE22 3HL
UK
e-mail: K.Xiao@derby.ac.uk

Dr Sergej Yendrikhovskij
Eastman Kodak Company
1700 Dewey Avenue
Rochester
NY 14650-1916
USA
e-mail: serguei.endrikhovski@kodak.com

Ms Silvia Zuffi
ITIM
National Research Council
Via Ampere 56
I-20131 Milano
Italy
e-mail: zuffi@itim.mi.cnr.it

Preface

The scope and importance of colour image science have grown rapidly in recent years, in parallel with the proliferation of consumer imaging products. As the range and capabilities of colour displays, printers and digital cameras have increased, so too has the availability of more sophisticated and accurate colour measuring instruments. The work of the CIE and national standards laboratories has been crucial in establishing reference standards and calibration procedures. But many issues remain to be resolved, not least the development of a fully comprehensive model of colour appearance, including spatial and temporal parameters, and how to make it work well for practical systems. New challenges for colour image science are emerging as cross-media image reproduction is applied in other colour imaging domains outside the graphic arts, including Internet and multimedia displays, motion pictures, digital television and augmented-reality systems.

This book is a companion volume to *Colour Imaging: Vision and Technology*. Again we take an interdisciplinary approach, combining aspects of human vision with image capture, processing and reproduction. We believe that colour image science will develop primarily through research directed to a deeper understanding of human colour vision and perception in all its aspects – spectral, spatial and temporal. Only through the application of colour image science will digital media achieve their full potential in the reproduction images that are both good-looking and effective.

We thank everyone who has made this book possible, particularly the contributors of the chapters, all of whom are experts of international standing in their fields. We are also indebted to our colleagues and staff at the Colour & Imaging Institute for their many helpful suggestions and assistance with the compilation and editing. Most important of all, we acknowledge the support and encouragement of our wives, Sandra and Hui-Min, without which none of this would have been possible.

Lindsay MacDonald
Ronnier Luo

PART 1

Colour vision

1

Perception of transparency

Caterina Ripamonti and Stephen Westland

1.1 INTRODUCTION

The colour appearance of surfaces in the world is an important property that allows us to identify objects. We are able to recognise an object even if its position has changed or it is seen under a different light source, or if it is partially covered by a transparent layer. The perception of transparency has been studied by vision scientists for more than 100 years. This chapter reviews the nature of physical and perceptual transparency and discusses the fact that physical transparency is neither necessary nor sufficient for perceptual transparency. The chromatic and figural constraints for perceptual transparency are outlined. Finally, we introduce and test a hypothesis that the chromatic constraints necessary for transparency perception are defined by simple ratios of cone excitations.

1.2 PHYSICAL TRANSPARENCY

When directional light interacts with a layer of dielectric material the light can be reflected, refracted, scattered, absorbed or transmitted. The difference in refractive index as the light passes from air to the layer will cause some light to be reflected back from the surface. Light that is not reflected will be refracted and pass into the layer. Light in the layer

Colour Image Science, edited by L.W. MacDonald and M.R. Luo.

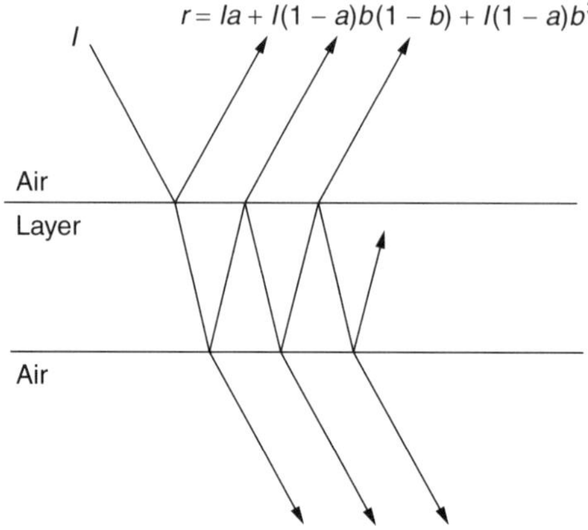

Figure 1.1 Schematic diagram to show the reflectance r and transmittance t for a non-scattering and non-absorbing layer suspended in air. The internal and external surface fractional reflectance factors are given by a and b respectively and the intensity of the incident light is given by I. The sum to infinity of the progressions for r and t are shown in equations (1.1) and (1.2).

can either be absorbed by pigment particles or dye molecules or it can be scattered by particles within the layer. Light that is absorbed is generally converted into heat or kinetic energy and is thus removed from the system. Light that is scattered is not removed from the system but the scattering process causes the light to change direction. Light within the layer that is not absorbed will eventually strike the upper or lower layer/air interface where it could either be reflected back into the system or be refracted through the interface. Figure 1.1 shows that for a layer (without absorption or scattering) suspended in air, light can either be reflected by the layer or transmitted.

The intensity of the reflected light, r, and the intensity of the transmitted light, t, are given by a sum of terms derived from multiple reflections within the layer. If we define the external surface reflectance of the layer by the fractional coefficient a and the internal surface reflectance of the layer by the fractional coefficient b, then the fractional layer reflectance and transmittance intensities are given by

$$r = a + b(1 - a)(1 - b)/[1 - b^2] \tag{1.1}$$

$$t = (1 - b)(1 - a)/[1 - b^2] \tag{1.2}$$

Since the layer does not absorb light, $r + t = 1$. We can define the layer to be physically transparent if $t > 0$ and opaque if $t = 0$. If we allow the layer to contain particles that scatter light then, since no light is actually lost from the system, it is still true that $r + t = 1$ and the system will be opaque if $t = 0$. However, if $t > 0$ we define the system to be translucent [1]. For transparent or translucent systems the layer can also contain dye molecules or pigment particles that absorb light and these absorption properties can be wavelength selective. When the layer absorbs light it is now the case that $r + t < 1$ since light that is absorbed is removed from the system. (We note that for fluorescent or phosphorescent layers some of the light that is absorbed may be re-emitted but subject to a bathochromic shift.) For layers that absorb or scatter light, equations analogous to (1.1) and (1.2) can be derived that include absorption and scattering terms that are functions of wavelength. Some workers would use the term 'transparency' to encompass both our definitions of transparency and translucency and therefore would simply define transparency by $t > 0$. However, although our work could easily be extended to account for translucency, our definition of physical transparency is $t > 0$ *and* zero (or negligible) scatter.

1.3 PERCEPTUAL TRANSPARENCY

It is important to note the distinction between physical transparency and perceptual transparency. Perceptual transparency is the phenomenon of seeing one surface behind another. Systems that are physically transparent may not give rise to perceptual transparency; moreover, systems that are perceptually transparent may not be physically transparent. Physical transparency is neither a necessary nor sufficient condition for perceptual transparency [2]. For example, in Figure 1.2(a) four opaque areas give rise to the perception of two opaque surfaces (large rectangles) seen behind a transparent filter (small rectangles).

Figures 1.2(b) and (c) show the same four opaque rectangles but in arrangements that do not give rise to perceptual transparency. Figure 1.2(b) does not satisfy the necessary figural constraints whereas Figure 1.2(c) does not satisfy the necessary chromatic constraints. Note that in this context the term refers to 'chromatic' constraints on the colour signals of surfaces rather than simply the chromatic components of those signals; chromatic constraints therefore equally apply to achromatic stimuli where the patches differ only by their luminance values. (We define the colour signal for an illuminated surface to be the product of the reflectance of the surface and the spectral energy distribution of the light source. Similarly, the colour signal of a self-luminous surface is the spectral energy distribution of the emitted radiation.) What is it about the nature of the colour signals of the surfaces in Figure 1.2(a) and (c) that cause (a) to be perceptually transparent and (c) to appear as four opaque surfaces? This is the key question that is addressed by this chapter.

Chromatic constraints are necessary but not sufficient conditions for perceptual transparency (Figure 1.2(b)). In order to perceive a transparent filter in front of opaque surfaces, figural conditions must also be met. Researchers have proposed three main figural conditions [2–4]: figural unity of the transparent region, continuity of the boundary line, and adequate stratification. If any one of these conditions is violated, no transparency will be perceived. Recent studies have proposed some general constraints for the perception of transparency. For example, it has been shown that the presence of X-junctions formed by the junctions of borders of opaque surfaces and transparent medium at the overlapping area is a necessary element in the image [5–7]. In order to have an X-junction a minimum of four areas are needed. Other studies have shown that perceptual transparency occurs even with only three areas [8].

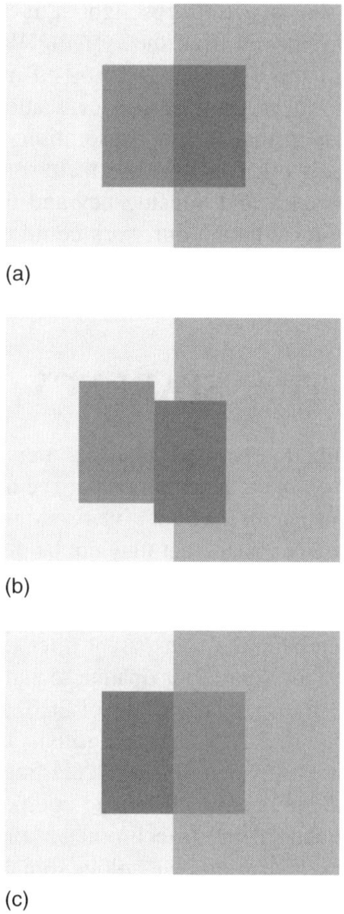

Figure 1.2 Schematic diagram to illustrate perceptual transparency: (a) is perceptually transparent; (b) lacks the necessary figural constraints for perceptual transparency; (c) lacks the necessary chromatic constraints.

For physically transparent systems that do appear to be perceptually transparent, the issue of whether it is possible to perceive both the colour of the filter and the colour of the opaque surface in the overlapping region has been a matter of controversy since the beginning of the nineteenth century when Helmholtz [9] described the perception of transparency as 'seeing through'. On the contrary, Hering [10] denied the possibility of perceiving one colour behind another and stated that the light reflected by two different colours and projected onto the same retinal region gives rise to one colour, called *fusion colour*. Also, Koffka [8, 11] stated that the filtered region is the area where we can simultaneously perceive both the filter and the opaque surface behind the filter. Moreover, according to Morinaga *et al.* [12] in the filtered region we see two surface colours one behind the other. However, recovering the colour of two surfaces from one set of cone excitations would seem to be intractable. Furthermore, if an opaque surface is partially covered by a filter whose colour is complementary (e.g. a red surface and a cyan filter), the filtered patch will appear black and the red and cyan surfaces will not seem to be simultaneously observed [13].

The first studies on transparency perception were qualitative investigations [5, 9, 10, 11, 14, 15]. The first quantitative model was Metelli's *episcotister* model [2–4]. The episcotister (E) is a wheel with open sectors rotating in front of two opaque surfaces A and B (Figure 1.3). During its rotation the episcotister colour is perceived to be a fusion colour between its sector colour and the background colour. Metelli described this colour in terms of Talbot's law of colour fusion. According to Talbot's law, the fusion of two colour reflectances x and y generates a third colour reflectance z:

$$z = \alpha x + (1 - \alpha)y \tag{1.3}$$

where α defines the proportion in which the two colours are mixed.

For the episcotister, if the reflectances of regions A, B, P and Q are given by a, b, p and q respectively, and t is the reflectance of the episcotister solid sectors, then the relationships given as (1.4) and (1.5) are valid:

$$p = \alpha a + (1 - \alpha)t \tag{1.4}$$

$$q = \alpha b + (1 - \alpha)t \tag{1.5}$$

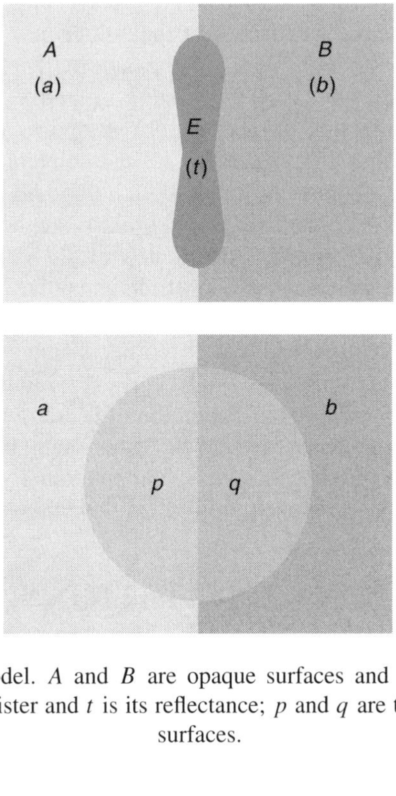

Figure 1.3 Episcotister model. *A* and *B* are opaque surfaces and *a* and *b* are their respective reflectances, *E* is the episcotister and *t* is its reflectance; *p* and *q* are the reflectances of the filtered surfaces.

According to Metelli, in order to perceive transparency, two chromatic constraints must be preserved. Specifically, the PQ region will be perceived to be transparent when the difference $(a - b)$ is greater than the difference $(p - q)$. Thus, $(a - b) < (p - q)$; the direction of contrast between opaque surfaces and filtered surfaces is the same. Thus, if $a > b$ then $p > q$.

Beck [16] presented an alternative model to the episcotister based on subtractive colour mixture instead of additive colour mixture. Subtractive colour mixture takes place when light is selectively absorbed. The model takes into account the percentage of transmission of each absorbing material as a function of the wavelength of the spectral power distribution of the light source. With achromatic colours a subtractive model of transparency makes the same predictions as an additive model [16].

With the exception of Beck, the episcotister model has been adopted more or less in its original formulation by most of the researchers investigating transparency. Minor changes have been suggested. For example, Gerbino *et al.* [17] proposed that the computations carried out by the visual system when perceiving transparency might be in terms of luminance values rather than reflectance values [4] or lightness values [18].

Although luminance relationships are necessary for the perception of transparency in achromatic images, they are not sufficient when the objects in the image do not have the same chromaticities. In fact, it has been shown [19–20] that the perception of transparency holds even when opaque and filtered surfaces have identical luminance and differ only in their chromaticities. D'Zmura *et al.* have suggested that in the case of colour transparency the colours of the filtered surfaces must converge to a point in colour space [19]. They show evidence that subjects are able to adjust the colour of a filtered surface in order to make the central region appear transparent. For example, if the tristimulus values of two opaque surfaces A and B are given by the vectors $\mathbf{x}_A$ and $\mathbf{x}_B$ respectively, the adjusted colours would lie on lines passing through $\mathbf{x}_A$ and $\mathbf{g}$, and $\mathbf{x}_B$ and $\mathbf{g}$, respectively, where $\mathbf{g}$ is a vector that defines the tristimulus values of the convergence point.

The convergence model defines chromatic conditions under which transparency perception can occur. The approach that we adopt similarly defines chromatic conditions for transparency perception and is broadly consistent with the convergence model. Furthermore, our hypothesis is that the chromatic constraints may be encoded by simple ratios of retinal signals that may easily be computed by the human visual system. We note, nevertheless, that the computations that lead directly to transparency perception are unlikely to take place in the retina and are more likely to be cortical. Moreover, the invariance of cone excitation ratios is only one possible representation of the chromatic constraints, and ratios of other signals (such as opponent channel activations) may provide equally appropriate cues. Our approach was inspired by a simple computational model of colour constancy based upon the invariance of cone excitation ratios developed by Foster *et al.* [21].

1.4 INVARIANT CONE EXCITATION RATIOS AND COLOUR CONSTANCY

An object's colour constancy can be defined as the maintenance of colour appearance despite variations in the colour of nearby objects and despite variations in the spectral power distribution of the ambient light [22–24]. A number of algorithms have been proposed for the purpose of modelling human colour constancy [25–33] but the underlying mechanism is still unknown.

One of the approaches to the colour constancy problem involves the estimation of the spectral power distribution for the light source and the spectral reflectance functions for the surfaces in the scene. This seems natural because although the colour signal reaching the eye depends upon properties of both the light source and the surfaces, the reflectance properties of surfaces are invariant to changes in the light source. The major problem in finding the colour constancy mechanism arises because the light in the visual image confounds two factors: the spectral power distribution of the ambient light and the surface reflectance of the objects in the scene. If there is only one unknown object illuminated by an unknown illuminant, the problem has an infinite number of mathematical solutions. As a consequence, all the algorithms must use information obtained from light reflected from different objects in the scene and make assumptions about the nature of the spectral properties of the surfaces and light sources. (The constraints are normally expressed in terms of linear models that allow surfaces and light sources to be represented by a small number of parameters.) However, although it is known that most natural surfaces and light sources are constrained to be smooth functions of wavelength [34], they do not seem to be sufficiently constrained to allow the recovery of the spectral properties from the responses of just three classes of cones.

Moreover, psychophysical measurements of classical colour constancy show that it is at best only approximate [35]. An alternative (operational) definition of colour constancy is to consider whether observers can differentiate between a change in illumination and a change in surface reflectance. To test operational colour constancy, observers are usually presented with two sequential displays (one followed by the other), each simulating a Mondrian illuminated by an illuminant. Typically, in 50% of the trials the second display represents the same Mondrian as in the first display but under a different illuminant; this is called illuminant change. In the other 50% of the trials the second display represents a different Mondrian; this is called surface change. The notion of invariant cone excitation ratios has been developed as a definition for operational colour constancy [21]. We note that the invariance of cone excitation ratios can alternatively be expressed by a diagonal matrix transform of a vector representing cone excitations to represent the illuminant shift [36]. Compensating for the illumination change by a purely diagonal scaling of the cone excitations is called the von Kries coefficient law [37]. The compensation of the illuminant change by a diagonal transform has also been investigated by Finlayson *et al.* [38], who have shown that a diagonal matrix transform accounts for psychophysical data from colour constancy experiments better when the cone-excitations are first transformed into a sharp sensor space.

Foster and Nascimento have shown that cone excitation ratios of pairs of surfaces seen under an unknown illuminant remain almost invariant when the same surfaces are viewed under a different illuminant [21]. To a first-order approximation it can be shown that the changes in the colour signals for surfaces that take place when the illuminant is changed are mathematically equivalent to the changes that occur when surfaces are covered by a physically transparent filter [39]; see Figure 1.4.

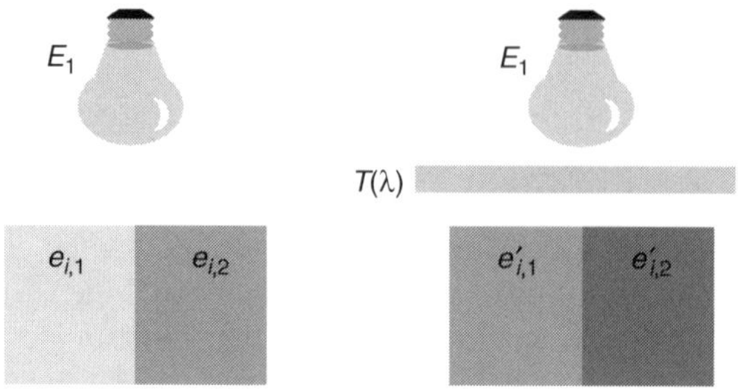

Figure 1.4 A change from light source E_1 to light source E_2 may be accomplished by filtering E_1. In certain circumstances, therefore, the changes in colour signals for surfaces illuminated by one light source then another, are approximately identical to the changes that occur when the surfaces are viewed under one light source then covered by a filter.

Note, however, that whereas the changes that occur when a surface is covered by a filter can be matched by a change in the light source, the inverse is not always true. That is, some changes in light source cannot be matched by simply filtering the first light source, if the filter is constrained to have transmittance in the range [0, 1].

1.5 INVARIANT CONE EXCITATION RATIOS AND PHYSICAL TRANSPARENCY

The light reaching the eye when an illuminant hits a surface is defined as the colour signal S. The spectral power distribution of S is computed by multiplying the illuminant E at each wavelength by the corresponding value of the surface reflectance function R. If the surface is partially covered by a transparent filter (Figure 1.5), the colour signal S' from

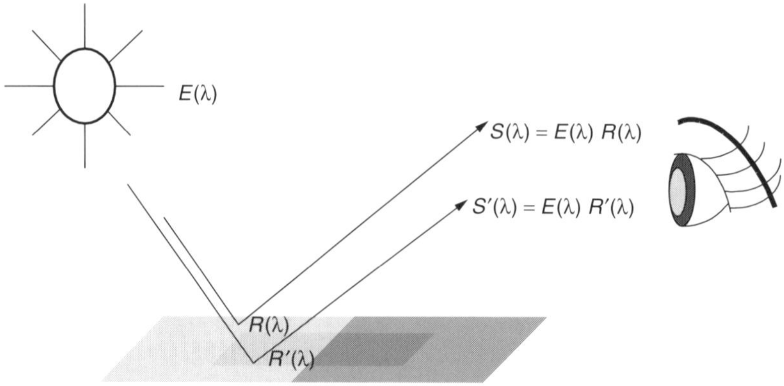

Figure 1.5 Colour signals for an opaque surface seen directly and under a transparent filter. $R(\lambda)$ is the reflectance of the opaque filter and $R'(\lambda)$ is the effective surface reflectance when it is covered by a transparent filter.

the filtered area is now different from the rest of the surface seen directly. The filtered or effective reflectance R' of the opaque surface can be expressed as the product of the spectral reflectance function R of the surface and the square of the transmittance t of the filter, thus $R' = Rt^2$.

However, such a simple relationship ignores the reflections that take place when the light passes from a medium of one refractive index to a medium of a different refractive index (see Figure 1.1) and a more realistic relationship [18, 39, 40] is given by

$$R'(\lambda) = R(\lambda)[T(\lambda)(1-b)^2]^2 \tag{1.6}$$

where b is the internal reflectance factor of the filter and T is an internal transmittance term that accounts for absorption of light by the filter.

Figure 1.6 illustrates two opaque surfaces ($e_{i,1}$ and $e_{i,2}$) covered by a simulated transparent filter. The cone excitation $e_{i,j}$ of cone class i (where $i \in \{L, M, S\}$ denoting long-, medium- and short-wavelength-sensitive cone classes) for a surface j seen directly is given by the integration of the product between the surface reflectance R, the illuminant E, and the cone sensitivity functions ϕ_i. Thus we have

$$e_{i,j} = \int E(\lambda)R(\lambda)\phi_i(\lambda)\delta\lambda \tag{1.7}$$

The term $R(\lambda)$ can be replaced by $R'(\lambda)$ from (1.6) in order to compute the cone excitation $e'_{i,j}$ for a surface j seen by cone class i through a filter defined by $T(\lambda)$ and b. A Monte Carlo simulation was carried out [39] to compute the invariance of cone excitation ratios for surfaces drawn randomly from the Munsell set [41] for filters defined by $T(\lambda)$ and b. Thus, explicitly, the equivalence

$$e_{i,1}/e_{i,2} = e'_{i,1}/e'_{i,2} \tag{1.8}$$

was tested. Note that when $T(\lambda)$ is defined by a wavelength-invariant constant (defining an achromatic filter) then (1.8) holds perfectly. For chromatic filters (defined by Gaussian-shaped transmission properties) the equivalence was found to hold approximately for

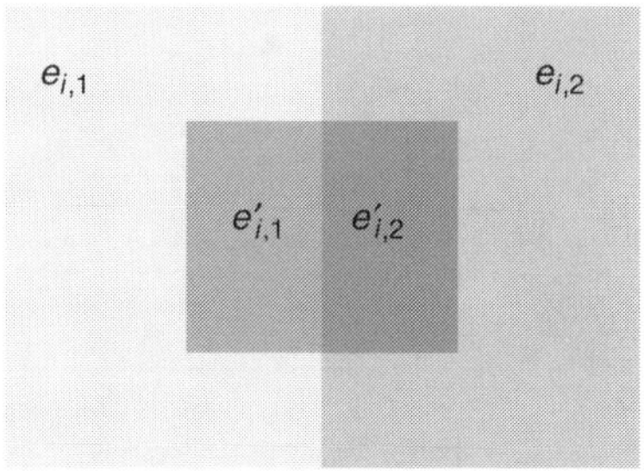

Figure 1.6 Two opaque surfaces covered by a homogeneous transparent filter; $e_{i,1}$, $e_{i,2}$ and $e'_{i,1}$, $e'_{i,2}$ are their corresponding cone excitations.

many filter parameters. Figure 1.7 shows scatterplots of ratios of cone excitations for short-, medium- and long-wavelength cone classes derived from pairs of Munsell surfaces considered to be viewed directly (abscissa) and through a typical filter (ordinate). Each point represents a pair of surfaces selected randomly and the plots show data for 1000 such points. If (1.8) held, then we would expect all of the points to lie on a straight line at 45°.

However, it was shown that the equivalence depends upon the transmission properties of the filter. For filters with broad spectral transmission properties the equivalence was strong, whereas for filters with narrow spectral transmission properties the equivalence

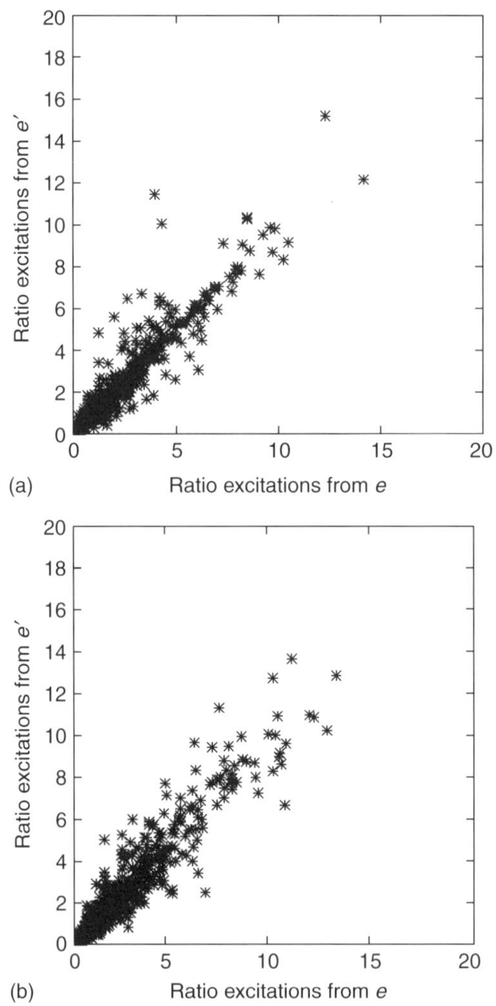

Figure 1.7 Scatterplots of ratios of cone excitations for (a) short-, (b) medium-, and (c) long-wavelength sensitive cone classes.

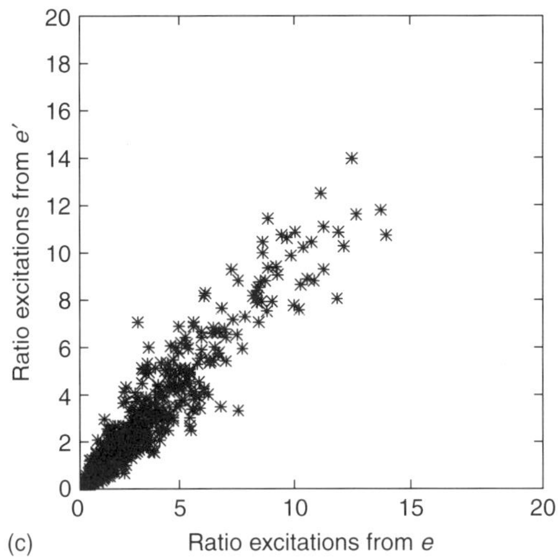

(c)

Figure 1.7 *(continued)*.

was much weaker [39]. It is clear that (1.8) is not sufficient to define physical transparency. Our hypothesis is that (1.8) defines the chromatic constraints that are necessary for perceptual transparency. The Monte Carlo simulation is consistent with this hypothesis since it seems reasonable to assume that the perceptual transparency of coloured filters with broad transmission spectra would be stronger than those with narrow transmission spectra.

1.6 INVARIANT CONE EXCITATION RATIOS AND PERCEPTUAL TRANSPARENCY

The hypothesis that the chromatic constraints required for transparency perception are defined by (1.8) has been tested by a series of psychophysical experiments [42–43]. The critical experiment is described in the following sections.

1.6.1 Introduction

Filters were defined by a spectral transmission T and an internal reflectance factor b. The transmittance function was given by

$$T(\lambda) = 0.4 + 0.6A\{\exp[-(\lambda - \lambda_m)^2/2\sigma^2]\} \tag{1.9}$$

where λ_m representing the peak of the filter) was selected from the range [400 nm, 700 nm], $b = 0.1$, σ as either 5 nm, 25 nm or 50 nm, and A was a scaling factor to ensure the area under the filter transmittance curve was independent of σ. Surface reflectances were drawn from a set of Munsell samples [41] and the effective reflectance of a surface covered by a filter was given by (1.6). Equation (1.7) was used to compute the cone excitations for the uncovered surfaces and an equation analogous to (1.7) (R being replaced by R') was used to compute the cone excitations for surfaces covered by a filter.

Mondrians, partly covered by a homogenous filter, were displayed on a CRT monitor display. The cone excitations of the filtered patches were modified to produce: (i) invariant cone excitation ratios; (ii) a control simulation (the two trials had the same cone excitation ratios); (iii) cone excitation ratios with 25% of noise; (iv) cone excitation ratios with 50% of noise. Observers were presented with two sequential displays and the task was to indicate which of the displays showed a transparent filter over a Mondrian. According to our hypothesis, in a discrimination task the filter generating invariant cone excitation ratios would be preferred to the other cases.

1.6.2 Equipment

A Sony Trinitron GMD500 colour monitor with 20″ diagonal, driven by a VSG2/3 video card in a personal computer was used for presenting the stimulus pattern. The display resolution was 1152 × 864 pixels and the frame rate was 120 Hz. The monitor had been characterised [44] using a Minolta spectroradiometer and was gamma corrected [45].

1.6.3 Stimuli

The stimuli consisted of a Mondrian (5.14° × 5.33°) partially overlaid by a simulated transparent filter (1.14° × 4.76°) displayed at the centre of a CRT monitor. The simulated illumination was D65. The opaque surfaces composing the Mondrian were selected from 1269 samples of the *Munsell Book of Color*. A preselection was made in order to choose only those surfaces that lay in the colour gamut of the monitor and thus could accurately be reproduced even when 50% of noise was added to them. Figure 1.8 shows the spectral reflectance R of a simulated opaque surface, the transmittance function T of one of the

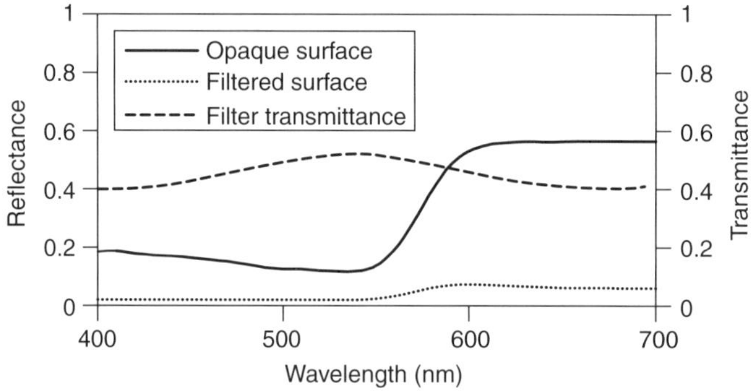

Figure 1.8 Example of a spectral reflectance function $R(\lambda)$ for one of the opaque surfaces simulated in the experiment and its effective reflectance $R'(\lambda)$ when covered by a filter of transmittance $T(\lambda)$.

filters used in the experiment, and the effective reflectance R' of the opaque surface after having been filtered.

1.6.4 Procedure

In a two-alternative forced choice (2AFC) task four naive observers viewed a simulation of a Mondrian partially overlaid by a transparent filter. In each trial a physically plausible filter was matched with one of four comparison filters. Three of those filters were a modification of the physically plausible filter and were obtained by making the short-, medium- and long-wavelength-sensitive cone classes of the filtered colour signal invariant (indicated here as perfect filter), or adding two different amounts of noise 25% (indicated here as 25% noise), and 50% (indicated here as 50% noise). Noise was added to the cone excitation ratios of the filtered surfaces by multiplying the cone excitations by a term $(1 + N)$ where N was randomly selected from a uniform variable in the range $[-0.25, +0.25]$ for 25% noise and in the range $[-0.50, +0.50]$ for 50% noise. The fourth comparison filter (indicated here as real) was almost identical to the physically plausible filter and was used as a control situation. Each presentation lasted 2 s on the screen. The next trial was not presented until the subject's answer was given. Filters had different orientations (vertical versus horizontal) in the two intervals, and their presentation order was randomised. The vertical and horizontal filters lay over different opaque surfaces (Figure 1.9); thus, even when a physically plausible transparent filter was compared with a real filter with a different orientation, their cone excitation ratios were not exactly the same.

Observers indicated whether a vertical or horizontal homogeneous transparent filter covered the Mondrian by pressing one of two buttons on a push-button switch-box. Each trial was repeated three times and the session of 72 trials was run three times. A training of 20 trials was given before each session and subsequently discarded. No feedback was provided during the experiment.

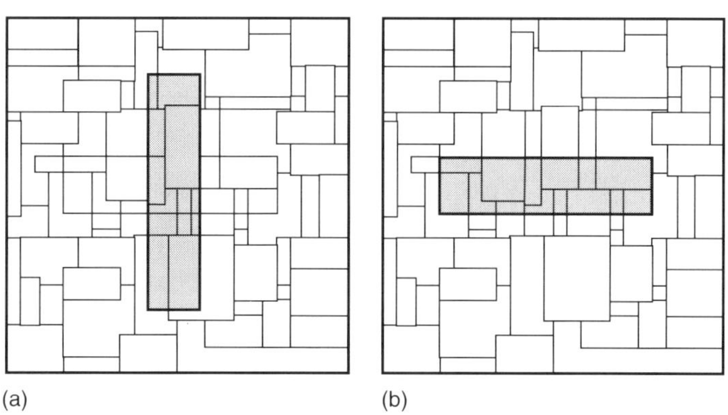

Figure 1.9 Simulation of two Mondrian patterns covered by (a) vertical and (b) horizontal transparent filters.

1.6.5 Results

Trials were classified according to the degree of deviation from the invariance in spatial cone excitation ratios for all the possible pairs of surfaces seen directly and under the filter displayed in each image. The degree of deviation was calculated as follows. For any pair of surfaces seen directly and under the filter three ratios of cone excitations can be defined: the ratio between their short-wavelength sensitive cones (for brevity r_s); the ratio between their medium-wavelength sensitive cones (r_m); the ratio between their long-wavelength sensitive cones (r_l). Mean deviations from an invariant ratio (i.e. ratio equal to 1) were then calculated for each single presentation separately for each of the three cone classes. Results are shown in Tables 1.1 to 1.3.

When the comparison filter is a perfect filter its cone excitation ratios are always equal to one and therefore its deviations are equal to zero. When the filter is physically plausible, its ratios vary according to the physical properties, which in the experiment have been controlled by varying its standard deviation. As the filter becomes more and more broadband, the cone excitation ratios approximate the invariance. This also means that narrowband filters deviate more from invariant ratios with respect to broadband filters. This can be seen in Tables 1.2 and 1.3, where deviations of real filters decrease more and more as the value of σ increases. An interesting result is that this does not apply to the short-wavelength sensitive cone.

Both the filter with 25% of noise and the filter with 50% of noise have ratios far away from invariance. As illustrated in the tables, this is accompanied by very high deviations in cone excitation ratio. We tested the ability to discriminate between a physically plausible filter versus any of the comparisons by measuring values of d'. In Figure 1.10 the mean values of d' for all the four conditions have been plotted against σ levels.

Four independent one-way ANOVAs were performed in order to test the variance in each condition as the filters became more and more broadband. No significant difference

Table 1.1 Mean deviations for the two presentations in each trial for the short-wavelength-sensitive cone class

σ	Real	Comparison	
5 nm	0.0035	Perfect	0.0000
	0.0012	Real	0.0038
	0.0012	Noise 25%	0.1685
	0.0044	Noise 50%	0.3527
25 nm	0.0025	Perfect	0.0000
	0.0043	Real	0.0074
	0.0077	Noise 25%	0.2021
	0.0032	Noise 50%	0.3773
50 nm	0.0048	Perfect	0.0000
	0.0029	Real	0.0023
	0.0059	Noise 25%	0.1387
	0.0027	Noise 50%	0.3803

Table 1.2 Mean deviations for the two presentations in each trial for the medium-wavelength-sensitive cone class

σ	Real	Comparison	
5 nm	0.0787	Perfect	0.0000
	0.0195	Real	0.1540
	0.0077	Noise 25%	0.2317
	0.0041	Noise 50%	0.6222
25 nm	0.0140	Perfect	0.0000
	0.0155	Real	0.0222
	0.0132	Noise 25%	0.1299
	0.0167	Noise 50%	0.6078
50 nm	0.0053	Perfect	0.0000
	0.0075	Real	0.0041
	0.0035	Noise 25%	0.1783
	0.0025	Noise 50%	0.5235

Table 1.3 Mean deviations for the two presentations in each trial for the long-wavelength-sensitive cone class

σ	Real	Comparison	
5 nm	0.0777	Perfect	0.0000
	0.0777	Real	0.0794
	0.04279	Noise 25%	0.2252
	0.0053	Noise 50%	0.2231
25 nm	0.0108	Perfect	0.0000
	0.0200	Real	0.0300
	0.0113	Noise 25%	0.1321
	0.0363	Noise 50%	0.7427
50 nm	0.004	Perfect	0.0000
	0.0126	Real	0.0036
	0.0041	Noise 25%	0.1016
	0.0034	Noise 50%	0.4864

was found in the discrimination task for any of the four conditions [$F_{2,22} = 0.21$, $p = 0.81$ for the perfect versus real condition; $F_{2,22} = 2.3$, $p = 0.12$ for the real versus real condition; $F_{2,22} = 0.41$, $p = 0.66$ for the noise 25% versus real condition; $F_{2,22} = 0.24$, $p = 0.79$ for the noise 50% versus real condition].

Since there was no effect of σ on performance, d' means were calculated and plotted according to the comparison filter in each condition. As shown by Figure 1.11, there is a significant trend ($F_{3,105} = 42.26$, $p = 0.00$) depending on the condition. In particular, when the physically plausible filter is compared to a filter with approximately the same

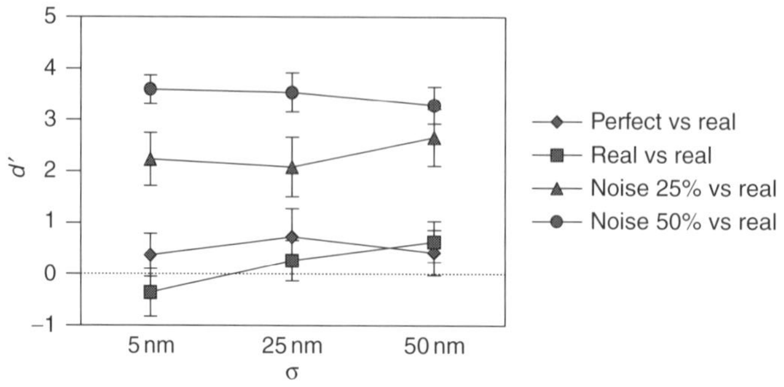

Figure 1.10 Mean values of d' for the four conditions plotted against different σ levels.

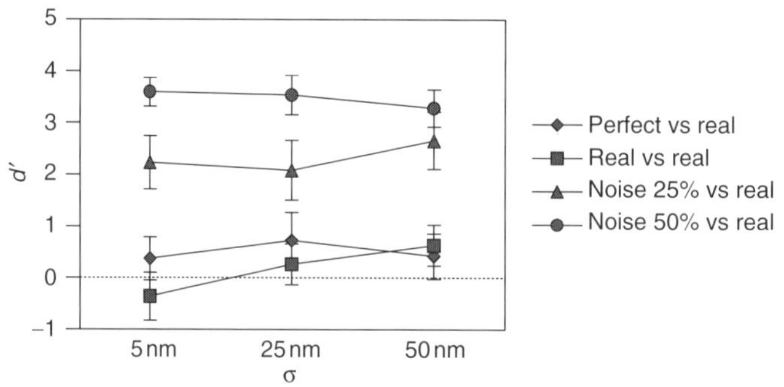

Figure 1.11 Mean values of d' for the four conditions.

deviations in cone excitation ratio, then the performance is random. This is the case of the perfect versus real condition ($t_{35} = 1.89$, $p = 0.07$) and the real versus real condition ($t_{35} = 0.71$, $p = 0.48$).

In the perfect versus real filter condition, the deviations in cone excitation ratio of the physically plausible filter are not sufficiently different from the invariance to be able to distinguish which filter is a homogeneous transparent layer. In the real versus filter with 25% of noise condition, subjects were able to discriminate between the two filters and choose the filter with the lower deviations from the invariance. A Student's t-test run for this condition showed that subjects' performance was significantly different from zero ($t_{35} = 7.48$, $p = 0.00$). In the real versus filter with 50% of noise condition, d' values were even higher than the previous condition. Also in this case the subjects' performance was significantly different from zero ($t_{35} = 17.98$, $p = 0.00$).

1.6.6 Discussion

Deviations of cone excitation ratios from invariance have been varied in a 2AFC task where presentations having zero deviations or close to zero deviations have been compared with presentations whose deviations were significantly different form zero.

Subjects' performance was random when zero deviations were compared. These were the perfect versus real filter condition and the real versus real filter conditions. The performance was above chance when cone excitation ratios between the surfaces seen directly and the surfaces under the filter gave rise to deviations far from the invariance. This was the case of the filters with 25% and 50% of noise.

It is still not clear how close to invariance the deviations have to be in order to give rise to a transparent percept. Also it is not known whether all three cone classes need to be invariant or whether the invariance of one cone class is enough to perceive transparency.

1.7 CONCLUSIONS

The perception of transparency seems to have some analogies with colour constancy. For the colour constancy phenomenon it has been proposed that cone excitation ratios for pairs of surfaces are almost invariant under changes in illumination and that these ratios offer a possible basis for perceptual colour constancy. In this chapter we have discussed modelling and psychophysical experiments and suggest that the invariance of cone excitation ratios is also a possible cue for the perception of transparency [39, 42, 43]. Specifically, the invariance of cone excitation ratios seems to define the chromatic conditions that are necessary for transparency perception. The figural conditions have not been considered in detail in these studies.

Our hypothesis requires that at least two opaque surfaces, each partly covered by a transparent filter, are required in order to satisfy the chromatic constraints, but does the percept of transparency increase with an increasing number of surfaces? Kasrai and Kingdom [46] note that for a filter defined by n parameters there is no unique set of values for the parameters that satisfy the chromatic constraints for transparency perception if the number of opaque surfaces is n or less. If Metelli's model is assumed to be correct then this would require at least three opaque surfaces for the filter parameters to be uniquely defined. Kasrai and Kingdom report psychophysical experiments using stimuli with three opaque surfaces partly covered by a filter where the observer is required to adjust the luminance of one of the filtered patches to cause the stimulus to appear homogeneously transparent. Although the results indicate a strong preference by the observers for one luminance setting, a wide range of luminance values for the adjusted patch was found to satisfy the requirements for perceptual transparency. Could this suggest that the number of parameters n required to define a physically transparent filter could be greater than two? Certainly, it would seem likely that at least three such parameters are required: an internal transmittance term and internal and external surface reflectance terms.

Our data strongly support the notion that the chromatic conditions necessary for transparency perception are defined well by the ratio of cone excitations. It seems reasonable, therefore, that such ratios (or some approximately equivalent measure) might be used as a cue by the visual system in the perception of transparency. For a homogeneously transparent system the more opaque surfaces that are partly covered by the filter, the more ratios are available to the visual system. Increased numbers of ratios may provide the visual system with increased information and a correspondingly stronger cue for transparency perception. We have previously reported experiments [47] to show that observers' ability to discriminate between displays whose cone excitation ratios are invariant and displays with perturbed cone excitation ratios, increases with the number of surfaces in the display.

Interestingly, increased performance with increased number of surfaces in the display has also been reported for experiments in colour constancy [33]. For computational models of perceptual transparency that make use of X-junctions and T-junctions [6, 48] the number of X-junctions also increases with the number of surfaces in the image. It is likely that the number of surfaces is one of several factors that could affect the strength of psychophysical cues; we might reasonably expect other factors to include the variance (e.g. [49]) of the surfaces and their spatial relationships. For real scenes we would expect many additional factors to be involved, such as surface specularity and the degree of spatial uniformity of surfaces [50, 51].

REFERENCES

1. M. H. Brill (1994) The perception of a colored translucent sheet on a background. *Col. Res. Appl.*, **19**, 34–36.
2. F. Metelli (1974) The perception of transparency. *Scientific American*, **230**, 90–98.
3. A. L. Gilchrist (1977) Perceived lightness depends on perceived spatial arrangement. *Science*, **195**, 185–187.
4. F. Metelli (1970) An algebraic development of the theory of perceptual transparency. *Ergonomics,* **13**, 59–66.
5. G. Kanizsa (1979) *Organization in Vision*. New York: Praeger.
6. P. Cavanagh (1987) Reconstructing the third dimension: interactions between color, texture, motion, binocular disparity and shape. *Computer Vision, Graphics, and Image Processing*, **37**, 171–195.
7. E. H. Adelson and P. Anandan (1990) Ordinal characteristics of transparency. *AAAI-90 Workshop on Qualitative Vision* (Boston), pp. 77–81.
8. S. C. Masin (1984) An experimental comparison of three- versus four-surface phenomenal transparency. *Perception and Psychophysics,* **35**, 325–332.
9. H. Helmholtz (1867) *Handbuck der Physiologishen Optik*. Leipzig: L. Voss.
10. E. Hering (1888) Ueber die Theorie des simultanen Kontrasten von Helholtz, 4. *Mitteilung, Pflugers Archiv*, **43**, 1–21.
11. K. Koffka (1935) *Principles of Gestalt Psychology*, New York: Harcourt, Brace, and World.
12. S. Morinaga, K. Noguchi and A. Ohishi (1962) Dominance of main direction in the apparent transparency. *Japanese Psychological Research*, **4**, 113–118.
13. O. Da Pos (1989) *Trasparenze*. Padua: Icone.
14. W. Fuchs (1923) Experimentelle untersuchungen uber das simultane Hintereinendersehen auf derselben Sehrichtung. *Zeitschrift für Psychologie*, **91**, 145–235.
15. W. Metzger (1956) Ueber durchsichtigkeits-erscheinungen (Fourlaufige Mitteilung). *Rivista di Psicologia, fascicolo giubilare*, pp. 187–189.
16. J. Beck (1978) Additive and subtractive color mixture in color transparency. *Perception & Psychophysics*, **23**, 265–267.
17. W. Gerbino, C. Stultiens, J. Troost and C. M. M. de Weert (1990) Transparent layer constancy. *Journal of Experimental Psychology: Human Perception and Performance*, **16**, 3–20.
18. J. Beck, K. Prazdny and R. Ivry (1984) The perception of transparency with achromatic colors, *Perception & Psychophysics*. **35**, 407–422.
19. M. D'Zmura, P. Colantoni, K. Knoblauch and B. Laget (1997) Color transparency. *Perception*, **26**, 471–492.

20. J. V. Chen and M. D'Zmura (1998) Test of a convergence model for color transparency perception. *Perception*, **27**, 595–608.
21. D. H. Foster and S. M. C. Nascimento (1994) Relational colour constancy from invariant cone-excitation ratios. *Proc. R. Soc. London*, **B257**, 115–121.
22. D. Brainard and B. Wandell (1986) Analysis of the retinex theory of color vision. *JOSA*, **A3** (10), 1651–1661.
23. P. Lennie and M. D'Zmura (1988) Mechanisms of color vision. *Crit. Rev. Neurobiol.*, **3**, 333–400.
24. D. Jameson and L. M. Hurvich (1989) Essay concerning color constancy. *Ann. Rev. Psychol.*, **40**, 1–22.
25. E. H. Land and J. J. McCann (1971) Lightness and the retinex theory. *JOSA*, **61**, 1–11.
26. L. T. Maloney and B. A. Wandell (1986) Color constancy: a method for recovering surface spectral reflectance. *JOSA*, **A3** (1), 29–33.
27. S. Tominaga and B. A. Wandell (1990) Component estimation of surface spectral reflectance. *JOSA*, **A** (7), 312–317.
28. D. H. Foster, B. J. Craven and E. R. H. Sale (1992) Immediate colour constancy. *Ophthalmic Physiol. Opt.*, **12**, 157–160.
29. B. J. Craven and D. H. Foster (1992) An operational approach to colour constancy. *Vision Research*, **32**, 1359–1366.
30. M. D'Zmura (1992) Color constancy: surface color from changing illumination. *JOSA*, **A9**, 490–493.
31. M. D'Zmura and G. Iverson (1993) Color constancy I. Basic theory of two stage linear recovery of spectral descriptions for lights and surfaces. *JOSA*, **A10**, 2148–2165.
32. M. D'Zmura and G. Iverson (1993) Color constancy II. Results for two stage linear recovery of spectral descriptions for lights and surfaces. *JOSA*, **A10**, 2166–2180.
33. S. M. C. Nascimento and D. H. Foster (1997) Detecting natural changes of cone-excitation ratios in simple and complex coloured images. *Proc. R. Soc. London*, **B264**, 1395–1402.
34. L. T. Maloney (1986) Evaluation of linear models of surface spectral reflectance with small numbers of parameters. *JOSA*, **A3**, 1673–1683.
35. L. Arend and A. Reeves (1986) Simultaneous colour constancy. *JOSA*, **A3**, 1743–1751.
36. B. A. Wandell (1995) *Foundations of Vision*. Sunderland MA: Sinauer Associates.
37. G. West and M. H. Brill (1982) Necessary and sufficient conditions for von Kries chromatic adaptation to give color constancy. *J. Math. Biol.*, **15**, 249–258.
38. G. D. Finlayson, M. S. Drew and B. V. Funt (1994) Spectral sharpening: sensor transformations for improved color constancy. *JOSA*, **A11** (5), 1553–1563.
39. S. Westland and C. Ripamonti (2000) Invariant cone-excitation ratios may predict transparency. *JOSA*, **A17** (2), 255–264.
40. G. Wyszecki and W. S. Stiles (1982) *Color Science: Concepts and Methods, Quantitative Data and Formulae*. New York: Wiley.
41. J. P. S. Parkkinen, J. Hallikainen and T. Jaaskelainen (1989) Characteristic spectra of Munsell colors. *JOSA*, **A6**, 318–322.
42. C. Ripamonti and S. Westland (1999) Colour signal constraints for the perception of transparency. *Perception*, **28**, 66.
43. C. Ripamonti and S. Westland (2000) Correlation between cone-excitation ratios invariance and perception of transparency. *Proceedings of Colour Image Science 2000*, Derby.
44. R. S. Berns Methods for characterizing CRT displays. *Displays*, **16**, 173–182.
45. D. L. Post and C. S. Calhoun (1989) An evaluation of methods for producing desired colors on CRT monitors. *Col. Res. Appl.*, **14**, 172–189.
46. R. Kasrai and F. A. A. Kingdom (2001) Precision, accuracy, and range of perceived achromatic transparency. *JOSA*, **A18**, (1), 1–11.
47. C. Ripamonti and S. Westland (2000) Invariant cone-excitation ratios predict the perception of transparency. *Investigative Ophthalmology and Visual Science,* **41** (4), S238 (ARVO abstract B623).

48. T. Watanabe, T and P. Cavanagh (1993) Transparent surfaces defined by implicit X Junctions. *Vision Research*, **33**, 2339–2346.
49. R. O. Brown and D. I. A. MacLeod (1997) Color appearance depends on the variance of surround colours. *Current Biology*, **7**, 844–849.
50. J. M. Kraft and D. H. Brainard (1999) Mechanisms of color constancy under nearly natural viewing. *Proceedings of the National Academy of Sciences USA*, **96**, 307–312.
51. L. T. Maloney and J. N. Yang (1999) Discounting the illuminant: what it means, how to do it. *Perception*, **28**, 19.

2

Investigation of colour memory

Peter Bodrogi and Tünde Tarczali

2.1 INTRODUCTION

Several different psychophysical methods have been found in the literature for investigation of human colour memory. In this chapter these methods are compared, classified and systematised, and some possible new experimental techniques are proposed. The results of experiments are reported for different versions of the so-called memory matching technique. A simple hypothesis is formulated to interpret the results and to help understand the characteristics of colour memory. Finally, theories of colour memory are described in Section 2.6.

Every experimental technique consists of two main steps. First, the observer whose colour memory is being examined is given a certain cognitive and/or perceptual *cue*, the so-called *colour memory cue*. Second, the observer has to find his or her memory colour based on the colour memory cue. In our system, the experimental methods for the investigation of human colour memory are classified based on the type of *colour memory cue* plus the type of psychophysical method [1] to find a colour stimulus equivalent to the memory colour. Four main types of *colour memory cues* have been defined:

1. The *abstract cue without image context* is the name of a familiar object. In this case observers are given a word or an expression only (e.g. 'green grass') and then they have to find their long-term memory colour corresponding to this word.

Colour Image Science, edited by L.W. MacDonald and M.R. Luo.

2. The *abstract cue with image context* is the greyscale picture of a familiar object. In this case observers are given a greyscale photorealistic image (e.g. a landscape) in which an area is left blank. Then they have to find their long-term memory colour that would best fit that blank area.
3. The *memory matching cue without image context* is a stand-alone uniform colour patch, which the observers can see as a so-called original colour (i.e. a colour that they have to memorise). 'Stand-alone' means that there is no visible image context (e.g. a photo depicting a familiar object) together with the original colour. After a time interval, they have to find their memory colour.
4. The *memory matching cue with image context* is a uniform colour patch (the original colour) which is part of a coloured or greyscale photorealistic image. In this case the observers have to memorise the original colour, and after a time interval they have to find their memory colour.

Three methods of finding the memory colour have been categorised. The first is a method of adjustment, the second and the third are constant methods [1]:

1. 'Mixing-up' the memory colour on a colour output device (a visual colorimeter or a colour monitor) by adjusting the hue, the chroma, and the lightness of a so-called 'actual' colour. Strengths of this method are that all colour shades can be 'mixed up' within the output device's gamut and exactly the same viewing condition can be ensured by using greyscale images (Section 2.3.2). The weakness is that it is sometimes difficult for the observer to use the tools to mix up the memory colour.
2. Selecting the memory colour from several constant colour patches. The strength of this method is that it is simple for the observer. The weakness is that there is a perceptual difference between the viewing situations of memorising and selecting (Section 2.3.3). In addition, the number of constant patches and thus the colour gamut from which to select is limited.
3. Deciding whether a just-presented colour patch is the memory colour or not. As this method has not yet been implemented by the authors and no literature references have been found, the strengths and weaknesses of this method are unknown. One might speculate that it may be very easy for the observer. A weakness may be that the consecutive presentation of many colour patches may confuse the observer and influence the short-term memory colour.

Four types of colour memory cues and three methods of finding the memory colour have been extensively studied and reported in the literature. Some types of cues and methods have also been studied by the authors. References are cited in Table 2.1.

The so-called preference task must be well distinguished from methods to investigate colour memory. In a 'preference task', observers are taught to look for the *preferred colour* of a just-seen or imagined object instead of trying to reproduce an original colour or a mean long-term memory colour [2, 3, 4]. The advantage of the preference task is that it represents better the everyday situation in which preferred or pleasing colour reproduction is sometimes more important than accurate colour appearance reproduction [3].

Table 2.1 References on the investigation of colour memory

	Method 1 Mixing up	Method 2 Selecting	Method 3 Deciding
Cue 1 Abstract cue without image context	Siple and Springer (1983) **	Newhall *et al.* (1957) Bartleson (1960) Pérez-Carpinell *et al.* (1998b)	**
Cue 2 Abstract cue with image context	Siple and Springer (1983) **		**
Cue 3 Memory matching cue without image context	Newhall *et al.* (1957) Jin and Shevell (1996) Nilsson and Nelson (1981) * **	Bartleson (1961) Pérez-Carpinell *et al.* (1998a) *	**
Cue 4 Memory matching cue with image context	Siple and Springer (1983) * **	*	**

*Previous studies by us.
**Intended studies by us.

2.2 REFERENCES ON COLOUR MEMORY

This section summarises references on colour memory. The first article dates back to 1922 when, from theoretical considerations, Wulf [31] expected a shift of memory of perceived hues toward unique hues. Adams [25] reported an experimental study of memory colour and related phenomena, in which observers attempted to match the colours associated with objects they had just directly perceived. Collins [28] reported some regular hue shifts in the red and green regions. Koffka [30] predicted increased saturation in memory colour and cited Katz's results in support [29]. Baker and Mackintosh [26] also favoured an increase in saturation. Hamwi and Landis [33] obtained greater saturation and less brightness for memory colours, and hue shifts for blue-greens and red-purples.

2.2.1 Newhall

Newhall *et al.* [18] compared two colour matching methods: successive and simultaneous (Table 2.1). Simultaneous or perceptual colour matching means modifying one of two simultaneously presented colours to make it visually match the other colour. Successive or delayed matching involves short-term colour memory and thus is memory matching, but 'it is only half memory in the sense that only one of the two compared colours has to be remembered'. They stated that successive matching was very common in everyday life.

They applied the following experimental paradigm: both simultaneous and successive matching were made in a test field of the same size, about 2° angular subtense. The colour temperature of the illuminant was 6500 K. For the perceptual matches, the test colour (in other words, the original colour) filled half of the central field and the observer adjusted the colour of the other half until a colour match was achieved. For the memory matches, the observer did the match from memory after the test colour had been replaced by an adjustable colour. There was a pause of 5 s after the removal of the test colour. There was no restriction upon the matching time. Each of three observers made 10 perceptual and 10 memory matches of each of the 25 test colours.

The results of these memory and perceptual matches were compared with respect to average matching colours and variability ellipses expected to contain 39% of the observers' judgements. The average area of the memory match ellipses turned out to be 6.2 times the average of the perceptual matches. Differences in shape and orientation of the variability ellipses were not generally significant. This greater variability of the memory matches was explained by the complete lack of juxtaposition, and 'appearance differences' between memory and perception. Averaging the matching colours indicated that systematic increases in saturation were required for the memory matching as compared with the perceptual matching of the same colours. The chroma increase was greater for more saturated colours, and averaged 1.7 Munsell chroma steps. No overall systematic changes in hue were apparent between perceptual and memory matches. There was a tendency for the memory matches to require more lightness than for the simultaneous matches. This tendency seemed to increase with increase in the lightness of the test samples. They remarked that 'the challenging problem of predicting remembered colours from perceived colours merits further attention in future studies'.

Newhall *et al.* [18] also reported results of a previous supplementary experiment carried out by Newhall and Pugh. In this experiment the observer viewed nearly the entire gamut of the Munsell 20-hue large book samples displayed simultaneously on a large table, and he was asked to select that sample which best represented the colour of a familiar absent object. There was no pictorial information in the visual field. Eight familiar objects or substances (brick, sand, grass, skin, dry grass, concrete, pine tree and weathered wood) were memory matched. Thirty observers took part in the experiment. The observations were carried out under artificial daylight. The memory matches of familiar objects were compared with perceptual matches or with colorimetric measurements of actual objects.

It was found that the hues of the memory colours exhibited a trend in the direction of the typical hues commonly associated with the actual objects. This is referred to as *typicality*, one of the three *cognitive effects* (Section 2.3.6) Brick appeared to be remembered as redder than the object, sand as more yellow, grass as greener, dry grass as more yellow, and pine trees as greener. Lightness of the memory colours, in all cases except brick, ran higher than in the object colour perceptions; as a general average, 1.1 extra Munsell value steps were required. On average, 0.95 Munsell steps more chroma were required. This supplementary experiment was concerned with memories of the colours of absent well-known objects (i.e. abstract cue without image context), whereas Newhall's main experiment (1957) was on short-term memory for coloured patches on a neutral background, i.e. memory matching cue without an image context.

2.2.2 Bartleson

At the beginning of his classic paper on the reproduction of *skin* colours, Bartleson [2], not included in Table 2.1, remarked: 'In theoretical discussions of the quality of photographic colour reproduction, it is frequently assumed that the objective of the photographic process is to reproduce exactly the chromaticities of the original objects ... It has often been recognised that chromatic fidelity may not be necessary or even desirable.' Thus his aim was to study what *skin* colours observers *prefer* in pictorial reproductions. Twelve prints of the same subject (a photo of a woman's face) were produced in which the chromaticities of the complexion areas were systematically varied. Ten observers performed paired comparisons: they were asked to indicate which print of each pair they preferred (preference task); see Section 2.1. Preferred skin colours were compared with memory colours of the abstract cue without image context of Newhall *et al.* [18]; with the memory colours of Bartleson [14], abstract cue without image context; and with measurements of average natural skin [5]. Some evidence was found that preferred skin colours were of the same hue and saturation as the memory colour with abstract cue for skin, and that preference contained more yellow than average measured skin colour.

Bartleson [14] studied the memory colours of ten familiar objects: skin, red brick, green grass, dry grass, blue sky, tanned skin, broad-leafed summer foliage, evergreen trees, inland soil, and beach sand. The experimenter named an object or a substance, and the observer examined a collection of Munsell colour samples. Thus he used an abstract cue without image context (Table 2.1). The observer indicated that patch which seemed to him to best represent the colour of the object. The object colours named by the experimenter were referred to in those terms cited above in quotation marks. Results indicated a considerable degree of consistency in the choice of memory colours for these 10 familiar objects.

The mean memory colours were compared with average measured data of the corresponding 10 natural objects. Mean memory colours had more saturation than the corresponding natural means except skin and tanned skin. Skin and tanned skin contained more unique yellow than natural skin or tanned skin. Sand and soil memory colours appeared to contain somewhat more unique yellow. Green grass and green foliage appeared to be remembered as more blue-green than yellow-green. The memory colour for blue sky was more cyan than the mean for natural skies.

The mean memory colours found by Bartleson [14] were compared with the findings of Newhall and Pugh. There was general agreement of the memory shifts of the two experiments. The closest agreement occurred in the memory colour for skin. Bartleson stated that 'skin, or more precisely, complexions, constitute an object-colour category with which all people have constant visual experience'. He concluded that 'in most cases there are hue shifts with memory in the direction of what is probably the most impressive chromatic attribute of the object in question'.

In a subsequent paper [27], Bartleson compared the memory colours obtained in 1960 with memory colours of patches obtained in the following experimental situation. Four colour patches (originals) without any pictorial information, having average measured natural colours [5, 6] of Caucasian skin, blue sky, beach sand, and green foliage, were used. Each of the seven observers had to view each of the four colour patches for 15 s on a neutral surround. Then the colour patch was removed and the observer searched an array of 931 Munsell chips in order to find the one that he felt best matched the original colour patch. (This is given in Table 2.1 as cue 3, method 2.) Mean hues of the memory colours of patches were not significantly different from the originals but chroma was always increased. The increment of chroma of the memory colours of patches can be interpreted by *exaggeration*; see the *cognitive effect hypothesis* in Section 2.3.6.

In another study [3], the *preferred colours* for Caucasian skin, blue sky and green grass were investigated. This was a so-called preference task which cannot be used directly to study colour memory. The first experiment dealt with Caucasian skin, the aim being to verify the results of Bartleson [2]. Each of 11 observers saw 19 pictures with changes of the colours of only their skin areas. These 19 skin colours were ranked by preference. The chromaticity of the mean memory colour obtained by the abstract cue for skin turned out to be located near the most preferred skin colour but at some distance from average measured natural skin colour. However, this tendency was not true for the pictures containing blue sky or green grass colours in the second, and third experiments. For these kinds of objects, the most preferred colour agreed rather with natural measured colours but not with the memory colours of the abstract cue. The following conclusion was drawn: 'It appears that one cannot assume simply that memory colours (with the abstract cue) represent a desirable reproduction aim for all object colours. It seems clear that the aim is not simply to attempt to reproduce the original chromaticities nor, except for skin at least, to attempt to match the memory colours (with the abstract cue).'

2.2.3 Pérez-Carpinell

In the first study [7], observers had to perform (A) simultaneous side-by-side colour matching and (B) memory matching without image context (Table 2.1) at three delay intervals ($t = 15$ s, 15 min, and 24 h). One of 20 comparison colour chips had to be selected to match a reference chip. There were 10 reference chips: violet, dark blue, blue, light green, green, yellow, chamois, orange, oxide red, and pink. The reference chip was either next to an arrangement of the corresponding 20 comparison chips (simultaneous matching, condition A) or observers had to memorise it and then, after the delay interval t, they had to select the chip corresponding to their later memory colour (memory matching, condition B). For the case of the simultaneous matching, the mean colour differences between the reference chip and the selected comparison colour chip were less than 1 CIELAB unit. For the case of the memory matching, memory shifts were between 4 and 11 CIELAB units with greater variability than for simultaneous matching. Light colours were remembered as being lighter, medium-light colours slightly lighter, and dark colours correctly or darker. For yellow and violet, an increase of chroma of $\Delta C^*_{ab} > 2$ was found. The chroma of green and light green was quite well remembered. The highest hue shifts were obtained for oxide red and yellow. The mean memory shift usually increased with delay time.

In the second study [8], the abstract cue without image context was applied. The observer was given the *name* of one of eight familiar objects (purple aubergine, green watermelon, green lettuce, yellow lemon, orange, pink rose, brown chestnut, and red tomato), then asked to examine ten comparison colour samples on a grey panel and choose the one that best represented the colour of a familiar *absent* object. The colour of each of the eight familiar objects was measured at ten different points of the object. Significant shifts were found between the measured colours and the memory colours. Dominant wavelength (related to hue) shifts depended on the kind of the familiar object considered. Colorimetric purity (related to chroma) increased for familiar objects with high purity and decreased or remained unchanged for familiar objects of mid-range and low purities.

2.2.4 Studies of image context

The effect of the *image context* has been studied in both memory tasks and preference tasks. In a study on semantic ratings of colours [9], subjects evaluated with 7-step ratings on five semantic scales a set of 13 colour chips and 5 sets of objects, each appearing in the same 13 colours. The five semantic scales were (1) beautiful–ugly, (2) elegant–vulgar, (3) loud–discreet, (4) masculine–feminine, (5) warm–cold. Taft's analysis indicated that generally few significant differences existed between chip and object ratings for the same colour. When such differences existed, the chip was always rated more beautiful, elegant, discreet, feminine, and warm than the object; and differences between chip and object ratings (i.e. effect of the image context) were confined to a limited number of colours. Ratings of yellow, red, and purple were most dependent on image context, whereas ratings of grey, brown, and beige were least affected by the image context. In these experiments, a colour chip or an object represented the absence or the presence of the image context, respectively.

Siple and Springer [4] used 18 observers to investigate memory shifts without image context, with shape context, and with texture context. Stimuli were made from sets of photos of six fruits and vegetables (carrot, maize, lettuce, lime, orange and peanut). They appeared in the centre of the photo on a neutral background surrounded by other fruits and vegetables not used as test items. Stimuli were constructed from these photos and from transparencies of the photos to allow for three conditions called disc (without image context), silhouette (with shape context), and texture. To produce the disk condition, the area of each fruit and vegetable was computed and circles of equal area were cut in the centres of the photos. Silhouette stimuli were constructed by cutting out the central object from one set of six photos. For the texture condition, a transparency of each photo was placed behind the appropriate silhouette so that the texture of the object could be seen through the hole.

First, observers were asked to mix up colours for the series of fruits and vegetables as they remembered their typical appearance to be (abstract cue). Observers could not preview the original colour. Thus the task was similar to Bartleson's naming experiment [14]. Mixing up was performed by adjusting a colorimeter. Discs, silhouettes, and transparencies were placed over the colorimeter such that they appeared over the viewing area. Second, observers were asked to mix up the colours they would prefer for the fruits and vegetables (preference task). In a final session, each item was measured by a visual colorimeter (original colours). Original colours were subtracted from the memory or preference colours to get hue, lightness, and chroma shifts.

Changes in the image context produced no change in the colour shifts. No significant hue shifts were found. Some items produced higher intra-subject variances (derived from three replications for each subject) than did others: memory hue for lettuce and preferred hue for peanut. The overall mean lightness shift did not vary from zero. Both memory chroma and preferred chroma were higher than the original. Items with mid-range chroma values (carrot, maize, and lime) showed greater shifts than did those with high (orange) and low (lettuce and peanut) saturation. This again can be explained by *exaggeration*; see Section 2.6.3. The data are in agreement with both Bartleson's [14] findings and Newhall's [18] findings.

2.2.5 Nilsson and Nelson

Nilsson and Nelson [17] measured the short-term memory for 16 monochromatic hues from 425 to 640 nm, after six delays ranging from 0.1 to 24.3 s. They investigated the effect of time on the hue shifts. The data were measured as the difference in wavelengths between the memorised stimulus and the stimulus that was adjusted by the observer to obtain a match. There was little difference in the hue matches of their observers, and no significant overall effect due to the length of delay interval in the above range. The hue shifts were small (1–2 just noticeable differences), but there was a consistent increase in the variances when the delay was increased. The delayed matches indicated that in short-term colour memory, blues tended to become greener and reds became yellower, whereas greens became yellower for delays less than 1 s but bluer at longer delays. The smallest shifts occurred for violets, for a 500 nm green-blue, and for yellow-oranges.

2.3 MEMORY MATCHING TECHNIQUES

The authors' data from a series of experiments [10–13] on human colour memory were based on memory matching techniques, i.e. using two types of colour memory cues, and two methods: *mixing-up* and *selecting*.

2.3.1 Memory shifts

In the memory matching techniques, observers memorise an original colour stimulus O in a first viewing situation. This becomes a so-called *instant memory colour* M. The term 'instant memory colour' is our own terminology. In traditional terminology [14], the term 'memory colours' refers to the colours that are recalled in association with *familiar objects* in *long-term memory*, i.e. using the *abstract cue*. After memorising O, during a given time interval t, the instant memory colour M may change in human colour memory. We have coined the term *later memory colour* M′ for the result of this change.

After the time interval t, observers compare M′ with one or more 'actual' *colours* A. The colour M′ is stored in the observer's memory. The colours A are seen in a second viewing situation which is usually different from the first viewing situation. In the second viewing situation, observers may modify the colour stimulus A until it matches M′ [13]. This is the mixing-up method of Section 2.1.

Alternatively, observers may be taught to select the colour stimulus A equivalent to M′ from several constant patches displayed in a second viewing situation. The set of these constant patches was called 'choice figure' [10]. This is the selecting method of Section 2.1. If the first and second viewing situations are not identical then the difference between the colour stimuli O (the original colour) and A (the 'actual' colour made equivalent to M′) may be due to perceptual artefacts in addition to the change between M and M′ in human colour memory. In order to explore the pure characteristics of the processes in colour memory that cause the change M–M′ in the time interval t, the first and second viewing situations must be the same. The difference between M and M′ is usually called *memory shift*. It is very important to keep in mind that memory shifts are not related to perceptual artefacts like viewing situation differences.

In our experiments, observers had to memorise many different original colour patches inside many photorealistic images depicting sky, skin, and plant. This is colour memory cue 4: *memory matching cue with image context* (Section 2.1). Our observers had to memorise the same original colour patches without the photorealistic image, as well. This is colour memory cue 3: *memory matching cue without image context*. A comparison of the memory shifts resulting from colour memory cues 3 and 4 may reveal the effect of the image context on the characteristics of colour memory.

Our aim was to analyse what memory shifts can be expected for the three types of image context: sky, skin, and plant. Particularly, we wanted to examine whether there was a systematic relationship between memory shifts and original colours within a given group of original colours: sky, skin, and plant. To do this, many photorealistic images and stand-alone colour patches were observed and memorised. They were displayed in several different shades of sky, skin, and plant colours.

Observers were given written instructions to read before the experiments. The images were displayed in a dark room, on a well characterised and calibrated colour monitor. First, observers had to practise their task by using two images different from those used in the main experiment. Each observer saw each original colour *only once* to avoid the effect of learning and to maintain naivety.

2.3.2 Mixing up the later memory colour

Memory matching with image context

For colour memory cue 4, the uniform colour patch of the original colour O was displayed together with the image context, i.e. it was displayed as a part of a photorealistic image. Examples are shown in Figure 2.2. Thus, to ensure that the second viewing situation (containing the actual colour stimulus A) would be the same as the first viewing situation (containing the original colour stimulus O), the photorealistic image surrounding the adjustable actual colour A should be the same as it was for the original colour O. So the colour of the proximal field of A would be *similar to the original colour* O because the colours of small areas do not change rapidly in photorealistic images. This would be a hint for the observer searching for the later memory colour M′. To cancel this hint, and to maintain at least approximately the same viewing condition, two methods were considered:

1. Displaying the image context as a greyscale image in the first viewing situation. An example is shown in Figure 2.1, which corresponds to the first coloured photo in the middle row of Figure 2.2. The only coloured patch in the photo is the uniform patch of the original colour O. To obtain a 'usual' picture, the lightness of O should be the same as the average of its proximal field in the greyscale image. This greyscale method has not yet been implemented but the authors are considering it for further study.
2. The other possibility is to display the image context as the same coloured photo in both viewing situations (Figure 2.2). To avoid any hint of the proximal field of A in the second viewing situation, it was recoloured with shades differing from the original colour O in hue, chroma, and lightness. In addition, the photorealistic image was blurred outside the patch of A. Thus the image surrounding A (Figure 2.3) became slightly different from the image surrounding the original colour O (compare with the corresponding photos in Figure 2.2) but it was assumed that this difference did not cause a perceptible difference in the viewing situation.

Each of 11 colour-normal subjects observed 20 different photorealistic images (designated by P) containing sky (so-called sky photos, each depicting a different scene, two examples

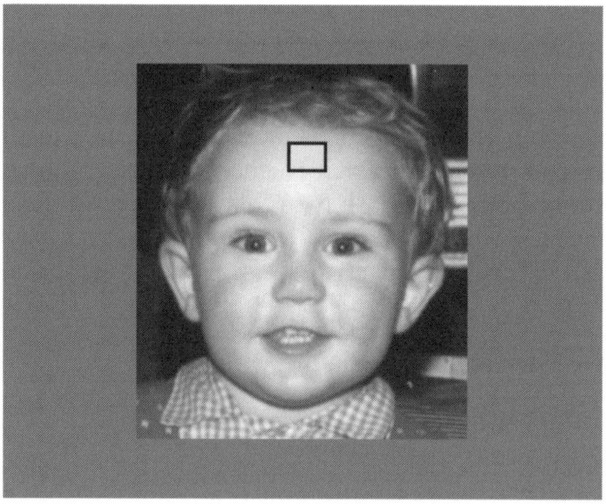

Figure 2.1 Displaying the image as a greyscale image in the first viewing situation. This example corresponds to the first colour photo in the middle row of Figure 2.2 The only colour patch in the photo is the uniform patch of the original colour O.

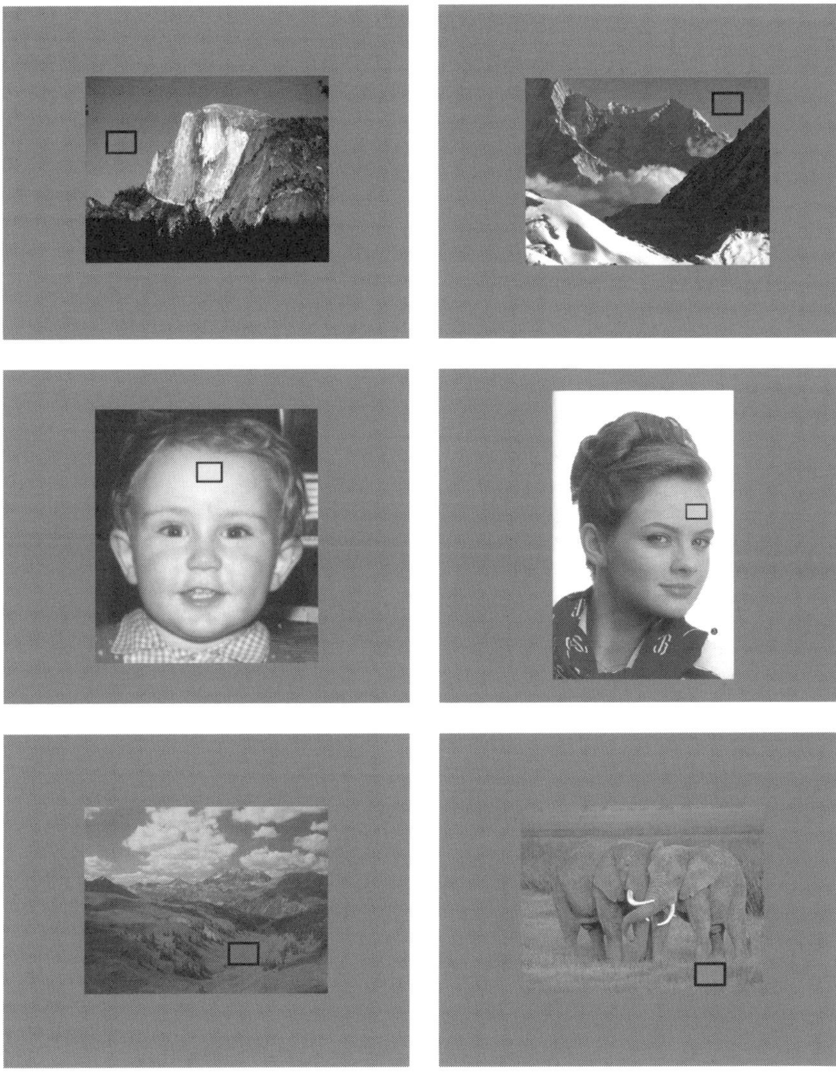

Figure 2.2 For colour memory cue 4, the uniform colour patch of the original colour O was displayed together with the image context, i.e. it was displayed as part of a photorealistic image. O is in a black frame. Top row, sky; middle row, Caucasian skin; bottom row, plant. Colour versions are shown in Plate 1 (top).

are shown in the first row of Figure 2.2) plus 20 different Caucasian skin photos (each depicting a different scene, two examples are shown in the middle row of Figure 2.2) plus 20 different plant photos (each depicting a different scene, two examples are shown in the last row of Figure 2.2). The presentation sequence of the photos was the following: sky, skin, plant, sky, skin, etc. First, a photo containing the original colour O was presented.

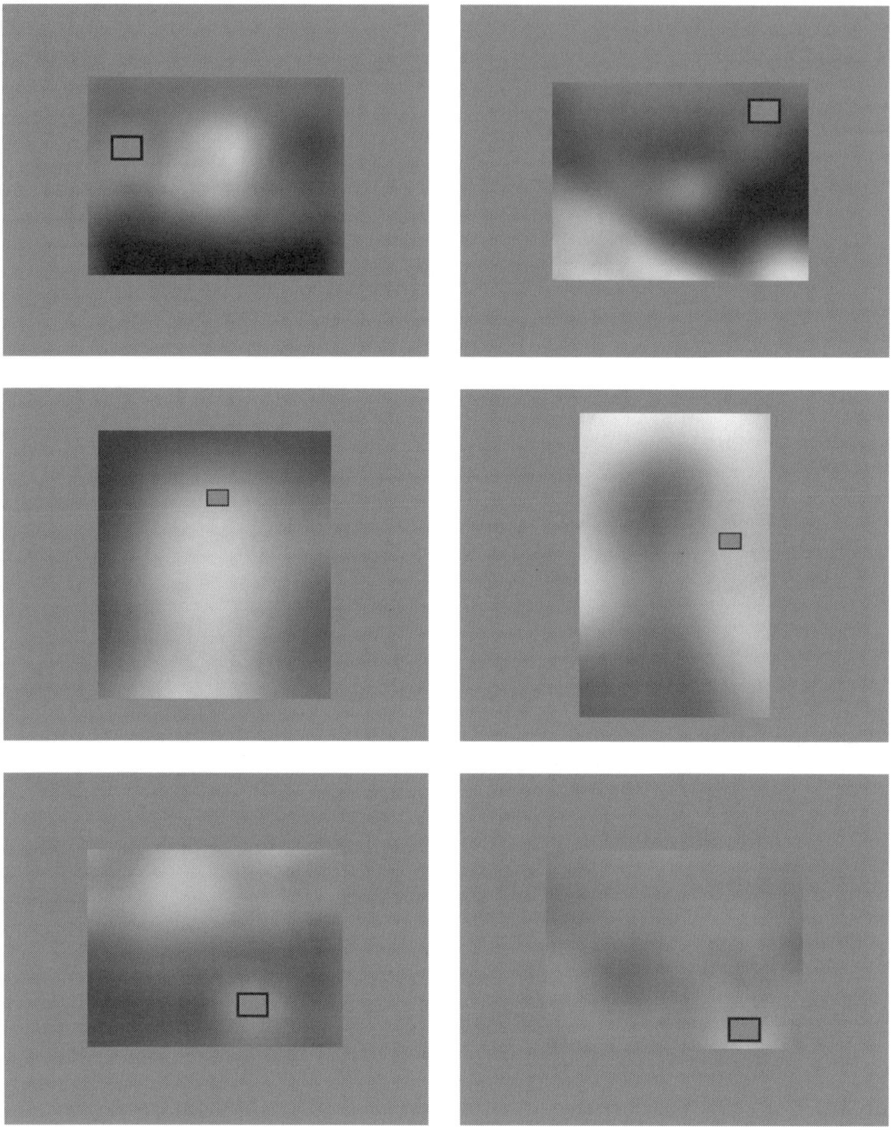

Figure 2.3 Blurred images corresponding to the photorealistic images of Figure 2.2.

The original colour O was a uniform rectangular patch (subtending typically $2^\circ \times 2^\circ$) in a black frame (Figure 2.2). There was no time limit to memorise it. After this, a full-screen uniform middle-grey (MG) image was displayed for 4 s. Then subjects were asked to adjust the hue, lightness, and saturation of the colour A on the blurred version of the photo. The adjustment was done by the aid of three sliders displayed at the top of the screen until the best match to their later memory colour M′ was achieved. The initial colour of the adjustable colour patch A was middle grey.

Memory matching without image context

For colour memory cue 3, each of 10 colour-normal subjects (all different from the previous 11 subjects) observed 3 × 20 *stand-alone colour patches* (designated SA) taken from the 3 × 20 photos of the implementation of the memory matching with image context. An example is shown in Figure 2.4. It corresponds to the first coloured photo in the middle row of Figure 2.2. The experiment was similar to the previous one except that: (a) all of the photo except the uniform rectangle of the original colour O in the black frame was substituted by middle grey (Figure 2.4); and (b) during the adjustment of the colour A, the blurred version of the photo was substituted by middle grey. Thus, for the invisible image context (i.e. colour memory cue 3) the identity of the first and second viewing conditions was achieved.

2.3.3 Selecting the later memory colour from several constant colour patches

Sixty-two observers took part in the experiment, of whom one-half (31) saw only *photorealistic images*, whereas the other half saw only *stand-alone colour patches* on a middle-grey (MG) background. The first viewing condition was similar to that described in Section 2.3.2. The observer had to look at the image and memorise the original colour O inside a black rectangular frame. The original colour was either part of a photorealistic image or a stand-alone colour patch on an MG background. After this, a full-screen uniform MG image was displayed for 2 s.

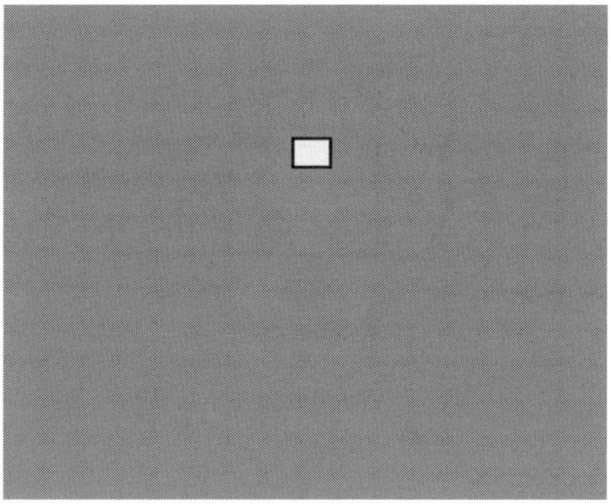

Figure 2.4 For colour memory cue 3, subjects observed stand-alone colour patches. This example corresponds to the first colour photo in the middle row of Figure 2.2. All of the photo except the uniform rectangle of the original colour O in the black frame was substituted as middle grey.

The second viewing condition was different from that described in Section 2.3.2. The observer saw a so-called *choice figure* with a 3×5 array of 15 colours each inside the same black rectangle frame as in the first viewing condition. An example is shown in Figure 2.5. It corresponds to a coloured photo in Figure 2.2. The observer had to choose from these 15 colours the one corresponding best to the later memory colour M′.

The original colour O was always among the 15 colours in the 3×5 array of the choice figure, but its location was randomly selected. The other 14 patches differed from O in hue, lightness, and saturation. Two of them were generated manually by trying to find out the typical colour of the object to be identified in the image. For example, in the image containing a road covered by snow, the original colour of the snow is a pale brownish shade. Thus in the choice figure a colour closer to white was included because the snow is known to be white, but a very clear white was avoided because this would have been suspicious for the observer. As can be seen, for the case of these two manually generated colours, the observer was directed towards a guessable long-term memory colour of the familiar object (Section 2.4). Twelve of the colours in the choice figure were generated computationally: either the hue angle, or the chroma, or the lightness was increased or decreased so that the overall colour difference between O and the colour was either $\Delta E^*_{ab} = 5$ or $\Delta E^*_{ab} = 10$.

A total of 21 different photorealistic images were used. They depicted different identifiable familiar objects (sky, skin, plant, and other objects such as sand, snow, brick, veneer). Each photorealistic image was assigned an image with a stand-alone uniform colour patch in the following way: all the photorealistic image was replaced by the medium grey except the colour element with the black rectangle frame (as seen in Figure 2.4).

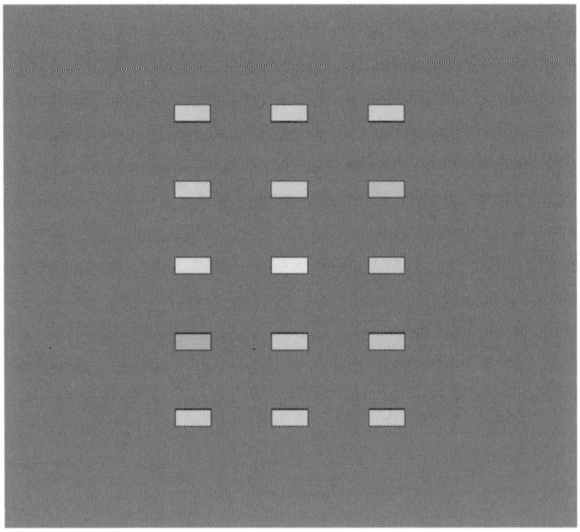

Figure 2.5 The choice figure. This example corresponds to a photo in Figure 2.2. The observer had to choose the colour patch corresponding best to the later memory colour M′. See also Plate 1.

2.4 RESULTS OF MEMORY MATCHING EXPERIMENTS

2.4.1 Mixing up the later memory colour

Original colours O and actual colours A corresponding to each observer's later memory colour M′ have been quantified in the CIELAB colour space. Memory shifts have been quantified by calculating: (a) CIELAB colour difference between O and A: ΔE^*_{ab}; (b) CIE 1976 *a*,*b* hue angle difference $\Delta h_{ab} = h_{abA} - h_{abO}$; (d) CIE 1976 *a*,*b* hue difference ΔH^*_{ab} between O and A; (d) CIE 1976 chroma difference $\Delta C^*_{ab} = C^*_{abA} - C^*_{abO}$; and (e) CIE 1976 lightness difference $\Delta L^* = L^*_A - L^*_O$.

General tendencies of memory shifts

Table 2.2 contains mean ΔH^*_{ab}, ΔC^*_{ab}, and ΔL^* values for sky, skin and plant photos, and mean values of the corresponding images with stand-alone colour patches. The following deductions can be made:

- ΔC^*_{ab} values tend to be greater than zero, indicating that the observers' later memory colours M′ tend to have more chroma than the instant memory colour M. This is in accordance with the findings of previous investigations.
- ΔL^* values were below zero for skin and sky. This means that observers' later memory colours M′ tend to be darker than the instant memory colour M. For sky, this tendency was stronger for photos than for stand-alone patches. ΔL^* values tend to be above zero for plant but this tendency is quite weak for stand-alone patches.
- ΔH^*_{ab} (and Δh_{ab}) values depend on the kind of the original colour: sky, skin or plant. For sky, subjects tend to find both positive and negative ΔH^*_{ab} values, indicating that their instant memory colour M shifted toward some kind of purple-blue. The sign of ΔH^*_{ab} depends on the hue of the original colour O. For skin, observers tend to find such M′ colours that contain more unique yellow than O. This tendency was stronger for photorealistic images (P) than for images with stand-alone colour

Table 2.2 Sky, skin and plant photos (P) and images with stand-alone colour patches (SA)

	ΔH^*_{ab} P	ΔH^*_{ab} SA	ΔC^*_{ab} P	ΔC^*_{ab} SA	ΔL^* P	ΔL^* SA
Sky	1.5	−0.2	7.2	6.1	−4.7	−1.3
Skin	5.1	2.5	8.0	7.6	−5.4	−6.5
Plant	5.0	2.7	8.0	5.4	2.8	1.4

Columns headed P contain the mean values of 11 observers × 20 photos, and columns headed SA contain the mean values of 10 observers × 20 images.

patches (SA). For plant, observers tend to find M′ colours containing more unique green than O.

Memory shift as a function of the original colour

Interesting tendencies were found by representing Δh_{ab} as a function of the hue angle of the original colours (h_{abO}) separately for sky, skin, and plant, as shown in Figures 2.6 to 2.8. Similar tendencies were found for photorealistic images and for images with stand-alone colour patches by depicting the mean ΔC^*_{ab} value as a function of C^*_{abO} and by depicting the mean ΔL^* value as a function of L^*_O.

'Constant' hue, chroma and lightness intervals

Arrows at the bottom of Figures 2.6 to 2.8 connect the smallest and largest h_{abO} values where there was a confidence interval overlapping the abscissa. These intervals have been called *constant hue intervals* because there was a tendency for no significant hue memory shift inside these intervals. Similarly, *constant chroma and lightness intervals* can also be defined. The hue, chroma and lightness values of the original colours inside the constant hue, chroma and lightness intervals have been called *constant hue, chroma, and lightness*. A numerical estimation of the constant hue intervals is given in Table 2.3.
The following general tendencies can be deduced from the above results:

- Constant intervals were broader for the images with stand-alone patches (SA) than for photos (P), especially for hue.

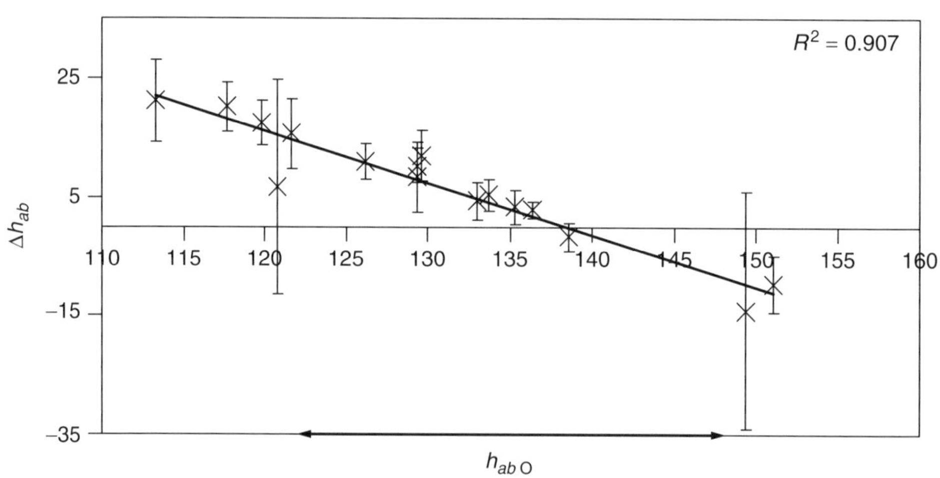

Figure 2.6 Hue angle component of the memory shift (Δh_{ab} in degrees) as a function of hue angle of the original colour (h_{abO} in degrees). Each cross depicts a mean Δh_{ab} value calculated from responses of 11 subjects observing one of the 20 plant photos. The graph also shows the 95% confidence intervals of the mean, a line fitted to the crosses, and a correlation coefficient (R^2).

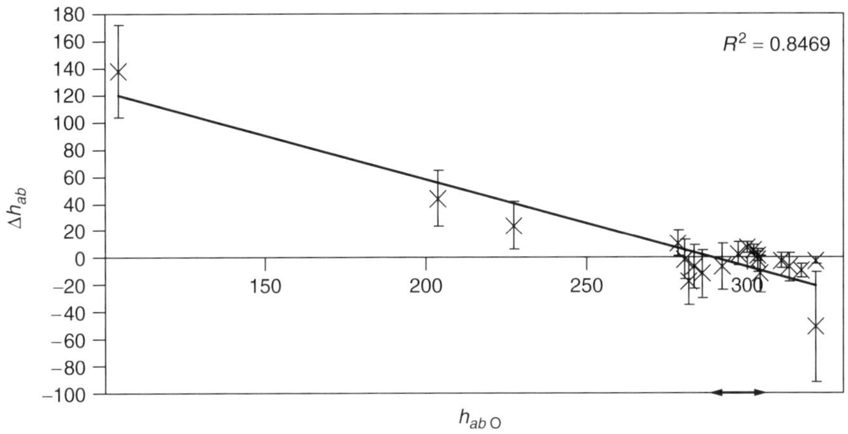

Figure 2.7 Hue angle component of the memory shift (Δh_{ab} in degrees) as a function of hue angle of the original colour (h_{abO} in degrees). Each cross depicts a mean Δh_{ab} value calculated from responses of 11 subjects observing one of the 20 sky photos. The graph also shows the 95% confidence intervals of the mean, a line fitted to the crosses, and a correlation coefficient (R^2).

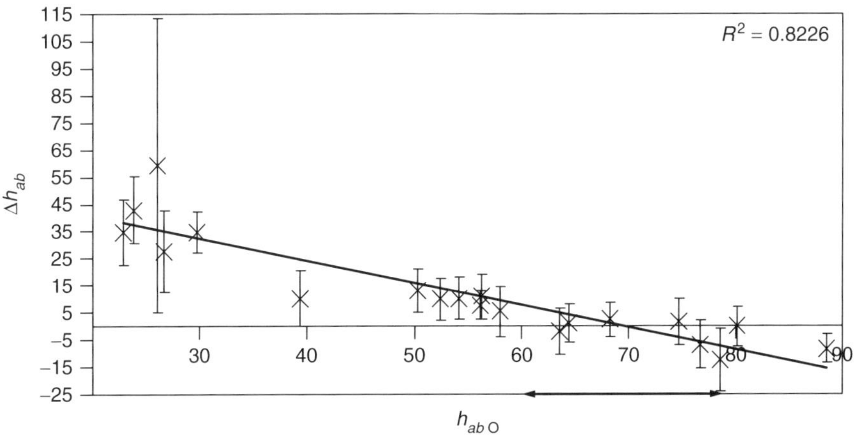

Figure 2.8 Hue angle component of the memory shift (Δh_{ab} in degrees) as a function of hue angle of the original colour (h_{abO} in degrees). Each cross depicts a mean Δh_{ab} value calculated from responses of 11 subjects observing one of the 20 Caucasian skin photos. The graph also shows the 95% confidence intervals of the mean, a line fitted to the crosses, and a correlation coefficient (R^2).

- All lines fitted to the diagrams had negative slopes. Correlation values (R^2) of the photos (P) were greater than those of the images with stand-alone patches (SA).
- The observers' mean Δh_{ab}, ΔC^*_{ab}, or ΔL^* values were positive before constant intervals and negative after them. In other words, memory shifts were directed toward constant intervals, especially for photos (P).

Table 2.3 Estimation of constant hue intervals h_{abO} (°)

		P	SA
Sky	Min	280	104
	Max	313	322
	Mean	297	213
Skin	Min	58	26
	Max	80	80
	Mean	69	53
Plant	Min	120	73
	Max	149	319
	Mean	135	196

2.4.2 Selecting the later memory colour from several colour patches

Observers selected the colour stimulus A equivalent to their later memory colour M′ from several constant patches of the choice figure (Section 2.3.3 and Figure 2.5).

General tendencies of the memory shifts

Table 2.4 contains mean ΔH^*_{ab}, ΔC^*_{ab}, and ΔL^* values for sky, skin and plant of photos, and mean values of the corresponding images with stand-alone colour patches. The values presented in Table 2.4 are smaller than those of Table 2.2. The reason may be the limited possibilities for the actual colour A in the choice figure. Using the 'mixing up' method (mean results are presented in Table 2.2), observers could produce any colour stimulus (within the imaging device's colour gamut) to represent their later memory colour M′. Similar to Table 2.2, mean ΔC^*_{ab} values tend to be greater than zero, indicating that the observers' later memory colours M′ tend to have more chroma than the instant memory colour M. The mean ΔL^* values are quite small.

Table 2.4 Sky, skin and plant photos (P) and images with stand-alone colour patches (SA)

	ΔH^*_{ab} P	ΔH^*_{ab} SA	ΔC^*_{ab} P	ΔC^*_{ab} SA	ΔL^* P	ΔL^* SA
Sky	−0.7	−0.2	1.2	1.6	0.9	−0.1
Skin	0.5	−0.6	0.2	1.9	0.0	0.0
Plant	2.4	0.9	3.6	2.2	1.0	−0.6

Sky: 31 observers × 3 images.
Caucasian skin: 31 observers × 6 images.
Plant: 31 observers × 4 images.

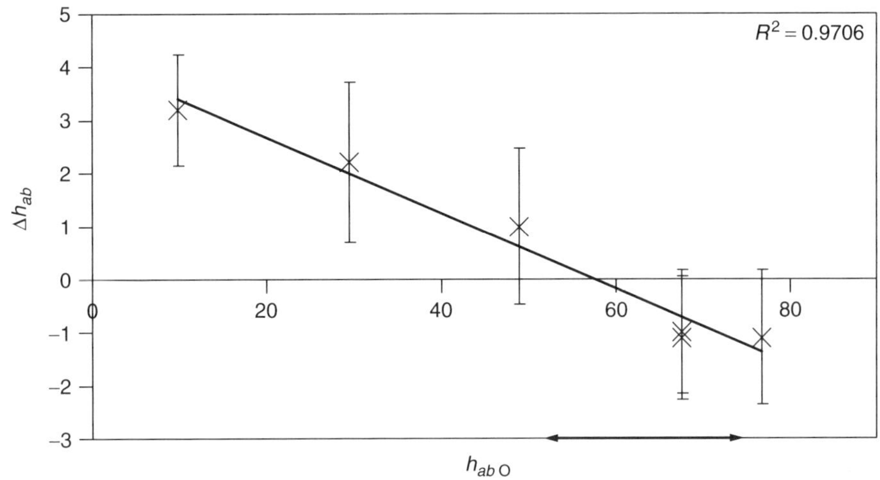

Figure 2.9 Δh_{ab} (degrees) as a function of hue angle of the original colour (h_{abO} in degrees) for Caucasian skin. Photorealistic images, method of 'selecting'. The arrow at the bottom of the figure indicates the constant hue interval [49°, 77°].

Memory shift as a function of the original colour

Representing the hue angle component of the memory shift (Δh_{ab}) as a function of the hue angle of the original colours (h_{abO}) for the six original colours of six photos depicting Caucasian skin (Figure 2.9), similar tendencies can be seen as in Figure 2.8. The constant hue interval was estimated to be [49°, 77°] (mean 63°) instead of [58°, 80°] (mean 69°) of Table 2.3.

2.4.3 Comparison of memory matching with other psychophysical techniques

It is interesting to compare the results from our memory matching experiments with the results from literature, including the most preferred colour, and an average instrumentally measured colour. Most of the comparable results from different techniques were found for Caucasian skin. They are presented in Table 2.5 and in the a^*b^* diagram of Figure 2.10. As can be seen from Table 2.5 and Figure 2.10, most memory colours of Caucasian skin (nos. 2–6) are lighter and contain more unique yellow than the average measured colour (no. 1). The mean chroma resulting from three memory matching techniques (nos. 4–6) was greater than the chroma of the average measured, most preferred, and abstract memory colours (nos. 1–3).

2.5 INTERPRETATION OF SYSTEMATIC MEMORY SHIFTS

Constant intervals have been defined as h_{abO}, C^*_{abO} or L^*_O value ranges between the smallest and largest h_{abO}, C^*_{abO} or L^*_O values associated with a 95% confidence interval

Table 2.5 Comparison of results from memory matching experiments with other techniques

No.	Technique	Reference	L^*	C^*_{ab}	h_{ab} (○)	a^*	b^*
1	Average measured	Buck and Froehlich (1948)	64	22	49	14.4	16.6
2	Most preferred colour	Bartleson and Bray (1962)	70	20	71	6.5	18.9
3	Abstract cue without image context Selecting method Mean finding	Bartleson (1960)	80	17	66	6.9	15.5
4	Memory matching cue with image context Selecting method Mean of the constant lightness, chroma, and hue intervals	Bodrogi (1998)	72	33	63	15.0	29.4
5	Memory matching cue without image context Selecting method Mean finding	Bartleson (1961)	76	31	49	20.3	23.4
6	Memory matching cue with image context Mixing-up method Mean of the constant lightness, chroma, and hue intervals, excluding 'tan skin'	Bodrogi and Tarczali (2001)	60	35	69	12.5	32.7

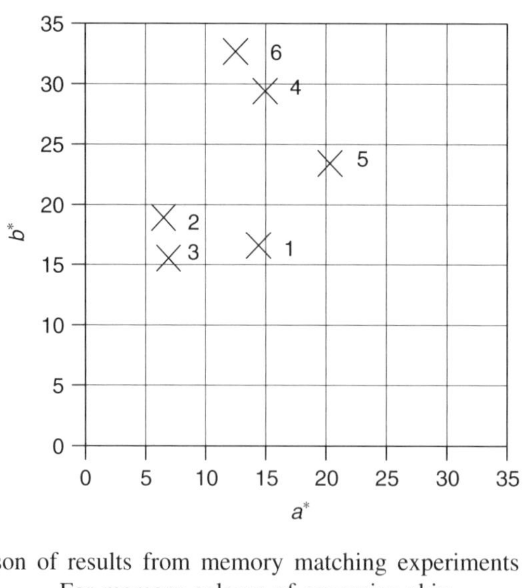

Figure 2.10 Comparison of results from memory matching experiments with other techniques. For memory colours of caucasian skin.

overlapping the abscissa (see the arrows at the bottom of Figures 2.6 to 2.9). Such a definition reveals an important property of memory colour shifts: there exist such hue, chroma and lightness intervals for original colours in which there is a tendency of no significant hue, chroma and lightness memory shifts.

Nevertheless, it seems worthwhile to mention the weak points of the concept of constant intervals:

- The range of the constant intervals depends on the range of original colours O used in the experiments.
- The size of the confidence intervals depends on the number of subjects who participated in the experiment.
- It is assumed that *all* memory shifts within the constant intervals are *not* significant, although there are *some* confidence intervals not overlapping the abscissa within certain constant intervals.

Considering only one type of object (sky or skin or plant), memory shifts seem to be *systematic* in the sense that they tend to be *directed toward constant intervals*, especially for photos (P). What might be the reason for this finding? To answer this question, we should examine the process happening in the time interval t (Section 2.3.1). Although the instruction given to the observer was to memorise the original colour and then try to express the colour in their mind, it is very likely that, during the time interval t, they were also *comparing* M with a *long-term memory colour* of the familiar object (sky or skin or plant).

For the *memory matching cue with image context*, i.e. for photorealistic images (P), the shape/texture of the familiar object was *observed* together with the original colour patch. For *memory matching cue without image context*, i.e. images with stand-alone patches (SA), it may be *possible* that the familiar object was *imagined* based on the original colour of the stand-alone patch (SA). The reason for this assumption is the similarity of the memory shift *tendencies* of the photos (P) and the images with stand-alone patches (SA). Long-term memory colours of familiar objects often seen in the past are also called *prototypical colours*. According to Yendrikhovskij *et al.* [15, 32], the perceived naturalness of a colour image is a result of a comparison between the perceived original colour O (or the instant memory colour M) and the prototypical colour. Departure from the prototypical colours causes naturalness to decrease.

From our point of view, observers tend to perceive an increased naturalness of M. In other words, observers tend to *shift* M toward the prototypical colour, resulting in the later memory colour M′. Note that observers seemed to *shift* the original colour toward the prototypical colour and *not to replace it* by the prototypical colour. If the original colour O is lying within a *tolerance bound* [15] of perceived naturalness around the prototypical colour, then naturalness will become acceptable and the hue, chroma and lightness shifts will not be significant, i.e. the original colour O will be in a constant interval.

For stand-alone uniform patches, the identification of the prototype may be indirect or missing because subjects do not see the image context (e.g. the shape of a face or the texture of grass) together with the colour patch to be memorised. That is why constant intervals of stand-alone uniform patches are broader than the constant intervals of the photographs.

2.6 THEORIES OF COLOUR MEMORY

The light entering the human eye evokes a colour perception and an instantaneous memory colour M. As described in Section 2.3.1, M is subject to changes in short-term colour memory from one viewing situation to the next. These memory shifts occur in all three perceptual colour dimensions: hue, chroma and lightness. Several authors agree that these memory shifts cannot be explained by sensory mechanisms or adaptation differences [4, 16–18].

2.6.1 Photoreceptor and surface reflectance hypotheses

Jin and Shevell [16] discussed the relationship between colour memory and colour constancy. They argued that because colour constancy is defined in terms of a change in illumination, it implies that the phenomenon occurs over some period of time. Therefore understanding memory shifts and the accuracy of colour memory are fundamental to understanding colour constancy. They tested two hypotheses of colour memory: (1) the *photoreceptor hypothesis*, which states that the colour recalled from memory 'reproduces' the light absorbed by each type of cone, and (2) the *surface reflectance hypothesis*, which states that the colour recalled from memory is based on an inferred spectral reflectance of a surface that does not depend on the spectral distribution of the illuminant. They were interested in whether or not the illuminant under which one learned a surface colour altered the colour produced from memory. Discounting of the illuminant in colour memory would then specify that the settings of colours from memory during the test phase would be the same regardless of the illuminant in the training phase.

Their experiments consisted of a training phase and a test phase. In the training phase, a central patch (test colour, there were six of them) that had to be memorised was surrounded by either a complex pattern composed of several coloured patches (first condition), or a uniform grey field at the chromaticity of the illuminant (second condition), or in a control condition, the test colour was presented on a dark background (third condition). These three conditions represented three different types of image context for the presentation of the test colour, but this type of image context was not pictorial information. In the test phase, the task of the subject was to adjust the colour of the central patch so that it looked the same as the colour they saw during the training phase.

The results from the third condition showed that the average recalled colour accurately reproduced the test colour. The results from the first condition were consistent with the *surface reflectance hypothesis*, i.e. with discounting of the illuminant used during the training phase of the experiment. There was much weaker discounting of the illuminant used during training with the second condition. In the first condition and in the third condition, memory shifts of the test colours occurred both in saturation and in hue. Jin and Shevell [16] argued that 'a possible explanation for larger memory shifts in the first condition concerns the representation of colour in memory'.

2.6.2 Adaptation and retention hypotheses

Newhall *et al.* [18] considered two alternative hypotheses to answer the question of why memory shifts occur: the *adaptation hypothesis* and the *retention hypothesis*. The *adaptation hypothesis* explained the memory shifts by the difference of the state of adaptation between the two viewing situations. In the Newhall experiment, this difference might have occurred because the observer was allowed to see the test colour for only 5 s but averaged 25 s in completing the subsequent memory task. These conditions would seem to guarantee greater adaptation to the matching colour than to the test colour because of longer time. The average memory matching time for each test colour was correlated with the average chroma and lightness shifts. The Pearson coefficient was not significantly above zero. This was not in accordance with the adaptation hypothesis. The Newhall and Pugh supplementary experiment (summarised in Section 2.2) also failed to favour the adaptation hypothesis because there was no experimental presentation of the test colours. Instead, observers were asked to match their own long-term memory colours of familiar objects by naming these objects.

Newhall *et al.* [18] explained their experimental results by the *retention hypothesis*, which stated that an (instant) memory colour was a selective result of the relative 'impressiveness' of various aspects of the original colour stimulus. Selection occurs during perception. More dominant, characteristic and attractive aspects tend to be more impressive and more prone to survival in short-term memory.

2.6.3 Cognitive effect hypothesis

Our so-called *cognitive effect hypothesis* is a modified and more detailed formulation of the retention hypothesis. The photoreceptor and surface reflectance hypotheses explain only how colour information is recalled from memory, but not memory shifts. The adaptation hypothesis was disproved by the existence of memory shifts even in identical viewing conditions. Our cognitive effect hypothesis states that memory shifts between the instant memory colour M and the later memory colour M′ result from one or more of three types of so-called cognitive effects: *exaggeration* (E), *focality* (F) and *typicality* (T).

The exaggeration effect (E) was deduced from the experimental fact that memory shifts tend toward more saturated colours or toward white to avoid storing a 'soiled' perception in short-term colour memory. Also a bright perception turns even brighter and a dark perception even darker in short-term colour memory. Thus observers tend to avoid storing 'medium' brightness or saturation in short-term colour memory.

The focality effect (F) was deduced from the fact that there are only 11 basic colour categories with *monolexemic* colour names, corresponding to distinct regions of colour space [19–21]. There is a *focal colour* in each region: the one named with the shortest response times and with consensus by many observers. The 11 regions of basic colours do not cover the whole colour space. In short-term colour memory, categorisation may occur: millions of perceptually different colours map into only 11 categories and observers may remember only the name of the colour category [22], e.g. 'orange'. This means that a discrete recoding of the perception [23] must be taking place. Focal colours are remembered more accurately than non-focal colours [24]. In short-term colour memory, an instantaneous memory colour M may be replaced by the focal colour to become a later memory colour M′, or M may shift toward the focal colour.

The typicality effect T is described in Section 2.5, whereby observers tend to *shift* M toward the prototypical colour.

The three types of cognitive effect described above may result from three abstraction levels of the colour information of actual objects. From the specific to the general, these three abstraction levels may be as follows:

1. From many objects of the same type (often seen in the past) a *prototypical colour* is deduced. Its semantic representation is the name of that object (e.g. grass). The corresponding cognitive effect is *typicality*.
2. From several similar types of object (e.g. foliage + grass + wood) a *focal colour* is deduced. Its semantic representation is a basic colour term [19]. The corresponding cognitive effect is *focality*.
3. From many different objects, two discrete attributes are deduced: lightness and chroma. The corresponding cognitive effect is *exaggeration*.

2.7 CONCLUSIONS

This chapter has compared and classified different psychophysical methods to investigate the characteristics of human colour memory. Some new experimental techniques were added to those found in the literature. Experimental data resulting from the different techniques have been compared. For a given type of image context (e.g. sky or skin or plant), systematic memory shifts have been found: the memory shift M–M′ was directed toward the long-term memory colour or prototypical colour of the given image context. Several theories of colour memory have been described.

ACKNOWLEDGEMENTS

One author (PB) acknowledges the support of the Hungarian OTKA, grant F025 169, the support of the US-Hungarian joint fund, and the support of the German Academic Exchange Service (DAAD).

REFERENCES

1. Guilford, J. P. (1954) *Psychometric Methods*. New York: McGraw-Hill.
2. Bartleson, C. J. (1959) Some observations on the reproduction of flesh colours. *Photographic Science and Engineering*, **3**, 114–117.
3. Bartleson, C. J. and Bray C. P. (1962) On the preferred reproduction of flesh, blue-sky, and green-grass colours. *Photographic Science and Engineering*, **6**, 19–25.

4. Siple P. and Springer R. M. (1983) Memory and preference for the colours of objects. *Perception & Psychophysics*, **34**, 363–370.
5. Buck, G. B. and Froelich, H. C. (1948) Colour characteristics of human complexions. *Illum. Eng.* **43**, 27–49.
6. Hendley, C. D., and Hecht, S. (1949) The colours of natural objects and terrains, and their relation to visual colour deficiency. *J. Opt. Soc. Am.*, **39**, 870–873.
7. Pérez-Carpinell J., Baldoví R., de Fez M. D., and Castro J. (1998a) Colour memory matching: time effect and other factors. *Col. Res. Appl.*, **23**, 234–247.
8. Pérez-Carpinell J., de Fez M. D., Baldoví R., and Soriano J. C. (1998b) Familiar objects and memory colour. *Col. Res. Appl.*, **23**, 416–425.
9. Taft, C. (1997) Colour meaning and context: comparisons of semantic ratings of colours on samples and objects. *Colour Res. Appl.*, **22**, 40–50.
10. Bodrogi, P. (1998) Shifts of short-term colour memory. PhD thesis University of Veszprém, http://knt.vein.hu/Bodrogi/phdeng12.doc.
11. Bodrogi P., Rehák R., Tenk K. and Schanda J. (1998) Cognitive factors of colour appearance. *Proc. Colour Imaging in Multimedia, CIM'98 Conference*, Derby, UK.
12. Bodrogi P. and Tarczali, T. (2000) Corresponding colours: the effect of colour memory. *Proc. Colour Image Science CIS'2000 Conference*, Derby, UK.
13. Bodrogi P. and Tarczali, T. (2001) Colour memory for various sky, skin, and plant colours: effect of the image context. *Col. Res. Appl.*, **26**, 278–289.
14. Bartleson, C. J. (1960) Memory colours of familiar objects. *J. Opt. Soc. Am.*, **50**, 73–77.
15. Yendrikhovskij S. N., Blommaert F. J. J. and de Ridder H. (1999a) Colour reproduction and the naturalness constraint. *Col. Res. Appl.*, **24**, 52–67.
16. Jin, E. W. and Shevell, S. K. (1996) Colour memory and colour constancy. *J. Opt. Soc. Am.*, **A13**, 1981–1991.
17. Nilsson T. H. and Nelson T. M. (1981) Delayed monochromatic hue matches indicate characteristics of visual memory. *J. Exp. Psychol.* **7**, 141–150.
18. Newhall S. M., Burnham R. W. and Clark J. R. (1957) Comparison of successive with simultaneous colour matching. *J. Opt. Soc. Am.*, **47**, 43–56.
19. Berlin, B. and Kay, P. (1969) *Basic Colour Terms: Their Universality and Evolution. Berkeley*: University of California Press.
20. Boynton, R. M. and Olson, C. X. (1987) Locating basic colours in the OSA space. *Colour Res. Appl.*, **12**, 94–105.
21. Lin, H., Luo, M. R., MacDonald, L. W., and Tarrant, A. W. S. (2001) A cross-cultural colour-naming study. Part II–using a constrained Method. *Col. Res. Appl.*, **26**, 193–208.
22. Boynton, R. M., Fargo, L., Olson, C. X. and Smallman, H. S. (1989) Category effects in colour memory. *Colour Res. Appl.*, **14**, 229–234.
23. Stalmeier, P. F. M. and de Weert, C. M. M. (1991) Large colour differences and selective attention. *J. Opt. Soc. Am.*, **A8**, 237–247.
24. Heider, E. R. (1972) Universals in colour naming and memory. *J. Exp. Psychol.*, **93**, 10–20.
25. Adams, G. K. (1923), *Am. J. Psychol.* **34**, 359.
26. Baker, K. E. and Mackintosh, I. (1955), *J. Exp. Psychol.* **49**, 281–286.
27. Bartleson, C. J. (1961) Colour in memory in relation to photographic reproduction. *Photographic Science and Engineering*, **5**, 327–331.
28. Collins, M. (1931/32) *Br. J. Psychol.*, **22**, 344–352.
29. Katz, D. (1935) *The World of Colour*. London: Kegan Paul, Trench, Trubner & Co.
30. Koffka, K. (1935) *Principles of Gestalt Psychology*. New York: Harcourt Brace and Co.
31. Wulf, F. (1922) *Psychol. Forsch.*, **1**, 333–373.
32. Yendrikhovskij S. N., Blommaert F. J. J. and de Ridder H. (1999b) Representation of memory prototype for an object colour. *Col. Res. Appl.*, **24**, 393–410.
33. Hamwi, V. and Landis, C. (1955) Memory for colour. *J. Psychol.*, **39**, 183–194.

3

Perception of colour differences in large printed images

Joan Uroz, Ronnier Luo and Ján Morovic

3.1 INTRODUCTION

Evaluation of colour difference is essential for colour quality control in the surface colour industries such as textile and paint. In fact, most of the advances in this field have been energised by the demands of these industries. Since the recommendation in 1976 by the CIE of the CIELAB and CIELUV colour difference formulae [1], many large-scale psychophysical experiments have been performed [2–5]. These have consisted of the visual evaluation of very large collections of uniformly coloured patches of a given size. The experimental data, revealing large discrepancies between the visual results and the predictions of the 1976 formulae, have been used to derive more advanced formulae such as CMC [6], BFD [7, 8] and CIE94 [9]. These all give much more accurate predictions to the experimental data than CIELAB and CIELUV. Currently CMC and CIE94 formulae have been adopted as ISO standards [10, 11] for evaluating colour differences for the textile and paint industries respectively; moreover, the new CIE Technical Committee TC1-47 was formed in 1997 to further investigate 'hue and lightness dependent correction to industrial colour difference evaluation'.

Colour Image Science, edited by L.W. MacDonald and M.R. Luo.

Unfortunately, advanced colour difference formulae still do not necessarily predict accurately the colour differences between complex stimuli such as photographic images. Digital colour reproduction systems have developed their capability to handle increasingly larger sizes and complex contents, with higher throughput and image quality. The need for better image quality leads to, but is not limited to, higher requirements of colour accuracy and repeatability. Just one example of the innovative use of colour reproduction technology is the National Gallery in London. To help in the restoration processes of Britain's collection of Western European paintings, they combine leading-edge digital image capture technology [12], image processing and large-format thermal inkjet printing as the means to print accurate reproductions of the paintings [13]. As the reproductions need to be viewed side by side with the original paintings, the requirements of colour accuracy and consistency for the colour reproduction system must be very strict. It is therefore of the greatest importance for the digital imaging industry in general, and digital printing in particular, to have models and formulae that correctly predict colour difference perception in complex images. In response to these needs, there is an increasing body of research in the subject. Also the CIE Technical Committee TC8-02 has been formed to study, develop and standardise methods to derive colour differences for images [14].

This chapter describes experiments to determine the magnitude of the just noticeable difference (JND) or threshold of perceptibility between colour stimuli when these stimuli are images printed using an inkjet printer. Psychophysical experiments of colour difference involving images are inherently more complex than those involving uniform colours, because of the varying size of the colour areas and perceptual interactions between them. Whether or not image content influences the perceptibility threshold of colour changes is a controversial issue. While some researchers have reported independence [15, 16], recent studies on printed media show that scene content influences the perceptibility of colour changes in photographic images [17, 18]. The subject is of very high practical importance, because if image composition did not influence the perceptibility threshold, then data from a small set of test images could be generalised to any image.

The choice of the colour transformations used in the generation of test stimuli is also important in practice. If the colour transformations used for the experiment corresponded to those likely to be induced by the colour reproduction system itself, conclusions relevant for the system design could be drawn from the experimental data. Most of the colour transformations reported in the literature are systematic variations in the perceptual colour dimensions of lightness, chroma and hue. Research on perception of colour differences in images has been most often based in the use of CRT monitors as the colour reproduction medium. Stokes used a CRT to present images with systematic changes in hue angle, chroma and lightness to a panel of 44 observers [15]. The nature of the colour changes corresponded to alterations that are likely to be introduced by CRT displays. The mathematical operations of addition or multiplication can be considered as corresponding to common characteristics of devices, such as colour shifts or gain. The behaviour of CRT displays can be correctly predicted by analytical models in which shift, gain, gamma or contrast are parameters [19].

Unfortunately, printers are difficult to model analytically. Therefore, the kind of transformations already exposed may not be as easily applied to meaningful printer characteristics. For reflection prints, other researchers have used colour transformations in a device-dependent space instead of in a device-independent space [20–22]. Further emulating likely device-dependent errors, it seems logical to consider transformations emulating some type of noise, which in more or less degree, affects all the components of any imaging system. The effect of random noise could be modelled by random changes in colour. McCann [23] studied colour reproduction preferences using Mondrian images, some showing large systematic colour differences and some showing exactly the same error magnitudes, but in random directions in CIELAB space (see also Chapter 11). Observers always rated the systematically shifted image as the preferred reproduction. Although his work was on preference (not perceptibility) of large colour errors, it could be an indication that the perceptibility thresholds of a random colour error are much smaller than those corresponding to systematic errors.

3.2 EXPERIMENT OVERVIEW

A colour reproduction system was implemented, and its ability to produce printed stimuli very close to each other in colour was quantified. Then a set of colour images was printed with increasing systematic differences in lightness or chroma, and increasing random differences in lightness, chroma and hue. For each modified image, a colour chart including its most prominent colours was printed, at the same time as the image itself. Since the colours that could be measured in the individual charts were the same as those

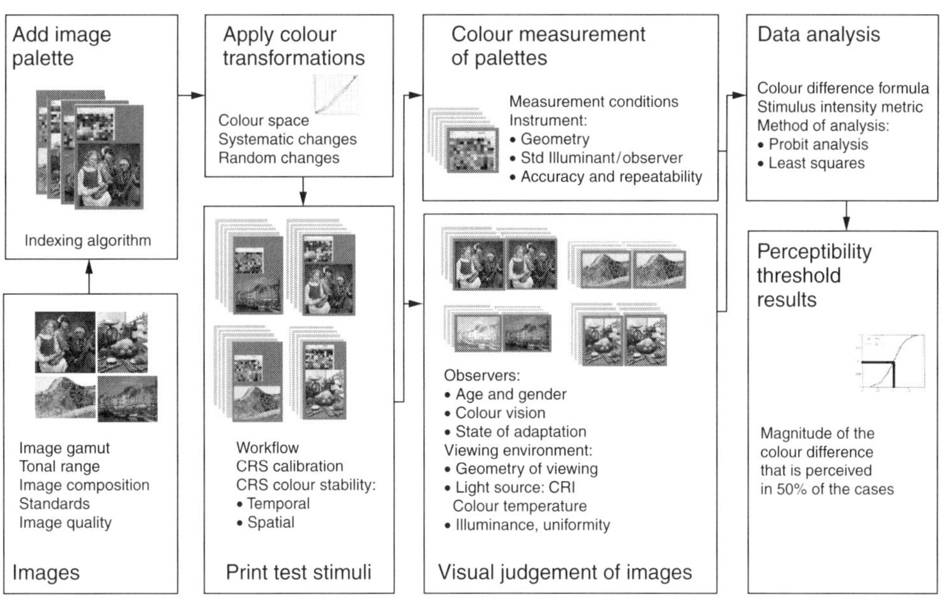

Figure 3.1 Block diagram of the experiments, indicating important factors that were considered during their design.

present in the individually modified images, accurate colorimetric calculations relative to the actual stimuli judged by the observers were possible.

Pairs of images showing various levels of colour difference were evaluated in two separate psychophysical experiments. In Experiment 1 only systematic colour changes were present. Experiment 2 was aimed at investigating perceptibility of random colour changes. Data were analysed using probit analysis. Figure 3.1 illustrates the workflow of the experiment.

Important experimental variables are discussed in detail through the following sections. They include the colour transformations, the choice of images, viewing environment, colour difference formulae and psychophysical methods.

3.3 COLOUR TRANSFORMATIONS

Most causes of colour variability in thermal inkjet (TIJ) printing are related to the variability in the size of the printed individual dots. Because of this, colours tend to change in chroma and/or lightness. Hue changes will generally only appear as loss of colour balance. The effects on printed colour of dot size variability were simulated by systematic changes in lightness and chroma applied to the original images. Noise is likely to affect colour reproduction systems. The effect of noise was modelled by random colour changes affecting lightness, chroma and hue, which result in generalised colour changes, including the loss of colour balance in the grey areas.

Colour changes can be applied in either an increasing or decreasing direction in a given perceptual colour dimension. Earlier studies demonstrated that the threshold levels of colour changes in the increasing direction of lightness or chroma were symmetrical to those in the decreasing direction [15]. Although these studies were on CRT media, it seemed at least reasonable to assume symmetry in this work. Thus, colour changes were only applied in the direction of gamut reduction. This had the additional benefit of reducing the possibility of transformed colours being out of the gamut of the printer.

3.3.1 Systematic transformations

Images with systematic variations of lightness were generated from the original images by applying the pixelwise power transformation given in equation (3.1), using six levels of the α parameter (Table 3.1). This transformation simulates the change in lightness due to a systematic variation in dot size in the printing system. The typical curves predicted by equation (3.1) are shown in Figure 3.2.

$$L^*_{\mathrm{out}} = L_K + (L_W - L_K)\left(\frac{(L^*_{in} - L_K)}{(L_W - L_K)}\right)^{\alpha} \tag{3.1}$$

where $L_K = 3$ is the L^* value of printed black, $L_W = 93$ is the L^* value of the white paper, L^*_{out} is the transformed value of L^*_{in}, $\alpha > 1$.

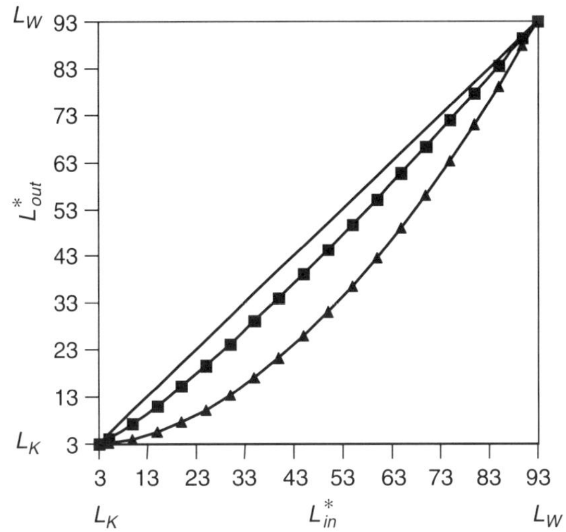

Figure 3.2 Power transfer function used to generate systematic lightness changes in the images: no change (solid line), $\alpha = 1.2$ (filled square), $\alpha = 1.5$ (filled triangle). When $\alpha > 1$ the L^* transformed values are smaller than the original L^* values. Note the two anchor points at $L^*_{in} = L_K$ and $L^*_{out} = L_W$.

Table 3.1 Colour difference between image palettes, versus values of the α, k and m parameters for the image Musicians

Chroma systematic transformation			Lightness systematic transformation			Random transformation		
k	Avg. ΔE^*_{ab}	99th pct ΔE^*_{ab}	α	Avg. ΔE^*_{ab}	99th pct ΔE^*_{ab}	m	Avg. ΔE^*_{ab}	99th pct ΔE^*_{ab}
0.967	1.89	4.53	1.05	1.42	2.62	0.5	1.22	2.19
0.963	2.19	5.47	1.10	2.49	5.90	1.0	1.59	2.70
0.900	2.79	7.27	1.15	3.60	8.48	1.5	1.92	3.52
0.867	3.49	9.16	1.20	4.83	10.76	2.0	2.41	3.99
0.833	4.42	11.28	1.25	5.67	13.24	3.0	3.61	5.82
0.800	5.19	13.05	1.30	6.78	14.77			

Images with systematic variations of chroma were generated from the original images by the pixel-to-pixel multiplicative transformation given in equation (3.2), using six levels of the k parameter:

$$C^*_{out} = kC^*_{in} \quad (k < 1) \tag{3.2}$$

Suitable values of α and k were determined in a pilot experiment. The objective was to generate a range of test stimuli that would likely include the perceptibility threshold level, while having enough resolution to avoid unanimous judgements. Table 3.1 contains the values used for the α and k parameters. Notice that $\alpha > 1$ and $k < 1$ values were used in order to transform pixels colour in the direction of a gamut reduction. Six levels of the α parameter were used to generate six lightness-altered versions of each of the four original images, therefore 24 prints showing systematic variations in lightness were produced in total. Six levels of the k parameter were used to generate six chroma-altered versions of each of the four original images, therefore 24 prints showing systematic variations in chroma were produced in total.

3.3.2 Random transformation

Randomly modified images were generated from the original ones by a point transformation. Every pixel in the modified image deviated from its corresponding pixel in the original image by a value $d\ \Delta E^*_{ab}$, whereby d was a random variable with chi-squared distribution of mean m. Increasing stimulus intensities were achieved by increasing levels of the mean m. The direction of change of the pixel's colour was also random. In a spherical coordinate system centred on the pixel, the direction of change was determined by the angles α and θ (Figure 3.3). These were random variables normally distributed with mean equal to the direction of the point $L^* = 50$, $a^* = 0$, $b^* = 0$; and with standard deviation equal to 15°. Hence 99.865% of the directions of change were limited to ±45° around the direction of the point $L^* = 50$, $a^* = 0$, $b^* = 0$. In summary, every transformed pixel was in a limited area on the surface of a sphere of radius d and centre in the original pixel. All transformed images used the same pixel direction transformation, but with increasing levels of m and hence ΔE^*_{ab}. The magnitudes of m as well as the ±45° limit for α and

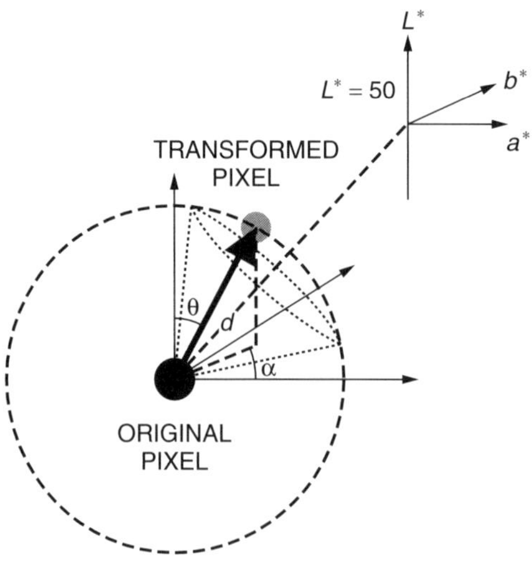

Figure 3.3 Random colour transformation in CIELAB colour space, centred on the pixel's colour coordinates.

θ were determined in a pilot experiment, in order to generate a range of stimuli with enough resolution around the probable threshold level. Colour changes were constrained to the 'inwards' direction, corresponding to gamut compression.

The values in or near the grey axis were also transformed; this was visible in the form of colour casts in the neutral colours. Five levels of the m parameter were used to generate five randomly altered versions of each of two original images, therefore 10 prints showing random variations in lightness, chroma and hue were produced in total (Table 3.1).

3.4 THE CIE 1976 AND 1995 COLOUR DIFFERENCE FORMULAE

In the CIELAB colour space, the colour difference between two points is defined as the Euclidean distance between them:

$$\Delta E^*_{ab} = (\Delta L^{*2} + \Delta a^{*2} + \Delta b^{*2})^{1/2} \tag{3.3}$$

where, for two colour points 1 and 2,

$$\Delta L^* = L^*_1 - L^*_2$$

$$\Delta a^* = a^*_1 - a^*_2$$

$$\Delta b^* = b^*_1 - b^*_2$$

ΔE^*_{ab} can also be expressed as a function of the differences in lightness, chroma and hue between the two colour points, in cylindrical coordinates, as

$$\Delta E^*_{ab} = (\Delta L^{*2} + \Delta C^{*2}_{ab} + \Delta H^{*2}_{ab})^{1/2} \tag{3.4}$$

where

$$\Delta L^* = L^*_1 - L^*_2$$

$$\Delta C^*_{ab} = C^*_{ab,1} - C^*_{ab,2}$$

but

$$\Delta H^*_{ab} \neq \Delta h_{ab} \qquad \Delta h_{ab} = \Delta h_{ab,1} - \Delta h_{ab,2}$$

because Δh_{ab} is expressed in degrees and therefore is incommensurate with ΔL^* and ΔC^*_{ab}.

There are several ways to calculate ΔH^*_{ab}; each has advantages and disadvantages. One of the best is proposed here [24]:

$$\Delta H^*_{ab} = s\left[2\left(C^*_{ab,1}C^*_{ab,2} - a^*_1a^*_2 - b^*_1b^*_2\right)\right]^{1/2}$$

$$s = 1 \quad \text{if } a^*_1b^*_2 < a^*_2b^*_1$$

$$s = -1 \quad \text{if } a^*_1b^*_2 > a^*_2b^*_1 \tag{3.5}$$

The CIE94 colour difference formula was published as a CIE technical report in 1995, and was recommended for the calculation of small to moderate colour differences. It provides a means of changing the relative contribution of lightness, chroma and hue, through the coefficients k_L, k_C and k_H in equation (3.6):

$$\Delta E^*_{94} = \left[\left(\frac{\Delta L^*}{k_L S_L}\right)^2 + \left(\frac{\Delta C^*_{ab}}{k_C S_C}\right)^2 + \left(\frac{\Delta H^*_{ab}}{k_H S_H}\right)^2\right]^{1/2} \tag{3.6}$$

$$S_L = 1$$

$$S_C = 1 + 0.045\left(C^*_{ab,1}C^*_{ab,2}\right)^{1/2}$$

$$S_H = 1 + 0.015\left(C^*_{ab,1}C^*_{ab,2}\right)^{1/2}$$

Under default conditions k_L, k_C and k_H are set to 1. Under specific experimental conditions, different values of k_L, k_C and k_H would optimise the correlation with visual results.

3.5 COLOUR REPRODUCTION SYSTEM

The test stimuli were generated using an HP DesignJet 2500CP large-format thermal inkjet printer. The HP DesignJet 2500CP can print on a variety of media using either dye-based or pigmented inks. Inks are contained in the replaceable cyan, magenta, yellow and black *printheads*. Ink droplets are ejected through the *nozzles* in the printhead's *nozzleplate* to hit the media, forming printed C, M, Y and K *dots*, at a maximum resolution of 600 dpi × 600 dpi. When the ink level in the printheads is low, these are *refilled* automatically from the *ink cartridges,* also inside the printer, through a valve system. The images used in the present work were printed on HP semi-gloss photo paper using dye-based HP CP inks.

Calibration is the process whereby a system or device is set to a known state, from which it can operate in a repeatable manner. The calibration procedure must take into account the causes of output variability and must provide the means, or specify the actions, needed to calibrate the device. The HP DesignJet 2500CP has a built-in closed-loop colour calibration system, designed to remove automatically most of the output colour variation without the need of user intervention. This system is appropriate for calibrating colour

Table 3.2 Colour difference between colour charts printed in close succession and after one week

Test chart	Number of colours	Close succession		Time interval one week	
		Avg ΔE^*_{ab}	95th percentile ΔE^*_{ab}	Avg ΔE^*_{ab}	95th percentile ΔE^*_{ab}
IT8.7/3 basic	182	0.50	1.53	1.06	2.40
Gaudi palette	128	0.24	1.45	1.09	1.97

under normal usage conditions. In order to produce images in which uncontrolled colour variability is reduced to well below threshold values, a more complex colour calibration procedure was used. This procedure is called the 'accurate calibration procedure' in the following paragraphs. The effectiveness of the calibration procedure is, i.e. the stablility of the calibrated state, is quantified indirectly by the long-term colour repeatability results in Table 3.2.

Important sources of colour output error considered were temporal stability, spatial uniformity, and short- and long-term repeatability. Colour accuracy was not taken into account, as we were only interested in measuring differences between colour stimuli. Whether the original images were accurate reproductions of some standard was less important for the purpose of this work.

3.5.1 Temporal stability

In order to characterise the temporal colour stability of prints, an IT8.7/3 basic colour chart, containing 182 colour patches, was printed. It was measured one hour after being printed, and successively at 1 day intervals over 18 days. While not being measured, the print was stored inside a cabinet. Most of the colour variation occurred during the first day, and colours in the chart remained much more stable afterwards (Figure 3.4 and Table 3.3).

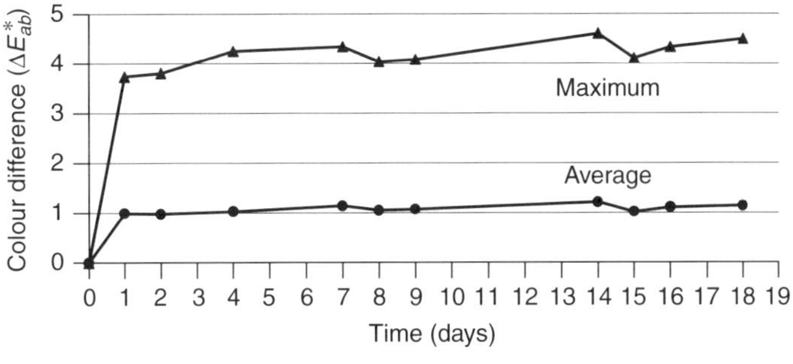

Figure 3.4 Average and maximum colour change over time of an IT8.7/3 basic target printed with an HP DesignJet 2500CP on HP semi-gloss photo paper and dye-based HP CP inks in conditions of no exposure to light.

Table 3.3 HP DesignJet 2500 CP characteristics, after calibration, on HP semi-gloss photo paper and CP inks

Characteristic	Avg. ΔE^*_{ab}	99th pct ΔE^*_{ab}
Temporal stability patchwise colour difference between successive measurements of an IT8.7/3 basic colour chart, in dark conditions	1.0	4.0
Spatial uniformity colour difference from patch colour to page mean colour, for a C40M40Y40K40 uniform input colour specification over a 90 × 72 cm page	0.5	0.8
Short-term repeatability patchwise colour difference from patch colour to patch mean colour, for in-gamut colours, for two consecutive prints	0.25	1.5
Long-term repeatability colour difference from patch colour to patch mean colour, for in-gamut colours, for two prints printed with an interval of 7 days	1.1	2.0

The implication for our experiment was that the visual evaluation of the photographic images and the measurement of the associated palettes could be uncorrelated if performed at different times. Correcting for colour deviations as a function of time was considered but rejected. The much more effective and accurate approach taken was to measure the palettes on the same day as the psychophysical experiments were performed.

3.5.2 Spatial uniformity

Colour spatial uniformity is the ability of the printer to print the same colour independently of the location on the page. Spatial uniformity was characterised as the ΔE^*_{ab} colour difference between the average page colour and the colour printed at each spatial location, when printing a uniform 40% C–40% M–40% Y–40% K (grayish) colour page. CIELAB coordinates of the average page colour were $L^* = 46.41$, $a^* = 1.66$, $b^* = -2.77$.

Printing the grey page just after a warm-up page, the average ΔE^*_{ab} colour difference between locations and the mean grey was 0.49 ΔE^*_{ab} and the maximum was 0.83 ΔE^*_{ab} (Table 3.3). Figure 3.5 illustrates the spatial distribution of the error.

According to these results, the accurate calibration protocol included sending a warm-up page at the beginning of every print session, and adding a grey frame to all printed images. In this way the colour error due to spatial non-uniformity could be limited to 0.49 ΔE^*_{ab} on average.

3.5.3 Short- and long-term repeatability

Colour repeatability is the ability of the printer to print the same colours when printing the same image several times. An IT8.7/3 basic chart and a palette made up of 128 colours present in the Gaudi image were printed twice in close succession, then a week later they were printed one more time. On both occasions the printer was calibrated using the accurate calibration procedure.

Short-term repeatability refers to the colour differences between the two successively printed charts. Long-term repeatability refers to the colour differences between the original

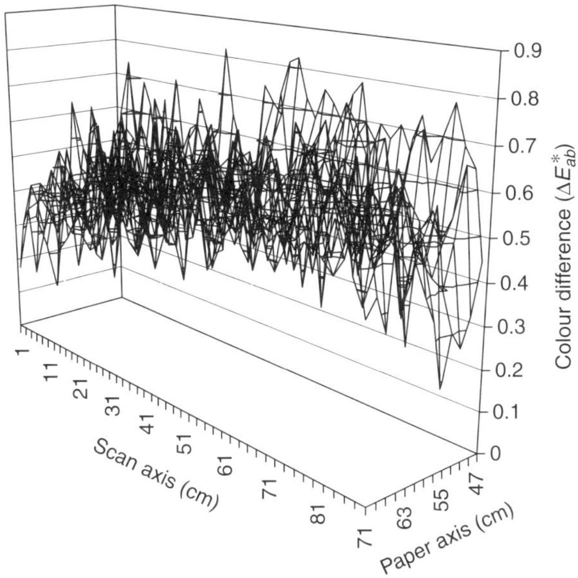

Figure 3.5 Magnitude of colour difference between spatial locations in a grey page and the average grey colour. The paper axis refers to the direction of advance of the paper; the scan axis refers to the direction of movement of the printheads.

charts and the charts printed one week later. Short- and long-term repeatability results are summarised in Table 3.2.

The repeatability error of a palette of colours contained in the Gaudi image represents better the magnitude of the error than that of the IT8.7/3 chart, because the latter covered colour regions that were not used in this experiment.

3.6 GENERATION OF THE TEST IMAGES

Important factors considered for the choice of the test images were colour gamut, object size, presence of memory colours, natural and man-made objects. The four images selected are represented in Figure 3.6. Fruit, Musicians and Harbor are well-known standards containing colours covering a wide range of lightness, chroma and hue [25, 26]. The Gaudi image was selected because it contains a variety of different hues, and because of the smaller size of the recognisable objects in the picture.

For each of the images, a single file was made up including the image itself and a palette containing its 128 most prominent colours. The adaptive palette indexing function in Adobe Photoshop was used to extract the palette colours. These resultant four original images could then be colour-altered to generate the test stimuli for the experiment. This arrangement was convenient to minimise the mismatch between visual measurements on the images and instrumental measurements on the palettes. By printing the image and its

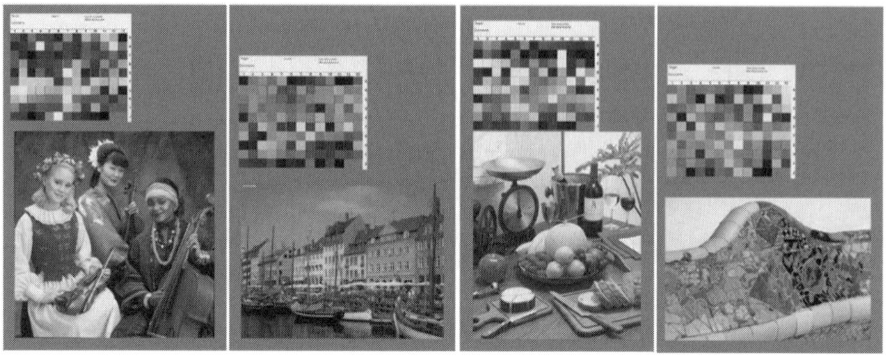

Figure 3.6 The four original test images. Left to right: SCID Musicians, SHIPP Harbor, Fruit, Gaudi. Image and palette were pasted into a single sheet (Photos N7 and N7A of ISO Standard 12640:1997, Figure 1, are reproduced with the permission of the International Organization for Standardization, ISO. This standard can be obtained from any ISO member and from the website of the ISO Central Secretariat at the following address: http://www.iso.org. Copyright remains with ISO. Colour versions are shown in Plate 2 (top). SHIPP Harbour and Fruit images: taken from K. Sakamoto, H. Urabe, Standard High Precision Pictures. The Fifth Color Imaging Conference: Color Science, Systems, and Applications 1997.

palette on the same sheet, undesirable colour mismatches between image and palette – due to printer repeatability – were minimised. By measuring the palettes on the same day as the visual judgements of images were performed, it was possible to minimise colour mismatch due to temporal stability of the printouts. Hence only short-term repeatability and spatial colour uniformity errors shown in Table 3.3 influenced the test images.

3.7 VIEWING ENVIRONMENT

The pairs of test images were judged inside a Macbeth SpectraLight II viewing cabinet placed in a dark room. The light source was filtered tungsten halogen (colour rendering index of 100), simulating the CIE standard illuminant D50. These are standard viewing conditions in the graphic arts industry [27, 28]. Observers adapted to the viewing conditions for 5 min before starting the test (Figure 3.7).

The four test images selected had various aspect ratios and orientations. They were printed at a size in which the maximum dimension was 420 mm. The viewing distance was fixed to 1 m so the angle subtended by the maximum dimension of a test image was approximately 24°. At this distance, the halftone texture was not considered to affect observers' judgements of colour. At 1 m, the angle subtended by a 600 dpi printed dot, having a nominal diameter of 42 μm, is about 9 seconds of arc. This is equivalent to a spatial frequency of 200 cpd (cycles per degree), which is far beyond the highest perceptible spatial frequency (at high luminance levels) of 50–60 cpd [29]. The stimulus

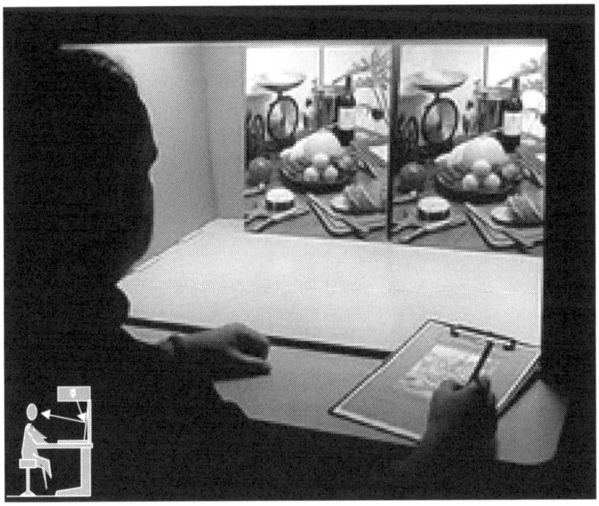

Figure 3.7 An observer evaluating a pair of Fruit images. The observer marks any perceived colour differences on the answer sheet.

size and viewing distance were chosen so that they subtended the same angle as a typical graphic arts print of size DIN A1, at a typical viewing distance of 2 m.

The viewing geometry was approximately 45/0, corresponding to the use of standard 45/0 geometry and D50 reference illuminant for the measurement of the colour charts.

3.8 PSYCHOPHYSICAL EXPERIMENTS

Psychophysics deals with establishing the relationship between measured stimulus intensities and the corresponding perceptual responses to these stimuli. Every time a stimulus of a given intensity is presented (trial) to a subject, a response to the stimulus occurs with some probability. In the present research, several pairs of printed images (stimuli) showing different levels of colour difference (stimulus intensity) were presented to a number of observers. As a result, positive responses ("Yes, I see these images are different.") or negative responses ("No they look the same.") occurred.

3.8.1 Method

A modified version of the single stimulus method was used [32]. A number of pairs of images were shown to observers in random order. Observers were asked to report (a) whether or not they could see the images in each pair to be different, and (b) where in the image the difference was perceived. For each image pair shown, an answer sheet was provided containing a sketch of the image. The observers identified the location of the colour differences seen, by marking in the answer sheet. A similar technique of collecting observer responses has been used by Zhang [30]. The duration of the judgement sessions was intended to be around 30 min, to avoid judgements to be influenced by observer fatigue. The number of pairs per session was 24 in Experiment 1, and 18 in Experiment 2. All observers had normal colour vision, as per the results of Ishihara and Farnsworth–Munsell tests. Observers 1 to 5 (three male and two female) were experienced in evaluating colour differences; their average age was 32 years. Observers 6 to 9 (one female, three male) were less experienced in colour difference evaluation; their average age was 30 years.

3.8.2 Data analysis

For each visual stimulus (pair of images), the following data was collected:

- The colour differences between the individual colour patches in the corresponding image palettes, computed using the CIELAB ΔE^*_{ab}, $\Delta E^*_{94}(1{:}1{:}1)$ and $\Delta E^*_{94}(2{:}1{:}1)$ colour difference formulae.
- The number of times that the colour difference of the images was perceived.

Data were analysed using probit analysis [15, 18, 30–32], performed by means of Minitab R.13 statistical software. In probit analysis the distribution of positive responses to stimulus intensities is fitted to a reference distribution. Since stimulus intensities could not take negative values, a lognormal distribution was used as the reference distribution in our case. The solution, rather than being optimal in a least squares (or other error criteria) sense, is the one that has the maximum probability to occur. The threshold stimulus intensity, that corresponding to 50% of positive responses, as well as its 95% confidence limits, can then be read from the fitted data (Figure 3.8).

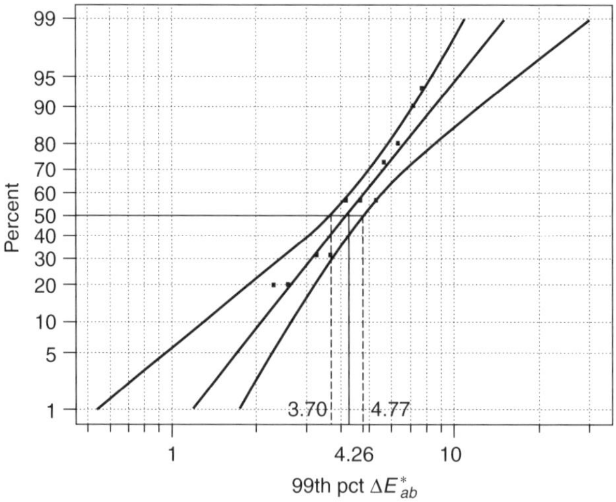

Figure 3.8 Probability of perception of systematic changes of chroma versus 99th percentile of CIELAB colour difference between image palette colours, plotted on normal probabilistic coordinates.

The statistical confidence on the results from probit analysis increases as the experimental data more closely follows the reference distribution. Minitab software provides a P-value to test the goodness of fit of the experimental data to the reference distribution. The P-value represents the probability of making a Type 1 error, which is rejecting the null hypothesis – that the experimental data follows a lognormal distribution – when it is true. The smaller the P-value, the smaller the probability that a mistake was made by rejecting the null hypothesis. $P < 0.05$ was used as a cut-off point for rejecting the null hypothesis.

3.8.3 Stimulus intensity metrics

Many different alternatives were possible for integrating patchwise colour differences between the pair's palettes into a single number representing the stimulus intensity. A first alternative was to use the arithmetic mean of patchwise colour differences. It did not seem an unreasonable starting point, as this criterion has been widely used in previous research [15, 17]. Another alternative was to use some kind of maxima, like the 95th or the 99th percentile of patchwise colour differences. The latter was suggested by an analysis of the observer comments and their behaviour during the psychophysical experiments. It seemed that their decisions were not triggered by a visual averaging process, but more likely they were unconsciously segmenting the image into recognisable features (apple, face, shirt, sky, etc.) and comparing these features one by one until they found *the first feature* that could be perceived as different.

Different distributions of experimental data would be obtained when describing stimulus intensity differently. The goodness of fit of experimental data to the reference distribution was generally better when using a high percentile of colour difference between palettes as stimulus intensity metric, than when using average colour difference. Hence the 99th percentile of colour difference between palette colours was preferred as the metric of perceptibility threshold of colour change in images.

3.9 EXPERIMENT 1: PERCEPTIBILITY THRESHOLDS OF INDEPENDENT LIGHTNESS OR CHROMA SYSTEMATIC CHANGES

Each of 4 original pictures was transformed in 6 increasing levels of either C^* or L^* changes, to obtain 24 L^*-modified and 24 C^*-modified prints. The palettes containing their 128 most significant colours were printed simultaneously with each. The process of generation of the images and palettes is described in Section 3.6.

From all possible pairs that could be formed with each image original plus its colour-altered copies, only 80 were chosen, including 40 lightness-altered and 40 chroma-altered. Pairs showing small and moderate colour difference were more numerous than pairs with higher colour difference. The reason for this was to obtain a higher number of judgements around the probable threshold level and to reduce the number of unanimous judgements, which provide little information about the threshold. They were judged in random order by 5 colour-normal observers, making a total of $80 \times 5 = 400$ observations (repetitions not included).

The colour differences between the corresponding patches in the image palettes for each of the pairs were computed using CIELAB ΔE^*_{ab}, ΔE^*_{94}(1:1:1) and ΔE^*_{94}(2:1:1) colour difference formulae. Three data items were collected for each pair:

- The 99th percentile of the colour differences between palettes (stimulus intensity)
- The number of times a pair was judged (number of trials)
- The number of times the difference could be perceived (number of successes)

Raw data were filtered before performing its analysis. Firstly, high-difference pairs whose colour difference was perceived unanimously by all observers were removed from the analysis. Secondly, data from individual pairs was categorised in classes where each class had its total number of trials and successes associated with the arithmetic mean of the individual stimulus intensities. For instance, the resulting classes for pairs showing systematic chroma differences are represented in Table 3.4.

The categorised data corresponding to the different cases (lightness or chroma changes, different colour difference formulae) were then fitted to a reference distribution using probit analysis. The threshold value and its confidence limits were extracted from each particular fit. For instance, the best fit for the data in Table 3.4 can be seen in Figure 3.8. The threshold values and confidence limits of all cases in Experiment 1 can be seen in Figure 3.9.

3.9.1 Comparison between colour difference formulae

With regard to its practical application, it would be highly desirable that the threshold of perceptibility of colour difference be independent of scene contents and colour dimension.

Table 3.4 Frequencies of perception of colour difference in image pairs with systematic changes in chroma, versus the magnitude of the difference, expressed in ΔE^*_{ab} units

Class	Number of pairs	Number of observations	Number of successes	$D = 99\% \Delta E^*_{ab}$
$D < 2.5$	1	5	2	2.32
$2.5 \leqslant D < 3.0$	2	10	1	2.59
$3.0 \leqslant D < 3.5$	5	25	9	3.29
$3.5 \leqslant D < 4.0$	2	10	2	3.70
$4.0 \leqslant D < 4.5$	1	5	4	4.15
$4.5 \leqslant D < 5.0$	4	20	11	4.65
$5.0 \leqslant D < 5.5$	7	35	19	5.28
$5.5 \leqslant D < 6.0$	3	15	11	5.67
$6.0 \leqslant D < 6.5$	1	5	5	6.39
$6.5 \leqslant D < 7.0$	2	10	7	6.65
$7.0 \leqslant D < 7.5$	2	10	9	7.24
$7.5 \leqslant D < 8.0$	3	15	14	7.73

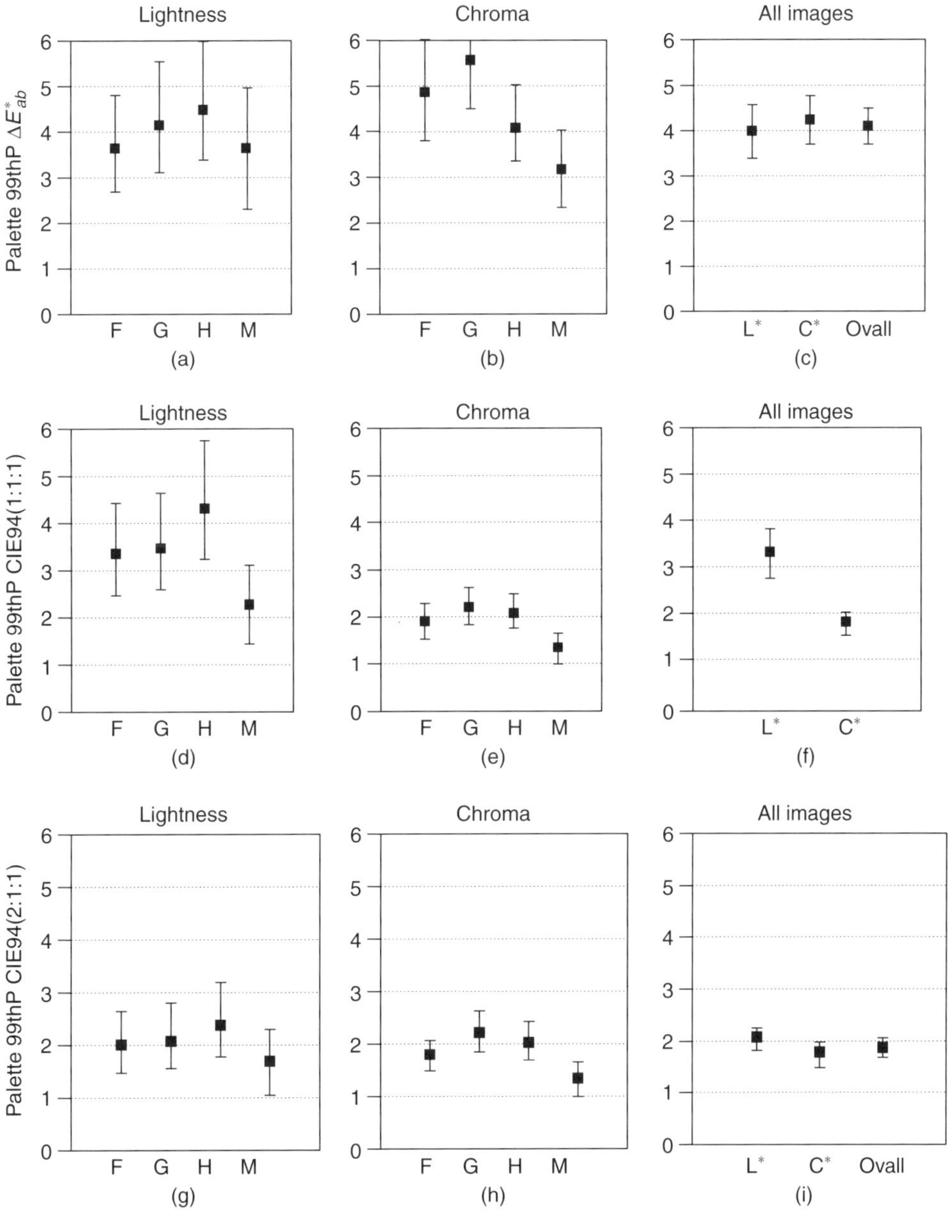

Figure 3.9 The T50 threshold perceptibility level of lightness or chroma systematic changes expressed as the 99th percentile of colour differences between palette colours. Colour differences in (a), (b), (c) are expressed in ΔE^*_{ab} units. Colour differences in (d), (e), (f) are expressed in CIE94(1:1:1) units. Colour differences in (g), (h), (i) are expressed in CIE94(2:1:1) units. The graphs in the first and second columns show the results individualised by image. The third column shows results for lightness, chroma or overall, integrating all images. The error bars correspond to the 95% confidence limits. F = Fruit, G = Gaudi, H = Harbor, M = Musicians.

The choice of colour difference formula is greatly influenced by this fact. From the results in Figure 3.9, the thresholds of perceptibility of systematic lightness changes are very similar, regardless the image, when colour differences are expressed in CIELAB ΔE^*_{ab}, or $\Delta E^*_{94}(2{:}1{:}1)$ units, but not in $\Delta E^*_{94}(1{:}1{:}1)$. This is because two results cannot be considered statistically different when the average of one falls within the error bar (95% confidence interval) of the other. In addition, the values of the lightness and chroma thresholds are very different when expressed in $\Delta E^*_{94}(1{:}1{:}1)$ units, therefore they cannot be assimilated into a single threshold value for generalised systematic changes (Figure 3.9(f)). The latter reasons make ΔE^*_{ab} or $\Delta E^*_{94}(2{:}1{:}1)$ colour difference equations more convenient than $\Delta E^*_{94}(1{:}1{:}1)$ for describing perceptibility thresholds of systematic colour changes in images.

A measure of dispersion of experimental results is the *coefficient of variation* (CV), defined as the standard deviation divided by the mean. Thus, it expresses the standard deviation as a proportion of the mean [31]. Table 3.5 compares the three colour difference formulae in terms of the CV value for lightness, chroma and overall. Again, $\Delta E^*_{94}(2{:}1{:}1)$ performed better overall, followed by ΔE^*_{ab}, although ΔE^*_{ab} performed worst for chroma. This is in contradiction to other research [15], in which ΔE^*_{ab} performed better than CIE94 for various weighting factors.

3.9.2 Overall perceptibility thresholds of lightness or chroma systematic changes

By fitting data from the lightness-altered images and the chroma-altered images, the overall perceptibility threshold corresponding to a 50% probability of perception is 4.12 ΔE^*_{ab} (99th percentile colour difference between the image palettes), with 95% confidence limits between 3.70 ΔE^*_{ab} and 4.50 ΔE^*_{ab} (Figure 3.10(a)). Previous research on CRT media situated the threshold at about 2 ΔE^*_{ab} arithmetic mean of all image pixels [15]. The arithmetic mean value that corresponds approximately to the palette 99th percentile reported here is 2.3 ΔE^*_{ab}. Therefore, the threshold level is very much in agreement, although the metric used is different. What is found in the present analysis is that the threshold of perceptibility of colour changes in images is better described by high percentile than by mean colour differences.

When expressed in CIE94(2:1:1) units, the overall perceptibility threshold corresponding to a 50% probability of perception is of 1.89 ΔE^*_{94} (99th percentile colour difference between the image palettes), with 95% confidence limits between 1.68 ΔE^*_{94} and 2.05 ΔE^*_{94} (Figure 3.10(b)).

Table 3.5 CV values of the results of Experiment 1, expressed as percentages

Colour dimension	Colour difference formula		
	CIELAB	CIE94(1:1)	CIE94(2:1)
Lightness	10	25	14
Chroma	23	20	20
Overall	18	38	17

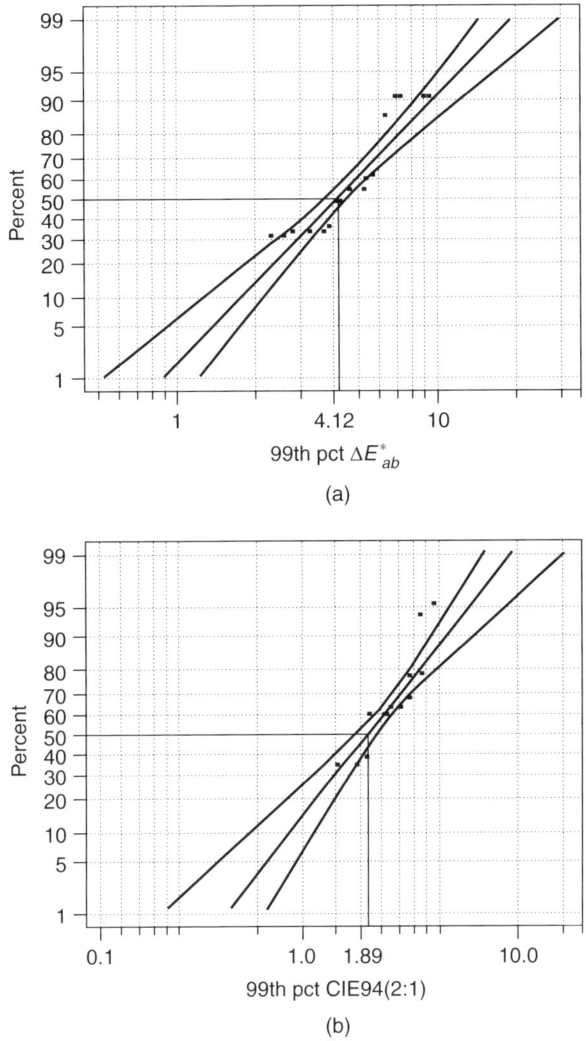

Figure 3.10 Probability of perception of systematic changes of colour in images versus the 99th percentile of colour difference between image palette colours, plotted on normal probabilistic coordinates: (a) ΔE^*_{ab} differences, (b) CIE94(2:1) differences.

3.10 EXPERIMENT 2: PERCEPTIBILITY THRESHOLD OF SIMULTANEOUS LIGHTNESS, CHROMA AND HUE RANDOM CHANGES

Two original pictures (Fruit and Musicians) were transformed by 6 increasing levels of random colour change, to obtain 12 randomly modified prints. The palettes containing

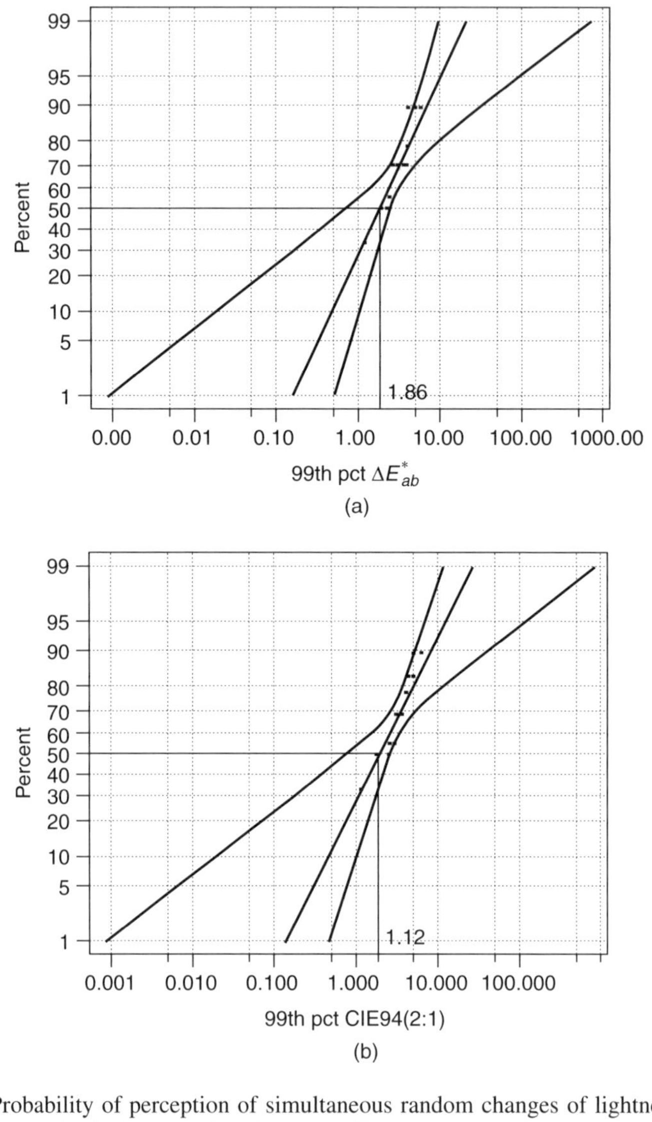

Figure 3.11 Probability of perception of simultaneous random changes of lightness, chroma and hue in images versus the 99th percentile of colour difference between image palette colours, plotted on normal probabilistic coordinates. The data shown correspond to all images: (a) ΔE^*_{ab} colour differences, (b) CIE94(2:1) colour differences.

their 128 most significant colours were printed simultaneously with each. From all possible pairs that could be formed with each image original plus its colour-altered copies, only 14 were chosen, again for similar reasons to those given earlier. They were judged in random order by 9 colour-normal observers, making a total of $14 \times 9 = 126$ observations (repetitions not included).

The colour differences between the corresponding patches in the image palettes for each of the pairs were computed using CIELAB ΔE^*_{ab} and $\Delta E^*_{94}(2{:}1{:}1)$ colour difference formulae. Following a similar procedure to that used in Experiment 1, data were fitted to a lognormal model using probit analysis, from which the 50% thresholds of perceptibility of random changes were found.

When expressed in CIELAB ΔE^*_{ab} units, the perceptibility threshold corresponding to a 50% probability of perception is 1.86 ΔE^*_{ab}(99th percentile colour difference between the image palettes), with 95% confidence limits between 0.73 ΔE^*_{ab} and 2.43 ΔE^*_{ab} (Figure 3.11(a)). When expressed in CIE94(2:1:1) units, the overall perceptibility threshold corresponding to a 50% probability of perception is 1.12 ΔE^*_{94} (99th percentile colour difference between the image palettes), with 95% confidence limits between 0.48 ΔE^*_{94} and 1.45 ΔE^*_{94} (Figure 3.11(b)).

Several effects were observable in the images in which the colour was altered randomly, effects that were not present in the images of Experiment 1, where the colour changes were systematic. First, the textures became grainier, as adjacent pixels could be of different lightness, chroma and hue altogether. Second, because of the hue changes, the lack of grey balance was noticeable.

3.11 SYSTEMATIC VERSUS RANDOM COLOUR CHANGES

When the results of Experiments 1 and 2 are compared (Table 3.6), it becomes evident, that the threshold of perceptibility of random colour changes is much smaller than the threshold of systematic colour changes; it is about half the value.

The reasons for this could be explained by the grain and colour balance effects present in the samples of Experiment 2. Increased sensitivity to grain is in accordance with the work of McCann [23], from which it can be established that, given adjacent areas in an image, observers are much more sensitive to differential changes between them than to the level of changes common to both. Also the correctness of hue and colour balance is the most important colour reproduction objective, because the sensitivity to hue changes is higher than the sensitivity to lightness or chroma changes [33].

Table 3.6 Values of the perceptibility thresholds of colour changes in images, for different types of colour transformations and colour difference formulae

Type of colour change	CIELAB	CIE94(2:1)
Systematic lightness	4.0	2.1
Systematic chroma	4.3	1.8
Systematic lightness or chroma	4.1	1.9
Random lightness, chroma or hue	1.9	1.1

3.12 THRESHOLD DEPENDENCE WITH IMAGE CONTENTS

The perceptibility thresholds of the individual images can be compared in Figure 3.9. When the threshold mean value of one image falls within the error bar of another image, those two thresholds cannot be considered statistically different. They can be considered statistically different otherwise. For instance, the perceptibility threshold of chroma systematic changes in the Gaudi image is different from that of Harbor or Musicians, when using CIELAB colour differences. Similar statement can be made about the Gaudi image versus Fruit or Musicians, when using CIE92(2:1) colour differences. These facts lead to the conclusion that in general the perceptibility threshold of colour change for a particular image would depend on its composition. In our case the Gaudi image was composed of smaller coloured areas than the others, therefore it is reasonable to expect that the perceptibility threshold should be higher. Musicians contains very large grey areas and a variety of skin tones, which would explain its resulting smaller threshold.

For practical purposes, the perceptibility threshold of colour change can be seen as the desirable lower bound of the magnitude of colour error allowed in an imaging device. It would not be desirable from an industrial view point to restrict colour errors in a printer below the level where they cannot be seen. For setting the worst-case colour accuracy and repeatability specifications of a new printer, or setting its production quality control limits, the presumably much higher acceptability thresholds (not studied in this work) would be appropriate. In spite of their dependence on image content, the overall perceptibility threshold levels found in this work would be a good indicator for industrial applications.

3.13 CONCLUSIONS AND FURTHER RESEARCH

At the earliest stages of this research, the capability of the selected printing system to reproduce input colour changes in a predictable way, even at the subthreshold level, was thought to be a key prerequisite. It has been demonstrated how tight control of the essential colour variability factors is possible, which makes the use of printed images in perceptibility threshold experiments feasible in practice.

The discrimination of colour difference between two images, when the magnitude of the difference is at the perceptibility threshold level, was found not to be a visual averaging process. Instead, the positive recognition of a pair of images as different in colour seemed to be triggered by the first recognisable feature that could be seen as different. This was supported by the fact that the mean colour difference of the palette colours (which corresponds well to mean image colour) correlated with visual data worse than the 99% percentile colour difference between palette colours (which corresponds to areas formed by groups of adjacent pixels in the image). Observers marked areas where they could perceive a colour difference between recognisable image features. Averaging implies the removal of spatial information; feature comparison involves some form of spatial and morphological processing.

As we claim that the positive perception of colour inequality in a pair of images is triggered by the worst-case difference in appearance of corresponding recognisable features in the pair, colour appearance models could be developed to predict image differences, based on the following hypotheses:

- The object is a recognisable area of variable size in the image.
- The background is the remainder of the image.
- The illumination and surround are common for the pair of images, if the comparison is simultaneous and not involving memory effects, as in the present research.

Colour differences expressed as ΔE^*_{ab} or $\Delta E^*_{94}(2{:}1{:}1)$ were found to describe the colour difference between two images more accurately than $\Delta E^*_{94}(1{:}1{:}1)$. Two reproductions of the same original will likely be perceived as different when their 99th percentile difference between predefined areas of pixels is greater than 4.1 ΔE^*_{ab}, when the colour changes have been produced by systematic causes. This result is in agreement with previous results from Stokes [15] on CRT media, but Stokes' results were expressed as mean colour differences.

When the colour changes are produced by random causes affecting lightness, chroma and hue, the 50% threshold is 1.86 ΔE^*_{ab}. This is significantly lower than the threshold values obtained when systematic changes were applied. A reason for this could be found in the fact that adjacent pixels or small areas in the same image can be much more different to each other than in the case of systematic changes. This is in accordance with work published by McCann [23].

As discussed in previous sections, image independence cannot be assumed for generalised systematic or random colour changes. Systematic colour changes have been applied in a single perceptual dimension at a time. That would not necessarily predict the perceptibility of simultaneous systematic changes in more than one dimension. While the results obtained from the current work have been useful as a first approximation to perceptibility of systematic colour changes in images, new experiments involving simultaneous systematic changes in lightness, chroma and hue would be necessary.

Acceptability studies (not addressed in this work) would be different from the perceptibility studies in that the test images would have to show much larger colour differences. More fundamentally, the set of observers would have to be appropriate for each particular market or application. While perceptibility comes from fundamental physiology, influenced by experience or training to the task, acceptability depends much more on cognitive, educational or professional factors.

Perceptibility and acceptability tolerances can be used in new product development, when setting product specifications, to understand the budget of colour error that can be assigned to every subsystem. For production, quality control in terms of final print allows for an evaluation of the whole system. In both cases tolerances derived from colour difference perception on complex images would be more realistic than those derived from uniform patches.

ACKNOWLEDGEMENT

This work has been supported by Hewlett Packard ICD in Barcelona.

REFERENCES

1. CIE (1986) *Colorimetry*, 2nd edn. CIE Vienna.
2. McDonald, R. (1980) Industrial pass-fail colour matching. Part I – Preparation of visual colour-matching data. *Journal of the Society of Dyers and Colourists*, **96**, 372–376.
3. Luo, M. R. and Rigg, B (1986), Chromaticity discrimination ellipses for surface colours. *Color Research and Application* **11**, 25–42.
4. Berns, R. S., Alman, D. H., Reniff, L., Snyder, G. D. and Balononrosen, M. R. (1991) Visual determination of suprathreshold color-difference tolerances using probit analysis. *Color Research and Application*, **16**(5), 297–316.
5. Witt, K. (1987) Three-dimensional threshold of color-difference perceptibility in painted samples: variability of observers in four CIE color regions. *Color Research and Application*, **12**, 128–134.
6. Clarke, F. J. J., McDonald, R. and Rigg, B. (1984) Modification to the JPC79 colour-difference formula. *Journal of the Society of Dyers and Colourists*, **100**, 128–132.
7. Luo, M. R. and Riggs, B. (1987) BFD(l:c) colour-difference formula, Part I – development of the formula. *Journal of the Society of Dyers and Colourists*, **103**, 86–94.
8. Luo, M. R. and Riggs, B. (1987) BFD(l:c) colour-difference formula, Part II – performance of the formula. *Journal of the Society of Dyers and Colourists*, **103**, 126–132.
9. CIE (1995) *Industrial colour-difference evaluation*. CIE, Vienna.
10. ISO 105-J03 (1995) Textiles. Tests for colour fastness – Part 3: calculation of colour differences.
11. ISO /DIS 7724 Part 6: Methods of test for paints. Determination of colour and colour difference.
12. MacDonald, L. W. (1993) Image representation and colour separation in the MARC project. *Electronic Imaging and the Visual Arts*, London.
13. http://www.hp.com/financials/99annrep/customerstories/nationalgallery.html
14. CIE (1999) Methods to derive colour differences for images. Draft V.03. CIE Technical Report. CIE Division 8 Technical Committee 8-02. http://www.colour.org/tc8-02/
15. Stokes, M. (1991) Colorimetric tolerances of digital images. MSc Thesis, RIT, University of Rochester.
16. Fedorovskaya, E., de Ridder, H., Blommaert, F. J. J. (1997) Chroma variations and perceived quality of color images of natural scenes. *Color Research and Application*, **22**(2), 96–110.
17. Farnand, S. P. (1996) The effect of image contents on color difference perceptibility. *Proceedings of the 4th IS&T/SID Color Imaging Conference.*
18. Uroz, J. (1999) Colour difference perceptibility for large-size printed images. MSc Thesis, Colour & Imaging Institute, University of Derby.
19. Berns, R. S. (1996) Methods for characterizing CRT displays. *Displays*, **16**(4), 173–182.
20. Attridge, G. G., Leverton, C., Pointer, M. R. and Jacobson, R. E. (1995) Colour reproduction indices and acceptability of prints at controlled density levels. *Journal of Photographic Science*, **43**(4), 144–151.
21. Attridge, G. G., Leverton, C., Pointer, M. R. and Jacobson, R. E. (1995) Measured colour difference and the acceptability of photographic colour prints. *Journal of Photographic Science*, **43**(5), 169–181.
22. Attridge, G. G., Pointer, M. R. and Jacobson, R. E. (1996) A summary of applications of colour reproduction indices to imaging systems. *Journal of Photographic Science*, **44**(6), 187–192.
23. McCann, J. J. (1996) A comparison of color metrics. *Proceedings of the 4th IS&T/SID Color Imaging Conference*.
24. Stokes, M. and Brill, M. H. (1992) *Color Research and Application*, **17**, 410.
25. ISO 12 640 (1995) Graphic technology. Prepress digital data exchange. Standard colour image data (SCID).
26. Sakamoto, K. and Urabe, H. (1997) Standard high precision pictures: SHIPP. *Proceedings of the 5th IS&T/SID Color Imaging Conference*.

27. ISO 3664:1998(E). Viewing conditions for graphic technology and photography. Working draft.
28. ANSI PH2.30-1989 (1989) Color Prints, Transparencies, and Photomechanical Reproductions – Viewing conditions. American National Standards Institute.
29. Wandell, B. (1995) *Foundations of Vision*. Sinauer Associates.
30. Finney, D. J. (1971) *Probit analysis*, 3rd edn. Cambridge University Press.
31. Berns, R. S., Alman, D. H., Reniff, L., Snyder, G. D. and Balononrosen, M. R. (1991) Visual determination of suprathreshold color-difference tolerances using probit analysis. *Color Research and Application*, **16**(5), 297–316.
32. Bartleson, C. J. (1984) Thresholds and matching. *Optical Radiation Measurement*, Vol. 5, Ch.7. Academic Press.
33. Hunt, R. W. G. (1995) *The Reproduction of Colour*, 5th edn. Fountain Press.

PART 2

Multispectral imaging

4

Evaluation of multispectral imaging

Yoichi Miyake and Kimiyoshi Miyata

4.1 INTRODUCTION

In recent years, digital imaging systems have achieved high-quality results in printing, artworks, telemedicine and Internet shopping. Silver halide photography, of course, can also achieve high image quality and has been widely used as recording material for a long time. Photographic film, however, cannot record and display images in real time, because of the time required for development. The image quality characteristics of film, such as colour and tone reproduction, are dependent on both the development chemistry and the taking conditions of the object. Furthermore, in the digitisation of photographs, scanner characteristics have a large influence on image quality, particularly on colour rendering.

Normal photographic film cannot record the true spectral reflectance of an object since it uses only three wavelength-sensitive materials to record the red, green and blue (R, G, B) portions of the visible spectrum. Charge-coupled device (CCD) cameras and scanners are also three-channel devices, generating RGB signals or CIE-XYZ tristimulus values, which are dependent on the characteristics of imaging devices and illuminant conditions. For a true record of a scene it is necessary to capture the reflectance spectra of every sample

Colour Image Science, edited by L.W. MacDonald and M.R. Luo.

point $O^{xy}(\lambda)$ independent of both the spectral sensitivity of the imaging system and the spectral power distribution of the illumination.

In this chapter, our recent researches on the evaluation, analysis and improvement of digital colour image quality are introduced and some experimental results are presented in the application areas of medical imaging and reproduction of artworks. From principal component analysis of the reflectance spectra of gastric mucous membrane [1] and skin colour [2, 3], we have shown that those reflectance spectra can be accurately estimated from the RGB signals of a CCD camera attached to an endoscope. We also showed that the information of five channels is necessary to estimate the reflectance spectra of oil paintings. On the basis of this experimental result, we have developed a five-band CCD camera [4] with 3120 (H) × 2160 (V) pixels and 14 bits dynamic range for recording the reflectance spectra of paintings and other artefacts. The reflectance spectra estimated by principal component analysis and Wiener estimation were applied to improve the colour reproduction of gastric mucous membrane, facial pattern, art paints, and so on.

Image quality of the CCD camera, especially its sharpness, are mainly determined by pixel number, pixel size, filter array and image processing such as interpolation. We used computer simulation to study the optimal design of a CCD array, based on the two-dimensional modulation transfer function (MTF) of human vision. Results showed that the honeycomb structure is significantly better than the conventional interline CCD array for image quality. This simulation result [5] gave theoretical support to quality evaluation for a new digital camera with honeycomb structure developed by Fuji Photo Film. We have also developed a Wiener filter to reduce graininess without degradation of sharpness for digital colour images [6].

4.2 MULTISPECTRAL IMAGING AND ITS APPLICATIONS

4.2.1 Principal component analysis and estimation of reflectance spectra

Figure 4.1 shows a colour reproduction system for an object with reflectance spectrum $O^{xy}(\lambda)$. The camera response v_i^{xy} $(i = 1, 2, \ldots)$ of the object can be represented as:

$$v_i^{xy}(\lambda) = \int_{400}^{700} E(\lambda)O^{xy}(\lambda)L(\lambda)f_i(\lambda)S(\lambda)\,\mathrm{d}\lambda \tag{4.1}$$

where (x, y) are the sampling coordinates of the object and λ is the wavelength of visible radiation from 400 nm to 700 nm, $O^{xy}(\lambda)$ is captured by CCD camera or colour film with spectral sensitivity $S_i(\lambda)$ through a lens with spectral transmittance $L(\lambda)$. In this equation we may consider that $S_i(\lambda)$ is represented by $S(\lambda)f_i(\lambda)$ where $f_i(\lambda)$ is spectral transmittance of the filter and $S(\lambda)$ is the sensitivity of a detector common to all channels. In digital imaging systems, V_i^{xy} is typically recorded in memory and then displayed onto a monitor or printed on paper after some image processing. In a conventional imaging system, $i = 3$, corresponding to channels R, G, B.

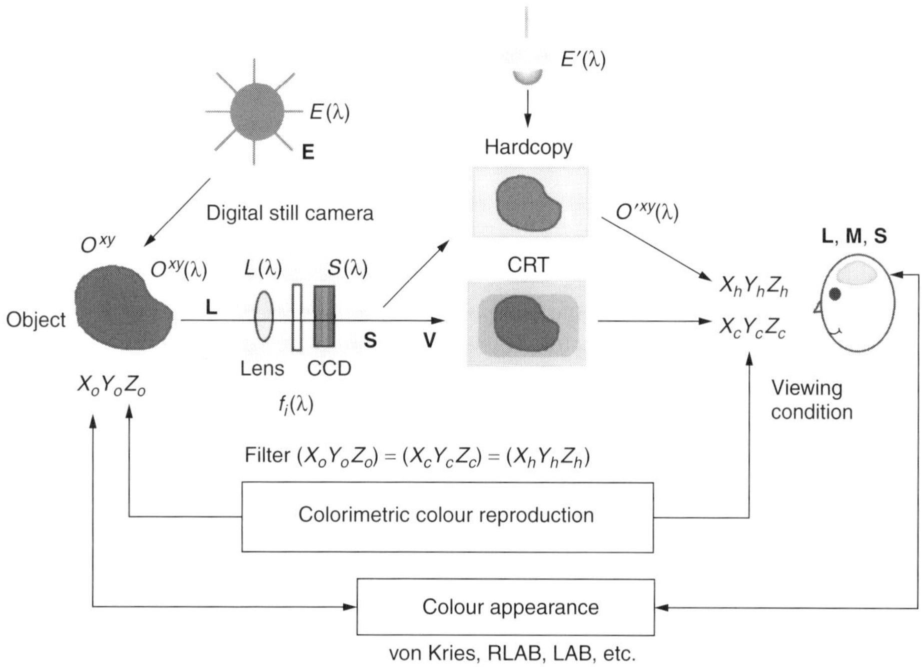

Figure 4.1 Colour reproduction systems.

Colorimetric colour reproduction is characterised by the original and reproduced colours having the same chromaticity values at each position, and is the objective for facsimile colour reproduction of images. The tristimulus values X_c,Y_c,Z_c of the reproduced digital image can be calculated as:

$$
\begin{aligned}
X_c &= \int_{400}^{700} E'(\lambda) O'^{xy}(\lambda)\bar{x}(\lambda)\,\mathrm{d}\lambda \\
Y_c &= \int_{400}^{700} E'(\lambda) O'^{xy}(\lambda)\bar{y}(\lambda)\,\mathrm{d}\lambda \qquad (4.2) \\
Z_c &= \int_{400}^{700} E'(\lambda) O'^{xy}(\lambda)\bar{z}(\lambda)\,\mathrm{d}\lambda
\end{aligned}
$$

where $E'(\lambda)$ is the spectral power distribution of the viewing illuminant and $O'^{xy}(\lambda)$ is the reflectance spectrum at each coordinate of the reproduced image corresponding to the camera response v_i^{xy}. This is determined by the spectral power distribution of an emissive reproduction device, such as a CRT or LCD monitor, or the spectral density distribution of dyes, inks or pigments of film or printer.

It is clear that the tristimulus values are dependent on both the taking and viewing illuminants, and on the spectral characteristics of all components in the imaging system.

They are therefore only a representation of how the object looks to the CIE standard observer in the given viewing environment, and not an absolute characteristic of the object itself. Therefore our research objective was to extract and record the true spectral reflectance of the object.

Equation (4.1) can be expressed using vector–matrix notation as follows:

$$\mathbf{V}_i^{xy} = \mathbf{ELSf}_i\mathbf{o}^{xy} = \mathbf{F}_i^{\mathrm{T}}\mathbf{o}^{xy} \quad i = 1, 2, \ldots \tag{4.3}$$

where **E**, **L**, **S** are vectors of the spectral power distribution of illuminant, spectral transmittance of imaging lens, and spectral sensitivity of sensor, respectively; $\mathbf{f}_i$ is the spectral transmittance of filter i, $\mathbf{o}^{xy}$ is the spectral reflectance of the object at co-ordinate (x, y); and $\mathbf{F}_i^{\mathrm{T}}$ is the overall spectral characteristic of the imaging system. The notation $\mathbf{X}^{\mathrm{T}}$ indicates the matrix transpose of **X**.

Then, using principal component analysis (PCA), $\mathbf{o}^{xy}$ can be expressed as follows:

$$\mathbf{o}^{xy} = \sum_{i=1}^{n} \alpha_i^{xy}\mathbf{u}_i + \mathbf{m}^{xy} \tag{4.4}$$

where α_i^{xy} are the coefficients (weighting values) at coordinate (x, y), $\mathbf{u}_i$ is an eigenvector of principal components, and $\mathbf{m}^{xy}$ is a constant.

Coefficients α_i can be calculated from the camera response. For example, when $i = 3$, they can be calculated as follows:

$$\begin{bmatrix} a_1 \\ \alpha_2 \\ \alpha_3 \end{bmatrix} = \begin{bmatrix} \mathbf{F}_R^{\mathrm{T}}\mathbf{u}_1 & \mathbf{F}_R^{\mathrm{T}}\mathbf{u}_2 & \mathbf{F}_R^{\mathrm{T}}\mathbf{u}_3 \\ \mathbf{F}_G^{\mathrm{T}}\mathbf{u}_1 & \mathbf{F}_G^{\mathrm{T}}\mathbf{u}_2 & \mathbf{F}_G^{\mathrm{T}}\mathbf{u}_3 \\ \mathbf{F}_B^{\mathrm{T}}\mathbf{u}_1 & \mathbf{F}_B^{\mathrm{T}}\mathbf{u}_2 & \mathbf{F}_B^{\mathrm{T}}\mathbf{u}_3 \end{bmatrix}^{-1} \left\{ \begin{bmatrix} V_R \\ V_G \\ V_B \end{bmatrix} - \begin{bmatrix} \mu_{Rm} \\ \mu_{Gm} \\ \mu_{Bm} \end{bmatrix} \right\} \tag{4.5}$$

where

$$\begin{bmatrix} \mu_{Rm} \\ \mu_{Gm} \\ \mu_{Bm} \end{bmatrix} = \begin{bmatrix} \mathbf{F}_R^{\mathrm{T}} \\ \mathbf{F}_G^{\mathrm{T}} \\ \mathbf{F}_B^{\mathrm{T}} \end{bmatrix} \mathbf{m} \tag{4.6}$$

and **m** is the mean vector calculated by reflectance spectra of samples.

Principal component analysis was employed to calculate eigenvectors $\mathbf{u}_i$ for the spectral reflectance of gastric mucous membrane, measured by an endoscopic spectrophotometer developed in our laboratories in cooperation with Olympus Optical Industry. Figure 4.2(a) shows three eigenvectors obtained from principal component analysis of 310 reflectance spectra of gastric mucosa samples. Figure 4.2(b) shows the cumulative contribution ratio of the principal components, indicating that 99% of the spectral reflectance of gastric

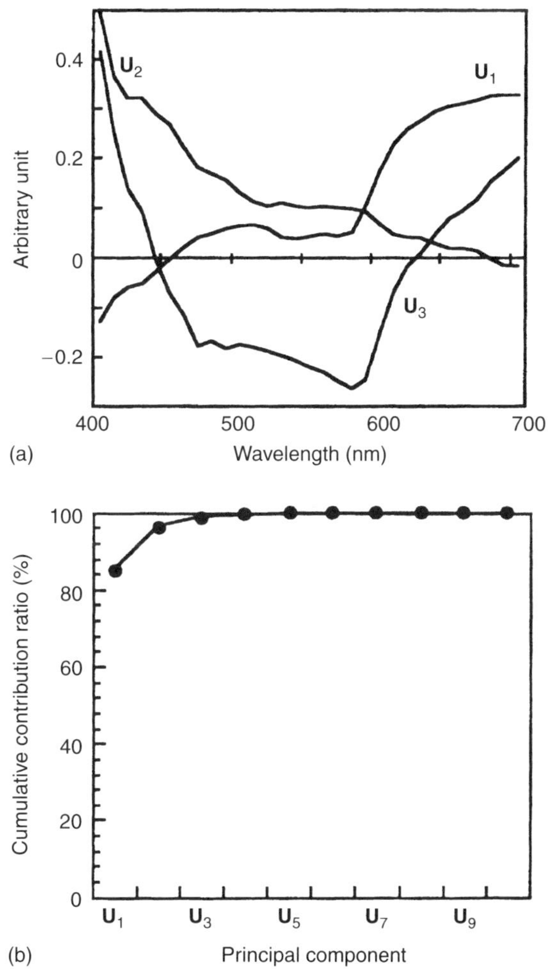

Figure 4.2 (a) Eigenvectors of the principal components for reflectance spectra of gastric mucous membrane. (b) Cumulative contribution ratio of the principal components.

mucous membrane can be estimated by the linear combination of only three eigenvectors (i.e. approximation error is less than 1%).

A related study showed that the spectral reflectance of human skin could also be accurately represented by three principal components. On the other hand, five principal components were found to be necessary to represent the spectral reflectance of oil paintings. Figure 4.3 shows five eigenvectors of principal components obtained from 148 reflection spectra of oil paints. Figure 4.4(a) shows those measured reflectance spectra. Figure 4.4(b) shows the relationship between the number of principal components and their cumulative contribution ratio. Figure 4.5 shows examples of estimated and measured reflectance spectra.

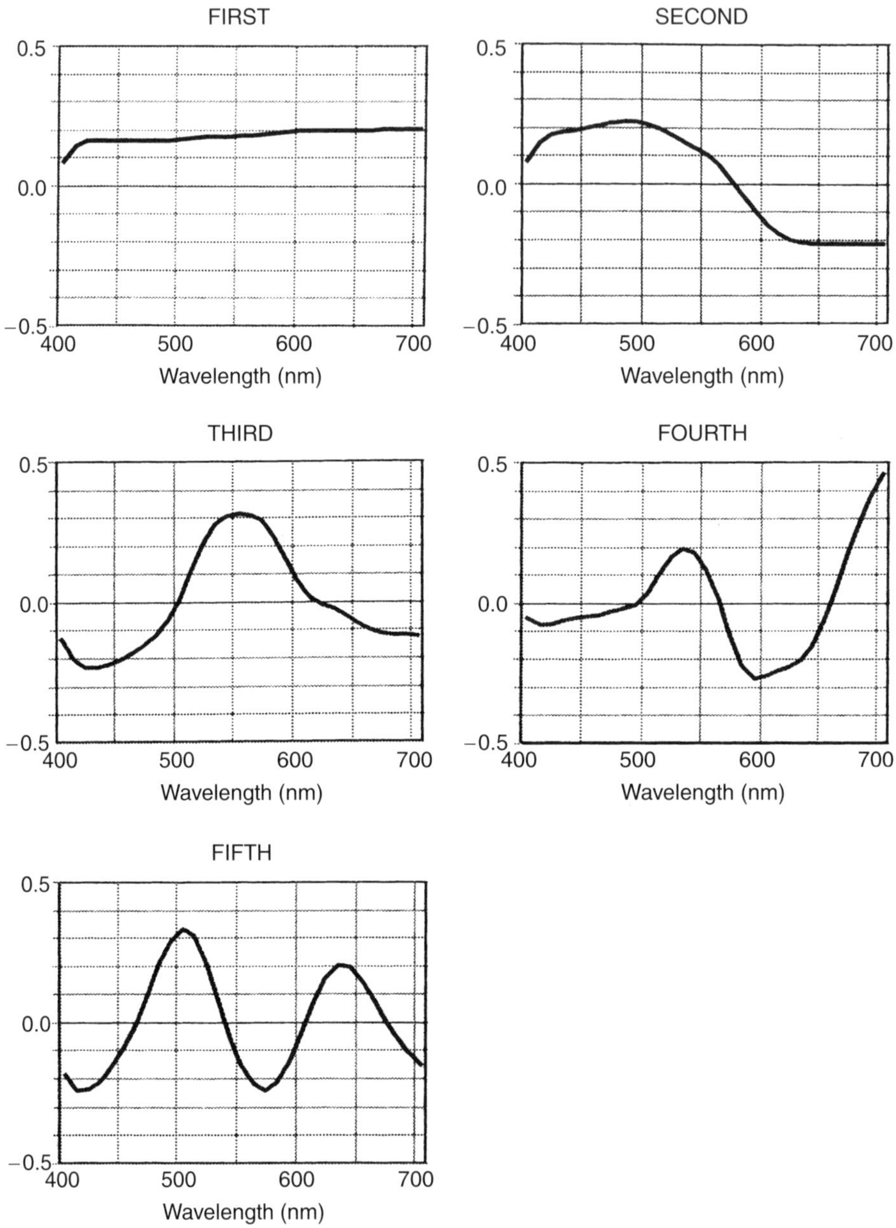

Figure 4.3 Eigenvectors of the principal components for reflectance spectra of oil paints shown in Figure 4.4.

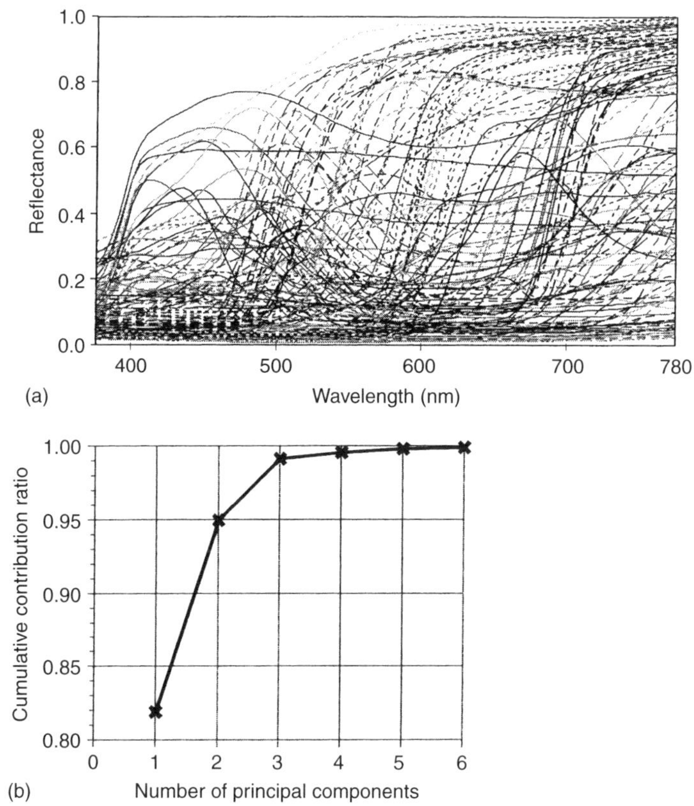

Figure 4.4 (a) Reflectance spectra of 147 oil paints; (b) Cumulative contribution ratio of the principal components shown in Figure 4.3.

4.2.2 Multispectral imaging systems for recording of art paints

The prevalence of virtual museums on the World Wide Web has increased rapidly in recent years. In the present systems, however, colour reproduction of paintings and 3D objects is highly dependent on the characteristics of recording and display devices. It would be far better to record and reproduce the colour of paintings or 3D objects in a device-independent way. For this purpose, we have developed a high-quality multispectral imaging system on the basis of principal component analysis. This system consists of a single-chip high-quality CCD camera (3120 × 2060 pixels, 14 bits) with a rotating colour wheel comprising eight colour filters (in the experiment five filters were used), high-quality CRT monitor and projection display, and personal computer. Three software modules – image digitiser, image estimator and image reproducer – control this system.

The image digitiser controls the rotating of filters, focusing of lenses, viewing angle and exposure settings. After capturing the image, processing operations for gamma correction, noise reduction and compensation of CCD pixel defects are applied. The image estimator estimates the reflectance spectra of the image based on principal component analysis and

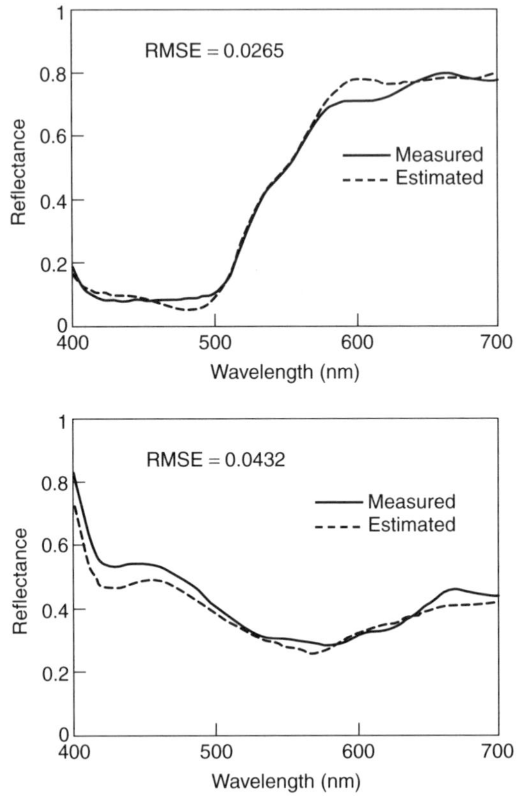

Figure 4.5 Examples of estimation of the reflectance spectra of two oil paints as linear combinations of the five principal components in Figure 4.3.

Wiener estimation from five image bands. The image reproducer reproduces the colour image from estimated reflectance spectra of the object, taking into consideration the CRT monitor characteristics and colour adaptation model. Figure 4.6 shows a schematic diagram of the multispectral image acquisition system and the appearance of the developed camera. Figure 4.7(a) is an example of an oil painting recorded by this system and Figure 4.7(b) shows the spectral reflectance of an arbitrary pixel, corresponding to the reflectance spectrum at the same location in the original oil painting.

4.2.3 Estimation of reflectance spectra of 3D objects

We introduced the goniospectral imaging method [7] to record the spectral reflectance of the surface of a 3D object using multispectral imaging systems. Five-band images were taken at different illumination angles as shown in Figure 4.8, where $f(r,\theta_i)$ represents the multispectral image at illumination angle θ_i. The dichromatic model was introduced for separation of body reflection and surface reflection; in other words, spectral reflectance of the object surface and spectral radiance distribution of reflected illuminant from the

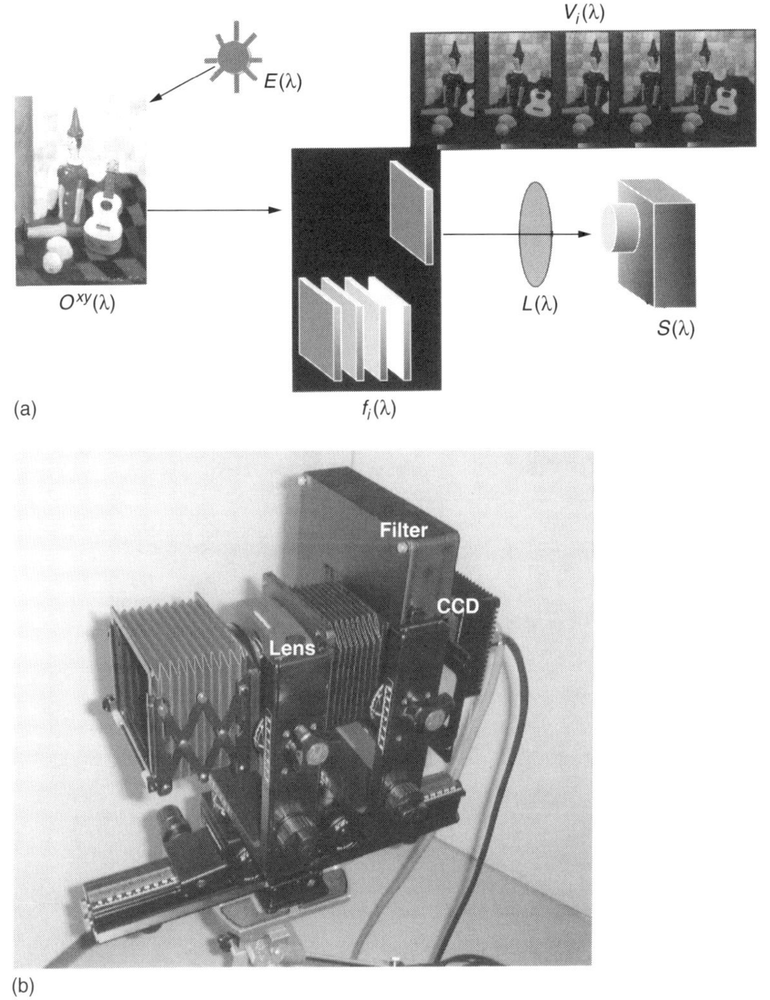

Figure 4.6 Multispectral camera: (a) schematic diagram, (b) appearance of developed camera.

obtained five-band images. The Phong model was also introduced to represent the goniophotometric angular distribution from the five-band images taken at different illuminant angles. The results showed that the proposed method is able to reproduce both colour and glossiness of the 3D object. We are developing goniophotometric imaging systems to combine the 3D shape and goniophotometric information [10].

4.2.4 Optimisation of taking illuminant in electronic endoscopes

As described above, we could estimate the reflectance spectra of an object O^{xy} (λ), and then simulate the colour reproduction of electronic endoscopic images taken with different

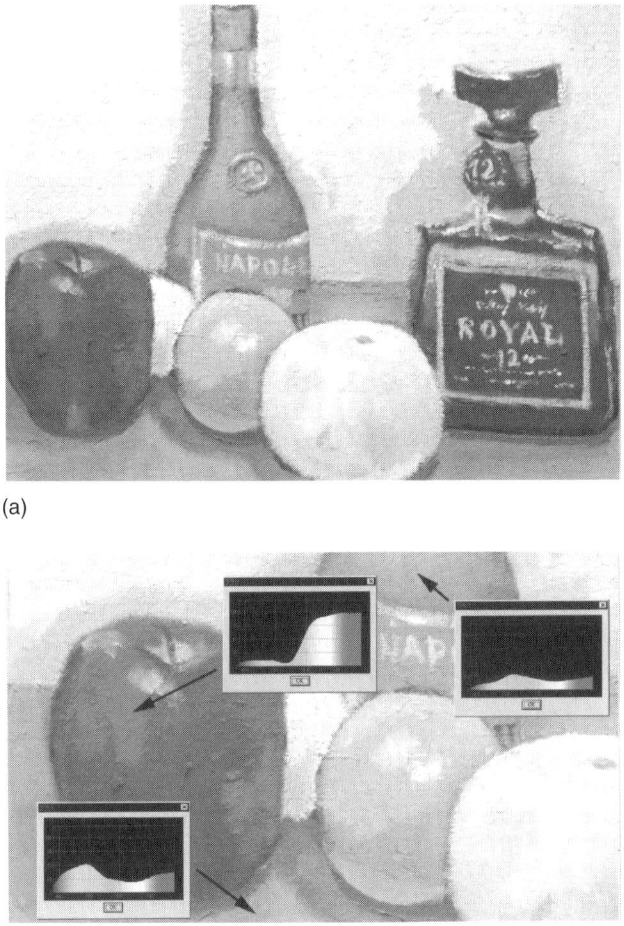

(a)

(b)

Figure 4.7 (a) Example of oil paint recorded by developed multispectral camera imaging system. (b) Recorded image has reflectance spectra information in each pixel. See also Plate 12.

kinds of illuminants. Physicians who specialise in endoscope image diagnosis evaluated these simulated images, which included cancer, early stage of chronic gastritis, chronic gastritis, advanced stage of chronic gastritis, and gastric ulcer. Figure 4.9 shows the polyp images estimated with 18 kinds of taking illuminant. In this evaluation, a xenon lamp was selected as the most preferred illuminant.

The projection onto convex set (POCS) method was also applied to design the optimum spectral radiance distribution of optical endoscopes [8]. POCS is an iterative algorithm to obtain a solution which holds simultaneously some predetermined conditions. Each condition must be defined so that its solution space forms a convex set. The solution for the optimisation of spectral radiance distribution of optical endoscopes can be

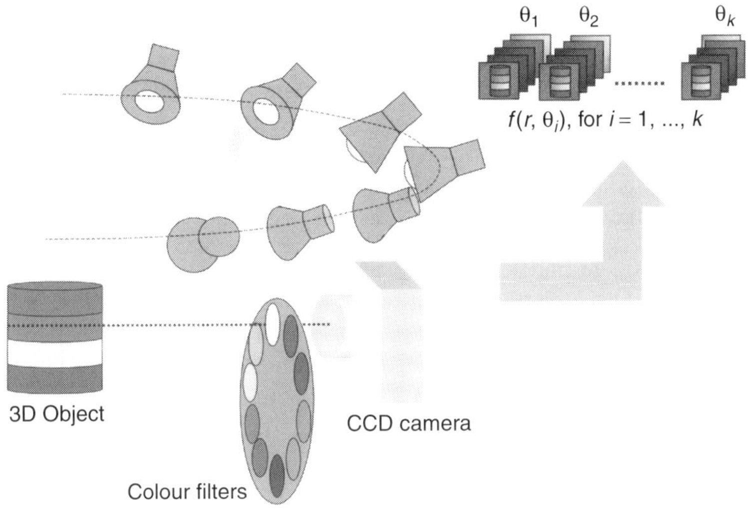

Figure 4.8 Goniophotometric imaging system.

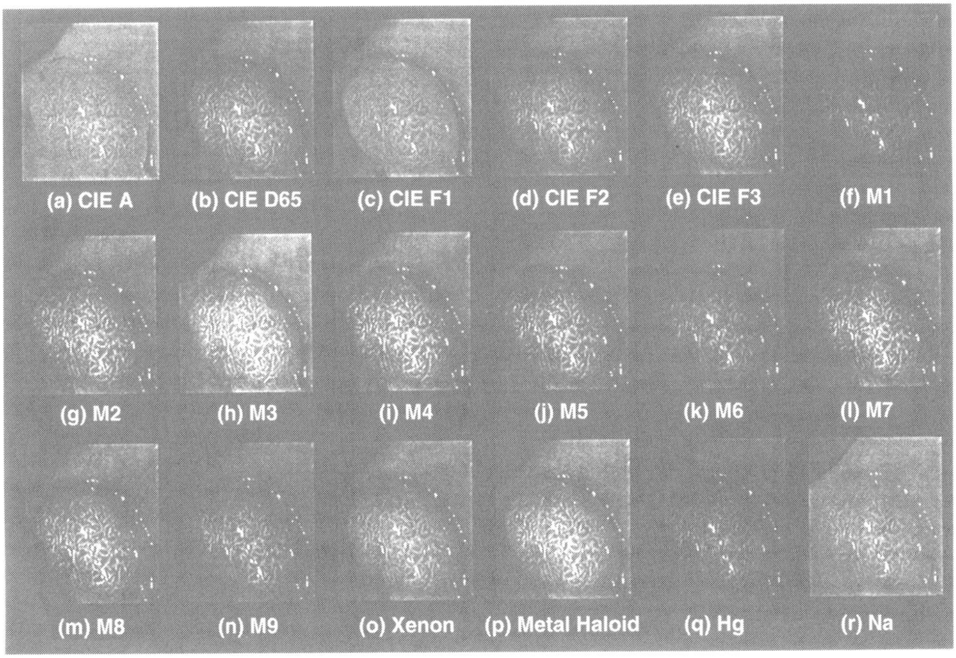

Figure 4.9 Simulated polyp images under 18 kinds of illuminant. Colour version is shown in Plate 2.

obtained by repeating the projections onto each subspace based on the following three constraints:

- The colour difference calculated from mucous membrane samples measured by endoscopic spectrophotometer is larger than the predetermined threshold.
- The light source has exactly the same whiteness (correlated colour temperature and colour rendering index) as the xenon lamp.
- The spectral radiance of the light source is non-negative.

These conditions were formulated and the POCS algorithm was applied to estimate the optimum spectral radiance distribution of the light source.

Figure 4.10 shows the spectral radiance distribution of the optimum light source for optical endoscopes estimated by this algorithm. The u^*v^* chromaticity values calculated from gastric mucous membrane illuminated by optimum lamp, xenon lamp, tungsten lamp and mercury lamp were analysed and compared. The result showed that the colour gamut obtained by the optimum light source based on the POCS algorithm is wider than the others.

4.2.5 Application to object segmentation

Transmittance spectra of fungi were estimated [9] by seven-band optical micrographs using the Wiener estimation method. The estimated transmittance spectra of fungi in each pixel were used as input vectors to the artificial neural network for the segmentation of fungal micrographs. This experiment showed the significance of the multiband imaging system compared with RGB and multispectral imaging systems.

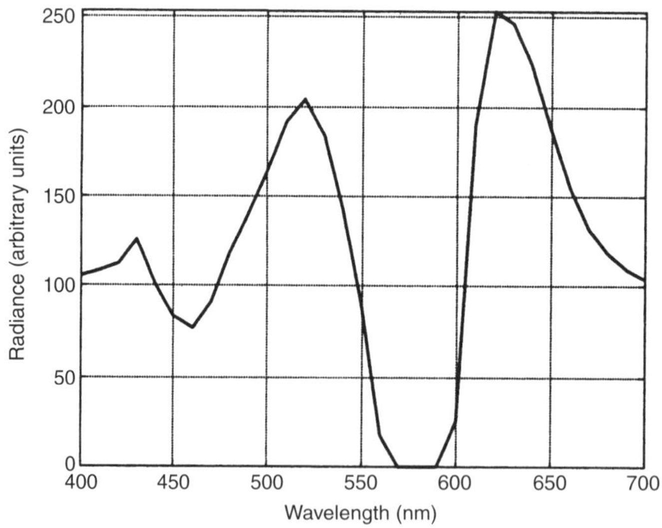

Figure 4.10 Optimum spectral radiant distribution of illuminant for optical endoscopes estimated by the POCS algorithm.

4.3 METHODS FOR QUALITY EVALUATION OF MULTISPECTRAL IMAGES

4.3.1 Image quality evaluation

Image quality should be considered in the context of the total imaging system, namely image acquisition, recording, transmission and reproduction. However, little has been studied on for reproduction systems for multispectral images. In this section we consider only the quality of acquisition of the multispectral image, which depends on both spatial and spectral resolution. Spatial resolution is mainly determined by the pixel number of the CCD sensor as described in Section 4.4. On the other hand, spectral resolution depends on the number of bands and the estimation algorithm of spectral reflectance, such as principal component analysis and Wiener estimation.

Two measures have commonly been used to evaluate the accuracy of the estimation of spectral reflectance of an object. The first is root mean square error (RMSE) between the measured spectral data and estimated spectral data from 400 nm to 700 nm. The second is a colour difference formula such as CIE $\Delta E_{a^*b^*}$ or ΔE_{94}. The RMSE is significant for handling the spectral data itself, and the colour difference is useful as a measure for the colour reproduction of the image. The results evaluated by RMSE and $\Delta E_{a^*b^*}$ do not always correspond well to each other.

4.3.2 Optimal filter design for multispectral camera

The measures mentioned above for evaluation of reflectance spectra of an object can be used as cost functions in the design of optimal filters for a multispectral camera. Estimation of spectral reflectance is considered as a problem to resolve ill-conditioned equations, since we must span the wavelength range from 400 nm to 700 nm measured at 10 nm or 5 nm intervals by a relatively small number of image bands. In other words, we must solve the full 31- or 61-dimensional equation from only 5-dimensional equations.

The reflection spectra of oil paint can be estimated by five principal components as described in Section 4.2.1. Therefore we have developed a five-band camera to record the reflection spectra of the object. The accuracy of recording spectra depends on the spectral transmittance of filters, which was calculated by the Wiener estimation method using the RMSE and colour difference $\Delta E_{a^*b^*}$ as a cost function. In this calculation we assumed the spectral transmittance of the filter is a Gaussian distribution with two parameters, mean (central wavelength) λ_c and variance w (half-width) as follows:

$$f_i(\lambda) = \exp\left[-\frac{(\lambda - \lambda_{ci})^2}{w_i^2}\right] \qquad (i = 1, 2, \ldots, n) \tag{4.7}$$

There are $2n$ unknown parameters if n different filters are used in the multispectral imaging system. Since this number of parameters was too large to determine by analytical methods, the simulated annealing technique was introduced to estimate optimal filter transmittance [10], in which the parameters were varied iteratively to minimise the cost function RMSE or $\Delta E_{a^*b^*}$. In the calculation, the central wavelength λ_c and half-width w of the filter were changed as follows:

$$\lambda_c = 380 + 5k \qquad (k = 0, 1, 2, \ldots, 80) \tag{4.8}$$

$$w = 20 + 5k \qquad (k = 0, 1, 2, \ldots, 80)$$

Figure 4.11 shows the spectral transmittance of five filters calculated using $\Delta E_{a^*b^*}$ as cost function. Figure 4.12 shows the estimation error of 147 oil paint samples shown in Figure 4.4(a). The estimation accuracy was verified by the finding that $\Delta E_{a^*b^*}$ was less than 0.62 for all samples.

In the calculation we assumed that the filter transmittance had a Gaussian distribution without any noise. However, in practical filter design we must consider the noise. Furthermore there is no guarantee that the optimal spectral distribution can be realized. Therefore, for the practical multispectral camera described in Section 4.2.2, we determined which five filters would minimise the cost function from 24 actual filters.

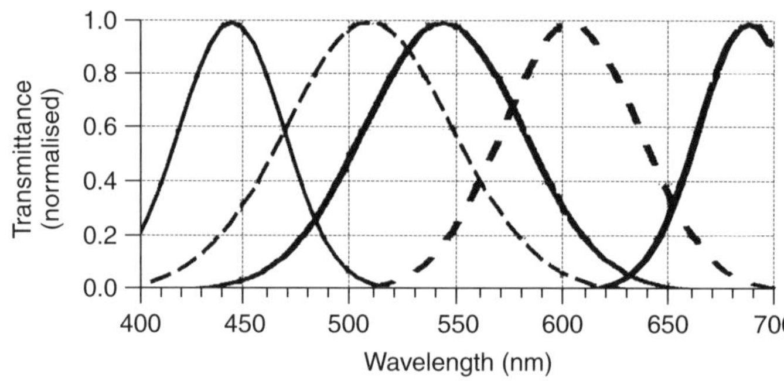

Figure 4.11 An example of optimised spectral transmittance of filters determined by $\Delta E_{a^*b^*}$ cost function.

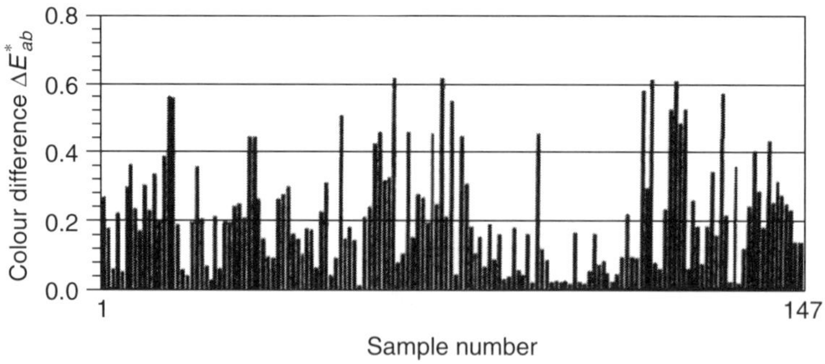

Figure 4.12 Colour difference $\Delta E_{a^*b^*}$ of 147 oil paint samples.

4.3.3 Evaluation of image compression

A multispectral image has far more information compared to an RGB image, and therefore occupies much more data storage. Hence it is important to compress the image data in both spatial and spectral dimensions. The JPEG compression method has been widely used to compress RGB images, and one simple way to compress multispectral image data is to apply JPEG compression to each image band independently. However, the multiband image has a strong correlation between each band image. Therefore we introduced principal component analysis (PCA) for every pixel corresponding to each band and discrete cosine transformation (DCT) for high compression ratio. In this process the principal components with lower contribution ratio were eliminated to reduce the volume of the multiband images, and then the compression by DCT was carried out. The proposed method was compared with conventional JPEG compression and the significance of the method was confirmed by both subjective and objective evaluation [11].

4.4 CCD ARRAY WITH HONEYCOMB STRUCTURE

Image quality of a CCD camera has frequently been equated by marketeers with the number of pixels generated. However, image quality is also dependent on many other factors such as structure of CCD, interpolation method, image processing, and so on. The image quality of two kinds of CCD camera with conventional interline and new honeycomb array structure was analysed and compared with computer simulation.

The Nyquist frequencies f_0 and f_{90} of both horizontal and vertical directions in a conventional CCD with interline structure are given by

$$f_0 = f_{90} = n/2L \tag{4.9}$$

On the other hand, Nyquist frequency f_{45} for the diagonal direction is given by

$$f_{45} = n/\sqrt{2}L \tag{4.10}$$

where $n \times n$ is the total pixel number, and L is the horizontal and vertical length of the CCD sensor Figure (4.13(a)). It is clear that the Nyquist frequency f_{45} is larger than f_0 and f_{90}. On the other hand, the Nyquist frequencies of the horizontal, vertical and diagonal directions in a honeycomb structure CCD (Figure 4.13(b)) are given by

$$f_0 = f_{90} = n/\sqrt{2}L \tag{4.11}$$

$$f_{45} = n/2L \tag{4.12}$$

Equations (4.11) and (4.12) show that, in the honeycomb structure CCD, the Nyquist frequency is larger in the horizontal and vertical directions than in the diagonal direction. It is well known that the modulation transfer function (MTF) of the human visual system does not have isotropic properties, insofar as the MTF in the vertical and horizontal

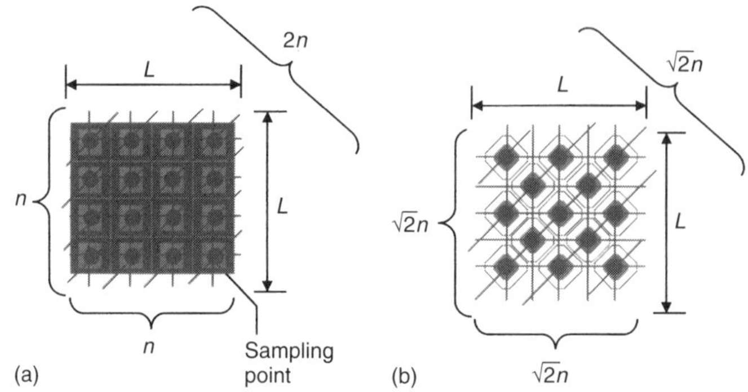

Figure 4.13 CCD structure with (a) interline array and (b) honeycomb array. Pixel number is $n \times n$ and size is $L \times L$.

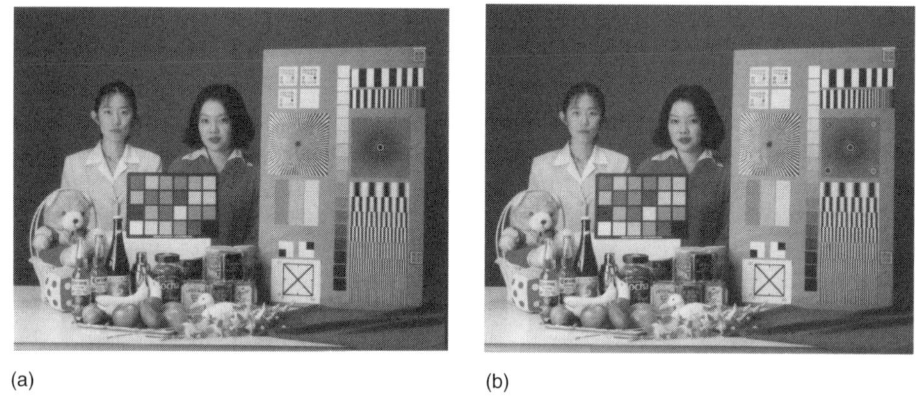

Figure 4.14 Examples of computer-simulated images: (a) interline CCD array, (b) honeycomb CCD array.

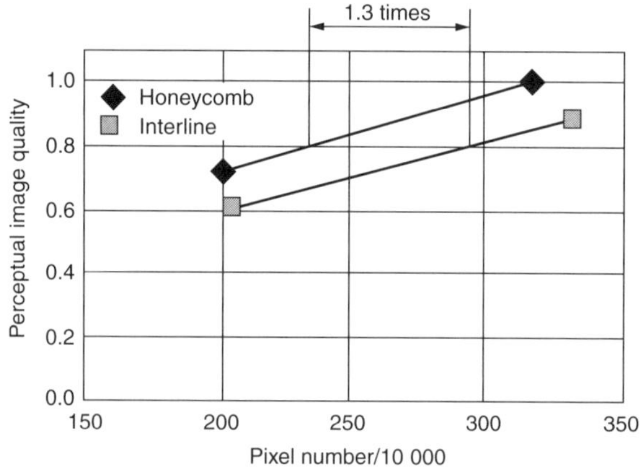

Figure 4.15 Relationship between observer rating value and pixel numbers for the images simulated by interline array and honeycomb array.

directions is superior to the MTF in the diagonal direction. Therefore we concluded that the honeycomb structure CCD is better than the interline CCD for image sharpness. Figure 4.14 shows the simulated images of (a) interline, and (b) honeycomb CCD arrays. This was confirmed by an experiment in which observers rated the images produced by the computer simulation (Figure 4.15).

4.5 QUALITY IMPROVEMENT OF NOISY IMAGES BY WIENER FILTER

A digital image captured by a CCD camera is usually degraded by many kinds of noise. It is important to reduce the noise without degradation of image sharpness and colour quality in various digital imaging processes. We have proposed a new Wiener filter, which can be calculated from the covariance matrices of the observed image on the assumption that the original image and noise have no correlation, and noise covariance can be estimated at the system characterisation stage or from a uniform density region within the image.

In the RGB colour space, the pixel vector of the observed image $\mathbf{g}_i$ is represented as the sum of the pixel vector of the original image $\mathbf{f}_i$ and the noise vector $\mathbf{n}_i$:

$$\mathbf{g}_i = \mathbf{f}_i + \mathbf{n}_i \tag{4.13}$$

where i denotes the pixel number ($1 \leqslant i \leqslant nm$); and n, m are the numbers of pixels in the horizontal and vertical directions, respectively. We represent the mean vector of the observed image as $\bar{\mathbf{g}}$, the pixel vector of the corrected image as $\hat{\mathbf{f}}_i$, and the mean vector of the corrected image as $\bar{\hat{\mathbf{f}}}$. Then these vectors can be related by the colour separation Wiener (CSW) filter $\mathbf{G}$ as:

$$\hat{\mathbf{f}}_i - \bar{\hat{\mathbf{f}}} = \mathbf{G}(\mathbf{g}_i - \bar{\mathbf{g}}) \tag{4.14}$$

The filter $\mathbf{G}$ is determined so as to minimise the mean square error between the original and corrected images:

$$E = \langle \|(\mathbf{f}_i - \bar{\mathbf{f}}) - \mathbf{G}(\mathbf{g}_i - \bar{\mathbf{g}})\|^2 \rangle \to \min \tag{4.15}$$

where the angle brackets denote the expectation operation with respect to i.

If the original image does not have any correlation with the noise, $\mathbf{G}$ is calculated from the covariance matrices of the original image and noise, as is well known. However, the covariance matrix of the original image, $\mathbf{C}_{ff}$, is generally unknown. On the other hand, the covariance matrix of the observed image, $\mathbf{C}_{gg}$, can be obtained as:

$$\mathbf{C}_{gg} = \langle (\mathbf{g}_i - \bar{\mathbf{g}})(\mathbf{g}_i - \bar{\mathbf{g}})^{\mathrm{T}} \rangle \tag{4.16}$$

If we assume that the original image and noise do not have any correlation, the covariance matrix of original image can be represented as:

$$\mathbf{C}_{ff} = \mathbf{C}_{gg} - \mathbf{C}_{nn} \tag{4.17}$$

Then the filter **G** is:

$$\mathbf{G} = (\mathbf{C}_{gg} - \mathbf{C}_{nn})\mathbf{C}_{gg}^{-1} \tag{4.18}$$

The CSW filter **G** calculated by (4.18) was found to be effective in reducing noise while preserving edges, compared to the conventional smoothing filter and median filter. We then designed a more effective filter for noise reduction and sharpness preservation. If the noise is white and uncorrelated to the original image, the CSW filter defined by (4.18) can be modified as follows. $\mathbf{C}_{gg}$ in (4.16) can be expanded using diagonal matrix $\mathbf{\Lambda}_g$:

$$\mathbf{C}_{gg} = \mathbf{P}_g \Lambda_g \mathbf{P}_g^{\mathrm{T}} \tag{4.19}$$

Here $\mathbf{\Lambda}_g$ has the eigenvalues in the diagonal components, and matrix $\mathbf{P}_g$ has eigenvectors of $\mathbf{C}_{gg}$ in the columns. Superscript T denotes transpose of the matrix. In the same manner, the covariance matrix of noise $\mathbf{C}_{nn}$ can be also expanded using matrices $\mathbf{\Lambda}_n$ and $\mathbf{P}_n$ as:

$$\mathbf{C}_{nn} = \mathbf{P}_n \Lambda_n \mathbf{P}_n^{\mathrm{T}} \tag{4.20}$$

An arbitrary orthonormal basis set can be selected as the eigenvectors of $\mathbf{C}_{nn}$ in the case of white noise. Thus we can determine $\mathbf{P}_n$ as follows:

$$\mathbf{P}_n = \mathbf{P}_g \tag{4.21}$$

Substituting (4.19), (4.20) and (4.21) into (4.18) we obtain:

$$\mathbf{G} = \mathbf{P}_g(\Lambda_g - \Lambda_n)\Lambda_n^{-1}\mathbf{P}_g^{\mathrm{T}} \tag{4.22}$$

Equation (4.22) can also be expressed using component representation:

$$\mathbf{G} = \mathbf{P}_g \begin{bmatrix} \dfrac{\sigma_{g^1}^2 - \sigma_n^2}{\sigma_{g^1}^2} & 0 & 0 \\ 0 & \dfrac{\sigma_{g^2}^2 - \sigma_n^2}{\sigma_{g^2}^2} & 0 \\ 0 & 0 & \dfrac{\sigma_{g^3}^2 - \sigma_n^2}{\sigma_{g^3}^2} \end{bmatrix} \tag{4.23}$$

where $\sigma_{g^1}^2$, $\sigma_{g^2}^2$, $\sigma_{g^3}^2$ and σ_n^2 are the eigenvalues of $\mathbf{C}_{gg}$ and $\mathbf{C}_{nn}$, respectively.

The operation with **G** can be interpreted as: (1) orthogonal transformation by $\mathbf{P}_g^{\mathrm{T}}$; (2) filtering using signal and noise variances; and (3) inverse transform by $\mathbf{P}_g$. Computer simulation based on the proposed method has been performed using samples made from the original images, ISO/JIS-SCID N1 to N8, degraded by additive white noise. In the simulation, noisy images are first classified into 10 colour classes. The covariance matrices $\mathbf{C}_{gg}$ of the observed images of each class are estimated from the neighbouring pixels, which are selected around the current pixel with a colour classification technique.

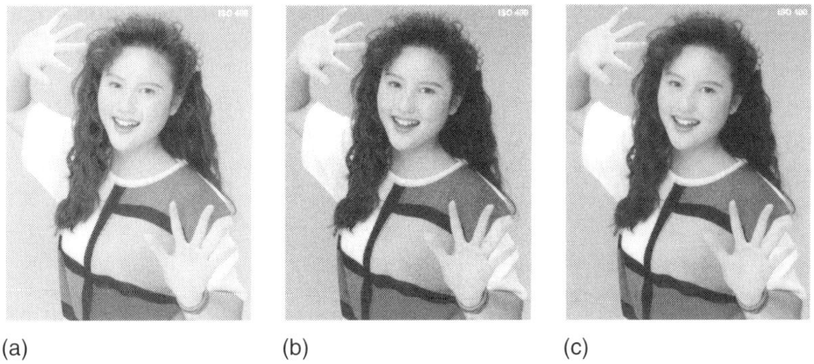

Figure 4.16 Improving a noisy image using the Colour Separation Wiener (CSW) filter of equation (4.22): (a) original image, (b) noisy image, (c) corrected image (Photos N1 and N1A of ISO Standard 12 640 : 1997, are reproduced with the permission of the International Organization for Standardization, ISO. This standard can be obtained from any ISO member and from the website of the ISO Central Secretariat at the following address: http//www.iso.org. Copyright remains with ISO).

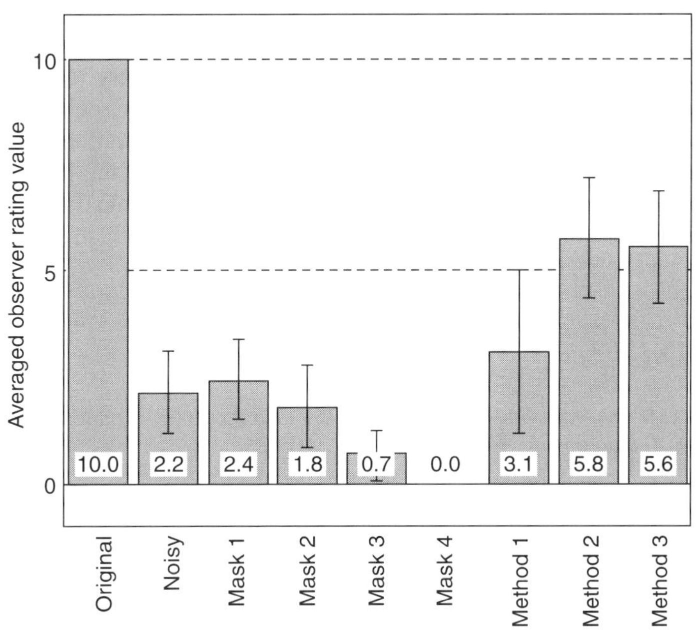

Figure 4.17 Result of observer rating values (average for 8 kinds of image by 20 observers) for original, noisy image and corrected images based on conventional smoothing filters, conventional Wiener filter (method 1), equation (4.18) (method 2), and equation (4.23) (method 3).

Figure 4.16(a) shows one of the original images used in the simulation. Figure 4.16(b) shows the image degraded by noise. Figure 4.16(c) shows the image corrected by the modified CSW filter processing.

Figure 4.17 shows the obtained observer rating value (ORV) for SCID images N1 to N8. The ORV means that a higher value corresponds to better image quality. The test images corrected by the CSW filter method showed higher ORV than the images corrected by any conventional convolution masks.

4.6 CONCLUSIONS

This chapter has reviewed recent research studies at Chiba University for the improvement of digital image quality. Spectral reflectance is an inherent attribute of any object. Therefore it should be used for image transmission, recording and reproduction and for computer simulation in design of imaging systems in the future. In colour reproduction, multispectral imaging systems with high accuracy have been developed and applied for the recording of art paintings. Dichromatic and Phong models were introduced to reproduce the colour and glossiness of 3D objects. It was also shown that the reflectance spectra of skin and gastric membranes could be estimated from three channel signals based on principal component analysis.

Furthermore, it was shown that a CCD array with honeycomb structure could significantly improve image sharpness. In the future it will be necessary to study the optimal design of digital imaging systems based on CCD array structure, colour filter transmittance, noise reduction, interpolation, and so on. The colour separation Wiener filter was also shown to be a useful means of reducing noise without reducing image sharpness.

Digital imaging has a great many capabilities and the introduction of multispectral image processing techniques and methods of image quality evaluation opens up many exciting new avenues for research and application.

REFERENCES

1. T. Shiobara, H. Haneishi and Y. Miyake (1996) Improved colour reproduction of electronic endoscopes. *J. Imaging Sci. Technol.*, **40**, 494–501.
2. F. H. Imai, N. Tsumura, H. Haneishi and Y. Miyake (1998) Improvement of incomplete chromatic adaptation model for facial pattern images. *J. Imaging Sci. Technol.*, **42**, 264–268.
3. N. Ojima, H. Haneishi and Y. Miyake (1993) The appearance of skin with make-up II (analysis on surface topology of skin with make-up). *J. Soc. Photo. Sci. Technol. Japan*, **56**, 264–269.
4. Y. Miyake and Y. Yokoyama (1999) Development of multi-band color imaging systems for recording of art paintings. *Proc. SPIE*, **3648**, 218–225.
5. M. Baba, T. Ishimaru, M. Tamaru, M. Inuiya, H. Haneishi and Y. Miyake (1999) Evaluation of image quality for CCD camera with honeycomb structure by computer simulation. *J. Soc. Photo. Sci. Technol. Japan*, **63**(4), 204–209.
6. K. Miyata, N. Tsumura, H. Haneishi and Y. Miyake (2000) Quality improvement of noisy images by Wiener filters designed in color space. *J. Soc. Photo. Sci. Technol. Japan*, **63**(1) 18–27 (in Japanese).
7. H. Haneishi, T. Iwanami, T. Honma, N. Tsumura and Y. Miyake (1998) Color and glossiness reproduction of 3D object surface. *Proc. IS&T*, 354–358.

8. H. Haneishi, T. Yamada, N. Tsumura and Y. Miyake (1998) Optimum design of spectral characteristics of light source for an optical endoscopes. *Kogaku*, **27**(3), 164–171.
9. M. Takeya, N. Tsumura, H. Haneishi and Y. Miyake (1999) Estimation of transmittance spectra from multiband micrographs of fungi and its application to segmentation of conidia and hyphae. *Applied Optics*, **38**(16), 3644–3650.
10. Y. Yokoyama, T. Hasegawa, N. Tsumura, H. Haneishi and Y. Miyake (1998) New color management system based on human perception and its application to recording and reproduction of art paintings (I). *J. Soc. Photo. Sci. Technol. Japan*, **61**(6), 343–355, (in Japanese).
11. W. Kondou, K. Miyata, H. Haneishi and Y. Miyake (2000) A new compression method of multispectral images based on principal component analysis. *Display and Imaging*, **8**, 301–307, (in Japanese)
12. Y. Miyake Introduction. *Proceedings of the International Symposium on Multispectral Imaging and Color Reproduction for Digital Archives*, University of Chiba (2000).

5

Spectral colour statistics of surfaces

Mitch Thomson and Stephen Westland

5.1 INTRODUCTION

Traditional image-capture devices such as scanners and digital cameras capture and represent information about real scenes or surfaces by means of three broadband sensors usually termed (often misleadingly) red, green and blue. The colorimetric information represented by the resulting RGB values will in general be device and illuminant dependent, and either dependency may make difficult the subsequent accurate representation of colorimetric information in the target. Device dependency often leads to a form of 'observer metamerism' – two physically different colour signals can be identical to the RGB system but not to the CIE observer, or conversely, two physically different colour signals can be identical to the CIE observer but not to the RGB system.

In fact, unless the device sensors happen to be equivalent to (i.e. identical to, or to a linear transform of) the CIE colour matching functions of the standard observer, there will be no one-to-one correspondence or mapping between device space and CIE xyz space and, since transforms of the latter are typically used as a reasonable working approximation to human perceptual space, this limits the usefulness of these devices. Illuminant dependency is potentially an even more serious problem: the human visual system is approximately

Colour Image Science, edited by L.W. MacDonald and M.R. Luo.

colour constant (surfaces retain their approximate daylight appearance when viewed under a wide range of different light sources), whereas the physics of colour imaging dictates that changes in illuminants' spectral energy distributions are just as able to change device RGB values as changes in surface spectral reflectance.

The limitations of these trichromatic imaging systems have inspired efforts to develop image-capture devices that record *spectral* information about surfaces. The ultimate aim when using such a device is usually to produce estimates of the spectral reflectance functions of target surfaces: spectral reflectance data are usually thought of as being both device and illuminant independent (although we discuss later some reasons why this may not be so in practice). The term *multispectral imaging* is typically used for image-capture devices that use 6 or more broadband sensors, whereas the term *hyperspectral imaging* is usually reserved for devices that use 30 or more narrowband sensors.

Whether the instrument uses 2 or 30 spectral channels, it must essentially perform a sampling of the colour signal spectra, and a key question is how many channels or measurements are required to determine these spectra to an acceptable degree of accuracy. The answer to this question depends critically upon the statistics of surface spectral reflectances (for both natural and man-made surfaces), the statistics of spectral energy distributions of light sources, and the definition of 'acceptable'. The aim of this study is to illustrate some of the issues that bear upon this question with some new spectral data gathered within the last few years. We begin with some mathematical preliminaries.

5.2 LINEAR MODELS FOR REPRESENTING COLORIMETRIC DATA

A *linear model* of a dataset is simply a set of N basis functions which, when added together in varying linear proportions, will represent any member of that dataset. One may say, for example, that a spectroradiometer provides a particularly simple linear model of colour signals, in that the sum of the fixed bases $R_i(\lambda)$ of the spectroradiometer (in this case the bases are simply the spectral equivalents of the well-known pointspread function), weighted by the measured spectral data σ_i, will represent a particular colour signal:

$$R(\lambda) = \sigma_1 R_1(\lambda) + \sigma_2 R_2(\lambda) + \cdots + \sigma_N R_N(\lambda) \tag{5.1}$$

Once the $R_i(\lambda)$ are known, a set of weights σ_i will be sufficient to specify any single colour signal. The only assumptions involved here are those of linearity; these bases must superpose linearly and a uniform scaling of the weights σ_i must scale $R(\lambda)$ linearly.

Typically, a number of information-theoretic constraints are applied to the choice of basis; for example, one might reasonably wish that, given a random dataset, the information carried by one weighted basis, say $\sigma_1 R_1$, provides absolutely no information at all about the information carried on a different weighted basis, say $\sigma_2 R_2$. In an ideal world, these two quantities would be orthogonal, i.e. for a set of random colour signals, $\mathrm{E}\{(\sigma_1 R_1)(\sigma_2 R_2)\}$ would be zero (where E is the expectation operator), but in real-world systems, the signals are almost always corrupted by noise, in which case the best one can do is to have bases which are orthogonal, i.e. $\mathrm{E}\{(\sigma_1 R_1)(\sigma_2 R_2)\} = \mathrm{E}\{\sigma_1 R_1\}\mathrm{E}\{\sigma_2 R_2\}$. In the example above, the spectroradiometer will provide an orthogonal, linear basis of a set of colour signals if the product of expectations of every pair of $\sigma_i R_i$ is zero (orthogonality does not require that the bases be non-overlapping). In spectroradiometry it is commonly assumed that the device achieves point sampling in the spectral domain, i.e. the spectral pointspread functions R_i are Dirac delta functions (in which case orthogonality is clearly satisfied), but in practice the device always has a finite spectral bandwidth, so orthogonality is far from guaranteed.

Alternatively, spectral data may be represented by a linear transform of the input space; for example, one might choose to compute the Fourier transform (FT) of the 'weights' (the σ_i), which simply rotates the coordinate system from one basis (the spectral domain, or the domain of wavelength) to another – the domain of Fourier transforms of wavelength, or the domain of *spectral frequency*. There are in effect an infinite number of such rotations; the space of Fourier transforms of sampled colour signals is just another linear basis for representing colour signals. Notice that since the basis functions of the FT (the R_i) are sine waves and cosine waves, these are mutually orthogonal, but the weighted bases (the $\sigma_i R_i$) may not be mutually orthogonal, since the original bases of the system (the spectral pointspread functions of the spectroradiometer) might not have been orthogonal in the first place.

Some statistical techniques, however, do not simply rotate the coordinate system; rather, they attempt to deduce from the input data set a class of linear, orthogonal bases which themselves are derived from the data. The members of this class of techniques differ slightly in respect of the metric they use and the precise way in which the bases are selected (usually so as to package the variance of the input dataset in a quite particular manner). Among these techniques are principal component analysis (PCA), characteristic vector analysis (CVA), eigenfunction analysis, Karhunen–Loeve transformation (KLT) and factor analysis. These data-dependent, multivariate statistical techniques typically allow the expression of large data sets by a small number of linear combinations of the original data and a corresponding set of known constants. CVA, the technique on which the present study is based, returns the eigenvectors and eigenvalues of the covariance matrix, which equates to the best-fitting linear model of the data under the criterion of least squares.

There is a natural relationship between some of these techniques and that of Fourier analysis. For example, if the statistics of the input data are exactly stationary, the bases returned by PCA will be sine waves and cosine waves – the bases of the Fourier transform. This is because Fourier *phase* is the parameter that distinguishes CVA-type analyses from Fourier analyses: it is represented explicitly in the Fourier transform but implicitly in CVA (i.e. it is incorporated into the shape of the basis functions). The phase values (in spectral frequency space) of a sample's spectrum play an important role in determining the position of that sample in chromaticity space.

Standard algorithms exist for computing both of these transformations: Fourier methods are generally based on the discrete fast Fourier transform algorithm, whereas CVA typically invokes standard packages for computing matrix eigenvectors and eigenvalues. Since both CVA and FT techniques change only the coordinate system in which the data are represented, both forms of linear model nominally require the same number of coefficients as in the original (wavelength) domain, i.e. the techniques produce no reduction in dimensionality *per se*. The motivation behind fitting these models, however, is often to reduce the dimensionality of the data, i.e. to represent N-dimensional data with fewer than N coefficients. This is accomplished by truncating the basis expansion, throwing away the last m terms; the linear model is then expressed as the weighted sum of $n = N - m$ bases plus a term $e(\lambda)$ which denotes the error incurred in discarding the last m terms:

$$R(\lambda) = \sigma_1 R_1(\lambda) + \sigma_2 R_2(\lambda) + \cdots + \sigma_n R_n(\lambda) + e(\lambda) \tag{5.2}$$

One fundamental distinction between Fourier analysis and CVA lies in the ordering of the bases: in an FT the bases are ordered by frequency, whereas in CVA the bases are ordered by 'variance accounted for', whereby the first basis function is the one that accounts for most of the variance in the ensemble, the second basis function is the one that accounts for most of the remaining variance, and so on. Thus, throwing away the last m terms in a CVA corresponds to throwing away the terms that account for the m smallest amounts of variance in the ensemble; for Fourier analysis, throwing away the last m terms corresponds to lowpass filtering or smoothing, since it is the highest-frequency terms that are lost. One may study the effects of these truncations by simply resynthesising every individual signal in the ensemble, using the above expression but without the error term $e(\lambda)$, and using an error metric to compare these truncated and resynthesised signals with the originals. In the case of CVA, this resynthesis is accomplished by multiple regression of each original spectrum onto the basis functions R_i under the criterion of least squares (typically by means of singular value decomposition) to yield the weights σ_i for that spectrum, i.e. by finding the σ_i that minimise the quantity:

$$\sum_{\lambda} [R(\lambda) - (\sigma_1 R_1(\lambda) + \sigma_2 R_2(\lambda) + \cdots + \sigma_n R_n(\lambda))]^2 \tag{5.3}$$

for each individual spectrum. Techniques such as Fourier analysis and CVA can provide useful mathematical descriptors of colour signal, reflectance or illuminant spectral data; they allow us to quantify the information loss incurred by representing the data with only n discrete coefficients within two different coordinate systems. In the next section we briefly review some studies that have investigated the effect of these truncations on the representation of colorimetric data as a means of elucidating constraints on the statistical structure of surfaces and illuminants.

5.3 PREVIOUS STUDIES

5.3.1 Smoothness and dimensionality

Several studies have investigated possible constraints on the nature of spectral reflectance functions of surfaces and/or spectral power distributions of illuminants. Two classes of constraints in particular have received much attention: smoothness constraints and dimensionality constraints.

Smoothness

It has been established that the spectral reflectance functions of most natural and man-made surfaces are lowpass functions (in the space of Fourier transforms of wavelength); that is, the Fourier power spectra of these functions are zero above a certain limiting spectral frequency (the band limit). For example, Maloney [1] has shown that the limiting spectral frequency of a set of Munsell surfaces is between 0.01 and 0.02 cycle per nanometre. Spectral reflectance data are thus essentially smooth functions of wavelength, and this smoothness reflects regularities in the world [2]: the limiting spectral frequency is probably the result of the fundamental mechanisms by which matter interacts with light at a molecular level [3]. Although it is mainly the phase of the spectral frequencies that determines the position of a sample in colour space, there is also a relationship between the limiting spectral frequency and the gamut [4]; for example, the chromaticities of all Munsell chips can be matched by functions of reflectance that are band-limited to 0.015 cycle per nanometre.

Dimensionality

Cohen's original analysis of 150 spectral reflectances of Munsell colour samples found that a linear model with only three parameters could account for 0.992 of the variance in the overall fit [5], and a more recent analysis of the 462 samples in the Nickerson–Munsell set found that 0.9916 of the variance could be accounted for by a linear model with only three parameters [1]. Several authors have since suggested that naturally occurring spectral reflectance curves are also well fitted by low-dimensional models with only a few parameters [1, 6, 7, 8]. Maloney analysed a set of 337 natural reflectance spectra (obtained by Krinov in 1947) and found that 0.9960 of the variance could be accounted for by a linear model with three parameters [1]. Parkinnen *et al.* [9] and Dannemiller [10] have, however, argued that as many as seven parameters may be required to represent the Munsell and natural spectral reflectance data respectively. It may even be true that, in general, the reflectance data of artificial surfaces are as smooth as those of natural surfaces; a linear model for representing reflectances has been developed from a group of 5574 samples of acrylic paint on paper [6], and it was found that seven linear components were necessary and sufficient to represent this data accurately. Dimensionality constraints have also been applied to illuminant data; it is well known, for example, that phases of natural daylight can be accounted for by a linear model with just three parameters [11]. More recently it has been shown that a seven-dimensional linear model can represent adequately the spectral energy distributions of artificial illuminants [12].

5.3.2 Model fitting

Although these two classes of constraint are almost certainly closely related in practice (for reasons related to the physical causes of colour), they are nominally quite distinct. For example, the spectral power distributions of artificial illuminants have been fitted successfully with a low-dimensional model [12] but the data set used in this study included fluorescent sources which have very non-smooth power distributions. The opposite case, where a data set is very smooth but not low-dimensional, would occur if each member of a data set was well modelled by a very low frequency sine wave having a specific phase: the limiting spectral frequency would be very low (since the data are so smooth) but one might need a many-parameter linear model (to represent the variation in the data caused by changing the phase terms).

The observation that most spectral reflectance data sets appear both smooth and low-dimensional is a property of the data, and is probably related to the fact that the physical causes of colour are finite in number and result in spectral bandpass phenomena. This is also true for illuminants; for example, it has been suggested that the three dimensions along which natural daylight varies have a clear physical basis [2]. The first variation is a light–dark direction which is affected by the intensity of the natural light source. Chromatically non-selective filtering can occur when light reaches a scene after being scattered by chromatically neutral surfaces (e.g. white clouds, grey cliffs). The second dimension of chromatic variation is yellow–blue and arises mainly as a result of Rayleigh scattering by small particles in the atmosphere. The third dimension of variation is red–green and this depends on the elevation of the sun and on the atmospheric burden of water vapour (long wavelengths are most absorbed by water).

5.4 ISSUES IN SPECTRAL CAPTURE AND MODELLING

In this section we discuss three important issues that affect spectral capture and modelling: the nature of the illuminant, the estimation of reconstruction error, and the precise manner of fitting the linear model.

5.4.1 Illuminant

Suppose one were able to capture a spectral reflectance function directly using a reflectance spectrophotometer. Since it measures *samples* of a signal, not the signal itself, one would need to consider the resolution of the spectrophotometer in wavelength space. Assuming it produces point samples in λ, basic principles of time series analysis may be used to quantify the accuracy of spectral capture. The uniform sampling theorem [13] states that 'if a signal is band-limited with no components at frequencies greater than f_h, then it is completely specified by samples taken at the uniform rate $f_s > 2f_h$.'

The minimum sampling rate or minimum sampling frequency, f_s, is called the *Nyquist rate* or the *Nyquist frequency*; thus, if the upper band limit is known for a given set of data, one may compute the necessary sampling rate that the device must have in order to capture the spectrum with no loss of information. Alternatively, this rate can be converted to the number n of samples that are required, by simply multiplying by the length of the signal W: the number of samples required is at least $2f_hW$: where the units of f_h are cycle per nanometre and the units of W are nanometre. For example, a typical W might be 300 nm, so if f_h was 0.01 cycle per nanometre, at least six samples would be required for lossless capture.

In most cases, however, the signal capture is performed by a spectroradiometer, so the captured signal is not the spectral reflectance S of a surface but rather the colour signal R; the two are related by the formula $R(\lambda) = S(\lambda)E(\lambda)$, where E is the spectral energy distribution of the light source and λ is wavelength. In colour and imaging science the assumption is often made that if $E(\lambda)$ can be determined (typically through spectroradiometric measurements of a white tile), then a simple pointwise division suffices to return $S(\lambda)$.

In practice things are not so simple, since one needs to consider how finely one must sample R in order to achieve lossless capture. It has been shown [1] that if the surface is a band-limited function with band limit p and the illuminant is a band-limited function with band limit q, then the resultant colour signal will also be a band-limited function with band limit $r = p + q$. Thus, the band limit of the colour signal must be strictly larger than the band limit of the spectral reflectance function, and for very unsmooth illuminants, q could be very large. For Munsell samples imaged under a fluorescent illuminant, q would be much larger than p. Since a given spectroradiometer will deliver a fixed resolution in wavelength space (and therefore a fixed r), one might say that the illuminant 'uses up' some of the bandwidth provided by the device; this effect is often ignored, particularly in computational work, since after dividing $S(\lambda)$ by $E(\lambda)$ the illuminant is usually conveniently forgotten about.

5.4.2 Estimation of reconstruction error

Recall from Section 5.2 that one may assess the success of a linear model for spectral data by comparing the truncated and resynthesised spectra with the original spectra. An important issue is exactly how these spectra should be compared. Almost all published studies report either the proportion of variance accounted for in the data by the models, or a closely related statistic, the root mean square (RMS) reconstruction error. But these measures do not easily allow the practical consequences of information loss to be assessed. Indeed, Maloney reports that, for the Krinov data, just two principal components will account for 99.2% of the variance, yet few of us would think of a two-dimensional colour vision system as providing an adequate representation of surface spectral reflectance.

Perhaps a more pertinent question is whether the two-parameter reconstructions of these spectra would be visually distinguishable from the original spectra (in this case almost certainly). Such a question could be addressed through the use of standard-observer colour difference metrics such as CIE ΔE [14, 15], although these themselves are quite imperfect (CIELAB space suffers from perceptibility variations of up to sixfold).

5.4.3 Fitting linear models

Some modifications to the standard linear modelling techniques are usually necessary to ensure sensible results. As Maloney points out [1], one should make the spectral data set zero mean (or else the CVA will return the mean spectrum as the first basis) and also normalise the spectra such that they are unit length vectors (otherwise higher absolute spectral values will contribute more to the error metric). Accordingly, as in [1], here the technique used is a variant of CVA proper, which does not include these modifications.

This CVA variant will find one particular orthogonal basis of the spectral data set, whereas there are in fact infinitely many orthogonal bases; all that is special about the CVA bases is the manner in which the expansion is ordered (by 'variance accounted for'). Notice also that the misgivings about error metrics voiced above apply not only to an *a posteriori* analysis of the bases produced; it is a least squares error metric that drives the CVA itself, and this also may be problematic. For example, the CVA algorithm may go to great lengths to reduce high RMS errors at wavelengths where human vision is very insensitive. Maloney [1] addressed this by weighting the error metric with the spectral sensitivity envelope of human colour vision (V_λ), but this could be a dangerous procedure in itself (since there may well be wavelengths where absolute spectral sensitivity is low yet around which discrimination is rather sensitive).

Fourier analyses of spectral data require that one contend with the fundamental problem of spectral estimation: the trade-off between bias and variance that depends on the choice of window in the wavelength domain. If no window is used (effectively a square window), the estimated signal will suffer from spectral broadening and the possible introduction of spurious high spectral frequencies (since the spectrum of the signal is convolved with the spectrum of the window, which for a square window is a sinc function). A standard spectrum estimation window (e.g. the Hanning window), will ameliorate both this effect and the problem of circularity (unmodified, the Fourier transform will treat the spectrum as circular in wavelength whereas it is of course linear) but at a cost of reducing the overall power of the signal.

In the rest of this chapter, we describe a new spectral data set and consider the application of linear models to this data set in the light of the issues discussed above.

5.5 COLLECTION AND MEASUREMENT OF DATA

A set of natural surfaces was obtained from the environs of Keele and Derby universities in the Midlands region of the UK. The spectral reflectance values of these were measured between 400 nm and 700 nm at 10 nm intervals using an Ihara S900 reflectance spectrophotometer (0/45 geometry). A total of 1154 reflectance spectra were thus obtained, called the *natural set*. For comparison purposes a set of 1269 Munsell reflectance spectra, called the *Munsell set*, were obtained [7, 9]. As discussed above, since there is a well-defined relationship between the gamut of the colours contained within these data sets and the parameters of the resulting models (this is true of both Fourier analysis and CVA), our aim when sampling the natural environment was to obtain as large as possible a gamut of colours *in order to avoid the possibility of generating overoptimistic linear models with overoptimistically few parameters*. In other words, it is much more important that our linear model's statistics reflect those of that linear model which would be derived from an unimaginably large database than it is for the probability distribution of our samples' spectra to reflect the corresponding real-world probability distribution. It has been pointed out to us that had we used the latter criterion, our collection of natural spectral reflectance functions would be dominated by the reflectance spectra of chlorophyll-pigmented surfaces.

5.6 REPRESENTATION OF REFLECTANCE DATA BY LINEAR MODELS

5.6.1 Dimensionality

CVAs were computed for both data sets independently (Figure 5.1). The components are different for the two sets but this most likely reflects the different weighting given to

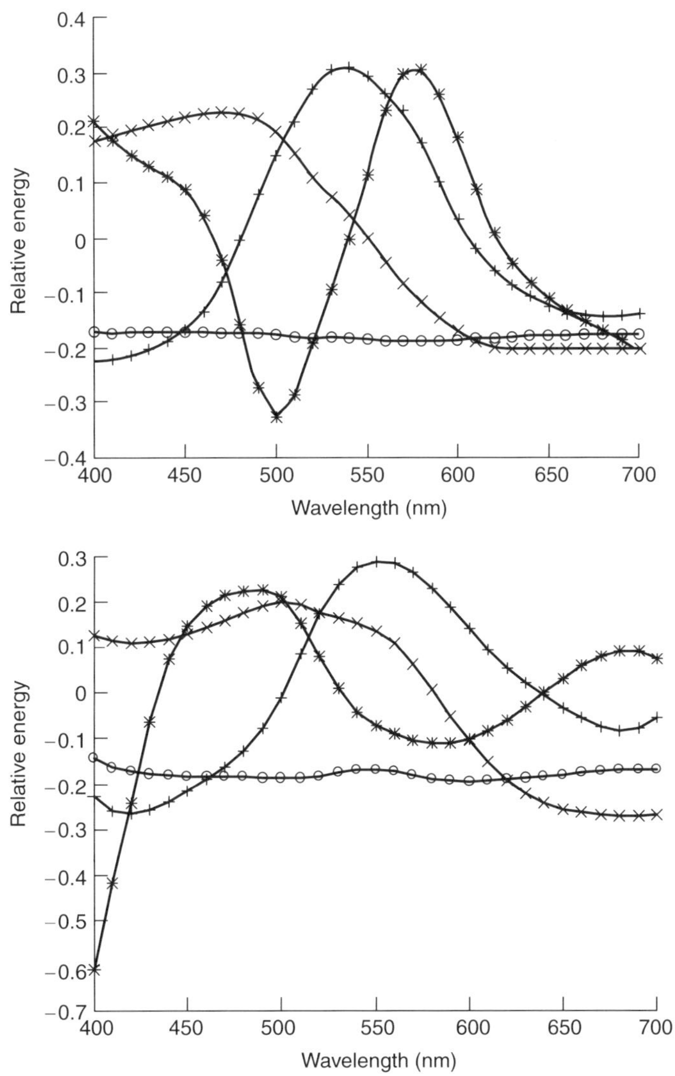

Figure 5.1 First four bases for (a) Munsell and (b) natural data sets: (○) first basis, (×) second basis, (+) third basis, (∗) fourth basis.

different areas of colour space caused by sampling. Specifically, recall that the position of a sample in colour space is determined largely by the *phase* of the coefficients in the Fourier transform of its spectral reflectance function; if there are indeed colour space sampling differences, one would expect the bases returned by the two CVAs to be of similar smoothness but to differ by linear shifts in their constituent Fourier components, and the shapes of the two plots in Figure 5.1 appear broadly consistent with this.

Differences in sampling characteristics are also evident in the mean spectral reflectance distributions for the two data sets (Figure 5.2).

In general, the bases of Figure 5.1 increase in their band limit and, in fact, become increasingly bandpass rather than lowpass. The band limits of the first three bases of the Munsell set are 0.005, 0.010 and 0.0250 cycle per nanometre, respectively. Table 5.1 lists the proportion of variance accounted for by increasing numbers of bases. It is tempting to conclude that both data sets can be adequately represented by a linear model with relatively few parameters and that the natural set is almost as low-dimensional as the Munsell data set.

The data in Table 5.1 may, however, be expressed in terms of perceptual colour differences: reconstruction errors may be computed as CIELAB colour differences between actual reflectance spectra and spectra reconstructed from n bases. The means of these reconstruction errors are presented for both data sets in Table 5.2.

Table 5.2 illustrates that approximately 5–7 components would be required to represent these reflectance spectra to the accuracy that would be required by many commercial applications. Comparing Tables 5.1 and 5.2 allows us to draw a number of conclusions. First, notice that 5–7 components in Table 5.1 corresponds to about 99.8% of the total variance; total variance is certainly not a good guide to accuracy of reconstruction in

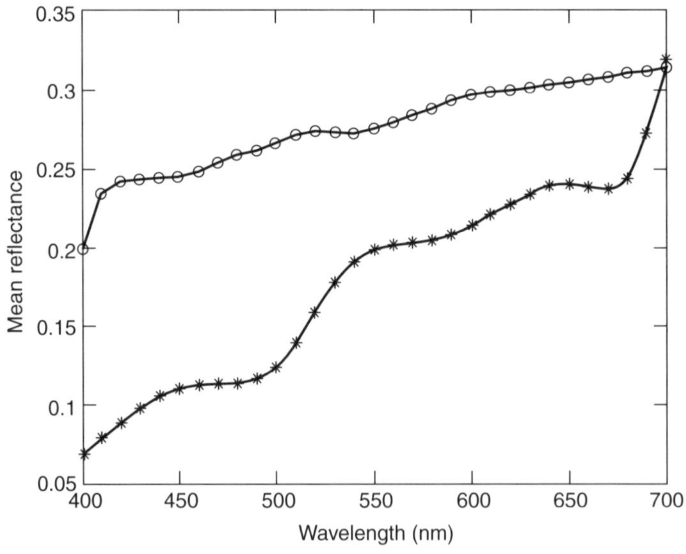

Figure 5.2 Mean reflectance for (○) natural and (∗) Munsell sets.

Table 5.1 Proportion of variance accounted for using n Bases

n	Munsell	Natural
1	0.757	0.733
2	0.921	0.861
3	0.985	0.963
4	0.993	0.987
5	0.996	0.994
6	0.998	0.997
7	0.999	0.998

Table 5.2 Mean CIELAB reconstruction errors for linear models with varying numbers n of parameters

	$n = 1$	$n = 2$	$n = 3$	$n = 4$	$n = 5$	$n = 6$	$n = 7$
Mean ΔE^*_{ab}							
Munsell	22.72	16.86	3.21	2.37	1.30	0.29	0.25
Natural	29.17	25.26	5.99	6.18	2.52	0.71	0.40

terms of human perception. Secondly, the ΔE measure does not necessarily decrease monotonically with variance accounted for; the four-component resynthesis of the natural data is actually worse than the three-component resynthesis by the criterion of ΔE^*_{ab}. This reflects how the different error metrics are used to drive the CVA (least squares) and to assess the accuracy of reconstruction (ΔE). Thirdly, the error values for the natural data set are generally appreciably higher than those for the Munsell data set, even though the statistics in Table 5.1 barely differ.

5.6.2 Smoothness

Table 5.3 shows the proportion of power contained by various candidate band limits in the Fourier power spectra. To generate the data in Table 5.3, each reflectance spectrum was multiplied by a Hanning window before computing the Fourier power spectrum using the fast Fourier transform. The proportion of power below each candidate band limit was computed separately for each spectrum and the median value computed across all spectra. Table 5.3 also shows comparative data obtained without using the Hanning window. From Table 5.3 we can conclude that 0.015 cycle per nanometre is a reasonable estimate of the band limit for both data sets. The band limit corresponds to a linear model with n basis vectors [13]. For both data sets, a reasonable estimate for n would be 9.

5.6.3 Illuminants

Figure 5.3 shows the spectral power distributions of three illuminants: D65, A and F11.

Table 5.3 Proportion of power below candidate band limits for natural and Munsell data set

Candidate band limit (cycles/nm)	Natural		Munsell	
	Hanning	No Hanning	Hanning	No Hanning
0.0025	0.9168	0.9612	0.9423	0.9876
0.0050	0.9876	0.9776	0.9946	0.9968
0.0100	0.9991	0.9863	0.9997	0.9986
0.0150	0.9999	0.9912	0.9999	0.9992
0.0200	1.0000	0.9935	1.0000	0.9994
0.0300	1.0000	0.9966	1.0000	0.9977

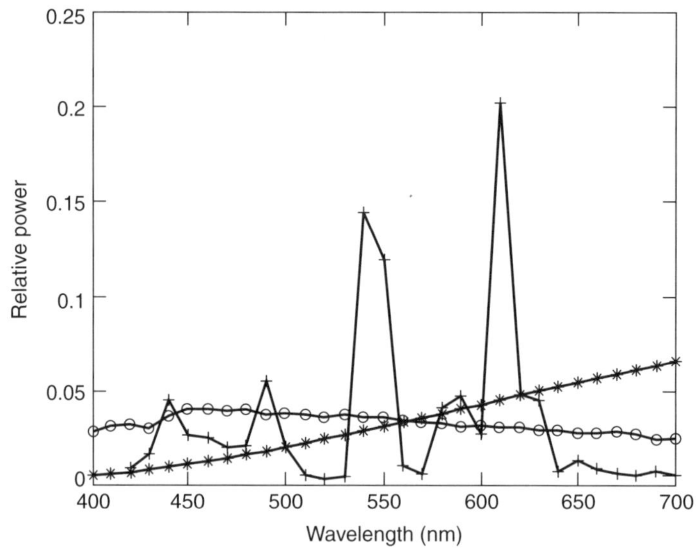

Figure 5.3 Relative spectral power distributions (normalised for equal total energy) for three illuminants (○) D65, (∗) A and (+) F11.

The band limits (corresponding to limiting spectral frequencies containing 99.9% of the Fourier power) were estimated as being 0.008, 0.015 and 0.05 cycle per nanometre for illuminants A, D65 and F11 respectively. But these estimates were computed from data sampled at 10 nm intervals and this imposes an upper value of 0.05 cycle per nanometre on the band limits; the true band limit of an F11 light source may be even higher than 0.05 cycle per nanometre.

5.6.4 Colour signals

Using these illuminant data and the spectral reflectance data described above, colour signals were simulated for the Munsell and natural data sets under each of the three

Table 5.4 Proportion of Fourier power contained by various candidate band limits (after limiting with a Hanning window)

Band Limit (cycles/nm)	Natural			Munsell		
	D65	F11	A	D65	F11	A
0.0025	0.9100	0.4755	0.9097	0.9391	0.5129	0.9313
0.0050	0.9814	0.5307	0.9878	0.9937	0.5602	0.9944
0.0100	0.9994	0.5610	0.9992	0.9995	0.5786	0.9997
0.0150	0.9996	0.6883	0.9999	0.9997	0.6978	0.9999
0.0200	0.9998	0.7888	1.0000	0.9998	0.7940	1.0000
0.0300	0.9999	0.9003	1.0000	0.9999	0.8866	1.0000

illuminants, and these colour signals were subjected to Fourier analysis. Table 5.4 lists the proportion of power contained by various candidate band limits for the colour signals derived for each of the two data sets under each of the three illuminants considered in this study.

The band limits for the natural colour signals under D65, A and F11 are 0.0300, 0.015 and >0.0500 and compared with 0.015 for the reflectance spectra alone. In the case of D65 the colour signal band limit is almost exactly the sum of the band limits for the reflectance spectra and illuminant spectrum, but this is not the case for the other illuminants. The band limits for the colour signals under illuminant A are not quite as high as expected from theory, and this may be due to an interaction between the Hanning window and the spectral characteristics of this illuminant (the shape of the window might compensate for the gradient in the illuminant's spectral power distribution (Figure 5.3), making it flatter and therefore reducing the band limit). Moreover, it is impossible to estimate the band limits for colour signals under illuminant F11, since the illuminant alone is beyond the band limit of the device. Thus, the band limits for the three sets of colour signals are clearly different and could not generally be predicted from Fourier theory alone. Similar results are shown for the colour signals derived from the Munsell samples.

5.7 CONCLUSIONS

We have reported Fourier and characteristic vector analyses of a new set of natural reflectance spectra. As previous studies have shown, the reflectance spectra of both natural and Munsell surfaces have been found to be highly constrained; for example, Fourier analyses have shown that both data sets are band-limited with a limiting spectral frequency of about 0.015 cycle per nanometre, in good agreement with previous estimates of this figure for both data sets [1, 4, 8]. The main novel findings fall into two categories.

CIELAB errors

In spite of the fact that three-dimensional linear models may account for as much as 99% of the variance in some spectral data sets, linear models may in general require as many as seven parameters in order to produce reconstruction errors of the order of 1.0 CIELAB units. CIELAB errors are not predictable from 'variance accounted for' measures and the two statistics may not even be related monotonically in n; CIELAB errors may also be more sensitive to the precise nature of the spectral data set. Thus, the choice of error metric is of prime importance in assessing the accuracy to which a set of surface spectral reflectance functions or colour signals can be subsequently recovered.

Choice of illuminant

Although the band limits of simulated colour signals were found to be greater than those of the corresponding reflectance spectra, in line with the theoretical assumption that band limits are additive when band-limited functions are convolved in Fourier (spectral) frequency space, theoretical predictions of colour signal band limits may be rather poor for important practical reasons. Thus, the statistical properties of light sources need to be considered carefully when colour signals are sampled by multispectral imaging systems. Indeed, before gathering important spectroradiometric data under a given illuminant, it may be advisable to check the statistics of the sampled colour signals to ensure that the spectral band limits are substantially lower than the limiting resolution of the measuring device; otherwise it may not be possible to recover accurate spectral reflectance functions from the colour signal data.

REFERENCES

1. Maloney L. T. (1986) 'Evaluation of linear models of surface spectral reflectance with small numbers of parameters'. *J. Opt. Soc. Am.* **A3**, 1673–1683.
2. Shepard R. N. (1997) 'The perceptual organization of colors: an adaptation to regularities of the terrestrial world'. In *Readings on Color*, Vol. 2, Byrne A. and Hilbert D. R. (eds).
3. Nassau K. (1983) 'The physics and chemistry of color: the fifteen causes of color'. Wiley, New York.
4. Buchsbaum G. and Gottschalk A. (1984) 'Chromaticity coordinates of frequency-limited functions'. *J. Opt. Soc.* **A67**, 885–887.
5. Cohen J. (1964) 'Dependency of the spectral reflectance curves of the Munsell color chips'. *Psychonomic Science*, **1**, 369–370.
6. García-Beltrán A., Nieves J. L., Hernández-Andrés L. and Romero J. (1988) 'Linear bases for spectral reflectance functions of acrylic paints' *Col. Res. Appl.* **23**(1), 39–45.
7. Jaaskelainen T., Parkkinen J. P. S. and Toyooka S. (1990) 'Vector subspace model for color representation'. *J. Opt. Soc. Am.* **A7**, 725–730.
8. Westland S., Shaw J. and Owens H. (2000) 'Colour statistics of natural and man-made surfaces'. *Sensor Review*, **20**(1), 50–55.
9. Parkkinen J. P. S., Hallikainen J. and Jaaskelainen T. (1989) 'Characteristic spectra of Munsell colors'. *J. Opt. Soc. Am.* **A6**, 318–322.
10. Dannemiller J L (1992) 'Spectral reflectance of natural objects – how many basis functions are necessary?' *J. Opt. Soc. Am.* **A9**(4), 507–515.
11. Judd D. B., McAdam D. L. and Wyszecki G. (1964) 'Spectral distribution of typical daylight as a function of correlated color temperature'. *J. Opt. Soc. Am.* **A54**, 1031–1041.
12. Romero J., Garcia-Beltran A. and Hernandez-Andres J. (1997) 'Linear bases for representation of natural and artificial illuminants'. *J. Opt. Soc. Am.* **A14**, 1007–1014.

13. Carlson G. E. (1998) *Signal and linear system analysis*. Wiley, Chichester.
14. Eem J. K., Shin H. D. and Park S. O. (1994) 'Reconstruction of surface spectral reflectances using characteristic vectors of Munsell colors'. *Proc. 2nd IS&T/SIDs Color Imaging Conference: Color Science, Systems and Application*. Scottsdale, AZ, pp. 127–131.
15. Vrhel M. J., Gerchon R. and Iwan L. S. (1994) 'Measurements and analysis of object reflectance spectra'. *Col. Res. Appl.*, **19**(1) 4–9.

6

A generalised method for spectral scanner characterisation

Friedhelm König and Patrick Herzog

6.1 INTRODUCTION

A method of scanner characterisation was previously proposed to determine a scanner's spectral properties by scanning a special test target with known spectral characteristics [1]. The method was based on a complex scanner model (called 1I3S-model) consisting of an illuminant, three all-positive physical sensitivities, a colour correction matrix and channel-specific non-linearities. Its main advantage was the separation of the scanner properties from those of the scanned medium, allowing both a better evaluation of the scanner and the calculation of profiles for an arbitrary medium with known spectral properties.

Up to now, the characterisation method was only applicable to scanners with a single illuminant. It is now extended to scanners that use different illuminants for each scanner channel. In this chapter an improved spectral scanner model (3I3S-model) is described, whereby the application of the characterisation method is demonstrated for a scanner with a single illuminant and different configurations of scanners with three illuminants.

Colour Image Science, edited by L.W. MacDonald and M.R. Luo.

The simplest configuration of a scanner with three illuminants uses a single sensor. The output signals of the scanner are acquired independently of each other. In more complex scanners the scanner signals may be buffered and processed using a linear 3×3 matrix to achieve a better approximation of the colorimetric RGB curves. An even more complex scanner configuration uses three illuminants and three sensors. The scanner signals are calculated from the three sensor signals by using a 9×3 matrix. Although this configuration is rather unlikely in practice, it is included as the most general configuration.

6.1.1 Conventional colour management

While the problems of the optimal reproduction of colour images are not yet solved completely, the introduction of modern colour management has led to a substantial improvement. This technique requires an ICC profile for each imaging device that is used for a given reproduction. Typically the reproduction of an image requires a scanner profile for image input and a printer profile for image output. Frequently, the image is edited or enhanced before image output, hence a monitor profile is required additionally.

Such an ICC profile is only valid under specific conditions. For example, the monitor profile is valid only for specific viewing conditions (e.g. dim surround), and the printer and scanner profiles are specific to a given *medium* (e.g. film material or the output of a specific printer). In this context, the term 'medium' is used to denote one combination of paper and inks. If more than three inks are used for a medium, the separation algorithm is also a factor influencing the image rendering characteristics of the medium.

6.1.2 Spectral characterisation

Spectral scanner characterisation was proposed as a method to divide a conventional ICC profile (scanner and medium specific) into a scanner-specific *spectral scanner profile* and a medium-specific *spectral medium profile* [1]. The spectral medium profile is determined only by the properties of the medium. The simplest implementation of a medium profile consists of the spectral reflectances of the corresponding IT8 target.

The spectral scanner profile is dependent only on the properties of the scanner. It allows us to calculate the output signals of the scanner for a given reflectance spectrum. Therefore, the spectral scanner profile can be considered as a mathematical model of the scanner. The simplest implementation of such a profile consists of the scanner's spectral sensitivities only. This simple implementation, however, is somewhat limited and a more complex model will be described in Section 6.2.

With the spectral characterisation approach, both the spectral medium profile and the spectral scanner profile are used to calculate a conventional profile every time an image is scanned. This profile is then used with a conventional colour management system to optimise the scanner output.

This approach has several advantages. First, in an environment that uses multiple media and multiple scanners, only one profile has to be changed, if either the properties of a medium or scanner change. Secondly, a spectral scanner profile can be used with a method such as the smoothing inverse [2] to create optimised generic profiles. Thirdly, an image provider such as a photographic studio can provide a medium profile with its images that can be used with any scanner.

Furthermore, a spectral profile can be used by the manufacturer or a third party to evaluate the scanner performance. Another advantage is that the spectral medium profile and the spectral scanner profile can be acquired at different locations, therefore the medium-specific test chart does not have to be transferred from the medium manufacturer to the scanner location.

At first glance, the need for two different profiles for one scan might seem like a drawback. Upon taking a closer look, however, one notices that only the medium profile has to be changed on a scan-by-scan basis. Therefore, it is possible to hide the scanner profile from the operator of the scanner, who will notice no difference from conventional colour management. Only the system administrator will have to deal with both types of profile, and the spectral approach will mean less work for him, if the scanner profile can be acquired in an easy way.

A note on notation

Spectral data will be represented by 31-dimensional vectors whose components represent equidistant sample values in the range 400–700 nm of the spectrum taken at the sample wavelengths λ_i ($\lambda_i = 400\,\text{nm} + i \times 10\,\text{nm}$, $0 \leqslant i \leqslant 30$). Furthermore, the notation $v_{(R,G,B)}$ will be used as an abbreviation for v_R, v_G and v_B, where v stands for any variable.

6.1.3 Linear programming

Linear programming is an optimisation method that will be used in Section 6.3 to determine the effective sensitivities of the scanner. This section is intended to give a brief and incomplete overview of this method. (Readers who are familiar with this technique should skip this section.)

Linear programming can be applied to any optimisation problem with a linear objective functions, which may be subject to linear constraints. Such an optimisation problem has a unique global optimum which is always found. Actually, this statement is a simplification, as there do exist problems that are unbounded; consider $\min(-x)$ such that $x > 5$. However, the problem considered here is not unbounded. A simple example is given by:

$$\min(0.5a + 2b + 3c + d)$$

$$\text{such that} \quad a + b \geqslant 2$$

$$c + d \leqslant 1$$

$$a + b + c = 3$$

Later on, constraints containing absolute values will be used. While such constraints are no longer linear, it is possible to formulate them as two linear constraints. This is demonstrated by the following equations:

$$\begin{aligned} &\min(3c) & & & &\min(3c) \\ &\text{such that } |a+b| = c & &\Longleftrightarrow & &\text{s.t.}\quad a+b \leqslant c \\ & & & & &\qquad -a-b \leqslant c \end{aligned}$$

A complete description of linear programming can be found in Schrijuv.

6.2 THE IMPROVED SCANNER MODEL

6.2.1 Earlier approaches to spectral scanner characterisation

The central aspect of spectral scanner characterisation is that spectral scanner profiles allow us to determine the scanner output data for any given reflectance spectrum. Therefore, a spectral scanner profile has to be based on a mathematical model of the scanner. This might be either a simple 'black box' model like a look-up table (LUT) or a more complex model that is based on knowledge about the scanner's design. The characterisation process is then used to parameterise the model.

Unfortunately, it turns out to be almost impossible to parameterise even a linear black box model where the scanner is described by a matrix, because of the high number of model parameters and the high dimensionality of the possible input vectors (here 31-dimensional). At the same time, it is difficult to find test spectra that make use of this high dimensionality. The characterisation process is consequently very sensitive to noise, compounded by the fact that scanner output is usually quite noisy.

For this reason, most spectral scanner characterisation methods proposed in the literature use mathematical scanner models that consist of three *effective* spectral sensitivities. These effective sensitivities account for the complete optical path of the scanner and contain the influence of the scanner illuminant, all lenses and other glass parts and also the sensitivity of the scanner sensor, usually a charge-coupled device (CCD) chip.

The use of such a scanner model leads to a 31×3 matrix. At first glance, this is identical to the linear black box approach. The advantage of this model, however, is the possibility to improve the results by using knowledge about spectral sensitivities to constrain the set of possible solutions. Feasible properties of the sensitivities are positivity, smoothness and unimodality. Spectral scanner characterisation methods using these properties to constrain the set of possible solutions have been published by Sharma and Trussell [3], Hardeberg *et al.* [4] and Finlayson *et al.* [5].

While these approaches work quite well in simulation and even in controlled environments, there are some difficulties with this approach. The first problem is that the scanner models proposed in the earlier papers are completely linear. Therefore, these models can be used only to describe linear behaviour. This is a problem, because scanners do not usually behave very linearly. In fact, most scanner drivers offer the possibility to adjust the gamma factor of the scanner to introduce a strong voluntary non-linearity. The simple model cannot account for this.

Furthermore, one has to question the validity of the proposed constraints. The constraint of unimodality is really hard to justify. From a colour science viewpoint we would usually like the sensitivities to be unimodal, but industrial scanner design is very often influenced by considerations other than colour science. If a CCD chip is offered, whose sensitivities are not unimodal but which is a lot cheaper than another CCD chip with unimodal sensitivities, we all know which chip will be chosen for a low-end scanner. Also, if one scanner is designed to measure XYZ values instead of RGB values, we would not even want the sensitivities to be unimodal.

The smoothness of the scanner sensitivities seems to be a much safer assumption, as CCD sensitivities are usually quite smooth. On the other hand, the effective sensitivities of a scanner describe the complete optical path, including not only the sensitivities of the CCD but also of the lenses and the illuminant of the scanner. Contrary to the CCD sensitivities, the illuminant spectra are seldom smooth and they contain spikes and peaks instead. This problem can of course be avoided by measuring the scanner illuminant and considering it separately, which has already been proposed by the authors of the previous papers.

At first glance, the positivity of the scanner sensitivities seems to be the constraint that is easiest to defend. After all, negative CCD sensitivities are a physical impossibility. Unfortunately, this does not take colour correction into account. Scanners frequently use internal colour correction matrices to improve their colour quality. This can lead to negative lobes of the effective sensitivities. In fact, negative lobes are frequently desired, because the optimal (colorimetric) RGB curves do contain negative lobes.

These drawbacks have been discussed in more detail in an earlier paper [1] and led to the development of an improved scanner model that is usable for a scanner with a single illuminant (Figure 6.1). It consists of the measured illuminant, three smooth and all-positive physical sensitivities, followed by a 3×3 colour correction matrix and channel-specific non-linearities implemented by fourth-order polynomials.

The scanner model is parameterised by measuring an appropriate test chart and applying an algorithm based on linear programming.

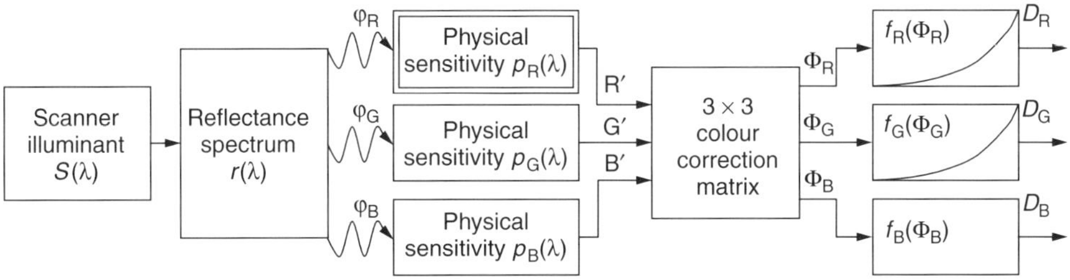

Figure 6.1 The lI3S scanner operates with a single illuminant. It uses a light source and three linear physical sensitivities (i.e. all positive). The measured values are transformed by a 3×3 colour correction matrix and then fed into channel-specific non-linearities. Figure 1.2 of 'spectral scanner characterization using linear programming' by Friedhelm König and Patrick Herzog SPIE Vol. 3963. Reproduced by permission of SPIE.

6.2.2 The test chart

Similar to all other approaches for spectral scanner characterisation, the parameterisation of the spectral scanner model relies on a carefully designed test chart with reflectances $r_{SC,i}$. An ideal test chart would consist of colours with linearly independent reflectance spectra. Unfortunately, such a set of test colours would require reflectance spectra with negative lobes and therefore is not available. Nevertheless, the spectra should be selected to maximise the spectral variability, which requires the use of a large variety of inks. Furthermore, it is important to differentiate between neighbouring wavelengths, so the test spectra should include at least one significant peak or slope. These characteristics are usually found in saturated colours. We use a test chart consisting of the primary colours of the HKS printing colour system.

Contrary to the earlier approaches, our model includes some non-linearities. The parameterisation of these non-linearities requires additional test patches. Contrary to the first set of test patches, the reflectance spectra $r_{\mathrm{GS},i}(\lambda)$ of these test patches should not be linearly independent, but span only a one-dimensional colour space. Mathematically this can be expressed as:

$$r_{\mathrm{GS},i}(\lambda) = k_i r_{\mathrm{GS},1}(\lambda) \tag{6.1}$$

where k_i is the scaling factor for the ith test patch spectrum. This condition allows us to separate the influence of the non-linear submodel from the linear submodel, because the output of the linear submodel $\Phi_{\mathrm{GS},i,\mathrm{R}}$ fulfils the condition:

$$\Phi_{\mathrm{GS},i,(\mathrm{R,G,B})}/\Phi_{\mathrm{GS},1,(\mathrm{R,G,B})} = k_i \tag{6.2}$$

due to its linearity. By setting $\Phi_{\mathrm{GS},1,\mathrm{R}}$ to a fixed quantity (e.g. $\Phi_{\mathrm{GS},1,\mathrm{R}} = 1$), we can use least squares fitting to parameterise the non-linear submodel.

6.2.3 Generalising the model

Here the scanner model (1I3S) from [1] is enhanced to deal with scanners that use three different illuminants. The improved model is shown in Figure 6.2. It combines three different illuminants $S_{\mathrm{R}}(\lambda)$, $S_{\mathrm{G}}(\lambda)$ and $S_{\mathrm{B}}(\lambda)$ with three physical sensitivities $p_{\mathrm{R}}(\lambda)$, $p_{\mathrm{G}}(\lambda)$ and $p_{\mathrm{B}}(\lambda)$ for a total of nine spectral channels $s_{\mathrm{RR}}(\lambda), \ \ldots, s_{\mathrm{BB}}(\lambda)$, where:

$$s_{xy}(\lambda) = S_x(\lambda) p_y(\lambda) \qquad x, y \in \{\mathrm{R,G,B}\} \tag{6.3}$$

Similar to the earlier scanner models, this scanner model is parameterised by scanning a test chart and extracting the average scanner response to each test patch. Then test patches that lead to saturated scanner responses have to be identified, as saturation leads to non-linear behaviour of the scanner. Unfortunately, the exact identification of saturated test patches is a rather cumbersome process that requires the examination of the histogram of each test patch. To simplify this process, a simple rule has been defined. Following this rule, all test patches that lead to average scanner responses below 4% or above 96% of the maximum scanner output are considered to be saturated. In the following steps of the characterisation process, these test patches are ignored.

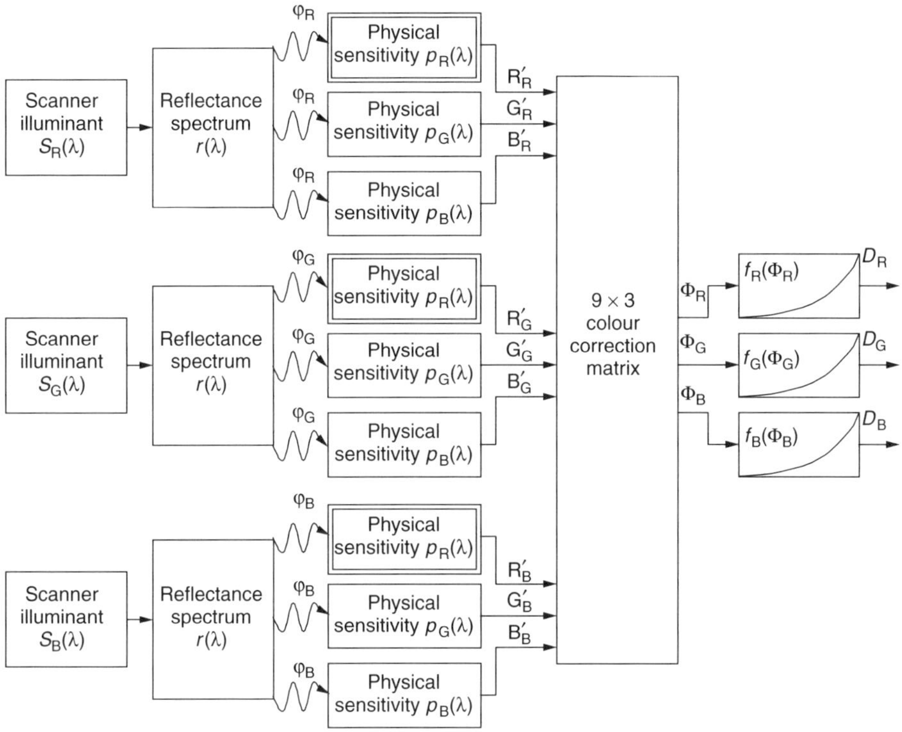

Figure 6.2 The 3I3S model generalises the 1I3S model in Figure 6.1. It uses three light sources and three linear physical sensitivities. The nine measured values are transformed by a 9×3 colour correction matrix and then fed into channel-specific non-linearities to calculate the digital output signals $D_{(R,G,B)}$.

After the removal of the saturated test patches, linear programming is applied to the average output values of the remaining patches. The linear program will be described in the following sections. Sections 6.2.4 and 6.2.5 focus on the different types of constraint. The objective function used for the linear programming approach will be given in Section 6.2.6. Finally, the scanner model's error definition used with the objective function of the linear programming approach depends on the scanner configuration; this will be discussed in Section 6.3.

6.2.4 Constraints for the physical sensitivities

A major component of the spectral scanner model is the set of physical sensitivities. The term 'physical' is used to imply that these sensitivities behave like real sensor sensitivities. It does not imply, however, that the physical sensitivities are the real sensitivities of the CCD, although ideally they are a linear combination thereof.

Like the CCD sensitivities, the three physical sensitivities must also be all-positive and smooth. The positivity of the physical sensitivities can be enforced by using the following linear constraints:

$$\begin{aligned} p_{\mathrm{R}}(\lambda_i) &\geqslant 0 \\ p_{\mathrm{G}}(\lambda_i) &\geqslant 0 \\ p_{\mathrm{B}}(\lambda_i) &\geqslant 0 \end{aligned} \tag{6.4}$$

Equation (6.4) is called the positivity constraint. Note that each inequality actually represents 31 inequalities, as the physical sensitivities have to be positive at each of the 31 sample wavelengths λ_i which are used to describe spectral data.

The smoothness of the physical sensitivities is somewhat more difficult to implement as a linear constraint. First, some way to measure smoothness is needed. One possibility is to measure smoothness by examining the curvature of physical sensitivities $p_{(\mathrm{R,G,B})}(\lambda)$. Smoothness can be enforced by limiting this curvature.

To evaluate the smoothness, our method uses the two measures $P_{i,(\mathrm{R,G,B})}$ and $P_{\max,(\mathrm{R,G,B})}$ for the curvature, defined by the following two equations:

$$\begin{aligned} |p_{(\mathrm{R,G,B})}(\lambda_i) - 2p_{(\mathrm{R,G,B})}(\lambda_{i+1}) + p_{(\mathrm{R,G,B})}(\lambda_{i+2})| &= P_{i,(\mathrm{R,G,B})} \qquad (1 \leqslant i \leqslant 29) \\ \max(P_{i,(\mathrm{R,G,B})}) &= P_{\max,(\mathrm{R,G,B})} \end{aligned} \tag{6.5}$$

The first of these smoothness measures, $P_{i,(\mathrm{R,G,B})}$, uses the second differences to calculate the local curvature of the respective sensitivity at the wavelength λ_{i+1}. This is equivalent to calculating the second derivative in a continuous system. The second measure, $P_{\max,(\mathrm{R,G,B})}$, is used to calculate the maximum curvature of each sensitivity. Small values of these quantities correspond to smooth sensitivities. Therefore, smoothness can be enforced by limiting the maximum curvature or by minimising the smoothness measures.

To use these smoothness quantities in a linear programming algorithm, the previous equations have to be formulated as linear constraints. This can be done by using the method described in Section 6.1.3:

$$\begin{aligned} p_{(\mathrm{R,G,B})}(\lambda_i) - 2p_{(\mathrm{R,G,B})}(\lambda_{i+1}) + p_{(\mathrm{R,G,B})}(\lambda_{i+2}) &\leqslant P_{i,(\mathrm{R,G,B})} \\ -[p_{(\mathrm{R,G,B})}(\lambda_i) - 2p_{(\mathrm{R,G,B})}(\lambda_{i+1}) + p_{(\mathrm{R,G,B})}(\lambda_{i+2})] &\leqslant P_{i,(\mathrm{R,G,B})} \qquad (1 \leqslant i \leqslant 29) \\ P_{i,(\mathrm{R,G,B})} &\leqslant P_{\max,(\mathrm{R,G,B})} \end{aligned} \tag{6.6}$$

Both measures, $P_{i,(\mathrm{R,G,B})}$ and $P_{\max}$, are introduced into the objective function (Section 6.2.6). This is explained in more detail in [1].

6.2.5 Colour correction matrix

The next stage of the scanner model is the reduction of the output signals of the nine spectral channels to a three-dimensional *light flux* vector containing the light flux signals Φ_{R}, Φ_{G} and Φ_{B}. To this end a 9×3 dimensional colour correction matrix $\mathbf{C}$ is used whose coefficients are denoted $c_{i,.j,k}$ ($i, j, k \in \{\mathrm{R,G,B}\}$). For example, the coefficient c_{RGB}

is used to denote the coefficient that combines the red illuminant channel $S_R(\lambda)$, the green physical sensitivity channel $p_G(\lambda)$ for the blue light flux Φ_B. After applying the colour correction matrix, the output RGB signals are calculated from the raw signals by applying channel-specific non-linear processing.

The scanner model is parameterised by linear programming. Since linear programming can only handle a linear objective function, only a linear error measure can be minimised. This error measure may not include the product of two unknown variables (i.e. the product of two model parameters). Hence the minimisation of the error has to take place in the nine-dimensional *raw data* space between the physical responses and the colour correction matrix. This requires us to calculate the output signals of the physical responses $R_R, \ldots, B_B$ from two different directions, firstly from the reflectance spectrum $r(\lambda)$ and secondly from the light flux Φ_{RGB}. The light flux calculation requires the inversion of the colour correction matrix **C**. Unfortunately, this is impossible with a 9×3 matrix, and a way to reduce this matrix to a 3×3 matrix has to be found.

The details of how this is done depend on the configuration of the scanner. In most scanner configurations some of the coefficients of the colour correction matrix **C** vanish. Often it is possible to reduce the matrix **C** to a 3×3 matrix $\mathbf{C}^*$ which can be inverted. In these cases, an inverse colour correction matrix $\mathbf{C}_{\text{inv}}$ can be calculated, allowing the use of a linear model error definition within the nine-dimensional raw data space. The actual error definition depends on the scanner configuration.

There are, however, two constraints that must be fulfilled regardless of the scanner configuration, if the inverse colour correction matrix $\mathbf{C}_{\text{inv}}$ is used:

$$\begin{gathered} c_{\text{inv},11} = c_{\text{inv},22} = c_{\text{inv},33} = 1 \\ c_{\text{inv},12}, c_{\text{inv},13}, c_{\text{inv},21}, c_{\text{inv},23}, c_{\text{inv},31}, c_{\text{inv},33} \leqslant 1 \end{gathered} \tag{6.7}$$

Their purpose is to avoid the trivial solution of the optimisation method, where both the physical sensitivities and the inverse colour correction matrix are all zero.

6.2.6 Objective function for linear programming

Besides the constraints of equation (6.7), spectral characterisation by linear programming requires an objective function. This objective function is a weighted sum that combines the smoothness measures $S_{i,(R,G,B)}$ and $S_{\max,(R,G,B)}$ with the scanner configuration dependent model error measures $E^*_{M,i,(R,G,B)}$ and $E^*_{M,\max,(R,G,B)}$.

$$\begin{aligned} \min \Bigg(& w_{E,\text{avg}} \sum_i E^*_{M,i,R} + w_{E,\max} E^*_{M,\max,R} + w_S \sum_j P_{j,R} + w_{S,\max} P_{\max,R} \\ & + w_{E,\text{avg}} \sum_i E^*_{M,i,G} + w_{E,\max} E^*_{M,\max,G} + w_S \sum_j P_{j,G} + w_{S,\max} P_{\max,G} \\ & + w_{E,\text{avg}} \sum_i E^*_{M,i,B} + w_{E,\max} E^*_{M,\max,B} + w_S \sum_j P_{j,B} + w_{S,\max} P_{\max,B} \Bigg) \end{aligned} \tag{6.8}$$

Here the $w_{E,\mathrm{avg}}$, $w_{E,\max}$, w_S and $w_{S,\max}$ are arbitrary weighting factors for the optimisation. The smoothness measures $P_{i,(\mathrm{R,G,B})}$ and $P_{\max,(\mathrm{R,G,B})}$ are defined by equation (6.2). The test patch specific model error measure $E^*_{\mathrm{M},i,(\mathrm{R,G,B})}$ depends on the configuration and is defined in Section 6.3.

Finally, the model error measure $E^*_{\mathrm{M},\max,(\mathrm{R,G,B})}$ is given by the constraint:

$$E^*_{\mathrm{M},\max,(\mathrm{R,G,B})} \geqslant E^*_{\mathrm{M},i,(\mathrm{R,G,B})} \tag{6.9}$$

where index i is used to denote the test patch of the test chart.

6.3 SCANNER CONFIGURATION, COLOUR CORRECTION MATRIX AND SCANNER MODEL ERROR DEFINITIONS

This section explains how to reduce the 9×3 colour correction matrix $\mathbf{C}$ to the 3×3 matrix $\mathbf{C}^*$. It discusses the advantages and disadvantages of several possible scanner configurations and the influence of the scanner configuration on the colour correction matrix.

6.3.1 Scanner with single illuminant and three sensitivities

A scanner with one single illuminant and three different sensitivities can either have one sensor using a mosaic filter or three different sensors with a beam splitter. The former leads to large colour errors if high spatial frequencies are examined, the latter is more expensive. The advantage of this configuration is that fluorescence is handled in the same way as in the human eye, keeping colour errors moderately low.

The scanner model is applied to this configuration by setting one of the model illuminants $S_{(\mathrm{R,G,B})}(\lambda)$ equal to the scanner illuminant $S(\lambda)$. Let us assume this illuminant is the green channel illuminant $S_{\mathrm{G}}(\lambda)$. In this case all the elements c_{Rxx} and c_{Bxx} of the characterisation matrix that are used for the other two illuminants are not needed and the model collapses into the simpler 1I3S model shown in Figure 6.1.

The 3×3 matrix $\mathbf{C}^*$ consists of the following elements:

$$\mathbf{C}^* = \begin{pmatrix} c_{\mathrm{GRR}} & c_{\mathrm{GRG}} & c_{\mathrm{GRB}} \\ c_{\mathrm{GGR}} & c_{\mathrm{GGG}} & c_{\mathrm{GGB}} \\ c_{\mathrm{GBR}} & c_{\mathrm{GBG}} & c_{\mathrm{GBB}} \end{pmatrix} \tag{6.10}$$

The model error $E^*_{\mathrm{M},i,\mathrm{R}}$ is given by:

$$E^*_{\mathrm{M},i,\mathrm{R}} = \left| \sum_{j=1}^{31} r_i(\lambda_j) S_{\mathrm{GR}}(\lambda_j) - \left[\Phi_{\mathrm{R},i} c_{\mathrm{inv},11} + \Phi_{\mathrm{G},i} c_{,\mathrm{inv},12} + \Phi_{\mathrm{B},i} c_{\mathrm{inv},13} \right] \right| \tag{6.11}$$

In this equation the index i is used to denote the test patches of the test chart. The model errors for the green and blue channels are defined in a similar way.

6.3.2 Scanner with three illuminants and single sensitivity

The second scanner configuration consists of three different illuminants $S_{(\mathrm{R,G,B})}(\lambda)$ with a single physical sensor sensitivity p_{G}. This configuration avoids the problems of the configuration described in Section 6.3.1. On the other hand, it is not suited for fluorescent colours and may lead to major desaturation.

For spectral characterisation, this configuration has another problem: it can be quite hard to measure the spectra of the scanner's light sources because of the flashing lights, e.g. with a rotating colour filter wheel. If the scanner illuminants $S_{(\mathrm{R,G,B})}(\lambda)$ cannot be measured, the only way to deal with that problem is to include the scanner illuminants into the unknown physical sensitivity $p(\lambda)$. This leads to three effective sensitivities $p_{(\mathrm{R,G,B})}(\lambda)$. In this case standard illuminant E (equi-energy) is used as the scanner illuminant. This is equivalent to the 1I3S model.

Otherwise, if the scanner illuminants can measured, the 9×3 colour correction matrix **C** can be reduced to a 3×3 matrix by setting two of the model sensitivities, e.g. $p_{\mathrm{R}}(\lambda)$ and $p_{\mathrm{B}}(\lambda)$, to 0. Then the 3×3 colour correction matrix $\mathbf{C}^*$ is given by:

$$\mathbf{C}^* = \begin{pmatrix} c_{\mathrm{RGR}} & c_{\mathrm{RGG}} & c_{\mathrm{RGB}} \\ c_{\mathrm{GGR}} & c_{\mathrm{GGG}} & c_{\mathrm{GGB}} \\ c_{\mathrm{BGR}} & c_{\mathrm{BGG}} & c_{\mathrm{BGB}} \end{pmatrix} \tag{6.12}$$

and thus the model error $E^*_{\mathrm{M},i,\mathrm{R}}$ can be calculated from:

$$E^*_{\mathrm{M},i,\mathrm{R}} = \left| \sum_{j=1}^{31} S_{\mathrm{R}}(\lambda_i) r_i(\lambda_j) P(\lambda_j) - \left[\Phi_{\mathrm{R},i} c_{\mathrm{inv},11} + \Phi_{\mathrm{G},i} c_{\mathrm{inv},12} + \Phi_{\mathrm{B},i} c_{\mathrm{inv},13}\right] \right| \tag{6.13}$$

If no colour correction is carried out within the scanner, the colour correction matrix $\mathbf{C}^*$ is reduced to the identity matrix:

$$\mathbf{C}^* = \begin{pmatrix} 1 & 0 & 0 \\ 0 & 1 & 0 \\ 0 & 0 & 1 \end{pmatrix} \tag{6.14}$$

In this case the model error $E^*_{\mathrm{M},i,\mathrm{R}}$ is given by:

$$E^*_{\mathrm{M},i,\mathrm{R}} = \left| \sum_{j=1}^{31} S_{\mathrm{R}}(\lambda_i) r_i(\lambda_j) P(\lambda_i) - \Phi_{\mathrm{R},i} \right| \tag{6.15}$$

6.3.3 Scanner with three sensitivities and three illuminants

The authors do not know of a scanner that combines three illuminants with three sensitivities. A scanner using this configuration combines all the problems of the two other configurations without offering a real advantage. Therefore a scanner with three sensitivities and three illuminants is only a theoretical case described here for the sake of completeness and to allow the exposition of a general method.

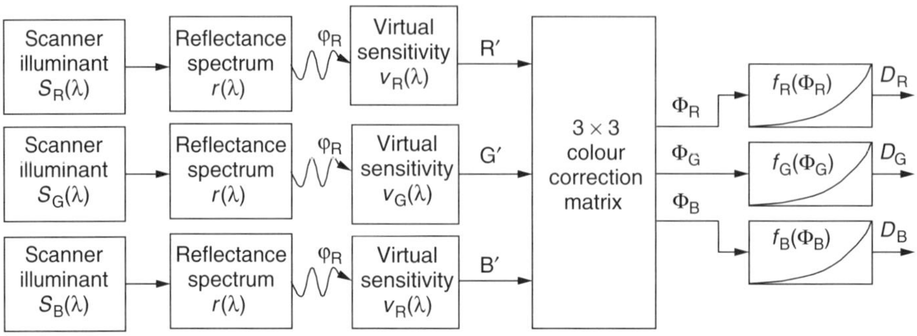

Figure 6.3 The 3I3V model uses three illuminants and three sensitivities. Unlike the physical sensitivities used in the other scanners, a virtual sensitivity might have negative lobes.

In this configuration the colour correction matrix is a 9×3 matrix and cannot be inverted. Therefore it is not possible to avoid the multiplication of two unknown variables, and linear programming cannot be applied. This problem can be avoided only if the scanner's colour correction matrix does not combine measurement results for different illuminants. This means for the output value of the red channel only, the sensor responses taken under the red illuminant are combined.

In this case the scanner can be modelled by using virtual sensitivities v_R, v_G and v_B. Each virtual sensitivity is a weighted sum of the three physical sensitivities:

$$\begin{aligned} v_R(\lambda) &= c_{RRR}\,p_R(\lambda) + c_{RGR}\,p_R(\lambda) + c_{RBR}\,p_R(\lambda) \\ v_G(\lambda) &= c_{GRG}\,p_R(\lambda) + c_{GGG}\,p_R(\lambda) + c_{GBG}\,p_R(\lambda) \\ v_B(\lambda) &= c_{BRB}\,p_R(\lambda) + c_{BGB}\,p_R(\lambda) + c_{BBB}\,p_R(\lambda) \end{aligned} \tag{6.16}$$

Note that the virtual sensitivities $v_{(R,G,B)}$ may contain negative lobes. Therefore the positivity constraint (6.4) does not apply to the virtual sensitivities.

Using the virtual sensitivities $v_{(R,G,B)}$, the scanner model is reduced to the 3I3V model shown in Figure 6.3. This configuration is quite similar to the one described in Section 6.3.2. The only difference is that the single physical sensitivity of section 6.3.2 is replaced by three virtual sensitivities. The resulting model error can be calculated from:

$$E^*_{M,i,R} = \left| \sum_{j=1}^{31} S_R(\lambda_i) r_i(\lambda_j) v_R(\lambda_i) - \left[\Phi_{R,i} c_{inv,11} + \Phi_{G,i} c_{inv,12} + \Phi_{B,i} c_{inv,13}\right] \right| \tag{6.17}$$

6.4 PARAMETERISING THE LINEAR SUBMODEL

Up to this point, everything that is necessary to parameterise the linear model has been discussed. Nevertheless, we feel that it might be helpful to summarise the necessary steps in one place, so here is the complete process broken into 10 steps.

1. The illuminants used by the scanner are measured. Depending on the scanner configuration, this may require one measurement or three measurements. If the illuminants cannot be measured, assume illuminant E and the scanner model with three sensitivities.
2. The scanner that is to be characterised is used to measure the test chart.
3. For each test patch, the average scanner response is calculated.
4. In the following, only test patches that lead to averaged scanner responses between 4% and 96% of the possible scanner output values are considered.
5. The non-linearities are parameterised. To this end, fourth-order polynomials are optimised to linearise the relationship between the colorimetric Y-values of the $r_{GS,i}$ test patches and the respective scanner output values.
6. The inverse non-linearities are used to calculate the light flux values $\Phi_{(R,G,B)}$ for each channel.
7. The linear program used for the parameterisation of the linear submodel is set up. This linear program is described as follows:
   a. Positivity constraints (6.4). Depending on the scanner configuration, there are either 31 constraints (single sensitivity) or 93 constraints (three sensitivities).
   b. Smoothness constraints (6.6). Depending on the number of sensitivities used, there are either 29 or 87 constraints.
   c. Colour correction matrix constraints (6.7). There are 9 constraints.
   d. Constraints to define the maximum error (6.9). This leads to a number of constraints, that is three times the number of test patches.
   e. Constraints to define the model error. Equation (6.11), (6.13), (6.15) or (6.17), depending on scanner configuration. This also leads to a number of constraints, that is three times the number of test patches.
   f. The objective function given by (6.8).
8. The linear program is executed to generate the model parameters.
9. The inverse colour correction matrix determined by the solution of the linear program is inverted to calculate the colour correction matrix.
10. Finished.

6.5 RESULTS

6.5.1 Summary of previous studies

In an earlier paper [1], experimental results for a scanner using one illuminant and three sensitivities have been published. To obtain these results, a Umax Powerlook scanner was characterised using the spectral characterisation method for a scanner with a single illuminant. The spectral profile was used to predict output values for a second test chart. The spectral characteristics of the second test chart were different from those of the test chart used to characterise the scanner (different substrate, different inks). The second test chart was also scanned using the same scanning options as during the scan used to parameterise the scanner model. The measured scanner responses were compared to the calculated ones. We found mean errors between calculation and measurement of the order of 1% of the maximum output of the device (8 bit resulting in a maximum output of 255) with maximum errors as large as 4.5%.

While these errors appear to be quite large, the results are in good agreement with results obtained by Knox [6] and Herloski [7, 8], who describe the integrating cavity effect (ICE) of desktop scanners. This effect is caused by multiple reflections between the image placed on the scanner and the reflector of the scanner's lamp. The reflections can cause considerable measurement errors; deviations of up to 11% have been reported.

To estimate the magnitude of the ICE for the examined scanner, the two additional scans were made. In both scans the same test patches were measured, once in front of a white background and once in front of a black background. The output values of the scan with the white background were up to 8.9% higher (again related to maximum output) than those measured with the black background. The average difference was 3.3%.

Because the ICE is caused by non-linear crosstalk between different pixels, it is impossible to correct for this effect in the context of a conventional pixel-based colour management system. From this viewpoint the ICE is perceived as noise. Therefore the performance of the spectral scanner model is perceived as adequate.

6.5.2 New characterisation study

An LED-based slide scanner [9] was characterised spectrally. Since the special test chart was not yet available in 35 mm format, we simulated the behaviour of the scanner. Earlier investigations showed that simulations can give very realistic predictions of the behaviour of real devices [10].

The LED slide scanner comprises three illuminants (light-emitting diodes) and a single CCD. The spectra of the LED illuminants and the spectral sensitivity of the CCD are shown in Figure 6.4 while the resulting effective spectral channels are given in Figure 6.5. These spectral curves were used to simulate the scanner response to the patches of the spectral characterisation target. The parameters of the spectral characterisation method were derived from the input and output data.

The performance of the spectral characterisation method was studied with known and unknown illuminants and with and without noise, making up a total of four experiments.

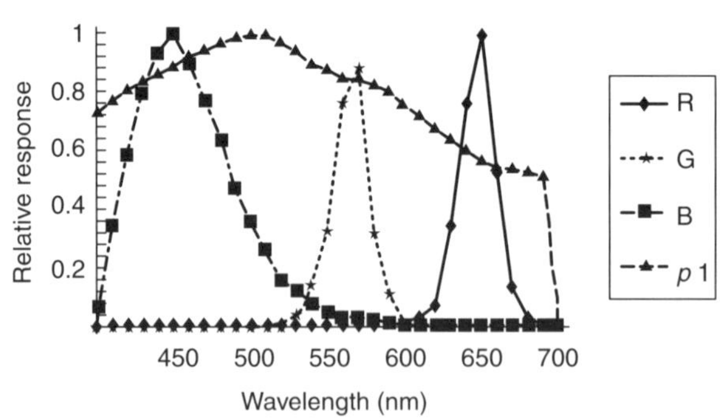

Figure 6.4 The power distribution of the three LED illuminants (R, G, B) and the sensitivity $p(\lambda)$ of the CCD of the simulated scanner.

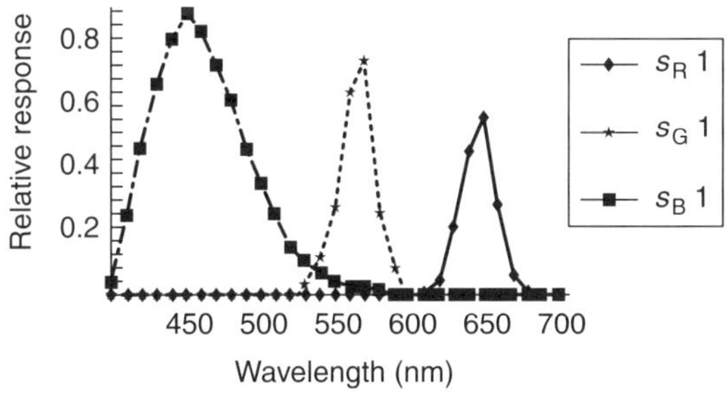

Figure 6.5 The effective spectral channels (s_R, s_G, s_B) of the simulated scanner.

In the noisy cases, a noise level of 5% equally distributed was assumed. Compared with the expected colour errors, this is a high level of noise, but the integrating cavity effect means it is not unrealistic. Although the deviations caused by this effect are systematic in nature if the complete test chart is considered, they appear to be random within the context of this paper. This is because standard colour management and International Colour Consortium profiles work on a pixel-by-pixel basis. Therefore the surroundings are unknown and it is impossible to account for these deviations at a profile level.

The result of these simulations were four spectral scanner profiles. Each profile was used to calculate scanner output for a test chart different from the one used to derive the profiles. These estimated scanner output data were compared to the scanner output data obtained from simulation of the real device. The results of these comparisons can be found in Table 6.1. The mean errors were calculated from the absolute values of the deviations.

For all cases the errors are quite small; all maximum errors are below 1.5% for the noiseless simulations and below 2.5% for the noisy simulations. There is a slight increase in the mean and maximum errors if the illuminants cannot be measured.

The results clearly show the excellent performance of the spectral scanner characterisation method. At first glance, it might seem peculiar that the errors of the spectral profiles are significantly below the 5% level of the noise. This is possible because the noise was only considered during the characterisation of the scanner.

Table 6.1 Percentile deviations between original scanner (3 illuminants/1 sensor) and values calculated from spectral profiles acquired under different assumptions (simulation)

	Known illuminants				Unknown illuminants			
	No noise		With 5% noise		No noise		with 5% noise	
	Mean	Max	Mean	Max	Mean	Max	Mean	Max
R channel	0.30	1.20	0.52	1.59	0.40	1.18	0.64	1.81
G channel	0.13	0.77	0.44	1.92	0.17	0.83	0.64	2.66
B channel	0.20	0.69	0.71	2.25	0.10	0.38	0.62	2.22

No noise was considered while calculating the output values that are compared in Table 6.1. Therefore these results only contain the errors due to the spectral profile. As these errors are significantly lower than the errors produced by the scanner itself, the spectral characterisation method can be considered to be very robust.

In the future these results should be verified by experiments. Here we expect somewhat larger errors due to the fact that noise cannot be avoided during the comparison between the calculated and the measured output data.

6.6 CONCLUSIONS

A spectral scanner characterisation method is proposed for scanners with more than one illuminant. This method allows the separate acquisition of scanner properties and medium properties. Therefore the spectral characterisation method can simplify the characterisation process significantly.

The spectral characterisation process is based on a spectral scanner profile. This profile is based on a complex mathematical model of the scanner that incorporates three illuminants, three linear sensitivities, a 9×3 colour correction matrix and channel-dependent non-linear adjustment functions. A method to parameterise the linear part of the spectral scanner profile was introduced. This method slightly depends on the scanner configuration. A variety of different configurations have been discussed.

Finally, simulation showed the good performance and robustness of the spectral characterisation process.

ACKNOWLEDGEMENTS

The authors thank Marc Röber for his help during the preparation of this chapter. We also thank Professor T. Jongen, Dr. Klaus Meer and Gabor Kun of Mathematics Section C at Aachen University of Technology for their help with linear programming.

REFERENCES

1. F. König and P. G. Herzog (2000) 'Spectral scanner characterisation using linear programming'. *Proc. SPIE* **3963**, 36–46.
2. P. G. Herzog, D. Knipp, H. Stiebig and F. König, (1999) Colorimetric characterisation of novel multiple-channel sensors for imaging and metrology. *J. Electron. Imaging*, **8**(4), 329–478.
3. G. Sharma and H. J. Trussell (1996) 'Set theoretic estimation in color scanner characterisation'. *J. Electron. Imaging*, **5**(4), 479–489.
4. J. Y. Hardeberg, H. Brettel and F. Schmitt (1998) 'Spectral characterisation of electronic cameras'. *Proc. SPIE* **3409**, 100–109.
5. G. D. Finlayson, S. Hordley, and P. M. Hubel (1998) 'Recovering device sensitivities with quadratic programming'. *Proc. 6th IS&T/SID Color Imaging Conference: Color Science, Systems and Applications*, pp. 90–95.

6. K. T. Knox (1996) 'Integrating cavity effect in scanners'. *Proc. IS&T/OSA Optics and Imaging in the Information Age*, Rochester NY, pp. 156–158.
7. R. P. Herloski (1997) 'Characterisation of ICE in document scanners using illumination analysis software'. *Proc. Optical Society of America Annual Meeting*, Paper TuQQ2.
8. R. P. Herloski (1998) Analytical computation of integrating cavity effect, *Proc. SPIE* **3482**.
9. B. Hill, and M.-C. Kim (1998) 'LED-illuminated CCD slide scanner with a new concept for color processing'. *Proc. SPIE* **3409**, pp. 110–117.
10. P. G. Herzog, D. Knipp, F. König, and H. Stiebig (2000) 'Performance of amorphous-silicon-based multiple-channel color sensors'. *Proc. SPIE* **3963**, pp. 60–69.

7

Webcam for interactive multispectral measurements

Hans Brettel, Jon Yngve Hardeberg and Francis Schmitt

7.1 INTRODUCTION

Highly accurate cross-media colour reproduction often requires spectrophotometric measurements of imaging targets. In a conventional laboratory set-up such measurements are done by manual or semi-automatic operation of a specific optical instrument, such as a spectroradiometer. Each individual measurement typically requires mechanical repositioning of the target with respect to the actual measuring spot of the instrument, and spatial resolution, speed and interactivity are severely limited.

Electronic cameras, on the other hand, are fast and provide high spatial resolution but they are generally limited to a given set of three spectral bands only. With regard to the growing interest in the development and application of multispectral image acquisition and analysis [1–5], several solutions to overcome the three-band-only limitation have been proposed. They are usually based on a combination of a monochrome or trichromatic digital camera with a suitable set of additional filters [6, 7]. In a typical set-up, a given number of interference filters is mounted on a filter wheel in front of a monochrome digital camera. The number of readily available spectral channels is therefore limited, and mechanical filter switching is required.

Colour Image Science, edited by L.W. MacDonald and M.R. Luo.

In this chapter we describe a system for multispectral image acquisition and analysis which uses an electronically tunable spectral filter and a monochrome digital CCD camera of photometric quality. The filter and the camera are controlled through Java servlets which allow for interactive operation of the multispectral camera across the Web. We also present two interesting applications, a *colorimetric webcam* that implements the spectral sensitivity functions of the CIE 1931 standard colorimetric observer [8, 9], and a camera that provides output signals required for a colorimetrically correct imaging chain using an ITU-R BT.709 [10] or sRGB [11] compatible display device.

7.2 MULTISPECTRAL IMAGE ACQUISITION

Each pixel of a multispectral image contains information about the spectral reflectance of the imaged scene. Multispectral images carry information about a number of spectral bands: from three components per pixel for RGB colour images to several hundreds of bands for hyperspectral images. Multispectral imaging is relevant to several domains of application, such as remote sensing [12], astronomy [13], medical imaging, analysis of museological objects [3, 14], cosmetics, medicine [15], high-accuracy colour printing [4, 16] and computer graphics [17].

In this section we present the different elements constituting a multispectral camera system called SpectraCam that we have set up in our laboratory.

7.2.1 Electronically tunable filter

The key element of our system is a liquid crystal tunable filter (LCTF) which allows for continuous tuning of its peak transmission wavelength over the full range of the visible spectrum. The spectral transmission profile is similar to a Gaussian function, and the LCTF is operated completely electronically, without any moving parts.

The optical principle of this type of spectral filter was introduced by Bernard Lyot in 1933, when he suggested using a series of birefringent plates between polarisers in order to set up a monochromatic filter [18]. Birefringent materials have slightly different refractive indices n_o and n_e for two orthogonal planes of polarisation, respectively known as the planes of the ordinary and the extraordinary rays. The refractive index n of a material is the ratio of the speed of light in vacuum c to the speed of light in that material $c_{material}$:

$$n = c/c_{material} \tag{7.1}$$

so an incident light wave with its electric field component in the polarisation plane of the ordinary ray travels through the birefringent material at a different speed from its orthogonally polarised counterpart. The difference $\Delta n = n_o - n_e$ leads to a phase lag between the ordinary and extraordinary rays. For a birefringent plate of thickness d_k, the phase lag δ between the two rays is:

$$\delta = 2\pi d_k \Delta n/\lambda \tag{7.2}$$

where λ is the wavelength in vacuum. A single stage of a Lyot filter consists of such a retarder plate between parallel linear polarisers; the plane of polarisation forms an angle of 45° with the n_o and n_e directions of the birefringent plate. This results in a circularly polarised wave propagating through the plate, and the angle of polarisation at the end of the plate is given by δ. For a wave of amplitude A, the second polariser lets pass only the parallel component $A_{\|}$:

$$A_{\|} = A \cos \delta \tag{7.3}$$

Since filter transmittance is defined as a ratio of light *intensities* I rather than amplitudes A, and:

$$I \propto A^2 \tag{7.4}$$

we conclude from (7.2) to (7.4) that the transmittance $\tau_k(\lambda)$ of a single Lyot stage of thickness d_k can be expressed as:

$$\tau_k(\lambda) = \cos^2(2\pi d_k \Delta n/\lambda) \tag{7.5}$$

The transmittance function (7.5) of a single stage shows a series of minima and maxima (Figure 7.1), and more selective filters consist of a series of such stages where the thicknesses d_k of the birefringent plates decrease progressively. In a Lyot filter, the thickness d_k of any individual stage is always a multiple of the thickness d_1 of the thinnest plate:

$$d_k = k\, d_1 \tag{7.6}$$

In a *tunable* spectral filter of the Lyot type, there is a liquid crystal cell added to each retarder plate in order to allow for an additional phase shift under control of an electric

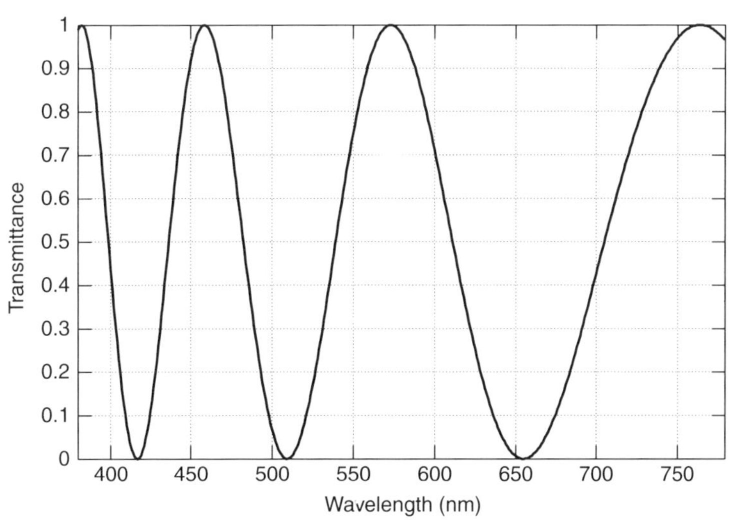

Figure 7.1 Theoretical spectral transmission function $\tau_k(\lambda)$ of a single stage of a Lyot filter.

signal [19]. The spectral width of the passband of such a filter is primarily determined by the thickest retarder plate whereas the other stages attenuate all but one of the multiple transmittance maxima of the thickest plate.

A theoretical model of this successive selection process is illustrated in Figures 7.1 to 7.3 for a four-stage Lyot filter. The spectral transmittance factors of the individual stages shown in Figure 7.2 are

$$\tau_k(\lambda) = \cos^2(2\pi k d_1 \Delta n/\lambda), \quad k = 1, 2, 3, 4 \tag{7.7}$$

and the resulting transmission function of the four-stage Lyot filter, shown in Figure 7.3, is given by the product

$$\tau_1(\lambda)\tau_2(\lambda)\tau_3(\lambda)\tau_4(\lambda) = \prod_{k=1}^{4} \cos^2(2\pi k d_1 \Delta n/\lambda) \tag{7.8}$$

A value of $d_1 \Delta n = 286$ nm was arbitrarily chosen in order to simulate a transmittance profile resembling one of those of the real filter shown in Figure 7.4.

We use a liquid crystal tunable filter (LCTF) VariSpec Model VIS2 (Cambridge Research & Instrumentation, Inc., Boston MA) with a nominal bandwidth of 30 nm and a nominal accuracy of the selected peak wavelength of 4 nm. This allows us to select about 80 significantly different tuning positions in the range 400–720 nm.

Figure 7.4 shows the measured transmittance curves of the LCTF of our SpectraCam system for nine peak wavelength positions. These curves reveal the desired Gaussian-like areas of high sensitivity, but they also show the minor sidelobes which could be

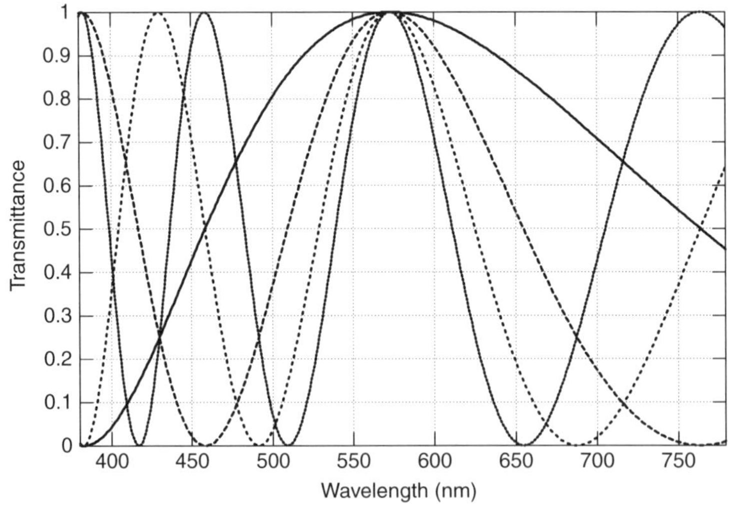

Figure 7.2 The theoretical spectral transmission functions $\tau_1(\lambda)$, $\tau_2(\lambda)$, $\tau_3(\lambda)$, $\tau_4(\lambda)$ of each element of a four-stage Lyot filter.

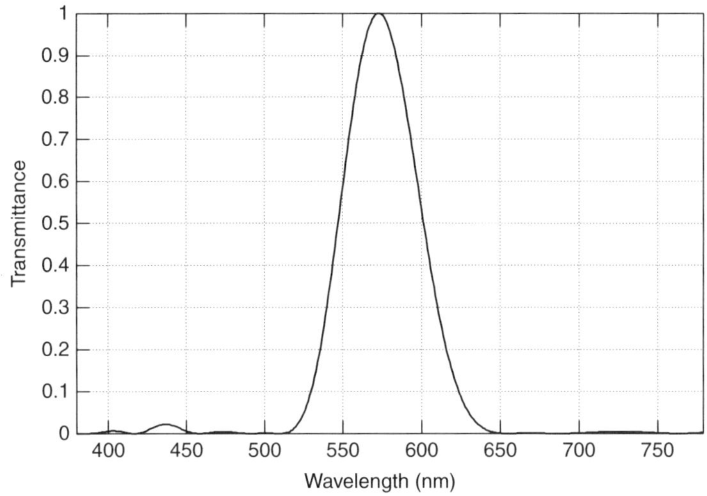

Figure 7.3 Theoretical spectral transmission function of a four-stage Lyot filter. The plotted curve shows the product of the four transmission functions, $\tau_1(\lambda)\tau_2(\lambda)\tau_3(\lambda)\tau_4(\lambda)$.

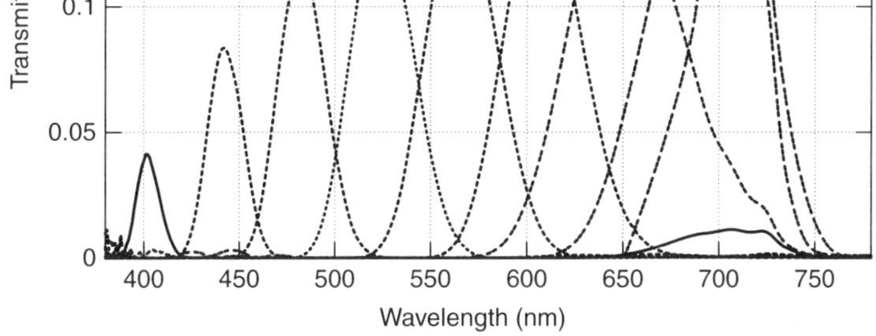

Figure 7.4 Spectral transmittance curves of the LCTF Varispec Model VIS2 (SN50346) for initially unpolarised light. The curves were measured using a Minolta CS-1000 spectroradiometer.

expected from the theoretical analysis presented above (Figure 7.3). The biggest sidelobe near 700 nm belongs to the filter profile which peaks near 400 nm. The four smaller sidelobes in the range 400–480 nm successively belong to the filter profiles peaking near 605, 650, 685 and 720 nm, respectively. These artefacts have to be carefully compensated in applications requiring spectral or colorimetric measurements of high accuracy.

7.2.2 Digital camera

Behind the tunable filter, a monochrome digital camera serves for image capture. We use a PCO SensiCam Model 370 KL camera with 1280×1024 pixels on a progressive scan CCD image sensor (PCO Computer Optics, 93 309 Kelheim, Germany). The CCD sensor is Peltier cooled to a temperature of -12°C for low-noise image acquisition and the output signal is 12-bit analogue-to-digital (AD) converted. The CCD camera features an electronic shutter and the exposure time can be varied in 1 ms steps over the range from 1 ms to 1000 s. The linearly 12-bit encoded pixel data are transferred by a high-speed serial link to a specialised PCI interface (PCO Interface Board 520KP).

The spectral sensitivity of the image sensor (Sony ICX085AL) has its maximum near 510 nm and shows about 10% variation in the wavelength range 450–580 nm. Figure 7.5 shows the effective spectral sensitivity functions of our multispectral webcam system for the most commonly used 13 channels. These curves were obtained by multiplying the spectral transmittance functions of the LCTF with the spectral sensitivity function of the monochrome digital camera.

7.2.3 Network link

In our system the tunable filter and the CCD camera are both controlled by a PC-type computer, which is linked via Ethernet to the campus-wide local area network (LAN) and the Internet as shown in Figure 7.6.

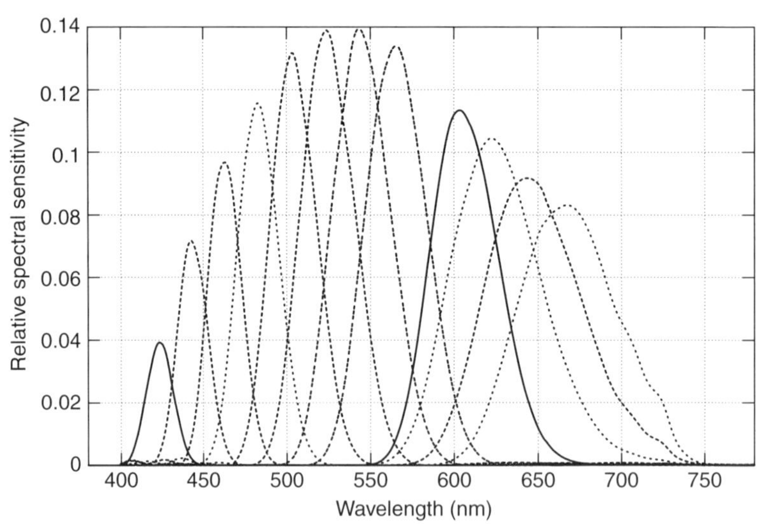

Figure 7.5 Effective spectral sensitivity functions of the most commonly used 13 channels of our SpectraCam system. These curves were obtained by multiplying the spectral transmittance functions of the LC tunable filter with the spectral sensitivity function of the monochrome camera.

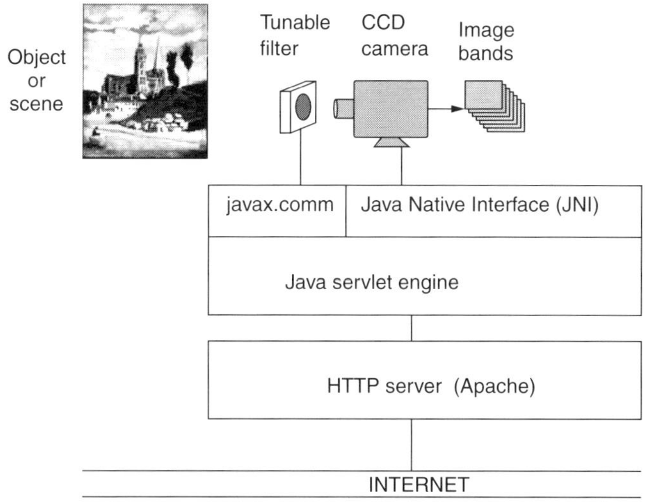

Figure 7.6 Schematic of our SpectraCam system. A monochrome CCD camera is used for image acquisition through a tunable spectral bandpass filter. The image stack on the right of the camera symbolically represents an example in which the image was captured at seven different peak wavelengths of the tunable filter. Both the tunable filter and the CCD camera are controlled by Java servlets which are accessible via the Internet through simple HTTP requests.

In order to allow for interactive use of this multispectral image acquisition system through the network, we developed a set of Java servlets which provide access to the system through Hypertext Transfer Protocol (HTTP) requests. The choice of HTTP as basis for client–server communication for our SpectraCam system was obvious since the HTTP is used by all web browsers and web servers on the Internet [20]. For the same reason, we chose the HyperText Markup Language (HTML) to deliver usage information and requested results from the SpectraCam server to the clients on the Internet [21]. The basic elements of user interaction are implemented through HTML 'form' actions and the standard Common Gateway Interface (CGI) mechanisms for client–server communication. Taken together, these design choices assure that the SpectraCam system is accessible from any web browser.

On the server side, we chose the Java servlet application programming interface (API) as standard for extending the basic web server functionality with the SpectraCam-specific services. Java servlets are commonly known as a versatile means to generate dynamic web pages, for example by adding specific information concerning a particular e-business transaction. But the major advantage of Java servlets for our application is the possibility of using all the features that the Java environment provides on the server computer.

The specific native functions required for the operation of the digital CCD camera were called through the Java Native Interface (JNI) [22]. The LCTF was controlled by means of the Java communications API, which contains support for RS-232 serial ports [23], and the Jama package [24] was used for the linear algebra operations for multispectral data processing, including matrix inversion and singular value decomposition.

7.3 COLORIMETRIC WEBCAM

For practical applications, it is interesting to implement specific types of spectral sensitivity functions on a multispectral webcam.

In the CIE 1931 standard colorimetric system [8, 25], the colorimetric properties of a stimulus of any spectral power distribution $\varphi(\lambda)$ are described by a tristimulus vector $[X, Y, Z]^{\mathrm{T}}$. The components of this vector, called tristimulus values, are obtained by numerical integration from the spectral power distribution $\varphi(\lambda)$ of the stimulus and three different spectral weighting functions $\bar{x}(\lambda), \bar{y}(\lambda), \bar{z}(\lambda)$ (Figure 7.7) which take into account the colour matching properties of the human observer [9]:

$$\begin{aligned} X &= k \int \bar{x}(\lambda)\varphi(\lambda)\mathrm{d}\lambda \\ Y &= k \int \bar{y}(\lambda)\varphi(\lambda)\mathrm{d}\lambda \\ Z &= k \int \bar{z}(\lambda)\varphi(\lambda)\mathrm{d}\lambda \end{aligned} \tag{7.9}$$

Here $\bar{x}(\lambda), \bar{y}(\lambda), \bar{z}(\lambda)$ are the CIE 1931 colour matching functions and k is a constant which determines the photometric unit. The luminance Y is obtained in photometric SI

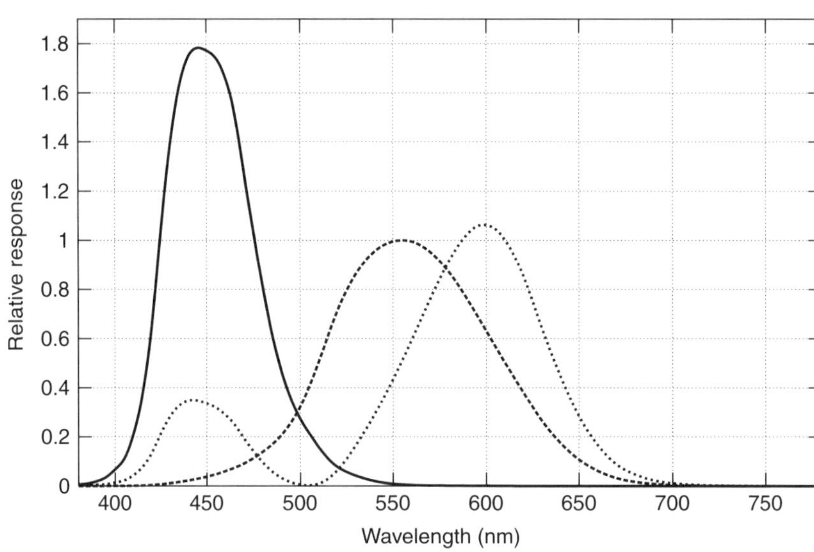

Figure 7.7 Colour matching functions of the CIE 1931 standard colorimetric observer in the XYZ system.

units if $k = K_m$ where $K_m = 683\,\mathrm{Lm\,W^{-1}}$. By using sampled versions instead of continuous spectral functions over the visible spectrum (360–780 nm), the integrals in (7.9) turn into sums:

$$X = k \sum_{\lambda_i=360\,\mathrm{nm}}^{780\,\mathrm{nm}} \bar{x}_{\lambda_i} \varphi_{\lambda_i}$$

$$Y = k \sum_{\lambda_i=360\,\mathrm{nm}}^{780\,\mathrm{nm}} \bar{y}_{\lambda_i} \varphi_{\lambda_i} \tag{7.10}$$

$$Z = k \sum_{\lambda_i=360\,\mathrm{nm}}^{780\,\mathrm{nm}} \bar{z}_{\lambda_i} \varphi_{\lambda_i}$$

which can be written in matrix notation:

$$\begin{bmatrix} X \\ Y \\ Z \end{bmatrix} = k \begin{bmatrix} \bar{x}_{\lambda_1} & \bar{x}_{\lambda_2} & \cdots & \bar{x}_{\lambda_N} \\ \bar{y}_{\lambda_1} & \bar{y}_{\lambda_2} & \cdots & \bar{y}_{\lambda_N} \\ \bar{z}_{\lambda_1} & \bar{z}_{\lambda_2} & \cdots & \bar{z}_{\lambda_N} \end{bmatrix} \begin{bmatrix} \varphi_{\lambda_1} \\ \varphi_{\lambda_2} \\ \vdots \\ \varphi_{\lambda_N} \end{bmatrix} \tag{7.11}$$

In (7.11) λ_i runs from $\lambda_1 = 360$ nm to $\lambda_N = 780$ nm, and the wavelength step size is given by the sampling interval. We adopt the usual convention of linear algebra to represent vectors by lower case boldface letters; **a** designates a column vector and its transpose $\mathbf{a}^{\mathrm{T}}$ is a row vector. With $\bar{\mathbf{x}} = [\bar{x}_{\lambda_1}, \bar{x}_{\lambda_2}, \ldots, \bar{x}_{\lambda_N}]^{\mathrm{T}}$, $\bar{\mathbf{y}} = [\bar{y}_{\lambda_1}, \bar{y}_{\lambda_2}, \ldots, \bar{y}_{\lambda_N}]^{\mathrm{T}}$, $\bar{\mathbf{z}} = [\bar{z}_{\lambda_1}, \bar{z}_{\lambda_2}, \ldots, \bar{z}_{\lambda_N}]^{\mathrm{T}}$, and $\boldsymbol{\varphi} = [\varphi_{\lambda_1}, \varphi_{\lambda_2}, \ldots, \varphi_{\lambda_N}]^{\mathrm{T}}$, equation (7.11) takes the form

$$\begin{bmatrix} X \\ Y \\ Z \end{bmatrix} = k \begin{bmatrix} \bar{\mathbf{x}}^{\mathrm{T}} \\ \bar{\mathbf{y}}^{\mathrm{T}} \\ \bar{\mathbf{z}}^{\mathrm{T}} \end{bmatrix} \boldsymbol{\varphi} \tag{7.12}$$

7.3.1 From camera channel responses to CIE colour matching functions

We now address the problem of how to approximate the $\bar{x}(\lambda)$, $\bar{y}(\lambda)$, $\bar{z}(\lambda)$ functions by linear combinations of the 13 spectral channels from Figure 7.5.

If we designate the number of individual spectral channels by M ($M = 13$ in our example), a multispectral recording of an original spectral power distribution $\boldsymbol{\varphi} = [\varphi_{\lambda_1}, \varphi_{\lambda_2}, \ldots, \varphi_{\lambda_N}]^{\mathrm{T}}$, will yield M components which can be written as a vector $[C_1, C_2, \ldots, C_M]^{\mathrm{T}}$:

$$\begin{bmatrix} C_1 \\ C_2 \\ \vdots \\ C_M \end{bmatrix} = \begin{bmatrix} c_{1\lambda_1} & c_{1\lambda_2} & \cdots & c_{1\lambda_N} \\ c_{2\lambda_1} & c_{2\lambda_2} & \cdots & c_{2\lambda_N} \\ \vdots & \vdots & \ddots & \vdots \\ c_{M\lambda_1} & c_{M\lambda_2} & \cdots & c_{M\lambda_N} \end{bmatrix} \begin{bmatrix} \varphi_{\lambda_1} \\ \varphi_{\lambda_2} \\ \vdots \\ \varphi_{\lambda_N} \end{bmatrix} \tag{7.13}$$

where each $c_{m\lambda_n}$ represents the effective spectral sensitivity of channel M at wavelength λ_n. By designating the sampled spectral sensitivity function of channel M by a vector $\mathbf{c}_m = [c_{m\lambda_1}, c_{m\lambda_2}, \ldots, c_{m\lambda_N}]^{\mathrm{T}}$, equation (7.13) reads

$$\begin{bmatrix} C_1 \\ C_2 \\ \vdots \\ C_M \end{bmatrix} = \begin{bmatrix} \mathbf{c}_1^{\mathrm{T}} \\ \mathbf{c}_2^{\mathrm{T}} \\ \vdots \\ \mathbf{c}_M^{\mathrm{T}} \end{bmatrix} \boldsymbol{\varphi} \tag{7.14}$$

Here the spectral sensitivities $\mathbf{c}_1, \mathbf{c}_2, \ldots, \mathbf{c}_M$ are given by the physical device characteristics of the multispectral camera.

In order to obtain a close approximation of CIE 1931 X,Y,Z values from the M channel outputs, we adopt a linear model approach in which *approximated* values $\tilde{X}, \tilde{Y}, \tilde{Z}$ are obtained by linear combinations of the output signals $C_m (m = 1, 2, \ldots, M)$ of the camera channels:

$$\begin{bmatrix} \tilde{X} \\ \tilde{Y} \\ \tilde{Z} \end{bmatrix} = \begin{bmatrix} a_{x1} & a_{x2} & \ldots & a_{xM} \\ a_{y1} & a_{y2} & \ldots & a_{yM} \\ a_{z1} & a_{z2} & \ldots & a_{zM} \end{bmatrix} \begin{bmatrix} C_1 \\ C_2 \\ \vdots \\ C_M \end{bmatrix} \tag{7.15}$$

If we express the *approximated* tristimulus vector $[\tilde{X}, \tilde{Y}, \tilde{Z}]^{\mathrm{T}}$ of (7.15) in the form of (7.12):

$$\begin{bmatrix} \tilde{X} \\ \tilde{Y} \\ \tilde{Z} \end{bmatrix} = k \begin{bmatrix} \tilde{\bar{\mathbf{x}}}^{\mathrm{T}} \\ \tilde{\bar{\mathbf{y}}}^{\mathrm{T}} \\ \tilde{\bar{\mathbf{z}}}^{\mathrm{T}} \end{bmatrix} \boldsymbol{\varphi} \tag{7.16}$$

and then substitute (7.16) and (7.14) into (7.15), we obtain

$$k \begin{bmatrix} \tilde{\bar{\mathbf{x}}}^{\mathrm{T}} \\ \tilde{\bar{\mathbf{y}}}^{\mathrm{T}} \\ \tilde{\bar{\mathbf{z}}}^{\mathrm{T}} \end{bmatrix} \boldsymbol{\varphi} = \begin{bmatrix} a_{x1} & a_{x2} & \ldots & a_{xM} \\ a_{y1} & a_{y2} & \ldots & a_{yM} \\ a_{z1} & a_{z2} & \ldots & a_{zM} \end{bmatrix} \begin{bmatrix} \mathbf{c}_1^{\mathrm{T}} \\ \mathbf{c}_2^{\mathrm{T}} \\ \vdots \\ \mathbf{c}_M^{\mathrm{T}} \end{bmatrix} \boldsymbol{\varphi} \tag{7.17}$$

Equation (7.17) is satisfied for arbitrary spectral distributions $\boldsymbol{\varphi}$ only if

$$k \begin{bmatrix} \tilde{\bar{\mathbf{x}}}^{\mathrm{T}} \\ \tilde{\bar{\mathbf{y}}}^{\mathrm{T}} \\ \tilde{\bar{\mathbf{z}}}^{\mathrm{T}} \end{bmatrix} = \begin{bmatrix} a_{x1} & a_{x2} & \ldots & a_{xM} \\ a_{y1} & a_{y2} & \ldots & a_{yM} \\ a_{z1} & a_{z2} & \ldots & a_{zM} \end{bmatrix} \begin{bmatrix} \mathbf{c}_1^{\mathrm{T}} \\ \mathbf{c}_2^{\mathrm{T}} \\ \vdots \\ \mathbf{c}_M^{\mathrm{T}} \end{bmatrix} \tag{7.18}$$

We now have to compute the required coefficients $a_{xm} (m = 1, 2, \ldots, M)$ by solving the least mean square problem:

$$\sum_{\lambda_i=360\,\text{nm}}^{780\,\text{nm}} (\bar{x}_{\lambda_i} - \tilde{\bar{x}}_{\lambda_i})^2 = \min \tag{7.19}$$

and, in the same way, the coefficients a_{ym} and a_{zm} by solving:

$$\sum_{\lambda_i=360\,\text{nm}}^{780\,\text{nm}} (\bar{y}_{\lambda_i} - \tilde{\bar{y}}_{\lambda_i})^2 = \min \tag{7.20}$$

and

$$\sum_{\lambda_i=360\,\text{nm}}^{780\,\text{nm}} (\bar{z}_{\lambda_i} - \tilde{\bar{z}}_{\lambda_i})^2 = \min \tag{7.21}$$

respectively. To formulate this problem more concisely, we use matrix notation with:

$$\mathbf{A} = \begin{bmatrix} a_{x1} & a_{x2} & \ldots & a_{xM} \\ a_{y1} & a_{y2} & \ldots & a_{yM} \\ a_{z1} & a_{z2} & \ldots & a_{zM} \end{bmatrix} \tag{7.22}$$

$$\mathbf{X} = k \begin{bmatrix} \bar{\mathbf{x}}^{\mathrm{T}} \\ \bar{\mathbf{y}}^{\mathrm{T}} \\ \bar{\mathbf{z}}^{\mathrm{T}} \end{bmatrix} = k \begin{bmatrix} \bar{x}_{\lambda_1} & \bar{x}_{\lambda_2} & \ldots & \bar{x}_{\lambda_N} \\ \bar{y}_{\lambda_1} & \bar{y}_{\lambda_2} & \ldots & \bar{y}_{\lambda_N} \\ \bar{z}_{\lambda_1} & \bar{z}_{\lambda_2} & \ldots & \bar{z}_{\lambda_N} \end{bmatrix} \tag{7.23}$$

$$\tilde{\mathbf{X}} = k \begin{bmatrix} \tilde{\bar{\mathbf{x}}}^{\mathrm{T}} \\ \tilde{\bar{\mathbf{y}}}^{\mathrm{T}} \\ \tilde{\bar{\mathbf{z}}}^{\mathrm{T}} \end{bmatrix} = k \begin{bmatrix} \tilde{\bar{x}}_{\lambda_1} & \tilde{\bar{x}}_{\lambda_2} & \ldots & \tilde{\bar{x}}_{\lambda_N} \\ \tilde{\bar{y}}_{\lambda_1} & \tilde{\bar{y}}_{\lambda_2} & \ldots & \tilde{\bar{y}}_{\lambda_N} \\ \tilde{\bar{z}}_{\lambda_1} & \tilde{\bar{z}}_{\lambda_2} & \ldots & \tilde{\bar{z}}_{\lambda_N} \end{bmatrix} \tag{7.24}$$

$$\mathbf{C} = \begin{bmatrix} \mathbf{c}_1^{\mathrm{T}} \\ \mathbf{c}_2^{\mathrm{T}} \\ \vdots \\ \mathbf{c}_M^{\mathrm{T}} \end{bmatrix} = \begin{bmatrix} c_{1\lambda_1} & c_{1\lambda_2} & \ldots & c_{1\lambda_N} \\ c_{2\lambda_1} & c_{2\lambda_2} & \ldots & c_{2\lambda_N} \\ \vdots & \vdots & \ddots & \vdots \\ c_{M\lambda_1} & c_{M\lambda_2} & \ldots & c_{M\lambda_N} \end{bmatrix} \tag{7.25}$$

With these designations, equation (7.18) reads:

$$\tilde{\mathbf{X}} = \mathbf{AC} \tag{7.26}$$

where the matrix $\mathbf{A}$ has to be determined such that $\tilde{\mathbf{X}}$ provides a close approximation of $\mathbf{X}$. The solution of this problem is given by means of the Moore–Penrose pseudoinverse $\mathbf{C}^+$ [26, 5] of the matrix $\mathbf{C}$ as:

$$\mathbf{A} = \mathbf{XC}^+ \tag{7.27}$$

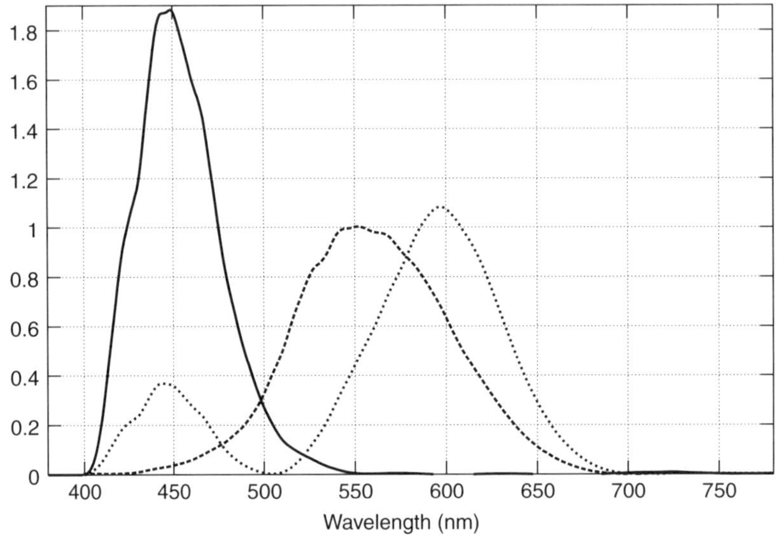

Figure 7.8 Approximation of the CIE 1931 XYZ colour matching functions obtained with the SpectraCam system by using linear combinations of the 13 spectral channels Figure 7.5.

Figure 7.8 shows the results obtained by this method if the CIE 1931 colour matching functions $\bar{x}(\lambda), \bar{y}(\lambda), \bar{z}(\lambda)$ are approximated by linear combinations of the 13 spectral channels from Figure 7.5.

7.3.2 Spectral sensitivities of an ideal colour camera

In an imaging chain, a colour camera has to provide three very specific signals which depend on the primary colours of the display device. To derive the requirements for a *colorimetrically correct* imaging chain, we consider a vector φ_{ORIG}, representing the spectral power distribution of light coming from a given position of the original scene, and a vector φ_{CRT} representing the spectral power distribution of the corresponding pixel on a cathode ray tube (CRT) image display.

Although φ_{ORIG} and φ_{CRT} will be generally different, they should be metamers, i.e. they should visually *match*. This is only the case if their tristimulus vectors $[X, Y, Z]^T$ as determined by (7.12) are identical:

$$\begin{bmatrix} \bar{\mathbf{x}}^T \\ \bar{\mathbf{y}}^T \\ \bar{\mathbf{z}}^T \end{bmatrix} \varphi_{ORIG} = \begin{bmatrix} \bar{\mathbf{x}}^T \\ \bar{\mathbf{y}}^T \\ \bar{\mathbf{z}}^T \end{bmatrix} \varphi_{CRT} \tag{7.28}$$

Since the light output φ_{CRT} of the CRT display is the result of additive colour mixing, it can be expressed as:

$$\varphi_{CRT} = R\varphi_{CRT\ R} + G\varphi_{CRT\ G} + B\varphi_{CRT\ B} \tag{7.29}$$

where $\varphi_{CRT\ R}$, $\varphi_{CRT\ G}$, and $\varphi_{CRT\ B}$ designate the spectral power distributions of the CRT primaries. The coefficients R, G, B are weighting factors which determine the relative contribution of each primary to the total light output φ_{CRT} of the display. The values of R, G, B lie between 0 (no contribution) and 1 (full contribution). Note that the coefficients R, G, B represent light quantities rather than video signal amplitudes; because of the non-linear relationship between video signals and CRT light output, they are linked to the video signal values by a non-linear function, commonly referred to by a power function with an exponent called γ (gamma).

Using the notation of linear algebra, (7.29) can be rewritten as the product of the Nrow $\times$ 3 column matrix formed by the three primary vectors $[\varphi_{CRT\ R}, \varphi_{CRT\ G}, \varphi_{CRT\ B}]$ with a column vector containing the coefficients R, G, B:

$$\varphi_{CRT} = [\varphi_{CRT\ R}, \varphi_{CRT\ G}, \varphi_{CRT\ B}] \begin{bmatrix} R \\ G \\ B \end{bmatrix} \tag{7.30}$$

By substituting φ_{CRT} from (7.30) into (7.28), we get

$$\begin{bmatrix} \bar{\mathbf{x}}^{\mathrm{T}} \\ \bar{\mathbf{y}}^{\mathrm{T}} \\ \bar{\mathbf{z}}^{\mathrm{T}} \end{bmatrix} \varphi_{ORIG} = \begin{bmatrix} \bar{\mathbf{x}}^{\mathrm{T}} \\ \bar{\mathbf{y}}^{\mathrm{T}} \\ \bar{\mathbf{z}}^{\mathrm{T}} \end{bmatrix} [\varphi_{CRT\ R}, \varphi_{CRT\ G}, \varphi_{CRT\ B}] \begin{bmatrix} R \\ G \\ B \end{bmatrix} \tag{7.31}$$

We can now use (7.12) to replace the matrix product on the right-hand side of (7.31) by a 3 $\times$ 3 matrix which contains the CIE XYZ tristimulus values of the CRT phosphors:

$$\begin{bmatrix} \bar{\mathbf{x}}^{\mathrm{T}} \\ \bar{\mathbf{y}}^{\mathrm{T}} \\ \bar{\mathbf{z}}^{\mathrm{T}} \end{bmatrix} \varphi_{ORIG} = \frac{1}{k} \begin{bmatrix} X_R & X_G & X_B \\ Y_R & Y_G & Y_B \\ Z_R & Z_G & Z_B \end{bmatrix} \begin{bmatrix} R \\ G \\ B \end{bmatrix} \tag{7.32}$$

Finally, the solution of (7.32) for $[R, G, B]^{\mathrm{T}}$ reads:

$$\begin{bmatrix} R \\ G \\ B \end{bmatrix} = k \begin{bmatrix} X_R & X_G & X_B \\ Y_R & Y_G & Y_B \\ Z_R & Z_G & Z_B \end{bmatrix}^{-1} \begin{bmatrix} \bar{\mathbf{x}}^{\mathrm{T}} \\ \bar{\mathbf{y}}^{\mathrm{T}} \\ \bar{\mathbf{z}}^{\mathrm{T}} \end{bmatrix} \varphi_{ORIG} \tag{7.33}$$

Equation (7.33) tells us how to obtain the colorimetrically correct CRT primary contributions R, G, B for any colour stimulus given by its spectral power distribution φ_{ORIG}. An ideal colorimetric camera, providing directly the R, G, B coefficients, would have to implement spectral sensitivities $\mathbf{c}_R$, $\mathbf{c}_G$, $\mathbf{c}_B$ such that:

$$\begin{bmatrix} R \\ G \\ B \end{bmatrix} = \begin{bmatrix} \mathbf{c}_R^{\mathrm{T}} \\ \mathbf{c}_G^{\mathrm{T}} \\ \mathbf{c}_B^{\mathrm{T}} \end{bmatrix} \varphi_{ORIG} \tag{7.34}$$

for any φ_{ORIG}. According to equation (7.33), we get:

$$\begin{bmatrix} \mathbf{c}_R^{\mathrm{T}} \\ \mathbf{c}_G^{\mathrm{T}} \\ \mathbf{c}_B^{\mathrm{T}} \end{bmatrix} = k \begin{bmatrix} X_R & X_G & X_B \\ Y_R & Y_G & Y_B \\ Z_R & Z_G & Z_B \end{bmatrix}^{-1} \begin{bmatrix} \bar{\mathbf{x}}^{\mathrm{T}} \\ \bar{\mathbf{y}}^{\mathrm{T}} \\ \bar{\mathbf{z}}^{\mathrm{T}} \end{bmatrix} \tag{7.35}$$

In other words, the requirement (7.28) can be satisfied for any φ_{ORIG} if and only if the spectral sensitivity functions of each of the camera's three colour channels are linear combinations of the colour matching functions of the human observer.

7.3.3 Implementation of an ideal colour camera for ITU-R BT.709 CRT primaries

In Section 7.3.1 we showed how to obtain CIE 1931 X, Y, Z colorimetric values from the output signals of a multispectral camera. Another interesting application of interactive multispectral image acquisition is the implementation of the spectral sensitivity functions of the blue, green and red colour channels of an ideal colour camera for a display using ITU-R BT.709 or sRGB primaries [10, 11].

The spectral sensitivity functions $\mathbf{c}_{R\ 709}, \mathbf{c}_{G\ 709}, \mathbf{c}_{B\ 709}$ of such an ideal camera are directly obtained from (7.35) if we use the CIE XYZ tristimulus values of the ITU-R BT.709 primaries in the 3×3 matrix:

$$\begin{bmatrix} \mathbf{c}_{R709}^{\mathrm{T}} \\ \mathbf{c}_{G709}^{\mathrm{T}} \\ \mathbf{c}_{B709}^{\mathrm{T}} \end{bmatrix} = k \begin{bmatrix} X_{R\ 709} & X_{G\ 709} & X_{B\ 709} \\ Y_{R\ 709} & Y_{G\ 709} & Y_{B\ 709} \\ Z_{R\ 709} & Z_{G\ 709} & Z_{B\ 709} \end{bmatrix}^{-1} \begin{bmatrix} \bar{\mathbf{x}}^{\mathrm{T}} \\ \bar{\mathbf{y}}^{\mathrm{T}} \\ \bar{\mathbf{z}}^{\mathrm{T}} \end{bmatrix} \tag{7.36}$$

The only remaining question is how to obtain the CIE XYZ values for the 3×3 matrix in (7.36) from the chromaticity coordinates of the ITU-R BT.709 reference primaries and of the CIE standard illuminant D65, given in Table 7.1.

The general definition of the chromaticies x, y, z are:

$$x = \frac{X}{X+Y+Z}$$
$$y = \frac{Y}{X+Y+Z} \tag{7.37}$$
$$z = \frac{Z}{X+Y+Z}$$

so for any colour stimulus i, it follows that:

$$\begin{bmatrix} X_i \\ Y_i \\ Z_i \end{bmatrix} = \begin{bmatrix} x_i \\ y_i \\ z_i \end{bmatrix} m_i \tag{7.38}$$

Table 7.1 CIE 1931 chromaticities for ITU-R BT.709 reference primaries and CIE standard illuminant $D65$

	Red R_{709}	Green G_{709}	Blue B_{709}	White D65
x	0.6400	0.3000	0.1500	0.3127
y	0.3300	0.6000	0.0600	0.3290
z	0.0300	0.1000	0.7900	0.3583

with:

$$m_i = X_i + Y_i + Z_i \tag{7.39}$$

On an ideal ITU-R BT.709 display device, equal 100% video signals on all three video inputs should produce a white stimulus with $D65$ chromaticity. In terms of CIE 1931 tristimulus vector components, this additive mixing can be expressed as:

$$\begin{bmatrix} X_{D65} \\ Y_{D65} \\ Z_{D65} \end{bmatrix} = \begin{bmatrix} X_{R\ 709} \\ Y_{R\ 709} \\ Z_{R\ 709} \end{bmatrix} + \begin{bmatrix} X_{G\ 709} \\ Y_{G\ 709} \\ Z_{G\ 709} \end{bmatrix} + \begin{bmatrix} X_{B\ 709} \\ Y_{B\ 709} \\ Z_{B\ 709} \end{bmatrix} \tag{7.40}$$

By substituting (7.38) for $i = R_{709}, G_{709}, B_{709}, D65$, into (7.40), we get:

$$\begin{bmatrix} x_{D65} \\ y_{D65} \\ z_{D65} \end{bmatrix} m_{D65} = \begin{bmatrix} x_{R\ 709} \\ y_{R\ 709} \\ z_{R\ 709} \end{bmatrix} m_{R\ 709} + \begin{bmatrix} x_{G\ 709} \\ y_{G\ 709} \\ z_{G\ 709} \end{bmatrix} m_{G\ 709} + \begin{bmatrix} x_{B\ 709} \\ y_{B\ 709} \\ z_{B\ 709} \end{bmatrix} m_{B\ 709} \tag{7.41}$$

which reads in matrix notation:

$$\begin{bmatrix} x_{D65} \\ y_{D65} \\ z_{D65} \end{bmatrix} m_{D65} = \begin{bmatrix} x_{R\ 709} & x_{G\ 709} & x_{B\ 709} \\ y_{R\ 709} & y_{G\ 709} & y_{B\ 709} \\ z_{R\ 709} & z_{G\ 709} & z_{B\ 709} \end{bmatrix} \begin{bmatrix} m_{R\ 709} \\ m_{G\ 709} \\ m_{B\ 709} \end{bmatrix} \tag{7.42}$$

The solution of (7.42) is given by:

$$\begin{bmatrix} m_{R\ 709} \\ m_{G\ 709} \\ m_{B\ 709} \end{bmatrix} = \begin{bmatrix} x_{R\ 709} & x_{G\ 709} & x_{B\ 709} \\ y_{R\ 709} & y_{G\ 709} & y_{B\ 709} \\ z_{R\ 709} & z_{G\ 709} & z_{B\ 709} \end{bmatrix}^{-1} \begin{bmatrix} x_{D65} \\ y_{D65} \\ z_{D65} \end{bmatrix} m_{D65} \tag{7.43}$$

where the only remaining unknown quantity is m_{D65}. To determine m_{D65}, we take the middle row of (7.38) for $i = D65$:

$$Y_{D65} = y_{D65}\, m_{D65} \tag{7.44}$$

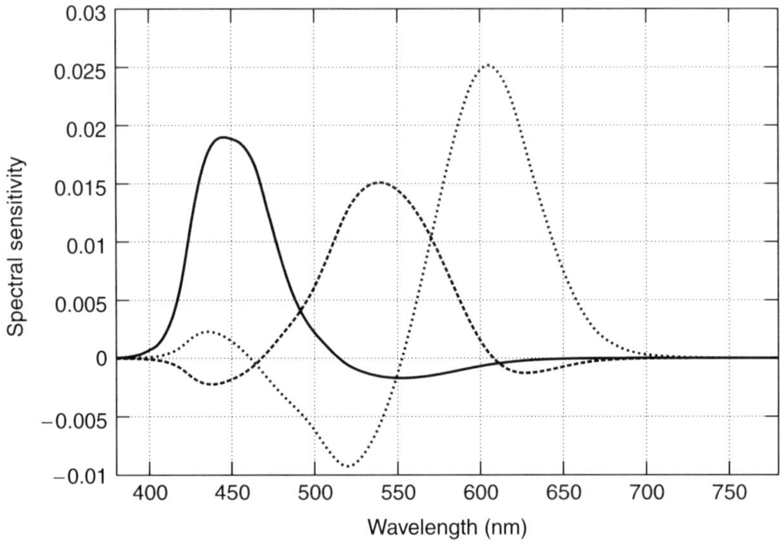

Figure 7.9 Theoretically correct spectral sensitivity functions of the blue, green and red colour channels of an ideal colour camera for a display using ITU-R BT.709 or sRGB primaries.

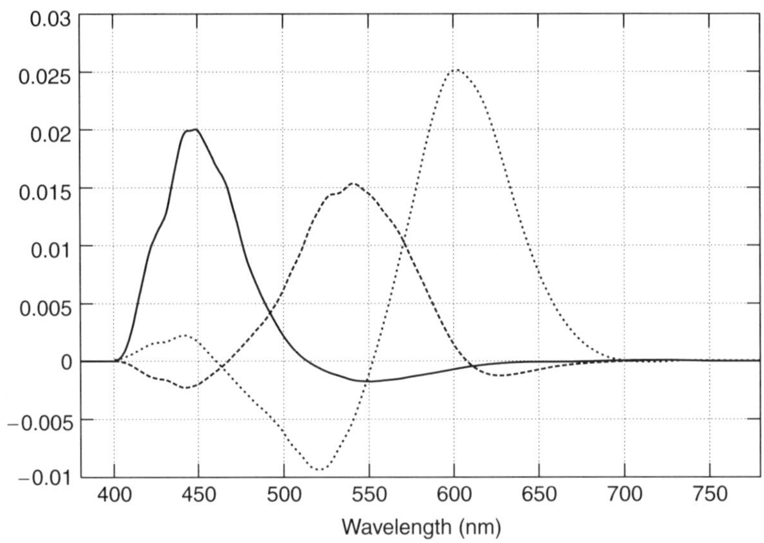

Figure 7.10 Approximation by our SpectraCam system of the spectral sensitivity functions of an 'ideal' colour camera for a display using ITU-R BR.709 primaries. This approximation is obtained by using linear combinations of the 13 spectral channels in Figure 7.5.

Here Y_{D65} represents the luminance of the nominal white stimulus as determined by a photometric measurement, and m_{D65} in (7.43) can therefore be replaced by:

$$m_{D65} = Y_{D65}/y_{D65} \tag{7.45}$$

Equation (7.43) is now completely determined, and we can use the resulting values $m_{R\ 709}, m_{G\ 709}, m_{B\ 709}$ to compute the CIE XYZ values of the ITU-R BT.709 primaries according to (7.38):

$$\begin{bmatrix} X_{R\ 709} & X_{G\ 709} & X_{B\ 709} \\ Y_{R\ 709} & Y_{G\ 709} & Y_{B\ 709} \\ Z_{R\ 709} & Z_{G\ 709} & Z_{B\ 709} \end{bmatrix} = \begin{bmatrix} x_{R\ 709} & x_{G\ 709} & x_{B\ 709} \\ y_{R\ 709} & y_{G\ 709} & y_{B\ 709} \\ z_{R\ 709} & z_{G\ 709} & z_{B\ 709} \end{bmatrix} \begin{bmatrix} m_{R\ 709} & 0 & 0 \\ 0 & m_{G\ 709} & 0 \\ 0 & 0 & m_{B\ 709} \end{bmatrix} \tag{7.46}$$

Figure 7.9 shows the resulting spectral sensitivity functions $\mathbf{c}_{R\ 709}, \mathbf{c}_{G\ 709}, \mathbf{c}_{B\ 709}$ of an ideal camera for ITU-R BT.709 primaries obtained by substituting the matrix of the CIE XYZ values (7.46) into equation (7.36).

To implement these ITU-R BT.709 spectral sensitivity functions on our interactive multispectral camera system, we again used linear combinations of the 13 spectral channels from Figure 7.5. The procedure was exactly the same as described in Section 7.3.1 and the results are shown in Figure 7.10.

7.4 CONCLUSIONS

This chapter presents a fully electronic system for multispectral image acquisition and analysis which allows for interactive operation across the web.

The key elements of the system are an electronically controlled liquid crystal tunable filter, a digital camera, and modular software components based on a client–server architecture. On the server side, Java servlets are used to implement access to the system through simple HTTP requests. Since only the standard Common Gateway Interface (CGI) mechanisms for client–server communication are used, the system is accessible from any web browser.

In its present form, the system provides real-time remote access on our intranet to reflectance spectra at any position on the target. The user typically first selects the reference 'white' position by means of the mouse cursor, and then interactively examines reflectance spectra, CIE XYZ tristimulus values, or CIELAB data for any region of interest. Application areas include the spectrophotometric analysis of fine art paintings and museum objects, the simulation of object appearance under different illuminants, and high-end multimedia colour imaging.

REFERENCES

1. B. A. Wandell (1987) The synthesis and analysis of colour images. *IEEE Transactions on Pattern Analysis and Machine Intelligence*, **9**, 2–13.

2. J. E. Farell (1996) Spectral based colour image editing (SBCIE). In *Proceedings of IS&T and SID's 4th Colour Imaging Conference: Colour Science, Systems and Applications*, Scottsdale, Arizona, pp. 104–108.
3. H. Maître, F. Schmitt, J.-P. Crettez, Yifeng Wu and J. Y. Hardeberg (1996) Spectrophotometric image analysis of fine art paintings. In *Proceedings of IS&T and SID's 4th Colour Imaging Conference: Colour Science, Systems and Applications*, Scottsdale, Arizona, pp. 50–53.
4. R. S. Berns, F. H. Imai, P. D. Burns and Di-Y. Tzeng (1998) Multi-spectral-based colour reproduction research at the Munsell Colour Science Laboratory. *Proc. SPIE*, **3409**, 14–25.
5. J. Y. Hardeberg, F. Schmitt, H. Brettel, J.-P. Crettez and H. Maître (1999) Multispectral image acquisition and simulation of illuminant changes. In L. W. MacDonald and M. R. Luo (eds), *Colour Imaging: Vision and Technology*, Wiley, pp. 145–164.
6. F. König and W. Praefcke (1998) The practice of multispectral image acquisition. *Proc. SPIE*, **3409**, 34–41.
7. Wencheng Wu, J. P. Allebach and M. Analoui (1999) Imaging colorimetry using a digital camera. In *Proceedings of IS&T and SID's 7th Colour Imaging Conference: Colour Science, Systems and Applications*, Scottsdale, Arizona, pp. 15–20.
8. CIE (1986) *Colorimetry*. Commission Internationale d'Eclairage, Vienna.
9. CIE (1986) *CIE Standard Colorimetric Observers*. Commission Internationale d'Eclairage, Vienna.
10. ITU (1997) Recommendation ITU-R BT.709-3. Parameter values for the HDTV standards for production and international programme exchange. International Telecommunication Union, Geneva.
11. M. Stokes, M. Anderson, S. Chandrasekar and R. Motta (1996) A standard default colour space for the Internet–sRGB. http://www.w3.org/Graphics/Colour/sRGB.html.
12. P. H. Swain and S. M. Davis (eds) (1978) *Remote Sensing: The Quantitative Approach*. McGraw-Hill, New York.
13. A. Rosselet, W. Graff, U. P. Wild, C. U. Keller and R. Gschwind (1995) Persistent spectral hole burning used for spectrally high-resolved imaging of the sun. *Proc. SPIE*, **2480**, 205–212.
14. H. Haneishi, T. Hasegawa, N. Tsumura and Y. Miyake (1997) Design of colour filters for recording art works. In *Proceedings of IS&T 50th Annual Conference*, pp. 369–372.
15. D. L. Farkas, B. T. Ballou, G. W. Fisher, D. Fishman, Y. Garini, W. Niu and E. S. Wachman (1996) Microscopic and mesoscopic spectral bio-imaging. *Proc. SPIE*, **2678**, 200–206.
16. R. S. Berns (1998) Challenges for colour science in multimedia imaging. In *Proc. CIM'98: Colour Imaging in Multimedia*, Derby, UK, pp. 123–133.
17. M. S. Peercy (1993) Linear colour representations for full spectral rendering. *Computer Graphics Proceedings*, pp. 191–198.
18. B. Lyot (1993) Un monochromateur à grand champ utilisant les interférences en lumière polarisée. *Comptes Rendus de l'Académie des Sciences*, **197**, 1593–1595.
19. T. Chrien, C. Chovit and P. Miller (1993) Imaging spectrometry using liquid crystal tunable filters. http://stargate.jpl.nasa.gov/lctf/rtf/.
20. W3C. HTTP – hypertext transfer protocol overview. http://www.w3.org/Protocols/.
21. W3C. HTML – hypertext markup language. http://www.w3.org/MarkUp/.
22. Sun Microsystems. The java tutorial: overview of the jni. http://java.sun.com/docs/books/tutorial/native1.1/concepts/index.html.
23. Sun Microsystems. The java communications api. http://www.javasoft.com/products/javacomm/.
24. The MathWorks and National Institute of Standards and Technology. Jama: a java matrix package. http://math.nist.gov/javanumerics/jama.
25. G. Wyszecki and W. S. Stiles (1982) *Colour Science*, 2nd edn. Wiley, New York.
26. A. Albert (1972) *Regression and the Moore–Penrose pseudoinverse*. Academic Press, New York.

PART 3

Image processing

8

Spotting colours

Georgina Kwei, Kobus Barnard and Brian Funt

8.1 INTRODUCTION

This chapter describes tests to evaluate the accuracy with which objects of a specific single colour can be identified in a complex image, and the effectiveness of the addition of colour constancy preprocessing. Although it is already known how well colour constancy algorithms perform in terms of RMS error [3], much less is known about how these error rates affect the likelihood of identifying a particular colour in a complex scene. There are numerous colour-based object recognition algorithms [12, 2, 13, 7] but the algorithms generally expect objects that have more than one colour. For example, Yuille, Snow and Nitzberg [13] perform the task of locating street signs using the two colours on the signs. Algorithms by Funt and Finlayson [7] and Ennesser and Medioni [2] use colour-edge histograms to do multicoloured object recognition.

Spotting one distinct and more or less uniform colour is basic to object recognition in both human and machine vision. For example, a lemon is an object that has the distinct uniform colour of yellow. Locating human skin in an image by looking for flesh tones is another example. Spotting a single colour presents different challenges from spotting a multicoloured object. In the case of multicoloured objects, the relationship between the colours remains quite stable under changes in the incident illumination. This fact has been used in several colour-based object recognition algorithms [7, 9]. These colour

Colour Image Science, edited by L.W. MacDonald and M.R. Luo.

relationship methods require there to be more than one colour in the image, otherwise they will not work. Since they identify objects based on the relationship between colours, rather than the colours themselves, the actual illumination-independent colours are not required. This means that colour constancy preprocessing can be avoided. However, in the case of spotting a single colour, where relationships between colours are not available, colour constancy processing is required to extract an illumination-independent colour representation.

Spotting colours is the task used here to measure the accuracy of several colour constancy strategies. The colour constancy methods tested are the neural network approach [4–6], greyworld, database greyworld and white-patch retinex. The control is the image taken under the known illuminant with no colour constancy preprocessing.

8.2 TEST IMAGES

The test images were taken from the object recognition image database used in Funt, Barnard and Martin [3] and have been adjusted against the camera calibration model described in that paper. They were derived from three test objects (Figure 8.1):

- Ball 1: a fuzzy, partially fluorescent, ball
- Ball 2: a shiny multicoloured ball
- Tide: a detergent box printed in colour

Ball 1 is fluorescent in the sense that it glows brightly under ultraviolet light.

These particular objects were chosen because they have fairly large areas of uniform and distinct colour that can be used for the spotting tests. From each image, one colour was segmented from the object and represented the single-colour object to be spotted in the later tests.

In the Ball 1 image, the blue and pink areas were used separately as the single-colour objects. In other words, the goal was not to identify Ball 1, but rather to identify one or other region in various images of Ball 1 taken under different illuminants. The white area

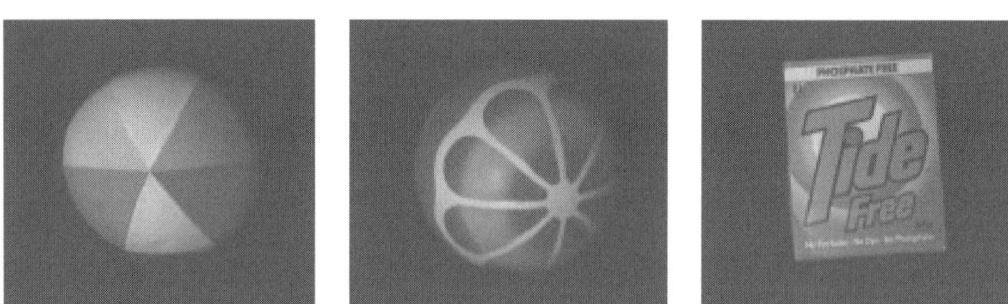

(a) (b) (c)

Figure 8.1 Test objects: (a) Ball 1, (b) Ball 2, (c) Tide.

Table 8.1 The five illuminants

Illuminant	Description
mb-5000	Macbeth 5000 K fluorescent tubes
mb-5000 + 3202	Macbeth 5000 tubes with Roscolux #3202 full blue filter
syl-cwf	Sylvania cool white fluorescent tube
Ph-ulm	Phillips Ultralume fluorescent tube
Halogen	Sylvania 75 W halogen bulb

was chosen from Ball 2 as the single-colour object, and the green lettering from the Tide image. This resulted in four 'objects' to spot.

Each original object was placed in a Macbeth Judge II light booth and an image was captured of the object under five different sources of illumination. The camera aperture was adjusted to prevent image clipping under the brightest lighting conditions for a given object, and not changed between illuminants. The five illuminants are listed in Table 8.1.

Images were taken of each object under each of the five illuminants. A copy of each image was kept unprocessed as a control image. Each image was then processed using each of the four colour constancy algorithms to generate 25 images per test object. In all, 100 images were used.

8.3 METHOD

8.3.1 Colour constancy processing

The images stored in the calibrated database had been averaged over numerous frames to reduce noise and increase dynamic range. In addition, they had been linearised and adjusted for camera black offset. The image data was stored in floating point format to preserve the accuracy of the multiframe averaging.

The greyworld algorithm estimated the illumination chromaticity by comparing the average of the image chromaticities to an ideal grey defined as $R = G = B$. The database greyworld compared the image average to the average of the chromaticities taken over all images in the database. The white-patch retinex algorithm estimated the illumination chromaticity as the chromaticity obtained from the maximum values in each of the channels.

The neural network method [4–6] was based on a two-layer feedforward network that estimated the chromaticity of the scene illumination from an image. It based its estimate on the gamut of colours present in the image. The neural network was a Perceptron [10] with one hidden layer and an input layer consisting of 1000–2000 binary inputs representing the chromaticity of the RGB values present in the scene. The hidden layer had a much smaller size, in the range 16–32 neurons, and the output layer was composed of only two neurons. Each image RGB from a scene was transformed into rg chromaticity space, as defined by (8.1), which was then coarsely but uniformly discretised and presented to the network's input layer. The input was binary, indicating either the presence or absence of the corresponding chromaticity in the image. The output layer of the neural network produced the values r and g (in the chromaticity space) of the illuminant. The output values were real numbers ranging from 0.0 to 1.0. The neural network was trained using the back-propagation algorithm without momentum [11] on thousands of images. During the learning phase, the network was provided with the image data together with the chromaticity of the corresponding scene illuminant.

8.3.2 Spotting

The spotting algorithm required as input a target colour (the colour being spotted) and a test image. The four target colours used for spotting are given in Table 8.2.

Intensity information was discarded, so the spotting algorithm compared colours in rg chromaticity space:

$$r = R/(R + G + B) \quad \text{and} \quad g = G/(R + G + B) \tag{8.1}$$

There are other ways of normalizing the RGB to eliminate the effects of intensity, such as $r = R/B$ and $r = R/(R^2 + G^2 + B^2)^{1/2}$ but experience from our tests indicates that (8.1) yields the most favourable results. That is, there was a higher degree of accuracy when this normalising method for RGB was used.

Before converting to chromaticity space, the test image was averaged using a 5×5 block of pixels. By smoothing the image in this way, the individual pixels were more representative of the true colour of the object and were less susceptible to noise.

The actual spotting task required determining whether the target colour existed in the test image. This was done by computing the Euclidean distance between each pixel value and the target spotting colour:

$$\sqrt{(\text{source } r - \text{target } r)^2 + (\text{source } g - \text{target } g)^2} \leqslant \text{tolerance} \tag{8.2}$$

If the result was below the specified tolerance, then the corresponding pixel was considered to be present (a hit). The tolerance was defined as a percentage of the maximum value of a pixel in the rg chromaticity space. The maximum value was used because it gave a fixed reference for comparing chromatic variation, but other metrics could have been chosen instead.

Table 8.2 The four target colours

Colour	Image	(T, g)
Pink	Ball 1	(0.605 147, 0.120 839)
Blue	Ball 1	(0.121 209, 0.372 324)
White	Ball 2	(0.412 187, 0.319 539)
Green	Tide	(0.315 499, 0.542 787)

The number of hits depended on the tolerance. As the tolerance was increased, more and more pixels were incorrectly identified as having the target colour. Therefore the spotting performance was analysed using receiver–operator characteristic (ROC) curves [8]. The true positive (TP) proportion was plotted against the false positive (FP) proportion for various possible thresholds. The TP proportion is defined as:

$$\text{TP} = \frac{\text{pixels identified as hits}}{\text{pixels in ideal region}} \tag{8.3}$$

The FP proportion is defined as:

$$\text{FP} = \frac{\text{pixels identified as hits outside the ideal region}}{\text{pixels outside the ideal region}} \tag{8.4}$$

Each of the nodes in the ROC curve represented a particular tolerance value. The tolerances used were 1%, 5%, 10%, 15%, ..., 50%. To determine the target spotting colour, the average colour value of a patch of the single-colour object was calculated. In the case of Ball 1 this was a 25×25 pixel patch, as shown in Figure 8.2.

Although the pixels of the single-colour object varied slightly from one another, the averaging of a patch on the object helped to select a representative target spotting colour. But a remaining concern was that due to shading variations across the image, the patch chosen would be a poor representation of the overall colour of the single-colour object. This could have had an adverse effect on the performance of the spotting algorithm. Thus, for each of the single-colour objects, we took five sample patches at different locations within the single-colour object to analyse the variation between the chromaticity values in Table 8.3.

As shown in Table 8.3, the standard deviation of chromaticity values of the sample patches was between 0.0006 and 0.006. Performing the spotting task on samples showed that the variation was sufficiently small that a random patch of the single-colour object yielded similar results to any other randomly selected patch.

After determining the target spotting colour for each of the single-colour objects, we defined the 'ideal' answer region within the image. In other words, this was the region of the image we considered to be correct, in that all of its pixels appeared to be the target colour. As an example, Figure 8.3(b) shows the region considered to be the correct

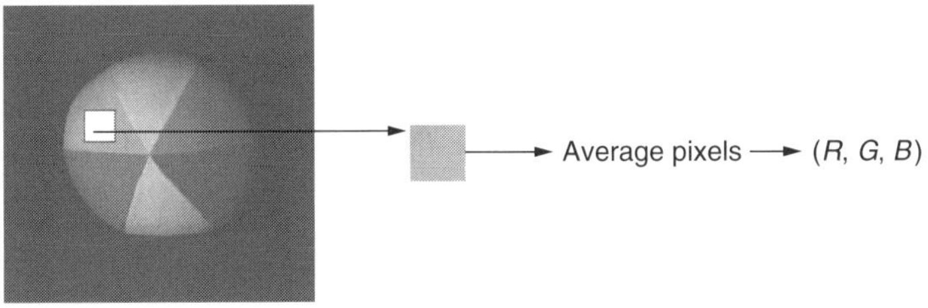

Figure 8.2 Determining the target spotting colour. See also Plate 3.

Table 8.3 Standard deviation of target spotting colours

		Sample 1	*Sample 2*	*Sample 3*	*Sample 4*	*Sample 5*	
Ball 1, pink area	*r*	0.614 492	0.605 147	0.620 408	0.609 581	0.609 950	Std dev = 0.005 785
	g	0.117 290	0.120 839	0.115 259	0.119 396	0.119 400	Std dev = 0.002 181
Ball 1, blue area	*r*	0.121 209	0.120 963	0.122 714	0.122 982	0.121 192	Std dev = 0.000 955
	g	0.372 324	0.371 319	0.371 341	0.372 665	0.371 180	Stn dev = 0.000 679
Ball 2, white area	*r*	0.412 187	0.413 473	0.403 474	0.411 394	0.413 821	Std dev = 0.004 248
	g	0.319 539	0.315 366	0.326 269	0.317 707	0.315 363	Std dev = 0.004 503
Tide, green area	*r*	0.315 499	0.314 403	0.323 186	0.314 637	0.318 649	Std dev = 0.003 714
	g	0.542 787	0.533 660	0.525 901	0.532 917	0.535 618	Std dev = 0.006 053

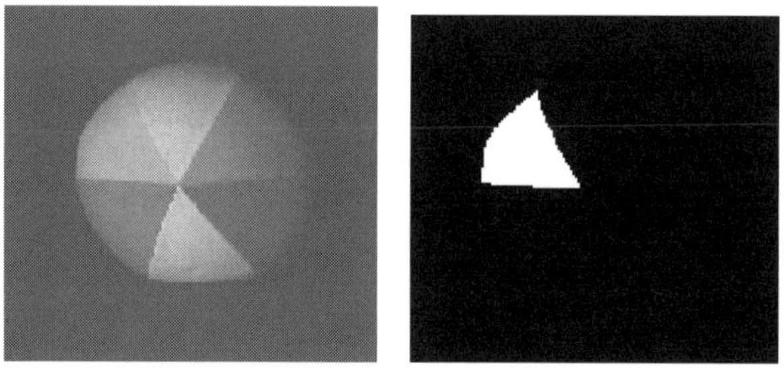

(a) (b)

Figure 8.3 Ideal region of the pink single-colour object in Ball 1.

answer when spotting for the pink colour in Ball 1. Pixels identified within this region were considered correct hits, those outside as incorrect hits.

8.4 RESULTS

The performance of each of the different colour constancy algorithms under different illumination conditions was analysed. We plotted (but do not show here) the ROC curves for each illuminant–object pair, and then combined the ROC curves for each algorithm to form the charts shown in Figures 8.4 to 8.7. Each ROC curve in the chart represents the combined results of a colour constancy algorithm under different illuminants. Each plotted point on a curve represents an increase in the tolerance value (1%, 5%, 10%, 15%, ..., 50%.) over the preceding point on the curve. With the exception of the blue in the Ball 1 image, the Macbeth 5000 with a blue filter caused the greatest difficulty for the colour constancy algorithms in terms of the ROC curves for each illuminant–object pair. Despite this, its results are included in the combined ROC curves for each algorithm.

For all the objects, colour constancy preprocessing appeared to give better results than no preprocessing at all. In fact, for the blue and pink objects in the Ball 1 image and the white object in the Ball 2 image, colour constancy preprocessing helped the spotting

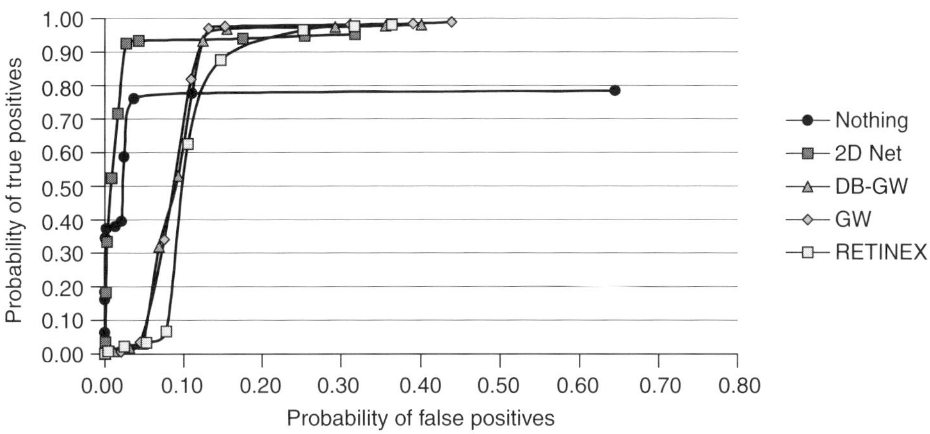

Figure 8.4 ROC curves for Ball 1: blue. Each entry along a curve represents an increasing tolerance, 1%, 5%, 10%, 15%, ..., 50%.

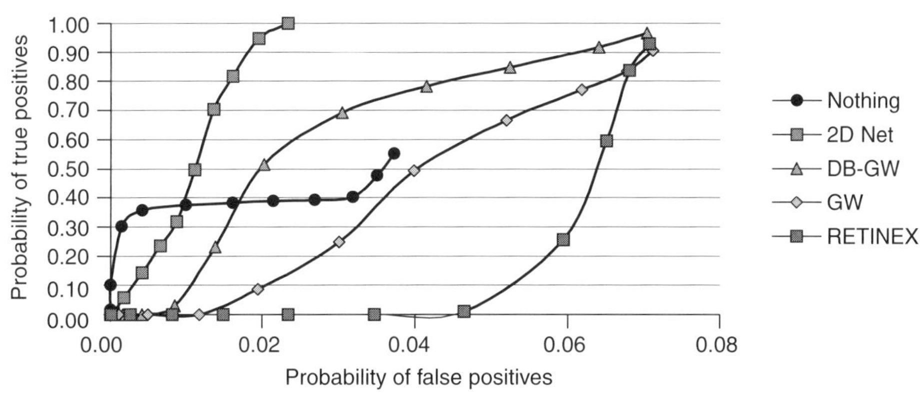

Figure 8.5 ROC curves for Ball 1: pink. Each entry along a curve represents an increasing tolerance, 1%, 5%, 10%, 15%, ..., 50%.

algorithm to achieve a TP proportion greater than 90% at a 50% tolerance. With no preprocessing, the spotting algorithm achieved at a 50% tolerance a TP proportion less than 80% for the blue object and less than 60% for the pink object.

Two of the four single-colour objects had a significant fluorescent component, namely the pink in the Ball 1 image and the green in the Tide image. Fluorescence of this sort is very common, especially in clothing laundered with detergents with added 'whiteners' and in printing substrates (white paper and card). It is known that fluorescent surfaces can adversely affect the performance of colour constancy algorithms [1]. The effect of fluorescence may explain why the 2D neural net and retinex algorithms generally performed

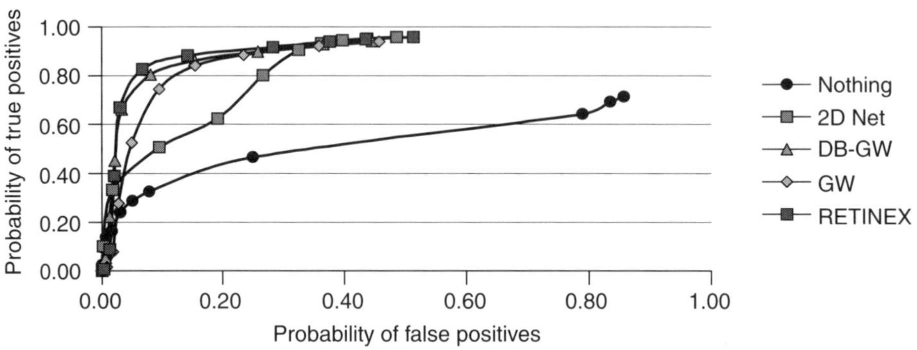

Figure 8.6 ROC curves for Ball 2: white. Each entry along a curve represents an increasing tolerance, 1%, 5%, 10%, 15%, ..., 50%.

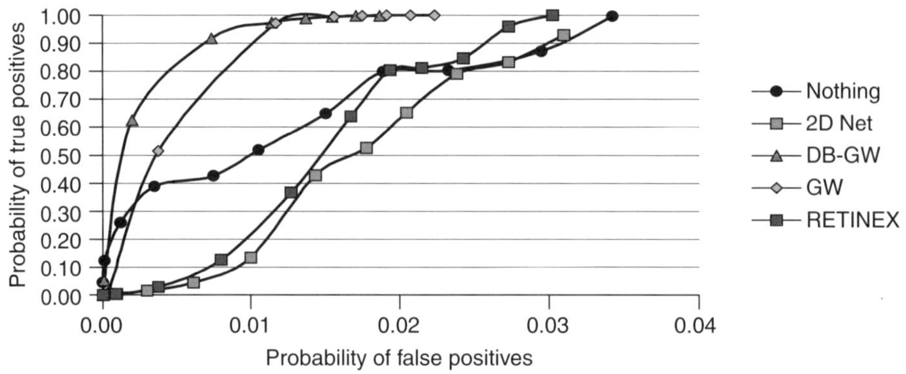

Figure 8.7 ROC curves for Tide: green. Each entry along a curve represents an increasing tolerance, 1%, 5%, 10%, 15%, ..., 50%.

worse than no preprocessing at all on the green object in the Tide image. On the pink object in the Ball 1 image, the retinex, greyworld, and database greyworld algorithms achieved a superior TP proportion but also had a larger FP proportion than when no preprocessing was used.

The maximum tolerance of 50% was sufficient for all the colour constancy algorithms to achieve a TP proportion approaching 1.00 (100%). This appears to be a sufficient maximum value. If a tolerance greater than 50% were required to attain a high TP proportion when spotting a colour, this would most likely indicate that the target colour was not sufficiently differentiated from the other colours in the image.

In our test cases, the range of FP values varied widely between the different scenes. At a tolerance of 50%, the blue object in the Ball 1 image (Figure 8.4) and the white object in the Ball 2 image (Figure 8.6) had an FP proportion of approximately 70% and

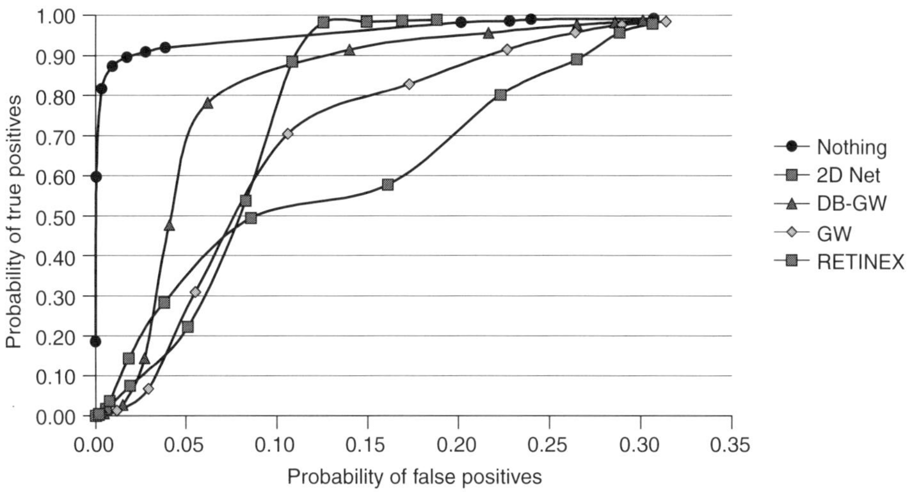

Figure 8.8 Average ROC curves. Each entry along a curve represents an increasing tolerance, 1%, 5%, 10%, 15%, ..., 50%.

90%, respectively. In contrast, the pink object in the Ball 1 image (Figure 8.5) had an FP proportion of approximately 7.5% and the green in the Tide image had an FP proportion of approximately 3.5% at a tolerance of 50% (Figure 8.7).

Spotting was also performed on images taken under the canonical illuminant but preprocessed using a colour constancy algorithm. Figure 8.8 shows the average ROC analysis results from each of the four images. As expected, all the algorithms adversely affected the spotting performance since the canonical illuminant contained the correct colours to begin with. The 'do nothing' case, in which the image was left untouched, did not yield good spotting results because of the presence of similarly coloured pixels in other parts of the image.

8.5 CONCLUSIONS

Machine colour constancy algorithms were tested to find out how well they performed when applied as a preprocessing step for the task of spotting colours. In particular, the task focused on the location of an object with one distinct and uniform colour. As one would hope, the colour constancy algorithms generally improved the spotting performance and usually resulted in a higher number of true positives (hits) and a reasonable number of false positives. In addition, the presence of fluorescent surfaces also appeared to have an effect on the success of the colour constancy preprocessing. The results show that colour constancy preprocessing appears to be beneficial for the task of spotting colours and can greatly improve the results, but it is not guaranteed to improve spotting performance in all cases.

REFERENCES

1. Barnard, K. (1999) Colour constancy with fluorescent surfaces *Proc. IS&T/SID 7th Color Imaging Conf.*, pp. 257–261.
2. Ennesser, F. and Medioni, G. (1995) Finding Waldo, or focus of attention using local color information. *IEEE Trans. on Pattern Analysis and Machine Intelligence*, 805–809.
3. Funt, B., Barnard, K. and Martin, L. (1998) Is machine colour constancy good enough? *Proc. ECCV98 Fifth European Conference on Computer Vision*, pp. 445–459. Image database at http://www.cs.sfu.ca/c̃olour/image_db/.
4. Funt, B., Cardei, V. and Barnard, K. (1996) Learning color constancy. *Proc. IS&T/SID 4th Color Imaging Conf.*, pp. 58–60.
5. Funt, B. Cardei, V. and Barnard, K. Neural network color constancy and specularly reflecting surfaces. *Proc. AIC Color 97*, Kyoto, Japan, Vol. **II**, pp. 523–526.
6. Funt, B., Cardei, V. and Barnard, K. (1999) Method of estimating chromaticity of illumination using neural networks. US Patent 5,907,629.
7. Funt, B. and Finlayson, G. (1995) Color constant color indexing. IEEE Trans. on Pattern Analysis and Image Processing **17** (5), 522–529.
8. Green, D. M. and Swets, J. A. (1966) *Signal Detection Theory and Psychophysics*. Wiley, New York.
9. Healey, G. and Slater, D. (1994) Global color constancy: recognition of objects by use of illumination invariant properties of color distributions. *J. Opt. Soc. Am. A.* **11** (11), 3003–3010.
10. Hertz, J., Krogh, A. and Palmer, R. G. (1991) *Introduction to the Theory of Neural Computation*. Addison-Wesley, Reading MA.
11. Rumelhart, D. E., Hinton, G. E. and. Williams, R. J. (1986) Learning internal representations by error propagation. In *Parallel Distributed Processing: Explorations in the Microstructure of Cognition*, Vol. 1, D. E. Rumelhart and J. L. McClelland (eds). MIT Press, Cambridge MA.
12. Swain, M. and Ballard, D. (1991) Color indexing. *Int. J. Computer Vision*, **7** 11–32.
13. Yuille, A. L, Snow, D. and Nitzberg, M. (1998) Signfinder: using color to detect, localize and identify informational signs. *Proc. Int. Conf. on Computer Vision ICCV98*, pp. 629–633.

9

Colour contrast in adjacent image regions

Alain Trémeau and Philippe Colantoni

9.1 INTRODUCTION

According to the phenomenon of colour constancy, the effects of the variability of image elements on colour appearance are, to some extent, less important than those described by the CIECAM97s model based on five circular visual fields [1]. This is the reason why, in the first version of this model, the proximal field was not taken into account [1–3]. Nevertheless, as the effects of simultaneous contrast and assimilation for very small stimuli are not negligible, we can expect in future a new version of this model which will incorporate the proximal field. Indeed the phenomenon of simultaneous contrast is all the more significant as the number of regions in a scene is almost infinitely variable.

Actually, colour appearance models, such as CIECAM97s, measure the colour contrast between two stimuli according to viewing fields surrounding them [1, 3, 4], but they are not adapted to measure the colour contrast between a stimulus and other stimuli surrounding it [5, 6]. The main contradictions between colour appearance models and inter-region colour contrast models are (1) the dissimilarity of geometrical configurations of viewing field components, (2) the dissimilarity of colorimetric specifications of proximal field component, and (3) the dissimilarity of colour appearance phenomena taken into account.

Colour Image Science, edited by L.W. MacDonald and M.R. Luo.

The main descriptors commonly used to characterise the colour appearance of a stimulus (e.g. [1]) or of an image (e.g. [7]) refer to lightness L, brightness, saturation S, chroma C, colourfulness c, hue angle H and hue quadrature h. It is less common to find descriptors which refer to the colour inhomogeneity of a stimulus or to its colour contrast relative to stimuli surrounding it.

We have shown in a previous study that colour image parameters based on the analysis of the colour distribution of image elements, and of the spatial distribution of colour image elements, could corroborate subjective judgement of colour appearance [18].

The aim of this chapter is to introduce new colour appearance descriptors based on colour contrast assessment and on colour uniformity assessment.

9.1.1 The colour appearance of a stimulus

According to the CIECAM97s model [1] to define the colour appearance of a stimulus it is necessary to specify the following quantities (Figure 9.1):

- (x_i, y_i, Y_i) the chromaticity and luminance factors of the stimulus i
- (x_b, y_b, Y_b) the chromaticity and luminance factors of the background
- (x_s, y_s, Y_s) the chromaticity and luminance factors of the surround
- (x_w, y_w, Y_w) the chromaticity and luminance factors of the white
- (x_r, y_r, Y_r) the chromaticity and luminance factors of the reference white

In the same way, it is necessary to quantify the following items:

- L_A the luminance of the adapting field (in $\mathrm{cd\,m^{-2}}$), i.e. the luminance of $\{sample, surround, background, periphery\}$

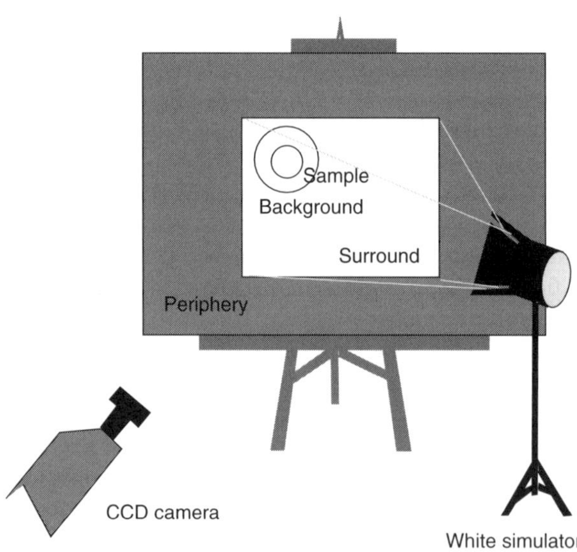

Figure 9.1 Image viewing conditions.

- L_v the average luminance of the viewing area (in cd m^{-2}), i.e. the average luminance of $\{sample, surround, background\}$
- L_p the luminance of the peripheral area (in cd m^{-2})

When an image is displayed on a monitor, we consider that the background of the screen represents the peripheral area, and the image area represents the viewing area. The luminance of the peripheral area is commonly lower than the average luminance of the image area. In the same way, the luminance of the monitor is commonly lower than the luminance of the room where the monitor is located. In our study, the subjects viewed a monitor of diagonal 30 cm (graphics resolution 640 × 480 pixels) at a distance of about 1.2 m. At this distance, the pixel size is about 1.12 minutes of arc, and the image size is about 11.5°(H) × 8.6°(V) of arc. Thus at this distance, the samples subtend less than 4° at the eye. Details concerning the surround and the angular subtense are all the more necessary to take into account as they determine the weight of surround parameters in the CIECAM97s model.

Considering that (1) the luminance of the adapting field L_A is low, (2) the white point of the monitor is similar to the reference white D65, and (3) the image has been acquired under the illuminant D65, we assume there is no chromatic adaptation.

9.1.2 The colour appearance of a set of stimuli

To characterise the colour appearance of a region in relation to the regions surrounding it, we have considered six fields of interest:

1. *Region under study*: a region with a uniform colour distribution. In our study, most of the colour elements of this region subtend less than 2°.
2. *Proximal field*: the set of adjacent regions which share a common edge with the region under study. It corresponds to an adjacency relation of first order (Figure 9.2(b)).
3. *Extended field*: the set of regions which are adjacent to the proximal field. Extended field corresponds to an adjacency relation of second order relative to the region under study (Figure 9.2(c)).
4. *Background*: the set of regions of the image which do not belong to the extended field (Figure 9.2(c)). In our study, the displayed images subtended less than 11.5° × 8.6°.
5. *Surround*: the field outside the background.
6. *Adapting field*: the total environment of the region under study, including the proximal field, the extended field, the background, the surround, and extending to the limit of vision (beyond the surround field corresponding to the monitor), in all directions.

Define the following variables:

- (x_p, y_p, Y_p) the chromaticity and luminance factor of the proximal field
- (x_e, y_e, Y_e) the chromaticity and luminance factor of the extended field

From an image point of view, we can make two assumptions:

- The proximal field is defined by a simple-connectivity relationship between adjacent regions (Figure 9.2(b))
- The extended field is defined by a second-order connectivity relationship (Figure 9.2(c))

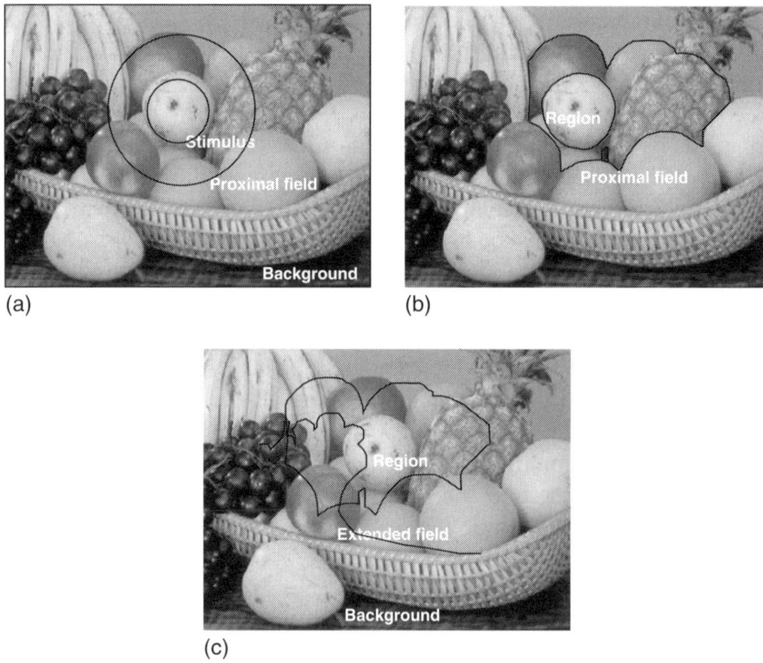

Figure 9.2 Areas of interest surrounding the region under study: (a) proximal field corresponding to the visual field model, (b) proximal areas corresponding to the proposed model, (c) extended areas surrounding proximal areas.

9.1.3 Image parameters

To characterise the colour appearance of a region in relation to the regions surrounding it, we propose to compute different parameters using a six-step process [5, 6]:

- *Step 1*: the image is segmented and then its region adjacency graph is computed (Figure 9.3).
- *Step 2*: to each vertex are associated several properties relevant to the colour distribution of the region under study. Such basic properties are linked to spatiochromatic features and colour statistic features.
- *Step 3*: a weighted colour distance is computed for each pair of adjacent regions. This colour distance is then associated with each edge of the graph.
- *Step 4*: colour distances are combined to define a colour contrast metric between a region and its adjacent regions.
- *Step 5*: a colour contrast metric is defined for each pair of adjacent regions in relation to the set of their neighbouring regions.
- *Step 6*: this measure is then used to define an emergence metric for each colour region in relation to the set of its neighbouring regions.

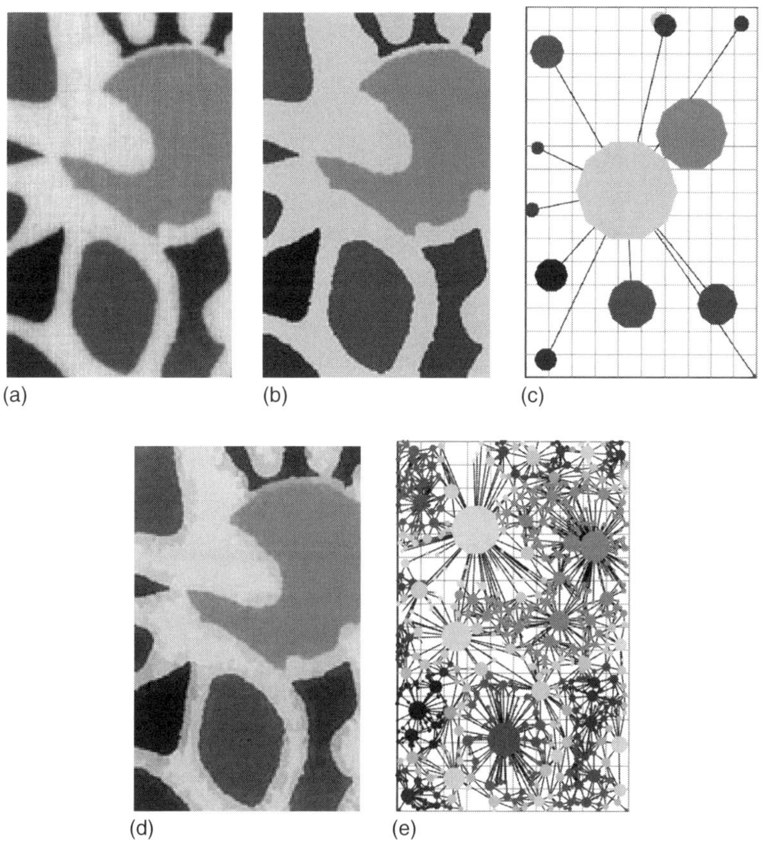

Figure 9.3 The higher an observer's visual attention, the higher his or her ability of spatial discrimination. One observer might discern only 12 regions on (a) but another might perceive tens of regions or even more. (a) Original image; (b) image segmented into 12 regions; (c) RAG of image (b); (d) image oversegmented into 150 regions; (e) RAG of image (d). See also Colour Plate 3.

9.2 PROPOSED METHOD

Step 1: Compute the region adjacency graph

An important task in image processing is image segmentation, which aims to partition the image into non-overlapped homogeneous regions. The level to which this subdivision is carried out depends on the problem being solved. To remove oversegmentation, a region merging process can be used. There are several methods to merge similar and adjacent regions; most of them based on region adjacency graph (RAG) processing [8–10].

One way to represent a region adjacency graph consists of associating a vertex at each region and an edge at each pair of adjacent regions. By definition, this region adjacency graph provides a simple-connectivity view of the image, such as Figure 9.4(a).

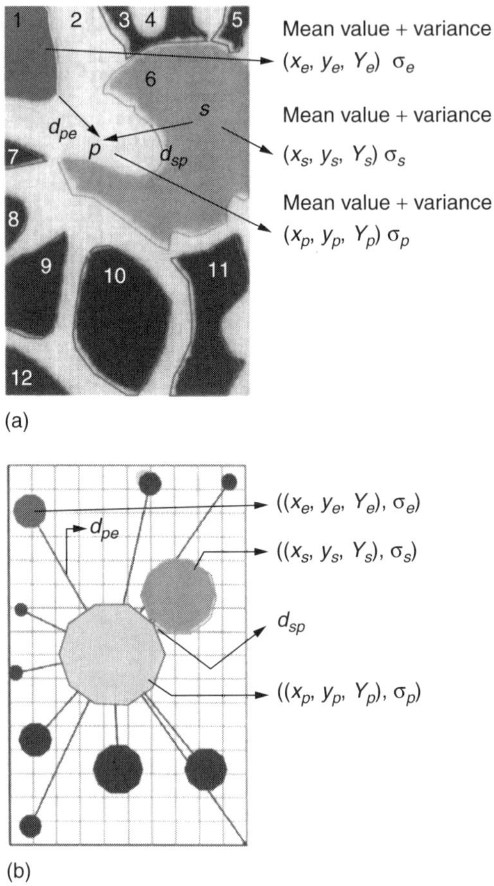

Figure 9.4 The inter-region colour contrast measure, which separates sample i of region p belonging to the proximal field of i, depends primarily on the colour distance d_{ip}, but to a lesser degree it also depends on the colour distance d_{pe} that separates sample i of region e belonging to the extended field of i. (a) Image areas under study, (b) corresponding areas in the RAG.

Beyond the simple-connectivity view, the graph gives also a high-level connectivity view of the image. We can see in Figure 9.4(a) that region 2 is adjacent to regions 6 and 1. Consequently, we can say there is a second-order connectivity relationship between regions 6 and 1. Note that the simple-connectivity view contains inherently all high-level connectivity relationships of the image.

Step 2: Add weighted values to the region adjacency graph

To each vertex v_i of the graph there correspond a region i and two colour values: the mean colour value $\vec{\mu}_i = (x_i, y_i, Y_i)$ and the variance value σ_i.

To each edge e_{ij} there correspond a pair of adjacent regions $\{i, j\}$ and a colour distance $d^2(i, j)$, which enables us to compare the colour distribution of these two regions. Commonly, the Fisher distance is used to quantify the colour distance between two regions [11]. Thus:

$$d^2(i, j) = \frac{(n_i + n_j)\|\vec{\mu}_i - \vec{\mu}_j\|^2}{n_i\sigma_i^2 + n_j\sigma_j^2} \quad \text{if } \sigma_i^2 \neq 0 \text{ and } \sigma_j^2 \neq 0 \tag{9.1}$$

$$d^2(i, j) = \|\vec{\mu}_i - \vec{\mu}_j\|^2 \quad \text{if } \sigma_i^2 = 0 \text{ and } \sigma_j^2 = 0 \tag{9.2}$$

where n_i is the size of region i.

Step 3: Compute the colour contrast between two adjacent regions

To decrease the weight of regions which have a small shared boundary connecting larger areas [11] in the colour contrast formula, we have defined a connectivity measure between adjacent regions that is computed as follows:

$$C_{ij} = \frac{4{P_{ij}}^2}{\min(P_i, P_j)\max(P_{\{i,j\}})} \tag{9.3}$$

where P_i and P_j are the perimeters of the regions i and j, P_{ij} is the length of the shared boundary between regions i and j, $\max(P_{\{i,j\}}) = \max\{P_{ik}/k \neq j, P_{kj}/k \neq i\}$ is the highest shared boundary length of a region adjacent either to region i or to region j. See the example i in Figure 9.5.

Next we combine this connectivity measure with the colour distance measure as follows:

$$WC_{ij} = d^2(i, j)C_{ij} \tag{9.4}$$

Since this measure, called weighted colour contrast is designed as a product of independent measures, it can be easily extended to include additional factors [12, 13].

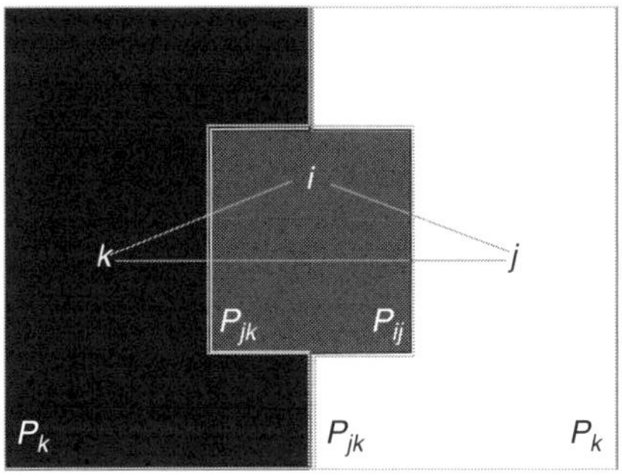

Figure 9.5 Example for which the most contrasted region is region i and the less contrasted regions are j and k.

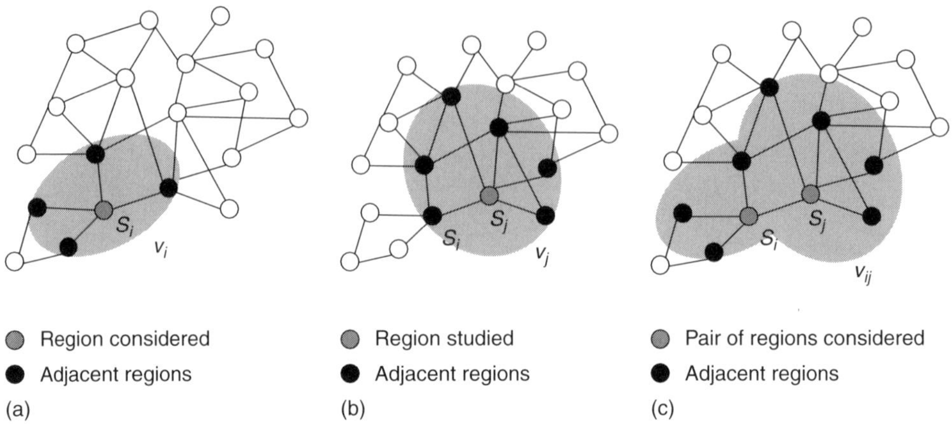

Figure 9.6 Connectivity relationships between adjacent regions in the RAG: (a) regions belonging to the proximal field of vertex v_i; (b) regions belonging to the proximal field of vertex v_j; (c) regions adjacent to vertices v_i and v_j.

To each region i there corresponds a set of adjacent regions $V_i = \{j/e_{ij} \neq 0\}$ as shown in Figure 9.6(a). Let $\mu(V_i)$ be the mean contrast value, $\max(V_i)$ the highest contrast value and $\sigma(V_i)$ the variance value of the set V_i.

To each edge e_{ij} there corresponds a pair of adjacent regions $V_{ij} = \{k \neq i, j/e_{ik} \neq 0$ or $e_{jk} \neq 0\}$. Let $\mu(V_{ij})$ be as shown in Figure 9.6(c) the mean contrast value, $\max(V_{ij})$ the highest contrast value and $\sigma(V_{ij})$ the variance value of the set V_{ij}.

Step 4: Compute the differential contrast between two adjacent regions

To assess the colour contrast between two adjacent regions, from the region adjacency graph, we define a new operator, called the differential contrast operator:

$$DC_{ij} = (\max(V_i) - WC_{ij}) + 2(\max(V_{ij}) - WC_{ij}) + (\max(V_j) - WC_{ij}) \quad \text{if } V_{ij} \neq 0 \tag{9.5}$$

$$DC_{ij} = 0 \quad \text{if } V_{ij} = 0$$

- $\max(V_i) - WC_{ij}$ = the difference in contrast between the pair of regions i and j, and the pair of regions i and the highest contrasted region of its proximal surround.
- $\max(V_j) - WC_{ij}$ = the difference in contrast between the pair of regions j and i, and the pair of regions j and the highest contrasted region of its proximal surround.
- $\max(V_{ij}) - WC_{ij}$ = the difference in contrast between the pair of regions i and j, and the pair of regions the most constrasted in the proximal surround of regions i and j.

An example is given in Figure 9.7(a). We can draw two conclusions:

- The more $DC_{ij} > 0$ the more the colour contrast between regions i and j seems to be perceptible in comparison with other colour contrast values of surrounding regions.

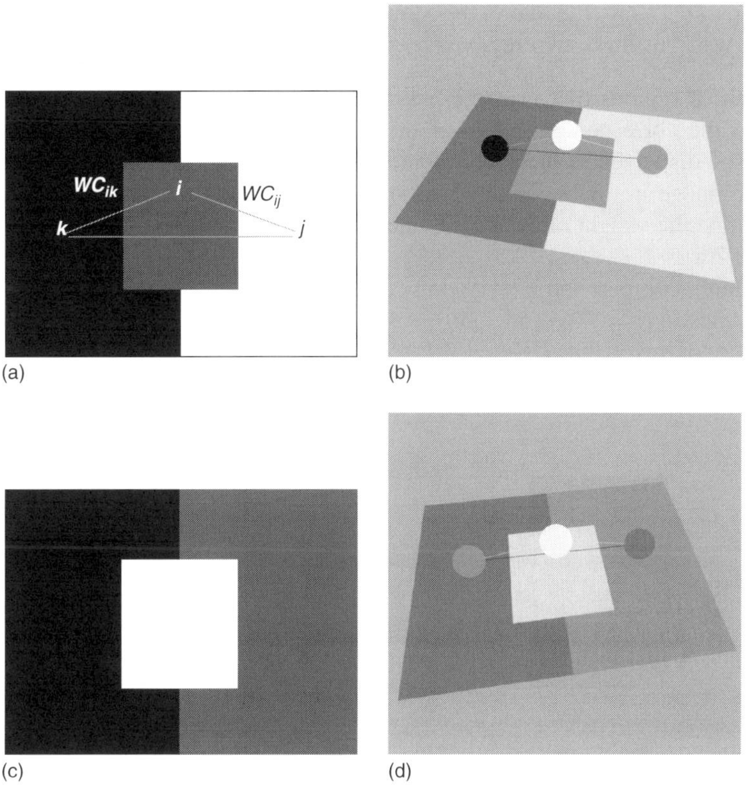

Figure 9.7 Examples for which the most contrasted region is the central region i and the less contrasted regions are j and k: (a, c) original image, (b, d) image of colour contrasts. The edges of the RAG represent the inter-region colour contrast values, and the vertices of the RAG represent the emergence value of each region. Parameter values are displayed in black and white from the smallest to the largest.

- The more $DC_{ij} < 0$ the more the colour contrast between regions i and j seems negligible in comparison with other colour contrast values of surrounding regions.

Step 5: Compute the inter-region contrast between two adjacent regions

From the previous operator, we define another operator, called the inter-region colour contrast operator:

$$RC_{ij} = WC_{ij} + DC_{ij} \tag{9.6}$$

This operator has been introduced to weight the colour contrast between two adjacent regions in relation to the variability of colour contrast of proximal region:

- The more $DC_{ij} > 0$ the more the surround of regions i and j enhances the colour contrast WC_{ij} of these two regions.

- The more $DC_{ij} < 0$ the more the surround of regions i and j reduces the colour contrast WC_{ij} of these two regions.

To each pair of regions there corresponds an inter-region colour contrast value which is assigned to the corresponding edge of the RAG. All these inter-region colour contrast values can be displayed in black and white, using a look-up table and a 3D viewer, with the original image in the background, as shown in Figures 9.7 and 9.8.

To illustrate the weight of each component of this operator, let us consider the example in Figure 9.7(a).

Let us firstly compute the inter-region colour contrast value between the red and white regions. As $\max(V_i) = WC_{ij}$, $\max(V_j) = WC_{ij}$ and $\max(V_{ij}) = WC_{ik}$, we have a differential colour contrast value $DC_{ij} = WC_{ik} - WC_{ij}$ that is negative. Consequently, due to

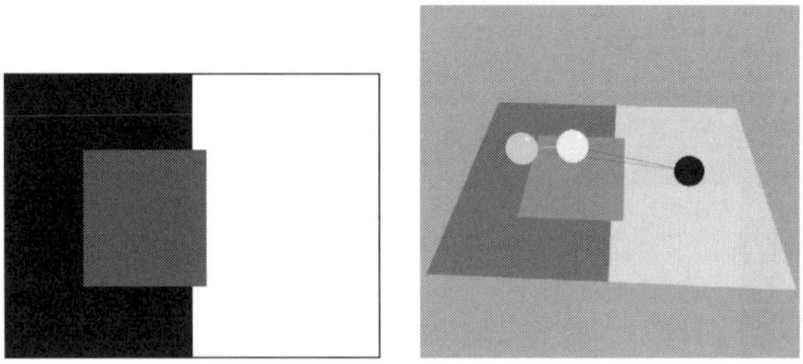

(a) (b)

Figure 9.8 Example for which the overlap between the most contrasted region i and the less contrasted region k is greater than those shown in Figure 9.7: (a) original image, (b) image of colour contrasts. The edges of the RAG represent the inter-region colour contrast values, and the vertices of the RAG represent the emergence value of each region. Parameter values are displayed in black and white from the smallest to the largest.

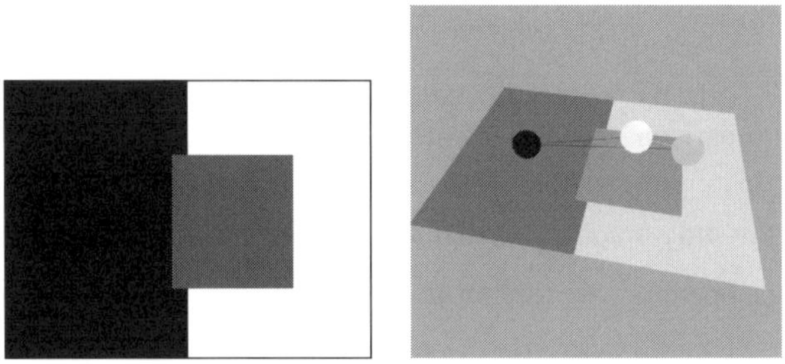

(a) (b)

Figure 9.9 Example for which the overlap between region i and region j is greater than those shown in Figure 9.7: (a) original image, (b) image of colour contrasts. The edges of the RAG represent the inter-region colour contrast values, and the vertices of the RAG represent the emergence value of each region. Parameter values are displayed in black and white from the smallest to the largest.

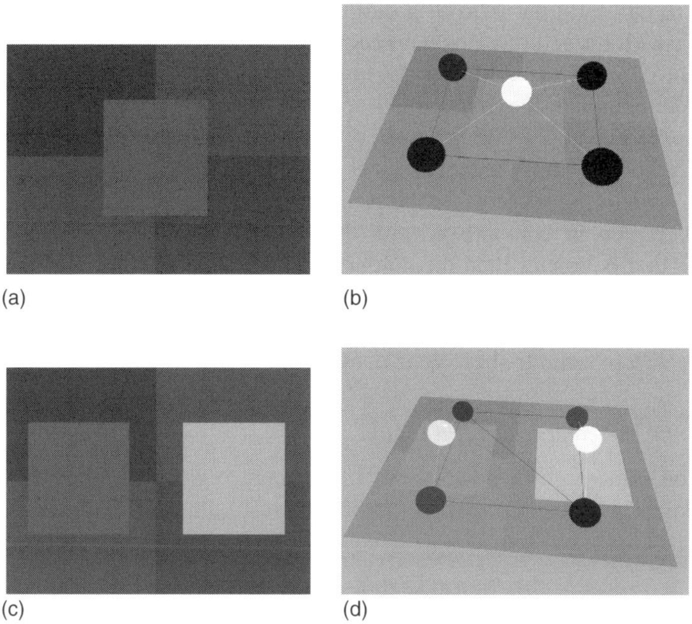

Figure 9.10 Examples of test images: (a, c) original image, (b, d) image of colour contrasts. The edges of the RAG represent the inter-region colour contrast values, and the vertices of the RAG represent the emergence value of each region. Parameter values are displayed in black and white from the smallest to the largest.

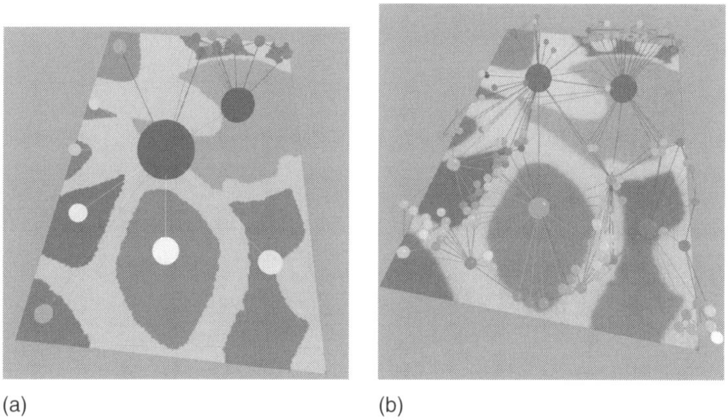

Figure 9.11 Image of colour contrasts computed from (a) the segmented image (see Figure 9.4) and (b) an oversegmented image. The edges of the RAG represent the inter-region colour contrast values, and the vertices of the RAG represent the emergence value of each region. Parameter values are displayed in black and white from the smallest to the largest.

the presence in the proximal field of a dark region less contrasted than the white region in comparison with the red one, we have an inter-region colour contrast value that is less than the colour contrast value initially estimated by WC_{ij}.

Let us now compute the inter-region colour contrast value between the red and dark regions. As $\max(V_i) = WC_{ij}$, $\max(V_k) = WC_{kj}$ and $\max(V_{ik}) = WC_{jk}$, we have a differential colour contrast value $DC_{ik} = (3WC_{kj} + WC_{ij}) - 4WC_{ik}$ that is positive. Consequently, due to the presence in the proximal field of a white region more contrasted than the dark region in comparison with the red one, we have an inter-region colour contrast value that is greater than the colour contrast value initially estimated by WC_{ik}.

Consequently, the more the regions belonging to the proximal field of the pair of regions (i, j) are contrasted in comparison with this pair of regions, the more the differential contrast value WC_{ij} weights the colour contrast value DC_{ij}.

Step 6: Compute the emergence of a region

To each region i there corresponds a set of adjacent regions V_i, then to each region i there corresponds a set of inter-region colour contrast values $\{RC_{ij}/j \in V_i\}$.

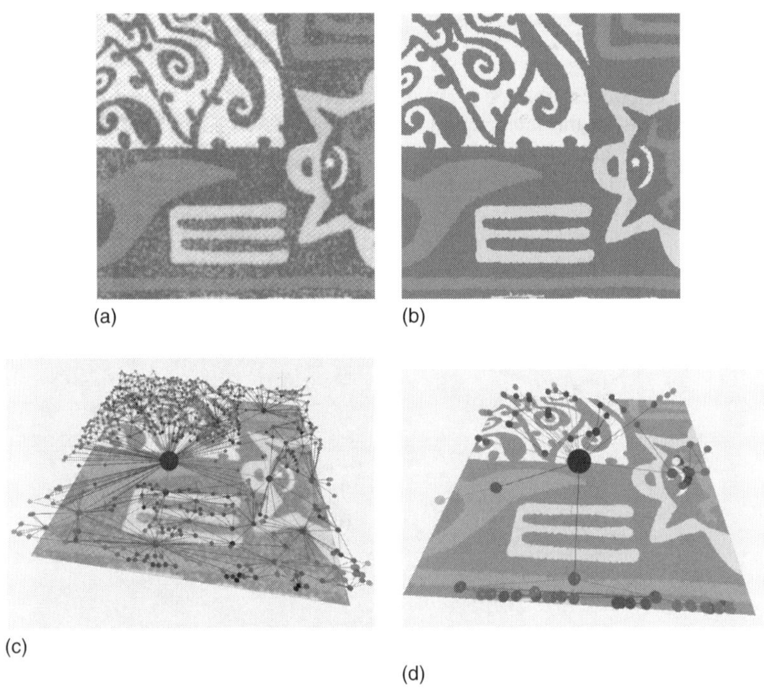

Figure 9.12 Complex image: (a) original image, (b) segmented image, (c) image of colour contrasts computed from an oversegmented image, (d) image of colour contrasts computed from the well-segmented image. The edges of the RAG represent the inter-region colour contrast values, and the vertices of the RAG represent the emergence value of each region. Parameter values are displayed in black and white from the smallest to the largest.

To analyse the emergence of a region i in relation to its surround [14], we compute the average value of the distribution of its set of inter-region colour contrast values:

$$RS_i = \frac{1}{\mathrm{card}(V_i)} \sum_{j \in V_i} RC_{ij} \tag{9.7}$$

Taking into account equation (9.7), we have:

$$RS_i = \mu(V_i) + (\max(V_i) - \mu(V_i)) + 2\left(\frac{1}{\mathrm{card}(V_i)} \sum_{j \in V_i} \max(V_{ij}) - \mu(V_i)\right) + \left(\frac{1}{\mathrm{card}(V_i)} \sum_{j \in V_i} \max(V_j) - \mu(V_i)\right) \quad \text{if } V_{ij} \neq 0 \tag{9.8}$$

$$RS_i = \mu(V_i) \quad \text{if } V_{ij} = 0$$

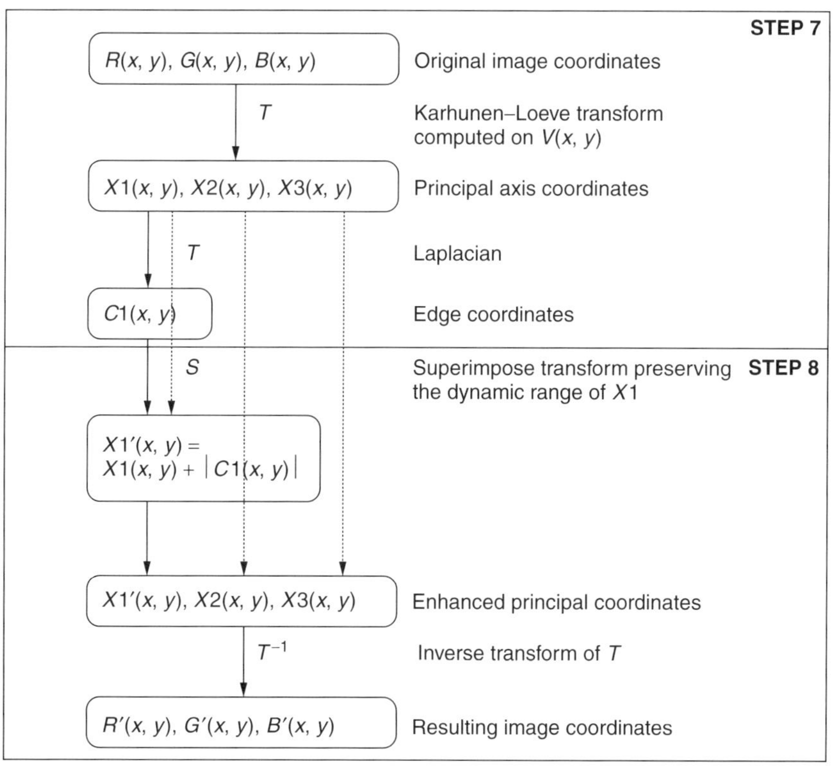

Figure 9.13 Process used for colour edge assessment and colour edge enhancement.

At each region the emergence value is assigned to the corresponding vertex of the RAG. All these emergence values can be displayed in black and white, using a look-up table and a 3D viewer, with the original image in the background, as shown in Figure 9.9.

9.2.1 Two extra steps

Step 7: Compute the edge contrast between adjacent regions

Edges of an image may be defined as a discontinuity or an abrupt change in the colour of adjacent pixels. Two types of discontinuity measurements can be considered at each pixel location (i,j) for performing directional differentiation from a parallel masking operation. The first-order directional edge operator corresponds to a gradient array. The second-order directional edge operator corresponds to a Laplacian array.

For the one-dimensional case, equation (9.1) shows the result of computing the second difference, from which a function $F(x)$ may be determined. This function is the difference

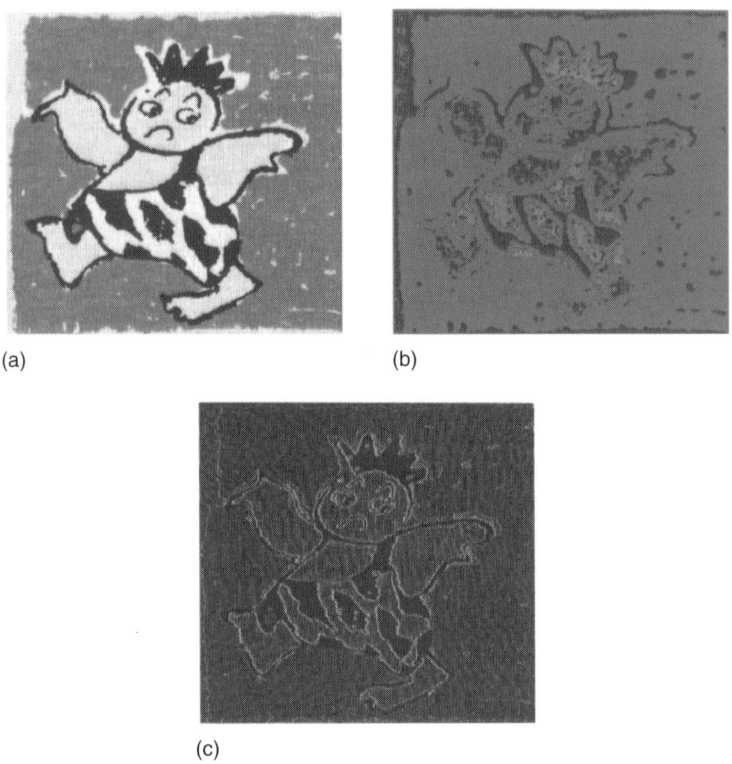

Figure 9.14 Example of edge assessment: (a) original image, (b) principal component, (c) Laplacian image using the Laplacian value of $X1$ at each location (i,j). In (b) each pixel (i,j) is associated with a vector that represents the direction of the principal component computed locally at location (i,j). To show the change in direction of the principal component $X1$, all these vectors are displayed in the RGB colour space.

of means of points on each side of (i,j) which are Δ pixels apart. Suppose the second difference $D^2(x)$ is given by:

$$D^2I(x) = I(x - \Delta) - 2I(x) + I(x + \Delta) \tag{9.9}$$

where $I(x)$ represents the intensity of pixel x.

Then $F(x)$ is defined by:

$$F(x) = \frac{1}{\Delta}\left[\sum_{i=1}^{\Delta} D^2I(x+i) - \sum_{i=1}^{\Delta} D^2I(x-i)\right] \tag{9.10}$$

All the figures in this chapter have been computed with $\Delta = 3$, i.e. at pixel location (i,j) the Laplacian has been computed from a mask $V(i,j)$ of size 7×7 centred on (i,j). An extension of this formula to the case of colour images can been found in [15] and [16].

To assess the edge contrast between regions as the human observer does [17], we have hypothesised that the more perceptible edge contrasts were those corresponding to the most abrupt changes of direction of the principal component $X1$.

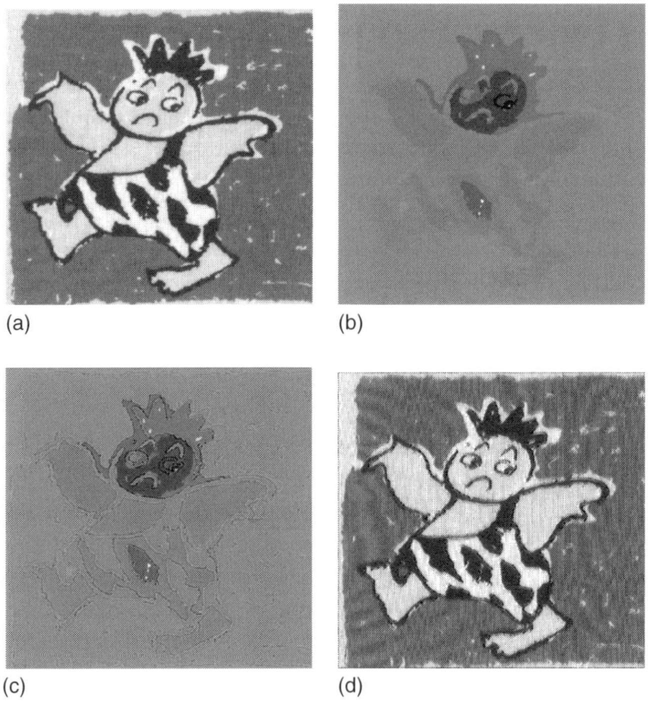

Figure 9.15 Example of colour contrast assessment: (a) original image, (b) colour contrast image, (c) colour edges superimposed on the colour contrast image, (d) colour edges superimposed on the original image. See also Colour Plate 12.

We have also hypothesised that in the neighborhood $V(i,j)$ of the pixel (i,j) there are at least two regions intersected. Consequently only one colour component (the principal component $X1$ corresponding to the two colour clusters involved) is significant to discriminate these two regions. For the other cases involving several regions, we consider that $X1$ is also the most relevant colour component to discriminate these regions. See the examples in Figures 9.10 to 9.12.

Taking into account these two hypotheses, we compute the Laplacian from the principal component computed locally from a mask $V(i,j)$ of size 7×7 centred on (i,j). This process can be described by a flow chart (Figure 9.13).

Step 8: Enhance the edge contrast between adjacent regions

To enhance edge contrast of the original image as a human observer does, we next compute the absolute value of the Laplacian, add this value to the image $X1$, and use the inverse transform T^{-1} to generate an RGB image for display (Figures 9.14 and 9.15).

This has been used only as an *a posteriori* process in this study to verify that edge contrast enhancement is well correlated with visual judgement.

9.3 CONCLUSIONS AND PERSPECTIVES

This chapter describes a step forward in the forward understanding of complex colour images from content-dependent parameters. It has introduced several image parameters based on the computation of colour contrast features from regions in the image:

- Colour contrast between two adjacent regions
- Differential contrast between two adjacent regions
- Inter-region contrast between two adjacent regions
- Emergence of a region
- Edge contrast between adjacent regions

We have also tested different cases. Figures 9.8 and 9.9 have been used to test the measure of connectivity. Figure 9.10 has been used to test the variability of the measure of inter-region colour contrast. Figures 9.11 and 9.12 have been used to test the effects of the presegmentation process from which the region adjacency graph is computed.

These parameters have been tested only with a few example images. There is no quantitative data to give a significant illustration of the proposed method's performance. Research continues into modelling complex images by content-dependent parameters.

Our investigation further analysed, from visual assessment experiments, the degree of correspondence between emergence features and perceptibility. The subjective perceptibility of regions has been measured on an arbitrary subjective image scale, and experiments have been conducted with a large variety of images. In these experiments, observers were asked to judge the chromaticness, lightness, colourfulness, texture, contrast and emergence

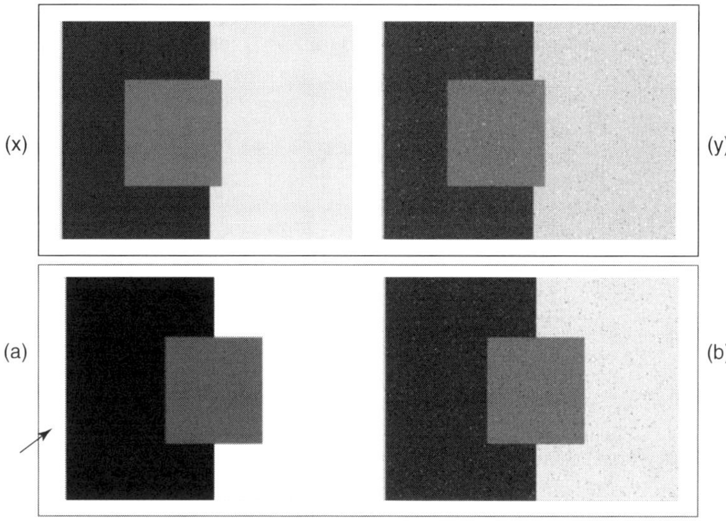

Figure 9.16 Step 1 of the subjective experiment performed to judge the perceptibility of regions in an image. The observer has selected the lower pair of images because he perceived the difference of emergence to be more pronounced for the lower pair than for the upper pair.

of each region of an image relative to a set of two pairs of two images (taken randomly among a set of 50 images), as shown in Figures 9.16 and 9.17 [18].

To extend this work to colour appearance models, we will need to examine carefully the theoretical rational and the consistency among perceptual measures of the various image parameters proposed. The main contradictions between colour appearance models and our colour contrast image model are (1) the dissimilarity of geometrical configurations of viewing field components, (2) the dissimilarity of colorimetric specifications of the proximal field component and (3) the dissimilarity of colour appearance phenomena taken into account in the models. This structural problem requires careful examination in order to improve colour image analysis models in the future.

Many interesting open questions are now under investigation:

- Which image parameters can be used to determine the colour inhomogeneity of a region, and how to combine these parameters with those previously used to measure the colour distance between two non-uniform colour regions?
- Which model can be used to determine the weight of the surround field in the colour contrast model that we have proposed to characterise the emergence of regions of an image?
- Which parameters can be used to determine the weight of viewing and illuminating conditions in the colour contrast model to predict the emergence of regions of an image?
- Which model can be used to determine the weight of edge data in the emergence assessment of a region?
- How to increase the degree of correlation between our colour contrast model and colour appearance models?

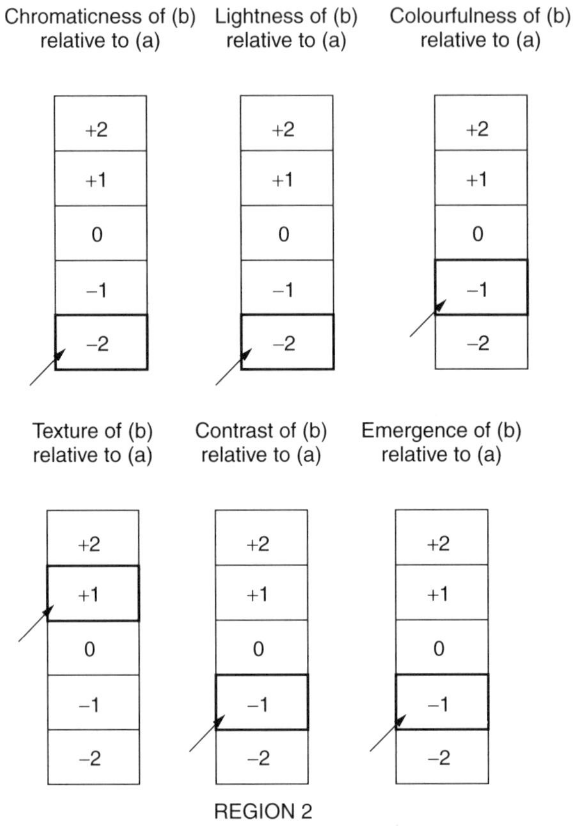

Figure 9.17 Step 2 of the subjective experiment performed to judge the perceptibility of regions in an image. For the pair of images selected in Figure 9.16, the observer has quantified the differences observed. In this example, image (a) is considered as the reference image and the central region (region 2) as the region under study. The grading scale used in this experiment is divided into five classes. Relative to the descriptor considered, 0 indicates that images (a) and (b) are close enough that visually their is no difference between them; +1 indicates that (b) is slightly more pronounced than (a) but still close enough to (a) to consider that visually their difference is just perceptible; −1 indicates that (b) is slightly less pronounced than (a) but still close enough to (a) to consider that visually their difference is just perceptible. The values ±2 indicate that visually their difference is really perceptible.

In this chapter we have outlined some of our current and future research directions for assessing the colour appearance of complex images from content-dependent parameters based on emergence features and edge features. The next stage will define a more complete set of parameters and will take into account both global and local visual features. In order to achieve this, we will study the goodness of the approximation between the computed colour appearance parameters and the mean opinion score (MOS). Visual assessment experiments will be conducted with strictly controlled viewing conditions, and will be based on the use of the grading scale previously defined. The colour appearance parameters will be defined so as to quantify all subjective factors which contribute to the colour appearance of complex images: chromaticness, lightness, colourfulness, texture, contrast and emergence.

ACKNOWLEDGEMENTS

This study was supported by Région Rhône-Alpes through financial assistance to the ACTIV programme. The authors are members of the French Colour Imaging Group.

REFERENCES

1. M. R. Luo and R. W. G. Hunt (1998) The structure of the CIE 1997 colour appearance model (CIECAM97s). *Color Research and Application*, **23**(3), 138–146.
2. CIE (1998) The CIE 1997 interim colour appearance model (simple version), CIECAM97s. Technical Report 131, CIE, Vienna.
3. M. D. Fairchild (1998) *Color Appearance Models*. Addison-Wesley, Reading MA.
4. H. Sobagaki, T. Yano, K. Hashimoto and Y. Nayatani (1999) On the field trials of CIECAM97s and its model structure. *Color Research and Application*, **24**(6), 439–456.
5. A. Trémeau (2000) *Color contrast parameters for analysing image differences. Proc. Colour Image Science 2000 Conference*, Derby, April 2000, pp. 11–23.
6. E. Favier, P. Colantoni and A. Trémeau (2000) *Color contrast parameters using edges data and sharpness data. Proc. Int. Conf. on Color in Graphics and Image Processing*, Saint-Etienne, France, October 2000, pp. 231–237.
7. E. A. Fedorovskaya, H. de Ridder and F. J. J. Blommaert (1997) Chroma variations and perceived quality of color images of natural scenes. *Color Research and Application*, **22**(2), 96–110.
8. K. Saarinen (1994) Color image segmentation by a watershed algorithm and region adjacency graph processing. *Proc. IEEE International Conference on Image Processing*, pp. 1021–1025.
9. X. Shen and M. Spann (1997) Segmentation of 2D and 3D images through a hierarchical clustering based on region modelling. *IEEE ICIP Proceedings*, **3**, 50–53.
10. A. Trémeau and P. Colantoni (2000) Regions adjacency graph applied to color image segmentation. *IEEE Transactions on Image Processing*, **9**(4), 735.
11. R. Schettini (1993) A segmentation algorithm for color images. *Pattern Recognition Letters*, **14**(6), 499–506.
12. A. Trémeau, J. Bousigue and B. Laget (1996) Cooccurrence shape descriptors applied to texture classification and segmentation. *Proc. SPIE*, **2665**, 135–147.
13. A. Trémeau, P. Colantoni and B. Laget (1996) On color segmentation guided by the cooccurrence matrix. *Proc. OSA Annual Conference on Optics and Imaging in the Information Age*, Rochester, October 1996, pp. 30–38.
14. A. Trémeau, E. Dinet and E. Favier (1996) Measurement and display of color image differences based on visual attention. *Journal of Imaging Science and Technology*, **40**(6), 522–534.
15. S. D. Zenzo (1986) A note on the gradient of a multi-image. *Computer Vision Graphics and Image Processing*, **36**, 1–9.
16. A. Cumani, P. Grattoni and A. Giuducci (1991) An edge-based description of color images. *Computer Vision and Image Processing*, **53**(1), 313–323.
17. G. A. Agoston (1979) *Color Theory and Its Application in Art and Design*, 2nd edn. Springer, New York.
18. A. Trémeau and C. Charrier (2000) Influence of chromatic changes on perception of color image quality. *Color Research and Application*, **25**(3), 200–213.

10

Indexing and retrieval in colour image databases

Raimondo Schettini, Gianluigi Ciocca and Silvia Zuffi

10.1 INTRODUCTION

Colour has been widely used for content-based image and video retrieval in multimedia databases. Much research has been devoted in recent years to the definition of effective and efficient tools for specifying visual queries and implementing retrieval strategies that satisfy some criteria of matching or pictorial similarity. The use of colour has been extensively investigated in various ways:

- *Colour matching* to find images containing specified colours in assigned proportions [8].
- *Similarity searches* to find a ranked list of images 'similar' to an image provided or hand sketched by the user [3, 33].
- *Region searches* to find images containing regions of colour as specified in a query [39, 69].
- *Target searches* to find a list of the images in which an object specified by the user appears [58, 71].

Colour Image Science, edited by L.W. MacDonald and M.R. Luo.

- *Semantic categorisation*, to group images in meaningful categories, such as graphics as opposed to photos, or indoor pictures as opposed to outdoor pictures [79].
- *Retrieving images* with certain colour-induced effects [15].

All these tasks depend upon the definition of robust and efficient colour features that can represent image contents. Unfortunately, there is no single 'best' representation of colour, but only multiple representations which characterise the colour feature from different perspectives. In any given context, however, the selected features will ideally present the following basic properties:

- *Perceptual similarity*: the feature distance between two images is large only if the images are not 'similar'.
- *Efficiency*: features and metrics can be rapidly computed.
- *Economy*: their dimensions are small in order not to affect retrieval efficiency.
- *Scalability*: the performance of the system is not influenced by the size of the database.
- *Robustness*: changes in the image capture conditions of the database images do not affect retrieval.

In matching images, a feature similarity/dissimilarity function must be coupled with the colour features. A distance d is defined as $d : \Im \times \Im \rightarrow \Re^+$ and must satisfy the following four properties for all images I, J and K in $\Im$:

$$\begin{aligned}
&\mathrm{P}_1 : d(I, I) = d(J, J) && \text{self-similarity}\\
&\mathrm{P}_2 : d(I, J) \geqslant d(I, I) && \text{minimality}\\
&\mathrm{P}_3 : d(I, J) = d(J, I) && \text{symmetry}\\
&\mathrm{P}_4 : d(I, K) + d(K, J) \geqslant d(I, J) && \text{triangular inequality}
\end{aligned} \tag{10.1}$$

Any function satisfying P_1, P_2 and P_4 is a metric. Any function satisfying P_1, P_2 and P_3 is a similarity measure.

A schematic description of the activities of a visual information retrieval (VIR) system is shown in Figure 10.1. During input, images are processed to compute the features selected to represent the image contents. This process, called *indexation* or *indexing*, assigns to each image a set of identifying descriptors, or indices, which will be used by the system in the matching phase to retrieve relevant images and reject extraneous ones. The indices are stored in the database, ideally designed for efficient retrieval. Different features (colour, shape, texture, size, distance, relative position, etc.) express different aspects of image contents, and may of course coexist [14]. Only colour-based features are considered here.

When an image query is posed, its colour features are extracted from the database, or computed using the same procedures applied to input images. Image retrieval is then performed by a matching engine, which compares the features of the query image with those of the stored images. The matching mechanism implements the retrieval according to the selected metric, or similarity measure. The images of the database are ranked

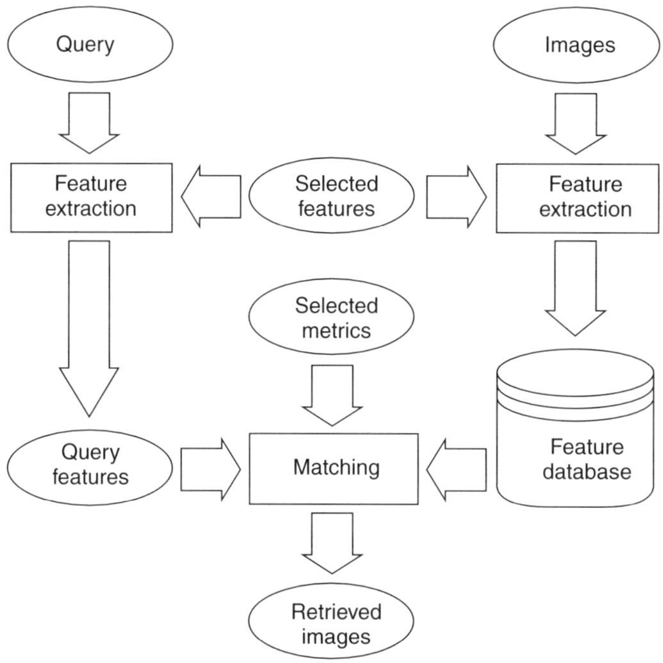

Figure 10.1 Schematic of a VIR system.

according to their similarity/match with the query, for evaluation by the user according to his or her information needs.

With very few exceptions, the effective and efficient computation of colour indices requires a drastic reduction in the number of colours used to represent the colour contents of an image. The algorithms employed for this are reviewed in Section 10.2. Once the number of colours has been sufficiently reduced, many different strategies for representing and comparing colour distributions can be used. These strategies are described in Section 10.3. Image retrieval based purely on colour distribution tends to include too many false positives when the database is large. The several possible extensions of global colour features to code local spatial information are described in Sections 10.4 to 10.6. In Section 10.7 the integration of colour-based features with other features is discussed. Methods for performance evaluation of image retrieval are discussed in Section 10.8. Our conclusions are presented in Section 10.9, together with an indication of what we see as the road map for future research.

10.2 COLOUR DISCRETISATION

The drastic reduction in the number of colours used to represent the colour image content that effective and efficient computation of colour indices usually demands is in general

Table 10.1 Quantisation methods

STATIC COLOUR DISCRETISATION
Most significant bits
Colour space partition
Colour space clustering
Reference colours
DYNAMIC COLOUR DISCRETISATION
Image segmentation

achieved by colour space quantisation, using a predefined colour palette (static quantisation), or by clustering and/or spatial segmentation (dynamic quantisation). Formally, we let C be a colour space, and $P = \{c_1, c_2, \ldots, c_i, \ldots, c_n\} | c_i \in C, n << \|C\|\}$, a subset of C called the quantisation space. A function Q that maps each colour in C to an element in P is called a *quantiser*, and is defined as:

$$Q : C \longrightarrow P \tag{10.2}$$

A schematic representation of the different quantisation methods is given in Table 10.1.

Several authors have used only a few (generally two) of the most significant bits of each of the RGB colour channels to reduce severely the number of image colours [55, 59]. But the lack of perceptual rules for colour mapping may cause considerable shifts in colour. Smith and Chang [69] have partitioned the HSV colour space into 166 bins, placing more importance on hue (18 levels) than on value and saturation (three levels each). Before computing the image index, a median filter is applied on each HSV colour component to eliminate outliers and emphasise prominent colour regions.

The QBIC system [33] makes it possible to compute a k-element colour histogram, where k can be set by the user (the default value is 64). Each RGB colour axis is initially quantised in 16 levels, obtaining an initial partition of the RGB colour space into 4096 cells. The coordinates of the centre of each cell in a modified Munsell colour space [54] are then computed, and a standard, greedy minimum sum of squares clustering is performed to obtain k 'super-cells'. A similar partition has been applied in the HSV colour space by Jain *et al.* [54, 79].

Ciocca *et al.* quantised the device colour space in two steps. First, a random sampling of few million colours is generated in the RGB colour space. These samples, assuming that they are coded in sRGB terms, are mapped into the CIELAB colour space, where a competitive cluster algorithm [78] is then applied to find the 64 most significant colours. The colours of the images to be indexed are mapped in the CIELAB colour space, and assigned to the nearest of the 64 centroids [14].

Syeda-Mahmood [70] proposed a quantisation method that partitions the RGB colour space into about 220 subspaces (categories) in which the colour remains perceptually the same and distinctly different from that of neighbouring subspaces. This partition was obtained by a 'rather informal but extensive psychophysical experiment', which systematically examined the device-dependent HSV colour space. A look-up table was used for the mapping between the RGB values and the colour categories.

Gagliardi and Schettini [29] proposed the use of multiple descriptions of colour in order to deal with the intrinsic variability in human evaluation of colour similarity. Their quantisation method partitions the gamut of feasible colours into equivalence classes corresponding to standardised linguistic tags. The CIELAB colour space is divided into 256 subspaces (categories), in each of which the colour remains perceptually the same, is labelled with its own linguistic tag, and is distinctly different from that of neighbouring subspaces. The colour stimuli representing the colour categories are derived from the ISCC-NBS colour naming system proposed in 1955 by the Inter-Society Colour Council (ISCC) and the National Bureau of Standards (NBS). The images quantised by this method are further clustered into a set of 13 equivalent classes representing basic colour terms (black, grey, white, red, orange, yellow, green, blue, violet, purple, pink, brown and olive) to produce a coarse but completely unsupervised image segmentation.

In their ImageRover system [67] Sclaroff *et al.* first transformed the RGB values into the CIELUV space, after which each colour axis was split into four equal-sized bins for a total number of 64 bins (theoretical, since very dark and very light colours cannot have a high chroma).

In order to achieve a more compact representation of colour images, Mehhre *et al.* [50] heuristically defined a small set of RGB reference colours in which all the colours in the application (trademark indexing) are approximately covered. Each pixel of the colour image is simply assigned to the nearest colour in the table. This type of discretisation must be performed very carefully, and requires a high level of user interaction. When a large subset of the image database is available, the colour space can instead be partitioned so that each discrete colour appears with approximately equal likelihood in order to maximise the information conveyed [37].

Gong *et al.* [32] roughly partitioned the modified Munsell colour space (the same used by QBIC) into 11 colour zones defined and validated empirically by different groups of examiners. A similar partition was proposed by Cox *et al.* in the PicHunter system in HSV [16], and by Ciocca *et al.* in the Quicklook system [14].

Other authors [8, 50, 64] have investigated the feasibility of image-dependent colour quantisation/segmentation by clustering. The main issues in this case are the strategy adopted to predict the number of valid clusters/regions in the image, the computational cost, and the need to have sophisticated measures for evaluating similarity. The resulting image signature may represent the colour image content very well. However, as is well known, unsupervised image segmentation is an ill-posed problem: when little is known about the images to be indexed and the clustering/segmentation parameters cannot be tuned accordingly, the risk of serious errors should not be underestimated.

Liu and Yang have proposed a function that does not require any user-set parameter or threshold values for the quantitative evaluation of the performance of algorithms for the segmentation of colour images [43]. Their function has been designed to incorporate, directly or indirectly, three out of the four heuristic criteria suggested by Haralick and Shapiro [34] for evaluating segmentation results without having to set threshold values for any of the subjective properties of region size, shape and homogeneity. The incorporated criteria are: (1) the regions must be uniform and homogeneous; (2) the interior of a region must be simple, without too many small holes; and (3) adjacent regions must present significantly different values for uniform characteristics. The authors, commenting on their experimental results, suggest that their function also takes into account, although indirectly, the smoothness of the boundaries (part of Haralick and Shapiro's fourth criterion, which includes boundary accuracy). The evaluation function is empirically defined as:

$$F(I) = \frac{1}{1000(N \times M)}\sqrt{R}\sum_{i=1}^{R}\frac{e_i^2}{\sqrt{A_i}} \tag{10.3}$$

where I is the segmented image, $N \times M$ the image size, and R the number of regions of the segmented image, while A_i and e_i are, respectively, the area and the average colour error of the ith region; e_i is defined as the sum of the Euclidean distances between the RGB colour vectors of the pixels of region i and the colour vector attributed to region i in the segmented image. Smaller values of $F(I)$ should give better segmentation results.

The equation is composed of three terms: the first is a normalisation factor which takes into account the size of the image; the second, $\sqrt{R}$, penalises segmentations that form too many regions; the third, the sum, penalises segmentations with non-homogeneous regions. Since the average colour error e_i of the region is significantly higher for large regions than for small ones, e_i has been scaled by the factor $\sqrt{A_i}$. The authors, who report a good match between function values and visual evaluation of the corresponding image segmentations, have used function F to select the best segmentation automatically, varying the colour space and the dissimilarity measure employed in their algorithm. Since this function tends to evaluate very noisy segmentations favourably, Borsotti *et al.* [10] have proposed an enhanced function that corresponds more closely to visual judgement:

$$Q(I) = \frac{1}{10\,000(N \times M)}\sqrt{R}\sum_{i=1}^{R}\left[\frac{e_i^2}{1+\log A_i} + \left(\frac{R(A_i)}{A_i}\right)^2\right] \tag{10.4}$$

where all the entities are as previously defined for F, while $R(A_i)$ represents the number of regions having an area equal to A_i. The body of the sum is composed of two terms: the first is high only for non-homogeneous regions (typically large ones), while the second is high only for regions with an area A_i equal to the area of many other regions in the segmented image (typically small ones). The design of this new term takes into account the fact that the number of regions of area A_i in a given image will probably be small if area A_i has a high value, in which case $R(A_i)/A_i$ contributes little to the sum. On the other hand, the number of regions of area A_i *may* be large, if the area A_i has a low value; here $R(A_i)/A_i$ contributes strongly to the sum. Heuristically it can be said that $R(A_i)$ is almost always 1 for large regions, and may be much larger than 1 for small regions. In any case, the denominator A_i drastically forces the term $R(A_i)/A_i$ to near zero for large regions, and allows it to grow for small regions.

A different approach has been proposed by Del Bimbo [19]. Image colours are first quantised on a palette of 128 reference colours by a competitive learning algorithm.

Region segmentation is then obtained by iteratively aggregating uniform colour patches, so as to minimise the following measures:

$$F = \sum_{i} \left(\alpha \frac{1}{A_{R_i}} + \beta D_{R_i} + \gamma \sum_{J} \frac{1}{D_{R_i - R_J}} \right) \tag{10.5}$$

where A_{R_i} is the area of region R_i, D_{R_i} is a measure of colour uniformity of region R_i, $D_{R_i - R_J}$ is a measure of the difference in colour between R_i and its adjacent regions R_j, and α,β,γ are control parameters. Colour regions are iteratively aggregated until a minimum of F is found; the values of α,β,γ are then adjusted, and the procedure repeated. The image segmentations produced by this process are then organised in a pyramidal schema (Figure 10.2).

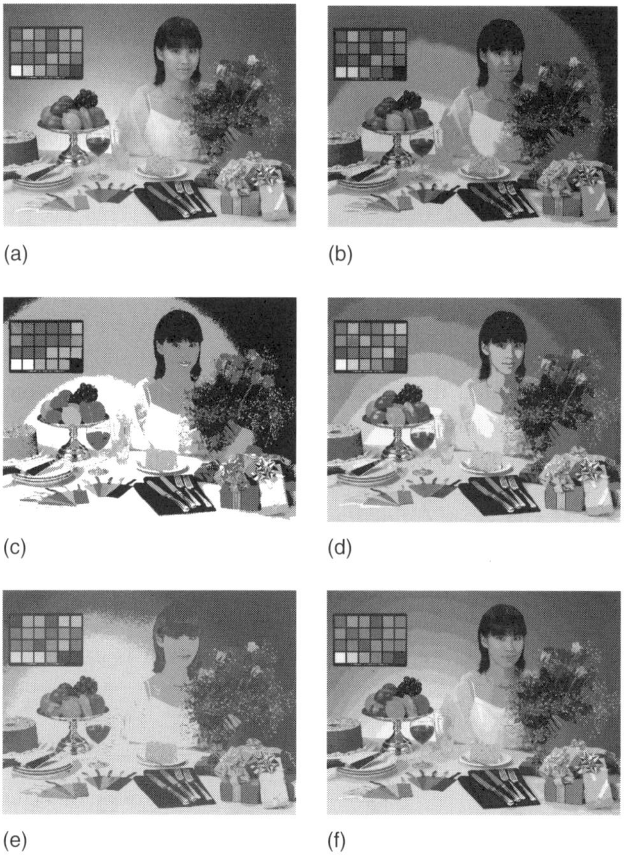

Figure 10.2 (a) Original image, (b) image quantised using 2 bits per colour channel, (c) image quantised using 11 colour classes corresponding to basic colour names, (d) image quantised by partitioning the HSV colour space into 64 bins, (e) image quantised in 64 colours using colour space clustering, (f) image quantised in 64 colours using a segmentation algorithm. See also Plate 4.

10.3 COLOUR INDICES

Once the number of colour images has been significantly reduced, they can be coded in many different ways in order to represent the image content. Very often colour is represented by histograms; in this case it is the matching strategy that most distinguishes the different retrieval methods. A colour histogram, **H**, is a vector $[h_1, \ldots, h_n]$ in which each bin h_j contains the number of pixels having the colour j in the image and can be considered the probability density function (PDF) of the colour values. If the images to be compared are of different sizes, but have been quantised on a common palette, their histograms can be compared as follows [4, 75]:

$$D(\mathbf{H}, \mathbf{H}') = \frac{\sum_i \min(h_i, h'_i)}{\sum_i h'_i} \tag{10.6}$$

If the images are of the same size (or the histograms have been scaled to the same size) and quantised on a common palette, their similarity is commonly measured using the sum of the squared differences (L_2 metric), or the sum of the absolute values of differences (L_1 metric). These metrics usually perform poorly, even for the simplest types of query (Figure 10.10).

To render the L metrics more stable with respect to quantisation (a slight change in lighting conditions may result in a corresponding shift in the colour histogram, causing these metrics to misjudge similarity completely, as shown in Figure 10.3), Stricker and Orengo [72] proposed the use of cumulative histograms. In order to use these histograms, the colours must first be ranked in the colour space.

Hafner *et al.* [33] suggested the use of a weighted distance between histograms that takes into account the 'crosstalk' between colours. However, these authors were mainly concerned with the efficiency of the solution, and only marginally with the necessity of coding the perceptual similarity between colours. According to Hafner, the distance between histograms **H** and **H**′ is defined as:

$$d_{\mathrm{H}}(\mathbf{H}, \mathbf{H}') = \sqrt{\sum_i \sum_j a_{ij}(h_i - h'_j)(h_i - h'_j)} \tag{10.7}$$

where a_{ij}, coding the similarity between the colour i and j, is expressed as:

$$a_{ij} = 1 - \frac{d_{ij}}{\max_{ij}(d_{ij})} \tag{10.8}$$

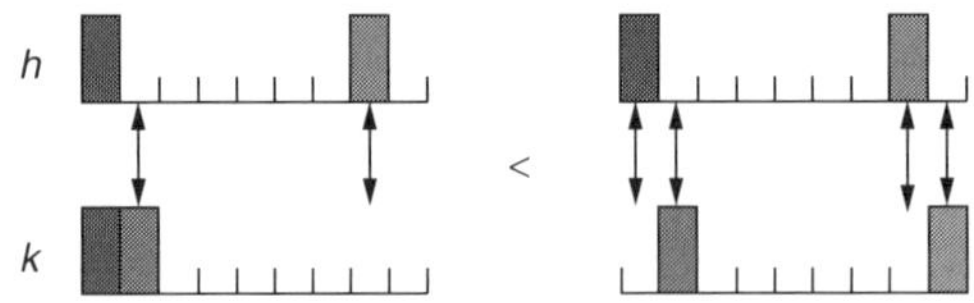

Figure 10.3 Misjudged similarity caused by colour shift.

and d_{ij} represents the Euclidean distance between the colours as defined in a variant of the Munsell colour space. They have also proposed an alternative a_{ij}:

$$a_{ij} = \exp(-\sigma(d_{ij}/d_{\max})^2) \tag{10.9}$$

for some positive constant value of σ.

In earlier studies, Binaghi *et al.* exploited perceptual correlates of the psychological dimensions of lightness, chroma and hue, defined in the CIELAB or CIELUV colour space to address colour range and image indexing [8]. Using a structured interview technique, these authors elicited three primary fuzzy sets corresponding to similarity in lightness (L^*), hue (h^*) and chroma (C^*) colour dimensions.

Each of the defined membership functions assigned a degree of similarity between two colours i and j as a function of the difference in a given colour feature, while the product of these three membership functions was used to define the global degree of similarity between the two colours considered. Extending these studies, the authors defined the similarity between two histograms as:

$$d_F(\mathbf{H}, \mathbf{H}') = \sqrt{\sum_i \sum_j \mu_{h^*L^*C^*}(i, j)(h_i - h_j)(h'_i - h'_j)} \tag{10.10}$$

Weighted versions of the L_2 metric may underestimate distances because they tend to accentuate the similarity between colour histograms presenting many non-empty bins. (Figure 10.4) and are also computationally expensive. Hafner *et al.* [33] proposed a simpler low-dimensional distance measure, called the average colour distance, which can be used to perform a sort of prefiltering before applying histogram matching. An alternative strategy for increasing retrieval efficiency is described in [6].

Stricker proposed two other approaches more efficient than those based on colour histograms, as they do not require colour quantisation, and produce more compact indices [73, 74]. In the first, instead of storing the complete 3D colour histogram, only the first three moments of the histograms of each colour channel are computed and used as an index; in the second, the image is represented only by the average and covariance matrices of its colour distribution.

The features of mean, variance and skewness can be computed for the ith colour channel as follows:

$$E_i(\tilde{I}) = \frac{1}{N} \sum_{x,y} \tilde{I}_i(x, y) \quad \text{(the average colour channel value)} \tag{10.11}$$

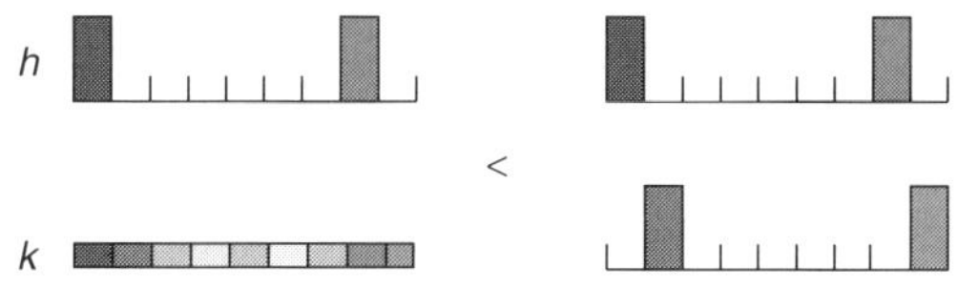

Figure 10.4 Overestimated similarity with histograms that lack well-defined modes.

$$\sigma_i(\tilde{I}) = \sqrt{\frac{1}{N}\sum_{x,y}(\tilde{I}_i(x, y) - E_i(\tilde{I}))^2} \quad \text{(the standard deviation)} \tag{10.12}$$

$$s_i(\tilde{I}) = \sqrt[3]{\frac{1}{N}\sum_{x,y}(\tilde{I}_i(x, y) - E_i(\tilde{I}))^3} \quad \text{(the third root of skewness)} \tag{10.13}$$

The similarity function used in these approaches for retrieval is a weighted sum of the absolute differences between the features computed. Each feature entry is weighted by a value, w_{i1}, w_{i2}, $w_{i3} \geqslant 0$, selected by the user, depending upon the specific application (Figure 10.11).

$$d_{\text{mom}}(\tilde{I}_1, \tilde{I}_2) = \sum_i (w_{i1}|E_i(\tilde{I}_1) - E_i(\tilde{I}_2)| + w_{i2}|\sigma_i(\tilde{I}_1) - \sigma_i(\tilde{I}_2)| + w_{i3}|s_i(\tilde{I}_1) - s_i(\tilde{I}_2)|) \tag{10.14}$$

If the images to be compared have been quantised on different colour palettes, none of the above metrics can be applied.

Rubner, Guibas and Tomasi defined the distance between two colour distributions as the minimum amount of work needed to transform one colour distribution into the other [64]. Alternatively, the Hausdorff distance can be applied. This provides the degree of mismatch between two colour signatures (A, B) as the maximum distance between the colours of A and those of B:

$$H(A, B) = \max(\max_{a\in A} \min_{b\in B} d(a, b), \max_{b\in B} \min_{a\in A} d(a, b)) \tag{10.15}$$

Androutsos *et al.* [2] designed a combinatorial distance measure, based on the angle between two vectors. It enables queries based on single and multiple colours and it allows the exclusion of certain colours.

All these methods neglect the spatial relationships of colour pixels; consequently, images that are actually different in appearance may be judged similar simply because they have a similar colour distribution. To complicate matters further, observers disagree in their evaluations of colour similarity, and a set of similar images found by browsing the original images may not coincide with that obtained by browsing the database version in which the colour distribution has been preserved but the original image structure has been changed at random [3].

10.4 COLOUR SPATIAL INDICES

The main weakness of all the indexing methods described above is the lack of spatial information in the indices. For example, all of the patterns shown in Figure 10.5 have the same colour proportions but different spatial distributions. Their appearance is clearly

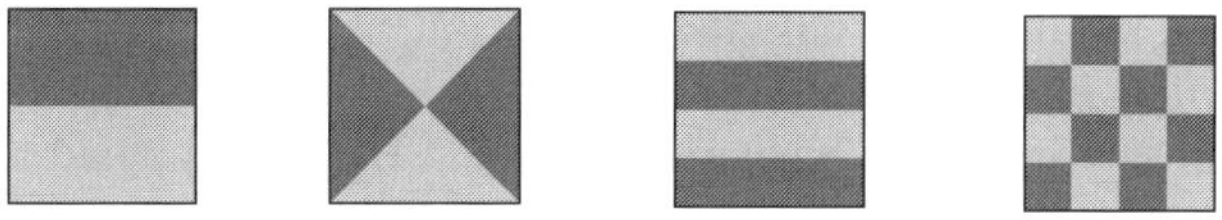

Figure 10.5 Some patterns having the same colour proportions but different spatial distributions.

quite different, so obviously we cannot assume that colour distribution always suffices to represent the pictorial content of an image.

Since in most applications complete segmentation implies a great deal of user interaction during database acquisition, this approach is not feasible for large image databases. The simplest way to provide spatial information is to divide the image into sub-images, and then index each of these. Gong *et al.* [32], for example, model the colour-spatial information of an image by splitting it into nine equal sub-images and representing each sub-area by a colour histogram. Although conceptually simple, this approach may still not provide accurate colour-spatial information, and is expensive both to compute and to store.

To facilitate the search of large-scale image collections, Smith and Chang used colour sets to approximate histograms. Colour sets correspond to salient image regions and they are represented by binary vectors to allow a more rapid search [69].

Stricker and Dimai [74] split the image into an oval central region and four corners. Their system evaluates and combines the colour feature similarity of each of these sub-images, attributing more weight to the central region. But this is a strictly domain-dependent solution: it could be effective for an archive of photographs, yet it might not work well in other imaging applications. Some region splitting strategies are shown in Figure 10.6.

Stricker [71] used boundary histograms to encode the lengths of the boundaries between different discrete colours, in order to take into account geometric information in colour image indexing. But this method may yield a huge feature space (for a discrete colour space of 256 elements, a boundary histogram of 32 768 bins is required), and is not robust enough to deal with textured colour images. Gagliardi *et al.* [29] investigated the integration of different colour information descriptions and similarity measurements to enhance the system's effectiveness. In their method, both query and database images are described in the CIELAB colour space with two limited palettes of perceptual significance, having 256 and 13 colours respectively. Indices of the image are constructed from (a) a histogram of the finer colour quantisation and (b) a histogram of the boundary lengths between two discrete colours of the coarser quantisation. While the former contains absolutely no

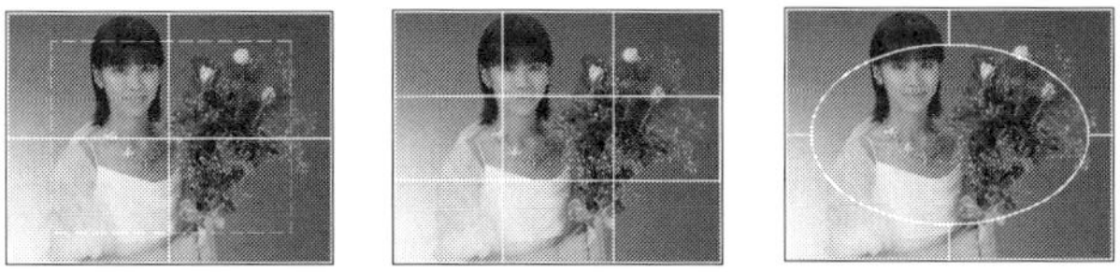

Figure 10.6 Examples of possible sub-image indexation.

spatial information, but describes only the colour content of the image, the latter provides a concise description of the spatial arrangement of the basic colours in the image. The similarity between two boundary histograms **BQ** and **BD** is computed as follows:

$$S_b(\mathbf{BQ}, \mathbf{BD}) = 1 - \frac{\sum_{i \in \{\text{allbins}\}} |\mathbf{BQ}_i - \mathbf{BD}_i|}{s(\mathbf{BQ}) + s(\mathbf{BD})} \tag{10.16}$$

where $s(\ )$ is the size of the histogram that is the sum of the edge lengths in the image. Normalisation is necessary as the size of the boundary histogram is not constant, but depends upon the image segmentation. Since the images are coarsely segmented, the boundary histogram is little influenced by minor image details and noise. Suitable procedures for measuring the similarity between histograms are then adopted, and the measures combined to model the perceptual similarity between the query and target images.

Pass, Zabih and Miller [59] also present a histogram-based method for comparing images that incorporates spatial information. They classify each pixel of the quantised image as either coherent or incoherent, depending upon whether or not it is a part of a ‘large’ similarly coloured region (a region is classified as large if its size exceeds a fixed user-set value). By counting coherent and incoherent pixels separately, the method offers a finer distinction between images than colour histograms alone can provide (Figure 10.12)

For each colour c_i the number of coherent pixels, α_{c_i}, and the number of non-coherent pixels, β_{c_i} are computed; each entry in the colour coherence vector (CCV) is thus a pair $(\alpha_{c_i}, \beta_{c_i})$, called a *coherence pair*. The whole coherence vector is defined as

$$CCV(\tilde{I}) = \langle(\alpha_c, \beta_c), \ldots, (\alpha_{c_i}, \beta_{c_i}), \ldots, (\alpha_{c_n}, \beta_{c_n})\rangle \tag{10.17}$$

The sum $\alpha_{c_i} + \beta_{c_i}$ is clearly the number of pixels of colour c_i present in the image; the set of the sums for $i = 1, 2, \ldots, n$ represents the colour histogram. The L_1 distance can be used to compare two CCVs:

$$\Delta CCV(\tilde{I}, \tilde{I}') = \sum_{i=1}^{n}(|\alpha_{c_i} - \alpha'_{c_i}| + |\beta_{c_i} - \beta'_{c_i}|) \tag{10.18}$$

Spatial chromatic histograms (SCHs) [12] take information about the location of pixels of similar colour and their arrangement within the image and combine it with information provided by the classical colour histogram. For every colour in the quantised image, the percentage of pixels having the same colour is calculated, and the spatial information summarised in the relative coordinate of the baricentre of their spatial distribution (b) and the corresponding standard deviation from the baricentre (σ). Given two spatial chromatic histograms **H** and **H**$'$ having c bins, a new distance function is computed as follows:

$$D(\mathbf{H}, \mathbf{H}') = \sum_{i=1}^{c} \min(h_{\mathbf{H}}(i) - h_{\mathbf{H}'}(i)) \left(\frac{\sqrt{2} - d(b_{\mathbf{H}}(i), b_{\mathbf{H}'}(i))}{\sqrt{2}} + \frac{\min(\sigma_{\mathbf{H}}(i), \sigma_{\mathbf{H}'}(i))}{\max(\sigma_{\mathbf{H}}(i), \sigma_{\mathbf{H}'}(i))} \right) \tag{10.19}$$

where $h(i)$ is the ratio of pixels having colour i.

Mitra *et al.* [55] proposed new colour features for image indexing called colour correlograms. These include the spatial correlation of colours, and can be used to describe the global distribution of the local correlations. They appear to tolerate large changes in the appearance of the same scene caused by changes in viewing position and background, partial occlusions, and camera zooms. The colour correlogram is a set of values $\gamma^{(k)}_{c_i,c_j}$ that gives the probability that a pixel of colour c_i lies at distance k from a pixel of colour c_j:

$$\gamma^{(k)}_{c_i,c_j} = \Pr_{p_1 \in I_{c_i}, p_2 \in I_{c_j}} [|p_1 - p_2| = k] \tag{10.20}$$

where p_1 and p_2 are two pixels, I is the image, and I_{c_i}, I_{c_j}, the set of pixels of colours c_i and c_j respectively. Computing the correlogram for a set of m distances k and given c colours of quantisation, the whole feature size is c^2m, which is rather high if the quantisation is not sparse. To overcome this problem, another feature, called the banded correlogram, is employed. This feature merges the results of the correlograms computed on different k:

$$\overline{\gamma}^{(k)}_{c_i,c_j} = \sum_{k'=kb}^{(k+1)b-1} \gamma^{(k')}_{c_i,c_j} \quad \text{for } 1 \leqslant k \leqslant b \tag{10.21}$$

The banded correlogram requires c^2m/b values. If only local information is needed, a small set of distances suffices to capture the spatial correlation of pixels, further reducing the dimensions of the feature.

Brambilla *et al.* [11] used a multiresolution wavelet transform in a modified CIELUV colour space to compute image signatures for content-based image retrieval applications, i.e. target search and similarity retrieval. Their multiresolution wavelet decomposition is based on Haar wavelet filtering applied consecutively along horizontal and vertical directions (Figure 10.7). The major features of the images are encoded in signatures of predefined lengths, which are compared in the retrieval phase by applying a similarity measure. The system has previously been trained for this similarity measure from a learning set of very similar, rather similar, not very similar, and different pairs of images, using a regression model for ordinal responses. This method is related to the work of Jacob *et al.* [35], in which a similar approach was employed to target image search, i.e. to seek a specific image in the database when only a roughly painted sketch or low-resolution

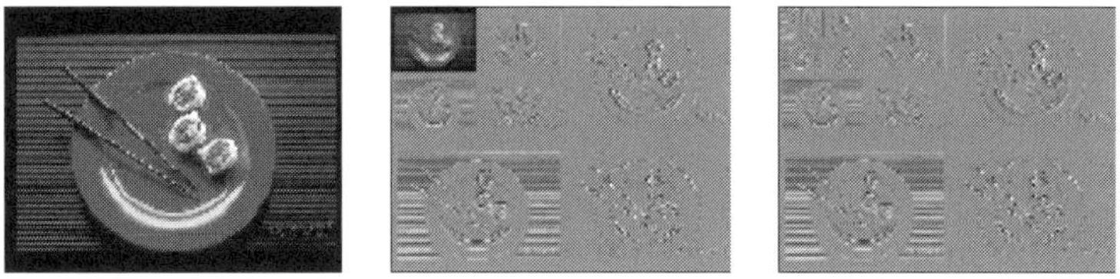

(a) (b) (c)

Figure 10.7 (a) Original image, (b) two-step multiresolution wavelet transform, (c) multiresolution wavelet transform.

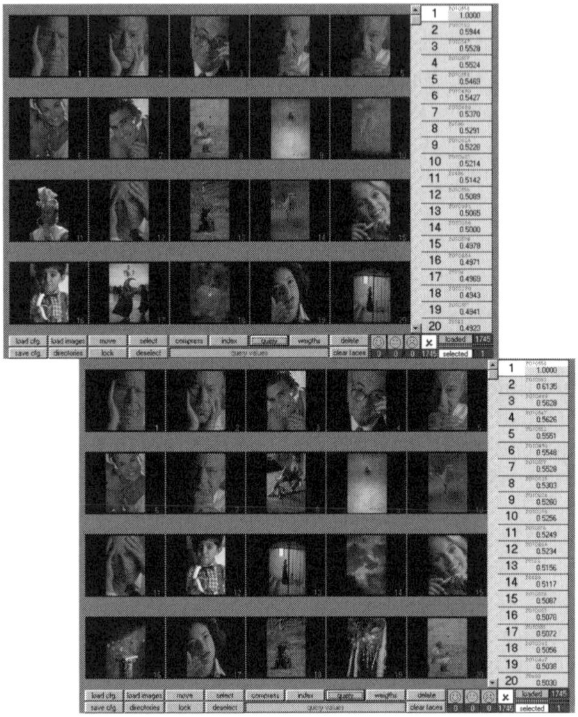

Figure 10.8 Examples of 64- and 128-coefficient wavelet-based image retrieval.

version of it is available. Figure 10.8 shows a sample query on a photo database of 1745 images. The first image is the query itself, and the other images are ranked from the most similar to the least similar in a left-to-right, top-to-bottom scan order.

10.5 COMPARING SEGMENTED IMAGES

Segmented images represented in the spatial domain are usually described by region adjacency graphs [58], or by multidimensional indices representing the spatial distribution of the colour clusters [18, 38, 69].

Binaghi *et al.* [8] have described the segmented image in terms of colour, spatial distribution, and coverage. During retrieval, feature differences are mapped to a reduced set of qualitative linguistic variables modelling the uncertainty in the colour description.

Smith and Chang [69] developed methods for automatically extracting and indexing significant colour regions from images. These use efficient indexing techniques for colour information, region sizes, and absolute and relative spatial locations to allow a wide variety of complex joint colour-spatial queries. However, they do not provide a general procedure for measuring the similarity between two images.

Kankanhalli *et al.* [39] combined colour and spatial clustering for image retrieval. Colour clustering is applied first, to obtain an initial segmentation; then a component labelling algorithm is applied to obtain spatial clustering. The spatial colour cluster is identified by the mean colour value, the fraction of the image the cluster constitutes, and the coordinates of the centroid. The similarity between two images is based on five heuristically weighted elements: the similarity between colour clusters, the relative frequency of pixels in corresponding clusters, the spatial distance between colour clusters, the relative frequency of pixels of the corresponding spatial colour clusters, and the spatial distance between spatial colour clusters.

The description of segmented images using 2D strings is brittle in the sense that minor changes in region location may greatly affect the comparison of two images. In [7, 17] the authors have introduced an original modelling technique for the quantitative representation and comparison of the mutual positioning of a pair of extended regions, which can account for the overall distribution of relationships among the individual pixels belonging to the two regions. In this approach, the relationship between two regions is represented by a finite set of equivalence classes (walk-throughs) among the dense sets of possible paths leading from any pixel in first region to any pixel in the second. Each equivalence class is associated with a weight which provides an integral measure of the set of pixel pairs connected by a path belonging to the class, thus accounting for the degree of truth with which the individual class represents the actual relationship between the two regions.

10.6 ILLUMINANT-INVARIANT COLOUR IMAGE INDEXING

We may assume that all the images stored in the database are described in terms of sRGB colour coordinates, but we cannot always assume constant imaging conditions during data acquisition (particularly when the database contains images collected from many different sources, such as material taken from the World Wide Web). In many cases the user may still be able to recognise the colours in the scene, but when the retrieval is based only on colour, we can only guess how effectively an image search engine will perform the same task, and at what cost.

Previous studies in the field of object recognition have drawn attention to how changes in illuminant conditions modify the colours of the image acquired, and affect the results of colour-based algorithms. Swain and Ballard [75] suggested the application of a colour constancy algorithm to cope with this problem. Their work has been followed by several attempts to provide for the effects of illuminant changes through the definition and use in indexing of illuminant-independent colour features.

10.6.1 Illuminant invariance achieved with descriptors

A method for deriving illuminant-independent colour descriptors was developed by Funt and Finlayson [28]. Starting from the assumption of the local constancy of illumination, they indexed the derivative of the logarithm of the image, which is in effect the ratio of neighbouring colours. The histogram of the derivatives of the logarithm of an image codes the lengths of the boundaries between colours, providing an illumination-independent description of the image. Experiments on small sets of synthetic and real images demonstrated that their *colour constant index* algorithm performs slightly worse than Swain's under fixed illumination, but substantially better than Swain's under illumination that varies both spectrally and spatially.

In a subsequent publication, Finlayson *et al.* [22] proposed the use of colour angular indexing to describe image similarity. In the angular indexing paradigm, objects are represented by the three colour angles. To these are added three colour texture angles, calculated after a linear filtering of the image. Using these six features the authors obtained illuminant invariance in indexing, while accelerating the matching process by drastically reducing the number of parameters, from the 4064 of Swain and Ballard's histogram to only 6. In experiments this method performed better than colour indexing [75] and colour-constant colour indexing [28] in the presence of changes in illumination.

Gevers and Smoulders proposed various colour models and checked their invariance under changing imaging conditions, including the presence of shadows and highlights [30, 31]. Tests were performed on a database of about 500 images. One of the colour models proposed assumes dichromatic reflection and white illumination, and is independent of the viewpoint, surface orientation, illumination direction and intensity, and highlights [31]:

$$\begin{aligned} l_1(R,G,B) &= \frac{(R-G)^2}{(R-G)^2+(R-B)^2+(G-B)^2} \\ l_2(R,G,B) &= \frac{(R-B)^2}{(R-G)^2+(R-B)^2+(G-B)^2} \\ l_3(R,G,B) &= \frac{(G-B)^2}{(R-G)^2+(R-B)^2+(G-B)^2} \end{aligned} \tag{10.22}$$

Another model which was demonstrated to be invariant for illuminant colour is:

$$m_1 = \frac{R^{x_1}G^{x_2}}{R^{x_2}G^{x_1}}, \quad m_2 = \frac{R^{x_1}B^{x_2}}{R^{x_2}B^{x_1}}, \quad m_3 = \frac{G^{x_1}B^{x_2}}{G^{x_2}B^{x_1}} \tag{10.23}$$

where R, G, B are the colour values in the RGB colour space and x_1 and x_2 are the locations in the image of two neighbouring pixels.

Berens and Finlayson [5] proposed a method that addresses simultaneously the problem of illuminant invariance in indexing and the dimension of colour histograms. Each (R, G, B) coordinate is transformed into a log-chromaticity space defined by:

$$(\ln(R/G), \ln(RG/B^2)) = (\ln R - \ln G, \ln R + \ln G - 2\ln B) \tag{10.24}$$

In this colour space, illuminant changes result in a translation of coordinates; consequently illuminant invariance can be accomplished by mean subtraction. To reduce the dimension of the matching problem, the authors coded the log-chromaticity distribution obtained by projecting it onto a PCA base. Using Funt's data set of 11 objects photographed under four different illuminants, they demonstrated how removing the mean from the log-chromaticity coordinates removes the effect of illuminant variance on the colour distribution.

Mandal *et al.* have presented a method to define illuminant-invariant moments [46]. Assuming that the change in illumination is uniform, and the illumination does not produce a non-linear effect on the image, the histograms of an image with varying lighting conditions can be approximated as a translated and scaled version of each other. This translation and scaling effect can be countered by using as image indexing, a set of moments of a translation and scale invariant (TSI) histogram. If we assume that the change in illumination has dilated the PDF of an image by a factor α, it can be demonstrated that the kth central moments and normalised central moments of the PDF of the changed image and those of the original image are related as follows:

$$\mu'_k = \alpha^{k\mu_k} \quad \text{and} \quad \beta'_k = \sigma\beta_k \tag{10.25}$$

From the normalised central moments, a set of TSI moments can be defined as:

$$\eta_k = \frac{\beta_k}{\beta_2} \quad (k > 2, k \in Z) \tag{10.26}$$

Since β_1 is equal to zero, the η_k can be considered moments of a PDF with the first moment set at zero and the second set at one, whatever the value of α that transformed the image's illumination. In [47] Mandal *et al.* defined a procedure to convert TSI moments to the corresponding Legendre moments as it has been shown that these perform better than central moments.

Mandal *et al.* [47] have proposed a method of image indexing using illumination-compensated standard deviations and shape parameters of highpass wavelet sub-images. They have demonstrated that the standard deviations of the coefficients of the wavelet sub-bands are related to each other by a linear function of the illuminant scale factor α:

$$\sigma'_{F_k} = \alpha\sigma_{F_k} \tag{10.27}$$

The histograms of highpass wavelet coefficients can be described using a generalised Gaussian density function which depends on a parameter γ, called *shape* [9]. The following relationship holds:

$$\gamma'_{F_k} = \gamma_{F_k} + c(1 - \alpha) \quad \text{with } c \text{ a positive constant} \tag{10.28}$$

The standard deviation and the shape parameter are used as indexing values. First, the scale factor α is estimated by comparing the β_2 moments of the histograms corresponding to the query and target image (see the TSI moments), then the new values are calculated from the above equations and used to evaluate the distance between the two images.

10.6.2 Illuminant invariance achieved by image preprocessing

All the previously mentioned studies addressed the definition of illuminant-invariant colour features. Funt and Barnard [26] instead compared five preprocessing algorithms for normalising images to a standard neutral illuminant and removing the effects of varying illumination conditions in the acquired scenes. The algorithms tested were white-patch retinex, greyworld, 2D gamut constraint and 3D gamut constraint and neural networks. They were run on 110 images of 11 objects viewed under 5 different illuminants and in 2 different positions. Apart from the obvious conclusion that colour constancy improved colour indexing when the target image was produced under an illuminant different from that used to acquire the corresponding image in the database, the results achieved by colour constancy algorithms were disappointing. The best performer was successful only 67% of the time, compared with the 92% when the illuminant was known.

Finlayson *et al.* [23] proposed a comprehensive image normalisation which removes image dependency on lighting geometry and illumination colour. Their approach alternates normalisation for illumination intensity and normalisation for illumination colour, iterating this process until a stable state is reached. If an RGB image of N pixels is represented by an $N \times 3$ matrix, the normalisation operators are defined as follows:

$$R(I)_{i,j} = \frac{I_{i,j}}{\sum_{k=1}^{3} I_{i,k}} \quad \text{(normalisation for illumination intensity)} \tag{10.29}$$

$$C(I)_{i,j} = \frac{\frac{1}{3} N I_{i,j}}{\sum_{k=1}^{N} I_{k,j}} \quad \text{(normalisation for illumination colour)} \tag{10.30}$$

where i, j indicates the ijth element of the matrix. The algorithm takes the following form:

1. $I_0 = I$ (initialisation)
2. $I_{i+1} = C(R(I_i))$ (iteration)
3. $I_{i+1} = I_i$ (termination condition)

The experiments were performed on a database of about 100 images.

The retinex theory was originally proposed by Land and McCann [41] in order to understand and emulate human colour perception. Many variations of the method have been developed in the last 30 years [48, 27]. Ciocca *et al.* [13] have recently examined the performance of various colour-based retrieval strategies when coupled with a prefiltering based on a Brownian look-up table retinex algorithm [48] to see whether, and to what degree, retinex improved the effectiveness of the retrieval, regardless of the strategy adopted.

The retrieval strategies implemented have included colour and spatial-chromatic histogram matching, colour coherence vector matching, and the weighted sum of the absolute differences between the first three moments of each colour channel (see Section 10.7 for a description of the retrieval algorithms). Experiments were performed on two databases, containing 310 paintings and 387 ceramic objects respectively: 15 images were randomly selected from each database, simulating for each of these a change in imaging conditions, using one of eight illuminants. These images were then used to query the corresponding database, employing one strategy at a time, first without any prefiltering, and then applying the retinex algorithm to both the query and the database images. The conclusion was that retinex prefiltering improved the effectiveness of all the retrieval strategies implemented. A simple comparison of the improvements in performance suggests that better results are obtained when retinex is coupled with colour quantisation.

Figure 10.9 shows the results of applying the Marini *et al.* version of retinex [48] and the version defined by Funt *et al.* [27]. The algorithms have been applied to images of the same scene under different illuminants.

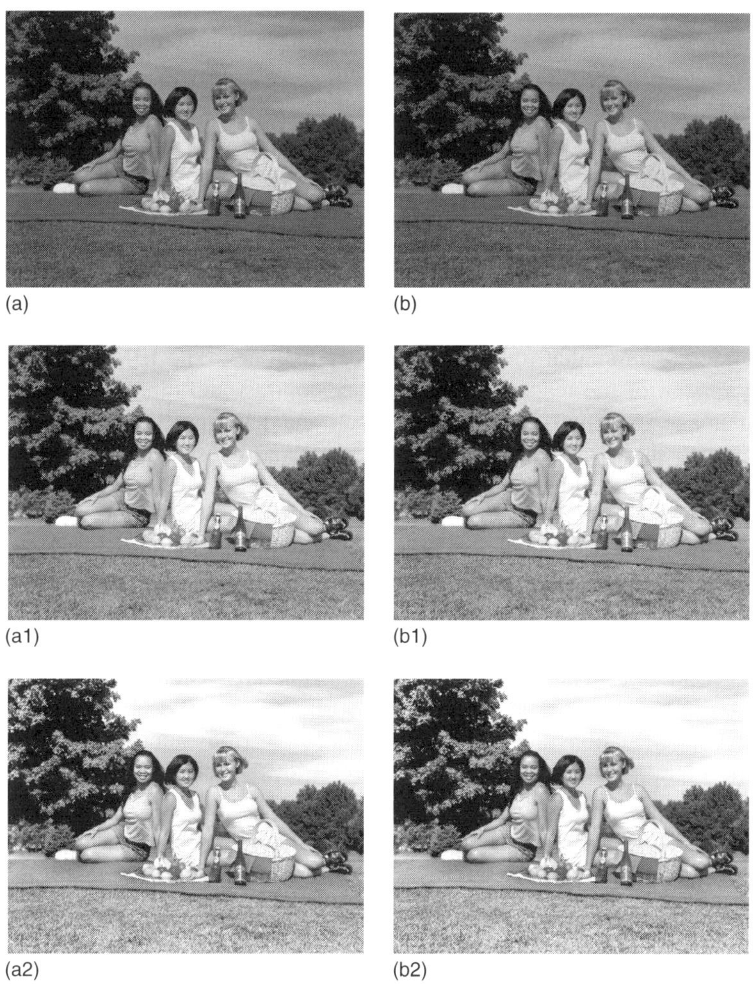

Figure 10.9 (a) Original image and (b) simulation of a warm illuminant: (a1) shows the retinex proposed by Marini *et al.* on image (a) and (b1) shows the same retinex on image (b); (a2) shows the retinex proposed by Funt *et al.* on image (a) and (b2) shows the same retinex on image (b). See also Plate 5.

10.7 INTEGRATION WITH OTHER FEATURES

Most content-based image retrieval systems do not exploit only colour and spatial-colour features for characterising image content. All the low-level features that could be computed automatically, i.e. without human assistance, could be computed and associated with the colour-based features described in the previous sections to index an image database. In many systems, colour-based features have already been coupled with texture and edge/shape features.

Texture has been widely studied in psychophysics, as well as in image analysis and computer vision. However, our understanding of texture is still very limited, compared with our knowledge of other visual features, such as colour and shape. Most of the computational methods available for describing texture provide for the supervised or unsupervised classification of image regions and pixels. Within these contexts, grey level textures have been processed using various approaches, such as Fourier transform, co-occurrence statistics, directional filter masks, fractal dimension and Markov random fields; for a review of the various methods, see [20] and [77].

Rao and Lohse designed an experiment to identify the high-level features of texture perception [62, 63]. Their results suggest that in human vision three perceptual features (repetitiveness, directionality, and granularity and complexity) concur to describe texture appearance. Consequently, the computational model applied in image indexing should compute features that reflect these perceptual ones. The IBM QBIC system uses a modified version of the features of coarseness, contrast and directionality proposed by Tamura for image indexing [76, 21]. Amadusun and King proposed another feature set corresponding to the visual properties of texture: coarseness, contrast, busyness, complexity and texture strength [1]. Picard and Liu, extending the work described in [24] and [25], proposed an indexing scheme based on word decomposition of the luminance field [44, 61] in terms of periodicity, directionality and randomness. Wavelet transform representations, also described in Section 10.4, have proved to be effective for texture annotation [45].

Shape features may provide the highest level of abstraction in describing image content, but they cannot always be used because they generally require that regions of interest in the images be segmented *a priori*, and as we have observed in Section 10.2, 'good' unsupervised segmentations are not always possible. Various approaches have been proposed in the literature for shape-based image retrieval. According to Del Bimbo [19], these can be distinguished by whether they employ feature-based representations (both boundary based and region based) or follow shape transformation techniques. Depending on the application, some shape representations must be invariant to translation, rotation and scaling, while others need not. Jain and Vailayata [36] defined a very simple and effective shape matching technique based on histograms of the direction of significant edges; this technique is invariant to translation and can also be made invariant for scaling and rotation. Mehtre *et al.* [52] and Scasselati *et al.* [68] reviewed and reported experimental comparisons of different methods of image retrieval based on shape similarity.

Although several general-purpose systems have been developed in recent years, the integrated management of the various image features remains complex and application dependent [57, 60]. Several factors may intervene when choosing the aggregation operator to integrate the results of a query based on many features [8]: different tasks in the same context deal with similarity at different levels of precision; similarity depends greatly on the nature of the objects to which it is applied, and on the features selected for their description; different users from different backgrounds may interpret image content differently, and the objectives of their queries may also differ. All these factors, which are interrelated, make it quite impossible to determine in advance the most suitable aggregation operator for the different similarity measures, e.g. [51]. This places on users the burden of formulating their information needs, which may be rather difficult to express as a weighted combination of the features actually employed for retrieval [65].

It is obvious that user feedback is a key element in the successful retrieval of multimedia information. The potential of relevance feedback in textual information retrieval has been widely studied. In image retrieval, it has been employed by Minka and Picard [53] and by Cox *et al.* [16] for target search, and by Rui *et al.* [66] and La Cascia *et al.* [40, 67] for similarity retrieval. Ciocca and Schettini [14] designed an algorithm which, through statistical analysis of the image feature distributions of retrieved images the user has judged relevant or not relevant, identifies the features the user has taken into account. It then modifies accordingly the contribution of different features to the overall evaluation of image similarity (Figures 10.10 to 10.14).

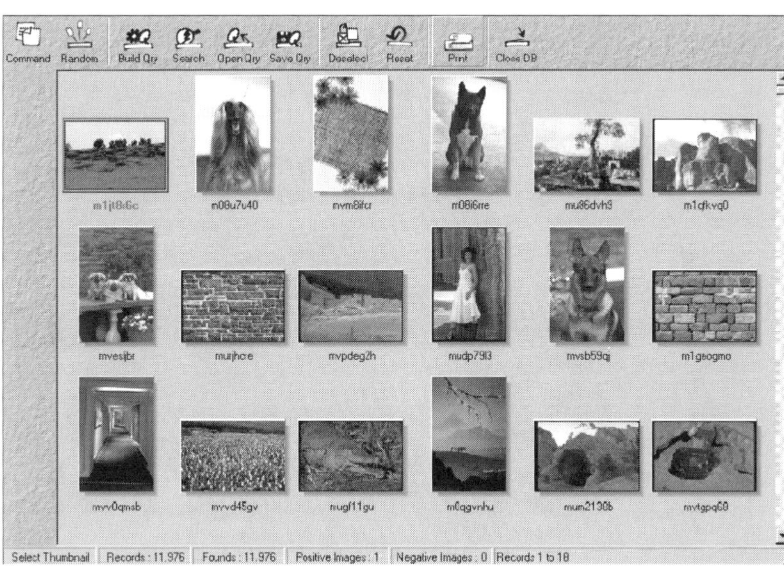

Figure 10.10 Retrieval results using the first three moments of each colour channel on a photo database of about 12 000 images.

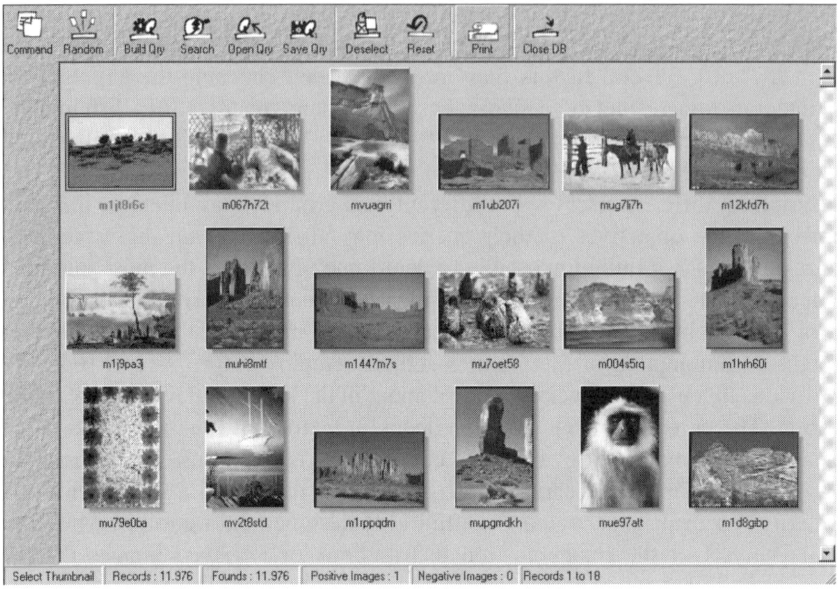

Figure 10.11 Retrieval results using histogram intersection (64 colours) on a photo database of about 12 000 images.

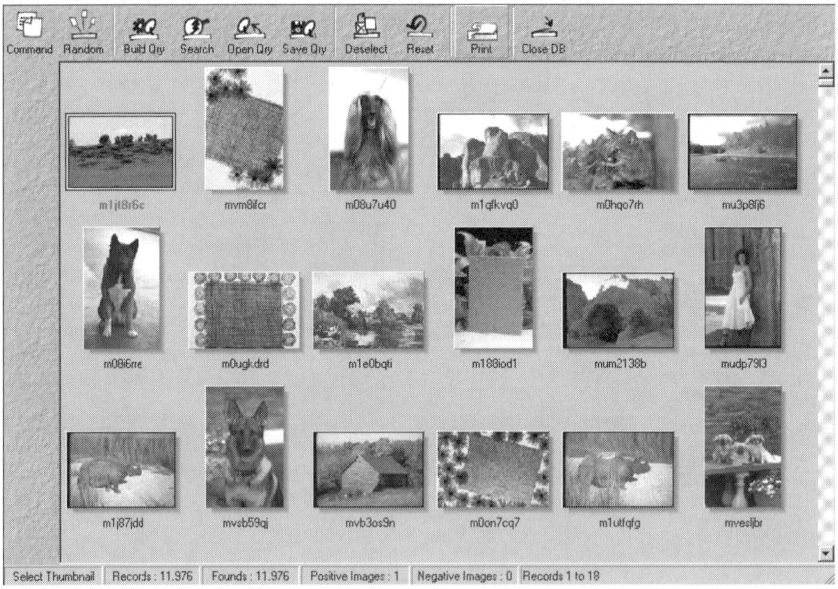

Figure 10.12 Retrieval results using colour coherence vectors (64 colours) on a photo database of about 12 000 images.

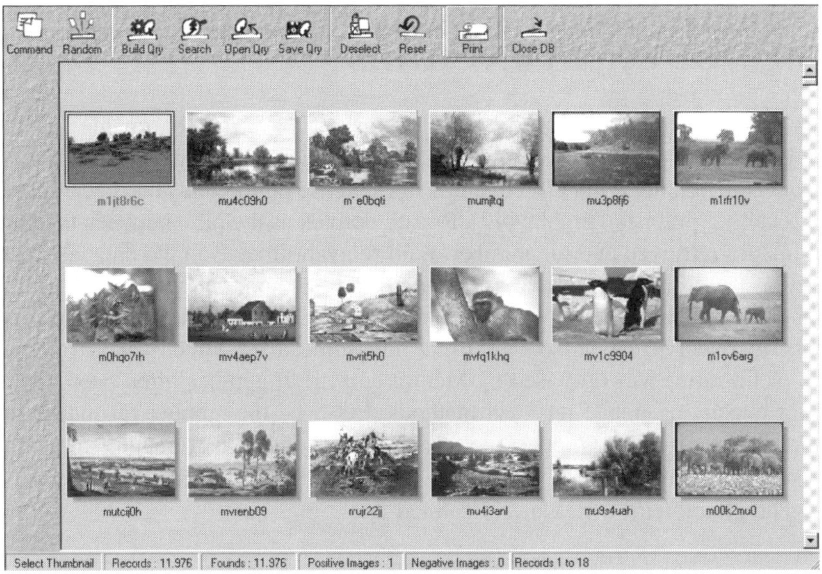

Figure 10.13 Retrieval results using multiple features search on a photo database of about 12 000 images.

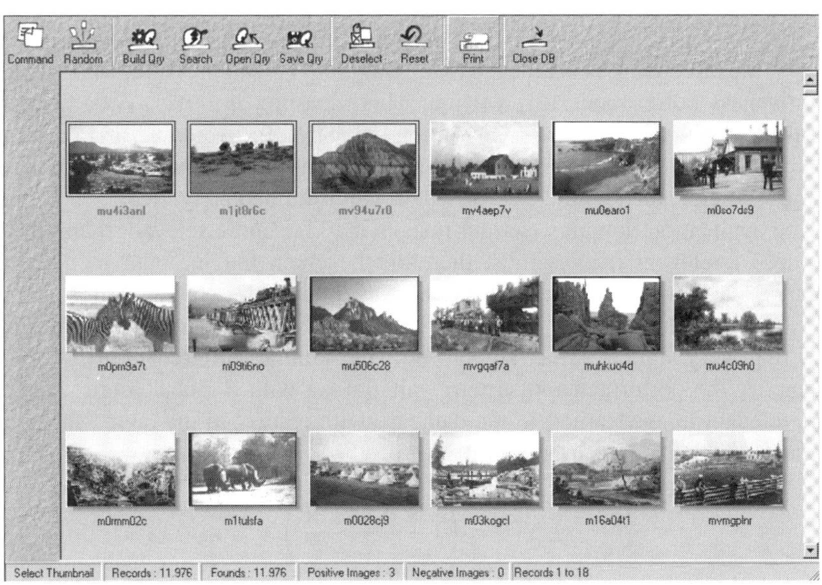

Figure 10.14 Retrieval results using multiple features search on a photo database of about 12 000 images.

10.8 PERFORMANCE EVALUATION OF IMAGE RETRIEVAL STRATEGIES

Although a host of measures can be used for evaluating retrieval strategies, in the great majority of papers, when there was more than one relevant image in the database with respect to a generic query, the effectiveness of the retrieval methods has been quantified in terms of recall vs. precision graphs [42]. Recall, defined as the ratio between the number of relevant images retrieved and the number of all relevant images in the database, quantifies the ability of the system to retrieve useful images. Precision, defined as the ratio between the number of relevant images retrieved and the number of retrieved images, measures the ability to reject irrelevant ones [56]. A measure called effectiveness (efficiency of retrieval, or fill ratio) was proposed by Mehtre *et al.* [50] and has often been applied [51, 52, 29] for evaluating image retrieval methods. Let S be the number of images retrieved in the shortlist when posing a query; let $R_{\mathrm{q}}^{\mathrm{I}}$ be the set of relevant images in the database; and let $R_{\mathrm{q}}^{\mathrm{E}}$ be the set of images retrieved in the shortlist (considered 'relevant' by the system). The effectiveness measure is defined as

$$\eta_{\mathrm{S}} = \begin{cases} \dfrac{|R_{\mathrm{q}}^{\mathrm{I}} \cap R_{\mathrm{q}}^{\mathrm{E}}|}{|R_{\mathrm{q}}^{\mathrm{I}}|} & \text{if } |R_{\mathrm{q}}^{\mathrm{I}}| \leqslant S \\[2ex] \dfrac{|R_{\mathrm{q}}^{\mathrm{I}} \cap R_{\mathrm{q}}^{\mathrm{E}}|}{|R_{\mathrm{q}}^{\mathrm{E}}|} & \text{if } |R_{\mathrm{q}}^{\mathrm{I}}| > S \end{cases} \tag{10.31}$$

If $|R_{\mathrm{q}}^{\mathrm{I}}| \leqslant S$, the effectiveness is reduced to the traditional recall measure, while if $|R_{\mathrm{q}}^{\mathrm{I}}| > S$, the effectiveness corresponds to precision. This measure, however, does not take into account the number of relevant images in the database. To overcome this drawback, the authors evaluate the effectiveness for different lengths of the shortlist S, producing an effectiveness vector, the significance of which is not immediately clear.

In some application domains, certain images may be 'more relevant than others', and the ranking of relevant images must therefore be taken into account in the design of performance metrics [29]. As even experts may find it difficult and tiresome to rank images exactly on the basis of similarity, a few equivalent classes of similarity can be provided (e.g. very similar, rather similar, not very similar, different) [29].

To quantify the performance of a retrieval strategy with a global score when there is only one relevant image (target) in the database with respect to the query, the success of target search (STS) index can be used:

$$\mathrm{STS} = \left(1 - \frac{\mathrm{rank} - 1}{N - 1}\right) \tag{10.32}$$

where *rank* is the retrieval position of the target image and ranges from 1 to N, the number of images in the database.

Since image retrieval is often an interactive process, other performance measures can be applied [42, 56], which may include the average number of processing stages required to achieve satisfactory results, computational complexity and other domain-specific indices [19].

10.9 CONCLUSIONS

Colour has been widely used for content-based image and video retrieval. Since the introduction of colour distributions as descriptors of image content, various research projects have addressed the problems of colour spaces, illumination invariance, colour quantisation and similarity functions. Many different methods have been developed to enhance the limited descriptive capacity of colour distributions. We have presented here the state of the art of colour-based methods that can be used to index and retrieve colour images.

The most surprising element that emerges from our study of colour indexing and retrieval is that most of the methods analysed do not address the problem of how to deal with colour in a device-independent way. Very seldom are details given, or references made to image acquisition and management in terms of standard colour coordinates, although it is reasonable to assume that the image database contains images acquired from many sources, and subjected to a number of processing steps before indexing and display. Quantisation and segmentation reduce acquisition noise, and may to some extent cope with changes in imaging conditions, but a more rigorous approach to colour imaging is surely desirable.

Several of the algorithms proposed have been designed to implement machine colour constancy, but their application in real-world conditions is still under investigation. Indeed the definition of machine colour constancy is still a matter for future research, rather than an effective tool that can be employed in current content-based image retrieval engines.

Most colour-based retrieval algorithms make it possible to perform searches for the presence of specific colours, but not, with very few exceptions [2], for their absence. Consequently, it would be desirable to modify retrieval methods so that users can specify which colours should be excluded from an image retrieval query.

The definition of feature similarity also plays a fundamental role in content-based retrieval, because images with ‘similar’ feature distributions are often considered to be similar in appearance without requiring any semantic expression of this.

Most of the methods described here have been tested on different databases, of very different sizes, ranging from 50 to 200 000 images, for different retrieval tasks. This makes it extremely difficult, if not impossible, to provide an absolute ranking of the effectiveness of the algorithms. We can make the general observation that colour alone cannot suffice to index large, heterogeneous image databases. The combination of colour with other visual features is a necessary approach that merits further study. Much more dubious are methods that assume that affordable, unsupervised image segmentation is always possible, and that the evaluation of image similarity can be dealt with as a graph matching problem, with a reasonable computational burden. The design of any content-based retrieval system for a large image database must address issues of efficiency in addition to those of effectiveness.

A promising direction for future research is, in our opinion, the exploitation of colour image similarity for image database navigation and visualisation [64] and the retrieval of colour images based on psychological effects [19]. We would also like to see a new generation of systems that support querying by similar emotions (e.g. melancholy, joy), and open-ended searches in the image database where similar images are located contiguously.

REFERENCES

1. Amadasun M. and R. King (1989) Textural features corresponding to textural properties. *IEEE Trans. on Systems, Man and Cybernetics*, **19**(5), 1264–1274.
2. Androutsos (1999) A novel vector-based approach to colour image retrieval using vector angular-based distance measure. *Computer Vision and Image Understanding,* **1/2**, 46–58.
3. Barolo B., I. Gagliardi and R. Schettini (1997) An effective strategy for querying image databases by colour distribution. *Computer and the History of Art Journal*, **7**(1), 3–14.
4. Berens J., G. D. Finlayson and G. Qiu (1999) Image indexing using compressed histograms. *Proc. on the Challenge of Image Retrieval.*
5. Berens J. and G. Finlayson (2000) Log-opponent chromaticity coding of colour space. *Proc. International Conference on Pattern Recognition*, Barcelona.
6. Berman A. P. and L. G. Shapiro (1999) A flexible image database system for content-based retrieval. *Computer Vision and Image Understanding*. **75**, 175–195.
7. Berretti S., A. Del Bimbo and E. Vicario (2000) Modeling spatial relationships between colour sets. *Proc. IEEE Workshop on Content Based Access to Image and Video Libraries CBAIVL'00*, June.
8. Binaghi E., I. Gagliardi and R. Schettini (1994) Image retrieval using fuzzy evaluation of colour similarity. *International Journal of Pattern Recognition and Artificial Intelligence*, **8**, 945–968.
9. Birney K. A. and T. R. Fischer (1995) On the modelling of DCT and subband image data for compression. *IEEE Trans. Image Processing*, **4**(2), 186–193.
10. Borsotti M., P. Campadelli and R. Schettini (1998) Quantitative evaluation of colour image segmentation results. *Pattern Recognition Letters,* **19**, 741–747.
11. Brambilla C., A. Della Ventura, I. Gagliardi and R. Schettini (1999) Multiresolution wavelet transform and supervised learning for content based image retrieval. *IEEE Multimedia Systems 99* Vol. I, pp.183–188, IEEE Computer Society.
12. Cinque L., S. Levialdi and A. Pellicano (1999) Colour-based image retrieval using spatial-chromatic histograms, *IEEE Multimedia Systems 99*, Vol. II, pp. 969–973, IEEE Computer Society.
13. Ciocca G., D. Marini, A. Rizzi, R. Schettini and S. Zuffi (2001) On pre-filtering with Retinex in colour image retrieval. In *Proc. Second Internet Imaging Conference*, G. Beretta and R. Schettini (eds).
14. Ciocca G. and R. Schettini (1999) A relevance feedback mechanism for content-based image retrieval. *Information Processing and Management*, **35**, 605–632.
15. Colombo C. and A. Del Bimbo (1999) Colour-induced representation and retrieval. *Pattern Recognition*, **32**, 1685–1695.
16. Cox I. J., M. L. Miller, S. O. Omohundro and P. N. Yianilos (1996) PicHunter: Bayesian relevance feedback for image retrieval. *Proc. ICPR'96*, pp. 361–369.
17. Del Bimbo A. and E. Vicario (1998) Using weighted spatial relationships in retrieval by visual contents. *Proc. Workshop on Image and Video Content-Based Retrieval*, Italian Chapter of the IAPR, Milan, February 1998.
18. Del Bimbo A., M. Mugnai, P. Pala and F. Turco (1998) Visual querying by colour perceptive regions. *Pattern Recognition*, **31**, 1241–1253.
19. Del Bimbo A. (1999) *Visual Information Retrieval*, Morgan Kaufmann, San Francisco.
20. Du Buf J. M. H., M. Kardan and M. Spann (1990) Texture feature performance for image segmentation. Pattern Recognition, **23**, 291–309.

21. Equitz W. and W. Niblack (1994) Retrieving images from a database: using texture algorithms from the QBIC system. IBM Research Division, Research Report 9805.
22. Finlayson G. D., S. S. Chatterjee and B. V. Funt (1998) Colour angular indexing and image retrieval. In *Image Description and Retrieval*, E. Vicario (ed.). Plenum, New York.
23. Finlayson G. D., B. Schiele and J. L. Crowley (1998) Comprehensive colour image normalisation *Proc. 5th European Conference on Computer Vision.*
24. Francos J. M., A. Z. Meiri and B. Porat (1993) A unified texture model based on a 2-D Word like decomposition. *IEEE Trans. on Signal Processing*, **41**, 2665–2678.
25. Francos J. M., A. Z. Meiri and B. Porat (1991) Modeling of the texture structural components using 2-D deterministic random field visual communication and image processing. *Proc. SPIE*, **1666**, 554–565.
26. Funt B., K. Barnard and L. Martin (1998) Is machine colour constancy good enough? *Proc. 5th European Conference on Computer Vision.*
27. Funt B., F. Ciurea and J. McCann (2000) Retinex in Matlab. *Proc. IS&T/SID Eighth Colour Imaging Conference*, Scottsdale, Arizona, pp. 112–121, November 2000.
28. Funt B. V. and G. D. Finlayson (1995) Colour constant colour indexing. *IEEE Trans. on Pattern Analysis and Machine Intelligence*, **17**, 522–529.
29. Gagliardi I. and R. Schettini (1997) A method for the automatic indexing of colour images for effective image retrieval. *New Review of Hypermedia and Multimedia*, **3**, 201–224.
30. Gevers T. and A. W. M. Smeulders (1996) A comparative study of several colour models for colour image invariant retrieval. *Proc. IDB-MMS'96.*
31. Gevers T. and A. W. M. Smeulders Colour based object recognition. *Pattern Recognition*, **32**, 453–464.
32. Gong Y., C. H. Chuan and G. Xiaoyi Image indexing and retrieval using colour histograms. *Multimedia Tools and Applications*, **2**, 133–156.
33. Hafner J., H. S. Sawhney, W. Esquitz, M. Flickner and W. Niblack (1995) Efficient colour histogram indexing for quadratic form distance functions. *IEEE Trans. on Pattern Analysis and Machine Intelligence*, **17**, 729–736.
34. Haralick R. H. and L. G. Shapiro (1985) Image segmentation techniques. *Computer Vision, Graphics, and Image Processing*, **29**, 100–132.
35. Jacob C., A. Frinkelstein and D. Salesin (1995) Fast multiresolution image query. Technical Report 95-01-06, University of Washington.
36. Jain A. K. and A. Vailaya (1998) Shape-based retrieval: a case study with trademarks databases. *Pattern Recognition,* **31**, 1369–1390.
37. Jaynes E. T. (1982) On the rationale of maximum-entropy methods. *Proc. IEEE*, **70**, 939–952.
38. Kankanhalli M. S., B. M. Methre and J. K. Wu (1996) Cluster-based colour matching for image retrieval. *Pattern Recognition*, **29**, 701–708.
39. Kankanhalli M. S., B. M. Mehtre and H. Y. Huang (1999) Colour and spatial feature for content-based image retrieval *Pattern Recognition Letters*, **20**, 109–118.
40. La Cascia M., S. Sethi and S. Sclaroff (1998) Combining textual and visual cues for content-based image retrieval on the World Wide Web. *Proc. IEEE Workshop on Content-Based Access of Image and Video Libraries*, June.
41. Land E. and J. McCann (1971) Lightness and retinex theory. *J. Opt. Soc. Am.*, **61**, 1–11.
42. Leung C. H. C. and H. H. S. Ip (2000) Benchmarking for content-based visual information search. *Advance in Visual Information Systems*, R. Laurini (ed.), pp. 442–456. Springer, Berlin.
43. Liu J. and Y.-H. Yang (1994) Multiresolution colour image segmentation. *IEEE Trans. on Pattern Analysis and Machine Intelligence*, **16**(7), 689–700.
44. Liu F. and R. W. Picard (1994) Periodicity, directionality and randomness: wold features for perceptual pattern recognition. MIT Vision and Modeling Lab, Technical Report 320.
45. Ma W. Y. and B. S. Manjunath (1995) A comparison of wavelet transform features for texture image annotation. *Proc. IEEE International Conference on Image Processing.*
46. Mandal M. K., T. Aboulnasr and S. Panchanathan (1996) Image indexing using moments and wavelets. *IEEE Trans. on Consumer Electron.*, **42**(3), 557–565.

47. Mandal M. K., T. Aboulnasr and S. Panchanathan (1998) Illuminant invariant image indexing using moments and wavelets. *Journal of Electronic Imaging*, **7**(2), 282–293.
48. Marini D., A. Rizzi and L. De Carli (2000) Multiresolution retinex: comparison of algorithms. *Proc. First International Conference on Colour in Graphics and Image Processing CGIP'2000*, Saint-Etienne, France, October.
49. McGill M. J. and Salton G. (1983) *Introduction to Modern Information Retrieval*. McGraw-Hill, New York.
50. Mehtre B. M., M. S. Kankanhalli, A. Desai Narasimhalu and G. C. Man (1995) Colour matching for image retrieval. *Pattern Recognition Letters*, **16**, 325–331.
51. Mehtre B. M., M. S. Kankanhalli and W. F. Lee (1998) Content-based image retrieval using a composite colour-shape approach. *Information Processing and Management*, **34**(1), 109–120.
52. Mehtre B. M., M. S. Kankanhalli and W. F. Lee (1997) Shape measures for content based image retrieval: a comparison. *Information Processing and Management*, **33**, 319–337.
53. Minka T. and R. W. Picard (1997) Interactive learning with a 'Society of Models'. *Pattern Recognition*, **30**(4), 565–581.
54. Miyahra M. and Y. Yoshida (1988) Mathematical transform of (RGB) colour data to Munsell (HVC) colour data. *Proc. SPIE Visual Communications and Image Processing*, **1001**, 650–657.
55. Mitra M., J. Huang and S. R. Kumar (1997) Combining supervised learning with colour correlograms for content-based image retrieval. *Proc. Fifth ACM Multimedia Conference*.
56. Desai Narasimhalu A. and M. S. Kankanhalli (1997) Benchmarking multimedia databases. *Multimedia Tools and Applications*, **4**, 333–356.
57. Nastar C., M. Mitschke, C. Meilhac and N. Boujemaa (1998) Surfimage: a flexible content-based image retrieval system. *Proc. ACM-Multimedia*, Bristol, September.
58. Park I. K., I. D. Yun and S. U. Lee (1999) Colour image retrieval using hybrid graph representation. *Image and Vision Computing*, **17**, 465–474.
59. Pass G., R. Zabih and J. Miller (1996) Comparing images using colour coherence vectors. *Proc. Fourth ACM Multimedia Conference*.
60. Pentland A., R. Picard and S. Sclaroff (1996) Photobook: tools for content-based manipulation of image databases. *International Journal of Computer Vision*, **18**(3), 233–254.
61. Picard R. W. and T. P. Minka (1995) Vision texture for annotation. *Multimedia Systems*, **3**, 3–14.
62. Rao A. R. and G. L. Lohse (1993) Identifying high level features of texture perception CVGIP. *Graphical Models and Image Processing,* **55**(3), 218–233.
63. Rao A. R. and G. L. Lohse (1993) Towards a texture naming system: identifying relevant dimensions of texture. IBM Research Division, Research Report 19 140.
64. Rubner Y., C. Tomasi and L. J. Guibas. (1998) A metric for distributions with applications to image databases. *Proc. IEEE ICPR*.
65. Rui Y. and T. S. Huang (1999) Image retrieval: current technologies, promising directions and open issues, *Journal of Visual Communication and Image Representation*, **10**, 39–62.
66. Rui Y., T. S. Huang, M. Ortega and S. Mehrotra (1998) Relevance feedback: a power tool in interactive content-based retrieval. *IEEE Trans. on Circuits and Systems for Video Technologies*, **8**(5), 644–655.
67. Sclaroff S., L. Taycher and M. La Cascia (1997) Image-Rover: a content-based image browser for the World Wide Web. *Proc. IEEE Workshop on Content-Based Access Image and Video Libraries*.
68. Scasselati B., S. Alexopoulos and M. Flickner (1994) Retrieving images 2D shape: a comparison of computational methods with human perceptual judgments. *Proc. SPIE Conf. on Storage and Retrieval for Images and Videos*.
69. Smith J. R. and S-F Chang (1995) Single colour extraction and image query. *Proc. ICIP*.
70. Syeda-Mahmood T. F. (1992) Data and model-driven selection using colour regions. MIT AI memo 1270.
71. Stricker M. A. (1992) Colour and geometry as cues for indexing. Technical Report CS92-22.
72. Stricker M. and M. Orengo (1995) Similarity of colour images. *Proc. Storage and Retrieval for Image and Video Databases*, Vol. III, pp. 381–392.

73. Stricker M. and A. Dimai (1996) Colour indexing with weak spatial constraints. *Proc. Storage and Retrieval for Image and Video Databases*, Vol. IV.
74. Stricker M. and A. Dimai (1997) Spectral covariance and fuzzy regions for image indexing. *Machine Vision and Applications*, **10**, 66–73.
75. Swain M. J. and D. H. Ballard (1991) Colour indexing, *Int. J. Computer Vision*, **7**, 11–32.
76. Tamura H., S. Mori and T. Yamawaky (1972) Textural features corresponding to visual perception. *IEEE Trans. on Systems, Man and Cybernetics*, **8**(6), 460–473.
77. Tuceryan M. and A. K. Jain (1994) *Texture Analysis Handbook of Pattern Recognition and Computer Vision*, C. H. Chen, L. F. Pau and P. S. P. Wang (eds), pp. 236–276.
78. Uchiyama T. and M. A. Arbib (1994) Colour image segmentation using competitive learning. *IEEE Transaction on Pattern Analysis and Machine Intelligence*, **16**, 1197–1206.
79. Vailaya A., A. Jain and H. J. Zhang (1998) On image classification: City images vs. landscapes. *Pattern Recognition*, **31**, 1921–1935.

11

A spatial colour gamut calculation to optimise colour appearance

John McCann

11.1 INTRODUCTION

The retinex model for estimating apparent lightness was proposed by Land and McCann in 1967 [1]. It was applied to colour constancy by McCann, McKee and Taylor in 1976 [2]. In the early 1980s Frankle and McCann [3] extended the ratio, product, reset, average, operation to highly efficient multiresolution image processing. Recently, retinex has been extended for use in calculating the closest colour appearance in situations in which the reproduction is made with media having a smaller colour gamut than the original [4].

This chapter describes the experiments that led up to the new gamut retinex calculation and discusses the results of a sample calculation. The central theme here is that the underlying mechanisms that control colour constancy can be used to advantage to make images in a small colour gamut resemble images in a large colour gamut. These colour constancy mechanisms are spatial comparisons between pixels. They show almost no dependence on the L, M, S triplet of radiance at a pixel. It suggests that colour gamut transformations calculated one pixel at a time produce poor colour reproductions, while those done using spatial comparisons can give better results.

Colour Image Science, edited by L.W. MacDonald and M.R. Luo.

Gamut mapping transformations are an essential part of trying to make images in print look like images on monitors despite large differences in the colour gamuts of the display and the print media. Morovic and Luo [5] have reviewed the extensive literature and described three generations of gamut mapping algorithms (GMA). Some of these GMAs are very complex. CARISMA applies different methods of empirical correction for each hue depending on the shapes of the two gamuts. The CIE Technical Committee 8–03 is working on guidelines for the evaluation of gamut mapping algorithms working to establish comparison techniques by unbiased observers [6]. It is beyond the scope of this chapter to provide blind comparisons of relative performance of spatial versus the many different pixel-based procedures. Further experimentation is required to establish the relative merits of the techniques in a complete image transformation system (spatial GMA). This chapter is limited to describing the ideas supporting spatial mechanisms for gamut mapping.

11.2 COLOUR GAMUT CALCULATIONS USING A TWO-AREA MONDRIAN

We can begin this discussion of colour gamut calculation with an analysis of calculation strategies. Figure 11.1 illustrates different choices of strategies used in calculating the

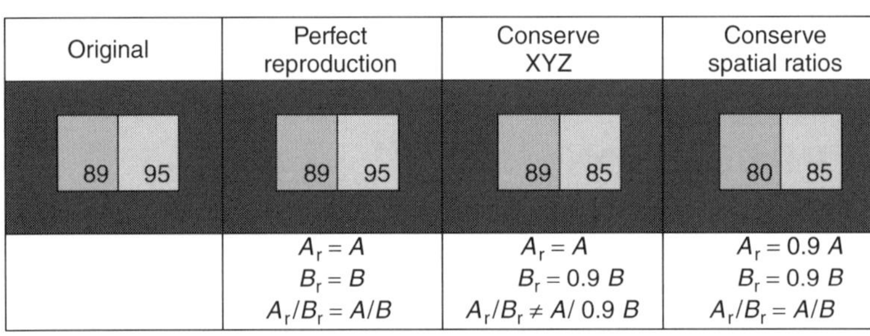

Figure 11.1 Different approaches to making reproductions. All four panels represent the middle-wave, or green, light coming to the eye from complete colour images. The first panel illustrates the original image with two areas having radiances A and B. The second panel illustrates a reproduction with the same colour gamut as the original. Here the two reproduction radiances, A_r and B_r equal those of the original. Conservation of X, Y, Z and conservation of spatial ratios are both successful. The third panel illustrates the approach of colorimetry. Here each area is treated separately The reproduction of the grey area, on the left, has the same radiance as the original ($A_r = A$). However, the gamut limit found in this example restricts B_r to 90% of B. The chroma of the blue area is limited by the unwanted absorptions of the cyan and magenta dyes. By selecting the best fit for the right area and the left area independently, we alter the ratio A_r/B_r compared to A/B. Now the reproduction reports that the left area is lighter than the right. The fourth panel illustrates the conservation of spatial ratios. Here the limit of 90% on area B is also applied to area A. The effect of keeping ratios constant is that we have made both areas darker. Despite this change in radiance, the relationship between areas A and B is the same. The thesis of this chapter is that conserving ratios makes a better reproduction than conserving X, Y, Z.

best colour compromise for a limited gamut reproduction [7]. For simplicity we will study only the combined green record seen by the observer. In other words, we will study the colour image as a colour densitometer would, isolating only the middle-wave, or green light from the combined, final colour image. (The same arguments apply to both the long- and short-wave records.) In principle the green record is controlled by only the magenta dye. In fact, the green record as seen by observers is controlled by the optical density of the magenta dye and the unwanted optical densities contributed by the yellow and cyan dyes. Monitors, using additive colour, have larger gamuts near white because there are no unwanted absorptions. The colour gamut of subtractive dye sets is controlled by the amount of unwanted absorptions. Dye sets with larger magenta gamuts have less absorption in the green by the yellow and cyan dyes. In this scheme, green radiance = 100 is the absence of any dye (reflecting all the green light), while green radiance = 0 is maximum dye (reflecting a minimum of green light). The first panel shows the original with radiance $A = 89$ from a light grey patch (left area) and radiance $B = 95$ from a bright blue patch (right area).

The second panel shows the case in which the colour gamut of the reproduction is as large as the original. In this fairly rare case, the reproduction radiances $A_r = A$ and $B_r = B$. That also means that $A_r/B_r = A/B$.

The third panel illustrates usual colour gamut transformations. Here the dye sets are such that reproduction radiance $A_r = 89 = A$ is in gamut. However, reproduction radiance $B_r = 85$ is the best possible in-gamut value compared to the original radiance, $B = 95$. This commonly occurs if A is close to white and B is a saturated colour with unwanted absorptions from the other dyes. In this example we substitute the closest value, namely 85. This approach conserves the colorimetric values X, Y, Z for area A. It leaves all in-gamut pixels unchanged, thus minimising the cumulative colour distance between original and reproduction for all areas. This choice has a highly adverse effect on the ratios. The original ratio is $A/B = 89/95 = 0.94$. The reproduction ratio has the value $A_r/B_r = 89/85 = 1.06$. The reproduction now reports that area A is lighter than area B, while the original reported that area B is lighter than area A. Such reproductions with distorted edge ratios make poor reproductions.

The fourth panel illustrates the principle of conserving spatial ratios. Here we have the same limitations on gamut. However, the limited gamut of $B = 85$ causes a shift of A to 80, so as to conserve spatial ratios. Here $A_r/B_r = A/B$ is the controlling principle. This mechanism requires an adjustment for the reproduced area A from 89 to 80 even though the 89 is in gamut. This strategy increases the cumulative colorimetric error distance for all areas between the original and the reproduction, yet preserves the information that $B > A$.

Although Figure 11.1 is a good illustration of the strategies, it may not convince the reader that one approach is better than the other. For that we need to study complex images.

11.3 SEARCH FOR A COLOUR METRIC

There are two histories of colour, one based on art and psychology of images and the other based on the physics of a pixel [8]. Leonardo, Goethe, von Guerica, Rumford, Helmholtz,

Chevreul and the Gestalt school all pointed out the role of the image. In the second half of the twentieth century, Campbell and Robson's paper on the visibility of sine wave gratings led to the entire field of spatial vision [9]. In a review paper, Braddick, Campbell and Atkinson [10] describe the wide range of experiments using gratings as visual stimuli. These experiments demonstrate the dependence of visual response on spatial properties of the stimulus. The paper begins with a description of receptive fields and channels, continues with periodic stimuli, and human responses to spatial frequency, orientation and temporal stimuli. This great wealth of data led to numerous spatial models [11, 12].

The "physics of a pixel" story of colour was established by Newton, Young and Maxwell. They described the eye's response at a point of light on the retina. During the twentieth century international standards were adopted for Maxwell's colour matching functions [8, 13]. Today, as a practical matter, colour differences are almost always described by ΔE^* in $L^*a^*b^*$ colour space. This space, defined by the 1976 CIE report [14], is calculated using the tristimulus values X, Y, Z, defined in the 1931 CIE report [15]. Further, a complex image is often evaluated by averaging the individual ΔE^* values to calculate a colour metric for the colour difference between two images.

Colorimetry provides easy-to-use equations for wavelength matches, derived from the properties of the retinal light receptors. However, these equations do not predict appearance representing the sensation image after spatial interactions in the human visual system [16]. Physical models of the image at the retina do not predict appearance in the brain's visual cortex. The question we are asking is whether the commonly used average ΔE^* metric is appropriate for predicting the quality of image reproductions or for evaluating the quality of gamut mapping. In other words, can colour differences between copy and reproduction be used to quantify the quality of the reproduction?

Although researchers are usually concerned with appearance matches across media, such as display to print, these experiments were restricted to single media to eliminate properties of materials and calibration variables. These experiments on identical media were aimed at observer preference of colour metric without confounding media issues. Initially, all experiments were performed on computer displays. Later, these experiments were repeated using print materials with the same results.

11.3.1 Select the better reproduction

The following series of demonstrations creates triplets of targets: Original, Copy A and Copy B (Figure 11.2) [16]. The colours in Copy A were selected to be significantly different from those in Original. Each area in Copy A is 10 units lighter, 10 units less red and 10 units yellower in $L^*a^*b^*$ space. The combined distance is $\Delta E^* = 17$. For each area the colour difference was $\Delta E^* = 17$ between Original and Copy A. Copy B was made with each area $\Delta E^* = 17$ compared to Original, but it was designed to have the colour shifts go in many different directions. Copy B significantly changed the local relationships, while Copy A preserved them.

The original demonstration was created on a computer CRT. Subsequently that the image was printed on a Fujix printer. Table 11.1 lists the measured $L^*a^*b^*$ values of the printed Original, Copy A and Copy B.

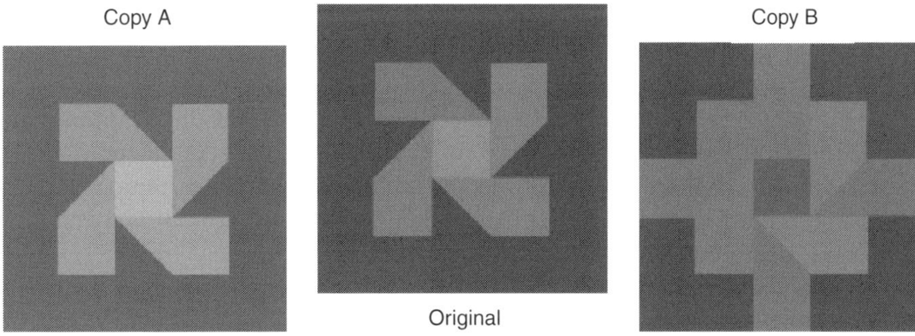

Figure 11.2 Copy A was made so that each area in Copy A was lighter ($\Delta L^* = +10$) and less red ($\Delta a^* = -10$) and yellower ($\Delta b^* = +10$) than Original. The first important observation is that Copy A is a fairly good reproduction, considering that it has $\Delta E^* = 17$ for each area. Copy B was made so that $\Delta E^* = 17$ changes were made in many different directions. In this case the ΔE^* were chosen to change the appearance of the display. The outer corner patches moved closer in colour to each other. The other, mid-side patches moved closer in colour to the inner areas. The net effect is that Copy B does not look at all like Original. It looks like a different display. Nevertheless, if judged by the ΔE^* colour metric, Copy B is exactly as good a reproduction as Copy A. See also Colour Plate 6.

Table 11.1 Measured L^*, a^*, b^* values for Original, Copy A and Copy B

Area	Original			Copy A				Copy B			
	L^*	a^*	b^*	L^*	a^*	b^*	ΔE^*	L^*	a^*	b^*	ΔE^*
1	54.4	0.6	−8.1	65.0	−7.3	−0.8	15.0	38.5	−1.1	−6.5	16.1
2	43.8	57.2	26.5	56.9	44.5	36.0	20.5	48.6	43.2	44.3	23.2
3	43.0	−31.5	48.4	50.6	−35.0	58.8	13.3	37.4	−49.1	33.1	24.0
4	35.4	−36.4	−23.7	54.1	−22.8	−14.2	25.0	43.9	−20.8	−22.4	17.8
5	42.5	41.6	−39.8	55.2	33.2	−34.6	16.1	44.0	23.2	−43.4	18.8
6	23.3	−25.0	1.5	29.3	−36.7	−8.7	16.6	42.6	−28.4	−0.9	19.8
7	23.9	−19.8	−12.9	33.0	−28.4	−8.4	13.4	24.8	−21.7	−22.0	9.3
8	24.4	−5.6	−24.6	35.2	−14.1	−19.4	14.6	24.8	−22.0	−21.6	16.7
9	24.4	13.6	−35.1	37.0	5.8	−29.9	15.7	45.2	12.3	−35.1	20.8
10	27.0	25.1	−29.3	37.8	16.4	−22.1	15.7	27.8	27.6	−16.7	12.9
11	26.1	32.5	−20.9	37.8	24.4	−16.1	15.1	27.2	29.8	−9.8	11.5
12	26.4	29.3	−9.1	37.9	21.4	−1.4	15.9	47.0	28.0	−8.9	20.6
13	25.0	41.3	25.9	36.7	36.4	39.5	18.6	27.6	28.3	25.2	13.3
14	27.0	16.9	26.8	38.1	9.8	41.3	19.6	28.0	29.2	30.9	1.3
15	26.8	−4.4	25.7	36.6	−12.2	39.7	18.8	46.8	−5.2	30.1	20.5
16	24.6	−16.9	19.4	33.4	−25.1	30.4	16.4	28.2	−6.6	29.2	14.7
17	23.3	−26.4	17.6	31.5	−35.5	28.0	16.0	27.2	−14.8	24.4	14.0
						Average	16.8			Average	16.9

Beside the $L^*a^*b^*$ data is the ΔE^* value measuring the colour difference between the copy and the original. The average distance was 16.8 for Copy A and 16.9 for Copy B. The printer measurements had more variability than those from the display, but on average the colour differences were close to the desired value of 17.

If average ΔE^* could be used as colour metric for quality of reproduction, half the observers would select Copy A as the best reproduction and half the observers would select Copy B. If spatial parameters, namely the relationship between different areas within the test target, were important then observers would select Copy A, preserving the spatial relationships. Observers were asked to pick the preferred reproduction.

The experiment consisted of asking people to choose the better reproduction. In a poster session at the Fourth IS&T/SID Colour Imaging Conference, all non-colour-blind observers said A was better than B.

Figure 11.3 plots the shifts in the a^* vs. b^* plane measured from the prints. In the Original vs. Copy A graph (Figure 11.3(a)) the vectors go in the same direction and have similar lengths. In the Original vs. Copy B graph (Figure 11.3(b)) the direction and magnitude of the shifts are different. If we compared plots of L^* vs. a^* and L^* vs. b^*, we would see the same pattern.

Observers selected Copy A, the image in which all areas had the same colour shift, as the better reproduction. Observers chose the image that maintained the ratios across edges. The fact that the displays had constant ΔE^* values was not apparent to the observers. Using this experimental design, we looked at a number of variations. In each case the observer preferred the systematic, constant ratio reproductions. These experiments support the other experiments pointing to the observation that colour appearance is a spatial calculation in humans. Obviously, the spectral sensitivity of the different receptors is very important, but falls far short of explaining the entire colour vision calculation. ΔE^* is a function of quanta catch of retinal receptors, but cannot be used to evaluate colour reproductions evaluated later in the visual system. Minimising ΔE^* searches for best matches independent of spatial information; but humans use spatial information to calculate contrast.

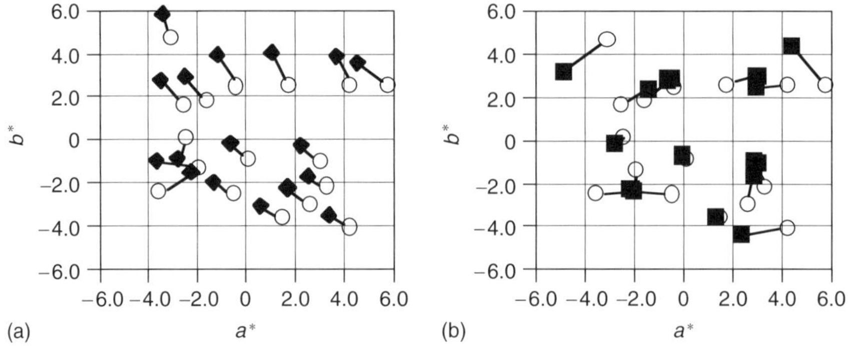

Figure 11.3 (a) Plot of the measured print b^* vs. a^* from Original (open circles) and Copy A (filled diamonds); the solid lines illustrate the shift in the a^*b^* plane caused by Copy A. With two exceptions (introduced by the printer) all the vectors go in the same general direction and have similar lengths. (b) Plot of the measured print b^* vs. a^* for Original (open circles) and Copy B (filled squares); the solid lines illustrate the shift in the a^*b^* plane caused by Copy B. All the vectors go in different directions and have variable length.

11.3.2 Spatial colour metric

Colour image reproduction needs a different kind of colour metric. It has to be based on the fundamental difference between imaging systems and human vision. All chemical and electronic imaging systems operate one pixel at a time. The exposure on a silver halide grain controls the concentration of metallic silver deposited at that pixel. The calories delivered to a thermal ribbon, the number of pulses delivered to the inkjet cavity, electrons delivered to the thin film transistor (TFT) cell of a display control the response of that pixel. The signal sent to other pixels far away from the pixel in question have no effect on it. Human vision at the receptor level behaves the same way. The rod and cone receptors respond to the quanta caught by the chromophores in the cell. This is modelled well by colorimetry. But appearance is the relative response of all the interconnected receptors across the field of view. The metric for colour appearance needs to build on colorimetry and accumulate relationships all across the image.

When printer and display technologies introduce different colour gamuts, the problem becomes more interesting. In fact, most displays have much larger gamuts than prints in high lightness at full saturation. Most printers have larger gamuts than displays in low lightnesses at full saturation. Typically one finds that the common volume of a three-dimensional colour space is half the combined display and printer volumes. A test image that populates all parts of display plus printer colour space will reproduce accurately only half the pixels on a printer or on a display. (See papers by Marcu [17] and Morovic and Luo [5] for specific data.)

An approach to solving the problem is to use the information learned from the comparison of Copy A with Copy B. The human eye cares more about the relationships of the parts of the image than it does about the absolute value of the match. Figure 11.4 shows Original with identification numbers. Area 1 is the grey square in the centre, the numbers are assigned in a clockwise spiral up to area 17 on the top left. The round black circle in the bottom right corner of area 1 represents the input information used in colorimetry to calculate the tristimulus values of area 1. Relative colorimetry compares the information from a single pixel to the ratio of media white to illuminant – information that cannot be derived from the image itself. The media white and the illuminant have to be independently measured.

The double-headed black arrows in Figure 11.4 show the 32 comparisons possible between adjacent areas in the image. This is the information the human eye uses to calculate colour appearance. We can propose a colour metric more like human vision by comparing X from one area with X' of an adjacent area in the same image ($X_{\text{Copy A}}/X'_{\text{Copy A}}$); see Figure 11.5.

We can calculate a corresponding spatial comparison for Original ($X_{\text{Original}}/X'_{\text{Original}}$). We can compare the two with a ratio:

$$\left[\left(X_{\text{Copy A}}/X'_{\text{Copy A}}\right) / \left(X_{\text{Original}}/X'_{\text{Original}}\right)\right]$$

The results calculated in X, Y, and Z for the 32 edges are plotted in Figure 11.6. Here we see that shifting all the colours by the same amount (Copy A, top right) has little effect in altering the 32 ratios across edges. The ratio of ratios is very close to 1.0 for all 32 edges

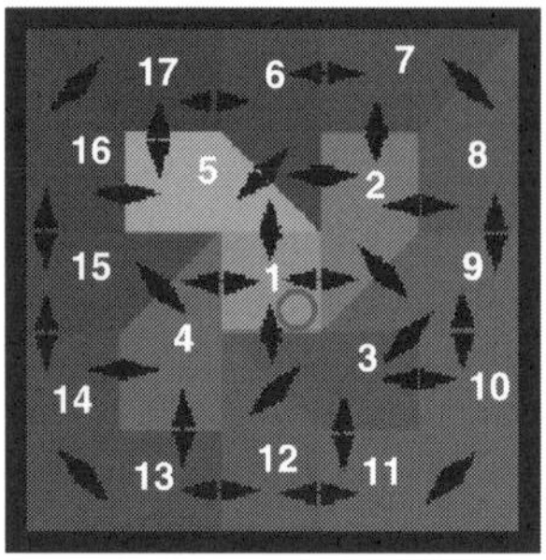

Figure 11.4 The 32 adjacent edges found in Original. The display has 17 different colour patches. The double-headed black arrows indicate edges between different patches in the image. The black circle represents the information in one pixel that is used to calculate tristimulus values of one area. The retinex colour metric for colour appearance compares the tristimulus values across each of these 32 edges to find the best reproduction of the entire image.

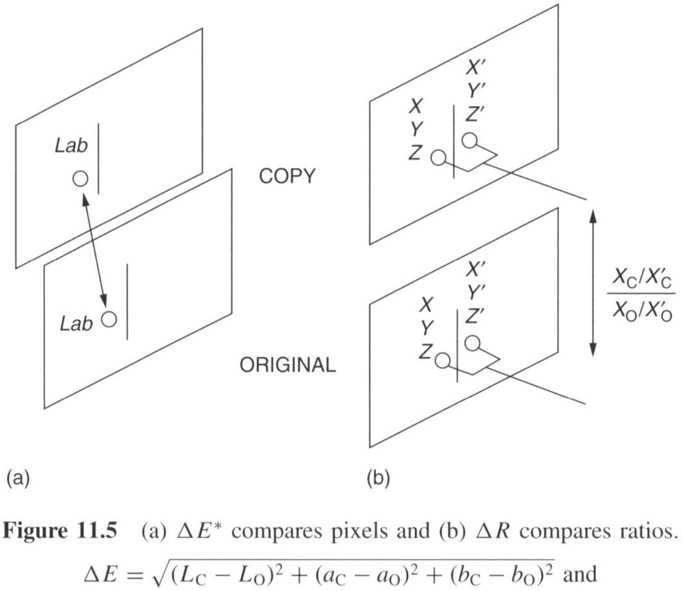

Figure 11.5 (a) ΔE^* compares pixels and (b) ΔR compares ratios.

$$\Delta E = \sqrt{(L_C - L_O)^2 + (a_C - a_O)^2 + (b_C - b_O)^2} \text{ and}$$

$$\Delta R \text{ is given by } \sqrt{\left(1 - \frac{X_C/X'_C}{X_O/X'_O}\right)^2 + \left(1 - \frac{Y_C/Y'_C}{Y_O/Y'_O}\right)^2 + \left(1 - \frac{Z_C/Z'_C}{Z_O/Z'_O}\right)^2}.$$

in X, Y, Z. In fact, the departures from ratios of 1.0 are experimental errors introduced by colour media limitations. Individual shifts that mimic separate pixel-by-pixel colour gamut mapping show significant shifts in the 32 spatial comparisons (Copy B, bottom right).

We use these ratios of ratios to formulate a spatial metric ΔR analogous to ΔE^* for pixels. We can calculate ΔR for each ratio in the image:

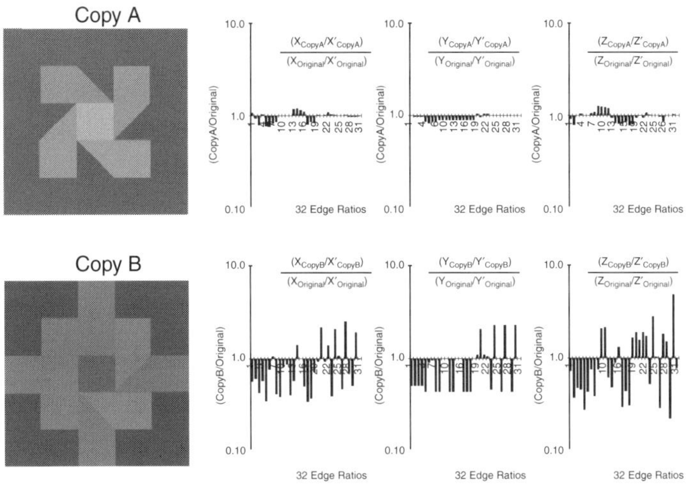

Figure 11.6 Results for the 32 edge ratios. A colour metric imitating human vision compares X of one area with X' of an adjacent area in the same display image ($X_{\mathrm{CopyA}}/X'_{\mathrm{CopyA}}$). The metric compares the corresponding ratio data for Original ($X_{\mathrm{Original}}/X'_{\mathrm{Original}}$). We can compare the two using $(X_{\mathrm{CopyA}}/X'_{\mathrm{CopyA}})/(X_{\mathrm{Original}}/X'_{\mathrm{Original}})$. The results X, Y and Z for the 32 edges are plotted. Results for Copy A (top row) show that all the comparisons of X/X' (left), Y/Y' (centre), Z/Z' (right) fall very close to 1.0. The same analysis of Copy B shows that the area comparisons are very different for Copy B and Original. The spatial metric can discriminate between Copy A and Copy B but colorimetry cannot.

$$\Delta \boldsymbol{R} = \sqrt{\left(1 - \frac{X_{\mathrm{Copy}}/X'_{\mathrm{Copy}}}{X_{\mathrm{Orig}}/X'_{\mathrm{Orig}}}\right)^2 + \left(1 - \frac{Y_{\mathrm{Copy}}/Y'_{\mathrm{Copy}}}{Y_{\mathrm{Orig}}/Y'_{\mathrm{Orig}}}\right)^2 + \left(1 - \frac{Z_{\mathrm{Copy}}/Z'_{\mathrm{Copy}}}{Z_{\mathrm{Orig}}/Z'_{\mathrm{Orig}}}\right)^2} \quad (11.1)$$

We can average ΔR to accumulate a net quantity that describes the entire image. Average ΔR for Copy A is 0.17 ± 0.11 and 1.05 ± 0.83. for Copy B. The spatial metric ΔR predicts that Copy A is six times better than Copy B. The displays were made to have equal ΔE^*. The spatial metric analysis of Copy A and Copy B corresponds with observer reports, namely that Copy A is significantly better than Copy B.

This particular spatial metric is very primitive. X, Y, Z are proportional to cone response, but are not isotropic in colour appearance. Further psychophysical experiments are needed to optimize the shape of an optimal spatial psychometric function. The point here is that spatial comparisons can discriminate between Copy A and Copy B whereas pixel comparisons cannot.

Figure 11.7 is a summary of the strategic ideas established so far. The central theme is the decision between evaluating colour one pixel at a time, as in colorimetry, as opposed to spatial comparisons. Original (top) is compared with Copy B reproduction (bottom) one pixel at a time. The data from the rest of the image is irrelevant. Retinex and field calculation advocate relative spatial information as the basis for colour appearance. Absolute intensity at a pixel is less important than spatial comparisons.

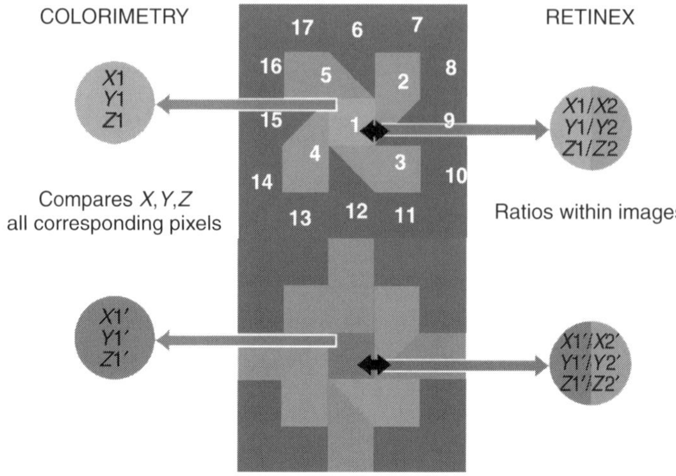

Figure 11.7 The different strategies used to calculate colour appearance. Original is the upper square in the central column and Copy B is the lower square. Colorimetry restricts input data to one pixel. Field calculations, such as retinex, use the ratios of radiances from different pixels. These images were created to have identical colorimetric differences but different edge ratios. The observer evaluations are consistent with human vision using spatial comparisons rather than colorimetric information.

The colour demonstration shown in Figure 11.2 was designed to have constant ΔE^*, and different edge ratios. When the edge ratios are nearly constant, Copy A makes a fairly good reproduction despite $\Delta E^* = 17$. When the edge ratios were distorted in Copy B, the appearance of the display changed. Figure 11.6 shows that ratios = 1.0 characterise a good copy. Ratios that depart from 1.0 characterise the bad copy. Local ratios provide an important tool in finding a meaningful colour metric.

The comparison of Copy A and Original shows an additional important point. Although Copy A has the same edge ratios as Original, it does not match Original. Edge ratios are an important tool for a successful metric, but not sufficient by themselves. Human vision normalisation depends on both spatial and absolute quanta catch information.

11.4 WORKING IN AN ISOTROPIC COLOUR SPACE

An important tool in the colour gamut calculation is minimisation of the discrepancy between the original and the copy. Minimisation programs are frequently used to find optimal compromises. The hard part is to provide the colour space that quantifies the colour mismatch. First, this space should be isotropic, that is equally spaced in appearance in all three dimensions. A forced compromise between hue, chroma and lightness must be made in a space that has been experimentally verified as isotropic in these dimensions. Second, it should be based on a large body of data across many observers and viewing surrounds. Third, it should include data from reflective surfaces and extrapolations to the spectrum locus. Displays using phosphors and light-emitting diodes (LEDs) emit colours on, or close to, the spectrum locus in x, y. Once the colour space has been shown to be appropriate, then a computer can reliably find the best compromise.

Except for lightness, CIE $L^*a^*b^*$ distorts the design principles of the Munsell book [18–21]. The Newhall *et al.* observers selected hue, chroma and lightness to be equally spaced [22]. To facilitate comparison between Munsell and $L^*a^*b^*$, we can convert the original Munsell notation by scaling chroma and hue proportional to lightness. The Munsell book uses chips that are spaced 1/ units apart in value. The Munsell real papers cover the range 9.5/ to 1.75/. L^* covers the range 100 to 0. It is convenient to set $ML = 10 \times$ Munsell value. The chips on a given page of the book have the chroma notation /2. To make them isotropic with value $MC = 5 \times$ Munsell chroma.

A Munsell designation of 5 Y8/10 becomes $ML = 80$, $Ma = 0$, $Mb = 50$ (MLab notation) [21, 17]. In other words, we will use the position in colour space selected by Munsell, but describe it using the same 3-space notation as $L^*a^*b^*$. If we assume that the experimentally based Munsell space is perceptually uniform, then departures from it introduced by $L^*a^*b^*$ can be described as errors introduced by the equations. Virtually all the errors are in the ab plane. We can evaluate their magnitude by measuring the distance between $[a, b]$, the CIE $L^*a^*b^*$ position, and $[Ma, Mb]$ the MLab position in the ab plane. In the upper right of Figure 11.8 we see a plot in the a^*b^* plane. The vector **C** from the origin to $[Ma, Mb]$ shows the position chosen by observer data. The vector **Er** shows the

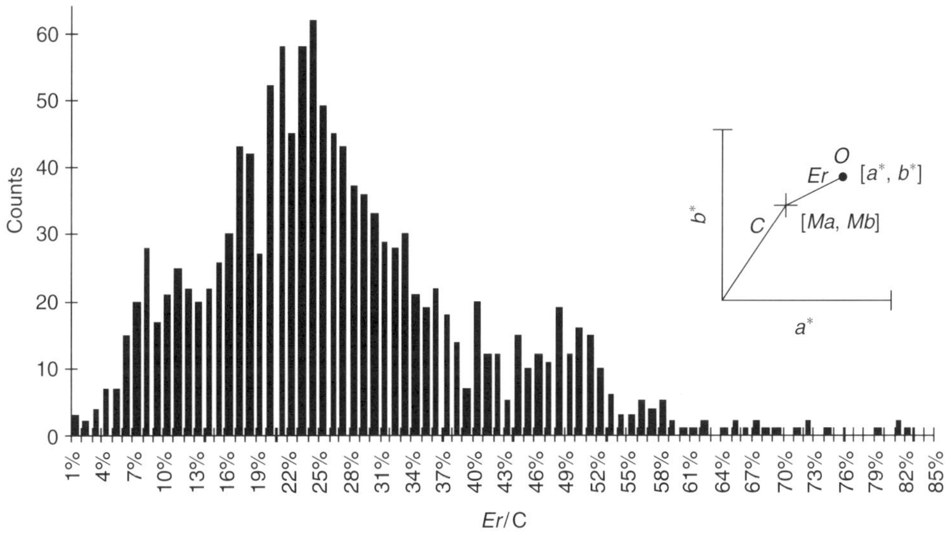

Figure 11.8 Histogram of the ratio Er/C for all 1731 real chips in the Munsell book. The maximum error is 82%, the minimum is 0.01%. The mean is 27%, the standard deviation is 13% and the median is 24%. The inset graph defines the vectors **C** and **Er**. The point (Ma, Mb) is the location in colour space selected by Nickerson's experiments. C is the distance from the origin to (Ma, Mb). The point O is at the coordinates assigned to the same X, Y, Z by CIE La^*b^*. The vector **Er** is the error introduced by La^*b^*.

magnitude of the error introduced by $L^*a^*b^*$. The ratio Er/C is plotted in Figure 11.8. The chroma error introduced by $L^*a^*b^*$ averages 27% [18].

11.5 EXPERIMENT IN MUNSELL SPACE

To remove any distortions in the demonstration shown in Figure 11.2, we can make new displays using Munsell notation, instead of $L^*a^*b^*$. To illustrate the point that colorimetric distance is a poor predictor of best colour appearance, we can study Figure 11.9 [7]. Here we have made a set of nine different 'umbrella' displays. The middle display (E) we call Original. All the others are reproductions. Which of the eight different reproductions are acceptable and which are not?

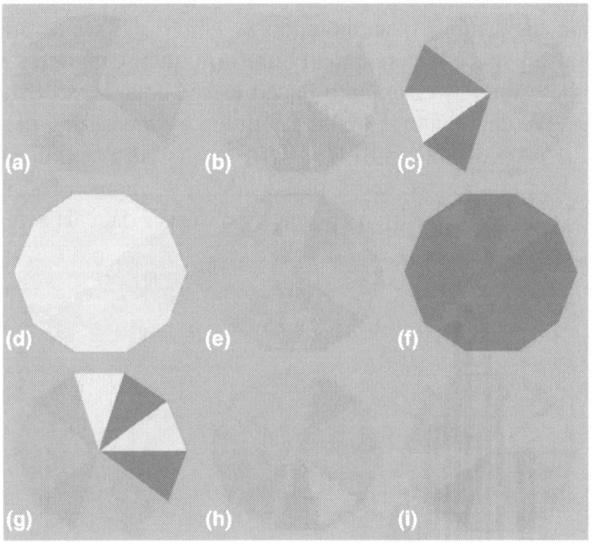

Figure 11.9 Original E is surrounded by eight reproductions. In all cases there are 10 pie-shaped colour patches. For all eight reproductions each individual patch differs from Original by one chip in the Munsell colour book. That means each individual chip is a constant distance from the original in Munsell uniform colour space. Thus, changes in lightness, chroma and hue are equal. Along the left to right axis (DEF), the original and reproductions vary only in lightness. All 10 patches in D are one Munsell chip lighter than the original. All 10 patches in F are one Munsell chip darker than the original. Along the top to bottom axis (BEH), the original and reproductions vary only in hue. All 10 patches in B are shifted counterclockwise by one Munsell chip from the original. All 10 patches in H are shifted clockwise by one Munsell chip from the original. Along the upper left to bottom right axis (AEI), the original and reproductions vary only in chroma. All 10 patches in A are one Munsell chip less saturated than the original. All 10 patches in I are one Munsell chip more saturated than the original. Reproductions A, B, D, F, H, I are still reasonable reproductions despite the one-chip colour shifts. Reproductions C and G are examples of individual colour shifts in hue, lightness and saturation. Unlike systematic shifts, individual shifts create unacceptable distortions of the original. An error of one Munsell chip is acceptable if it is global but not if it is local. See also Colour Plate 6.

11.5.1 Design of umbrella targets

The specifications for all areas are in Munsell notation. This avoids the problems introduced by the inconsistencies found in $L^*a^*b^*$ spacing [18]. 'Original' has 10 triangular areas. The top area has the same $L^*a^*b^*$ values as Munsell paper 5R 7/6. The remaining nine areas are all 7/6, each of them are four pages apart [5YR, 5Y, 5GY, 5G, 5BG, 5B, 5PB, 5P, 5RP]. Thus we have placed the 10 areas in a circle of constant lightness and chroma in colour space.

All 10 colours in all the remaining eight targets differ from the original by only one chip in the Munsell Book. The DEF series varies in lightness. Each corresponding area in D is 8/, and is 6/ in F. This change in stimulus is a global shift. It produces noticeable but acceptable changes in appearance. The changes for all 10 areas are about the same magnitude.

The AEI series varies in chroma. Here all 10 papers have /4 in A and /8 in I. The changes are noticeable but the displays are regarded as acceptable reproductions.

The BEH series varies in hue. Here 5R is replaced with 2.5R in B and 7.5R in H. The same shift was applied to all 10 areas. The chroma /6 was chosen so that one hue page in the Munsell book equals one chip in lightness value and one chip in chroma. Here the change in colour appearance is small, but noticeable and acceptable as good reproductions.

So far all the changes have been global shifts. All 10 papers have moved in the same direction in colour space. Such uniform movement is reminiscent of the changes found in colour constancy experiments in which the paper display is constant, while the intensity and colour of the illumination changes. In colour constancy experiments we are familiar with this kind of result, namely that colours change very little with large global shifts in illumination. Also, it is common practice in photographic systems to find small apparent changes with large global density shifts, while local changes of the same magnitude are clearly visible.

The final CEG series shows the effect of pseudorandom colour shifts. As above, each colour patch is one Munsell chip different from Original. Nevertheless, independent changes produce both large and small visual changes in appearance. These local area changes make for poor reproductions. They distort the appearance of the original in ways that make them unacceptable reproductions.

The analogy to colour constancy is very compelling. Changing the colours independent of the neighbours disrupts the spatial ratios (Figure 11.1). Changing the local ratios in the context of a colour constancy experiment is the same as changing the reflectances of the areas. Changing reflectances of individual papers (local shifts) cause big changes in appearance, while changes in illumination (global shifts) cause small changes. Note that changing the spectral character of the illumination is not the direct analogue of changing lightness, hue and chroma, as we did in the umbrella experiment. The direct analogue of colour constancy experiments would be uniformly to lower or raise the long-wave reflectances of all the papers, and make analogous changes to the middle- and short-wave reflectances. However, we began this experiment with the intention of substituting paper of known differences of colour appearance. That has been provided by the Munsell book data. Shifting long-, middle- and short-wave reflectances may be a better experiment, but equal colour difference data is not available.

Evans describes a 'consistency principle' for colour reproductions. He says, "As long as the chromatic relations within a given scene are consistently like those of the original scene, the colours will actually seem to be the same in both, unless of course, direct point-for-point comparisons are made. The actual discrepancies can be enormous, providing there is no inconsistency" [25]. Evans attributes this observation to poor colour memory. By introducing spatial comparisons we can add computational properties to Evan's principle. The suggestion from these experiments is that colour gamut calculations, using spatial comparisons, can lead to better in-gamut reproductions. Colorimetrically they will have larger colour difference errors, but they should look better. The same colour constancy mechanism that reduces large physical shifts in illumination to small appearance changes, could be employed to make gamut-limited reproductions look better.

11.6 RETINEX: A SPATIAL CALCULATION

There has been little change in the fundamental operation of the retinex model since it was proposed in 1967 at Land's Ives Medal Address to the Optical Society of America [1]. Figure 11.10(a) documents the details of the retinex model. There are only four operations: ratio, product, reset and average. Ratio makes spatial comparisons. Product propagates local comparisons in nearly global ones. Reset performs a normalisation process relative to the maxima in the image. Average combines the different reports of spatial information from different locations. In implementing these calculations we convert the input to log radiance. The consequence is that ratio and product operations are simplified to subtraction and addition. Reset is a simple logical operator that normalises the image.

The model, which evolved from the study of Mondrian patterns, can also calculate appearances in colour constancy experiments, high dynamic range real-life scenes and gestalt phenomena. Examples of these images can be found in a recent summary publication [16]. The details of the spatial calculations, along with sample Matlab code can be found in Funt, Ciurea and McCann [23].

11.6.1 Colour gamut calculation

The hypothesis connecting the experiments in this chapter is that humans calculate colour using spatial comparisons. The above experiments show that the sum of errors (distances in colour space) is a very poor predictor of the quality of a reproduction. In fact, good reproductions make all their errors in similar directions [7].

If that premise were true, then spatial comparisons could be helpful in finding a set of in-gamut colours that look like the out-of-gamut original. Figure 11.11 illustrates the colour gamut retinex calculation. For gamut mapping we begin with two input images, instead of one. We have Goal, the image that has the large, original gamut. Second, we have Best, the image that represents the limited gamut of the reproduction media. If the

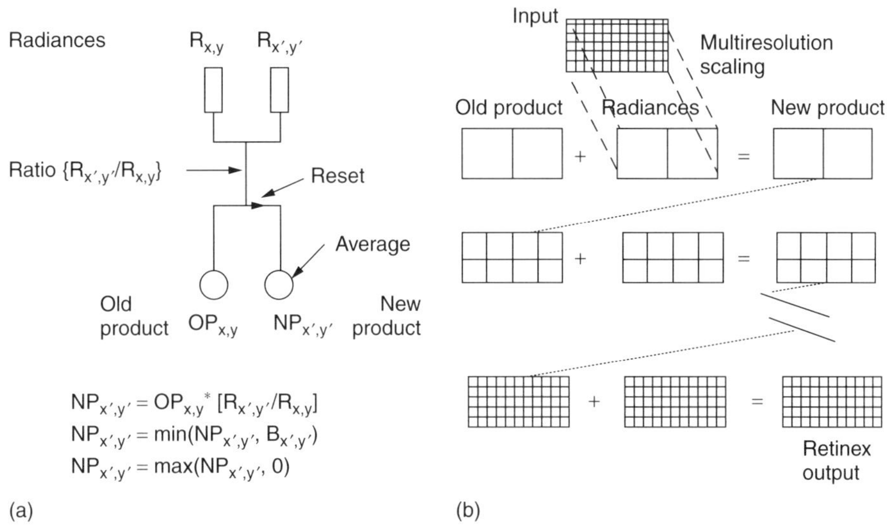

Figure 11.10 (a) Explanation of the ratio, product, reset, average operation. We calculate the new product (NP) for the output pixel x', y'. We begin at the starting pixel x, y using the old product (OP). All OPs are initialised with the value in the best image (Bx, y) for that waveband. The product of the radiance ratios with OP is reset if it is greater than Bx, y and averaged with the previous NPs. (b) The multiresolution aspect of the retinex calculation [23]. The calculation uses three data planes. The old product is initialised to the best image. The original full-resolution image is illustrated as input at the top. The input is averaged to make a series of multiresolution planes ending with two pixels. This average image, Radiance, is the second data plane. The third data plane is for the output of each iteration and is called the new product. Starting with two pixels, we multiply the old product at the starting pixel and multiply it by the ratio of Radiances for the starting and output pixels. That product is reset to the Bestin old product value, if it exceeds it. It is then averaged with previous old product values at the output pixel. To get to the next level, the new product is interpolated to twice the size and placed in the old product data plane. The Radiance data plane uses the next larger (8×2) average of the input. The ratio, product, reset, average calculation in part (a) is repeated. The process continues until the new product at full resolution is complete and is used as one retinex separation. The same process is carried out for each of the three RGB separations.

shape of the limited gamut is complicated, we may substitute a three-dimensional look-up table (LUT) for Best. Again, we begin by averaging down each of the R, G, B separations to a small number of pixels for both Goal and Best (Figure 11.10, right). We take Old Product initialised to maximum and multiply by the Goal ratio; this gives us New Product. New Product is reset to the Best image or the Best data LUT. This process is repeated and the New Product values from this resolution are interpolated up to the next resolution. The same process is carried out for R, G, B.

The gamut retinex process takes the spatial comparisons from Goal and limits the product by Best (Figure 11.11) [4, 24, 30]. The iterative process keeps reinforcing the ratios found in Goal while the reset forces New Product to migrate toward an image with all the

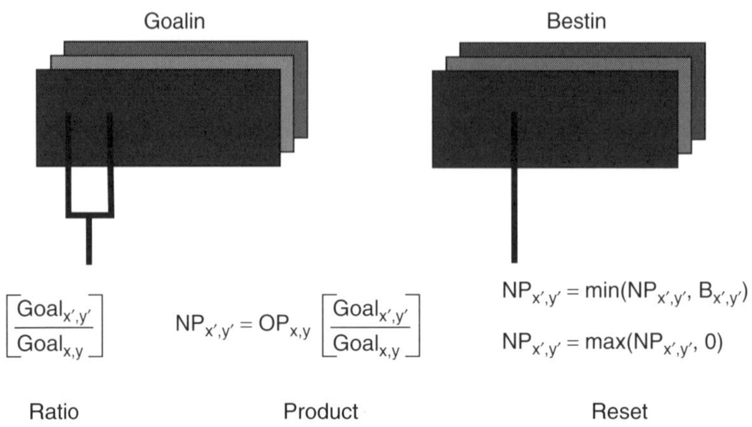

Figure 11.11 Schematic diagram of the colour gamut retinex calculation. This calculation creates long-, middle- and short-wave separations for Goalin and Bestin. It uses the ratios from Goalin and the reset from Bestin to introduce spatial comparisons into the search for best reproduction using a limited gamut.

same ratios, regardless of the absolute input values of Goal. The resulting image, NewProductOut, shows a big improvement in appearance compared to Best (Figure 11.11). The data shows that this new image is in gamut.

A demonstration of the process can be found in Figure 11.12. The Goalin.tiff image is a scanned photograph of a Jobo photographic test chart. In Photoshop the six colour patches have been replaced with the most saturated colours available. Red digits are [255, 0, 0], green digits are [0, 255, 0], blue digits are [0, 0, 255], yellow digits are [255, 255, 0], magenta digits are [255, 0, 255], cyan digits are [0, 255, 255].

The Bestin.tiff image was created in Photoshop from the modified Goalin.tiff image using the Toyo (uncoated) profile. The Toyo (uncoated) gamut is much smaller than the display. The NewProductOut image is the output of the calculation described in Figures 11.10 and 11.11.

In understanding these results it is helpful to study both the colour rendition and the *R*, *G*, *B* separation images. The Goalin, Bestin and NewProductOut images are shown in Figure 11.12 and Colour Plate 7a (top left). Figures 11.12(b), (c), (d) show the *R*, *G*, *B* separations.

In the blue separation (Figure 11.12(b)) the Goalin colours of [blue, green, red] are [white, black, black], whereas [yellow, magenta, cyan] are [black, white, white]. The Bestin image is much lower in contrast. All the blue separation values are nearly the same. The spatial gamut retinex process [NewProductOut] finds in-gamut combinations that maintain, as well as possible, the lightness differences for each colour. In this blue record, the Goalin whites have been limited to NewProductOut light greys. However, the blacks associated with red, green and yellow have remained black. The comparison with the Bestin image is very interesting. The Toyo ink profile found blue separation values much lower in contrast, in fact all the lightnesses are close to middle grey.

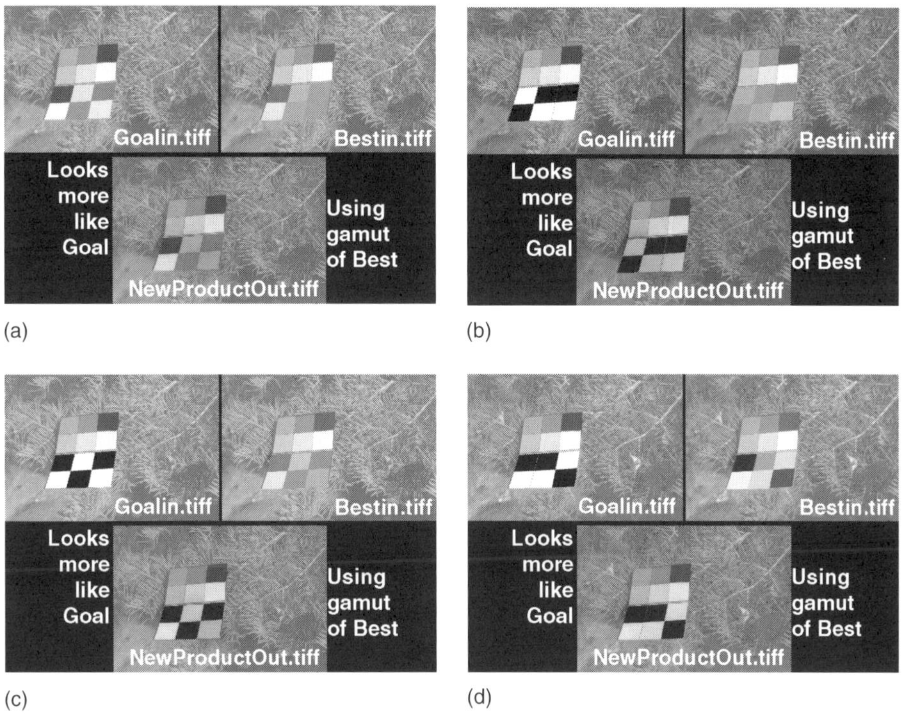

Figure 11.12 Goalin, Bestin and NewProductOut. (a) The three colour images: NewProductOut looks much closer to Goalin than to Bestin; both Bestin and NewProductOut are within the limited gamut of the Toyo inks (uncoated). (b, c, d) Blue, green and red colour separation images. By comparing NewProductOut with Goalin, we can see that the gamut retinex product preserved the spatial relationships in each separation. The gamut Toyo profile that modified Goalin to make Bestin adjusted each pixel independent of all the others. NewProductOut used spatial comparisons and gamut information to calculate the value at each pixel. The improvement in matching appearances can be seen by studying the three sets of colour separations. In each image the 12-patch Jobo target shows the rendition of six grey areas in the top two rows and the colours blue, green and red above yellow, magenta and cyan in the bottom two rows. See also Colour Plate 7.

In the green separation (Figure 11.12(c)) the Goalin colours of [blue, green, red] are [black, white, black], whereas [yellow, magenta, cyan] are [white, black, white]. Again the spatial gamut retinex process finds in-gamut combinations that maintain, as well as possible, the lightness differences in each colour separation. In this record the Goalin whites have been limited to NewProductOut light greys for green and cyan. However, the separation values associated with red, blue and magenta have remained very close to black. The comparison with the Bestin image shows that the non-spatial, Toyo profile generated a green separation with much lower contrast.

In the red separation (Figure 11.12(d)) the Goalin whites have been limited to NewProductOut light greys for yellow and light-middle grey for red and magenta. The rendition

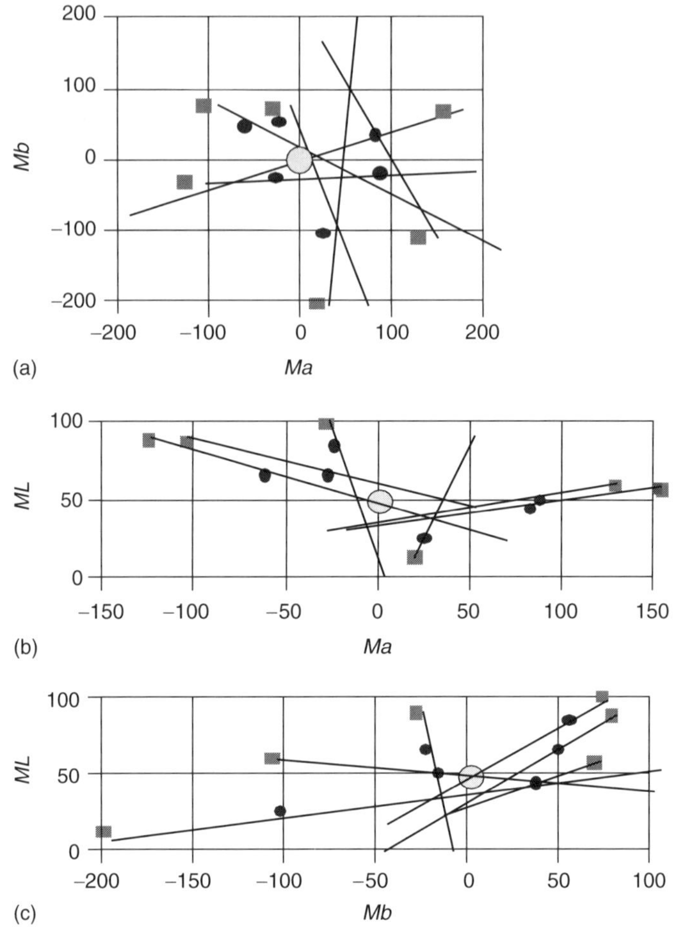

Figure 11.13 (a) Plot of the six Goalin to NewProductOut vectors in (a) the Ma vs. Mb plane, (b) the ML vs. Ma plane and (c) the ML vs. Mb plane. The central spot plots the coordinates $ML = 50$, $Ma = 0$, $Mb = 0$. The square grid represents equal distances in $MLab$ space. Key to symbols: (square) Goalin, (circle) NewProductOut.

of the other colours is close to black. The comparison with the Bestin image shows that the Toyo profile generated green-patch values much lighter than desired.

Figure 11.13 plots the Goalin and NewProductOut values of the six coloured areas in ML, Ma, Mb space. The Goalin values are plotted as large solid squares; the NewProductOut values are plotted as solid circles. The solid lines are drawn between Goalin and the NewProductOut values. These lines are beyond the NewProductOut values. Figure 11.13(a) plots the data in the Ma, Mb plane. Here many of the vectors pass near the central point ($Ma = Mb = 0$) but do not intersect there. Figure 11.13(b) plots the data in the ML, Ma plane. Here the vectors pass near the central point ($ML = 50$, $Ma = 0$)

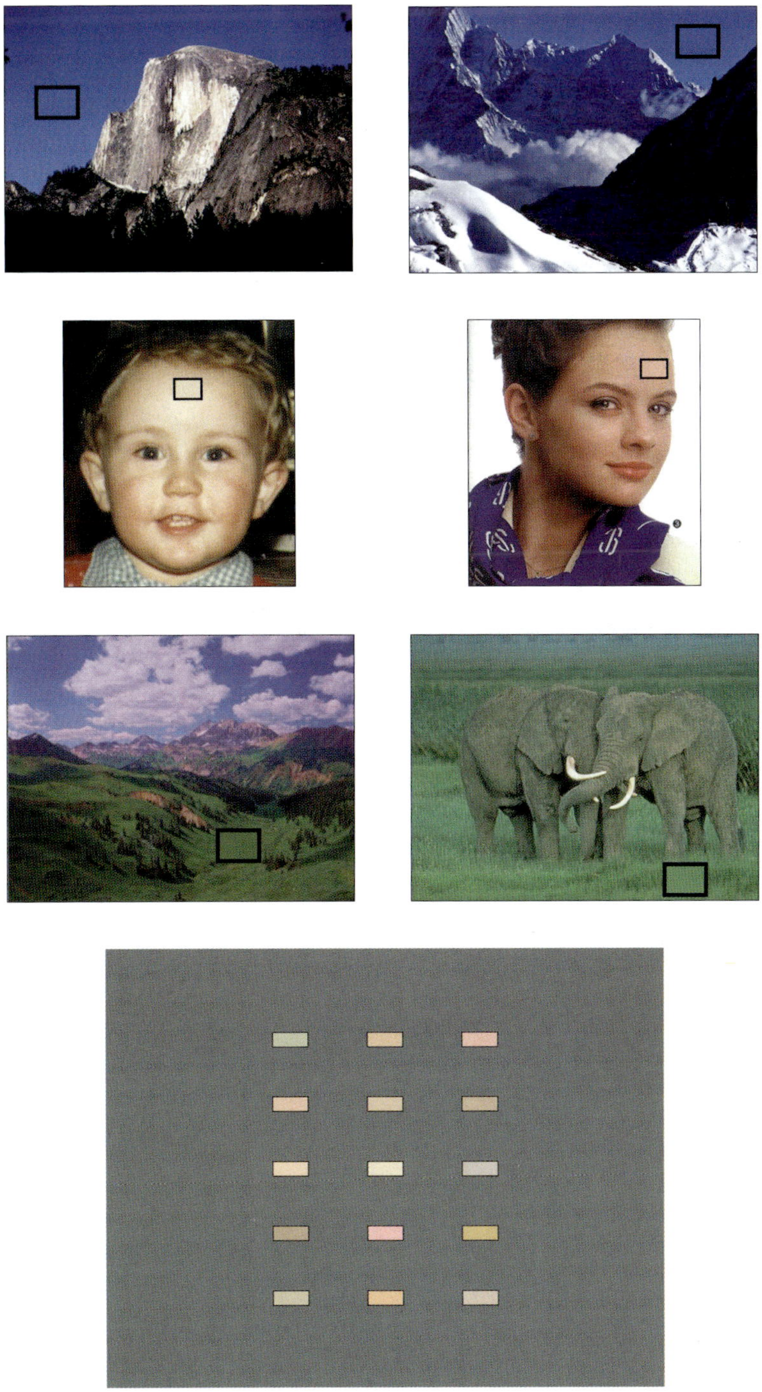

Plate 1

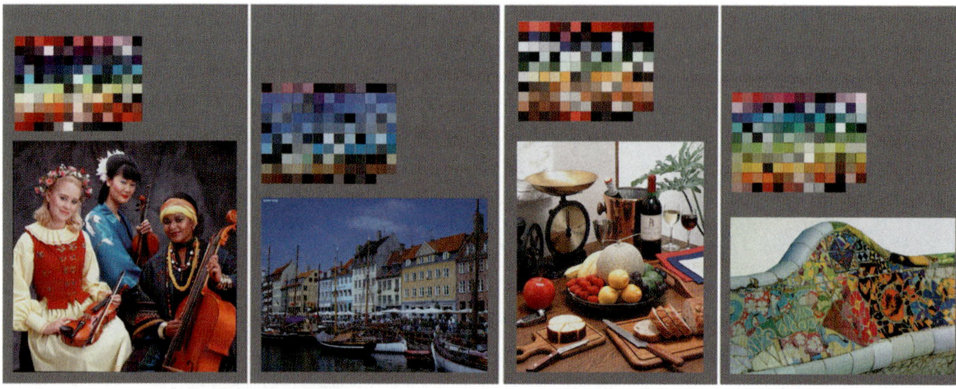

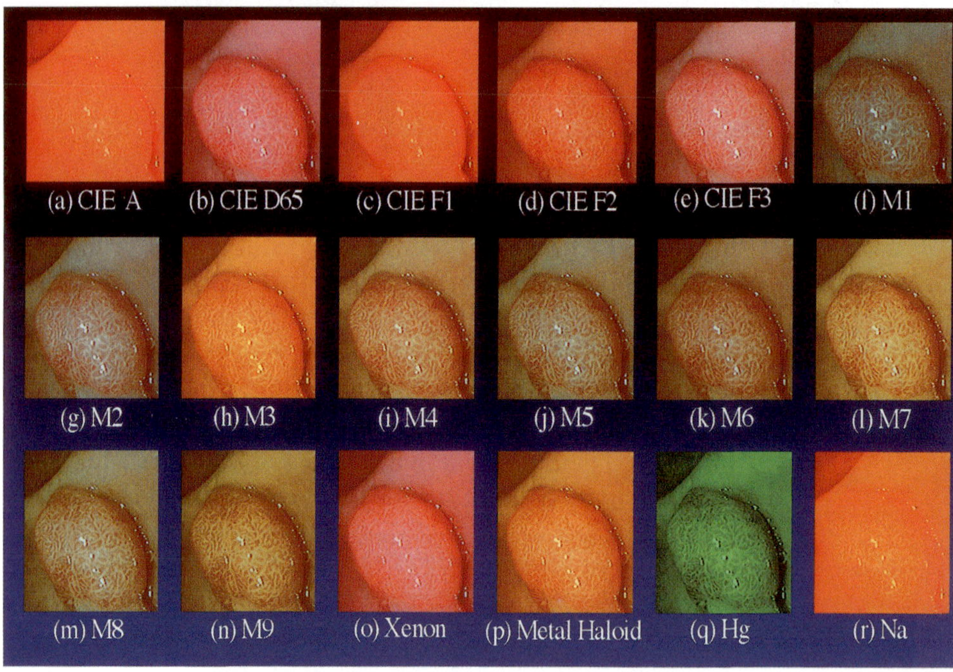
(a) CIE A
(b) CIE D65
(c) CIE F1
(d) CIE F2
(e) CIE F3
(f) M1
(g) M2
(h) M3
(i) M4
(j) M5
(k) M6
(l) M7
(m) M8
(n) M9
(o) Xenon
(p) Metal Haloid
(q) Hg
(r) Na

Plate 2

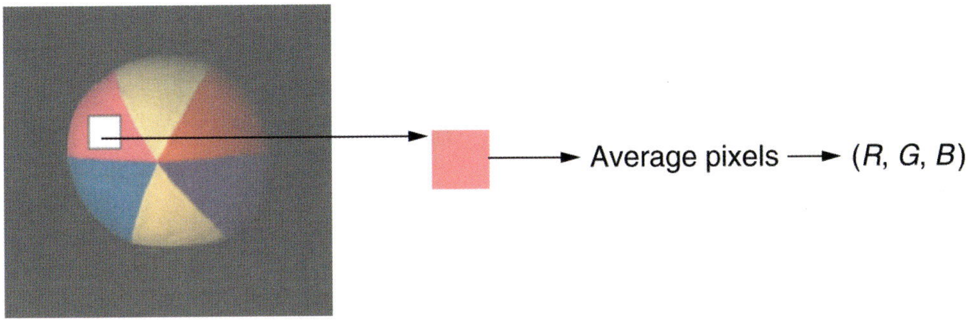

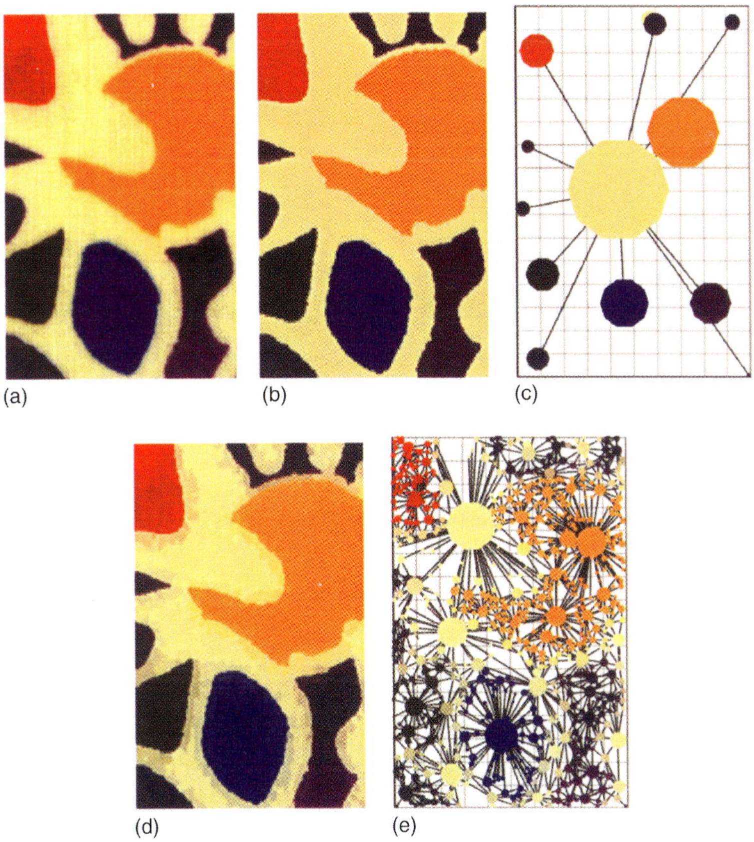

Plate 3

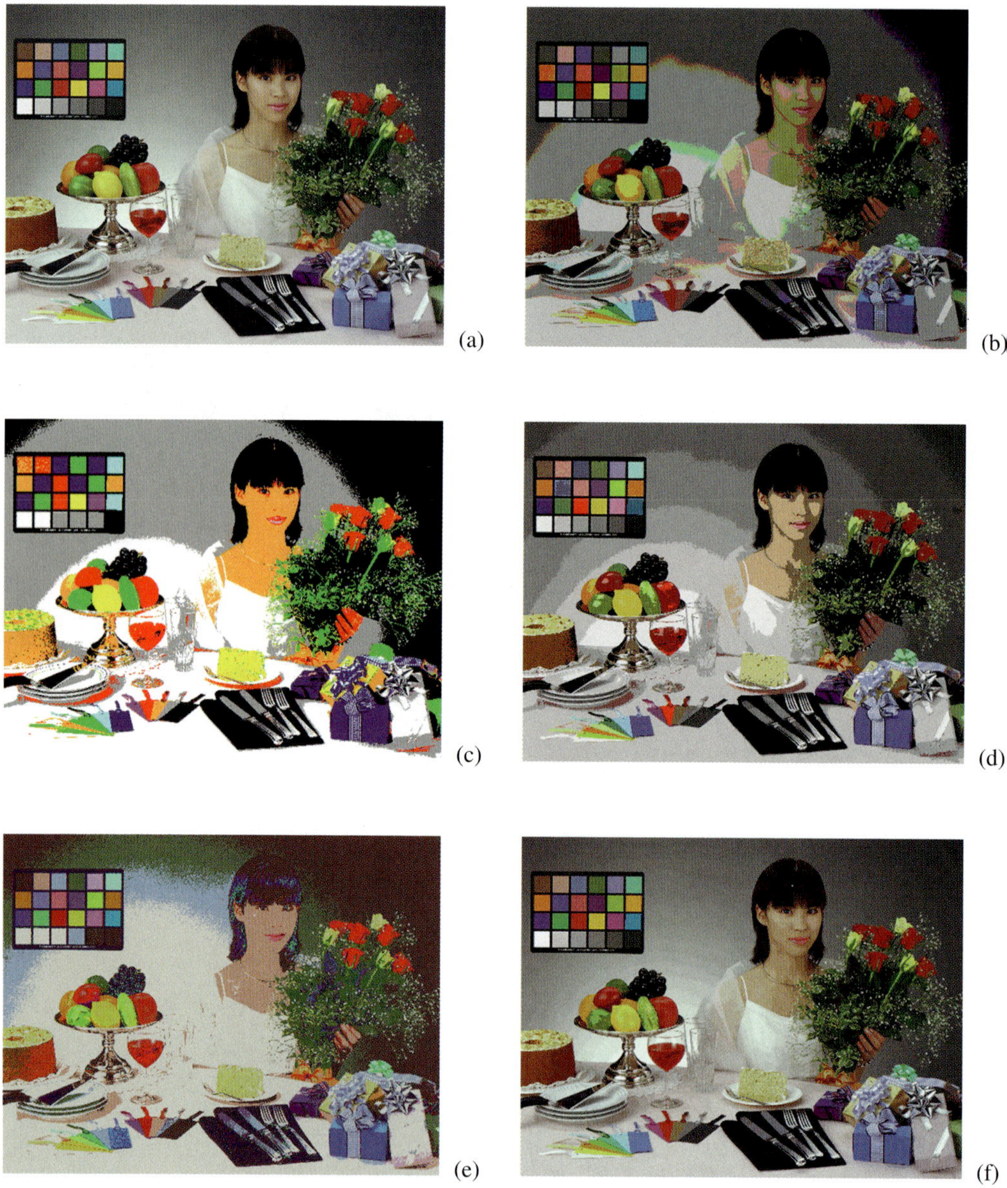

Plate 4

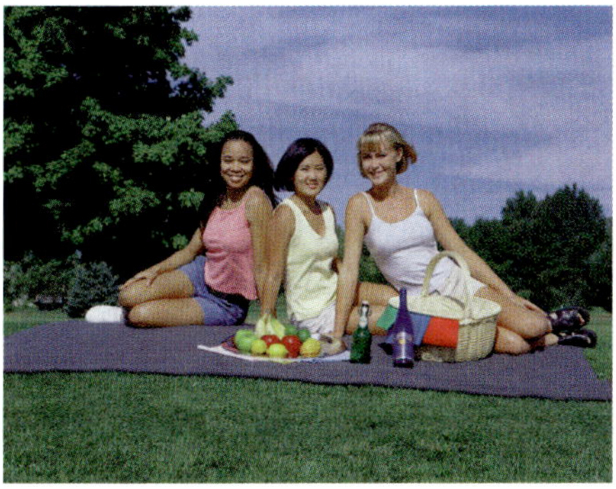
(a)

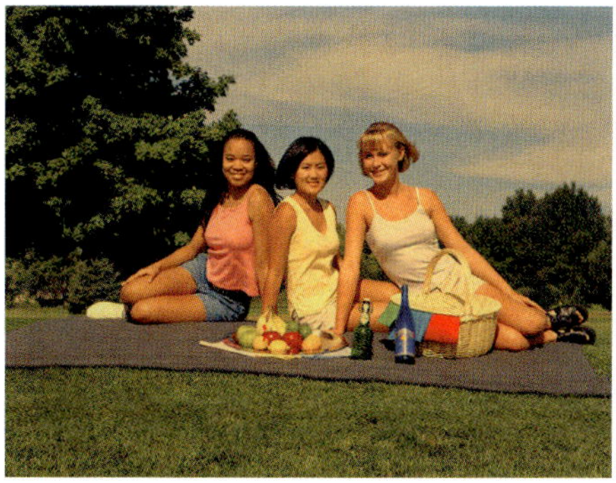
(b)

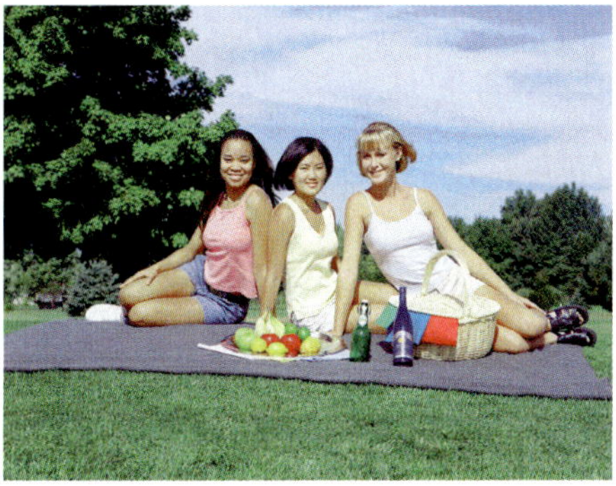
(a1)

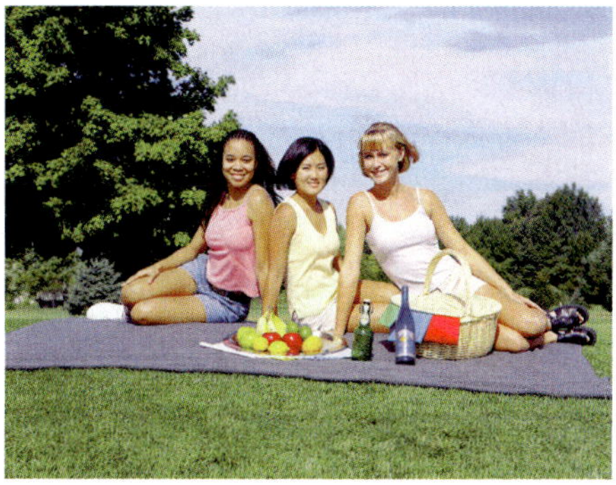
(b1)

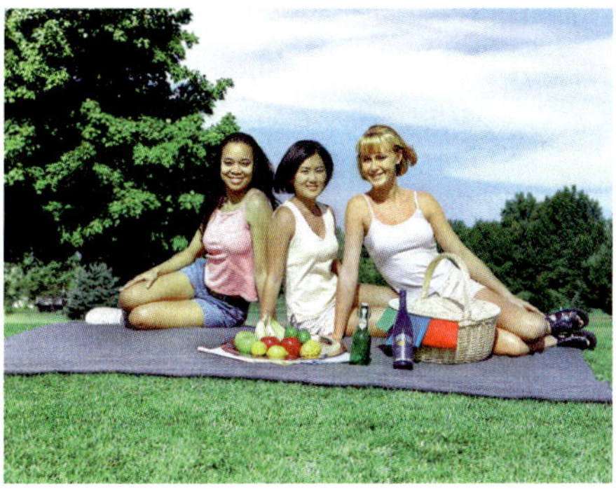
(a2)

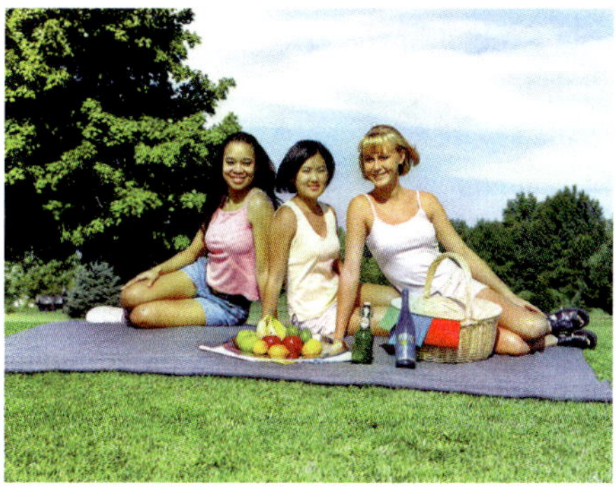
(b2)

Plate 5

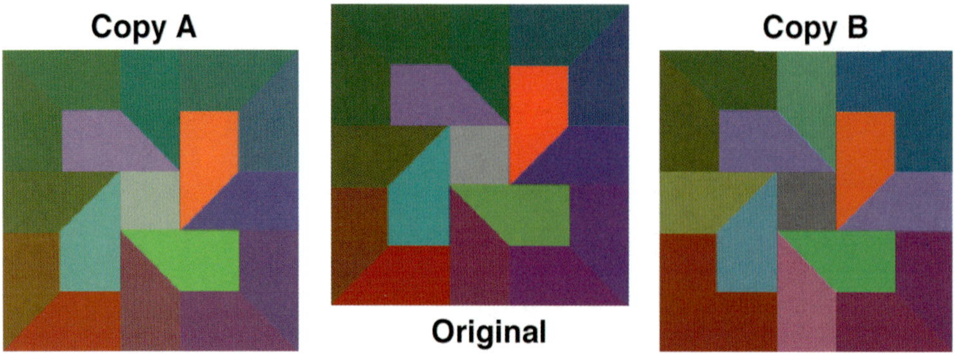

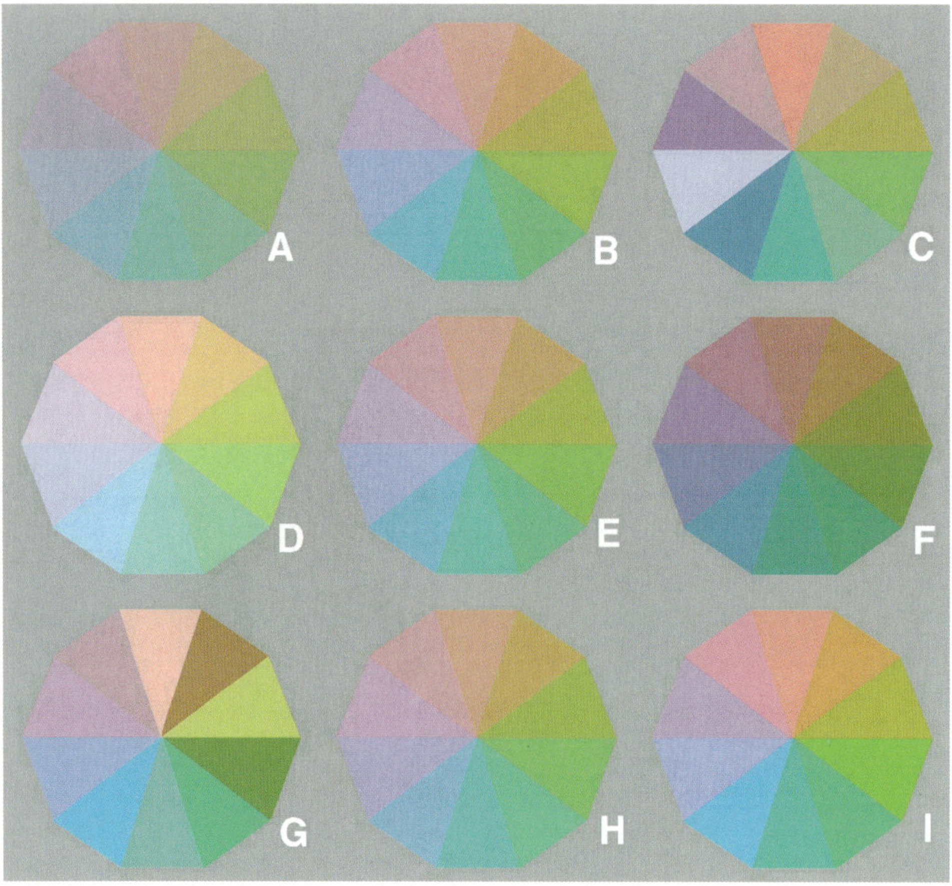

Plate 6

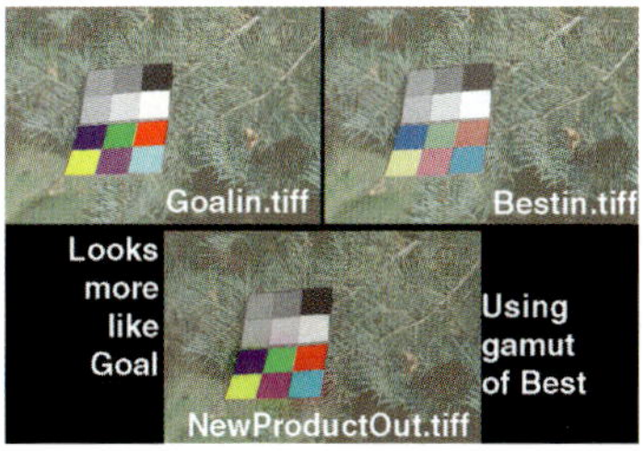

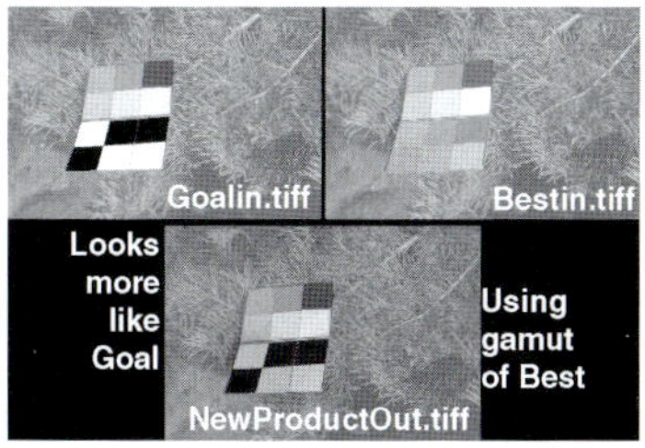

Blue Separation

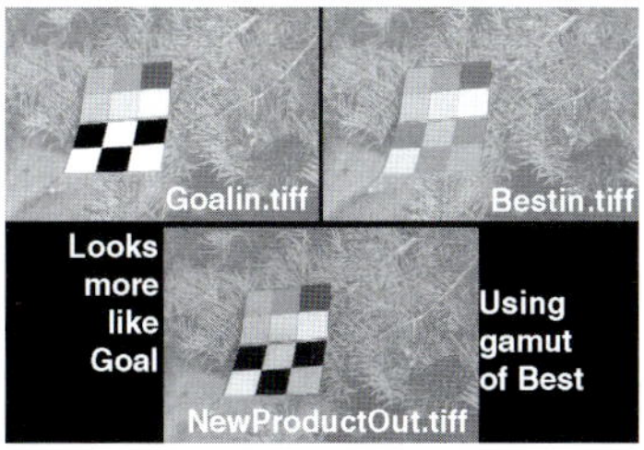

Green Separation

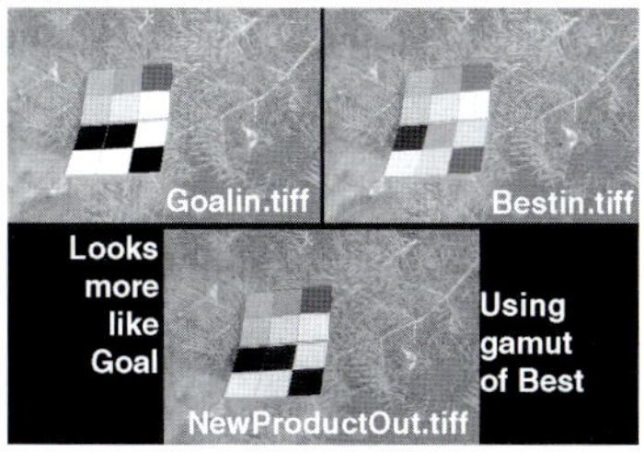

Red Separation

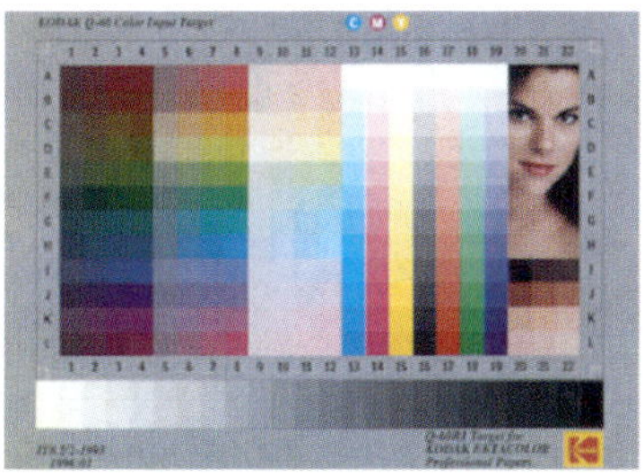

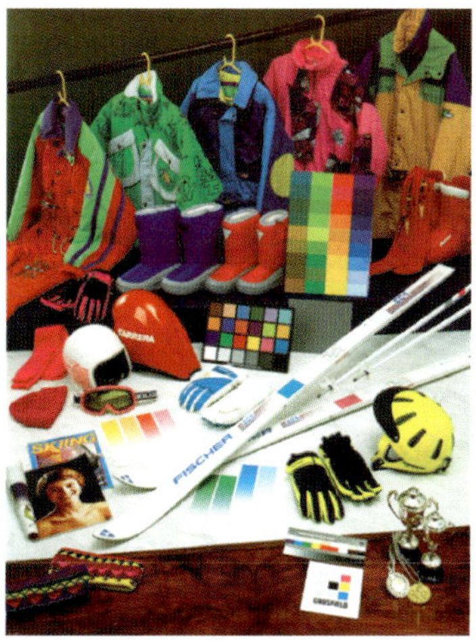

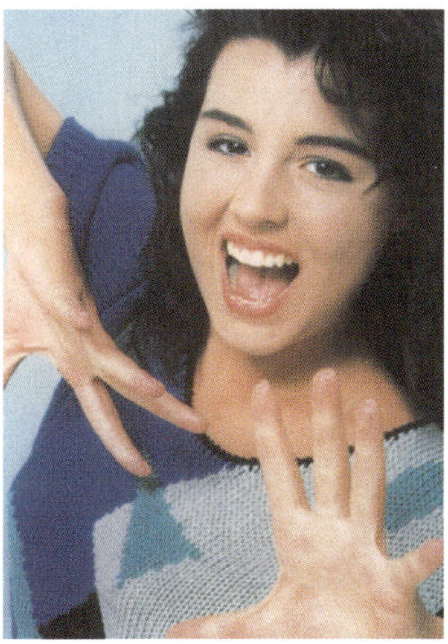

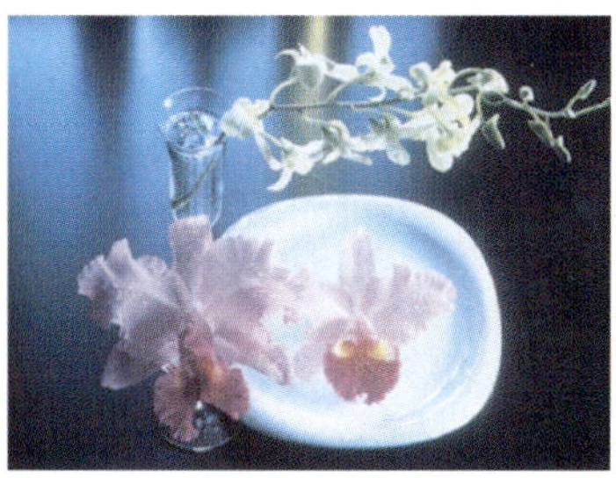

Plate 7

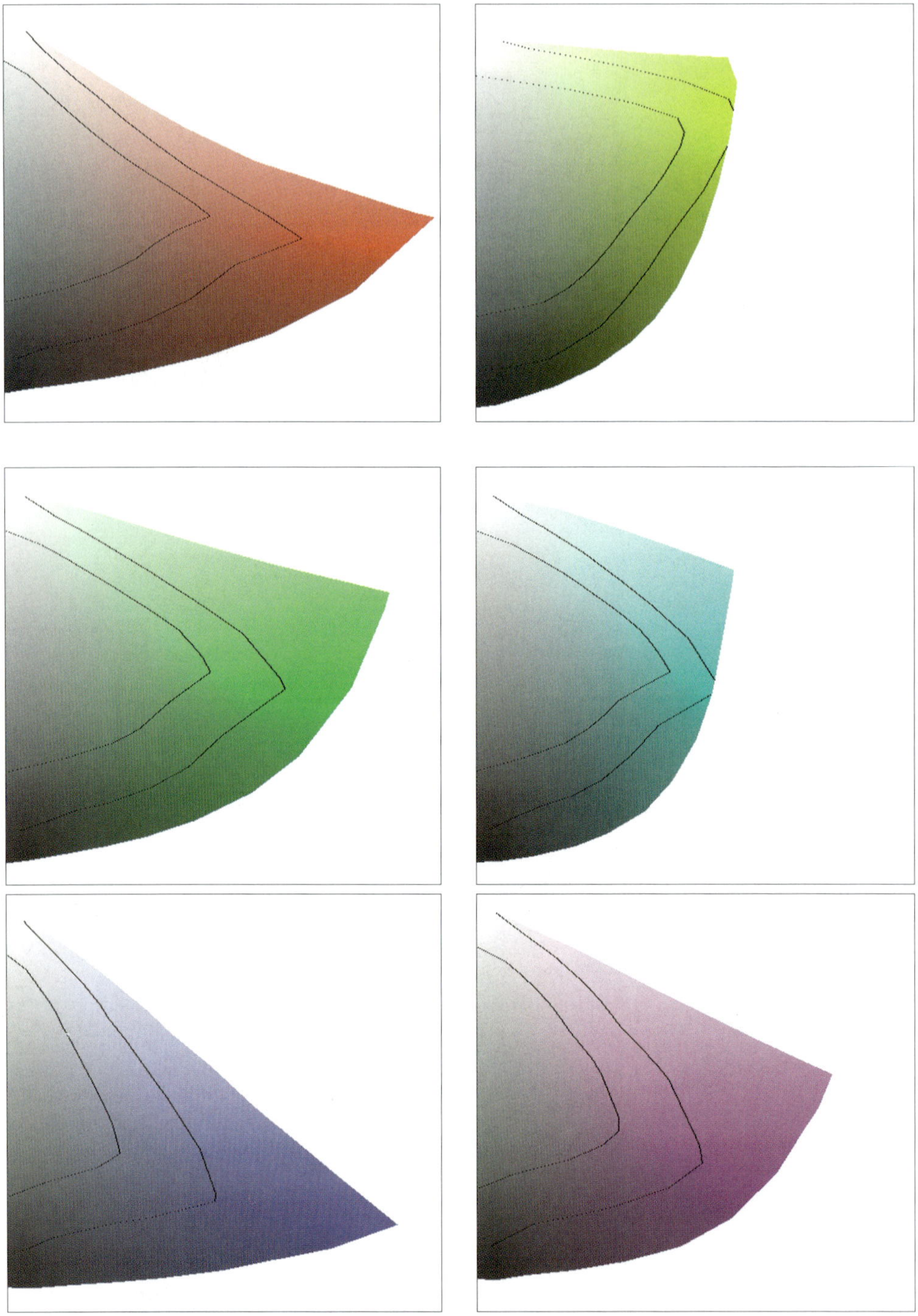

Plate 8

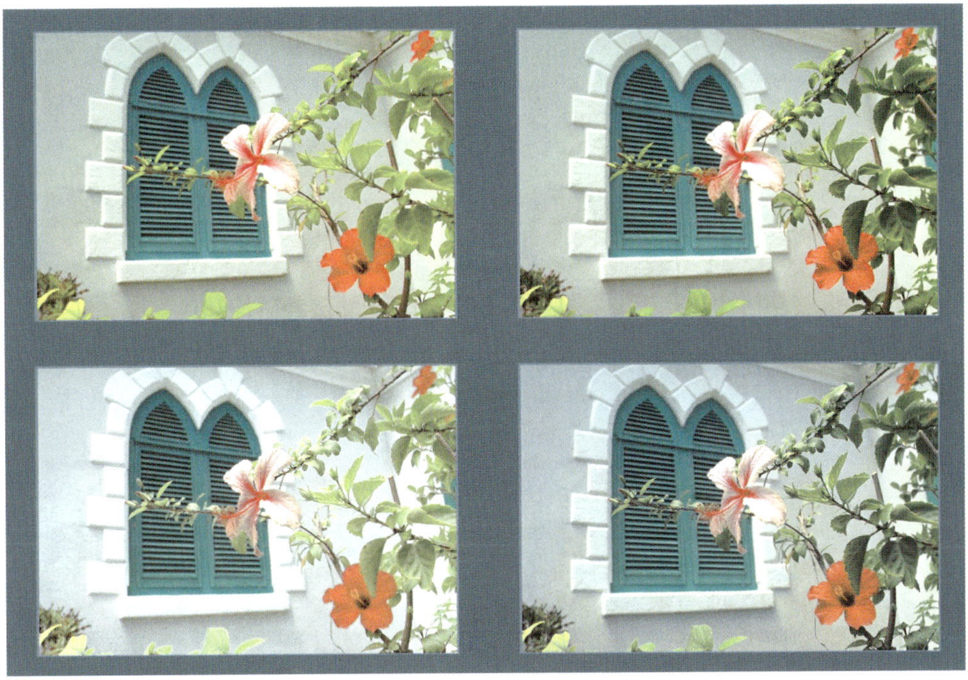

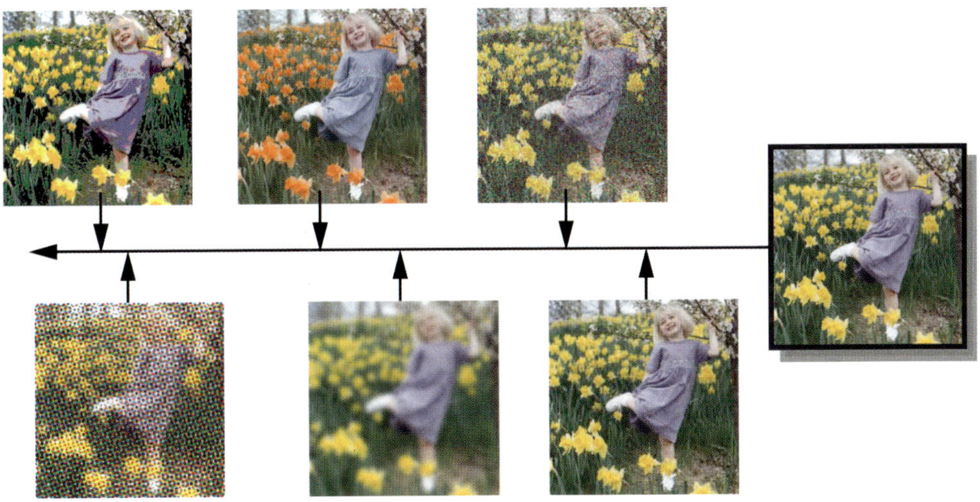

Plate 9

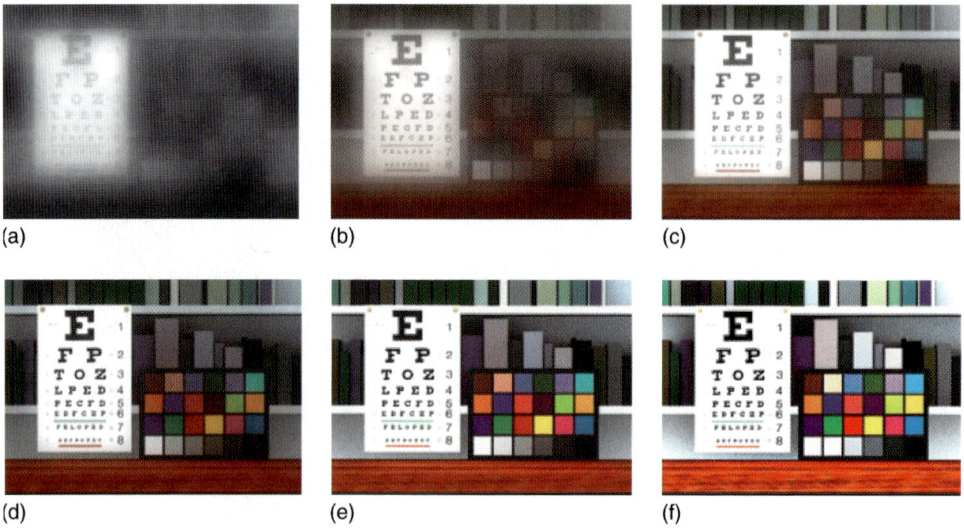

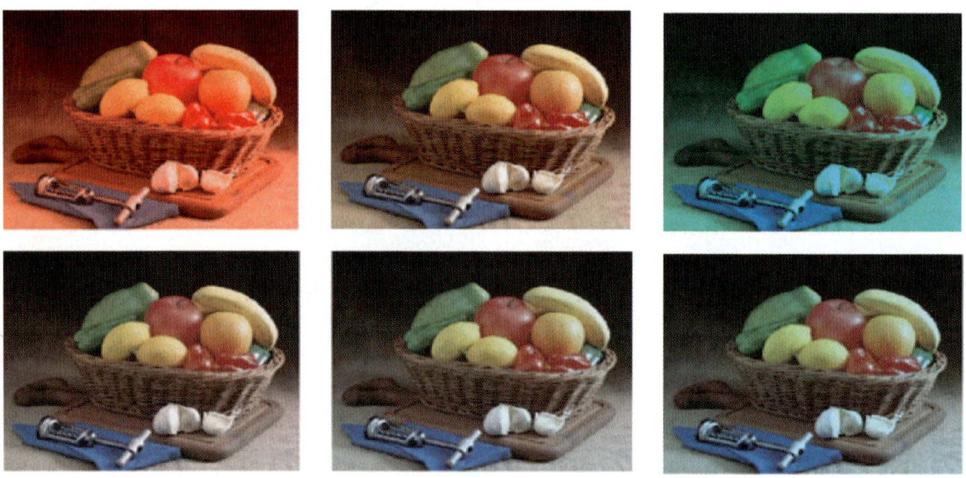

Plate 10

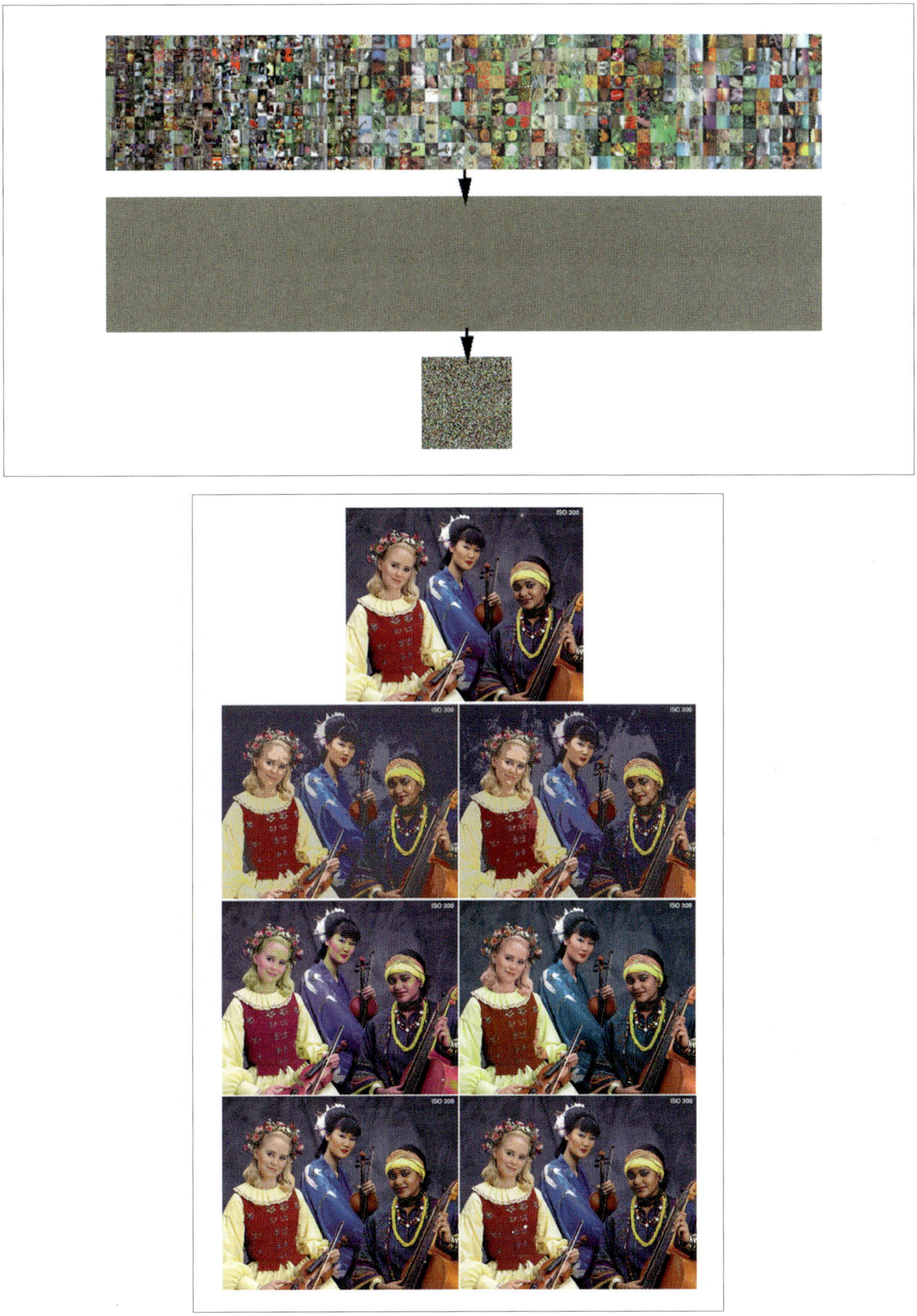

Plate 11

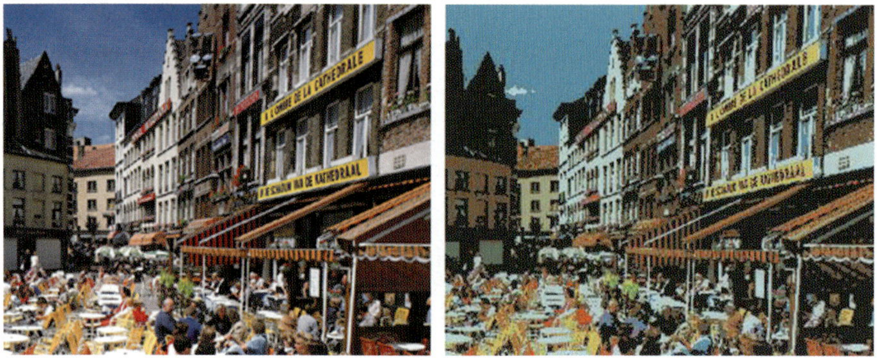

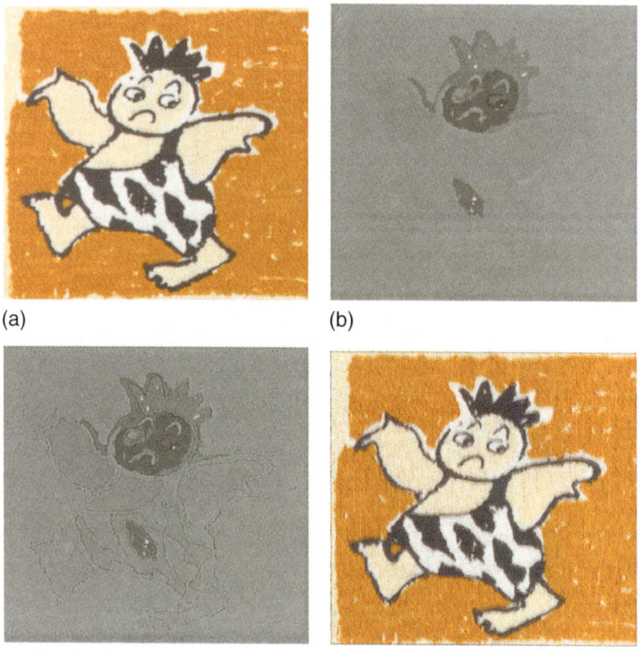

(a) (b) (c) (d)

Plate 12

but do not intersect there. Figure 11.13(c) plots the data in the ML, Mb plane. Here the vectors pass below the central point ($ML = 50$, $Mb = 0$). These graphs show that the improved colours seen in NewProductOut are not caused by simple colour space projections as reduction in chroma (Figure 11.13(a)), projecting toward middle grey (Figure 11.13(b) and (c)). NewProductOut was created by optimising spatial comparisons. Such a process is somewhat similar in that the results project in the vicinity of middle grey ($ML = 50$, $Ma = 0$, $Mb = 0$). However, their projections sweep out a substantial, asymmetrical volume. This is an argument that the gamut retinex process is fundamentally different from a single, 3D colour space transformation.

The lack of convergence to a single point in colour space is similar to projections generated by the CARISMA and Lee [26] algorithms. CARISMA used empirical non-global transformations. Further, it is based on how experienced printers would treat images on small-gamut media. Printers are trained to interpret images in terms of the quality of their ink colour separations. As we saw in Figure 11.12, the gamut retinex calculation retains the appearance of objects in their separations and hence does well in colour.

Kang, Cho, Morovic and Luo [27] recently described experimental matches to find the observers' choice of best compromise for each colour independently (see Chapter 13). Their data led to a model with three ranges. In the upper level (high lightnesses) there is a high point of convergence, in the middle level (middle lightnesses) there is no point of convergence, in the lower level (low lightnesses) there is a lower point of convergence. MacDonald, Morovic and Xiao [28] described their recent addition to models for gamut mapping algorithms (see Chapter 14). Here they described three zones. The first is the region between small gamut and large gamut. The third is the region in colour space close to the grey axis (vertical axis in $L^*a^*b^*$ space) that is unchanged by the GMA. The second is the region between the two that is shaped by the GMA. MacDonald *et al.* have described a new method that introduces a different point of convergence for different lightnesses. Green and Luo [29] extended CARISMA to the conversion of transparency to newsprint workflows (see Chapter 16). They included comparisons of CARISMA with algorithms by Lee and Kang.

A common property between CARISMA, Lee's algorithm, Kang's algorithm and MacDonald's observations and models is that there is no single projection to a single convergence point in colour space. The 'out-of-gamut to in-gamut' transforms get their speed and efficiency from the fact that there is only one rule to project all the out-of-gamut points to a common convergence point, such as $L^* = 50$, $a^* = 0$, $B^* = 0$. Observers prefer multiple endpoints and complex transforms. The more complex the transform, the greater the colorimetric error between the large-gamut original and the optimal small-gamut reproduction.

11.6.2 Best colour gamut compromise

A familiar gamut mapping process is to evaluate the absolute colorimetry of a pixel, see whether it is in gamut, and then replace it with the nearest in-gamut colour. This process distorts colour appearance. Take two areas next to each other. Let us assume that one area is in gamut and the other is not. If we leave the in-gamut pixel value unchanged, while changing the out-of-gamut pixel, we have replaced the ratio of these two areas with a new ratio and a new colour relationship [30]. This chapter has argued that it is better to change both pixel values, so as to leave the spatial comparisons constant. The best reproduction is the one that reproduces the most spatial comparisons.

11.7 CONCLUSIONS

Retinex calculations extended to the problem of gamut-limited reproductions show promise. The argument states that global shifts in colour similar to those found in colour constancy produce much smaller changes in image appearance than local, individual colour shifts. Further, this chapter argues that colour gamut transformations using spatial comparisons can generate in-gamut reproductions that look more like the original, because they employ the benefits of human colour constancy processing. These reproductions may have a greater colorimetric difference between original and reproduction, but look better. Colour is a spatial calculation in human vision.

ACKNOWLEDGEMENTS

I thank Norbert Herzer, Mike McGuire, Irwin Sobel, Paul Hubel, and Mary McCann for their thoughtful discussions and suggestions.

REFERENCES

1. E. H. Land and J. J. McCann (1971) Lightness and retinex theory. *J. Opt. Soc. Am.*, **61**, 1.
2. J. J. McCann, S. P. McKee and T. Taylor (1976) Quantitative studies in retinex theory: a comparison between theoretical predictions and observer responses to color Mondrian experiments. *Vision Res.*, **16**, 445–458.
3. J. Frankle and J. J. McCann (1983) Method and apparatus of lightness imaging. US Patent 4,384,336.
4. J. J. McCann (1999) Lessons learned from Mondrians applied to real images and color gamuts. *Proc. 7th IS&T/SID Color Imaging Conference*, pp. 1–8.
5. J. Morovic and R. Luo (1999) Developing algorithms for universal color gamut mapping. In *Color Imaging: Vision and Technology*, L. W. MacDonald and M. R. Luo (eds), pp. 253–282. John Wiley, Chichester.
6. Members of CIE Technical Committee 8-03. Ján Morovic, chairman (Color & Imaging Institute, UK), Peter Bodrogi (Veszprem University, Hungary), Gus Braun (Eastman Kodak, USA), Fritz Ebner (Xerox, USA). Mark D. Fairchild (Rochester Institute of Technology, USA), Phil Green (London College of Printing, UK), Patrick Herzog (RWTH, Germany), Tony Johnson (UK), Byoung-Ho Kang (ETRI, Korea), Naoya Katoh (Sony, Japan), M. Ronnier Luo (Colour & Imaging Institute, UK), Marc Mahy (Agfa, Belgium), Gabriel Marcu (Apple, USA), John McCann (USA), Ethan Montag (Rochester Institute of Technology, USA), Hideto Motomura (Matsushita Research Institute, Tokyo, Japan), Todd Newman (Canon Information Systems, USA), Raimondo Schettini (Italian National Research Council, Italy), J. A. Stephen Viggiano (RIT Research Corporation, USA), Geoff J. Woolfe (Eastman Kodak, USA). See the website www.colour.org/tc8-0.3.
7. J. J. McCann (1999) Making reproductions of masterpieces: managing all the colors within the gamut. *Proc. International Symposium on Multispectral Imaging and Color Reproduction for Digital Archives*, Chiba.

8. J. McCann (1973) Human color perception. In *Color Theory and Imaging Systems*, R. Eynard (ed.), p. 1. Society of Photographic Scientists and Engineers, Washington.
9. F. W. Campbell and J. G. Robson (1968) Application of Fourier analysis to the visibility of gratings. *J. Physiol. (Lond.)*, **197**, 551–566.
10. O. Braddick, F. W. Campbell and J. Atkinson (1978) Channels in vision: basic aspects. In *Handbook of Sensory Physiology VII*, R. Held, H. W. Leibowitz and H. Teuber (eds), pp. 3–38. *Publisher, Town*.
11. J. J. McCann (1978) Visibility of gradients and low-spatial frequency sinusoids: evidence for a distance constancy mechanism. *J. Photogr. Sci. Engng*, **22**, 64–68.
12. H. R. Wilson and J. R. Bergen (1979) A four mechanism model for threshold spatial vision. *Vision Res.*, **19**, 19–32.
13. R. Luo (1999) Color science: past, present and future. In *Colour Imaging: Vision and Technology*, L. W. MacDonald and M. R. Luo (eds), pp. 381–404. John Wiley, Chichester.
14. CIE (1971) Recommendations on uniform color spaces, color difference equations: psychometric color terms. Supplement 2 of CIE Publication 15 (E-1.3.1). CIE, Paris.
15. CIE (1932) *CIE Proceedings 1931*, p. 19. Cambridge University Press, Cambridge.
16. J. J. McCann (1998) Color theory and color imaging systems: past, present and future. *J. Imaging. Sci. Technol.*, **42**, 70.
17. G. Marcu (1998) Gamut mapping in Munsell constant hue sections. *Proc. 6th IS&T/SID Color Imaging Conference*, Scottsdale AZ, p. 159.
18. J. J. McCann (1999) Color spaces for color mapping. *J. Electronic Imaging*, **8**, 354–364.
19. J. J. McCann (1999) Color gamut measurements and mapping: the role of color spaces. *Proc. SPIE*, **3648**, 68–82.
20. J. J. McCann (1999) Uniform color spaces: 3D LUTs vs. algorithms. *Proc. 2nd IS&T PICS Conference*, Vol. 2, pp. 204–208.
21. J. McCann and M. Stokes (1998) Color spaces and image quality. *Proc. IS&T PICS Conference*, Vol. 1, pp. 140–144.
22. S. M. Newhall, D. Nickerson and D. B. Judd (1943) Final report of the OSA subcommittee on spacing of the Munsell colors. *J. Opt. Soc. Am.*, **33**, 385.
23. B. Funt, F. Ciurea and J. J. McCann (2000) Retinex in Matlab. *Proc. 8th IS&/SID Color Imaging Conference*, Scottsdale AZ, pp. 112–121.
24. J. J. McCann, Using color constancy to advantage in color gamut calculations. *Proc. 3rd IS&T PICS Conference*, Vol. 3, pp. 169–176.
25. R. M. Evans (1974) *The Perception of Color*, p. 205. John Wiley, New York.
26. C. S. Lee, K. Sim, E. J. Lee and Y. A. Ha (1999) Gamut mapping using variable anchor points. *Proc. SPIE*, **3648**, 126–130.
27. B. Kang, M. Cho, J. Morovic and R. Luo (2000) Gamut compression algorithm development on the basis of observer experimental data. *Proc. 8th IS&T/SID Color Imaging Conference*, Scottsdale AZ, pp. 183–196.
28. L. MacDonald, J. Morovic and K. Xiao (2000) A topographic gamut mapping algorithm based on experimental observed data. *Proc. 8th IS&T/SID Color Imaging Conference*, Scottsdale AZ, pp. 311–317.
29. P. Green and R. Luo (2001) Color gamut measurements and mapping: the role of color spaces. *Proc. SPIE*, **4300**, 139–149.
30. J. J. McCann (2001) Color gamut mapping using spatial comparisons. *Proc. SPIE*, **4300**, 126–130.

PART 4

Gamut mapping

12

How different are colour gamuts in cross-media colour reproduction?

Ján Morovic and Pei-Li Sun

12.1 INTRODUCTION

The gamuts of colour media are important parameters in the reproduction of colour images. Their assumed magnitudes directly influence the degree to which colours are modified and hence the relationship between an original and its reproductions. In the vast majority of practical and sometimes also theoretical applications, however, the gamuts of colour reproduction media are established under a standard set of conditions (e.g. those implicit in the measuring procedure).

The aim of this chapter is primarily to be pedagogic and motivational rather than to present a new phenomenon. It is pedagogic in terms of illustrating more clearly what is implicitly the case in that which is theoretically known and it is motivational in terms of aiming at initiating a change of practice with respect to what colour gamuts are considered to be and what it is that colour gamuts are attributed to. These twin aims will be pursued first by way of a theoretical discussion and then by the illustration of the theoretical conclusions by means of measurements taken of actual colour gamuts.

Before discussing the nature of colour gamuts, it is useful first to look at a context within which its understanding is of importance. Arguably the most important context in

Colour Image Science, edited by L.W. MacDonald and M.R. Luo.

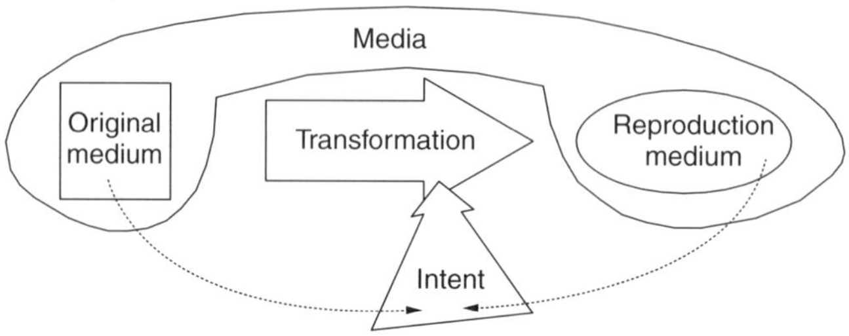

Figure 12.1 Elements of cross-media colour reproduction [1].

which an understanding of colour gamuts is crucial is *cross-media colour reproduction*, which will here be defined as 'the process by which colour information from an original medium is transferred to a reproduction medium so as to achieve a predetermined relationship between them' [1]. Such a definition entails that there are four elements involved in colour reproduction (Figure 12.1): colour information, colour reproduction media, cross-media transformation and the intended relationship between original and reproduction (i.e. rendering intent).

Colour gamuts are involved in the first two of these elements (i.e. colour information and colour reproduction media), whereby one can consider the colour gamut of the information (e.g. an image, a set of colours) and the gamut of the medium in which the image is encoded. Colour gamuts are also present in the transformation element, but with a parametric rather than a characteristic role, i.e. they influence the nature of the transformation rather than being its property. The characteristics of the first two elements are parameters of the third, and the accurate determination of colour gamuts will therefore directly influence how colour information will be transformed between original and reproduction media.

Colour gamuts are parameters of the gamut mapping stage of a cross-media reproduction transform, which can be considered to consist of six stages [2] made up of

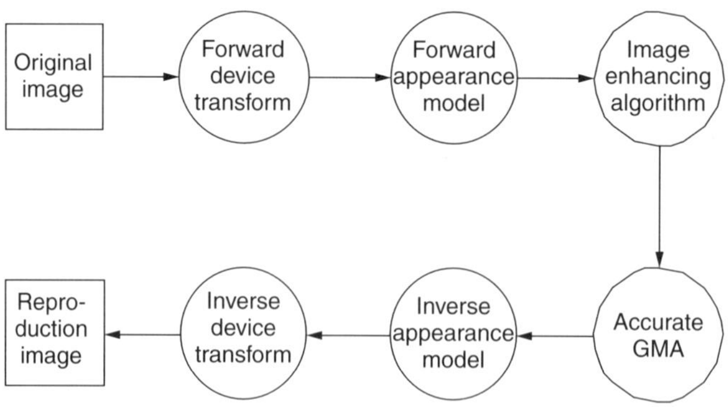

Figure 12.2 Six-stage cross-media colour reproduction transform.

the following elements (Figure 12.2): *device characterisation* (the modelling of the relationship between device-dependent data and resulting visual stimuli); *colour appearance modelling* (the prediction of appearance attributes of visual stimuli); *image enhancement* (sharpening, contrast enhancement, etc.); and *gamut mapping* (the assignment of colours in a reproduction medium to colours of an original medium or image).

Now that the cross-media colour reproduction context has been introduced, a more systemic approach to understanding the nature of a colour gamut can be attempted. The next section considers the nature of colour gamuts and what objects possess them. Section 12.3 contains details of an experimental set-up used to investigate these questions. Section 12.4 gives the experimental results and the final section draws some general conclusions.

12.2 DETERMINING GAMUT BOUNDARIES

12.2.1 Terminology

Three key gamut-related terms are defined as follows [3]:

- *Colour reproduction medium*: a medium for displaying or capturing colour information, e.g. a CRT monitor, a digital camera or a scanner. In printing, the colour reproduction medium is not the printer but the combination of printer, colorants and substrate.
- *Colour gamut*: a range of colours achievable on a given colour reproduction medium (or present in an image on that medium) under a given set of viewing conditions; it is a volume in some specified colour space.
- *Colour gamut boundary*: a surface determined by a colour gamut's extremities (Figure 12.3).

Note that the above terminology is that used by CIE Technical Committee 8–03 on gamut mapping [4], hence it represents the consensus of a number of researchers investigating the subject.

12.2.2 Theoretical implications of definitions

The definitions in Section 12.2.1 have two important implications, which are often overlooked. First, the most crucial factor is that viewing conditions are intrinsic to colour gamuts, i.e. one can only talk about the colour gamut of a set of stimuli if the corresponding viewing conditions are specified. This follows directly from our general understanding of colour, whereby it can be seen as a phenomenon that arises when all of the following are present: *stimulus*, *observer* and *viewing conditions* (illumination, geometry, surround, etc.). If this is the case for individual colours, it is necessarily also the case for a colour gamut, which is the range of colours that can be produced by a physical medium. Hence it is essential to specify the details of all three components when talking about a colour gamut. It is meaningless to talk about the colour gamut of a set of stimuli in general (e.g.

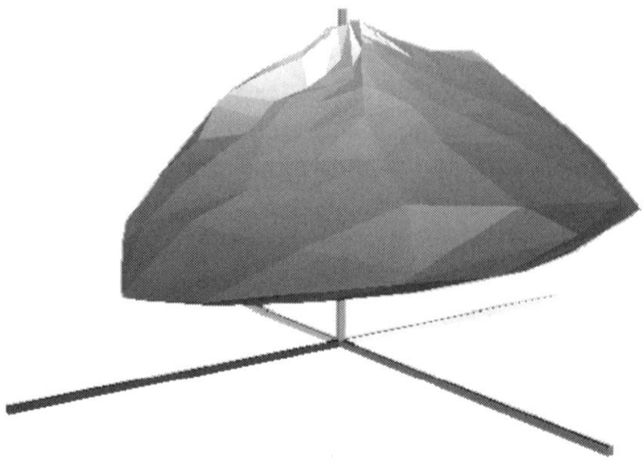

Figure 12.3 CAM97s2 gamut of a print made with a colour printer, illuminated by D50 with 100 cd m^{-2} luminance of reference white and seen against a mid-grey background by the CIE standard colorimetric observer (2°).

the set of colours displayable on a given CRT). Such a set only has a colour gamut when seen by some specific observer under some specific viewing conditions.

Considering that the colour gamut of a colour reproduction medium is nothing but the colour gamut of the set of stimuli it is capable of displaying or capturing, it is essential to specify viewing conditions and observer details. For example, talking about the colour gamut of a printed image is meaningless, as it could assume a number of forms subject to viewing conditions and observers, i.e. a printed image has a set of possible colour gamuts rather than a single one. Looking at such an image in the dark gives a zero-volume gamut (to use an extreme example), different levels of illumination result in different gamut volumes, illumination chromaticity changes gamut shape as well as volume, and viewing distance and flare in the environment make a difference too. Hence the question 'What is the gamut of this print?' cannot be answered and should instead be rephrased as 'What is the gamut of this print under viewing conditions X for observer Y?' This point will be illustrated in Section 12.4 to show that understanding colour gamuts in this way is necessary rather than dismissable as overly pedantic.

Second, colour reproduction media can be divided into two categories with very different gamut characteristics. For media that capture colour information (scanners, digital cameras, etc.) and can therefore be seen as *input media*, the determination of colour gamuts involves determination of the range across which they can capture variation in colour information. This results in significant difficulty from a practical viewpoint, as it necessitates the availability of stimuli from a larger gamut than that of the input gamut to be determined. A further issue arises when input media are characterised from a set of specific samples and their colour gamuts are estimated on the basis of the characterisation model. In this case the result is not necessarily the gamut of the medium itself but of the intersection of the medium's gamut and the gamut of the characterisation samples. (But if the medium gamut is a subset of the characterisation set's gamut then the result is the medium gamut.)

Output media do not suffer from this difficulty as their gamuts can be determined if their input can be sampled in its entirety, which is not a problem for digital devices that have a finite and known range of possible inputs. However, a different issue arises in conjunction with output media whereby some *colour reproduction devices* are media while others are not. CRT monitors, for example, are direct colour reproduction media. Printers, on the other hand, are not themselves colour reproduction media; rather, they can give rise to a range of printed media using a range of substrates and colorants, to be viewed under various types of illumination. Hence the question of a printer's gamut cannot be answered even if the details of viewing condition and observer are supplied. Only prints can have colour gamuts.

In addition to these factors influencing colour gamuts, the colour space in which they are computed and visualised also plays a crucial and well-recognised role.

12.2.3 Implications for characterisation and profiling

The definitions given above have important practical implications that are habitually overlooked. Any system including device characterisation must be interpreted as having medium characterisation, and this must be determined for each individual combination of observer and viewing condition (OVC). It is not possible to characterise a medium in general. If, for example, a CRT is to be used as a colorimetric medium, its characterisation needs to be determined under the OVC under which it is going to be used. Characterising a CRT under one set of conditions and then using the characterisation to predict colour appearance under another set of conditions is invalid.

A prominent example of systems relying on characterisation are colour management systems, such as those based on the ICC framework [5]. In this context it is essential that each medium is characterised under the OVC for which the resultant device profile will be used. Characterising a CRT in a dark, flare-free environment, for example, and then using the results to predict colour appearance under typical office conditions is invalid and will result in substantial error and mistrust of the system.

The implication is that either a large number of profiles need to be generated for each medium, or that the system has the ability to transform a standard OVC profile to predict appearance under a range of specific OVCs. While it is not within the scope of this chapter to investigate the latter and more ideal of these options, the experimental data presented here is intended to be a motivation for embarking on a more systemic modelling of medium appearance as a function of OVC change.

12.2.4 Gamut boundary calculation

Given particular OVCs, the gamut of a set of colours, which could represent either a colour reproduction medium or an image encoded within it, can be described using a number of methods [6–9]. This study employed the *segment maxima* method for calculating *gamut boundary descriptors* (SMGBD) [9], in which the gamut boundary of a set of colours is described by a matrix containing the most extreme colours for each segment of colour space. The segmentation is carried out in terms of spherical coordinates calculated from orthogonal CAM97s2 [10] coordinates using the following formulae:

$$r = [(J - J_E)^2 + (a - a_E)^2 + (b - b_E)^2]^{1/2} \quad (12.1)$$

$$\alpha = \tan^{-1}((b - b_E)/(a - a_E)) \quad (12.2)$$

$$\theta = \tan^{-1}[(J - J_E)/((a - a_E)^2 + (b - b_E)^2)^{1/2}] \quad (12.3)$$

where a and b are the orthogonal coordinates corresponding to CAM97s2's cylindrical C and h coordinates. E is defined as a point inside the gamut and can be obtained by averaging the coordinates of the points used for calculating an SMGBD (here $E = [50, 0, 0]$ in terms of Jab), r is the distance of a colour from E, α is an angle having a range of 360° and θ is the angle in a plane of constant α having a range of 180° (Figure 12.4(a)).

The SMGBD matrix is calculated by first dividing colour space into $n \times n$ segments ($n = 16$ was used here) in terms of α and θ (Figure 12.4(b)). Then the CAM97s2 coordinates of each of the given set of colours are transformed into spherical coordinates using (12.1) to (12.3). From these, the colour with the largest r is stored for each of the $n \times n$ segments whereby for a given segment we store not only r but also the corresponding spherical angles. Values for segments in which there are no colours are linearly interpolated between the nearest SMGBD matrix entries. The result is a bilinear surface describing the set of colours without the constraint of convexity.

Given such an SMGBD, the gamut boundary for any hue angle can be obtained using the *flexible sequential line gamut boundary* method [9] and *gamut volumes* can also be calculated by summing the volumes of tetrahedra formed by E and sets of three points from the SMGBD triangles on the gamut boundary surface.

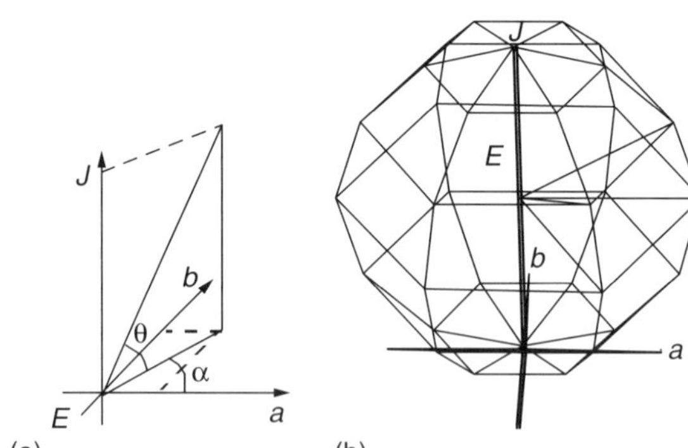

Figure 12.4 Overview of SMGBD in CAM97s2: (a) spherical coordinates, (b) sphere segmented in α and θ (6 × 6 segments used for illustration, one segment highlighted).

12.3 EXPERIMENTAL METHOD

The data gathered for illustration of the two main points in the previous theoretical section are measurements of colours from a number of media taken under several viewing conditions. Differences between observers and the relative spectral power distributions of the illumination were not considered in this study (*CIE standard colorimetric observer* (2°) [11] was used throughout) and the background and surround were kept constant at 20% reflectance for all setups. Table 12.1 shows the mnemonics and descriptions of the media used in the experiment.

All media were measured using a Minolta CS-1000 telespectroradiometer (TSR) under a range of levels of illumination in terms of $X_L Y_L Z_L$ [12] where Y_L is the luminance in cd m^{-2}. The Projector images were projected from a distance of 2 m and measured from a distance of 3 m under two levels of illumination resulting from having the diffuse ceiling lights on and off respectively in a room with blackened windows. For the other media, a 1 m measuring distance was used under four levels of illumination, resulting in the following luminances for the perfect diffuser at the location where colours were measured: 350, 240, 130 and 55 cd m^{-2}. The different levels of illumination were obtained by illuminating the various media using combinations of ceiling lights and an overhead projector (OHP) as well as using filters to vary the output of the projector. Measurements were taken orthogonal to the media surfaces (i.e. at 0°) and the OHP projector was positioned at 45° relative to the surface of the media so as to avoid specular reflection at the location from which measurements were taken. All illumination was diffuse. Note that while care was taken to minimise white point differences between the media, this was not completely possible. Although it would be desirable to have a set of data with identical white points for all media, the present set exhibits gamut differences similar to those of the more optimal set.

To obtain SMGBDs for the above set of media under these viewing and measuring conditions, a set of 26 colours was generated and measured per medium-viewing condition. These colours on the gamut surface were determined by device-dependent coordinate combinations of the 0, 50% and 100% levels. CAM97s2 coordinates were then calculated from perfect diffuser normalised *XYZ* values obtained from measurements made under a number of conditions. Based on the 26 original colour samples, which evenly cover the surface of the RGB gamut cube, 3456($= 12 \times 12 \times 4 \times 6$) simulated gamut boundary colours were generated for the gamut boundary calculation in CAM97s2 *Jab* colour

Table 12.1 Overview of media used in the experiment

Mnemonic	Description
Laser	Prints made on plain paper using HP Color LaserJet 5
Thermal	Prints made on glossy substrate using Tektronix Phaser 440 with cyan, magenta and yellow colorants only
CRT	Apple 21 in Studio Display with white point calibrated to D50
LCD	TFT LCD of Acer Extensa 367T notebook with white point set to D65
Projector	Images projected using a Sanyo PLC–5605B TFT LCD projector

Table 12.2 CAM97s2 parameters for combinations of medium, viewing technique and viewing condition

Medium	Viewing technique	Perfect diffuser (cd m^{-2})	Background (% adopted white)	Luminance of adapting field	Surround conditions
			(% adopted white)		
Laser	Isolated	350, 240, 130, 55	20	20	Average
Thermal	Isolated	350, 240, 130, 55	20	20	Average
Thermal and CRT	Simultaneous	350, 240, 130	20	20	Average
		55	20	20	Dim
CRT	Isolated	350, 240, 130	20	20	Average
		55	20	20	Dim
		0	20	20	Dark
LCD	Isolated	350, 130	20	20	Average
		0	20	20	Dark
Projector	Isolated	350, 240, 130, 55	20	20	Average
		0	20	20	Dark

space. A bilinear interpolation technique was used for simulating 12×12 colours within each square consisting of 2×2 original samples. RGB distances between the interpolated colour and the four original samples were regarded as the weights for the interpolation in *Jab* space.

For all calculations the background (CAM97s2 Y_b) had a luminance which was 20% of the luminance of the adopted white. When colour appearance was calculated for media viewed in isolation, surround conditions were set to 'average' and the adopted white was taken to be the medium white point (i.e. the substrate for Thermal and Laser and $R = G = B = 100\%$ for CRT, LCD and Projector) as measured under actual viewing conditions. The luminance of the adapting field (CAM97s2 L_A) was set to 1/5 of the adopted white. When calculating appearance for media viewed simultaneously, the adopted white was taken to be the medium white point with the higher luminance (i.e. the Thermal white point for the three highest illumination levels and the CRT white point for the 55 cd m^{-2} level). The CAM97s2 surround conditions were set to 'average' for the three highest illumination levels and to 'dim' for the lowest. Table 12.2 summarises the CAM97s2 parameter values.

12.4 EXPERIMENTAL RESULTS

The measurements taken under the conditions described in Section 12.3 can yield numerous insights about the relationship of the colour gamuts of various media under a range of viewing conditions. As the aim of this chapter is primarily to look at gamut differences, we first consider the nature of the difference between the gamuts of the CRT and Thermal media under a range of illumination conditions. This will then be followed by analysis of how the gamuts of individual media change with illumination level.

12.4.1 Comparison of CRT and Thermal gamuts

The relationship between displays and prints is very often of concern to users of colour management systems, so we first consider the CRT and Thermal gamuts. The difference between them can be considered from two viewpoints: (1) if the two media were viewed *simultaneously* under different illumination levels; (2) if they were viewed *separately* under the same or different viewing conditions. The first of these scenarios would result in a single adopted white (i.e. the medium white point with higher luminance) whereas in the second the adopted whites would be the white points of the individual media. Note that in all cases the medium white points were measured by a telespectroradiometer under the actual viewing conditions.

We first look at gamut differences when the two media (CRT and Thermal) are measured by conventional means (i.e. the way they would be measured if one were to make a single device profile for each). The CRT was measured as described in Section 12.3 but in a dark room which resulted in very little environmental flare and the setting of surround parameters to 'dark' in CAM97s2. The Thermal printer was measured using a GretagMacbeth *Spectrolino* spectrophotometer, and *XYZ* values were calculated for standard illuminant D50. Surround parameters were set to 'average' and the background (CAM97s2 Y_b) had a luminance of 20% of the luminance of the adopted white. The luminance of the adapting field (CAM97s2 L_A) was set to 1/5 of the CRT white's luminance for both media. The gamut differences resulting from this data are shown in Figure 12.5 and the gamut volumes under these conditions were 512 935 and 700 656 cubic CAM97s2 *Jab* units for the Thermal and CRT media respectively. Note that all *ab* plots in this chapter are projections onto the *ab* plane whereas *Ja* plots show the intersection of a gamut boundary and the *Ja* plane.

We now turn to consideration of the simultaneous scenario with data collected under actual viewing conditions. Gamut differences for the CRT–Thermal pair are shown in

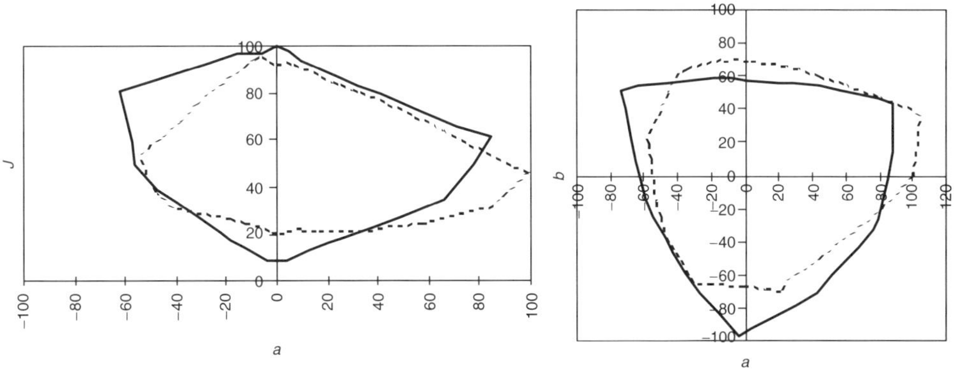

Figure 12.5 CRT gamuts (solid) and Thermal gamuts (dashed) under 'standard' conditions.

Figure 12.7 and the corresponding gamut volumes in Figure 12.6. As pointed out when discussing the 'standard' data, the key point to note is that the given pair of media can result in a number of gamut differences varying in magnitude and nature. What these figures show most clearly, and what would be the case even if they did not exhibit some white point chromaticity differences (which here most affect the 55 cd m^{-2} set-up), is that the CRT and Thermal media change in opposite directions with changes in the level of illumination. While the Thermal gamut decreases with a decrease of illumination level, the CRT gamut increases.

For the levels examined, this suggests that a CRT to Thermal gamut mapping procedure would require little compression at one end of the range (indeed it could even make use of expansion), while at the other end there would be significant need for compression and virtually no room for expansion. Viewing these media under any of the actual conditions considered here would result in dramatic differences between what is seen to be the gamut difference and what gamut difference is suggested by the 'standard' gamuts. The point is not a criticism of the standard gamuts but that a single gamut representation cannot match the range of possible gamut differences between a set of media. The gamuts calculated under any of the actual illumination levels considered here would represent the actual levels equally as badly as would the standard gamuts.

So far the gamuts of the CRT and Thermal media were considered from the viewpoint of simultaneous viewing, which represents cases where images on these two media are compared side by side. For example, if an image on the CRT is to be reproduced on the Thermal medium and this reproduction is held next to the CRT for comparison, then the two images could have a range of gamut differences as illustrated in Figures 12.6 and 12.7.

Next we consider the possible gamut differences between these two media when viewed separately. This corresponds to gamut comparisons between the gamuts of sets of colours seen under different viewing conditions by a single observer at different times or by multiple observers at either single or multiple times. Going back to the cross-media reproduction example from the simultaneous scenario, in this separate viewing scenario it would correspond to being only the CRT or only the Thermal medium present in an

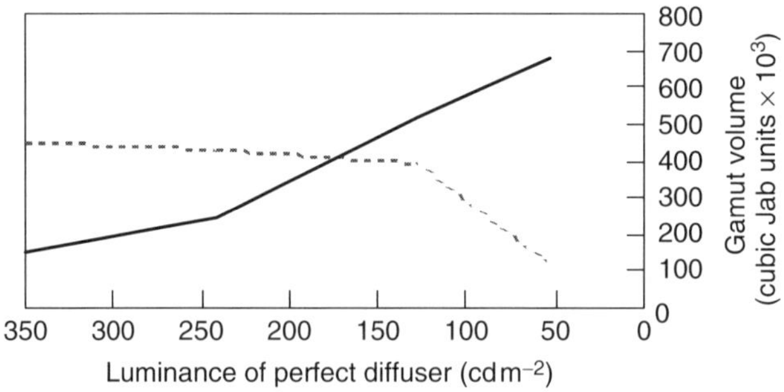

Figure 12.6 Gamut volumes for CRT (solid line) and Thermal (dashed) viewed simultaneously under viewing conditions resulting in different perfect diffuser luminances.

observer's field of view. For example, if one person views the CRT image under one set of conditions (e.g. in a graphics studio) and another person views the Thermal image under a different set (e.g. outdoors), then there are two gamuts corresponding to these two media being viewed under these two conditions, hence their difference should be considered.

Given the four levels of illumination used above, there are 16 (4×4) gamut difference possibilities if the two media are viewed separately. The result of such a comparison of gamuts is shown in Figures 12.8 to 12.10.

From the figures showing gamut boundaries of the CRT and Thermal media as seen in isolation under different viewing conditions, we can again see the same trend as exhibited in the data obtained from their simultaneous viewing. The Thermal gamut decreases with perfect diffuser luminance while the CRT gamut exhibits an increase. It can also be seen that gamut differences are smaller in general under these separate viewing conditions, while still having a significant variation in the possible differences due to differences in illumination level. Viewing the CRT medium under 55 cd m^{-2} conditions and the Thermal

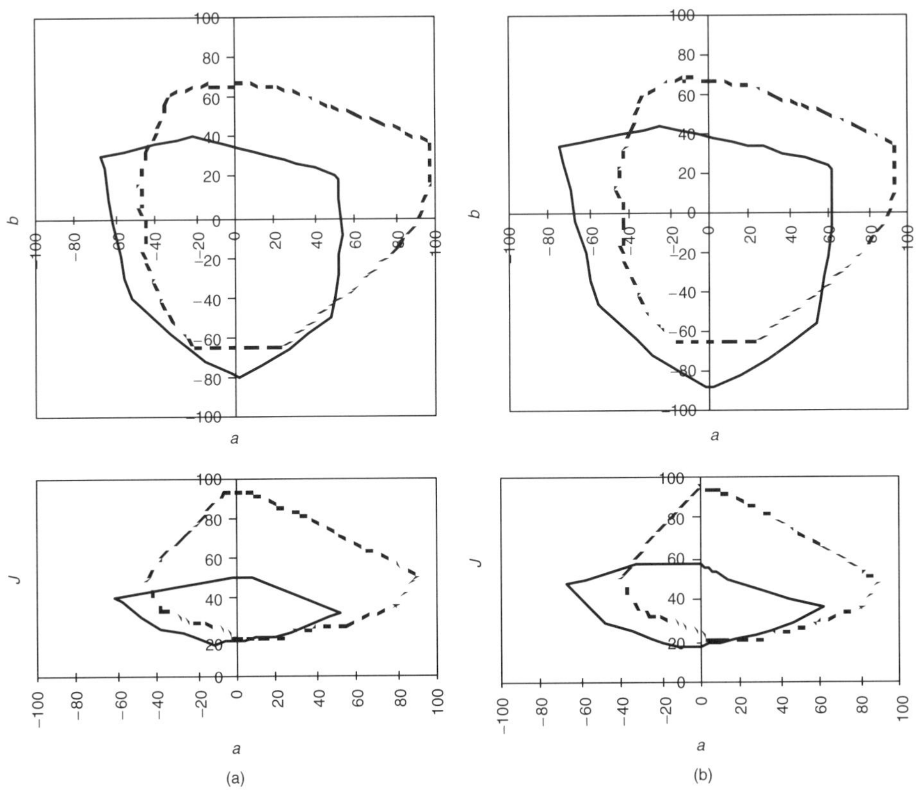

Figure 12.7 CRT gamuts (solid) and Thermal gamuts (dashed) viewed simultaneously under a range of illuminations; the a and b axes range from -100 to 100 and the J axis ranges from 0 to 100: (a) 350 cd m^{-2}, (b) 240 cd m^{-2}, (c) 130 cd m^{-2}, (d) 55 cd m^{-2}.

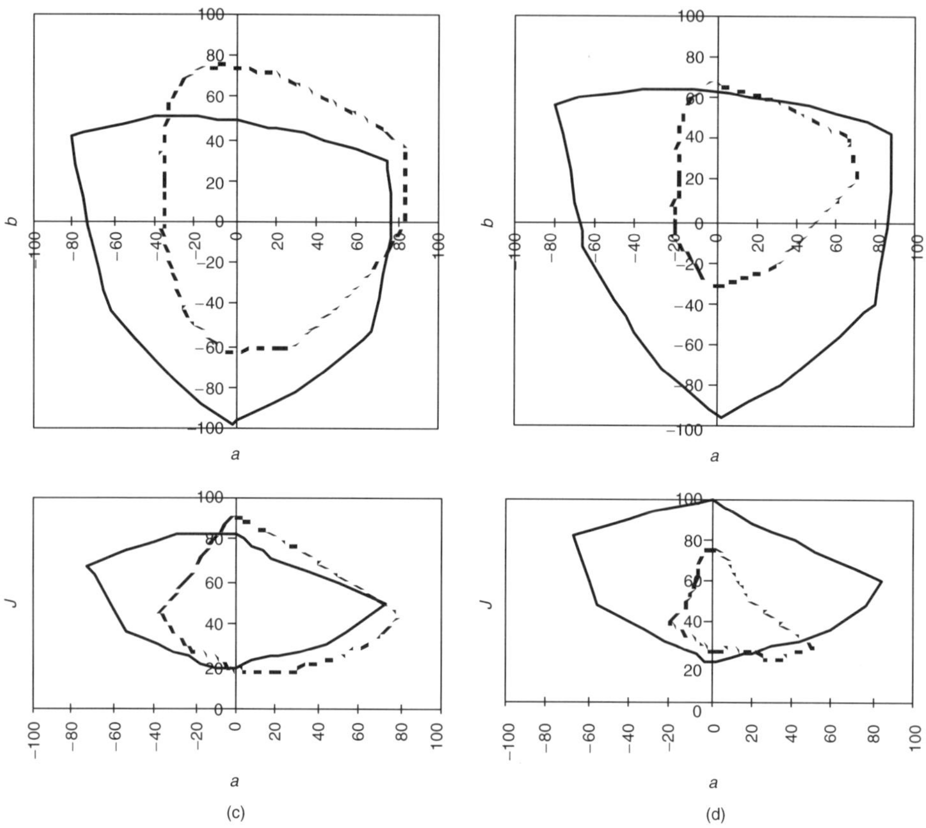

Figure 12.7 *(continued).*

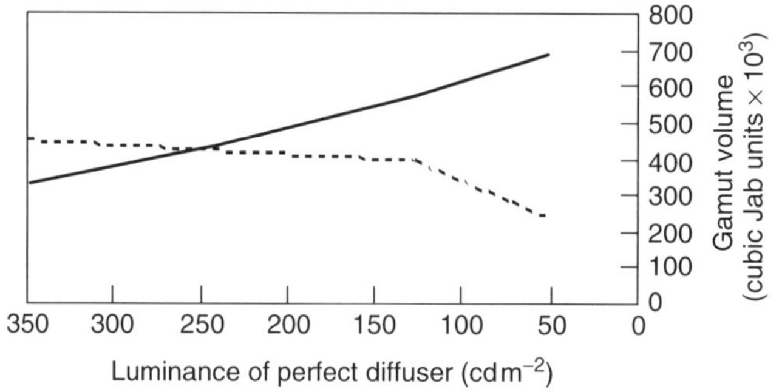

Figure 12.8 Gamut volumes for CRT (solid line) and Thermal (dashed) viewed separately under viewing conditions resulting in different perfect diffuser luminances.

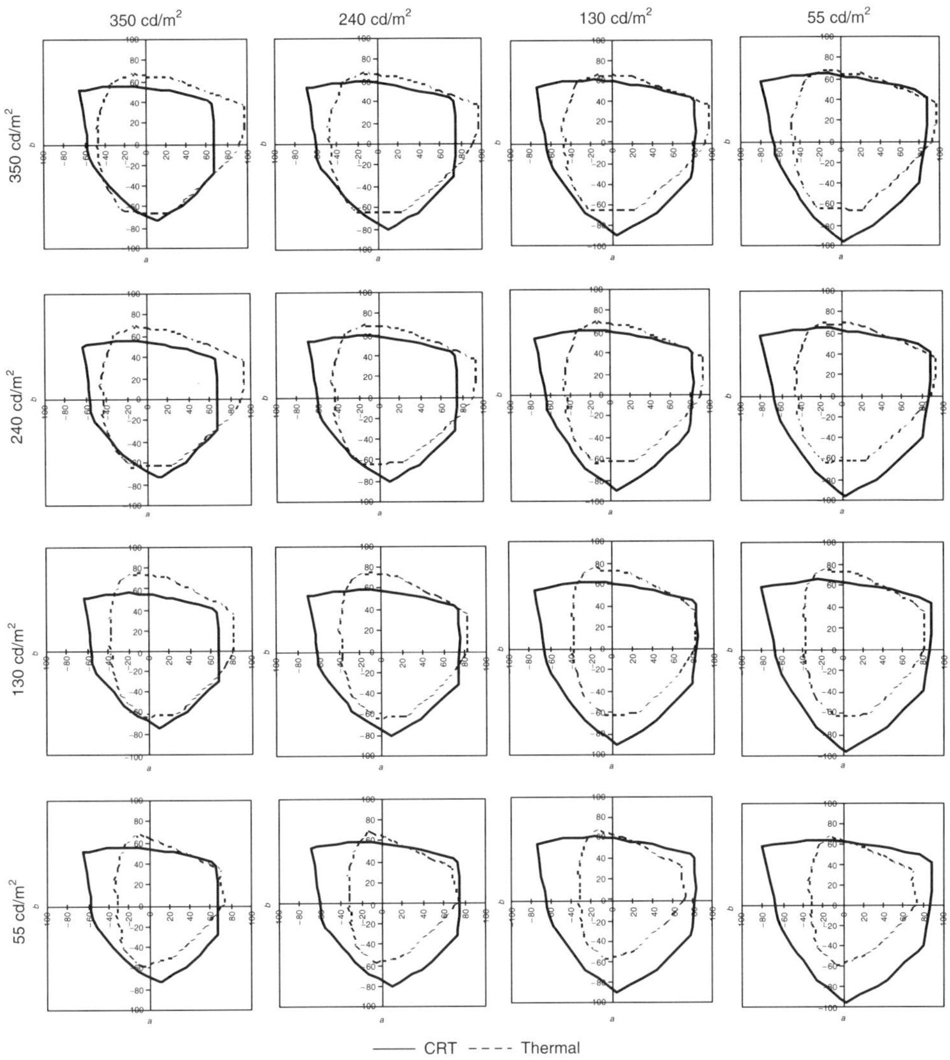

Figure 12.9 CRT gamuts (solid) and Thermal gamuts (dashed) viewed separately under four illumination levels. The horizontal direction shows four levels of luminance for the CRT (highest on left to lowest on right). The vertical direction shows four levels of illumination of the Thermal points (highest at top to lowest at bottom).

under 350 cd m^{-2} conditions results in the two media having a very large overlap between their gamuts. Viewing both media under 240 cd m^{-2} conditions yields very similar gamut volumes with a difference of only 2224 cubic CAM97s2 *Jab* units. The largest difference in this range of illumination levels results from having both media under the 55 cd m^{-2} condition where the gamut volume difference is 429 954 cubic units.

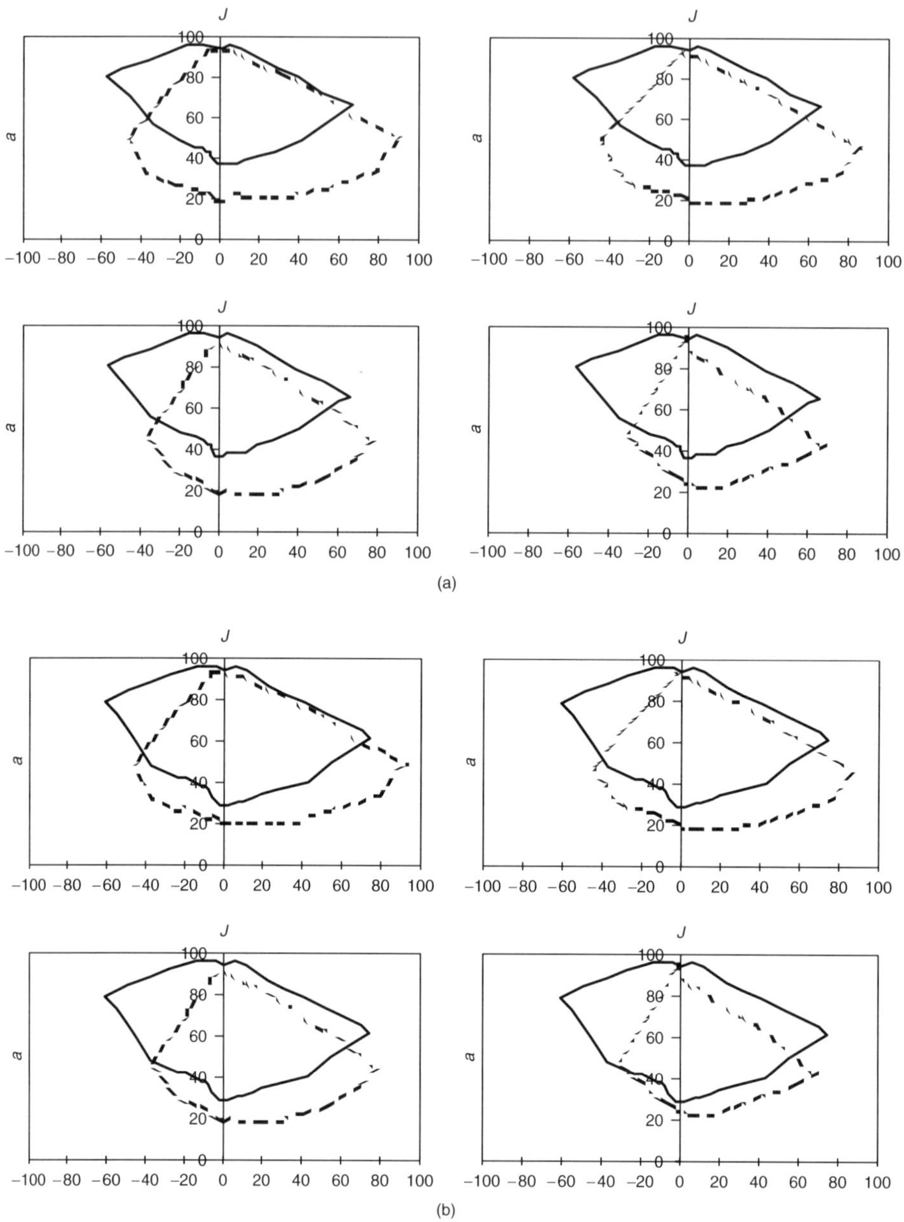

Figure 12.10 CRT gamuts (solid) and Thermal gamuts (dashed) viewed separately under a range of illuminations; the a and b axes range from -100 to 100 and the J axis ranges from 0 to 100: (a) $350\,\text{cd}\,\text{m}^{-2}$, (b) $240\,\text{cd}\,\text{m}^{-2}$, (c) $130\,\text{cd}\,\text{m}^{-2}$, (d) $55\,\text{cd}\,\text{m}^{-2}$.

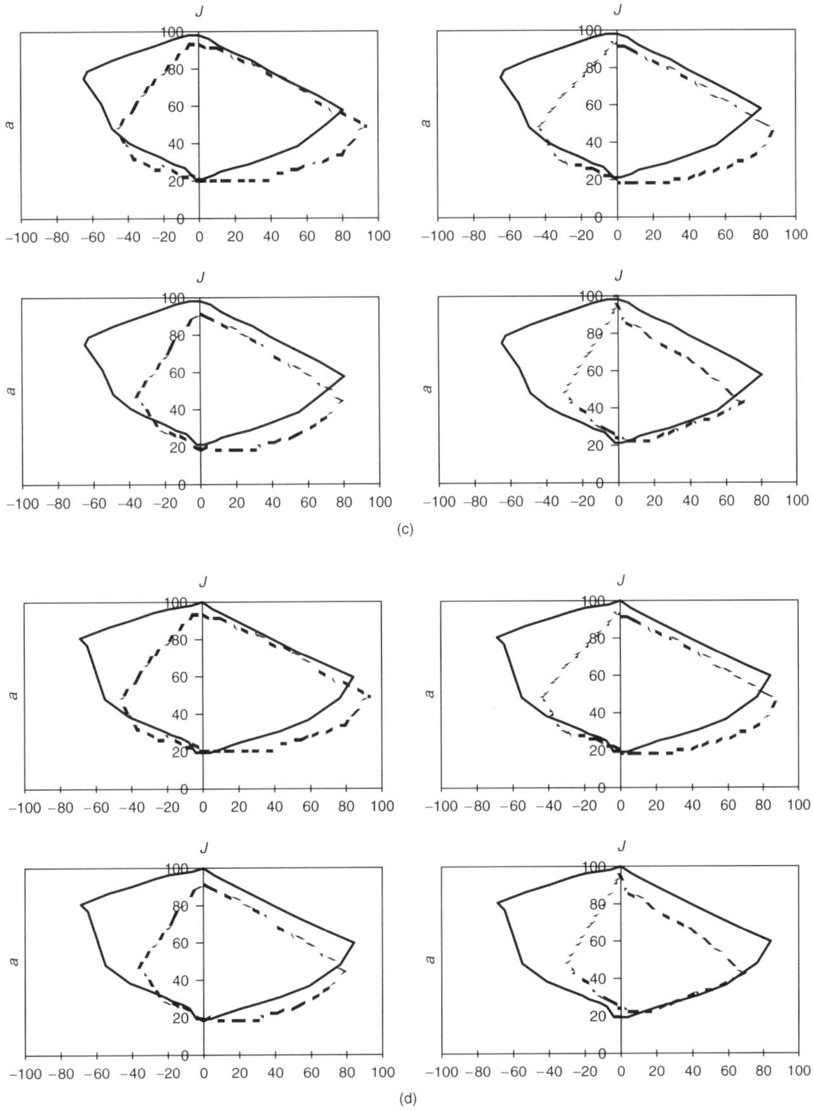

Figure 12.10 *(continued)*.

To put this figure into perspective, we can see that it is two orders of magnitude larger than the smallest difference and almost twice the gamut volume of the Thermal medium under these conditions (i.e. 251 609). Hence the answer to the question of how large the difference can be between the CRT and Thermal gamuts can range from 'almost the same' to 'the CRT gamut is almost three times as large as the Thermal gamut'. It all depends on viewing conditions and, as can be seen from this data, their influence is dramatic. Trying to describe colour reproduction media using single gamuts cannot accommodate the wide range of perceived gamuts they can exhibit. This will further be illustrated by seeing how the gamuts of individual media seen in isolation vary with changes in illumination levels.

12.4.2 CRT and thermal gamuts in isolation

Figures 12.11 and 12.12 show the CRT and Thermal gamuts for the range of four viewing conditions considered in the previous section. They show that the two media change in opposite directions with a change of illumination level and that the Thermal medium is subject to far less change than the CRT medium. This is due to the appearance of all colours from the Thermal medium being determined solely by the intensity of illumination whereas the appearance of the CRT medium is the result of a combination of its constant output and varying external illumination levels. Because the surface of the CRT is glossy, different levels of illumination result in changes in flare in the environment and hence different levels of lightness for the medium's black point. In other words, changes in illumination levels primarily introduce a scaling to the Thermal medium's colours in tristimulus terms, whereas they result primarily in an offset for the CRT, hence they have a different impact on the respective lightness ranges.

12.4.3 Laser gamut

The Laser medium is similar to the Thermal medium since both are prints, and the same trend as for the Thermal gamuts can be seen for the Laser gamuts (Figure 12.13). Overall

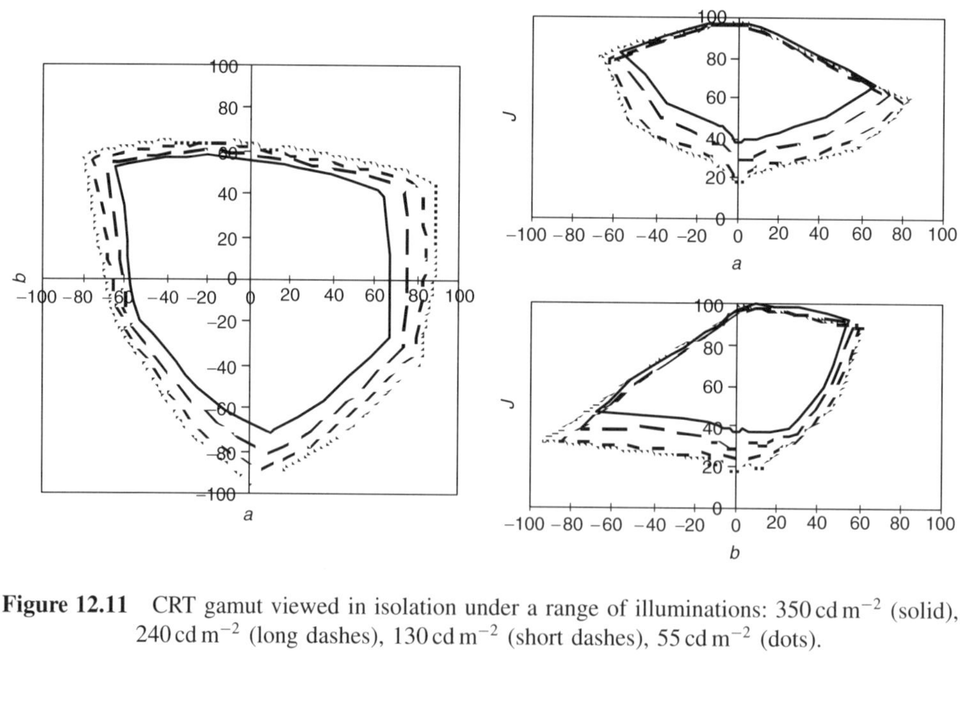

Figure 12.11 CRT gamut viewed in isolation under a range of illuminations: 350 cd m^{-2} (solid), 240 cd m^{-2} (long dashes), 130 cd m^{-2} (short dashes), 55 cd m^{-2} (dots).

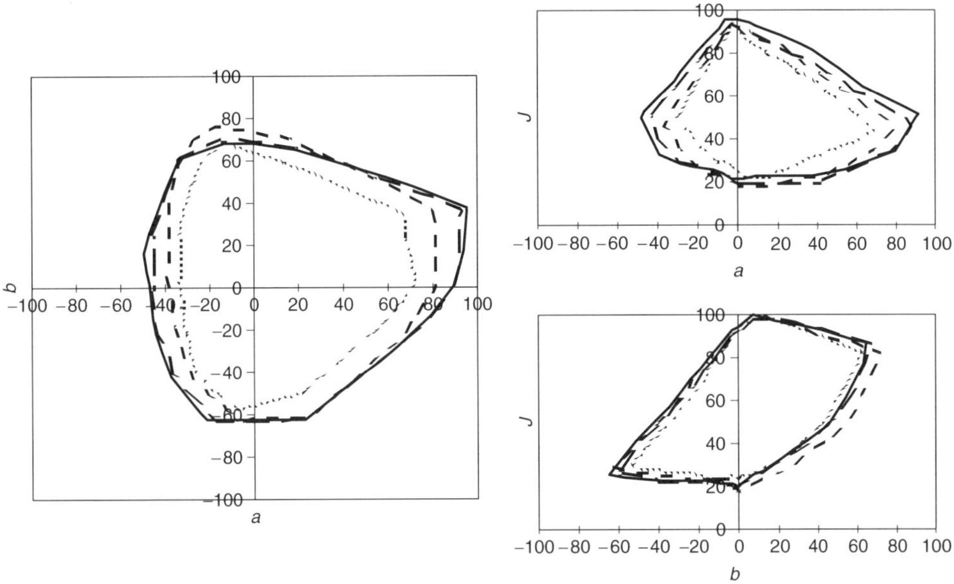

Figure 12.12 Thermal gamut viewed in isolation under a range of illumination levels: 350 cd m^{-2} (solid), 240 cd m^{-2} (long dashes), 130 cd m^{-2} (short dashes), 55 cd m^{-2} (dots).

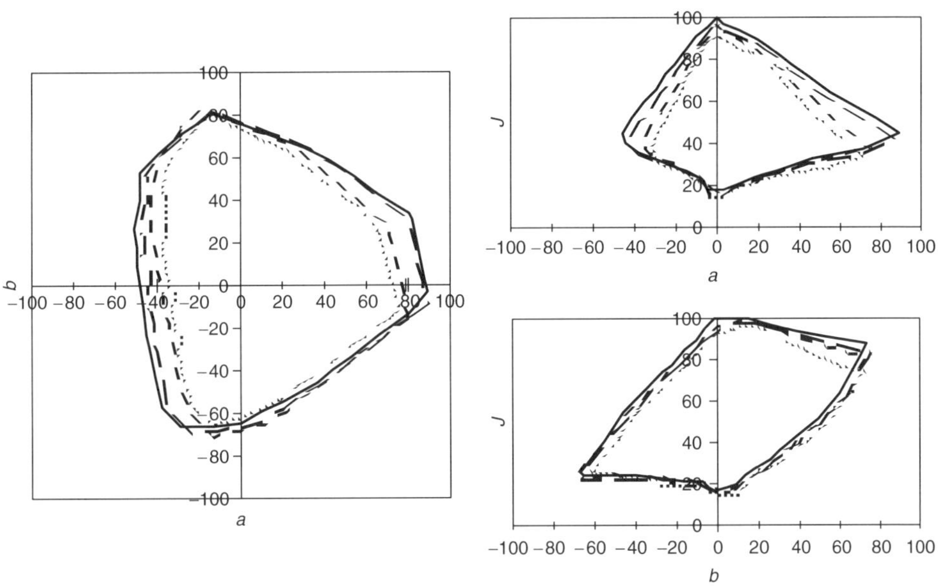

Figure 12.13 Laser gamut viewed in isolation under a range of illuminations: 350 cd m^{-2} (solid), 240 cd m^{-2} (long dashes), 130 cd m^{-2} (short dashes), 55 cd m^{-2} (dots).

the gamut does not change significantly with change of illumination level. Moreover, the lightness range stays virtually identical and changes in chromatic range are due primarily to changes in the redness–greenness direction.

12.4.4 LCD gamut

The gamuts of the LCD medium shown in Figure 12.14 are far less dependent on viewing conditions than the gamuts of the other media considered so far. This is probably due to the LCD medium's matte surface properties combined with it being self-luminous. The matte surface properties also account for there being minimal flare effects for the LCD medium between the two levels of illumination.

12.4.5 Projector gamut

Finally, the gamut of the Projector medium (Figure 12.15) very strongly dependent on illumination, as it produces colours by reflecting its projected light from a surface (the screen). If there is other (achromatic) light reflected from that surface then we have a similar situation as with the CRT medium. The reason for the stronger effect for projection is that, at $R = G = B = 0\%$ input, the illumination of the CRT medium results only in a first surface reflection from the glass faceplate in front of a black background, whereas the same input to the Projector medium results in a reflection of the external illumination from the highly-reflecting (white) screen surface.

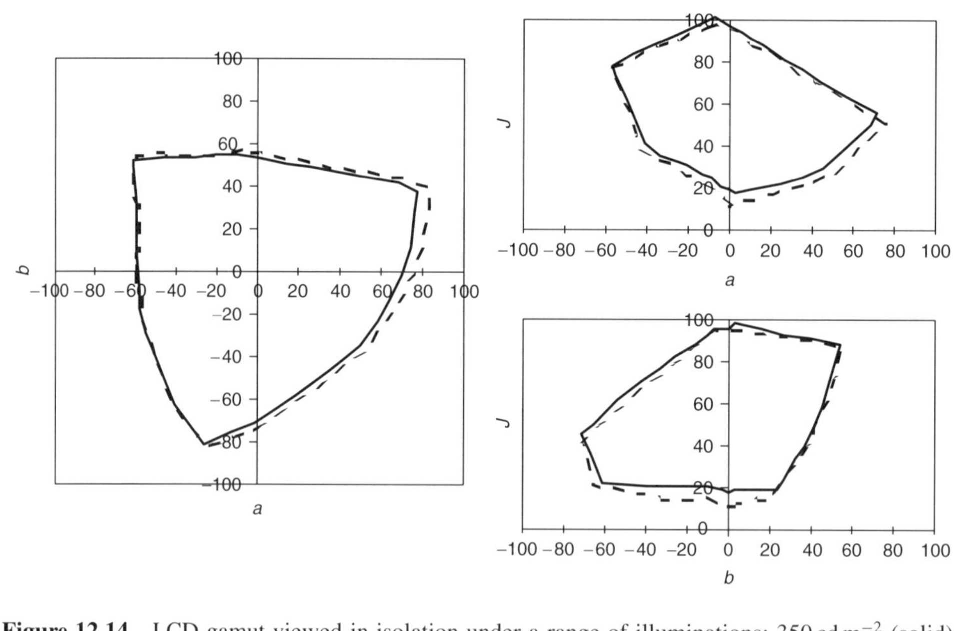

Figure 12.14 LCD gamut viewed in isolation under a range of illuminations: 350 cd m^{-2} (solid), 130 cd m^{-2} (dashed).

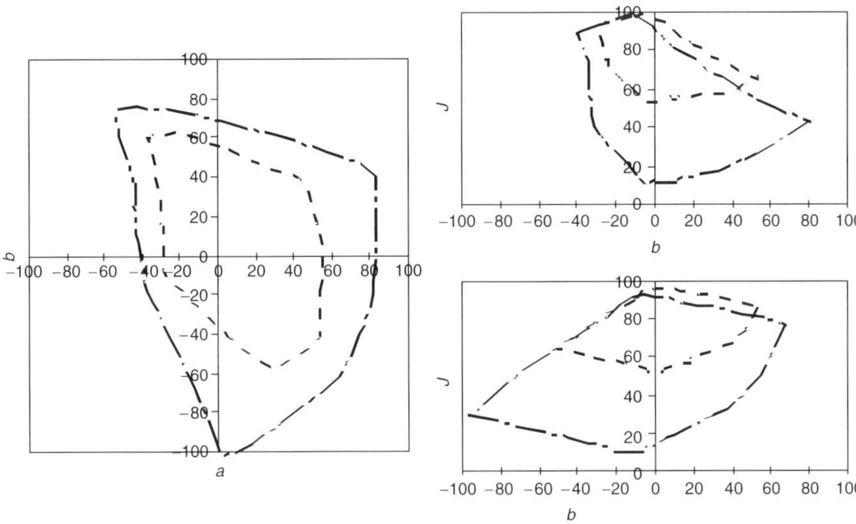

Figure 12.15 Projector gamut viewed in isolation under a range of illuminations: 130 cd m^{-2} (dashed), 0 (chain dotted).

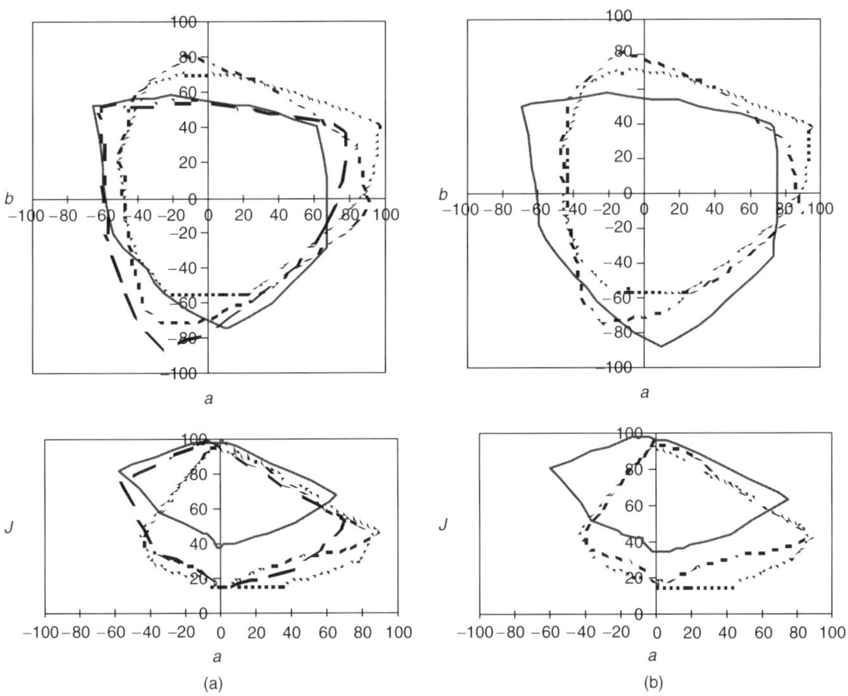

Figure 12.16 Gamuts seen in isolation under different illuminations: (a) 350 cd m^{-2}, (b) 240 cd m^{-2}, (c) 130 cd m^{-2}, (d) 55 cd m^{-2}. Key to gamuts: CRT (solid), Laser (short dashes), LCD (very long dashes), Projector (long dashes), Thermal (dots).

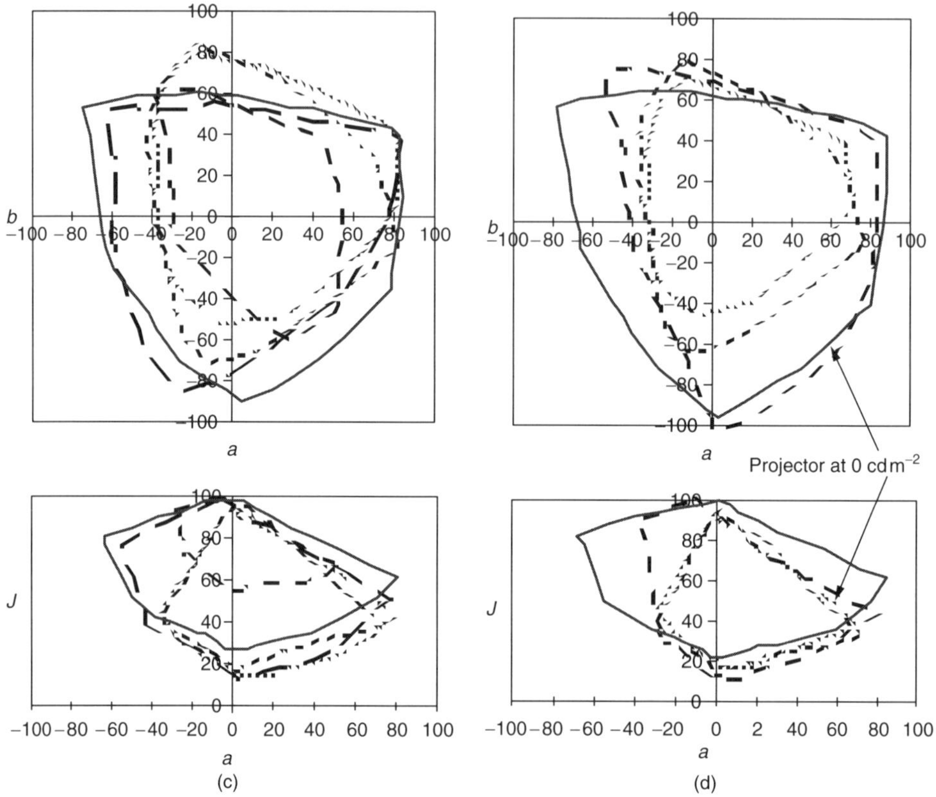

Figure 12.16 (*continued*).

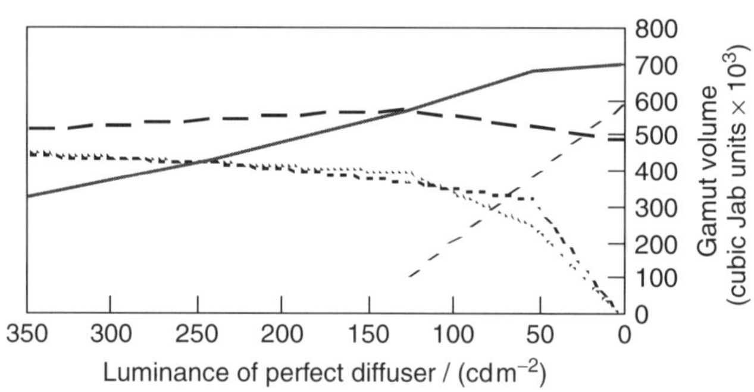

Figure 12.17 Gamut volumes: CRT (solid), Laser (short dashes), LCD (very long dashes), Projector (long dashes), Thermal (dots).

12.4.6 Overview

To allow for easier comparison between the media considered in the previous sections, their gamut boundaries and gamut volumes are shown together in Figures 12.16 and 12.17. The same trends can be observed as noted for the media individually.

12.5 CONCLUSIONS

Colour reproduction media are strongly affected by changes in illumination as a result of different methods of producing colours, including self-luminance and reflection, and a variety of surface properties ranging from the gloss of glass to the matte of uncoated paper. These differences necessarily and sometimes dramatically influence the corresponding colour gamuts, hence necessitate a description of medium gamuts dependent on viewing condition. Describing a colour reproduction medium using a single gamut boundary inevitably leads to mismatch between what that gamut boundary suggests and how the gamut of the medium is seen under different conditions.

While one solution to the mismatch problem is to generate a number of gamut boundaries for each combination of medium-viewing conditions, this would result in an explosion of gamut boundary descriptors even if only for standardised observer and viewing conditions, and it would always result in some degree of inflexibility. Alternatively and preferably, the relationship could be modelled, leading to the possibility of having a single reference gamut per medium which could then be modified to suit particular viewing conditions. As can be seen from Figure 12.17, medium gamuts can be affected to different degrees ranging from virtually no difference for the LCD medium, to a sixfold change for the Projector medium. The most important point to be taken from this chapter is that instead of a medium having a single gamut, it has a multitude of gamuts.

ACKNOWLEDGEMENTS

This research was inspired by an exchange of emails initiated by Michael Stokes (Microsoft) and later also involving Naoya Katoh (Sony) in February 1999. We would like to thank them both for bringing up this useful topic. Thanks also go to Julian Shaw for his comments.

REFERENCES

1. J. Morovic (1999) Colour reproduction – past, present and future. *Proceedings of the 5th National Congress on Colour*, Terrassa, Spain, June 1999, pp. 9–15.
2. J. Morovic (1999) Gamut mapping and ICC rendering intents. *Proceedings of the International Colour Management Forum*, Derby, UK.
3. J. Morovic and M. R. Luo (1999) Developing algorithms for universal colour gamut mapping. *Colour Imaging: Vision and Technology*, L. W. MacDonald (ed.). John Wiley, pp. 253–282.
4. http://www.colour.org/tc8–03/
5. http://www.color.org/

6. W. Kress and M. Stevens (1994) Derivation of 3-dimensional gamut descriptors for graphic arts output devices. *TAGA Proc.*, 199–214.
7. G. J. Braun and M. D. Fairchild (1997) Image lightness rescaling using sigmoidal contrast enhancement functions. *Journal of Electronic Imaging*, **8**(4) 380–393.
8. J. Morovic and M. R. Luo (1997) Gamut mapping algorithms based on psychophysical experiment. *Proceedings of the 5th IS&T/SID Color Imaging Conference*, pp. 44–49.
9. J. Morovic and M. R. Luo (2000) Calculating medium and image gamut boundaries for gamut mapping *Color Research and Application*, **25**, 394–401.
10. C. J. Li, M. R. Luo and R. W. G. Hunt (1999) The CAM97s2 model *Proceedings of the IS&T/SID 7th Color Imaging Conference: Color Science, Systems and Applications*, pp. 262–263.
11. CIE (1986) 2nd edn *Colorimetry*, CIE.
12. R. W. G. Hunt (1995) *Measuring Colour*, 2nd edn Ellis Horwood.

13

Gamut compression algorithms based on experimental observer data

Byoung-Ho Kang, Maeng-Sub Cho, Ján Morovic and Ronnier Luo

13.1 INTRODUCTION

In cross-media colour image reproduction, each medium can produce only a subset of the visible colour space, known as the *medium gamut*. Hence it needs to be ensured that all colours of the original image are transformed to colours that can be reproduced on the output medium. The process of mapping colours from the gamut of a source medium to fit the gamut of a reproduction medium is called *gamut mapping*. In the usual case where the source gamut is larger than the reproduction gamut, there are two major types of gamut mapping. *Gamut clipping* alters only out-of-gamut colours so as to render them reproducible, whereas *gamut compression* is applied to all original colours and can modify even colours which would be reproducible so as to distribute gamut differences across the entire range [18].

Gamut mapping techniques can be systematically categorised in terms of the mapping methods used for individual colour attributes, primarily lightness and chroma. Numerous gamut mapping approaches have been proposed and examined in the past. In most studies,

Colour Image Science, edited by L.W. MacDonald and M.R. Luo.

algorithms were first defined and then evaluated by observers making judgements about the suitability of algorithms for a given reproduction intent. Table 13.1 categorises gamut mapping into different categories.

An alternative approach is to have observers adjust image colours so as to make them a better representation of the original. This approach was taken by Ebner and Fairchild [4], who asked observers to adjust the colour of uniformly coloured simple images from a smaller gamut so as to make them more similar to corresponding original images from a larger gamut. A colorimetrically characterised computer-controlled CRT display was used

Table 13.1 Categorisation of gamut mapping methods

		Methods		**References**
Lightness mapping	Media based	Linear scale		[24], [28], [14], [19], [20], [16], [17]
		Soft clipping		[7], [16]
		Hard clipping		
	Image based	Homomorphic filtering Histogram equalisation Modified histogram equalisation		[15]
	Chroma weighted			[20], [21]
Chroma mapping	Mapping function	Clipping	Minimum distance Straight Cusp Centroid	[24], [5], [23], [8], [11], [12], [16], [4]
		Scaling	Soft clipping	[6], [7], [26]
			Three-piece Linear	[5]
			Knee	[5], [16], [7], [3].
			Linear	[16], [5], [3].
	Mapping directions	Constant lightness		[5], [23], [13], [19], [16], [29].
		Cusp point		
		Centroid		
		Constant saturation		
	Device and image based	Device dependent Image dependent		
Regional mappings				[29], [25], [22], [20], [21]
Gamut expansion				[25]

to determine the closest perceptual colour matches of 25 colours. To specify a reproduction gamut, a Xerox 4920 color laser printer was characterised. Twenty-one observers were involved in a colour matching experiment between out-of-gamut colours and those on the artificial gamut boundary, represented in the CIE $L^*a^*b^*$ colour space. Four different business graphics images were employed. Here is a summary of the results:

- Observers did not make simple matches of the kind assumed in gamut mapping experiments to date. Using the experimental data, three simple models were optimised against the observer match data and found to fit the match vectors acceptably, and they were used to create a clipping or compression-type gamut mapping that would create perceptually closest matches to out-of-gamut colours. Based on the resulting data, they analysed the Katoh and Ito [11] model and found it to be quite acceptable.
- There was no statistically significant difference in any of the gamut mapping decisions of the 25 colours.
- The CIE $L^*a^*b^*$ space is not uniform enough in hue angle to make adequate matches, particularly in the blue-magenta region.

Although deriving a GMA technique on the basis of direct experimental data, there are some limitations in the Ebner and Fairchild study. First, mapping was determined only by reproduction gamut. When larger differences between original and reproduction gamuts are to be overcome, mapping should be determined not only by the reproduction gamut but also by the original gamut and by the nature of the relationship between the two. Second, a limited number of sample colours (25) was used. The evaluation of image gamut compression requires the use of complex and multicolour images in order to work under all possible conditions.

As far as gamut compression is concerned, the most similar kind of data comes from the study of Johnson *et al.* [9], which analysed reproductions made by skilled scanner operators and then attempted to model the results. This approach to investigating gamut mapping was to 'get experienced (scanner) operators to reproduce images and see what they do to them'. A Kodak Q60 Ektachrome transparency – on which the IT8.7/1 chart (ANSI, 1993) is based – was given to five colour reproduction companies in the UK and the USA. Scanner operators were then asked to scan the transparency with their 'standard' set-up and also to edit the set-up to give a better reproduction if they felt it was necessary. A gamut mapping algorithm was then developed on the basis of the resulting reproductions. The interesting characteristics of this algorithm (known as CARISMA) are that it suggests changes to hue in addition to lightness and chroma, and that it uses different mapping methods for different hues depending on the relative shapes of the original and reproduction gamuts.

Braun and Fairchild [2] allowed subjects to control (user interface) sliders that dynamically updated the parameters of a sigmoidal lightness remapping function. Their results revealed the preferred contrast enhancement curves. It is common sense that a reliable gamut mapping should be capable of producing a match to the original scene. Hence it is important to maintain the perceived lightness contrast of the original image, by compensating for the loss that occurs when an image from a device with large dynamic range (such as a CRT display viewed in a dark room) is scaled into the more limited dynamic range of a destination device (such as an inkjet colour print on paper). Sigmoidal remapping functions were selected on the basis of an empirical contrast enhancement model, developed from the results of a psychophysical experiment. Subjects could control sliders to update the values of sigmoid centre and slope, i.e. to control the forms of the sigmoidal remapping function dynamically. Each subject was asked to adjust the image in reduced dynamic range conditions in order to match the appearance of the full dynamic range of the original image. Adjustments were made for each of six images at four different minimum lightness levels.

There has previously been no study in which observers interactively adjusted reproductions of complex images and thereby explored the possibilities of gamut compression. One of the reasons for the absence of direct experimental data for gamut compression is the complexity of the task in comparison with that of gamut clipping. First, gamut compression is determined not only by the reproduction gamut (as is the case for gamut clipping) but also by the original gamut and by the nature of the relationship between the two. Second, the evaluation of gamut compression requires the use of complex, multicolour images and it is not applicable to the reproduction of single colours. Third, the functionality requires an experimental apparatus to allow observers interactively to adjust the nature of gamut compression [10].

There were two aims in the study described in this chapter: (1) to develop an interactive experimental tool for the creation and acquisition of experimental data; and (2) to evaluate existing and derive new gamut compression algorithms (GCAs) based on the experimental data. Two experiments were performed. The first was an matching experiment with two images displayed side by side on a CRT, in which observers were asked to match an original image (within a CRT gamut) by adjusting a second image (within a printer gamut, which was much smaller than that of CRT) using the interactive tool. Eleven observers took part in the experiments in which they modified the colours of four images processed through an existing GCA. Based on analysis of the data, three new gamut compression algorithms were developed, consisting of non-linear lightness/chroma compression and cusp compressions in three different regions of the L^*C^* plane. The second experiment evaluated the performance between the newly derived GCAs and some existing GCAs such as LCLIP (linear lightness mapping and chroma clipping), LCUSP (linear lightness mapping followed by chroma compression toward cusp), GCUSP (Gaussian lightness mapping followed by chroma compression toward cusp), SLIN (simultaneous linear lightness and chroma mapping toward $L^* = 50$), LLIN (linear lightness mapping followed by linear chroma compression), CLLIN (chroma linear mapping and linear lightness mapping) [17] together with an average image based on the results of observers from the first experiment.

13.2 AN INTERACTIVE TOOL

An interactive GUI (graphical user interface) was developed for modifying the colour appearance of pictorial images displayed on a monitor. This was performed by altering colours of their pixels depending on the region of colour space into which they belonged. The colour space used was CIE $L^*a^*b^*$, but other colour spaces could have been used instead.

At the beginning of each experiment, the initial reproduction image (to be adjusted) was created by using the LCLIP algorithm, and this image is referred to as the *initial image*. Using the tool, observers first inspected which part of the reproduction image gave the most unsatisfactory match. They then selected the corresponding colours in CIE $L^*a^*b^*$ space using the *colour region selector* (CRS), and adjusted all image pixels from that region using *colour appearance adjuster* (CAA) controls.

The GUI was developed using the Microsoft C^{++} compiler on an IBM-compatible personal computer with 64 megabytes of main memory. The object-oriented-programming (OOP) technique allowed for individual functions to be grouped into different classes in terms of their procedural characteristics.

13.2.1 Menu design

The menu of the experimental GUI consisted of seven components: (1) File, (2) GMA, (3) Control, (4) CRS, (5) CAA, (6) Process and (7) HELP. Figure 13.1 shows this structure and Table 13.2 describes the individual submenus and their corresponding functionality. Figure 13.2 shows the functions of the control menu. Two different images, the *original* and the *initial* reproduction, were displayed side by side for comparison during the experiment. Each image size was made as large as possible on the screen and the background colour was set to a mid-grey ($L^* = 50.0, a^* = b^* = 0.0$). The white border of an image can have a large impact on the appearance of the test images, due to chromatic adaptation, i.e. the change in colour appearance due to the change in white point (our eyes adapt to this white as an illuminant). However, it is difficult to determine which border colour to use, generally values of L^* used in practical applications range from 70

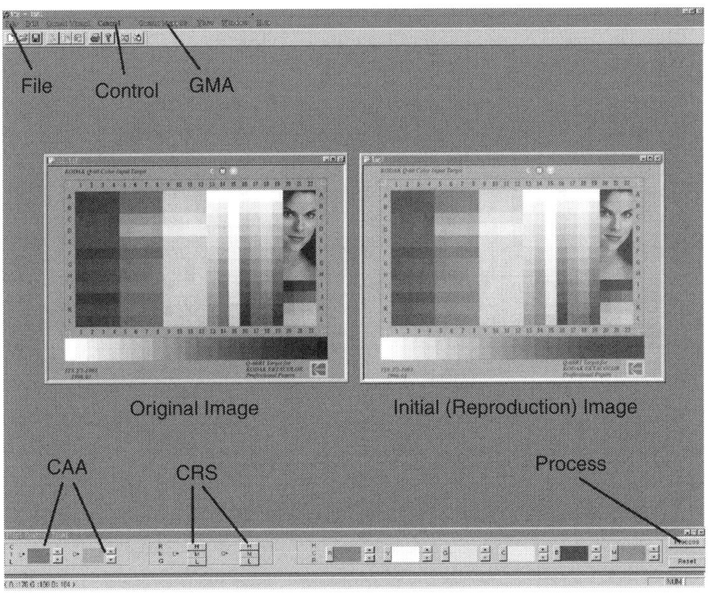

Figure 13.1 Graphical user interface for the experiments.

Table 13.2 Descriptions of menus (experimental tool)

MENU	SUB MENU		FUNCTION	FORM
File	Open		Open image files (*.bmp, *.tif)	Pull down
	Save		Save final processed image file (*.bmp, *.tif)	Pull down
	Save as		Save image file with different name	Pull down
	Exit		Exit the application	Pull down
GMA	LCLIP		Generate an *initial* image via linear lightness and clipping GMA	Pull down
Control	Dialogue		Visualise CRS and CAA dialogue menu	Pull down
	Snapshot		Take snapshot of image in memory at time t_3, (Figure 13.2)	Pull down
	Restore		Come back from t to t_3.	Pull down
	Undo restore		Come back again to t	Pull down
	Initialisation		Come back to time 0	Pull down
	Undo		Retrieve image from t to t_1	Pull down
CRS	L^*	High(65–100)	Select high range of lightness	Button
		Middle (35–65)	Select middle range of lightness	Button
		Low (0–35)	Select low range of lightness	Button
	C^*	High (50–)	Select high range of chroma	Button
		Middle (25–50)	Select middle range of chroma	Button
		Low (0–25)	Select low range of chroma	Button
	h_{ab}	Red (357–59)	Select hue range of red	Button
		Yellow (59–128)	Select hue range of yellow	Button
		Green (128–181)	Select hue range of green	Button
		Cyan (181–226)	Select hue range of cyan	Button
		Blue (226–291)	Select hue range of blue	Button
		Magenta (291–357)	Select hue range of magenta	Button
CAA	L^*	Up	Increase lightness of selected area	Spin button
		Down	Decrease lightness of selected area	Spin button
	C^*	Up	Increase chroma of selected area	Spin button
		Down	Decrease chroma of selected area	Spin button
	h_{ab}	Up	Increase hue angle selected area	Spin button
		Down	Decrease hue angle selected area	Spin button
Process	Apply sum of transforms to the reproduction image			
Help	Give instructions to observers			

to 85. In this study, $L^* = 85.0$ was applied, and the width of the border was set to 5 mm. Graphics options in Windows 98 were adjusted to give as small as possible an effect on colour appearance.

CRS, CAA controls

Figure 13.3 shows the CRS and CAA control buttons. Using the GUI, observers first inspected which part of the reproduction image gave the poorest match. Next they selected

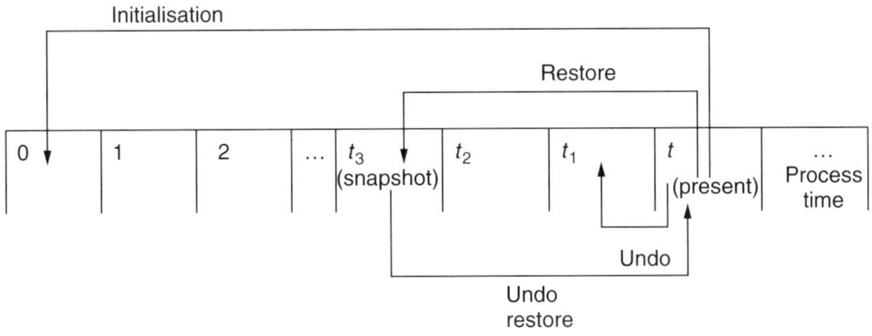

Figure 13.2 Functions of the control menu (in time sequence).

the corresponding colours in CIE $L^*a^*b^*$ space via the CRS controls, and then adjusted all image pixels from that region using the CAA controls. As shown in Figure 13.3, the CRS tool included selectors for lightness, chroma and hue. Figure 13.4 shows the structure of CRS and CAA clearly. For the lightness and chroma controls, CAA and CRS are divided into two region, labelled (1) and (2), and the CAA and CRS control buttons are combined into one region (3) for changing hue. For example, suppose an observer sees that the high-key neutral colours in an image are too dark and have a yellow tint. He or she first needs to select the high-lightness and low-chroma region in CIE $L^*a^*b^*$ (pressing buttons a and f) and adjusting it to be lighter (keep pressing g) and bluer (keep pressing l).

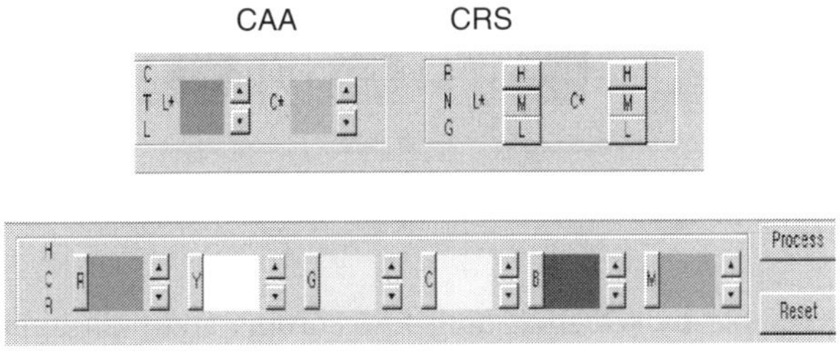

Figure 13.3 CRS and CAA control buttons.

Lightness and chroma were each divided into three colour regions – the high, medium and low ranges, i.e. L^* of 0–35, 35–65 and 65–100, and C^* of 0–25, 25–50 and 50 to the maximum achievable chroma respectively. Hues, on the other hand, were divided into six different sectors: red, yellow, green, cyan, blue and magenta, ranging from 356.5–59.0, 59.0–128.0, 128.0–180.5, 180.5–226.0, 226.0–291.0, and 291.0–356.5 degrees respectively, whereby this division was based on the angles of the unique hues.

The CAA controls allowed observers to modify colours by increasing or decreasing a particular colour attributes in steps of two units for lightness and chroma, and one unit for hue. Observers could select and modify colours using a single attribute, e.g. first select high-chroma region and increase or decrease its chroma. They could also use more than

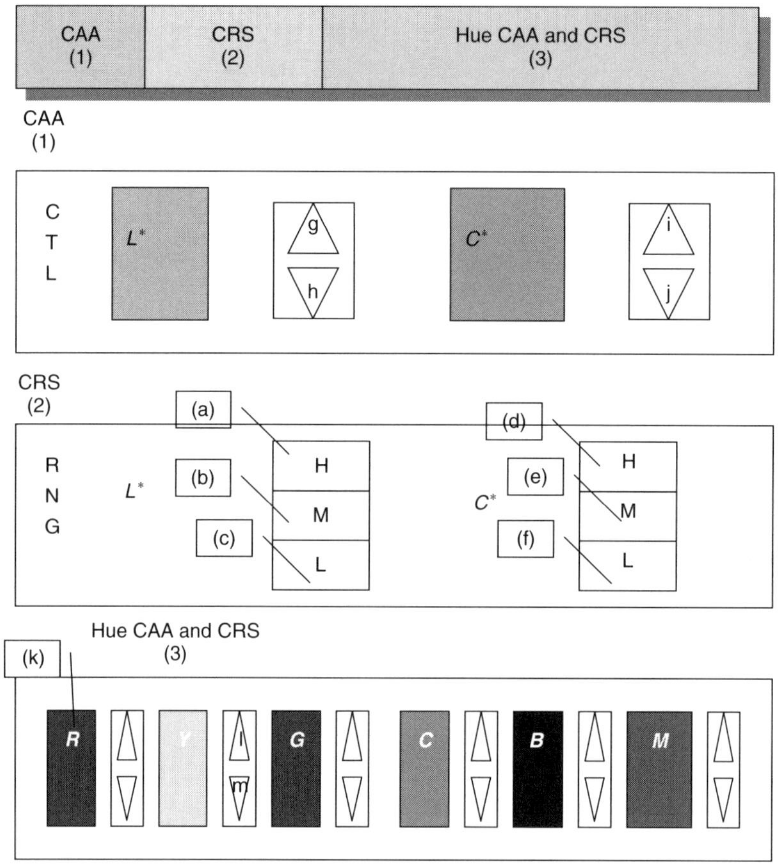

Figure 13.4 Structure of CRS and CAA.

one attribute, for example by selecting both low-chroma and high-lightness regions, and increasing or decreasing one of three attributes (i.e. lightness, chroma and hue).

The colours of control panel buttons were visually changed so as to indicate the extent of changes by observers. For example, if an observer increased lightness by clicking the CAA lightness control, the button colour was automatically adjusted to become lighter. When an observer requested an increase of hue angle in the yellow region, the button colour changed from yellow to yellow-green. Once the operating procedure for modifying a colour region was completed, the observer pressed the Process button. This led to the gamut-mapped test image being processed and displayed to replace the previous version. On average, it took 10–15 s to update the test image.

13.2.2 Control procedure

The flow chart in Figure 13.5 shows the typical control of the experimental GUI. First a test image, known as the ‘original’ image, is retrieved using the File-Open menu. Then,

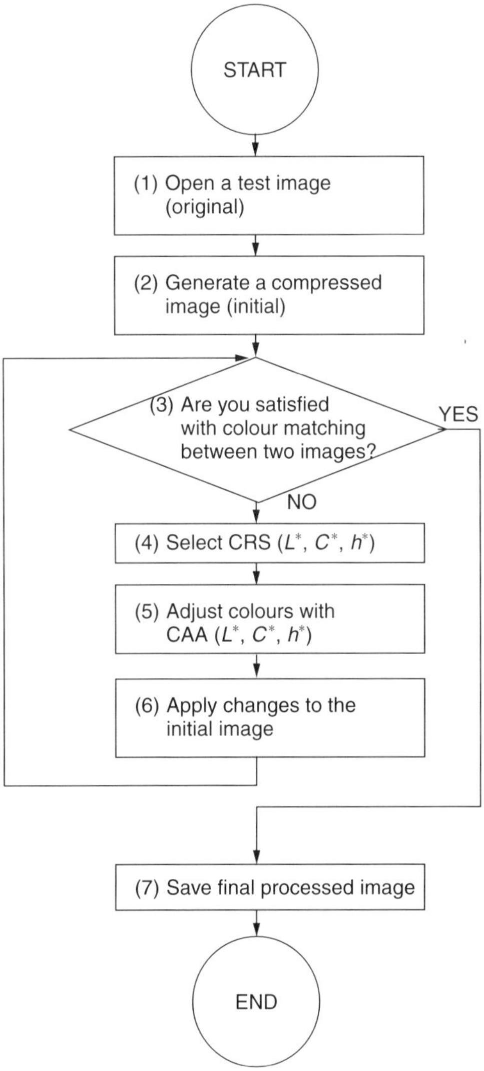

Figure 13.5 Control flow chart.

using the GMA menu, the original image is transformed pixel by pixel using the LCLIP algorithm into the 'initial' image. The observer then inspects the most unsatisfactory colour region in the initial image and selects it using the CRS controls. The selected colour region is transformed by increasing or decreasing an attribute using the CAA buttons. There are 60 combinations possible using the CRA and CAA controls. Colour transforms via CAA and CRS controls are iterated until the colour appearance of the reproduction is as close to the original as possible. When an observer is satisfied with the colour match, the final reproduction image is saved for further analysis.

Data processing

Image data transformations using the experimental software are described in the following discussion. The flow chart in Figure 13.6 specifies the data processing flow (following steps 1 to 8).

- *Step 1*: Image *RGB* data is obtained from an original image.
- *Step 2*: *RGB* values are converted to *XYZ* data via a monitor (forward) device characterisation model.

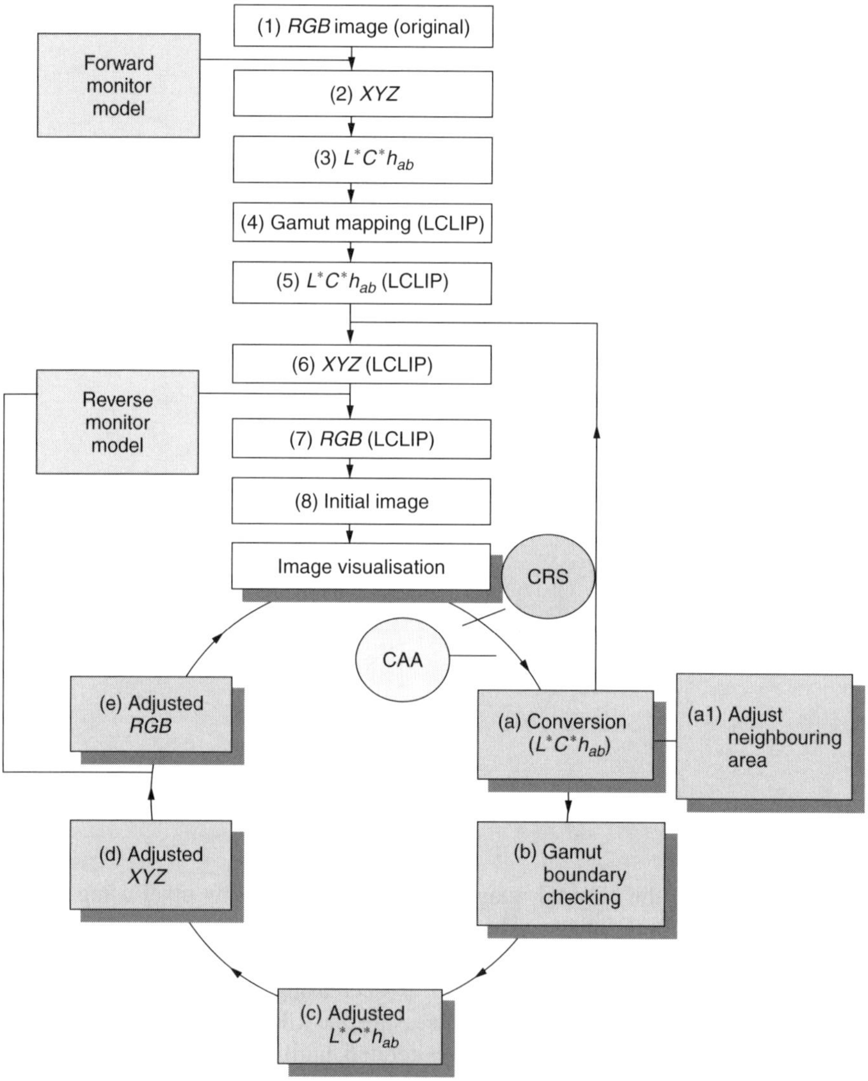

Figure 13.6 Data processing flow of experimental GUI.

- *Step 3*: *XYZ* data is converted to $L^*a^*b^*C_{ab}{}^*h_{ab}$ data.
- *Step 4*: Gamut mapping is performed using the LCLIP algorithm. For colours outside the reproduction gamut, chroma is clipped onto the reproduction gamut boundary along the same lightness level.
- *Steps 5 to 8*: $L^*a^*b^*C_{ab}{}^*h_{ab}$ data are converted to new *XYZ* values (after LCLIP). Finally an initial image is obtained and displayed.

13.3 THE FIRST EXPERIMENT

Four test images, designated IT8, Ski, Orchid and Smile (Figure 13.7) were used in this study. The original and reproduction images were arranged side by side on a CRT display as shown in Figure 13.1 and had very different image gamuts.

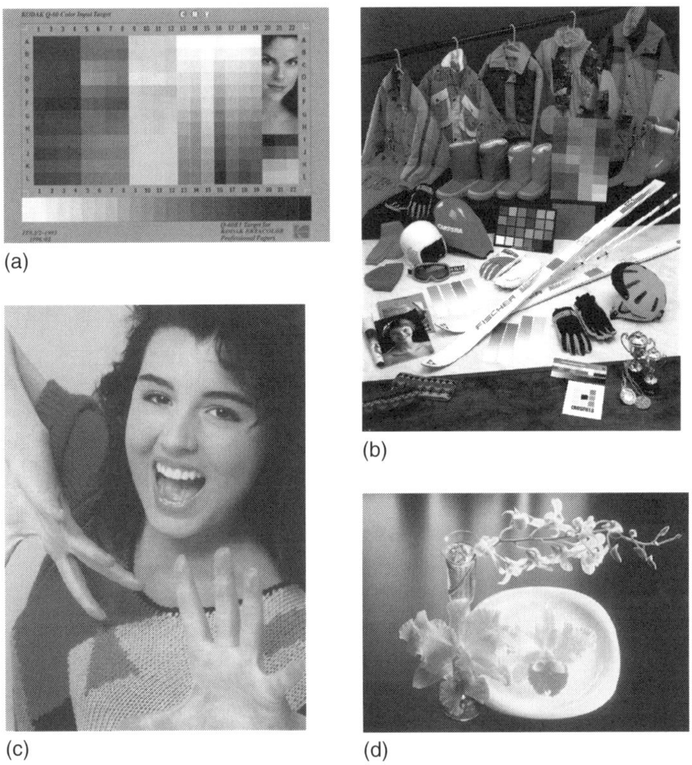

Figure 13.7 Four test images: (a) IT8, (b) Ski, (c) Smile, (d) Orchid (IT8 is reproduced by permission from Eastman Kodak Company. Ski is reprinted by permission of Fujifilm Electronic Imaging Limited. Smile: photos N1 and N1A and N6 and N6A of ISO Standard 12640 : 1997, Figure 1, are reproduced with the permission of the International Organization for Standardization, ISO. This standard can be obtained from any ISO member and from the website of the ISO Central Secretariat at the following address: http//www.iso.org. Copyright remains with ISO). See also Colour Plate 7.

The image gamut boundaries for each image are depicted in Figure 13.8, and Table 13.3 gives statistical information about the gamut volume of each image. These statistics are useful for analysing GCA experimental data. Mean chroma is the average chroma of image pixels. Out of printer gamut indicates the number of image pixels beyond the gamut boundary of the printer. Relative image chroma range to CRT (or printer) gamut

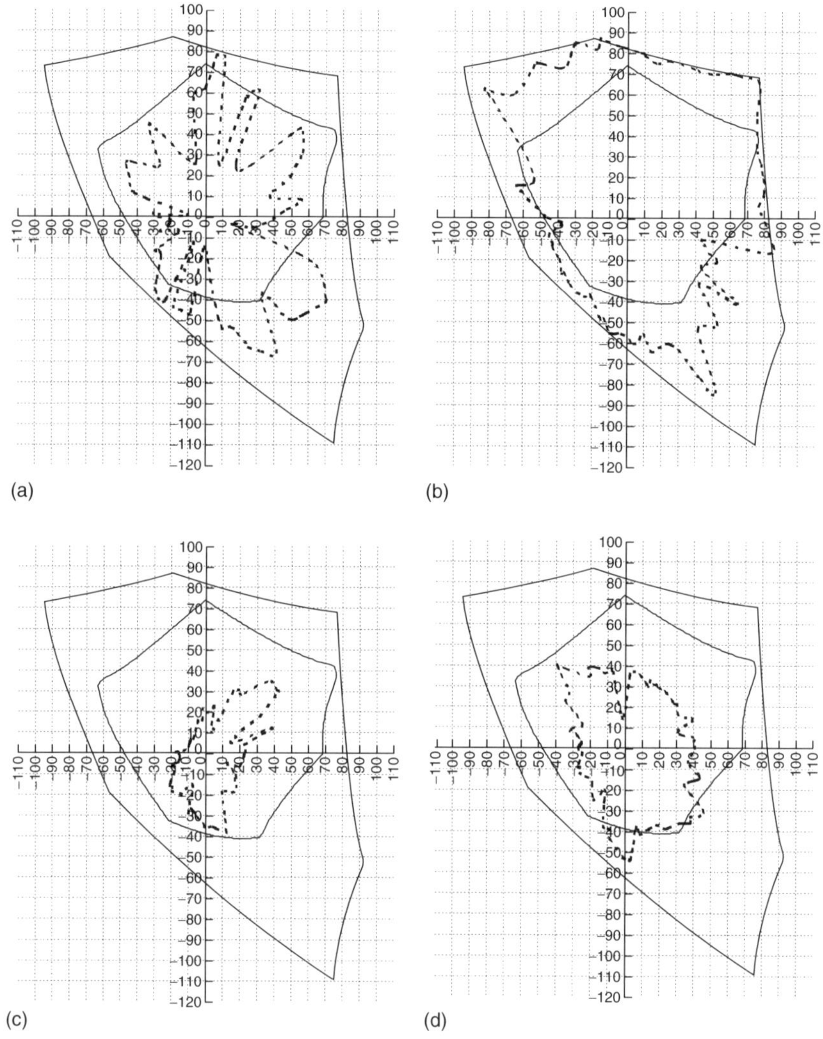

Figure 13.8 Image gamut boundaries on the CIE a^*b^* plane: (a) IT8, (b) Ski, (c) Smile, (d) Orchid. The image gamut is shown by the dotted line, relative to the CRT gamut (outer solid line) and printer gamut (inner solid line).

Table 13.3 Image statistics in terms of CIE $L^*a^*b^*$

	(1) Mean chroma	(2) Out of printer gamut (%)	(3) Relative image chroma range to CRT gamut (%)	(4) Relative image gamut chroma range to printer gamut (%)	(5) Out of monitor gamut (%)
IT8	22.94	22.57	37.98	76.38	0.87
Ski	33.35	37.36	46.07	108.65	2.07
Orchid	23.70	42.11	50.79	111.62	1.38
Smile	20.67	3.31	32.07	50.29	0

compares the chroma value of the image pixel to that of corresponding media (CRT or printer) gamuts. Average values for the whole image are represented in columns (3) and (4) of Table 13.3. Column 5 represents percentage of pixels for each image out of CRT gamut.

(1) Mean chroma $= \frac{1}{N}\sum_{i=0}^{N} C_i^*$ where N is number of pixels

(2) Out of printer gamut $= K/N$ where K is the sum of pixel number out of printer gamut

(3),(4) Relative chroma range with media gamut $= \frac{1}{N}\sum_{i=0}^{N} \frac{C_{i\ \text{image}}^*}{C_{i\ \text{media}}^*}$

The original gamut was that of a Sony Trinitron CPD display and the reproduction gamut that of an IBM LexMark 4097 inkjet printer. Figure 13.9 shows the gamut boundaries for each of the primary and secondary colours plotted on an L^* versus C^* diagram. All figures show that the gamuts of the two devices are quite different not only in volume but also in shape. The CRT gamut is much larger than that of the printer, except in the cyan region.

An LMT C1210 colorimeter was used to measure the CRT, and the GOG model developed by Berns *et al.* [1] was applied, with the white point set to D65. The characterisation was verified by comparing the measured and predicted results, based on 729 test colours which covered the entire colour gamut. The results showed an average colour difference of 0.6 with a maximum of $3.7\Delta E_{\text{CMC}(1:1)}$ units (Table 13.4).

For characterising the printer, tristimulus values of a set of test patches were measured by an X-rite 938 spectrophotometer. A third-order masking equation was derived between *CMY* and *XYZ* values of the printer. Verification was carried out using 729 colours. The results showed a mean prediction error of 2.6 with a maximum of $7.1\Delta E_{\text{CMC}(1:1)}$ units under D65 and the CIE 1931 standard colorimetric observer (Table 13.5). This degree of accuracy is considered to be reasonable, especially as the printer characterisation model was only used for calculating the simulated reproduction gamut boundary.

Eleven observers, all staff of the Computer Software Research Laboratory (CSRL) at the Electronics Telecommunications Research Institute (ETRI) took part in the experiment

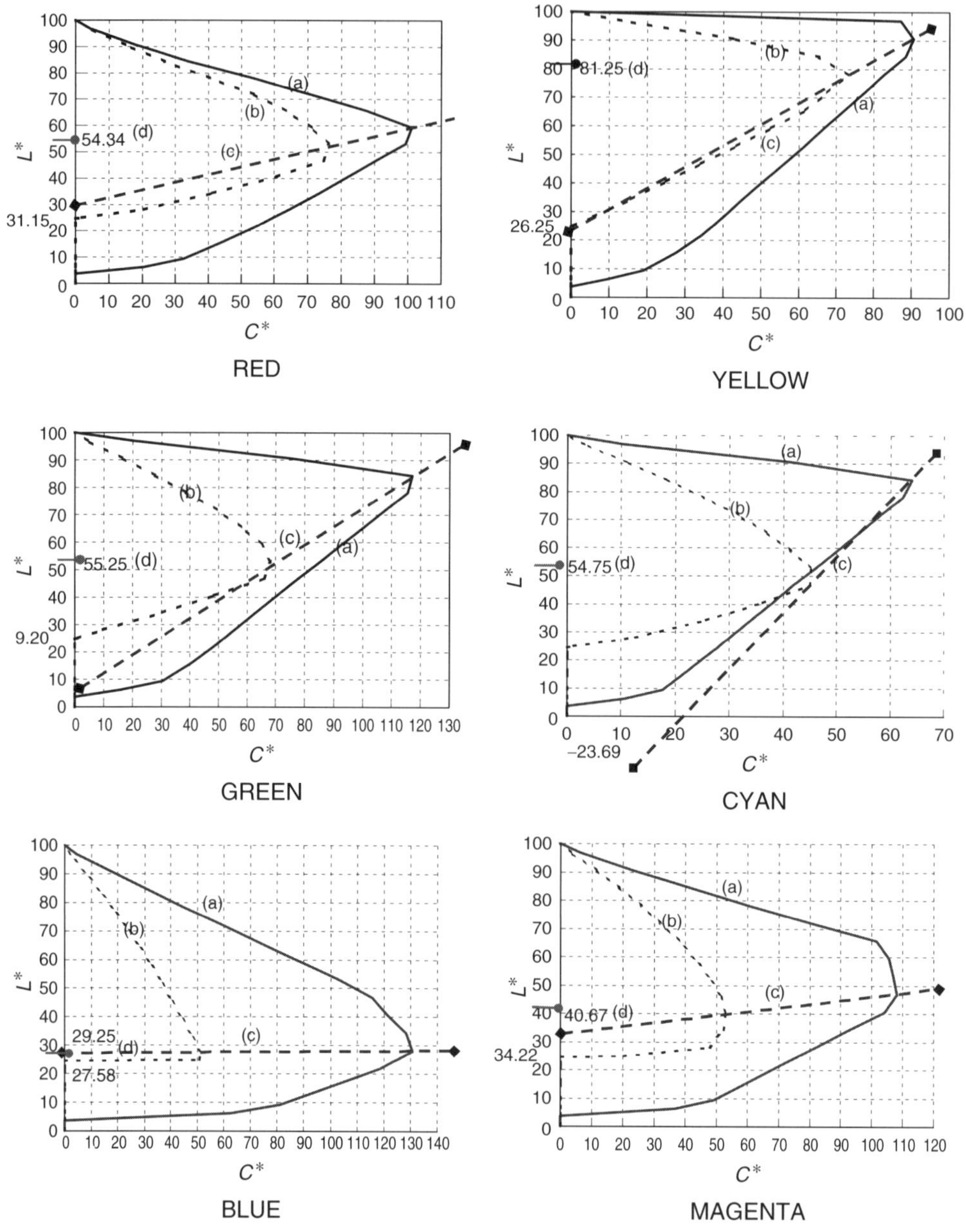

Figure 13.9 Media gamut boundaries at six hue angles: solid line (a) is the monitor gamut; dashed line (b) is the printer gamut; (c) is the connecting line between two cusps; (d) is the lightness of the cusp of the reproduction gamut.

Table 13.4 GOG modelling errors in terms of $\Delta E_{CMC(1:1)}$ and coefficients

Model/sampling	21	11	8	Mean
Mean	0.58	0.57	0.58	0.58
Max	3.71	3.73	3.95	3.77
Median	0.45	0.44	0.44	0.44
95th Percentile	1.51	1.50	1.51	1.51
$R(\gamma$, offset)	2.34, 1.06	2.34, 1.05	2.35, 1.05	
$G(\gamma$, offset)	2.30, 1.08	2.30, 1.08	2.31, 1.07	
$B(\gamma$, offset)	2.37, 1.06	2.37, 1.06	2.37, 1.06	

The 11-sample case was used in the main experiments.

Table 13.5 Forward modelling errors in terms of $\Delta E_{CMC(1:1)}$ for printer device characterisation

Sample	Min	Median	Mean	Max	95th Percentile	Standard deviation
			SECOND-ORDER MODEL			
27	0.47	3.98	4.65	16.06	11.23	3.17
125	0.31	3.75	3.96	11.32	7.77	2.06
729	0.65	3.76	3.89	11.34	7.53	2.11
			THIRD-ORDER MODEL			
27	0.09	2.64	3.22	7.71	6.53	1.84
125	0.51	2.36	2.64	7.08	6.09	1.57
729	0.14	2.24	2.66	7.96	6.46	1.74

which was carried out in a darkened room (Table 13.6). The observer group took a training session prior to the real experiment. They all passed the Ishihara colour deficiency test. In the real experiment, each observer performed the adjustments twice for each image. These results were used to investigate observer repeatability. On average, each image took about 30–60 minutes to complete. Table 13.7 shows experimental viewing conditions.

Table 13.6 Information on observers

Average age (age range)	Duration per image	Sex (M/F)
	FIRST EXPERIMENT	
28 (25–37)	30–60 min	11/0
	SECOND EXPERIMENT	
23 (21–33)	30–40 s	6/6

Table 13.7 Experimental viewing conditions

Screen	Viewing distance	Angular subtense[a]	Ambient lighting[b]
Width = 40 cm Height = 30 cm	50–55 cm	15–20°	$x = 0.31$ $y = 0.28$ $Y = 0.03$

[a]For observing two images simultaneously.
[b]Ambient light was measured at the CRT surface under experimental condition, darkened room.

13.4 RESULTS

13.4.1 Observer variation

In the first experiment, 11 observers adjusted four different test images twice using the tool. Finally, four averaged images were obtained through 22 experiments, averaging in the device-independent space (CIE $L^*a^*b^*$). These four averaged images, representative of all experimental results, were used in the subsequent algorithm development. To analyse observer behaviour, observer accuracy and repeatability were calculated, as given in Table 13.8. Observer accuracy is measured by the mean colour difference between individual images and observer average image. Repeatability is measured by the mean colour difference between two experiments carried out by one observer.

Table 13.8 Observer accuracy and repeatability (first experiment) $\Delta E_{CMC(1:1)}$

	Observer accuracy	Observer repeatability
Min	1.43	1.35
Median	2.83	3.86
Mean	2.94	3.88
Max	6.55	7.09
Std dev	0.99	1.43

The results in Table 13.8 show that observer accuracy was lower than repeatability in mean, maximum, medium and standard deviation, so that the variances across experimental results are not too high to prevent the results being used in algorithm development. Figure 13.10 shows observer accuracy and repeatability in $\Delta E_{CMC(1:1)}$ units for individual observers. Observer (mean) accuracy values are about 3.0. Figure 13.11 shows the observer accuracy of individual observers in terms of $|\Delta L^*|$, $|\Delta C^*|$ and $|\Delta h|$. Chroma differences were higher than the other two differences, though the values were less than 3.0.

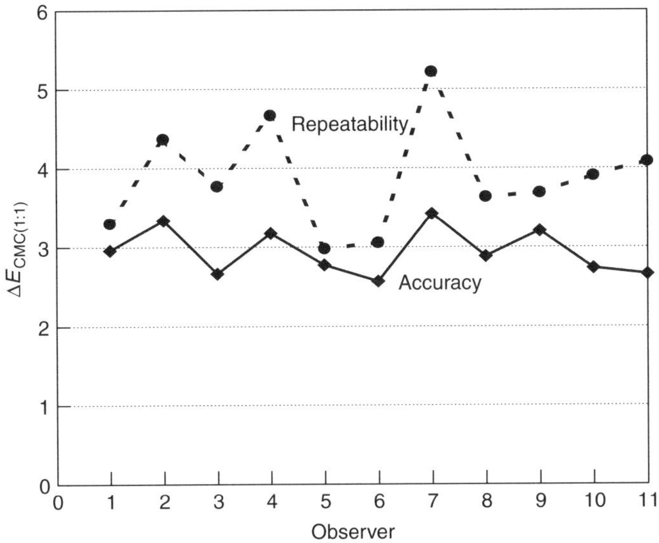

Figure 13.10 Observer accuracy and repeatability for individual observers (mean $\Delta E_{CMC(1:1)}$).

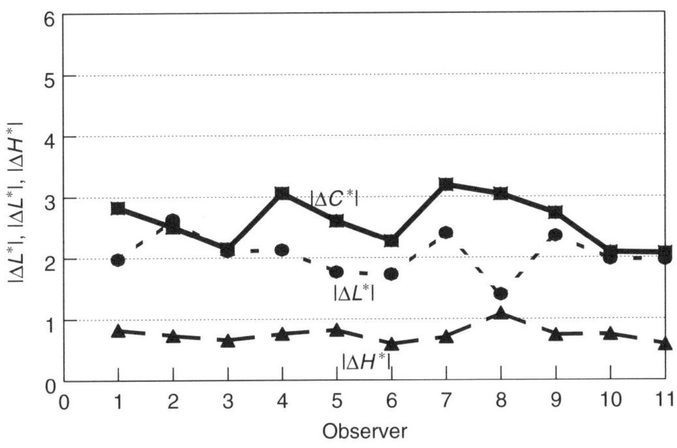

Figure 13.11 Observer accuracy for individual observers (mean $|\Delta L^*|$, $|\Delta C^*|$, $|\Delta h|$).

13.4.2 Qualitative analysis

Qualitative analysis was carried out by generating plots to visualise the relationship between the original and reproduction images. The reproduction images were calculated by averaging each observer's pixel-by-pixel data for each image, whereby these images represent the mean visual results.

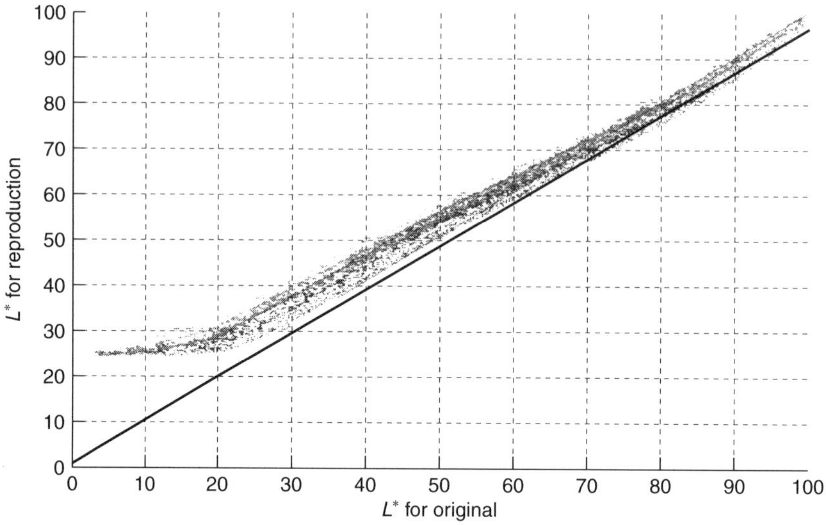

Figure 13.12 Lightness (L^*) mapping: original versus reproduction.

Lightness comparison

The L^* values of the original and reproduction colours are given in Figure 13.12, where the L^* value of 100 for the original and reproduction devices corresponds to the normalised white point of the monitor and the paper substrate of the printer, respectively. The solid line indicates a perfect agreement between the original and reproduction results. As shown in Figure 13.12, almost all data were adjusted to make the reproduction image brighter. There is a distinct curve for colours close to the dark end. This is caused by the limitations of dark colours for the printer devices, i.e. the black is not dark enough and suggests that contrast was considered to be more important than maintaining differences between lightness levels.

Chroma comparison

Figure 13.13 shows a plot of C^* (original) versus C^* (reproduction) for all four images. Again, the 45° line indicates a perfect agreement between original and reproduction. This relationship will be used to develop GCAs later on. Large scattering of C^* (original) versus C^* (reproduction) can be found in Figure 13.13. Chroma compression patterns are quite different across test images, and data of C^* (original) versus C^* (reproduction) from four test images were added into one. Many C^* (reproduction) values corresponding to one value of C^* (original) from various levels of lightness and hue are observed in the figure. In the first experiment, observers were asked to adjust individual colour attributes of test images, comparing reproduction images to original images. Due to limitations of the reproducible gamut (reproduction boundary) in lightness and hue levels, different adjustments of chroma occurred. In addition, the gamut of individual images seemed to influence the large scattering. From one original chroma value, Figure 13.13 shows

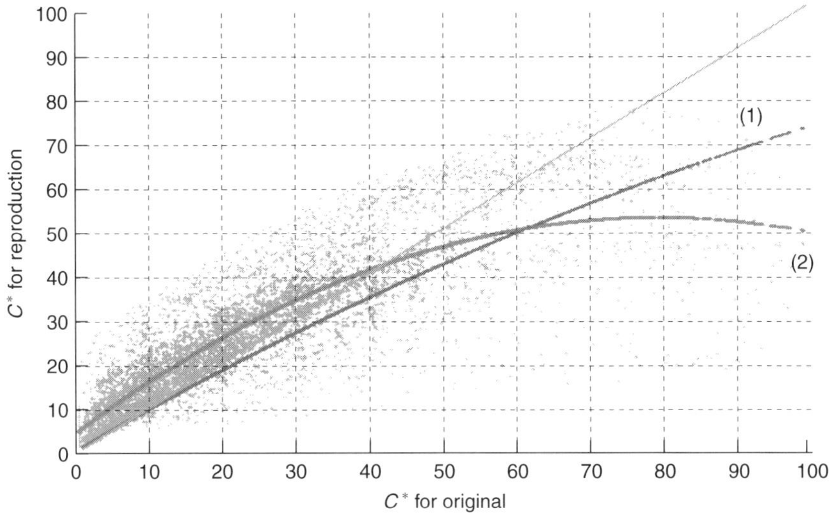

Figure 13.13 Chroma (C^*) mapping: original versus reproduction. The curves (1) and (2) correspond to functions fitted in algorithms GCA-2 and GCA-3.

that there could be many diverse chroma adjustments because observers made different adjustments for different original images.

Hue comparison

A systematic trend for hue changes is shown in Figure 13.14. Notice that colours were adjusted mainly in three hue areas (see the three peaks in the Figure 13.14): red to be

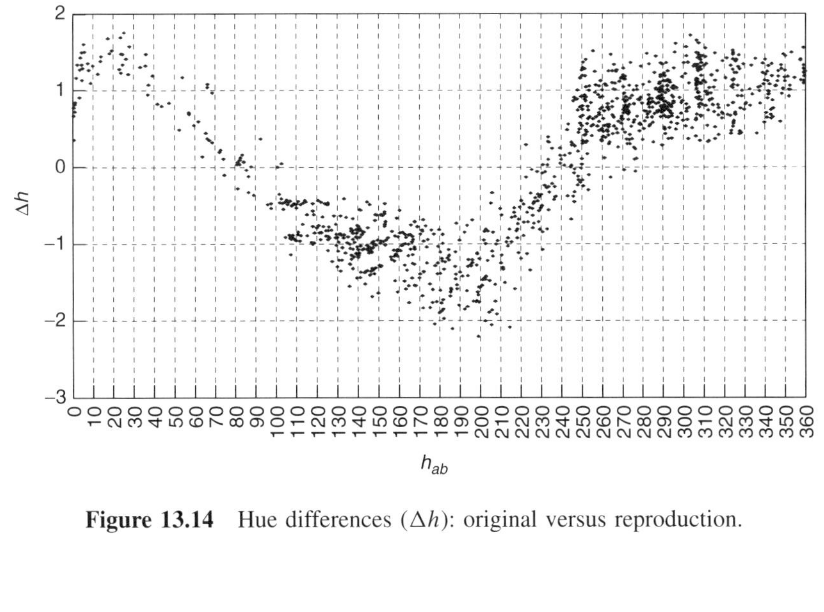

Figure 13.14 Hue differences (Δh): original versus reproduction.

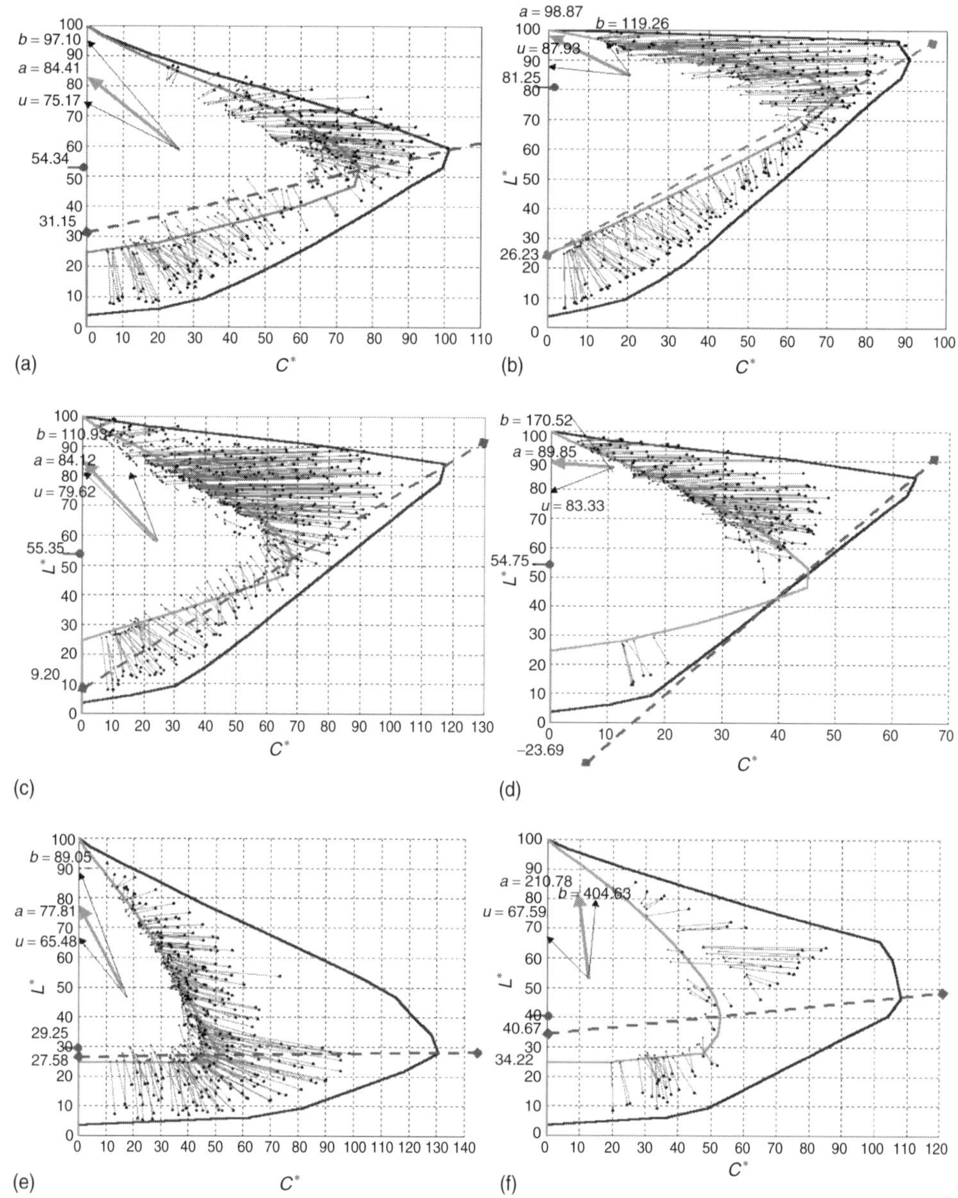

Figure 13.15 Colour gamut differences between the original (CRT, outside) and reproduction (printer, inside) devices for hues (a) red, (b) yellow, (c) green, (d) cyan, (e) blue and (f) magenta. The dashed line joins the cups of the two gamuts. The arrow indicates the average convergence point on the L^* axis. The filled circle represents L^* of the reproduction cusp.

bluer, green to be bluer, and magenta to be bluer. There were only small changes for the other colours such as yellow, green and cyan. The trend was consistent for all images. The mean hue angles for all images were 24, 187 and 329 for red, green and magenta, with standard deviation values of 8.4, 15.5 and 21.9 respectively. The amounts of hue change expressed by Δh were quite small, never exceeding 3 units.

Converging points in L^* vs. C^* plots

Plotting the data in L^* versus C^* diagrams for each of the primary and secondary hues has proven very useful for analysing the results. A vector was drawn between each pair of corresponding original and reproduction colours. These plots are shown in Figure 13.15 for red, yellow, green, cyan, blue and magenta hues, respectively, for the image Ski. For each vector, the convergence point (intercept with the L^* axis) was also calculated. In addition, the L^* value of the cusp from the reproduction gamut and the intercept between the cusps of the two gamuts are also shown. The data displayed in each figure make it easier to compare the current results with the GCAs proposed by Morovic and Luo [19].

13.5 DEVELOPMENT OF ALGORITHMS

13.5.1 Algorithm 1 (GCA-1)

The first attempt at developing an algorithm was modifying the CLLIN algorithm [19]. The chroma mapping procedure of CLLIN is:

$$C_r^* = \begin{cases} C_o^* \left(\dfrac{C_{cusp,r}^*}{C_{cusp,o}^*} \right) & C_{cusp,o}^* \geqslant C_{cusp,r}^* \\ C_o^* & C_{cusp,o}^* < C_{cusp,r}^* \end{cases} \tag{13.1}$$

where subscripts o and r denote the original and reproduction gamuts respectively.

Comparing images modified by observers in the experiment and data transformed via the CLLIN algorithm, it was found that the lightness compression followed a linear function but that the chroma compression was not linear. Hence the aim of GCA-1 was to include this observer non-linearity in chroma mapping. First chroma was compressed by the following non-linear function:

$$C_r^* = \begin{cases} C_r^* = (1-\alpha)C_o^* + \alpha \left[C_{cusp,r}^* - (C_{cusp,o}^* - C_o^*) \left(\dfrac{C_{cusp,r}^*}{C_{cusp,o}^*} \right) \right] \\ \qquad C_{cusp,o}^* \geqslant C_{cusp,r}^* \\ C_o^* \qquad C_{cusp,o}^* < C_{cusp,r}^* \end{cases} \tag{13.2}$$

where:

$$\alpha = 1.0 - (1 - \alpha_{min})e^m \tag{13.3}$$

and with the following parameters:

$L_\alpha = 0.797\ L^*$ of reproduction medium cusp
$C_\alpha = 0.563\ C^*$ of reproduction medium cusp
$\alpha_{min} = 1.84\ C_\alpha/C^*$ of original medium cusp
$m = 22.0$ (arbitrary disperse parameter)

Next the lightness was mapped linearly along lines of constant chroma using:

$$L_r^* = L_{r2}^* + (L_o^* - L_{o2}^*)(L_{r1}^* - L_{r2}^*)/(L_{o1}^* - L_{o2}^*) \tag{13.4}$$

where the subscripts $o1$ and $o2$ denote respectively the maxima and minima of the original gamut and $r1$ and $r2$ denote those of the reproduction.

Derivation of the chroma compression formula depends on the assumptions that (1) observer chroma compression follows a non-linear trend relative to the gamut boundaries; and (2) this non-linear function follows the normal distribution determined by three different parameters, namely chroma, lightness and α. Formulae for determining $L_\alpha, C_\alpha, \alpha_{min}$ were derived by observing the relationship between α and the lightness or chroma of the cusps in the experimental plots. The primary shortcoming of this algorithm was that the procedure used for deriving it was too heuristic and complex.

13.5.2 Algorithm 2 (GCA-2)

Further observing the L^*C^* plots showing the relationship between original and observer data, it was found that compression results were grouped into three different patterns in terms of their converging vectors towards the L^* axis. Figure 13.16 shows the modelling of this phenomenon. Chroma compression between original and observer data was analysed again, and a non-linear relationship was found (Figure 13.13). Based on this analysis, GCA-2 was derived as follows.

Step 1: Lightness mapping

The lightness mapping function was derived by modelling the relationship between the lightness of original and observer data (Figure 13.12). This modelling took into account the media used in the experiment by having as parameters the minimum L^* point A (in this case 3.68: minimum of original, and 24.67: minimum of reproduction), point B, which is the point where the slope is changed (i.e. 19.96, 26.03), and the maximum L^* point C (100.0: maximum of original, 100.0: maximum of reproduction). A piecewise linear interpolation function, connecting these three points, was then derived to model the relationship:

$$L_1^* = L_{min,o}^* + ((16.9/A)(L_{max,o}^* - L_{min,o}^*)) \tag{13.5}$$

if $L_{min,o}^* \leqslant L_o^* < L_1^*$

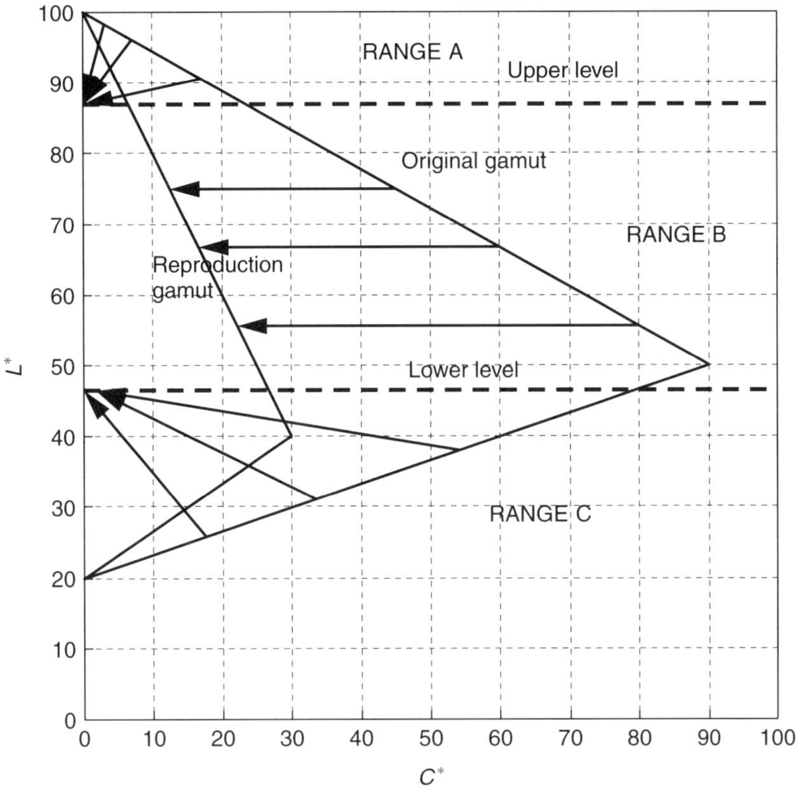

Figure 13.16 Three different compression patterns and two convergence points.

then

$$L_r^* = \left[L_{min,r}^* + \frac{1.8}{A}\left(L_{max,r}^* - L_{min,r}^*\right)\right]$$

$$-\frac{10.65}{A}\left[\left(L_{min,o}^* - L_o^*\right)2 + \frac{16.9}{A}\left(L_{max,o}^* - L_{min,o}^*\right)\right]\frac{L_{max,r}^* - L_{min,r}^*}{L_{max,o}^* - L_{min,o}^*}$$

else if $L_1^* \leqslant L_o^* \leqslant L_{max,o}^*$

then

$$L_r^* = L_{max,r}^* - 1.18\left(L_{max,o}^* - L_o^*\right)\frac{L_{max,r}^* - L_{min,r}^*}{L_{max,o}^* - L_{min,o}^*} \tag{13.6}$$

Step 2: Determining the convergence points

Investigating L^*C^* plane plots, observer compression was grouped into three patterns in terms of their converging vectors on the L^* axis. To derive a function describing this relationship, convergence lightness points depending on the above plots and the L^* of the original medium's cusp were utilised as parameters. The following formulae describe how to determine these two convergence points, i.e. lower and higher points in L^*.

- *Lower convergence point*: if original medium cusp's $L^* \leqslant 30.0$ then lower convergence point $= 31.54(L^*)$, else lower convergence point $= 19.42 + 0.404 \times$ original cusp's L^*.
- *Higher convergence point*: if original medium cusp's $L^* \leqslant 49.0$ then higher convergence point $= 70.12(L^*)$, else lower convergence point $= 49.297 + 0.425 \times$ original cusp's L^*.

Figure 13.17 shows this relationship between higher convergence point versus the original cusp's L^*.

Step 3: Chroma compression

Comparing chroma as transformed by LLIN with the chroma of observer data, the relationship shown in Figure 13.18 was obtained. This shows that observer chroma was maximised at $C^* = 11.93$, which was 17% of the original cusp's chroma, and where it

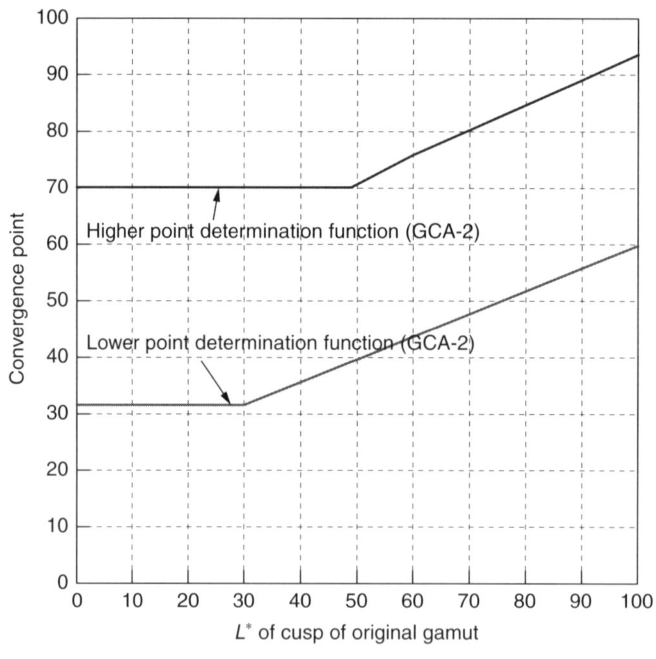

Figure 13.17 Convergence point determination functions.

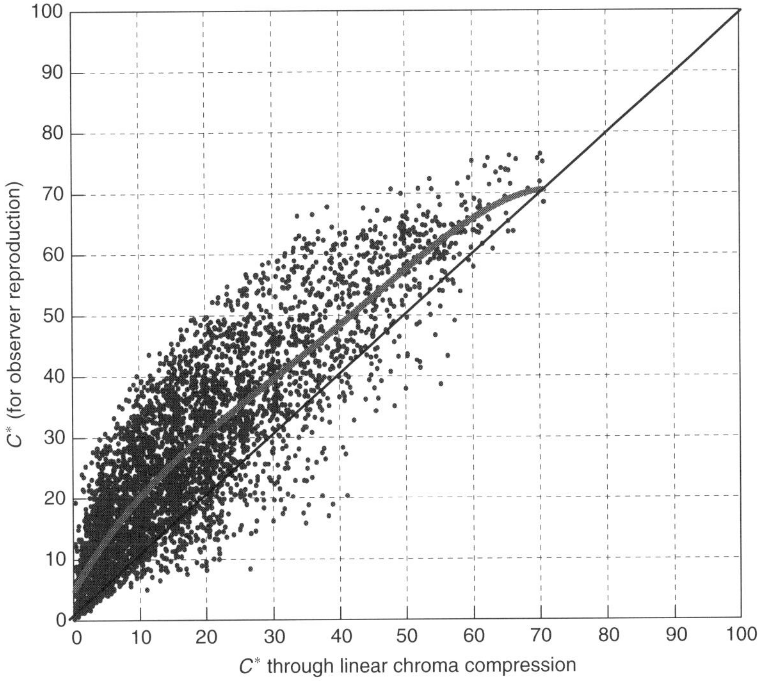

Figure 13.18 Chroma compression function of GCA-2.

was about 1.9 times greater than that of LLIN. Hence the chroma compression of GCA-2 follows this non-linear relationship:

$$C^*_{3\text{-}1} = f(C^*_o) \tag{13.7}$$

where:
$f(x)$ = function of linear compression towards convergence points from step 2
$C^*_{3\text{-}1}$ = value compressed by function $f(x)$
C^*_o = original chroma value

$$\begin{aligned} C^*_r &= C^*_{3\text{-}1} g(s(C^*_{3\text{-}1})) \\ s(C^*_{3\text{-}1}) &= 100(C^*_{3\text{-}1}/C^*_{cusp}) \\ g(x) &= \begin{cases} 0.118x & 0 \leqslant x < 17 \\ -0.023x + 2.291 & 17 < x \leqslant 100 \end{cases} \end{aligned} \tag{13.8}$$

where:
C^*_r = reproduction chroma value
C^*_{cusp} = chroma value at cusp of original gamut

In summary, GCA-2 consists of three steps: (1) piecewise linear lightness mapping, (2) convergence point determination, and (3) lightness-chroma compression in a non-linear manner along either lines of constant lightness or lines towards fixed convergence points. In terms of accurately modelling observer experimental data, GCA-2 outperforms GCA-1, but some shortcomings still exist:

- Unwanted artefacts were found particularly in the darker blue areas in the image Ski. From this it can be seen that the lower convergence point determination function needs some modification, taking into account lower lightness image regions.
- The chroma compression function does not properly fit the observer's compression behaviour, especially in the region of higher chroma (Figure 13.13).

13.5.3 Algorithm 3 (GCA-3)

The formulation of GCA-3 is identical to that of GCA-2 except for some modifications to steps 2 and 3.

Step 2

To circumvent the problems of GCA-2, the distance between lower and higher convergence points was extended, increasing the higher convergence point and decreasing the lower point. To achieve this, the following equations were defined:

- *Lower convergence point*: if original medium cusp's $L^* \leqslant 30.0$ then lower convergence point $= 28.0(L^*)$, else lower convergence point $= 45.0 \times (\text{original cusp's } L^*/100.0)^2 - 2.80(\text{original cusp's } L^*/100.0) + 24.8$
- *Higher convergence point*: if original medium cusp's $L^* \leqslant 30.0$ then lower convergence point $= 75.0(L^*)$, else lower convergence point $= 67.0 \times (\text{original cusp's } L^*/100.0)^2 - 51.97(\text{original cusp's } L^*/100.0) + 84.8$

Step 3

The following chroma compression function was derived directly from the relationship between C^* (original) versus C^* (observer) data using linear regression analysis:

$$C_{compressed} = -\left(\frac{7.8}{B}\right)(C^*)^2 + \left(\frac{122.78}{B}\right)(C^*) + 3.409 \quad (13.9)$$

where $B = 1000$ (constant).

Figure 13.13 shows that this function (2 in the plot) fits the observer data more accurately than that of GCA-2.

13.6 THE SECOND EXPERIMENT

Twelve observers including six females and six males took part in the second experiment using a pair comparison method. Four images used in the first experiment were again employed. The average observer data acquired in the first experiment was the basis for algorithm performance evaluation, although if other images and/or media had been employed for the evaluation then this data could not have been used. Before the GCA developed in this study can be applied generally, it needs to be tested on many more media and test images.

The images used in the second experiment were transformed through the three newly derived algorithms plus six existing algorithms (i.e. LCLIP, LCUSP, GCUSP, LLIN, CLLIN and SLIN) together with an average image based on the results in the first experiment. The LCLIP algorithm consists of linear lightness compression followed by chroma clipping along lines of constant lightness. The LCUSP algorithm includes linear lightness compression and chroma compression towards the lightness of reproduction cusp. GCUSP is the same as LCUSP except that the lightness compression depends on a Gaussian function of chroma. LLIN consists of linear lightness and linear chroma compression. SLIN is a simultaneous transformation towards the midpoint of the lightness axis ($L^* = 50$). CLLIN is described in Section 13.4.

In the experiment, an original image was shown to the observer for 20–30 s, then two images generated by different compression algorithms were displayed. The task was to judge which of the two was closer to the original. If the observer could not make a decision immediately, then the original was shown again. Based on Thurstone's law of comparative judgement [27], the overall z-score (accuracy) results were calculated, as shown in Figure 13.19.

From these results it can be seen that the newly derived algorithms together with the observer average image significantly outperform the existing algorithms. Among the new algorithms, GCA-3 performed better than the others and even better than the observer average image. In terms of existing algorithms, GCUSP outperformed the other five.

The results in terms of z-scores are given in Figures 13.20–13.23: (a) algorithms by test image, (b) test images by algorithm, (c) algorithms by colour region, (d) colour regions by algorithm. The z-score indicates the degree of colour matching accuracy; the higher

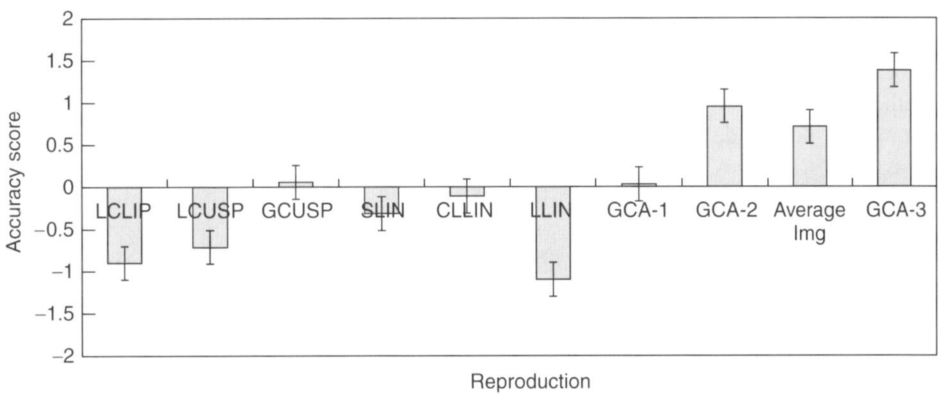

Figure 13.19 Overall z-scores averaged for four images (error bars represent 95% of population distribution).

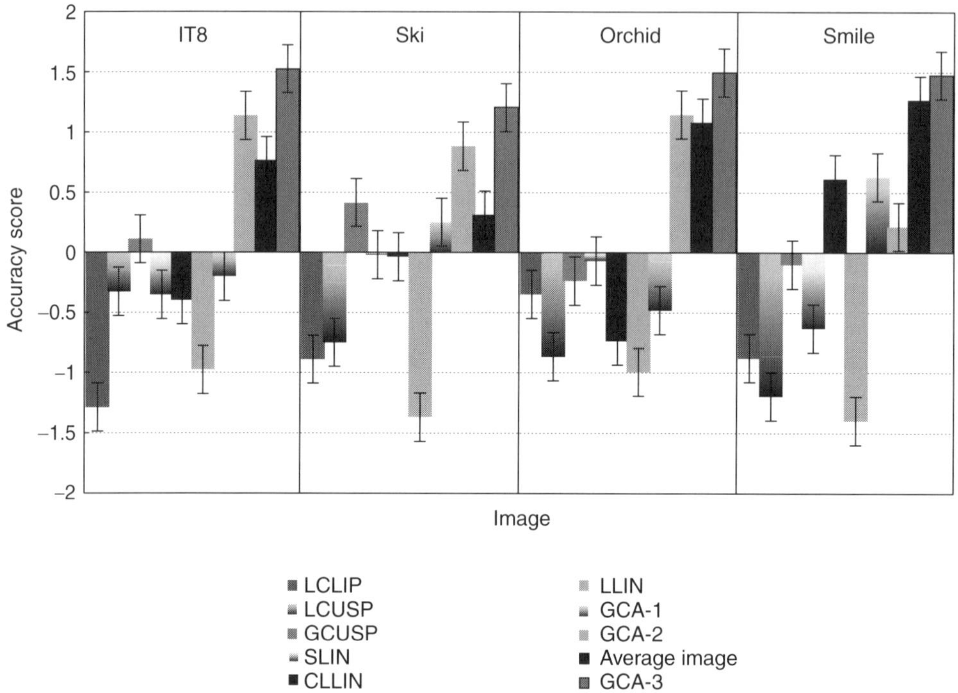

Figure 13.20 The z-score results of the second experiment (algorithm by test image).

the z-score, the higher the degree of colour matching as judged by observers. The 95% confidence interval for each z-score was calculated and is plotted. An important characteristic of any generally usable algorithm is the variance of its colour matching performance, which should be as small as possible covering a wide range of the different image content and colour regions.

The result of the overall case was generally similar to that of individual images. Good performance was exhibited by the newly developed algorithms (GCA-3, GCA-2, GCA-1) together with observer average image and the worst performance by LCLIP and LLIN. Among the newly developed algorithms, GCA-3 was evaluated as the best technique across all test images, and its variance of 0.15 was also lowest. Overall, the results in Figures 13.20 and 13.21 show a similar pattern for the accuracy scores of algorithms for the four different test images.

Note that some algorithms did not perform well for particular test images. CLLIN, GCA-1 and GCA-2 were less stable than other algorithms, with standard deviations of 0.58, 0.49 and 0.44 respectively. As GCA-1 is a modification of CLLIN (applying a non-linear chroma compression), these two algorithms had a strong correlation in the accuracy scores. CLLIN and GCA-1 performed well for Smile followed by Ski, IT8 and Orchid. This order was very similar to that of image gamut size (see relative image chroma range to CRT gamut, Table 13.3), which indicates a possible link between the size of an

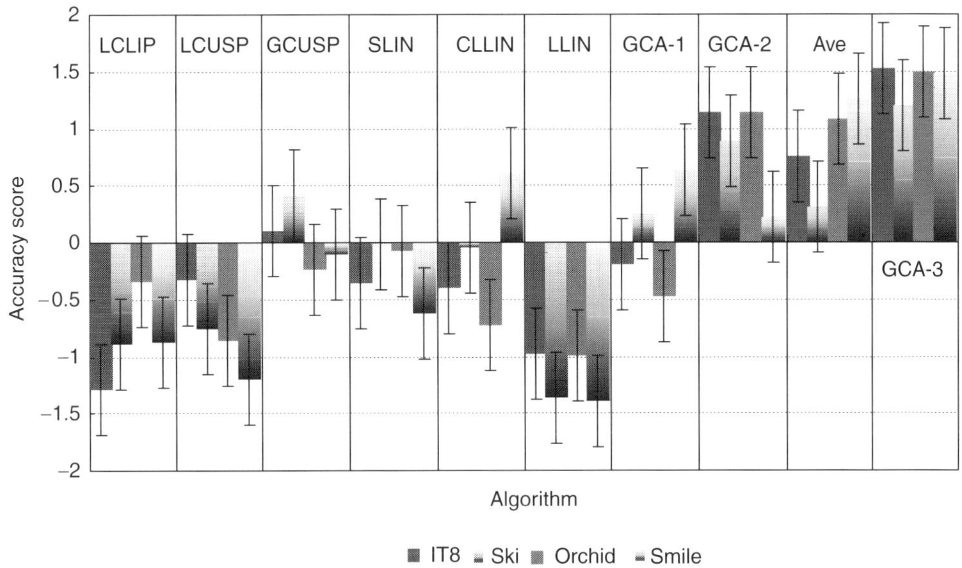

Figure 13.21 The z-score results of the second experiment (test image by algorithm).

image gamut and the performance of algorithms in which chroma mapping is followed by lightness mapping. GCA-2 did not give a better result for Smile. This implies that the non-linear chroma compression function used in GCA-2, which was modified in GCA-3, could not properly reproduce lower chroma colours, e.g. the skin colour of Smile.

From the observer data on Ski in the first experiment, it can be seen that observers did not sufficiently adjust chroma for some regions (e.g. the yellow helmet). Poor accuracy scores for observer average image of Ski may have been caused by this problem. This may explain the observer behaviour in the experiments. As the CRS is divided into only three ranges, observers may have felt unwilling to increase very high chroma colours in high lightness, for example the bright yellow colours in the helmet of Ski.

Over the experiments in general, observers do not seem to have had much difficulty in adjusting colours, although in some colour areas, limitations were found in the experimental tool. A particular issue concerned memory colour, for example the skin regions in Smile. Observers did not wish to adjust skin colours fully because the skin tone was changed very quickly (due to the small image gamut) in comparison with the prototypical colour in their minds. See Chapter 2.

As can be seen from Figures 13.22 and 13.23, the results for individual algorithms were not significantly influenced by colour region in comparison to variances across the images. The range of accuracy scores did not depend on a particular colour region. GCA-2 had a lower accuracy score than GCA-3, particularly in skin and grey colours. This was because GCA-2 does not properly fit the chroma compression preference of observers, particularly in the lower chroma regions. GCA-3 generally outperformed the other algorithms and did not have a higher variance between the accuracy scores of colour regions.

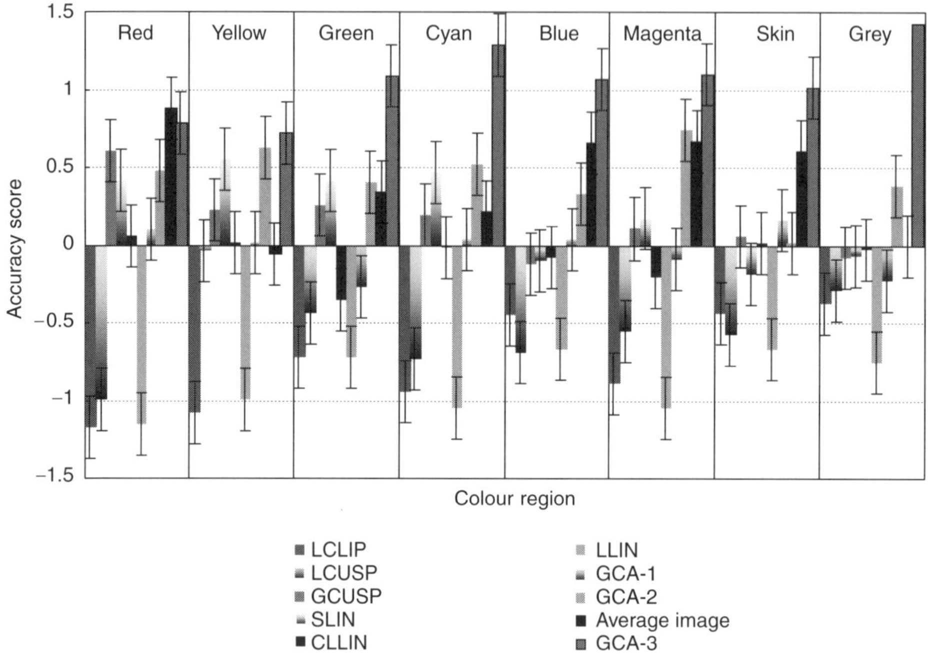

Figure 13.22 The z-score results of the second experiment (colour region by algorithm).

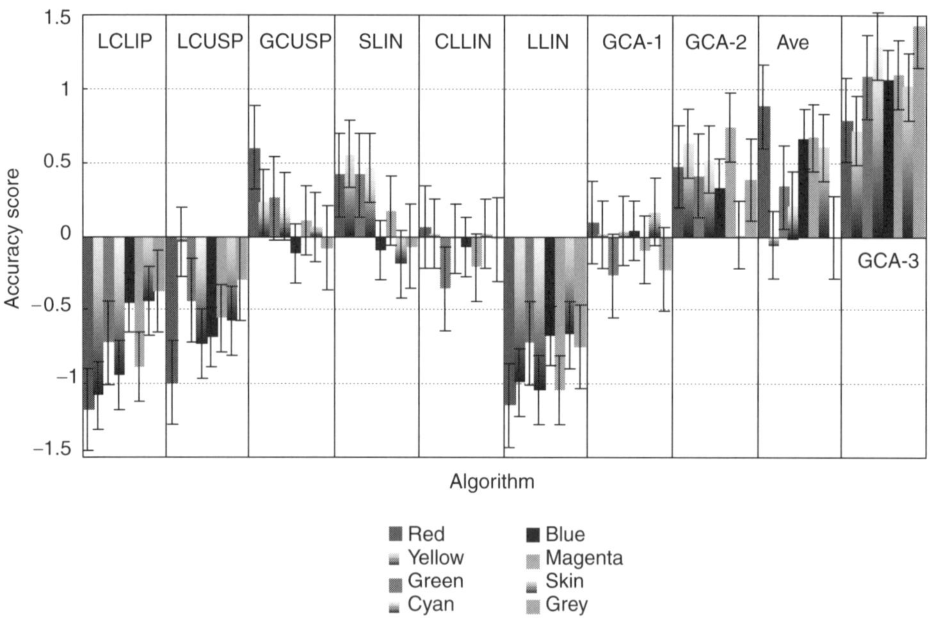

Figure 13.23 The z-score results of the second experiment (algorithm by colour region).

13.7 CONCLUSIONS

The interactive tool developed in this study allowed experimental subjects to select a particular colour region of a pictorial image in CIE $L^*a^*b^*$ colour space and to modify this image in comparison with the original image using colour controls based on CIE $L^*a^*b^*$ attributes. The original and reproduction images were rendered according to the colour gamuts of a CRT and an inkjet printer and the results were used for investigating and developing different gamut compression algorithms (GCAs). Observer experimental data were obtained by comparing original and reproduction images and their relationship analysed. Three new algorithms were developed on the basis of the data obtained using this tool. Based on Thurstone's law of comparative judgement, the newly derived algorithms outperformed existing methods in general.

REFERENCES

1. Berns R. S., Gorzynski M. E. and Motta R. J. (1994) CRT colorimetry part II: metrology. *Color Research and Application* **18**, 315–325.
2. Braun G. J. and Fairchild M. D. (1999) Image lightness rescaling using sigmoidal contrast enhancement functions. *Proc. SPIE*, vol., 96–107.
3. Braun G. J. and Fairchild M. D. (1999) General-purpose gamut mapping algorithms: evaluation of contrast-preserving rescaling functions for color gamut mapping. *Proc. 7th Color Imaging Conference*, pp. 167–182.
4. Ebner F. and Fairchild M. D. (1997) Gamut mapping from below: finding the minimum perceptual distances for colors outside the gamut volume. *Color Research and Application*, **22**(6), 402–413.
5. Gentile R. S., Walowit E. and Allebach J. P. (1990) A comparison of techniques for color gamut mismatch compensation. *Journal of Imaging Technology*, **16**, 176–181.
6. Herzog P. G. and Müller M. (1997) Gamut mapping using an analytical color gamut representation. *Proc. SPIE*, **3300**, 118–128.
7. Hoshino T. and Berns R. S. (1993) Color gamut mapping techniques for color hard copy images. *Proc. SPIE*, **1909**, 152–164.
8. Ito M. and Kato N. (1999) Three-dimensional gamut mapping using various color difference formulae and color spaces. *Proc. SPIE*, **3648**, 83–85.
9. Johnson A. J., Luo M. R., Lo M. C., Xin J. H. and Rhodes P. A. (1998) Aspects of colour management, part II: characterisation of four-colour imaging devices and colour gamut mapping. Working paper, CII, Derby University.
10. Kang B. H., Cho M. S., Morovic J. and Luo M. R. (1999) Gamut compression analysis based on observer experimental data. *Proc. 7th Color Imaging Conference*, pp. 295–300.
11. Katoh N. and Ito M. (1996) Gamut mapping for computer generated images (II). *Proc. 4th IS&T/SID Color Imaging Conference*, pp. 126–129.
12. Katoh N. and Ito M. (1999) Applying non-linear compression to thc three-dimensional gamut mapping. *Proc. 7th IS&T/SID Color Imaging Conference*, pp. 155–159.
13. MacDonald L. W. (1993) Gamut mapping in perceptual colour space. *Proc. 1st IS&T/SID Color Imaging Conference*, pp. 193–196.
14. MacDonald L. and Morovic J. (1995) Assessing the effects of gamut compression in the reproduction of fine art paintings. *Proc. 3rd IS&T/SID Color Imaging Conference*, pp. 194–200.
15. Meyer J. and Barth B. (1989) Color gamut matching for hard copy. *SID Digest*, **89**, 86–89.
16. Montag E. D. and Fairchild M. D. (1998) Evaluation of chroma clipping techniques for three destination gamuts. *Proc. 6th Color Imaging Conference: Color Science, Systems, and Applications*, pp. 57–61.

17. Morovic J. (1998) To develop a universal gamut mapping. PhD thesis, University of Derby, UK.
18. Morovic J. (1999) Gamut mapping and ICC rendering intents. *Proc. International Colour Management Forum*, pp. 107–116.
19. Morovic J. and Luo M. R. (1997) Gamut mapping algorithms based on psychophysical experiment. *Proc. 5th Color Imaging Conference*, pp. 44–49.
20. Morovic J. and Luo M. R. (1998) Developing algorithms for universal colour gamut mapping. In *Colour Imaging: Vision and Technology*, L. W. MacDonald and M. R. Luo (eds), pp. 50–55. John Wiley, Chichester.
21. Morovic J. and Luo M. R. (1998) Verification of gamut mapping algorithms in CIECAM97s using various printed media. *Proc. 6th Color Imaging Conference*, pp. 53–56.
22. Motomura H., Yamada O. and Fumoto T. (1997) Categorical color mapping for gamut mapping. *Proc. 5th IS&T/SID Color Imaging Conference*, pp. 50–55.
23. Pariser E. G. (1991) An investigation of color gamut reduction techniques. *Proc. 2nd IS&T Symposium on Electronic Publishing*, pp. 105–107.
24. Sara J. J. (1984) The automated reproduction of pictures with non-reproducible colors. PhD thesis, MIT, Cambridge MA.
25. Spaulding K. E., Ellson R. N. and Sullivan J. R. (1995) UltraColor: a new gamut mapping strategy. *Proc. SPIE*, **2414**, 61–68.
26. Stone M. C. and Wallace W. E. (1991) Gamut mapping computer generated imagery. In *Graphics Interface*, pp. 32–39.
27. Thurstone L. L. (1927) A law of comparative judgement. *Psychology Review*, **34**, 273–286.
28. Viggiano J. A. S. and Wang J. (1992) A comparison of algorithms for mapping color between media of differing luminance ranges. *TAGA Proc.*, **2**, 959–974.
29. Wolski M., Allebach J. P. and Bouman C. A. (1994) Gamut mapping, squeezing the most out of your color system. *Proc. 2nd IS&T/SID Color Imaging Conference*, pp. 89–92.

14

A topographic gamut mapping algorithm

Lindsay MacDonald, Ján Morovic and Kaida Xiao

14.1 INTRODUCTION

It remains a significant problem how best to reproduce the colours of an image that lie outside the colour gamut of a given device or medium. There can be no single optimal method, because various conflicting demands must be taken into account:

- Achieve a specified reproduction objective or *rendering intent*;
- Make best use of the available colour gamut of the output device;
- Not introduce any visible artefacts, such as contouring, into the image;
- Minimise computational complexity for efficient processing.

Developments in colour imaging techniques over the past decade have separated the problem into three areas – device characteristics, colour appearance and gamut mapping – enabling each to be studied in greater detail. Gamut mapping algorithms (GMAs) in particular have steadily become more sophisticated since the crude 'clip to range limits' methods of early computer graphics. Studies by Morovic and Luo [1] and

Colour Image Science, edited by L.W. MacDonald and M.R. Luo.

Braun *et al.* [2] have indicated that different algorithms are preferred by observers not only for different device colour gamuts, but also for different regions of colour space. Also the characteristics of individual images are crucial; generally much better results can be achieved by analysis of the distribution of colours within an image than by applying a generic algorithm [3, 4].

It is generally agreed that gamut mapping should be performed in a perceptually uniform colour space such as CIELAB or CIECAM97s [5]. This provides more control over the appearance of the image, and allows the techniques of Cartesian geometry to be applied to equally scaled dimensions of lightness, chroma and hue. The CIECAM97s colour model yields superior uniformity and independence of media and viewing conditions, although it is more complex to compute. Throughout this chapter we shall assume that a uniform colour space is employed, and denote the lightness and chroma axes by L and C respectively.

14.2 GAMUT MAPPING ALGORITHMS

Various methods of gamut compression have been proposed, from the basic clipping of colours onto the nearest point on the gamut boundary to complex transformations of colour space in which lightness, chroma and sometimes hue are modified. Good results for pleasing reproduction of scenes have been obtained by the CARISMA algorithm, first proposed by Johnson [6] and further developed by Morovic and Luo [1] and Green and Luo [7]. A recent evaluation by Pirrotta *et al.* [8] confirmed that it performs well for photographic images but not very well for business graphics and illustrations.

One of the problems with the majority of previous algorithms, is that they attempt to map all colours in the LC plane (at constant hue) toward a single convergence point, or 'centre of gravity', based on the coordinates of the cusps (points of maximum chroma) of the original and reproduction gamuts. An example is the SLIN algorithm [1], in which colours are mapped toward the point $L = 50$ on the lightness axis. Different rules may be employed for different cases (e.g. the relative lightness and chroma of the two cusp points), and the transformations may be non-linear, but usually all the points in the plane are governed by a single mapping formula. Such methods can result in unnecessarily large changes in the lightness of colours at the extremities of the lightness axis (notably in light yellow and dark blue-violet hues), and hence in significant changes to the overall image appearance.

Recent investigation by Kang *et al.*, as described in Chapter 13, has produced some interesting insights into gamut mapping in general and gamut compression in particular. In a series of experiments, observers were asked to make interactive adjustments to an image to achieve the most satisfactory match to a simulated inkjet print, adjacent on the CRT display. Observers were able to adjust lightness and chroma independently in three regions (high, medium and low) and hue in six regions (red, yellow, green, cyan, blue and magenta). The results indicated clearly the trend of the translation vectors from original (CRT gamut) to reproduction (simulated print gamut), as shown in Figure 13.15 for various hue angles. Inspection of Kang's results suggests the following aspects of observer preferences in gamut mapping:

- The chords between corresponding colours in the original and destination are of lengths proportional to the local distance between the two gamut boundaries. The directions of the chords change as a function of lightness, but they do not converge to a single point. Instead they are approximately normal to the destination gamut boundary for dark colours (below the destination cusp), horizontal for lightnesses between the two cusps, and inclined at an angle for light colours (above the source cusp).
- The colours within the reproduction gamut are largely untouched, but the mapping does extend a little inside the boundary, by about 10% at medium lightness values near the destination cusp. This suggests that the observers intuitively adopted a 'soft clipping' technique, in which chromatic gradations are preserved for colours near the gamut boundary while all other interior colours within a 'core gamut' are unchanged. Some variation in the thickness of the region between core and destination gamuts is evident when different hue angles are examined.

14.3 DESCRIPTION OF THE TOPO ALGORITHM

The TOPO algorithm transforms values from a source colour gamut into a destination colour gamut, preserving the relationships between source and destination in a reversible manner. The colour coordinate space is assumed to be perceptually uniform, such as CIELAB or CIECAM97s, with dimensions of hue, lightness and chroma. Hue angle is assumed to be invariant, so that the transformation maps pixel values within the lightness–chroma plane. The aim of the algorithm is to preserve the lightness and chroma differences of the source gamut, as far as possible, by means of an adaptive procedure applied consistently throughout the entire colour space.

The algorithm accommodates both gamut compression and gamut expansion, for three different cases:

- *Compression*: the destination gamut is entirely enclosed within the source gamut
- *Expansion*: the source gamut is entirely enclosed within the destination gamut
- *Mixed*: the source and destination gamut boundaries cross over

The algorithm is defined in four steps:

1. Construct the boundary of a 'core gamut', within which no colours are altered.
2. Define a distance metric along the source and core gamut boundaries.
3. Construct a set of mapping chords, connecting corresponding points.
4. Perform the gamut compression along the chords, with a soft-clip function.

14.3.1 Construct the core gamut boundary

Let the source and destination gamuts be expressed in a plane of constant hue, as shown in Figure 14.1. Assume that both the source and destination gamuts are convex. The maximum lightness (white point) of both gamuts is normalised to 100. Define L_S and L_D to be the minimum lightness (black point) of the source and destination gamuts respectively.

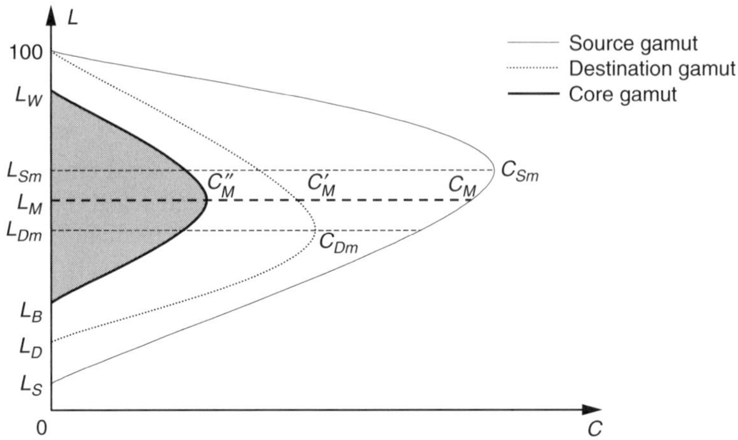

Figure 14.1 Gamut boundaries in the *LC* plane. The shaded region is the core gamut.

Let L_{Dm} be the lightness corresponding to the maximum chroma $C_{Dm} = \max_L(C_D)$, i.e. the cusp point, on the destination gamut, and let L_{Sm} be the lightness corresponding to the maximum chroma $C_{Sm} = \max_L(C_S)$ on the source gamut, as shown in Figure 14.1. Define the upper source cusp point L_{U_S} to be the lightness of the source cusp having the highest lightness over all hue angles (normally in the yellow region):

$$L_{U_S} = \max_h(L_{Sm}) \tag{14.1}$$

Define the upper destination cusp point L_{U_D} to be the lightness of the destination cusp having the highest lightness over all hue angles (normally in the yellow region):

$$L_{U_D} = \max_h(L_{Dm}) \tag{14.2}$$

Define the core white point L_W to be the lesser of the upper source and destination cusp points:

$$L_W = \min(L_{U_S}, L_{U_D}) \tag{14.3}$$

Similarly, define the lower source cusp point L_{L_S} to be the lightness of the source cusp having the lowest lightness over all hue angles (normally in the blue region):

$$L_{L_S} = \min_h(L_{Sm}) \tag{14.4}$$

Define the lower destination cusp point L_{L_D} to be the lightness of the destination cusp having the lowest lightness over all hue angles (normally in the blue region):

$$L_{L_D} = \min_h(L_{Dm}) \tag{14.5}$$

Define the core black point L_B to be the greater of the lower source and destination cusp points:

$$L_B = \max(L_{L_S}, L_{L_D}) \tag{14.6}$$

The core gamut boundary is constructed to lie within the smaller of the source and destination gamut boundaries. The relationship is determined by the black points of the two gamuts and the relative magnitude of the chroma of their respective cusps. Note that this may vary for different hue angles. If the destination gamut is not significantly larger than the source gamut (normal compression case) then the core gamut follows the shape of the destination gamut. Only if the destination gamut is significantly larger than the source gamut (expansion case) does the shape of the core gamut follow that of the source gamut.

Compression: $L_D > L_S$ *or* $C_{Dm}/C_{Sm} \leqslant 1.2$

Define chroma scaling factor χ to be the chroma of the destination cusp divided by the chroma of the source cusp. It is limited to a minimum of 0.5 to ensure that the core gamut is not too small and to a maximum value of 0.75 to ensure sufficient latitude for the mapping procedure. Note that χ may vary for different hue angles:

$$\chi = \max(0.5, \min(0.75, C_{Dm}/C_{Sm})) \tag{14.7}$$

Let the chroma of the destination gamut boundary be expressed as $C_D(L)$, a continuous single-valued function of L for $L_D \leqslant L \leqslant 100$. Then define the core gamut boundary $C_C(L)$ on the interval $L_B \leqslant L \leqslant L_W$ as follows:

$$C_C(L) = \chi C_D\left(L_D + (L - L_B)\frac{100 - L_D}{L_W - L_B}\right) \tag{14.8}$$

This function has a maximum value (cusp point) at lightness:

$$L_M = L_B + (L_{Dm} - L_D)\frac{L_W - L_B}{100 - L_D} \tag{14.9}$$

Expansion: $L_D \leqslant L_S$ *and* $C_{Dm}/C_{Sm} > 1.2$

Define chroma scaling factor χ to be the chroma of the source cusp divided by the chroma of the destination cusp. It is limited to a minimum of 0.5 to ensure the core gamut is not too small and to a maximum value of 0.75 to ensure sufficient latitude for the mapping procedure. Note that χ may vary for different hue angles:

$$\chi = \max(0.5, \min(0.75, C_{Sm}/C_{Dm})) \tag{14.10}$$

Let the chroma of the source gamut boundary be expressed as $C_S(L)$, a continuous single-valued function of L for $L_S \leqslant L \leqslant 100$. Then define the core gamut boundary $C_C(L)$ on the interval $L_B \leqslant L \leqslant L_W$ as follows:

$$C_C(L) = \chi C_S\left(L_S + (L - L_B)\frac{100 - L_S}{L_W - L_B}\right) \tag{14.11}$$

This function has a maximum value (cusp point) at lightness:

$$L_M = L_B + (L_{Sm} - L_S)\frac{L_W - L_B}{100 - L_S} \tag{14.12}$$

14.3.2 Define a distance metric along the gamut boundary

A key aspect of the new algorithm is its reliance upon a distance metric, or path length, along the boundary of each gamut in the hue plane. Let the horizontal line $L = L_M$ intersect the source, destination and core gamut boundaries at points C_M, C'_M and C''_M respectively, as shown in Figure 14.1. Define the parametric variable λ along the upper source gamut boundary on the interval $L_M \leqslant L \leqslant 100$, i.e. the light tonal region:

$$\lambda = \frac{L - 100}{L_M - 100} \tag{14.13}$$

Let the gamut boundary be represented by chroma function $g(\lambda)$, $0 \leqslant \lambda \leqslant 1$, and let the path length along the source gamut boundary be represented by ξ. Then for a small change $\Delta\lambda$ in parametric lightness, the corresponding change in distance $\Delta\xi$ along the source gamut boundary is:

$$\Delta\xi = \sqrt{\Delta\lambda^2 + (g(\lambda + \Delta\lambda) - g(\lambda))^2} \tag{14.14}$$

When the gamut boundary is represented as a series of n straight-line segments, connecting points $P_i = (\lambda_i, g_i)$ for $i = 0, \ldots, n$ along the boundary, each increment in path length can be conveniently calculated as the length of one segment, as shown in Figure 14.2. The total length of the source gamut boundary from L_M to 100 is then approximated as:

$$\xi_S = \sum_1^n \Delta\xi_i = \sum_1^n \sqrt{(\lambda_i - \lambda_{i-1})^2 + (g_i - g_{i-1})^2} \tag{14.15}$$

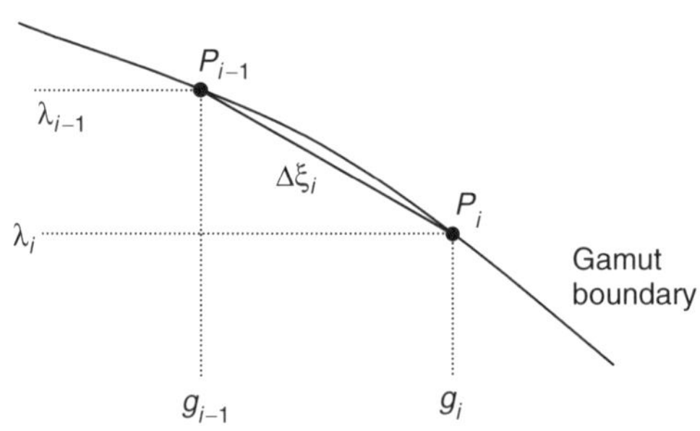

Figure 14.2 Approximation of gamut boundary path length by straight-line segments.

In the limit as $\Delta\lambda_S \to 0$ the path length can be expressed by the Riemann integral:

$$\xi_S = \int_0^1 \sqrt{1 + \left(\frac{dg_S}{d\lambda_S}\right)^2}\, d\lambda_S \tag{14.16}$$

Similar functions can be defined along the lower source gamut boundary on the interval $L_S \leqslant L \leqslant L_M$, i.e. the dark tonal region, by defining the parametric variable:

$$\lambda' = \frac{L - L_S}{L_M - L_S} \tag{14.17}$$

Other similar functions can be defined for the upper and lower regions of the core gamut boundary, i.e. above and below the line $L = L_M$.

14.3.3 Construct the mapping chords

The LC plane is divided into two regions, by range of lightness, as shown in Figure 14.3. The mapping chords, which define the local vector directions (or flow lines) of gamut mapping, are constructed separately in each region and generally have positive slopes in the upper region and negative slopes in the lower region.

Lower Region $L \leqslant L_M$

Locate $n + 1$ points (L_{Si}, C_{Si}) for $i = 0, \ldots, n$ at equal intervals of length ξ_S/n along the source gamut boundary. Similarly, locate $n + 1$ points (L_{Ci}, C_{Ci}) for $i = 0, \ldots, n$ at equal intervals of ξ_C/n along the core gamut boundary. Typically $n = 16$.

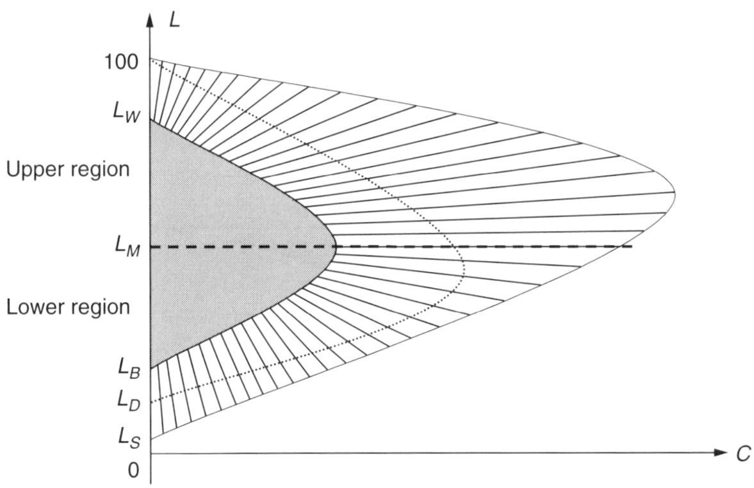

Figure 14.3 Chord directions in the two regions of gamut mapping.

Construct $n+1$ chords connecting each (L_{Si}, C_{Si}) with the corresponding (L_{Ci}, C_{Ci}). The first chord $(i=0)$ will be vertical, connecting L_S with L_B along the L axis. The last chord $(i=n)$ will be horizontal, connecting C_M with C''_M along the line $L = L_M$.

Upper Region $L \geqslant L_M$

Locate $n+1$ points (L_{Si}, C_{Si}) for $i = 0, \ldots, n$ at equal intervals of length ξ_S/n along the source gamut boundary. Similarly, locate $n+1$ points (L_{Ci}, C_{Ci}) for $i = 0, \ldots, n$ at equal intervals of ξ_C/n along the core gamut boundary. Typically $n = 16$.

Construct $n+1$ chords connecting each (L_{Si}, C_{Si}) with the corresponding (L_{Ci}, C_{Ci}). The first chord $(i=n)$ will be horizontal, connecting C_M with C''_M along the line $L = L_M$ (this duplicates the last chord of the lower region). The last chord $(i=0)$ will be vertical, connecting 100 with L_W along the L axis.

14.3.4 Perform the gamut mapping

A point P in the source gamut with coordinates (L_P, C_P) is to be mapped to a point P' in the destination gamut with coordinates $(L_{P'}, C_{P'})$. The core gamut boundary represents the common subset of the two gamuts, within which no mapping occurs. Thus $P' = P$ for all points within the core gamut.

Points outside the boundary of the core gamut are mapped as follows (Figures 14.4, 14.5 and 14.6):

1. Find the two nearest mapping chords constructed in step 3 on either side of P and, if not parallel, project them to intersect at point X.
2. Construct a new chord from X through P, intersecting the source, destination and core gamut boundaries at points P_S, P_D and P_C respectively.
3. In the case where the two nearest mapping chords are parallel, construct a new chord through P parallel to the other two.
4. Map P to P' along the chord using a suitable soft-clip mapping function.

It is required to construct a smoothly continuous function of x that lies between the upper bound of $f(x) = x$ and the lower bound $f(x) = x/s$, as shown in Figure 14.4,

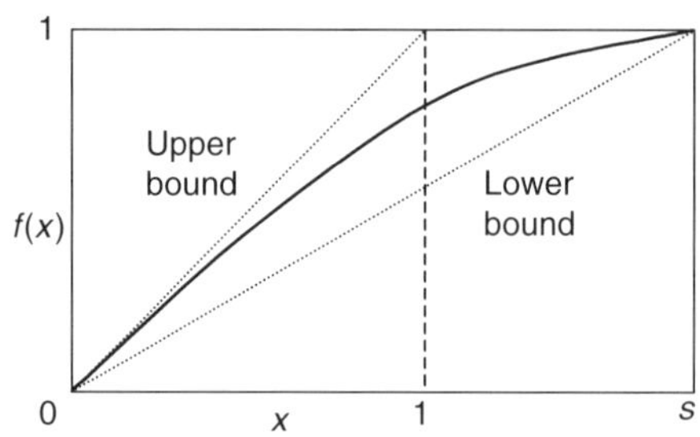

Figure 14.4 Soft-clip mapping function.

where for convenience the scalar variable $x = |P - P_C|/|P_D - P_C|$ and constant $s = |P_S - P_C|/|P_D - P_C|$. A suitable function and its first derivative are given by:

$$f(x) = kx^{\alpha} + x$$
$$f'(x) = k\alpha x^{\alpha-1} + 1 \tag{14.18}$$

To determine the coefficients k and α, we observe the constraints that $f(s) = 1$ and $f'(s) = m$, where $m > 0$ is the terminal slope of the curve. Hence:

$$f(s) = 1 = ks^{\alpha} + s \Rightarrow k = \frac{1 - s}{s^{\alpha}}$$
$$f'(s) = m = k\alpha s^{\alpha-1} + 1 \Rightarrow k = \frac{m - 1}{\alpha s^{\alpha-1}} \tag{14.19}$$

In the limiting case where $s = 1$ (corresponding to $P_S = P_D$), we have $k = 0$ and (14.18) reduces to $f(x) = x$ and $f'(x) = 1$. Solving (14.19) for α, we obtain:

$$\alpha = \frac{s(1 - m)}{(s - 1)} \tag{14.20}$$

Note that α is undefined when $s = 1$.

Compression: $|P_D - P_C| \leqslant |P_S - P_C|$

Define the scalar variable ζ as follows (Figure 14.5):

$$\zeta = \frac{|P - P_C|}{|P_D - P_C|} = \frac{\sqrt{(L_P - L_{P_C})^2 + (C_P - C^2_{P_C})}}{\sqrt{(L_{P_D} - L_{P_C})^2 + (C_{P_D} - C_{P_C})^2}} \tag{14.21}$$

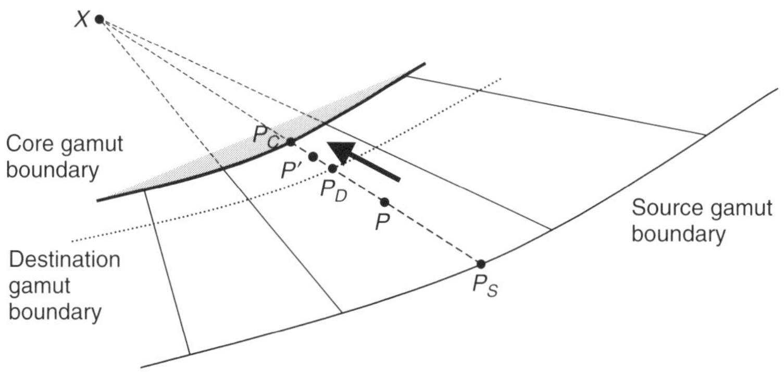

Figure 14.5 Compression: construction of mapping chord.

Define the parameters s, m, α and k as follows:

$$\begin{aligned} s &= |P_S - P_C|/|P_D - P_C| \\ m &= 0.5/s \\ \alpha &= \frac{s(1-m)}{(s-1)} = \frac{(s-0.5)}{(s-1)} \\ k &= (1-s)/s^{\alpha} \end{aligned} \tag{14.22}$$

For compression we have $s > 1$ and $k < 0$ and the trend of the curve is downward, as shown in Figure 14.6. The terminal slope m of the curve should be partway between zero (clipping case) and s (linear compression case), and the choice of 0.5 times the linear slope $1/s$ is somewhat arbitrary. (Values in the range 0.3–0.5 give good results.) In the limiting case when $P_S = P_D$ (no compression), we have $s = 1$, $k = 0$ and α is undefined.

The mapping function is then:

$$P' = \begin{cases} P & \text{for } P \leqslant P_C \\ P_C + (P_D - P_C)(k\zeta^{\alpha} + \zeta) & \text{for } P_C \leqslant P \leqslant P_S \end{cases} \tag{14.23}$$

Equation (14.23) can be implemented for mapping the L and C components of P' as:

$$\begin{aligned} L_{P'} &= L_{P_C} + (L_{P_D} - L_{P_C})(k\zeta^{\alpha} + \zeta) \\ C_{P'} &= C_{P_C} + (C_{P_D} - C_{P_C})(k\zeta^{\alpha} + \zeta) \end{aligned} \tag{14.24}$$

In the rare case where $P_C = P_S$ (core and source boundaries intersect, resulting in a zero-length mapping chord), set $\zeta = 0$ so that $P' = P$.

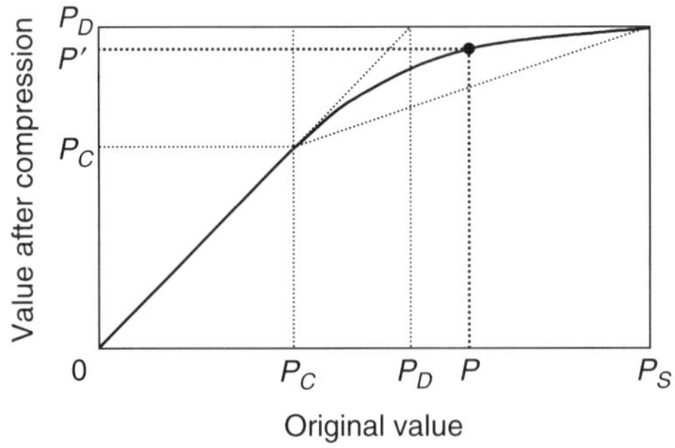

Figure 14.6 Soft-clip gamut compression function.

Expansion: $|P_D - P_C| > |P_S - P_C|$

Define the parameters s, m, α and k similar to (14.22) as follows (Figure 14.7):

$$\begin{aligned} s &= |P_S - P_C|/|P_D - P_C| \\ m &= 2/s \\ \alpha &= \frac{s(1-m)}{(s-1)} = \frac{(s-2)}{(s-1)} \\ k &= (1-s)/s^{\alpha} \end{aligned} \tag{14.25}$$

For expansion we have $s < 1$ and $k > 0$ and the trend of the curve is upward, as shown in Figure 14.8. The terminal slope m of the curve should be partway between s (linear

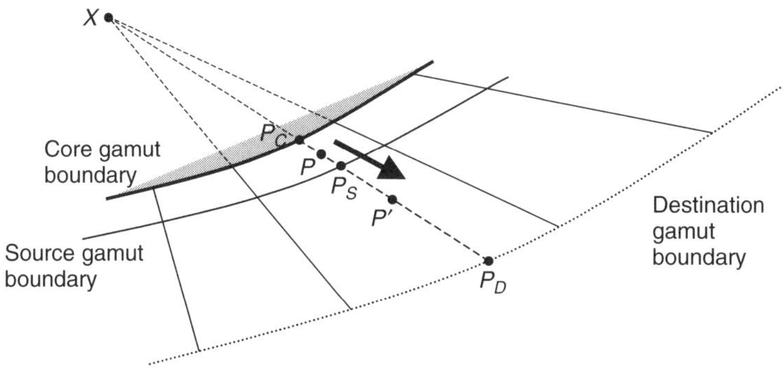

Figure 14.7 Expansion: construction of mapping chord.

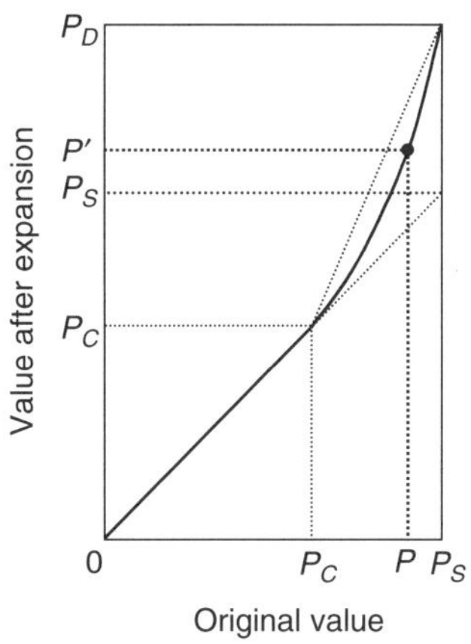

Figure 14.8 Soft-clip gamut expansion function.

expansion case) and vertical, and the choice of 2 times the linear slope $1/s$ is somewhat arbitrary. (Values in the range 2–3 give good results.) For computational reasons, and to ensure invertibility, it is important that the terminal slope should not be too large. In the limiting case when $P_S = P_D$ (no expansion), we have $s = 1$, $k = 0$ and α is undefined.

The mapping function is identical to (14.23) and can be implemented for mapping of the L and C components of P' by (14.24). In the rare case where $P_C = P_S$ (core and source boundaries intersect, resulting in a zero-length mapping chord), set $\zeta = 0$ so that $P' = P$.

14.4 DISCUSSION

The algorithm is described as topographic because of the way it delineates and preserves the local features of the source and destination gamut boundaries. The objective is to map colours between corresponding points of the two gamuts, while preserving the rendering of gradations in lightness and chroma to the greatest degree possible. In compression the range of colours in the source gamut is compressed into the smaller range of colours available in the destination gamut. In expansion the range of colours in the source gamut is expanded into the larger range of colours available in the destination gamut. Compression is an interpolation process, whereas expansion is an extrapolation and therefore may have the effect of amplifying noise or other gradations between colours in the image. The technique is in some ways comparable to the mapping along curved lines proposed by Herzog and Büring [9], as described in Chapter 16, but is more closely attuned to the actual conformations of both source and destination gamut boundaries.

The concept of the 'core gamut' is not entirely new. Spaulding *et al* proposed a 'gamut morphing' technique [10], in which a football-shaped volume in the centre of the source colour space was constrained to be reproduced using a colorimetric model. This volume was selected to include the convex hull of typical skin tone colours. Katoh and Ito proposed an 'onion-peel' method [11], in which an invariant colorimetric region lies at the core of a series of virtual gamut boundaries. This region was defined by scaling the destination (printer) gamut by a constant, the knee point of the chroma compression function, and was coterminous with the destination gamut at both black and white points. Their results from experiments with four test images appeared to show a slight observer preference for a core gamut of scale 50%, although the trend was very dependent on image content. Sakamoto and Urabe also defined an 'original colour region' in a similar manner [12], but their compression knee point was determined by analysis of the chroma histogram.

The definition of the core gamut is critical to the effectiveness of the algorithm. We found in our initial trials that elevating the black point of the core gamut was important in preserving gradations in the shadow regions (dark tones) of the image. The region between the lower surfaces of the core and destination gamuts is where the dark colours are mapped from a source device having significantly lower black point than the destination device. If this region is too narrow, as may happen when the core and destination gamut black points are coterminous, the shadow detail is greatly reduced or lost, and may result in contouring of the reproduced image.

The soft-clip functions shown in Figures 14.6 and 14.8 preserve all colours unchanged within the core gamut, while mapping colours proportionally in the region between the core gamut and source gamut boundaries. This technique was first proposed for compression by Stone and Wallace [13] and has since been employed by various researchers [11, 14, 15]. Values on the source gamut boundary are mapped onto the destination gamut boundary. The monotonic 1 : 1 mapping preserves the relationships between values and is thus invertible, subject to the quantising of the image coding. The mapping is constrained to lie between the clipping and linear compression bounds.

The factors L_W, L_B and χ determine the size and shape of the core gamut, which is crucial for obtaining the best results. L_B is the darkest tone of the destination gamut that remains unchanged after gamut mapping, whereas L_W is the lightest tone of the destination gamut that remains unchanged after gamut mapping. χ controls the radius of the core gamut, and may vary with hue.

The TOPO algorithm assumes that the source and destination gamut boundaries are known *a priori*, and that they can be accurately represented at each hue angle. Each gamut boundary should be well behaved, i.e. the chroma C should be expressible as a smooth and continuous single-valued function of the lightness L. Implementation should account for cases where the maximum chroma of the source gamut occurs at higher, equal and lower values of lightness than the maximum chroma of the destination gamut. Intermediate hue angles should be interpolated between LC planes of known hues, which should be at intervals of no greater than 30° (i.e. at least 12 hue angles defined in the full hue circle).

Implementation of the algorithm should accommodate cases where the gamut boundaries cross over, resulting in gamut expansion in some regions and gamut compression in others. In principle a test should be made during the construction of every mapping chord (Figures 14.5 and 14.7) to determine the relative distances from core to source and core to destination gamut boundaries.

14.5 IMPLEMENTATION

The topographic gamut mapping algorithm (TOPO) was implemented in the ANSI C language in the Microsoft Visual C++ programming environment. Images were converted into the CAM97s2 colour space [16], and the gamut mapping performed in the perceptual dimensions of lightness (J) and chroma (C). The source device was a Barco Calibrator V monitor, characterised by the Berns GOG model [17]. The reproduction device was a Hewlett Packard 895c inkjet printer, characterised by fitting third-order polynomials to colorimetric densities measured from $9 \times 9 \times 9$ printed colour patches [18]. Device gamut boundaries were described using the flexible sequential line gamut boundary (FSLGB) method developed by Morovic [1].

The black point for the source gamut it was $L_S = 3.2$ and for the destination gamut it was $L_D = 12.6$. To construct the TOPO core gamut we used $L_W = 90.8$ and $L_B = 27.1$, corresponding to source gamut hue angles 93° and 271° respectively; L_W comes from (14.3) and L_B from (14.6). The ratio χ (14.7) ranged from 0.54 to 1.03 for different hue angles, as shown in Table 14.1. The gamut boundary descriptors were calculated for 1°

Table 14.1 Ratio of maximum chroma (destination/source) for different hue angles

Colour	Hue angle	Chroma of destination cusp	Chroma of source cusp	$C_{D\,max}/C_{S\,max}$
Red	26.1	81.3	115.5	0.70
Yellow	103.7	71.3	69.5	1.03
Green	143.5	76.5	103.6	0.74
Cyan	198.2	66.6	68.9	0.97
Blue	267.1	56.7	105.5	0.54
Magenta	332.8	60.6	94.7	0.64

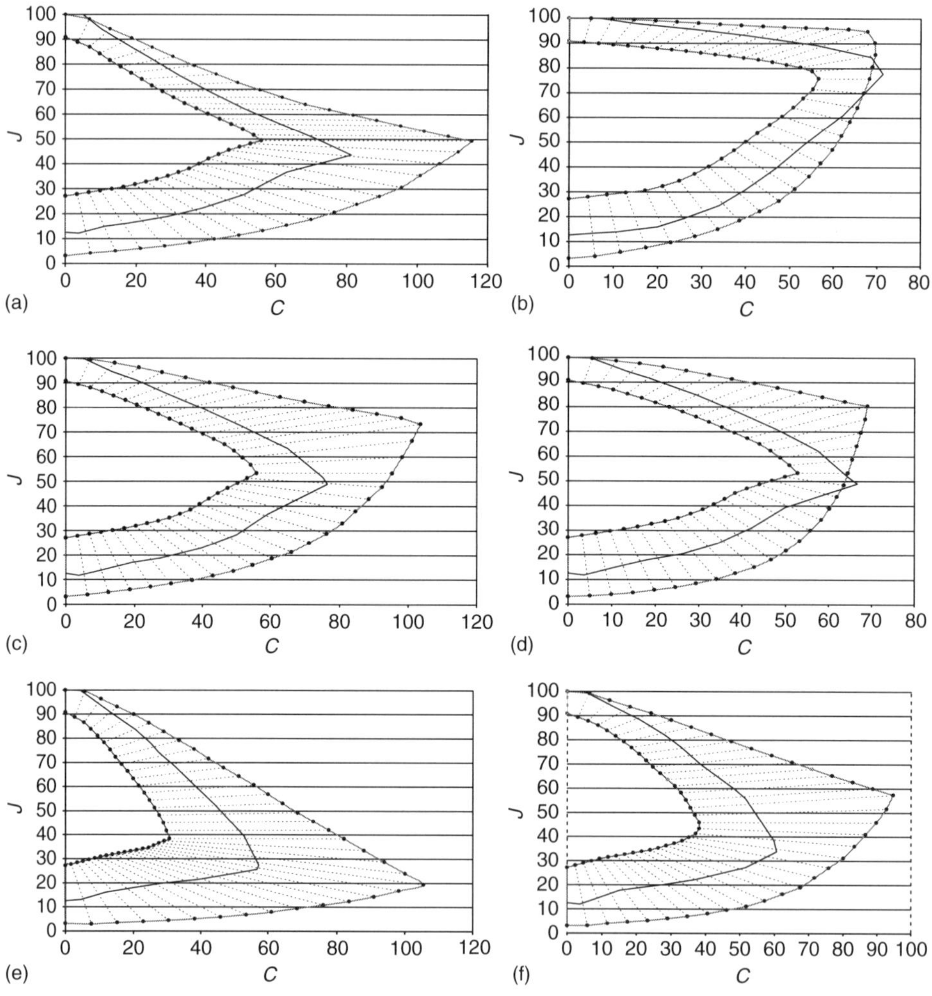

Figure 14.9 Construction of core gamut and mapping chords for six hue angles: (a) red, (b) yellow, (c) green, (d) cyan, (e) blue, (f) magenta.

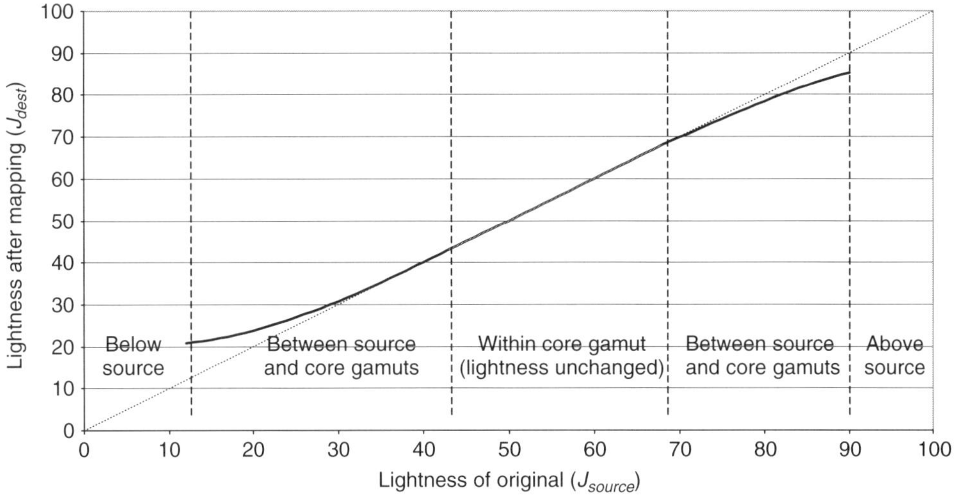

Figure 14.10 Lightness mapping function in green hue plane for chroma = 41.6.

intervals of hue angle. The mapping chords generated by the TOPO algorithm for six principal hue angles are shown in Figure 14.9. In the few cases where the destination gamut extended beyond the source gamut (yellow and cyan hue angles) the colours were limited to the source gamut, because this earlier version of the algorithm did not support gamut expansion.

The behaviour of the algorithm was verified by examination of the colours in the printed *JC* plane for six hue angles, as shown in Colour Plate 8. This shows the colours resulting from the gamut compression calculation for all combinations of *J* and *C* within the source colour gamut. The dotted lines indicate the positions of the destination and core gamuts, within which the colours remain unchanged. This type of visualisation is a very sensitive test both for any gamut mapping algorithm to reveal bugs in the program code, which may appear as contours or dropouts, and problems in the formulation of the algorithm, which may appear as distortions in the lightness and chroma gradations.

It is interesting to consider the effect of gamut mapping on the rendering of both lightness and chroma of the image. A facsimile reproduction would obviously be identical to the original in both respects, but this is impossible to achieve when compressing a larger source colour gamut to a smaller destination gamut. An effective GMA must strike the right balance between the extremes of preserving lightness unchanged by compressing only chroma and preserving chroma by compressing only lightness, both of which lead to poor image rendering.

The lightness mapping function of the TOPO algorithm is illustrated in Figure 14.10 for a line of constant chroma ($C = 41.6$) in the green hue plane (shown in Figure 14.9). Within the core gamut the lightness is reproduced unchanged (output = input), but at the white and black ends of the lightness range there is a smooth roll-off to the maximum and minimum lightness achievable in the reproduction gamut at the specified chroma.

This is the result of the soft-clip mapping function in the regions between the source and core gamuts and gives rise to a monotonic sigmoidal (S-shaped) curve. It is not dissimilar to the type of tone reproduction curve used in the graphic arts, except that in this case the contrast gradient remains fixed at 1.0 within the core region. On the lightness axis ($C = 0$) the curve for greyscale reproduction has a similar roll-off to the destination black point, but extends as a straight line up to the white point ($J = 100$) where the normalised source and destination gamuts are coterminous.

14.6 FIRST EXPERIMENT

The performance of version 2 of the TOPO algorithm was evaluated [19] using the same experimental technique and test images employed previously by Morovic and Luo [1]. Three other gamut mapping algorithms used in the previous study were also applied to each test image, employing a common gamut boundary data set:

- MDE: minimum ΔE clipping to gamut boundary, preserving hue (in *JC* plane)
- LLIN: linear compression of lightness and chroma
- GCUSP: chroma-dependent lightness compression and linear compression to cusp

The images were simultaneously viewed side by side, as shown in Figure 14.11, with the source image displayed on the CRT and two reproduction prints in a Verivide viewing booth under a simulated D65 light source, meeting the ISO 3664 viewing condition P2. Both the white point and the grey background on the CRT were carefully matched to the corresponding colours in the booth, based on spectroradiometric measurement. The printed

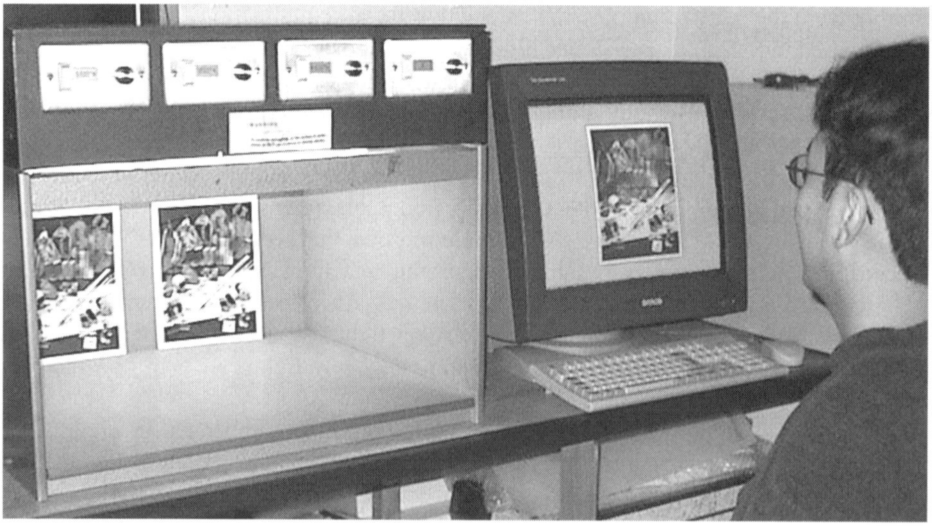

Figure 14.11 Viewing arrangement for the first experiment.

images were approximately 20 cm in width and subtended a visual angle of approximately 12° to the observer, viewed from a distance of 1 m. The observer position was chosen so that the angle subtended by both printed and displayed images was approximately equal. The images were viewed in a darkened room (lights off). Other conditions were as described in the evaluation guidelines under development for CIE Technical Committee 8-03 [20].

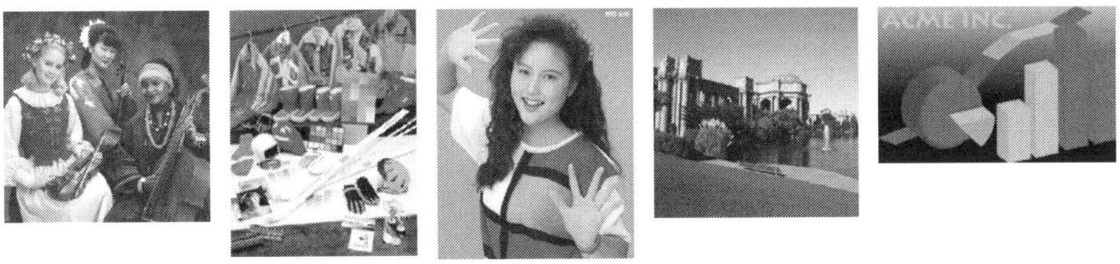

Figure 14.12 The five test images: MUS, SKI, GIRL, NAT, BUS (MUS: photos N7 and N7A, GIRL: photos N1 and N1A of ISO Standard 12640 : 1997, are reproduced with the permission of the International Organization for Standardization, ISO. Copyright remains with ISO. Standard 12640 : 1997 can be obtained from any ISO member and from the website of the ISO Central Secretariat at the following address: http//www.iso.org. Copyright remains with ISO. SKI is reprinted by permission of Fujifilm Electronic Imaging Limited. BUS: MacDonald/Luo: Colour Imaging, 1999 © John Wiley & Sons, Ltd Reproduced with Permission).

Five test images were chosen to contain a range of different types of pictorial content and tonal and chromatic variety, as shown in Figure 14.12. Twenty prints were produced (5 images × 4 algorithms). Twelve observers, all students and staff of the Colour & Imaging Institute with normal colour vision and ages ranging from 20 to 38, took part in the experiment. Each observer was required to make ${}^4C_2 = 6$ pairwise comparisons per image, a total of 30 comparisons per session. The observer's task was to decide which of the two prints in the viewing booth was the better overall match to the original (source) image displayed on the CRT.

Table 14.2 Pair comparison z-scores for each image and algorithm

Image	TOPO2	GCUSP	MDE	LLIN
MUS	0.58	0.11	−0.36	−0.33
GIRL	0.25	−0.18	0.70	−0.77
SKI	0.22	0.66	−0.57	0.45
NAT	−0.44	0.61	−0.46	0.30
BUS	−0.49	0.98	0.15	−0.63
Overall	**0.02**	**0.32**	**−0.08**	**−0.14**

For each image, the 4 × 4 matrices of comparison results for each observer were averaged over the 12 observers and transformed into z-scores. Using case V of the method proposed by Thurstone [21], the standard deviation of the z-score values is assumed to be $\sigma = 1/\sqrt{2}$ and the 95% confidence interval (CI) of a z-score value A can therefore be calculated [1] as:

$$CI = A \pm 1.96\frac{\sigma}{\sqrt{N}} \tag{14.26}$$

For the number of images and observers used in the first experiment, CI was calculated to be ±0.40 for the individual images and ±0.18 overall. The results are given in Table 14.2 and the overall z-scores for the four algorithms are plotted in Figure 14.13.

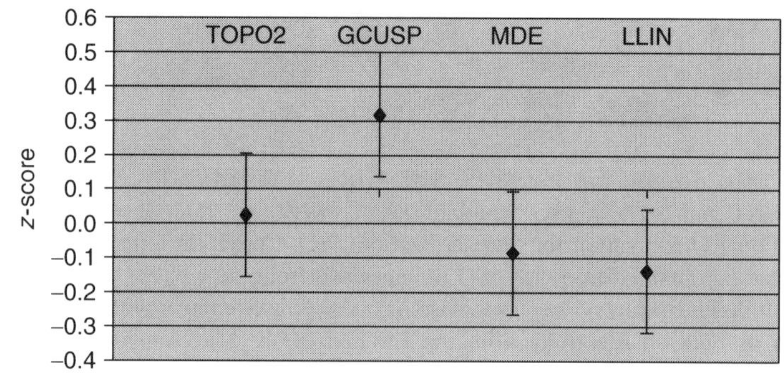

Figure 14.13 Overall z-scores for the four algorithms.

Table 14.3 gives the ranking of the performance of the four algorithms for the five test images. GCUSP was best overall and TOPO v2 second best. TOPO was ranked highest for MUS, in which it preserved the lightness rendering better than the other algorithms, especially in the skin colours. TOPO performed poorly for NAT, because observers judged the blue sky to be too dark, and also for BUS, because the loss in chroma was too great. Curiously, the MDE algorithm was ranked best for GIRL because it had little effect on the skin colours, which were largely inside the printer gamut boundary. It is clear that the performance of the various algorithms was very dependent on image content.

Table 14.3 Ranking of algorithm performance for each image (1 = best, 4 = worst)

Image	TOPO2	GCUSP	MDE	LLIN
MUS	1	2	4	3
GIRL	2	3	1	4
SKI	3	1	4	2
NAT	3	1	4	2
BUS	3	1	2	4
Overall	**2**	**1**	**3**	**4**

14.7 SECOND EXPERIMENT

The TOPO algorithm was revised and improved, based on the results of the first experiment. Version 3 was evaluated in a second experiment [22]. The same three gamut mapping algorithms as before were used for reference, but a different experimental technique was employed, with two simulated prints displayed alongside the original on the CRT, instead of real prints in the viewing cabinet, as shown in Figure 14.14. The white point of the simulated prints and the grey background were checked to be the same as for the white point of the real prints and the walls of the viewing cabinet, respectively, in the first experiment by measurement with a telespectroradiometer.

The simulated prints were generated by applying the gamut mapping algorithm to each image in *JCh* (polar coordinate transformation of *Jab*) colour appearance space, then applying the inverse CAM97s2 model using the display viewing conditions to obtain a colorimetric (*XYZ*) image, as shown in Figure 14.15. The GOG model [17] was used to convert the image to display RGB signals. The images were viewed in a darkened room (lights off).

Eight test images were chosen to contain a range of tone, chroma and pictorial content, as shown in Figure 14.16. Four of the images (top row) were the same as used in the first experiment. The second group of images (bottom row) was selected from the recent Japanese SHIPP standard [23].

Thirty-two versions of the simulated prints were produced (8 images $\times$ 4 algorithms). Twenty-one observers, all students and staff of the Colour & Imaging Institute with normal colour vision and ages ranging from 21 to 50, took part in the experiment. Each observer was required to make ${}^4C_2 = 6$ pairwise comparisons per image, a total of

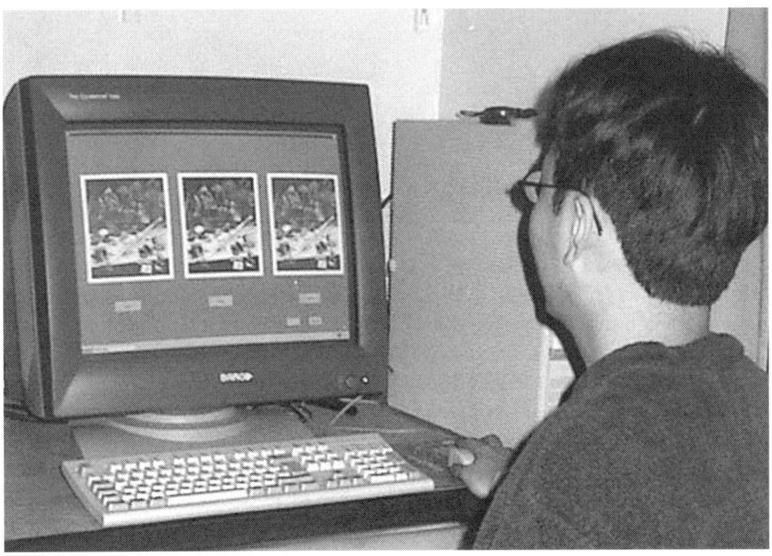

Figure 14.14 Viewing arrangement for the second experiment.

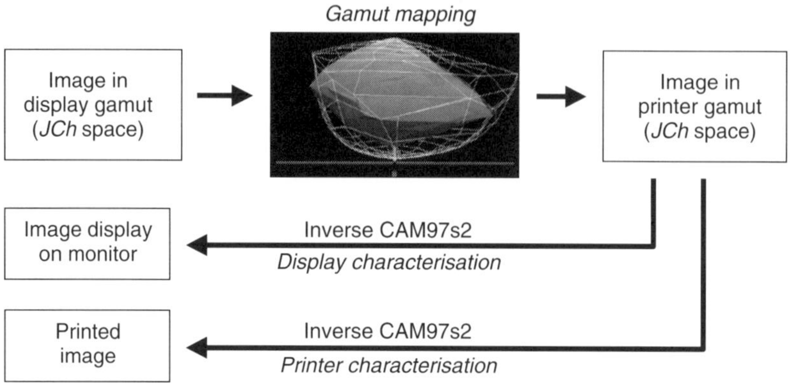

Figure 14.15 Processing of simulated and real prints.

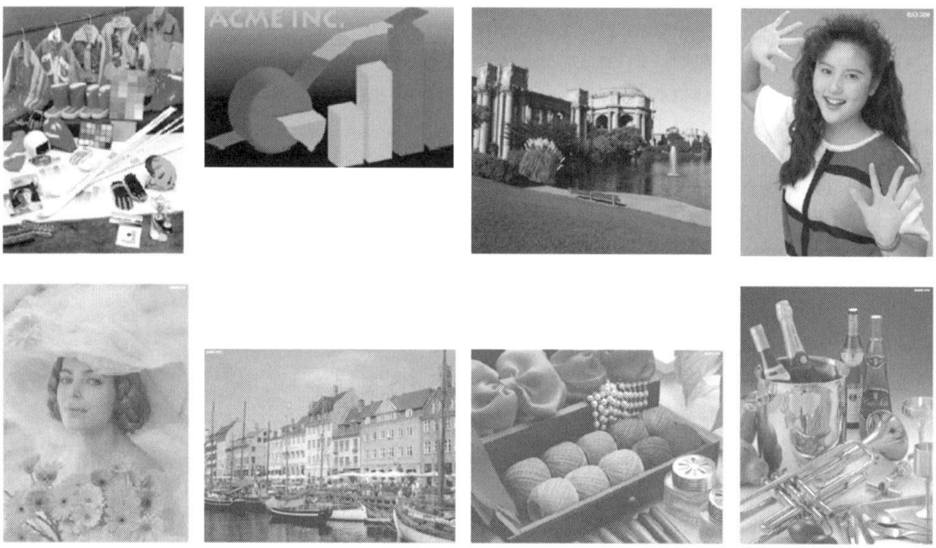

Figure 14.16 The eight test images: (top) SKI, BUS, NAT, GIRL; (bottom) Bride, Harbour, Textile, Metal (MUS: photos N7 and N7A, GIRL: photos N1 and N1A of ISO Standard 12640 : 1997, Figure 1, are reproduced with the permission of the International Organization for Standardization, ISO. Copyright remains with ISO. Standard 12640 : 1997 can be obtained from any ISO member and from the website of the ISO Central Secretariat at the following address: http//www.iso.org. Copyright remains with ISO. SKI is reprinted by permission of Fujifilm Electronic Imaging Limited. SHIPP: taken from K. Sakamoto, H. Urabe, Standard High Precision Pictures. The Fifth Color Imaging Conference: Color Science, Systems, and Applications 1997. BUS: MacDonald/Luo: Colour Imaging, 1999 © John Wiley & Sons, Ltd Reproduced with Permission).

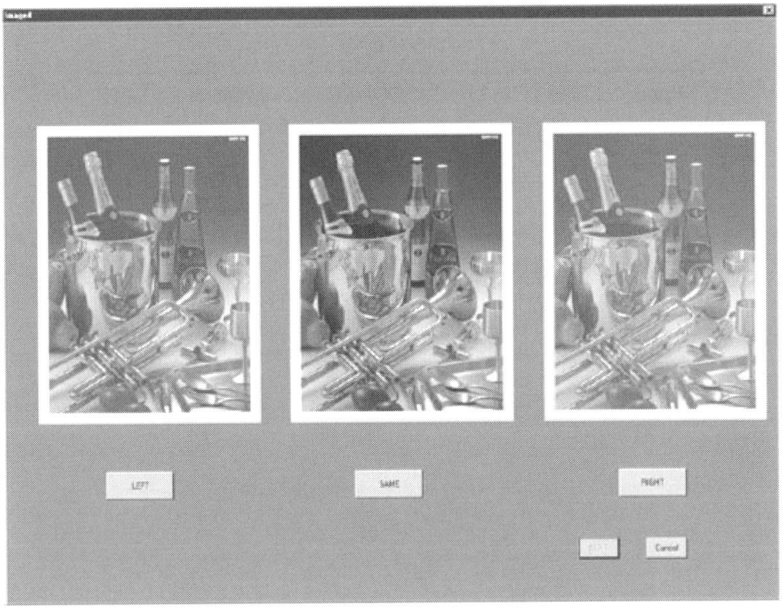

Figure 14.17 Experimental set-up for comparison of the original image (centre) with simulated prints (left and right).

48 judgements per session. The observer's task was to decide which of the two simulated prints displayed on the CRT was the better overall match to the displayed original image. Figure 14.17 shows a typical test screen. Automatic control software presented the pairs of images in random order, recorded the observer's selections (from point-and-click on left or right test image), and computed the z-scores on completion of each session.

For each image, the 4×4 matrices of comparison results for each observer were averaged over the 21 observers and transformed into z-scores. The 95% confidence interval (CI) was calculated to be ± 0.30 for the individual images, and ± 0.11 overall. The results are given in Table 14.4 and the overall z-scores for the four algorithms are plotted in Figure 14.18.

Table 14.5 gives the ranking of the performance of the four algorithms for the eight test images. TOPO was ranked highest for the four SHIPP images and second for the other four images. GCUSP and LLIN generally performed poorly, except for the BUS image, where GCUSP achieved the best compromise between maintaining chroma and rendering the surfaces of the solids. The MDE algorithm performed well overall, and was ranked best for SKI, NAT and GIRL. This can be explained for NAT and GIRL because it had little effect on the skin and landscape colours, which were largely inside the printer gamut boundary. For SKI, which has many high-chroma colours near the gamut surface, observers evidently preferred the preservation of chroma by the MDE algorithm to the graduated rendering of the other algorithms.

Table 14.4 Pair comparison z-scores for each image and algorithm

Image	TOPO3	GCUSP	MDE	LLIN
SKI	0.21	−0.04	0.24	−0.42
GIRL	0.90	−0.83	1.14	−1.22
NAT	0.75	−0.88	0.98	−0.85
BUS	0.46	0.69	−0.47	−0.68
Bride	0.98	−1.05	0.76	−0.69
Harbour	1.23	−1.07	1.18	−1.34
Textile	0.67	−0.94	0.13	0.15
Metal	0.92	−0.94	0.82	−0.80
Overall	**0.59**	**−0.42**	**0.40**	**−0.57**

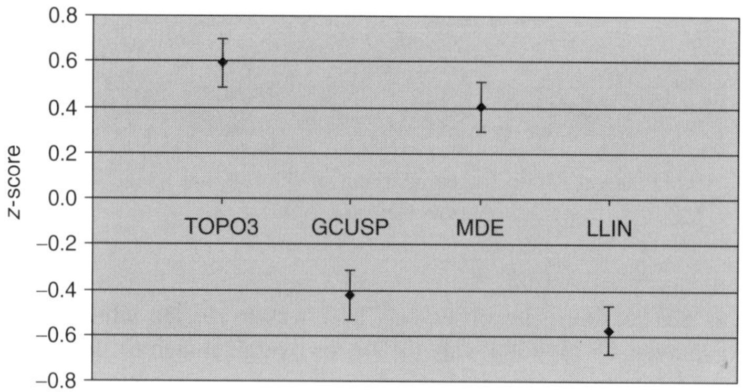

Figure 14.18 Overall z-scores for the four algorithms.

Table 14.5 Ranking of algorithm performance for each image (1 = best, 4 = worst)

Image	TOPO3	GCUSP	MDE	LLIN
SKI	2	3	1	4
BUS	2	1	3	4
NAT	2	4	1	3
GIRL	2	3	1	4
Bride	1	4	2	3
Harbour	1	3	2	4
Textile	1	4	2	3
Metal	1	4	2	3
Overall	**1**	**3**	**2**	**4**

14.8 COMPARISON OF ACTUAL AND SIMULATED MEDIA

The two experiments described in the previous sections were conducted to evaluate different versions of the TOPO algorithm and these experiments differed in a significant way. In the first experiment, the gamut mapping algorithms (GMAs) were evaluated by having originals on a CRT medium and reproductions on a printed medium, whereas in the second experiment both the originals and the reproductions were displayed on a CRT, with their gamuts restricted to the gamut of the printed medium used in the first experiment. Thus in the first experiment there was an actual (or real) difference between the two media whereas in the second experiment the difference was simulated (or virtual).

One might ask whether the difference in approach in the two experiments was significant, especially as the colour gamuts used in the present study were relatively similar. Figure 14.9 reveals that the vast majority of the printed medium's gamut was inside the gamut of the CRT and that even the two regions (around yellow and cyan) in which the printed medium had a larger gamut were of very small volume. With such gamuts, one would expect that simulation would yield results similar to those for actual media. The assumption underlying simulation is that if a visual stimulus corresponding to certain tristimulus values is seen under given viewing conditions, then its appearance should not be influenced significantly by the medium. This assumption is fundamental to our understanding of vision – colour appearance depends on how the eye responds to a stimulus and on the context in which it is seen. One would therefore expect good correspondence between the results of the actual and simulated experiments. If this were the case then one would be inclined to use simulation, due to the greater ease of displaying than printing images and the greater speed with which simulated experiments could be conducted. The situation, unfortunately, is not so simple.

In a survey of past literature on the experimental evaluation of GMAs, one can clearly see a divide between those that use actual media and those that use simulation, as well as a corresponding divide between the kind of results reported. Studies using real media carried out by Ito and Katoh [24], Morovic and Luo [25] and Kang *et al.* [26] have tended to conclude that gamut compression and/or linear lightness mapping outperformed gamut clipping. On the other hand, studies using simulation by Gentile *et al.* [27], Pariser [28], Montag and Fairchild [29], and Braun and Fairchild [30] have reported better results for clipping and/or knee function compression and non-linear lightness mapping. While it is conceivable that these different results could be due to other factors, such as the test images used or the magnitude of gamut differences, one should also investigate the issue of actual versus simulated media when trying to explain the divide between the respective results.

As the present study included experiments of both kinds, the data gathered could shed some light on the difference between the two approaches. In the simulation experiment, the gamut boundary to which reproduction images were restricted was that of the printed medium used in the initial experiment having real media. The close correspondence between simulated and actual reproduction gamuts was verified by measuring the white and black points in both cases (i.e. of the print in the viewing cabinet and the simulated print on the CRT).

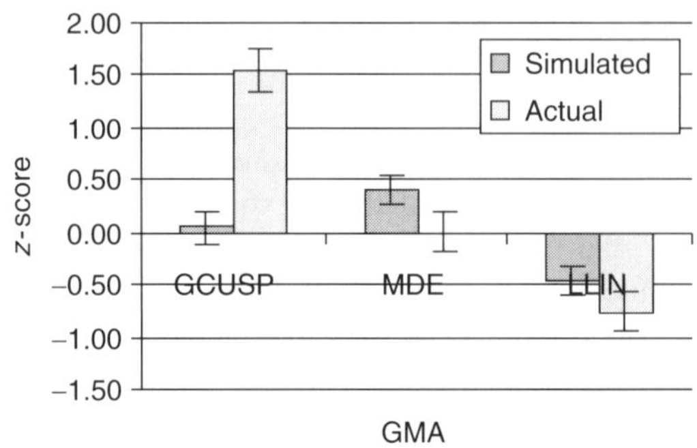

Figure 14.19 Overall results for experiments with actual and simulated media.

To make the comparison as fair as possible, only the observer judgements for the three algorithms (i.e. GCUSP, MDE, LLIN) and four images (i.e. SKI, BUS, NAT, GIRL) that were used in both experiments are considered. The overall results (Figure 14.19) show that the experiments did give very different results, particularly for the GCUSP algorithm, and also that the magnitude of differences between algorithms was smaller in the simulated experiment.

Considering the scores for these three algorithms and four images, the correlation between the actual and simulated sets is very low ($R = 0.19$), which shows that evaluating GMAs under either of these conditions does not lend itself to predicting what would have happened under the other. A closer look at the data also reveals that there was considerable variation between the correlation of scores for the different images, from as high as 0.99 for BUS, to as low as 0.25 for SKI and even negative (−0.82) for NAT. The correlation of scores for GMAs between the two conditions was also quite varied: 0.46 for GCUSP, 0.04 for MDE and 0.19 for LLIN. Plotting all accuracy scores from the two experiments against each other in Figure 14.20 further shows their weak relationship.

These results are especially intriguing given that in the pair of experiments for TOPO the match between simulated and actual gamuts was even verified at both extremes of the lightness range by measurements in situ with a telespectroradiometer.

One further step in understanding the present results would be to scrutinise the correspondence between actual and simulated reproduction media gamuts more closely to see whether there are discrepancies. The next aspect that could be considered is a comparison of the colour appearance of stimuli generated using different media under conditions which differ only in the type of medium used (i.e. two configurations having identical white point and viewing conditions but using different media to generate stimuli that match in colorimetric terms).

Although the present data does not lend itself to gaining a deeper understanding of why these difficulties occur with simulation, it shows very clearly that simulated and actual reproduction media can give rise to very different results when evaluating GMAs. A systematic investigation of these differences would therefore be a very worthwhile undertaking, as it might shed light on why previous studies have differed in their findings and might lead to an understanding that would help improve the quality of simulation.

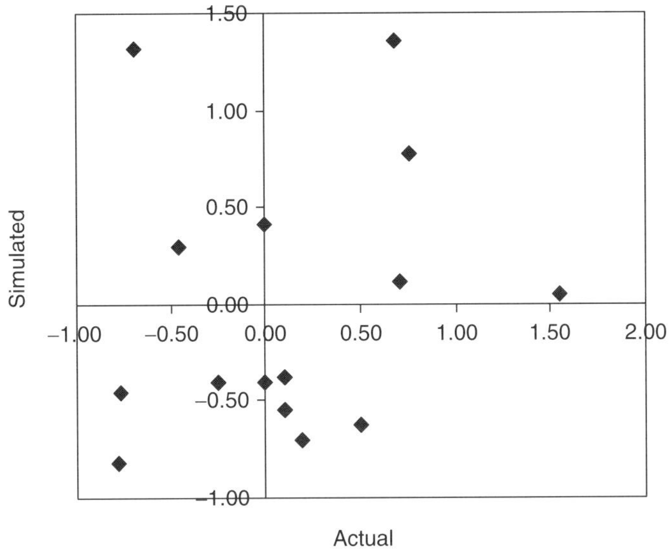

Figure 14.20 Accuracy scores for simulated versus actual media.

14.9 CONCLUSIONS

In summary, a new gamut mapping algorithm has been developed, based on topographic transformation from source colour gamut to destination colour gamut. It produced very pleasing visual results for a range of images when compressing the colour gamut from CRT display to inkjet printer. Its performance was particularly impressive for images containing large areas of high chroma colours, such as the textile image, but it also gave very good results for images of lower average chroma because it maintained optimum contrast. Only for the business graphics image, which contains large regions of colour near the gamut boundary, was its performance marginal because the mapping chords for medium to high lightness were too close to horizontal (e.g. red and blue hues in Figure 14.9), causing a substantial reduction in the chroma of the reproduction.

We believe that the TOPO algorithm has potential for further refinement in several ways. Improved definition of the core gamut will facilitate adaptation to the relative sizes and shapes of the source and destination gamut boundaries. Increase of contrast within the core gamut region may enhance the appearance of the reproduced image, using a variant of the sigmoidal lightness mapping function [30] shown in Figure 14.10. Knowledge of the statistics of individual images should permit the algorithm's behaviour to be optimised by mapping only those colours in an image falling outside the destination gamut boundary. The performance of the algorithm for gamut expansion will permit chroma to be increased in regions of colour space where the destination gamut is larger than the source gamut, and will raise fundamental questions about preferences and naturalness in colour image reproduction.

REFERENCES

1. J. Morovic and M. R. Luo (1999) Developing algorithms for universal colour gamut mapping. In *Colour Imaging: Vision and Technology*, L. W. MacDonald and M. R. Luo (eds), pp. 253–282. John Wiley, Chichester.
2. K. M. Braun, R. Balasubramanian and R. Eschbach (1999) Development and evaluation of six gamut-mapping algorithms for pictorial images, *Proc. 7th IS&T SID Color Imaging Conference*, pp. 144–148.
3. L. W. MacDonald and J. Morovic (1995) Assessing the effect of gamut compression in the reproduction of fine art paintings. *Proc. 3rd IS&T SID Color Imaging Conference*, pp. 194–200.
4. J. Morovic and P. L. Sun (1999) Methods for investigating the influence of image characteristics on gamut mapping. *Proc. 7th IS&T break SID Color Imaging Conference*, pp. 138–143.
5. L. W. MacDonald (1993) Gamut mapping in perceptual colour space. *Proc. 1st IS&T SID Color Imaging Conference*, pp. 193–196.
6. A. J. Johnson *et al.* (1992) Colour appearance research for interactive system management and applications (CARISMA). *Colour gamut compression* (Report WP2-19).
7. P. J. Green and M. R. Luo (2000) Developing the CARISMA gamut mapping model. *Proc. Colour Image Science 2000*, University of Derby, pp. 244–256.
8. E. Pirrotta, T. Newman and L. Lavendel (2000) A 'universal' gamut mapping algorithm? *Proc. Colour Image Science 2000*, University of Derby, pp. 313–320.
9. P. G. Herzog and H. Büring (2000) Optimizing gamut mapping: lightness and hue adjustments. *J. Image Sci. Technol.*, **44**(4), 334–342.
10. K. E. Spaulding, R. N. Ellson and J. R. Sullivan (1995) Ultracolor: a new gamut mapping strategy. *Proc. SPIE*, **2414**, 61–68.
11. N. Katoh and M. Ito (2000) Applying non-linear compression to the three-dimensional gamut mapping. *J. Image Sci. Technol.*, **44**(4), 328–333.
12. K. Sakamoto and H. Urabe (1999) Development of XYZ/sRGB-SCID and color gamut compression. *Proc. 7th IS&T SID Color Imaging Conference*, pp. 212–216.
13. M. C. Stone and W. E. Wallace (1991) Gamut mapping computer generated imagery. *Graphics Interface '91*, pp. 32–39. Canadian Information Processing Society, Toronto.
14. T. Hoshino and R. S. Berns (1993) Color gamut mapping techniques for color hard copy images. *Proc. SPIE*, **1909**, 152–164.
15. E. Granger (1995) Gamut mapping for hard copy using the ATD color space. *Proc. SPIE*, **2414**, 27–35.
16. C. Li, M. R. Luo and R. W. G. Hunt (2001) The CAM97s2 model. *Proc. 7th IS&T SID Color Imaging Conference*, pp. 262–263.
17. R. S. Berns (1996) Methods for characterizing CRT displays. *Displays*, **16**(4), 173–182.
18. T. Johnson (1996) Methods for characterizing colour printers. *Displays*, **16**(4), 193–202.
19. L. W. MacDonald, J. Morovic and K. Xiao (2000) A topographic gamut mapping algorithm based on experimental observer data. *Proc. 8th IS&T SID Color Imaging Conference*, pp. 311–317.
20. http://www.colour.org/tc8-03/.
21. L. L. Thurstone (1927) A law of comparative judgement. *Psychol. Rev.*, **34**, 273–286.
22. L. W. MacDonald, J. Morovic and K. Xiao (2002) A topographic gamut compression algorithm. *J. Image Sci. Technol.*, **46**(3), 228–236.
23. K. Sakamoto and H. Urabe (1997) Standard high precision pictures: SHIPP. *Proc. 5th IS&T/SID Color Imaging Conference*, pp. 250–244.
24. M. Ito and N. Katoh (1995) Gamut compression for computer generated images. In *Extended Abstracts of SPSTJ 70th Anniversary Symposium on Fine Imaging*, SPSTJ, Tokyo, Japan, pp. 85–88.
25. J. Morovic and M. R. Luo (1997) Cross-media psychophysical evaluation of gamut mapping algorithms. *Proc. AIC Color 97*, Kyoto, Japan, Vol. 2, pp. 594–597.

26. B. H. Kang, M. S. Cho, J. Morovic and M. R. Luo (2000) Gamut compression algorithm development on the basis of observer experimental data. *Proc. 8th IS&T/SID Color Imaging Conference*, pp. 268–272.
27. R. S. Gentile, E. Walowit and J. P. Allebach (1990) A comparison of techniques for color gamut mismatch compensation. *J. Imaging Technol.*, **16**, 176–181.
28. E. G. Pariser (1991) An investigation of color gamut reduction techniques. *Proc. 2nd IS&T Symposium on Electronic Publishing*, pp. 105–107.
29. E. D. Montag and M. D. Fairchild (1997) Psychophysical evaluation of gamut mapping techniques using simple rendered images and artificial gamut boundaries. *IEEE Trans. Image Processing*, **6**, 977–989.
30. G. J. Braun and M. D. Fairchild (1999) General-purpose gamut mapping algorithms: evaluation of contrast-preserving rescaling functions for color gamut mapping. *Proc. 7th IS&T SID Color Imaging Conference*, pp. 167–172.

15

Gamut mapping for high quality print reproduction

Phil Green and Ronnier Luo

15.1 INTRODUCTION

Colour reproduction media tend to have different ranges of reproducible colours (gamuts), depending on factors such as the spectral properties of the colorants used and the methods of imaging them on a substrate. For hard-copy printing systems, different substrates and colorants may be possible, thus extending the range of possible gamuts. Methods of mapping between media with different colour gamuts remain the subject of continuing interest, particularly with the formation of CIE Technical Committee 8-03 to address this problem.

Most studies of gamut mapping have assumed that hue should be preserved unchanged. In the CARISMA project, however, it was observed that pre-press workers commonly adjusted the hue of an original to exploit the greater chroma available at the primary colorants of the printing process and their secondary overprints.

It has commonly been found that, for matching surrounds, the lightness of the achromatic axis should be mapped linearly between the original and the reproduction. In most cross-media mapping contexts this includes a mapping of the media white and black points of the original media to the reproduction media to preserve perceived contrast. An

Colour Image Science, edited by L.W. MacDonald and M.R. Luo.

alternative approach which has been shown to give good results is to apply a media- and image-dependent rescaling function for lightness [1, 2].

After mapping the achromatic axis, clipping or compression in lightness and chroma is applied. This can be performed sequentially in lightness and chroma, or simultaneously in both attributes. The latter type of model has been shown to perform significantly better [3]. In simultaneous lightness/chroma compression, a convergence point is determined in the plane of constant hue (most frequently on the achromatic axis), and colours are compressed towards this point.

The CARISMA project [4] modelled the high-quality reproductions achieved by skilled pre-press operators (Figure 15.1). Five pre-press houses were asked to make reproductions of a Kodak Q60 input target (which enable the mapping strategies to be defined colorimetrically) at their 'baseline' set-up and at the settings that resulted in what they judged to be an optimum reproduction.

The gamut mapping strategy that emerged from the CARISMA project has the following features:

- Map the white and black points of the original to the reproduction gamut and scale lightness linearly.
- Map the primary and secondary colours of the original by translating them to those of the reproduction media, and apply a proportional shift to intermediate colours.
- Compress lightness and chroma linearly as follows:
  - If one gamut encloses the other, compress towards the point on the achromatic axis which has the same lightness as the cusp of the reproduction media gamut (unless the lightness of the original and reproduction media cusps are not similar, in which case the compression is the intercept on the achromatic axis of a line through the two cusps).
  - If one gamut does not enclose the other, compress towards the point where $L^* = 0$ and C^* equals half the chroma of the reproduction media cusp.

Morovic tested a comprehensive series of gamut mapping algorithms in mapping between a CRT display and a hard-copy print [3]. He concluded that a modified CARISMA model

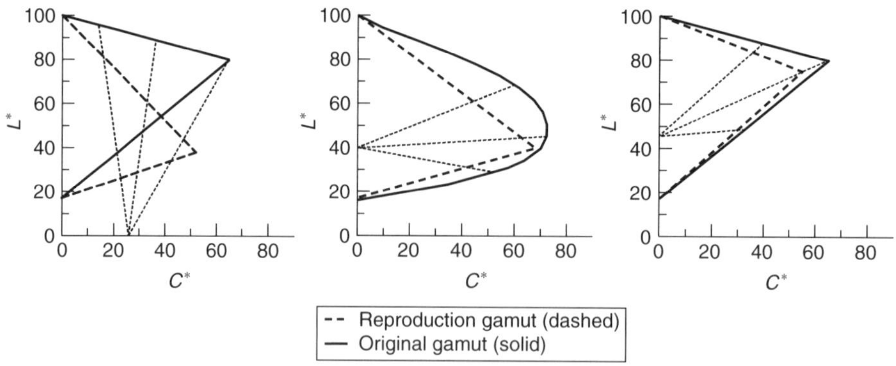

Figure 15.1 CARISMA gamut mapping: original gamut (solid) and reproduction gamut (dashed).

(in which the hue shift is chroma dependent and is only half that proposed in [4]) gave the best performance in terms of accuracy, along with the GCUSP algorithm. He found that of the algorithms tested, those that maintained relatively more chroma tended to produce more accurate reproductions and make smaller changes between the colours of the original and the reproduction. His results also suggested that the magnitude of difference between original and reproduction gamuts significantly affects the relative performance of different mapping algorithms.

15.2 REPRODUCTION AND MEASUREMENT OF TEST IMAGES

A research project is in progress to test the CARISMA model using natural instead of synthetic images plus a wider range of substrates, and if necessary to modify it in a way that improves performance. The approach of deriving gamut mapping strategies from empirical data, based on high-quality professional colour reproductions, is retained. Although operators are often constrained to work in CMYK print densities, they have extensive experience of producing pleasing reproductions to satisfy the most discriminating customers, and it is felt that taking advantage of this experience could save a considerable amount of time in psychophysical testing.

15.2.1 Test images

Five test images were selected for the derivation of mapping strategies. These were kindly supplied by Fujifilm Electronic Imaging and Eastman Kodak.

- Magic: a range of high-chroma content with a good contrast range
- Shoot: an image with detail in three-quarter tones
- Table: a predominantly high-key image with some high-chroma content
- Towels: predominantly high-chroma content
- Camera: relatively little high-chroma content but lots of detail in deep shadows

All were supplied as 10 cm × 12.5 cm transparencies, except for the medium-format (6 cm × 6 cm) Camera image. The first three images are shown in Figure 15.2, together with their lightness and chroma histograms and the distribution of colours (with one marker representing 60 pixels) relative to the media gamut boundaries.

15.2.2 Reproductions

In the first phase of the project, six pre-press houses (members of the London-based Pre-press Association) carried out a cross-media reproduction. A set of Ektachrome test transparencies of natural scenes was scanned on high-end drum scanners (largely Crosfield and Hell models, now maintained by Fujifilm EI and Heidelberg), output to film at a screen frequency of 54 lines per centimetre (150 lpi) and proofed photomechanically on

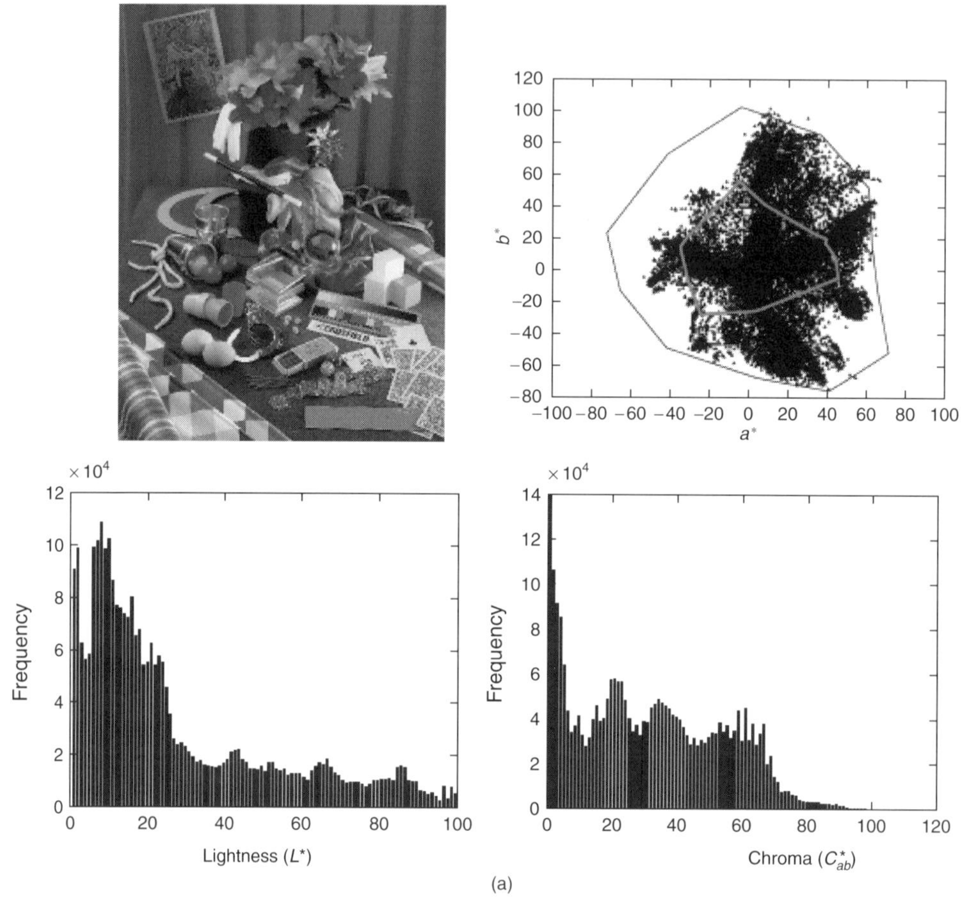

Figure 15.2 Test images with their lightness and chroma histograms and plots of the distribution of colours in a^*b^* projection: (a) Magic, (b) Shoot, (c) Table. The a^*b^* projections show gamut boundaries of Ektachrome and newsprint media; they indicate that in the red region there is a lack of agreement between the image gamut and the gamut boundary calculated for the media (Reproduced by kind permission of Fujifilm Electronic Imaging).

Cromalin ATM targeting sheet-fed offset litho on coated stock. A standard IT8.7/1 target was scanned at the same settings as each transparency to enable the mapping methods to be defined colorimetrically. Operators were asked to make an initial scan in which the white and black points were set for the individual image, followed by a corrected scan in which they used their judgement to make the best possible reproduction of each transparency.

All the resulting proofs were of high quality and visually very similar to each other. Owing to slight variations in the way that some of the sites performed the task, the initial analysis was limited to the reproductions made by three of the sites. Comparison

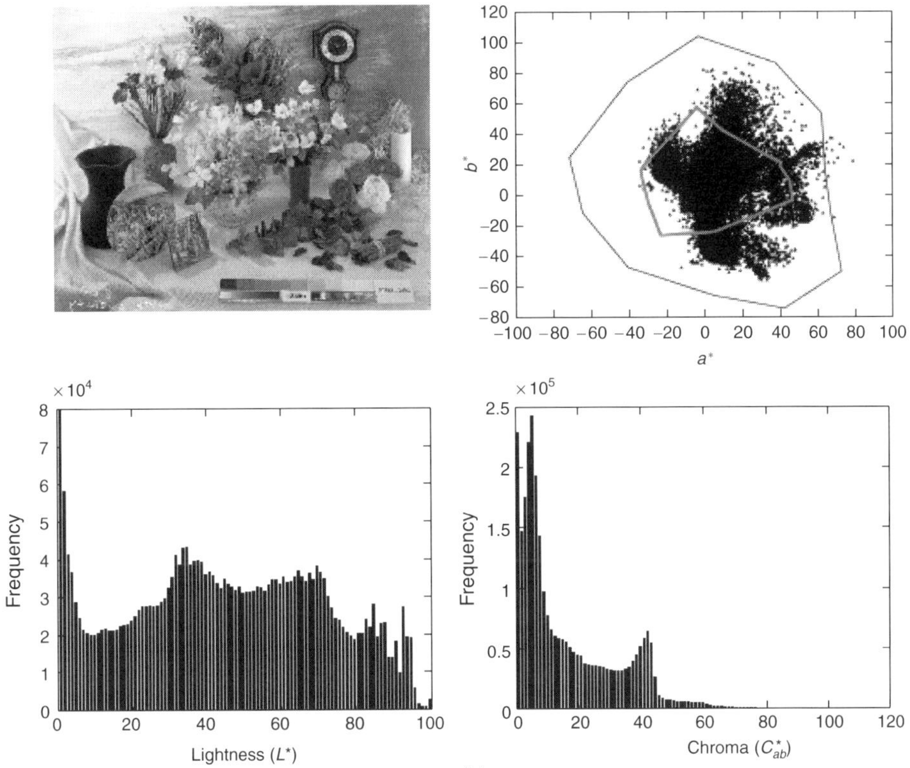

(b)

Figure 15.2 (*continued*).

of the colorimetric results showed that, for reasonably gamut-filling images, the difference between the initial and corrected reproductions was small.

This reproduction task has also been carried out using Digital Cromalin proofs targeting cold-set offset litho on newsprint. The proofing system is high-resolution inkjet, using the tone curves and news stock specified by a UK national newspaper.

15.2.3 Measurement

The colour patches of the IT8.7/1 chart [5] were measured on the Cromalin proofs to define the colorimetric characteristics of the reproduction. The instrument used was a Gretag Spectrolino with a 4 mm aperture and 0/45° geometry. All measurements were made in accordance with ISO 13655 [6], and the computation of CIELAB values was made with using the 1931 standard colorimetric observer and D50 illuminant.

Preliminary tests were undertaken to verify the repeatability of the instrument. After calibrating to a reference white diffuser, a series of four solid colour patches were each measured 10 times at the same position. The maximum variation from the mean was 0.33 ΔE^*_{ab} units, with a mean variation of 0.08 and a standard deviation of 0.07.

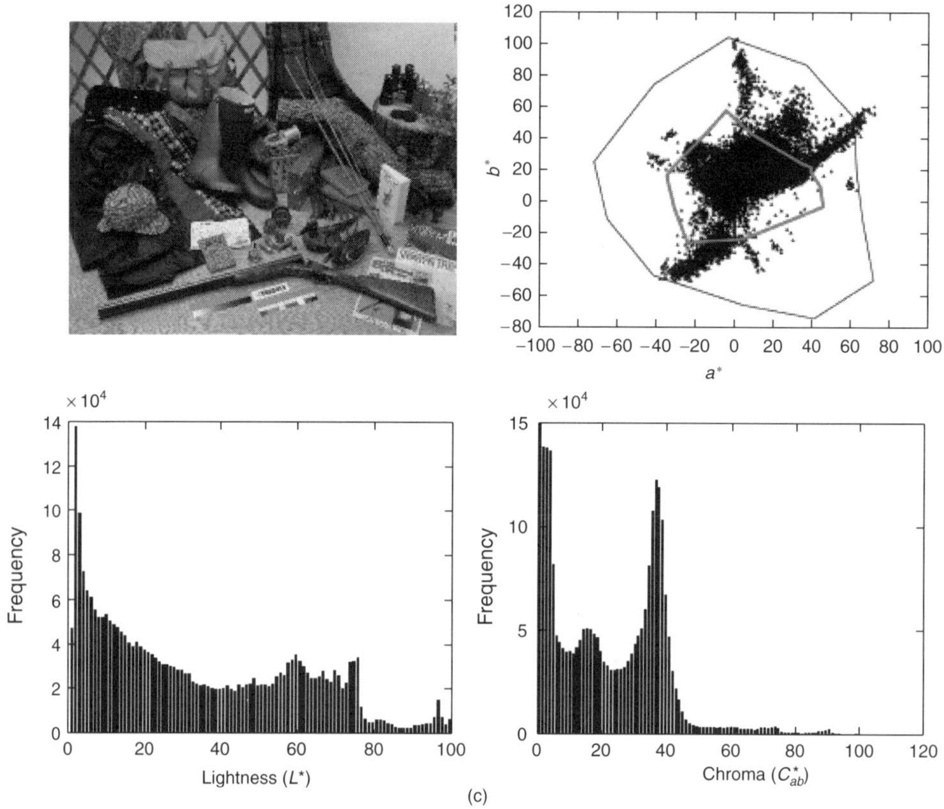

Figure 15.2 (*continued*).

Measurements for the IT8.7/1 transparency were taken from Kodak batch measurement data for the target. This data file represents batch average measurements, for which permissible deviations are defined in ISO 12 641 [5].

Measurement data for all media were converted to media-relative for the purposes of comparison. The $D_{\min}$ (GS0) patch of the IT8.7/1 target was treated as the Ektachrome media white point for this purpose.

15.2.4 Gamut boundary

When considering strategies for mapping between different media, it is important to have valid information about the relative shape of the gamuts. Methods of deriving gamut boundary descriptors using a characterisation model have been described, e.g. [7, 15, 16].

The boundary of the Ektachrome media was initially defined with the Kodak characterisation data for the Ektachrome product. However, it was found that this product data differed somewhat from the measurement data for the target used, and the dye scales

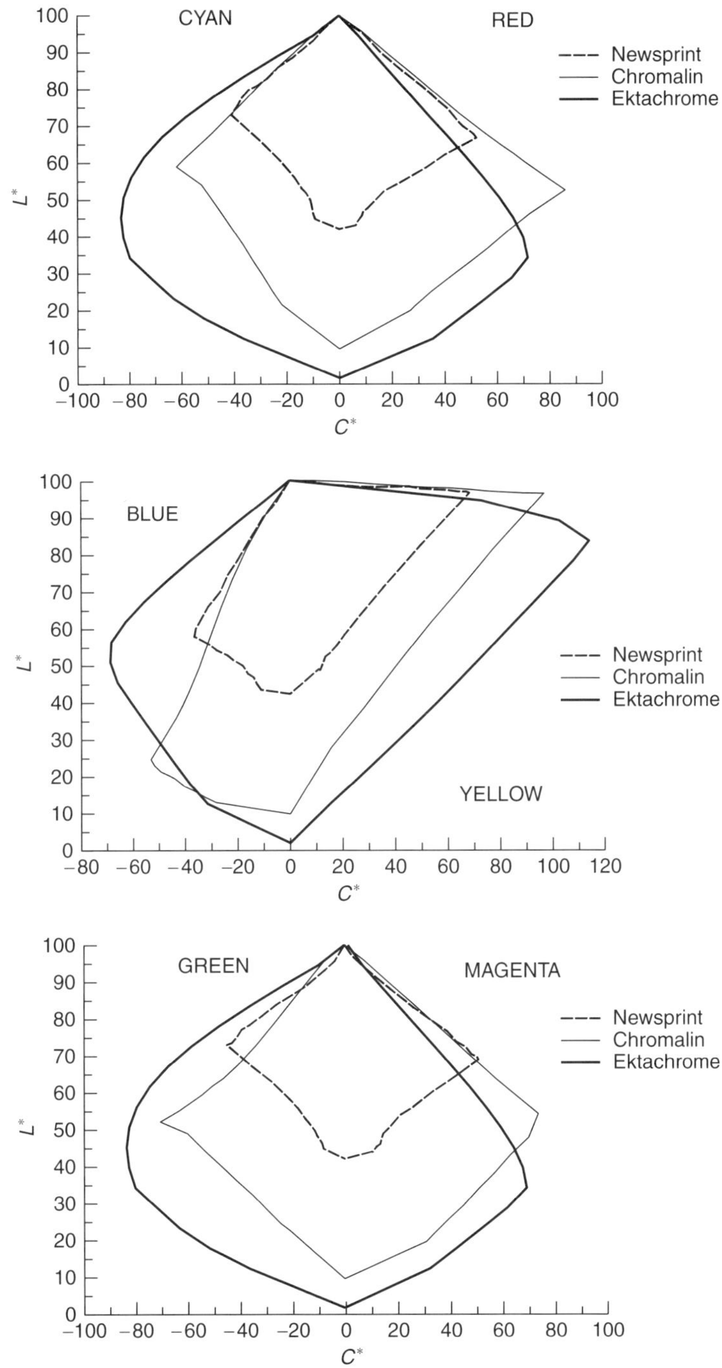

Figure 15.3 Gamut boundaries at three cross-sections through CIELAB colour gamuts for Ektachrome, Cromalin and newsprint: (dashes) newsprint, (thin solid) Cromalin, (thick solid) Ektachrome.

in columns 13–15 and 17–19 of the IT8.7/1 target were taken as defining the effective boundary at the colorant primaries.

The boundary for the Cromalin process was defined for the colorant primaries and secondaries by printing a test target with a 21-step scale for each colour ranging from white through solid colorant to black. The resulting gamut boundaries in planes of constant h_{ab} hue angle are compared in Figure 15.3.

The Ektachrome boundaries are more rounded and convex at the gamut cusp, unlike the Cromalin media whose cusps are more angular. This is typically the case for dye and pigment media. Transparencies and proofs are likely to follow the general shape of the boundaries shown in Figure 15.3, despite manufacturing variations in colorants or their densities.

15.3 BASELINE REPRODUCTIONS

15.3.1 Sheet-fed coated target media

There was remarkably good agreement among the results analysed from the three sites. Each site considered the highest and lowest densities of all five test transparencies sufficiently similar that there was no need to adjust white and black points separately. The first scans of each site were very similar in their treatment of lightness, hue and chroma, and it can probably be assumed that there is an underlying model for full-contrast originals. This we will denote as the baseline model. Taking the mean reproduction of the first scans of all three sites as representing this baseline model, the agreement between the different sites is summarised in Table 15.1. The attributes of the baseline reproduction of lightness, hue and chroma are described below.

Lightness

The achromatic axis of the original was mapped in a largely linear way to the reproduction. There was a very slight sigmoidal character to the baseline mapping of achromatic

Table 15.1 Mean variation between individual sites and the baseline mapping for the 265 patches of the target

	$\|\Delta L^*\|$	$\|\Delta C^*\|$	$\|\Delta h_{ab}\|$	$\|\Delta E^*\|$
		MEAN VALUES		
Site 1	1.04	1.97	1.83	3.21
Site 2	1.55	2.19	1.70	3.63
Site 3	1.23	1.17	1.59	2.61
		MAXIMUM VALUES		
Site 1	5.17	7.01	7.42	9.54
Site 2	6.77	11.07	10.67	12.13
Site 3	4.04	8.94	7.88	9.84

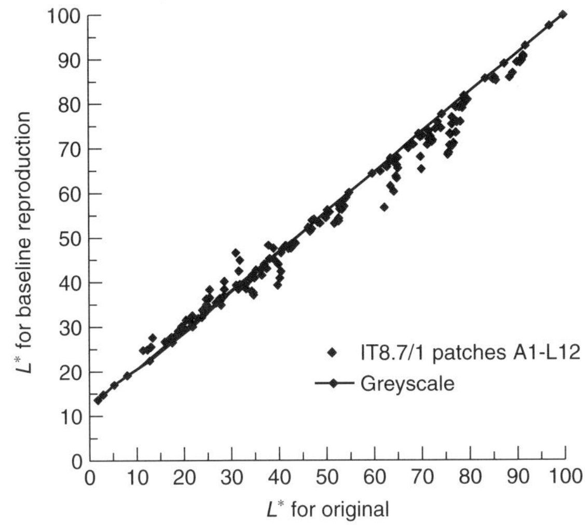

Figure 15.4 L^* of original plotted against L^* of reproduction for all IT8.7/1 colours.

lightness, particularly in the darkest colours. The reproduction of the target greyscale is shown by the solid line in Figure 15.4. A more sigmoidal lightness rescaling was performed for those images that were not gamut filling, suggesting that this may have been an image-dependent adjustment rather than a media mapping strategy.

Outside the achromatic axis, there were somewhat larger shifts in lightness. These were hue- and chroma-dependent: at a given hue angle they appear to be affected by the location of the cusps, and they generally take the form of a compression in lightness to the lightness of the cusp which increases at higher levels of chroma. This suggests a need for simultaneous compression of lightness and chroma.

Hue

The dye scales of the primary colorants and their overprints are shown in Figure 15.5, with the resulting baseline reproductions. The dye scales are formed on the transparency media by varying the density of the primary colorants. When plotted in the CIELAB a^*b^* projection of Figure 15.5, they do not form lines of constant hue angle, largely as a result of the hue shift that occurs as colorant concentration is increased but also possibly (particularly in the blue region) as a result of the lack of hue uniformity of CIELAB.

Systematic angular hue shifts of the original media colorants in the direction of the reproduction media primaries can clearly be seen in this plot. The CARISMA algorithm as modified by [7] would give a good prediction of these shifts, particularly in the blue region.

Figure 15.6 shows the hue shifts for all chromatic colours in the IT8.7/1 target (those with a C^* chroma less than 10 have been removed as the effect of hue shifts is exaggerated in the achromatic region). The average magnitude of the shift is about 10 ΔH^* units.

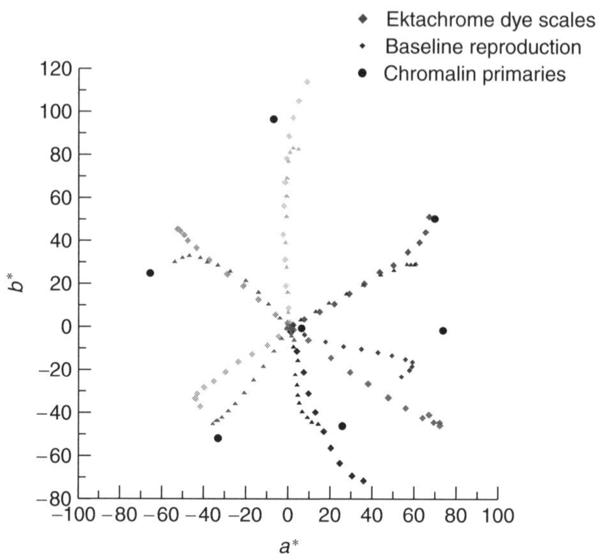

Figure 15.5 Hue shift of dye scales in the CIELAB a^*b^* diagram.

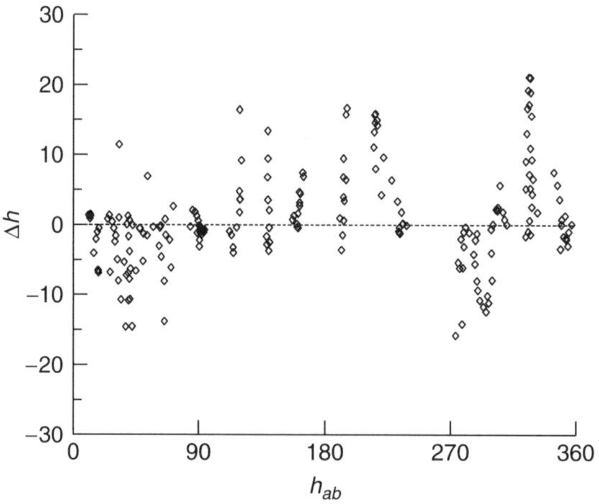

Figure 15.6 Plot of Δh against h_{ab}.

Chroma

There is a high degree of scatter in the plot of the chroma of the original versus the baseline reproduction (although possibly less than that observed in the CARISMA data) as shown in Figure 15.7. The regression line that can be fitted through the data using a second-order polynomial suggests a non-linear compression of chroma, but not a simple

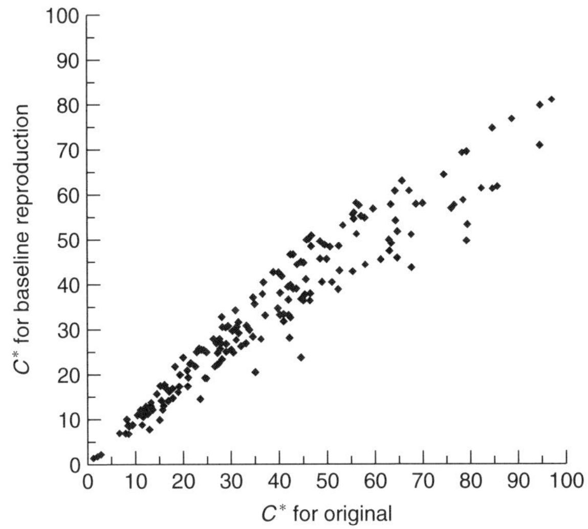

Figure 15.7 Twelve reproduction patches at a hue angle of about 41° in the L^*C^* diagram.

clipping to the gamut boundary. The low correlation between the original and reproduced chroma suggests that compressing chroma independently of lightness in a sequential compression algorithm could give rise to large differences between the model and the empirical data.

Lightness and chroma of chromatic colours

When simultaneous compression of lightness and chroma are performed, a convergence point is usually defined. Although the general tendency in the baseline data is for a compression towards the achromatic axis, it is not possible to define a general rule that uses the relative media gamut cusps to determine a single convergence point for each hue angle that fits well with this data. A variable convergence point may thus be needed to optimise the fit to the data.

The following observations can also be made:

- Compression tends to be greater at those hue angles where the gamut boundary of the original medium is particularly convex relative to the reproduction medium boundary.
- Chroma tends to be preserved or even increased in many patches between the region of the achromatic axis and the region of the cusp.
- In cases where the reproduction medium gamut is not enclosed by the original medium gamut, there tends to be an increase in chroma so that the available area is occupied.
- Compression of chroma is greater in dark colours.

Figure 15.8 shows the mapping of patches A1 to A12 of the IT8.7/1 target after lightness scaling to the media white and black points.

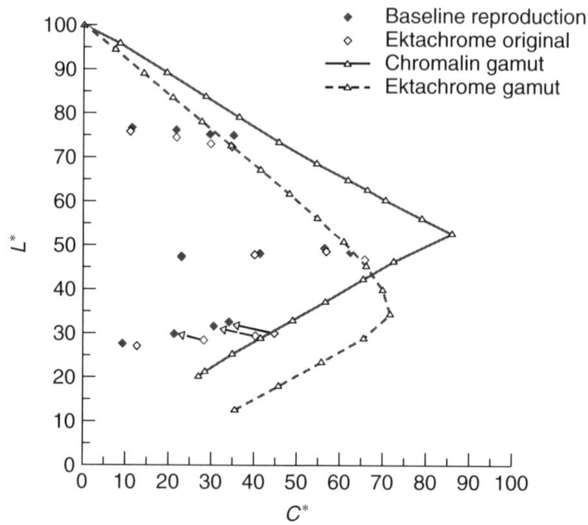

Figure 15.8 C^* of original versus reproduction for all IT8.7/1 colours.

In summary, the results for high-quality gloss reproduction on Cromalin proofing media suggest the need for CARISMA-like hue shifts, an initial linear (or slightly sigmoidal) lightness mapping, followed by a simultaneous lightness/chroma compression with a variable convergence point.

15.3.2 Newsprint target media

The results for the Digital Cromalin proof on newsprint media have the following characteristics:

- Hue angle shifts are broadly similar to those seen in the baseline reproduction on gloss coated media (Figure 15.9).
- Lightness mapping at the achromatic axis is more or less linear, with an increased sigmoidal characteristic in the dark tones (Figure 15.10).

A clearer pattern can be seen in the convergence points for simultaneous lightness and chroma compression. Varying the convergence point between $L^* = 50$ where $C^*_{ab} = 0$ to $L^* = L_{\text{Cusp}}$ where $C^* > C^*_{\text{Cusp\_out}}$ produces a very good fit to the data at almost all hue angles.

Figure 15.11 shows the mapping of patches from a single hue angle of the IT8.7/1 target after lightness scaling. Figure 15.12 shows a high degree of scatter in the mapping of chroma. Trends in chroma mapping are easier to identify in plots showing the mapping in constant-hue planes of lightness and chroma (such as Figure 15.11).

The results for newsprint media thus tend to confirm the main findings for the baseline gloss reproduction, despite the large differences in relative gamuts between the two media. The chroma increases in the baseline gloss reproduction are not repeated on newsprint;

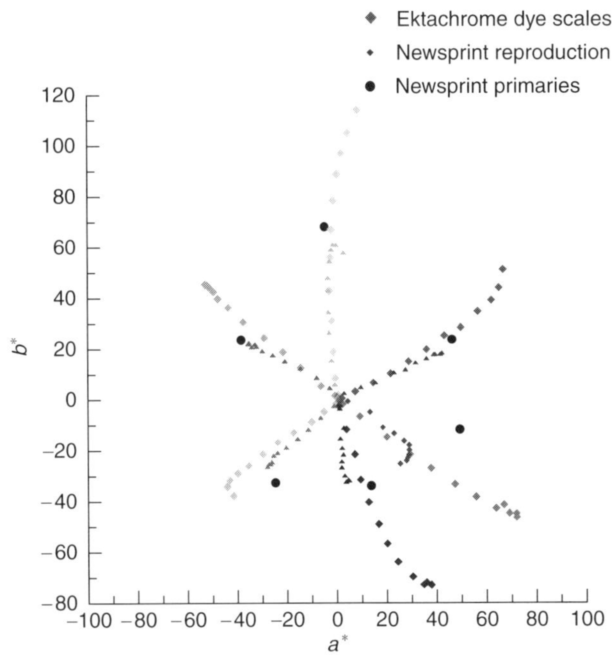

Figure 15.9 Reproduction of dye scales in the CIELAB a^*b^* diagram.

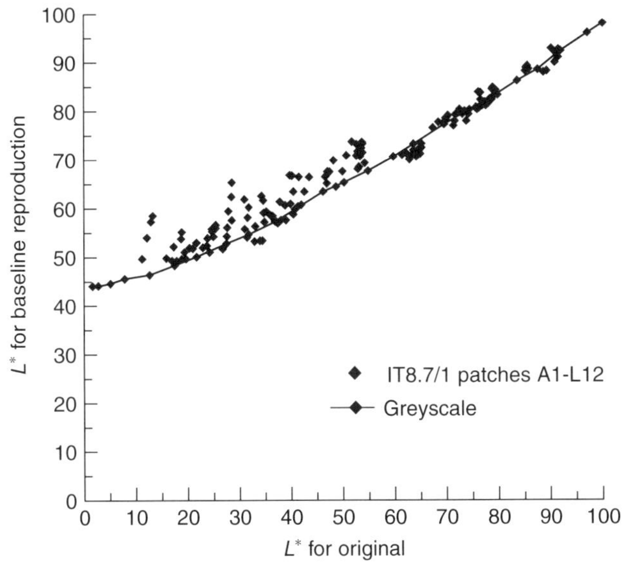

Figure 15.10 L^* mapping between the Ektachrome and newsprint media.

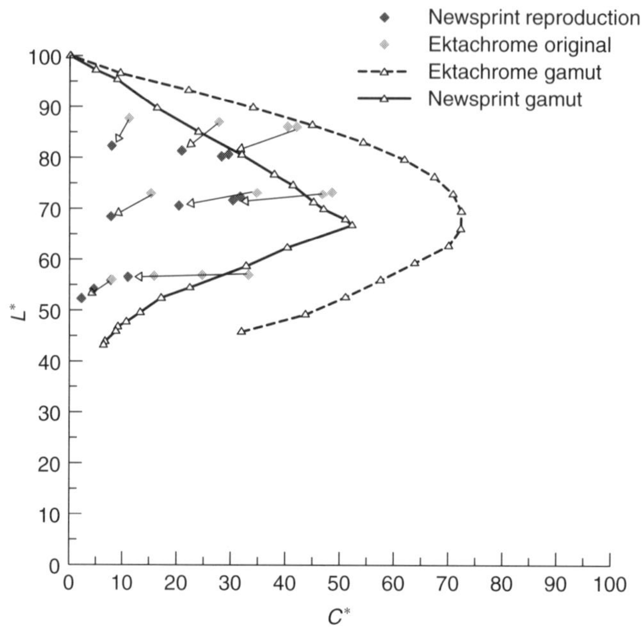

Figure 15.11 Twelve reproduction patches at a hue angle of about 41° in the L^*C^* diagram.

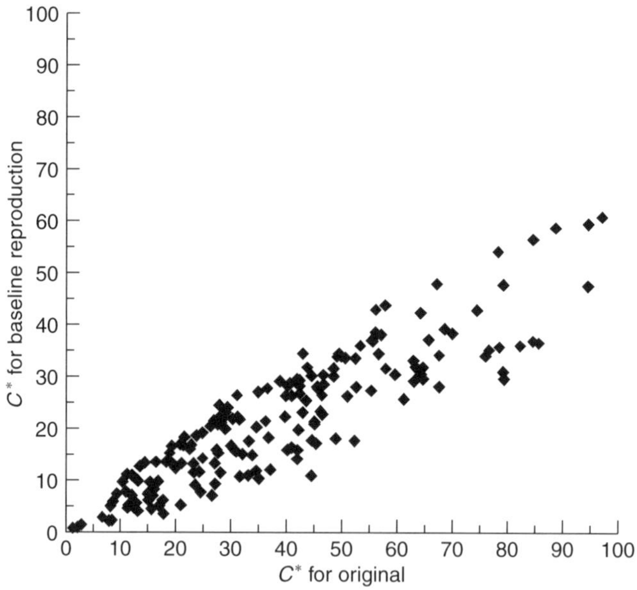

Figure 15.12 C^* mapping between the Ektachrome and newsprint media.

chroma is compressed in all patches, even in the light magenta region where the chroma of the reproduction is larger than that of the original.

15.4 EXTENDING THE CARISMA MODEL

The results of the empirical mapping data were used to establish the elements of a gamut mapping strategy that could be tested. Three models were defined, assuming hue shift and linear lightness mapping between the white and black points of original and reproduction media.

15.4.1 CUSP2CUSP model

The first model maps the cusp of the original medium at each hue angle to that of the reproduction medium. It does this in two stages. First the lightness of the original medium is scaled so that its cusp equals the lightness of the reproduction medium while the achromatic axis remains unchanged, as shown in Figure 15.13(a). Compression can then take place towards the point on the achromatic axis with the same lightness, as in Figure 15.13(b). This model is called CUSP2CUSP:

$$L_{\mathrm{d}} = L_{\mathrm{p}} + 100 - L_{\mathrm{p}}(L_{\mathrm{Black\_in}} - L_{\mathrm{Black\_out}})/100 \tag{15.1}$$

$$L_{\mathrm{c}} = L_{\mathrm{d}} + (L_{\mathrm{Cusp\_in}} - L_{\mathrm{Cusp\_out}})(C_p/C_{\mathrm{Cusp\_in}})$$

$$C_{\mathrm{c}} = C(C_{\mathrm{Cusp\_out}}/C_{\mathrm{Cusp\_in}})$$

where L_{d} is the lightness after mapping into the dynamic range of the reproduction medium, L_p and C_p are the lightness and chroma of the colour being mapped, L_{Black} is the lightness of the medium black point, L_{Cusp} and C_{Cusp} are the lightness and chroma of the medium cusp, and L_{c} and C_{c} are the lightness and chroma after CUSP2CUSP mapping (Figure 15.13).

15.4.2 CPOW model

The second model uses a non-linear compression of lightness and chroma towards a convergence point on the achromatic axis. The convergence point is defined as the point midway between $L^* = 50$ and $L^* = L_{\mathrm{Cusp}}$ for the hue angle. This model is called CPOW (CARISMA with power function).

The compression ratio r in CPOW is non-linear:

$$r' = r(C_{\mathrm{o}}/C_{p\mathrm{o}})^{\exp} \tag{15.2}$$

where $C_{p\mathrm{o}}$ is the chroma value of the point on the original medium gamut boundary that intersects with the line that passes through the colour being mapped and the convergence

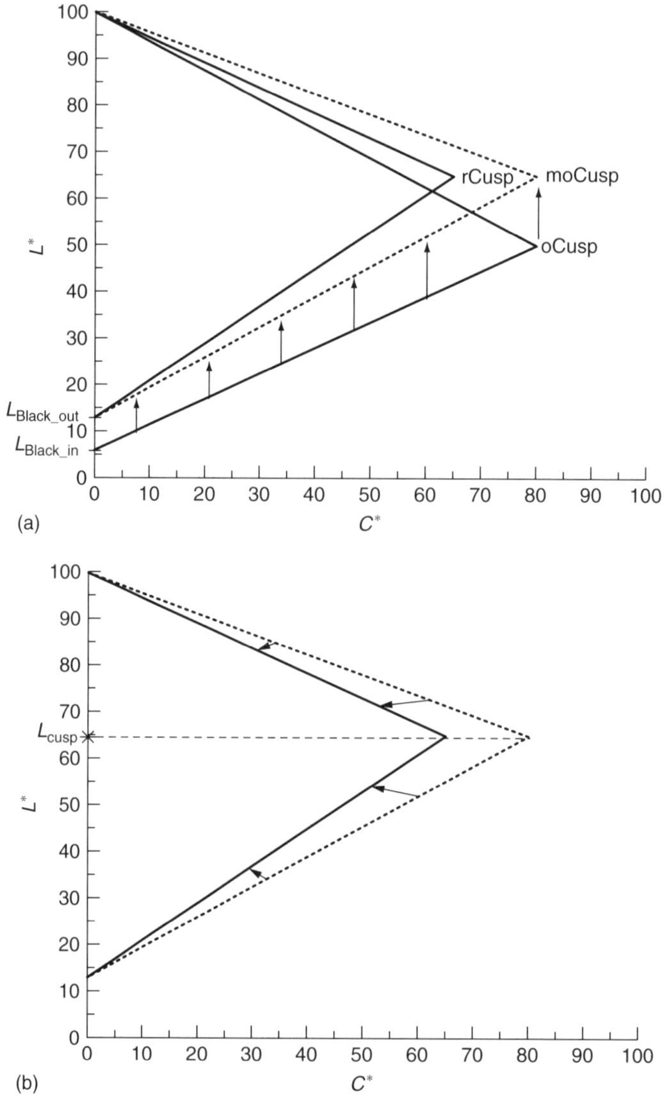

Figure 15.13 CUSP2CUSP mapping: (a) Lightness is scaled so that the cusp of the original equals lightness of cusp of reproduction medium; (b) Compression of lightness and chroma towards the convergence point (∗) on the achromatic axis.

point, and $exp = 2.5$. This value of *exp* gives the best fit to the baseline data, but has the disadvantage that for compression ratios (r) less than 0.69 the compression function becomes non-monotonic. This can be overcome by reducing the value of *exp* for media where the destination gamut is much smaller than the original gamut. Alternatively it could be replaced by a knee function.

Figures 15.14(a) and (b) show the effects of the non-linear compression for original medium intersection points whose C^*_{ab} chroma values are 40 and 70 respectively. Notice that the function is always relative to the media gamut boundaries on the line of compression to the convergence point, unlike chroma compression functions such as GamCom [8] which depend solely on the ratio of C^*_{ab} chroma at the original and destination media cusps.

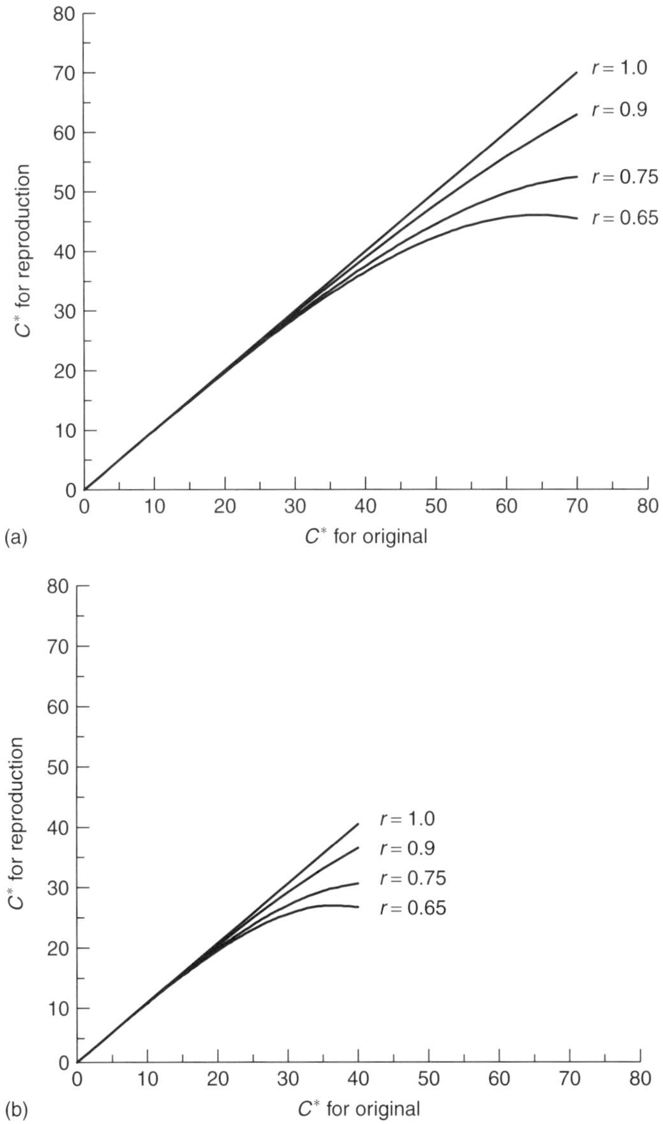

Figure 15.14 Non-linear compression in CPOW model: (a) Intersection point at $C^*_{ab} = 70$; (b) Intersection point at $C^*_{ab} = 40$.

15.4.3 CPAR model

The third method uses parameters that describe the relative shape of the two gamuts. This model is called CPAR (parametric CARISMA). Here are the parameters:

- M is the convexity of the source gamut relative to the destination
- N is the concavity of the destination medium gamut below the cusp
- O is a transfer function for chroma that partially models the empirical baseline results
- P is an expansion of chroma where the destination cusp lies significantly outside the source cusp.

The parameters M and N are hue dependent and they need to be selected for a given medium or computed from a small number of patches on a test object. The parameters of the CPAR model enable the effect of different mapping strategies to be investigated, including the effect of modelling the gamut boundary and linear versus non-linear compression.

Convexity

Modify the compression factor by a convexity parameter that depends on the relative shape of the original and reproduction media gamuts:

$$r' = rM \tag{15.3}$$

where the value of M is between 1.0 and 1.5; it is 1.0 if the original and reproduction gamut boundaries make similar angles at their cusps and it is 1.5 if the original medium gamut boundary is highly convex relative to the reproduction medium.

Chroma increase

If the original gamut does not enclose the reproduction gamut, increase the chroma of colours in the region where the reproduction gamut is larger. In our initial experiments we have done this by simply inverting the compression ratio for these colours:

$$T'' = 1/T' \qquad (C_{p^{\mathrm{T}}} > C_{p^{\mathrm{o}}}) \tag{15.4}$$

where $C_{p^{\mathrm{T}}}$ and $C_{p^{\mathrm{o}}}$ are the chroma values of the points on the original and reproduction media gamut boundaries that intersect with the line which passes through the colour being mapped and the convergence point. The compression of lightness is performed using r' not $1/r'$, and is thus unchanged by the expansion of chroma.

Concavity

Modify the chroma by a concavity parameter N to increase compression for colours whose lightness is below the cusp. The modification takes a Gaussian form similar to the compression of lightness in the GCUSP model [7], and enables the mapping to preserve lightness in dark colours.

$$C' = C[1 - (L_{\mathrm{rCusp}} - L)^3]/[(L_{\mathrm{rCusp}} - L)^3 + N \times 10^5] \qquad (L < L_{\mathrm{rCusp}}) \tag{15.5}$$

Chroma transfer function

Modify the chroma so it is increased at low values of C^* chroma and further compressed at higher values:

$$C_r = O_1 C' - O_2 C'^2$$

where $O_1 = 1.1$ and $O_2 = 0.003$.

15.5 EVALUATION AND DEVELOPMENT

The ability of the CUSP2CUSP, CPOW and CPAR models to predict the empirical baseline data has been tested [9], and it was found that those models incorporating non-linear compression and the parameters modelling the gamut boundary (CPAR and CPOW) gave better results than those that did not (CUSP2CUSP and compression of chroma without alteration of lightness).

In the CARISMA model, the media gamut boundaries can be defined solely by the white and black points and the primary and secondary solid colorants. The model linearly interpolates the compression ratios and convergence points from these reference points. This approach was followed in the models tested above, but the improvement in performance achieved by introducing parameters to model the boundary shape suggests that a more fine-grained gamut boundary descriptor would be better than a simple interpolation from the cusps.

It was further observed from the empirical data for both gloss and newsprint media that the convergence point at a given hue angle was not constant (as suggested in most models) but tended to have a higher lightness (L^*) as the lightness and chroma of the source colour increased.

In the next phase of this research, the features of the CPOW and CPAR models were incorporated into a more general algorithm which also included a new gamut boundary descriptor and a lightness- and chroma- dependent convergence point. The gamut boundary descriptor is based on the direct measurement of up to 432 colours on the gamut boundary, for which a new test target was devised [10]. To enable compression of lightness and chroma towards the convergence point, a method of calculating the gamut boundary on a line from the convergence point through the colour being mapped was also developed. The boundary descriptor and gamut boundary calculation method give similar results to the SMGBD + FSLGB method [11] when the boundary descriptors were derived from the same data.

The non-linear compression function was adjusted to make it more general across the different media in the study. By using the following equations, colours are compressed towards a convergence point on the achromatic axis whose L^* value is KL:

$$C_r = C_o^* cr$$

$$L_r = L_o - (1 - cr)^* (L_o - KL) \qquad (15.6)$$

where cr is the compression ratio, C_o and C_r are the original and reproduction chroma, L_o and L_r are the original and reproduction lightness, and KL is the lightness of the convergence point.

The compression ratio cr in the new model is:

$$cr = 1 - dr^f(1 - C_{\mathrm{LGBout}}/C_{\mathrm{LGBin}}) \tag{15.7}$$

where C_{LGBin} is the chroma of the original media boundary on the line from the convergence point through the colour being mapped, C_{LGBout} is the corresponding chroma for the reproduction media, and dr is given by C_{LGBout}

$$dr = C_o/C_{\mathrm{LGBin}} \tag{15.8}$$

The exponent f has a value between 1.0 and 1.8.

The role of dr is to scale the compression ratio by the distance of the point being mapped from the achromatic axis, thus reducing the compression of low-chroma colours. When (15.8) is used there is some clipping of high-chroma colours, and the proportion of colours which are clipped can be controlled by adjusting the parameter f.

The convergence point KL was found as follows:

$$KL = K_{\mathrm{LL}} + K_{\mathrm{CL}} \tag{15.9}$$

where

$$K_{\mathrm{LL}} = L_{\mathrm{Cusp}} - \frac{L_{\mathrm{Cusp}} - L}{L_{\mathrm{Cusp}}}(L_{\mathrm{Cusp}} - L_{\mathrm{Black\_out}})$$

and

$$K_{\mathrm{CL}} = 32(C/C_{\mathrm{Cusp}})^{0.25} - 25$$

where K_{LL} is the lightness-weighted convergence, K_{CL} is the chroma-weighted adjustment, L_{Cusp} and C_{Cusp} are the lightness and chroma of the cusp at the hue angle of p, and $L_{\mathrm{Black\_out}}$ is the lightness of the reproduction media black point.

When a fixed convergence point is used, there is a compression in lightness towards the convergence point that has a more significant effect in high-chroma colours where compression is greatest. A lightness-dependent convergence point helps to maintain the lightness contrast of the original, which previous studies of contrast-preserving mappings have found to be important [12]. Including a chroma-dependent element as shown in (15.9) has the effect of further increasing contrast, particularly in achromatic areas, and also of increasing the lightness of the most chromatic colours.

The new model incorporating non-linear compression, lightness and chroma-weighted convergence point, and method of determining the gamut boundary, is called the graphic arts media mapping algorithm (GAMMA). In a test on newsprint reproductions [13], the following methods of finding the convergence point were compared, together with linear compression versus the non-linear compression of (15.6):

- Fixed for each hue angle using the method defined in the CARISMA model
- Lightness dependent

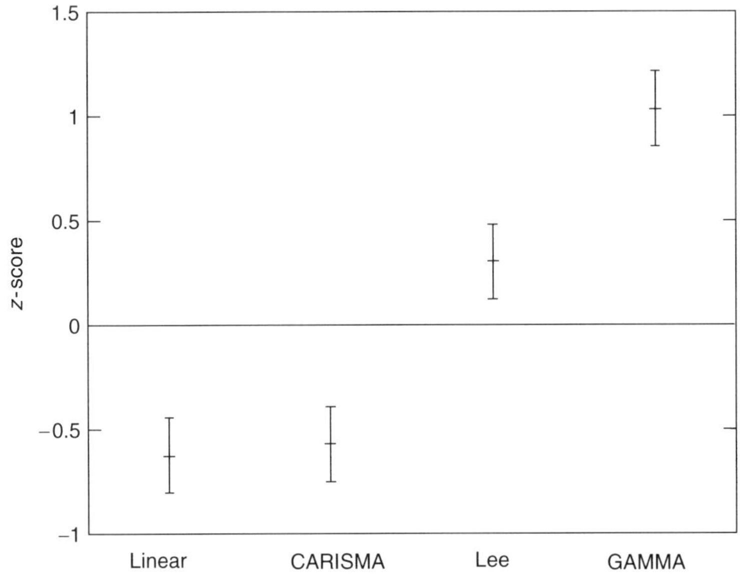

Figure 15.15 Results of the pair comparison experiment.

- Lightness and chroma dependent using (15.9)
- Lightness and chroma dependent using a three-zone method [14].

Two images with a significant amount of high-chroma detail were used (MAGIC and SKI) in order to explore the effect of gamut compression where the gamuts of the two media are very different and the images are reasonably gamut filling. The lightness-dependent algorithm produced some artefacts in dark neutral colours, so it was dropped from the subsequent testing.

Figure 15.15 shows the mean z-scores and confidence intervals resulting from a pair comparison experiment with a total of 15 observers. It can be seen that non-linear compression and lightness- and chroma-dependent convergence points performed better than fixed convergence and linear compression.

15.6 CONCLUSIONS

This project investigated the gamut mapping methods used by professional pre-press houses in high-quality reproductions of transparency originals to proofs simulating gloss coated reproductions. The results were sufficiently similar to define a baseline reproduction for images that are reasonably gamut filling and of good contrast. This baseline reproduction largely verified the conclusions of the CARISMA project in the fundamental strategies required to map colours between two media. In particular, it supported the mapping of hues towards the colorant primaries, and linear (or near-linear) mapping of lightness between media white and black points. These conclusions were further verified in reproductions made on newsprint.

A relatively simple model has been defined which predicts many of the features of the baseline reproduction. Its performance in predicting the baseline reproduction is broadly similar to the LLIN model, although the prediction of baseline lightness is somewhat worse. Two additional models have also been described in this phase of the work. The first used, a non-linear compression towards a variable convergence point on the achromatic axis; took the second the different cases of the CARISMA algorithm and replaced them with parameters that depend on the relative gamut shapes. These models gave a good prediction of the empirical baseline data, and thus demonstrated that it is desirable to have more information about the shape of the gamut boundary.

These results led to the development of a new gamut mapping model, which incorporates non-linear compression towards a variable convergence point. Known as GAMMA, the model was tested in a transparency-to-newsprint reproduction workflow, in which it was compared with other methods of finding a convergence point and a linear compression. The results of this test were encouraging, and further work will be done to test the model using a larger number of images and other colour reproduction workflows.

ACKNOWLEDGEMENTS

The authors thank Professor Tony Johnson and Dr Ján Morovic for their helpful advice and suggestions, and Trinity Mirror, Keene Repro and Rapida Group for their help in preparing proofs and prints.

REFERENCES

1. Braun, G. and Fairchild, M. (1999) Gamut mapping for pictorial images. *Proc. TAGA*, 645–660.
2. Braun, G. and Fairchild, M. (1999) General-purpose gamut mapping algorithms: evaluation of contrast-preserving rescaling functions for colour gamut mapping. *Proc. 7th IS&T/SID Colour Imaging Conference*, pp. 167–172.
3. Morovic, J. (1998) To develop a universal gamut mapping algorithm. PhD thesis, University of Derby.
4. Johnson, A. J. *et al.* (1992) Colour appearance research for interactive system management and application (CARISMA). Colour gamut compression (Report WP2-19).
5. ISO 12641:1997 Graphic technology – Pre-press digital data exchange –colour targets for input scanner calibration.
6. ISO 13655:1996 Graphic technology – Spectral measurement and colorimetric computation for graphic arts images.
7. Morovic, J. and Luo, M. R. (1997) Gamut mapping algorithms based on psychophysical experiment. *Proc 4th IS&T/SID Colour Imaging Conference*, pp. 44–49.
8. Schlapfer, K. (1997) Testing the colour rendering quality of a colour management system. IFRA Special Report 2.22.
9. Green, P. J. and Luo, R. M. (2000) Developing the CARISMA gamut mapping model. *Proc. Colour Image Science 2000*, University of Derby, pp. 244–256.
10. Green, P. J. (2001) A test target for defining media gamut boundaries. *Proc. Color Imaging: Device-Independent Color, Color Hardcopy and Graphic Arts*, **6**, pp. 105–113.

11. Morovic, J. (ed.) (2000) Guidelines for the evaluation of gamut mapping algorithms, 7th draft. CIE TC 8-03.
12. Braun, G. and Fairchild, M. (1999) Gamut mapping for pictorial images. *Proc. TAGA*, 645–660.
13. Green, P. J. and Luo, R. M. (2001) Testing the performance of an extended CARISMA gamut mapping model. *Proc. Color Imaging: Device-Independent Color, Color Hardcopy and Graphic Arts*, **6**, pp. 129–141.
14. Lee, C. S., Sim, K. M., Lee, E. J. and Ha, Y. H. (1999) Gamut mapping using variable anchor points. *Proc. Color Imaging: Device-Independent Color, Color Hardcopy and Graphic Arts*, **4**, pp. 139–149.
15. Braun, G. and Fairchild, M. D. (1997) Techniques for gamut surface definition and visualization, *Proc. 5th IS&T/SID Colour Imaging Conference*, pp. 147–152.
16. Morovic, J. and Luo, M. R. (2000) Calculating medium and image gamut boundaries for gamut mapping. *Col. Res. App.*, **25**, 394–401.

16

Gamut mapping along curved lines

Hendrik Büring and Patrick Herzog

16.1 INTRODUCTION

In the past, various gamut mapping algorithms have been proposed. Many of them differ with regard to the direction in which out-of-gamut colours are mapped, ranging from keeping lightness constant to mapping towards a focal point on the lightness axis. In each case the cross-section between the gamut boundary and the mapping vectors must be found. All methods require gamut boundary descriptions that are matched to the direction of mapping, or else iterative ray tracing must be applied.

In a preliminary psychophysical experiment [1, 2], the relative lightness change (RLC) method was evaluated with various parameterisations and compared with other techniques. The output medium was simulated on the original medium (CRT), hence no lightness scaling was performed.

It was shown that:

- The RLC method with a moderate degree of lightness change outperformed all other techniques, including the CUSP/GCUSP method published by Morovic [3].
- A mapping type near or equal to clipping yields the best visual results. This was also shown in an earlier study where lightness and hue were kept constant [4].

A new class of mapping functions described in this chapter has the advantage of being straightforward in the convenient perceptual attributes lightness, chroma and hue angle.

Colour Image Science, edited by L.W. MacDonald and M.R. Luo.

The mapping direction is approximately that of mapping towards a focal convergence point with negative chroma. In a first step, the lightness of a given colour is modified, depending on the lightness distance from the cusp and on the chroma distance from the gamut boundary. Therefore, the new technique is called the *relative lightness change* (RLC) method. The second step is chroma compression. Note that the mapping is carried out along curved lines. Research has been carried out to verify previous results (where no lightness scaling had to be applied) in real monitor-to-print cross-media experiments with different lightness scaling methods.

16.2 LIGHTNESS SCALING METHODS

Gamut mapping of images can be performed in two steps:

1. The lightness range of the source device must be mapped onto that of the destination device. This is called lightness scaling.
2. Assuming constant hue angle, some kind of chroma mapping (with or without constant lightness) has to take place. This mapping has a certain *direction* with a given mapping *type* from linear compression to clipping.

Since the lightness range of the source device (a CRT in the present study) does not match that of the reproduction device (thermal sublimation printer), some kind of lightness scaling has to be applied. Note that the task here is *not* to proof the appearance of a printed image on a monitor, but to reproduce an image displayed on a CRT using a printer. Since 'white' is to be reproduced as blank paper, *relative* colorimetry is used; the white point of both devices is set equal to $L^* = 100$ (with $a^* = b^* = 0$). Assuming that the black point of the printer equals $L^*_{\mathrm{min}} > 0$, the lightness of the original must be adjusted.

Figure 16.1 depicts some widely used scaling functions among gamut mapping methods. Only the soft-clip function was used in our experiments due to the drawbacks of the linear functions. Figure 16.2 shows the first derivative of the lightness scaling functions, i.e. the local contrast gradient.

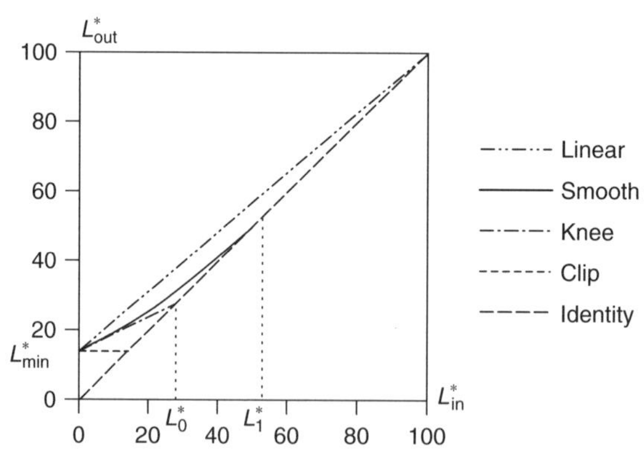

Figure 16.1 Lightness scaling functions.

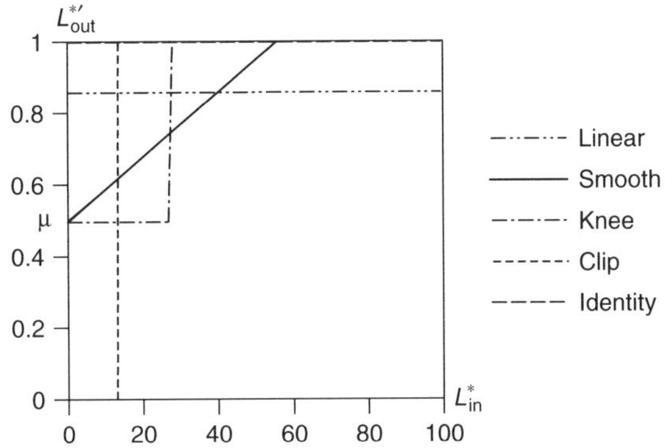

Figure 16.2 Local contrast determined by lightness scaling.

16.2.1 Clipping

A very simple method of lightness 'scaling' is clipping. The lightness range above L^*_{min} is left unchanged, but the range below is compressed entirely to the new black point. Therefore the contrast of the brighter parts of the image is preserved, whereas in the shadows it is lost completely. This kind of lightness modification could therefore be useful only for high-key images, in which little significant image content occurs in the shadow regions.

16.2.2 Linear compression

Linear compression is slightly more complex. The black points are mapped onto each other, and the complete lightness range is linearly adjusted to the range $[L^*_{min}, 100]$. This method has two drawbacks:

- The contrast of the image is reduced by a factor $(1 - L^*_{min}/100)$, making it look dull or foggy.
- The overall image lightness is increased while chroma is kept constant, which results in a desaturated appearance of the image.

Because of these unwanted changes to image appearance resulting from the linear compression algorithm, some kind of compromise has to be found. One solution is the development of a soft-clip scaling technique.

16.2.3 Soft-clip knee function

As a first step, a piecewise linear function (Knee in Figure 16.1) could be applied. The contrast of the darker colours is reduced by a factor μ, whereas the brighter parts above a breakpoint $L^*_0 = L^*_{min}/\mu$ are left unchanged.

At first sight, this kind of scaling makes the image look much better, since more saturation is preserved. But given a smooth lightness gradation to be reproduced, the discontinuity of the knee introduces artefacts (because of the local contrast gradient jumping from μ to 1) which can be detected by the human eye as unwanted edges or contours.

16.2.4 Smooth soft-clip

To avoid the edge artefacts, the knee function must be approximated by a smooth curve. For this purpose, a simple function consists of a quadratic parabola and its tangent:

$$L^*_{out}(L^*_{in}) = \begin{cases} aL^{*2}_{in} + bL^*_{in} + c & 0 \leqslant L^*_{in} \leqslant L^*_1 \\ L^*_{in} & L^*_1 \leqslant L^*_{in} \leqslant 100 \end{cases} \tag{16.1}$$

Given the following boundary conditions:

$$L^*_{out}(0) = L^*_{min} \tag{16.2}$$

$$L^{*'}_{out}(0) = \mu \tag{16.3}$$

$$L^*_{out}(L^*_1) = L^*_1 \tag{16.4}$$

$$L^{*'}_{out}(L^*_1) = 1 \tag{16.5}$$

where $L^{*'}_{out}(L^*_{in})$ denotes the derivative of $L^*_{out}(L^*_{in})$. Solving for a, b, c yields:

$$L^*_{out}(L^*_{in}) = L^*_{min} + \mu L^*_{in} + \frac{(1-\mu)^2}{4L^*_{min}} L^{*2}_{in} \quad (0 \leqslant L^*_{in} \leqslant L^*_1) \tag{16.6}$$

$$L^{*'}_{out}(L^*_{in}) = \mu + \frac{1-\mu}{L^*_1} L^*_{in} \quad (0 \leqslant L^*_{in} \leqslant L^*_1) \tag{16.7}$$

$$L^*_1 = \frac{2}{1-\mu} L^*_{min} \tag{16.8}$$

A plot of this kind of lightness compression with the parameters $L^*_{min} = 14$ and $\mu = 0.5$ is shown by Smooth in Figure 16.1. Note that this curve is similar to the sigmoidal remapping function derived by Braun and Fairchild for normal to high-key image content [5].

16.3 GAMUT MAPPING DIRECTION

Two mapping directions were used in our experiments: focal and relative lightness change. Both were evaluated in psychophysical experiments, where no lightness scaling was applied.

16.3.1 Focal mapping

Focal mapping has been widely used in other studies, with the focal convergence point located on the achromatic axis at the lightness of the cusp (i.e. the point of maximum

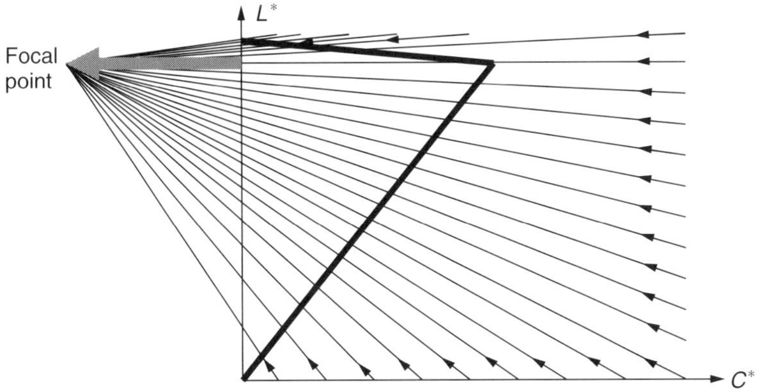

Figure 16.3 The focal point is moved away from the lightness axis. This mapping direction only moderately changes lightness.

chroma for the hue angle being considered). Since the amount of lightness change in the image seemed to be unnecessarily large, we considered moving the focal point away from the lightness axis towards 'negative' chroma (Figure 16.3). A spherical coordinate system with the origin at the focal point is used, in which the intersection of the mapping vector with the gamut boundary can be found simply using the spherical radius. A second intersection (with the L^* axis) is needed to limit chroma to non-negative values.

16.3.2 Relative lightness change mapping

This method was recently developed as an approximation of focal mapping. It is parameterised to allow various lightness change levels and uses the perceived attributes of lightness and chroma rather than a spherical coordinate system which must be different for each setting of the direction parameter. Note that there is no longer any convergence point. The algorithm is straightforward without the need for any iterations. If $C^* < \lambda \hat{C}_{out}(L^*, h^*)$ or $\hat{C}_{in}(L^*, h^*) < \hat{C}_{out}(L^*, h^*)$ then do nothing, else

$$L^*_{mod} = L^* + \frac{\alpha}{100} \frac{(L^*_{cusp}(h^*) - L^*)(C^* - \lambda \hat{C}_{out}(L^*, h^*))}{(C_{ref} - \lambda \hat{C}_{out}(L^*, h^*)} \tag{16.9}$$

$$C^*_{mod} = \lambda \hat{C}_{out}(L^*_{mod}, h^*) + (1 - \lambda)\hat{C}_{out}(L^*_{mod}, h^*) \frac{C^* - \lambda \hat{C}_{out}(L^*_{mod}, h^*)}{\hat{C}_{in}(L^*, h^*) - \lambda \hat{C}_{out}(L^*_{mod}, h^*)} \tag{16.10}$$

where $\hat{C}_{in}(L^*, h^*)$ and $\hat{C}_{out}(L^*, h^*)$ are the boundaries of the image and the reproduction gamuts, respectively; $L^*_{cusp}(h^*)$ is the lightness of the cusp at a given hue angle. C_{ref} is a parameter that influences the curvature of the mapping direction and must be greater

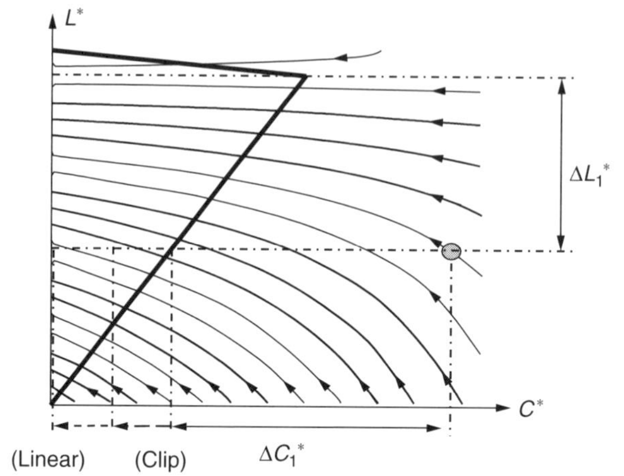

Figure 16.4 Mapping direction using the RLC method. The curvature is a result of a lightness change proportional to $\Delta L_1^* \Delta L_2^*$. There is no convergence point.

than the largest possible chroma, e.g. $128\sqrt{2}$ for TIFF-CIELAB images; λ is the degree of soft clipping (Section 16.3.3) and α gives the degree of lightness change (0–100%).

Figure 16.4 shows the RLC curvature for the linear compression type of mapping. ΔC_1^* depends on the chosen mapping type since the gamut boundary is scaled down from clipping (factor 1) to linear compression (factor 0). No lightness modification is performed inside the scaled boundary.

16.3.3 Mapping type

The mapping type used in this chapter, already published in a previous study, is called a knee function. It turned out that rounding the knee by use of a smooth function did not improve the mapping results.

As can be seen in Figure 16.5, the degree of clipping can be varied between 0 (linear compression) and 1 (pure clipping) using the parameter λ. Note the difference between λ

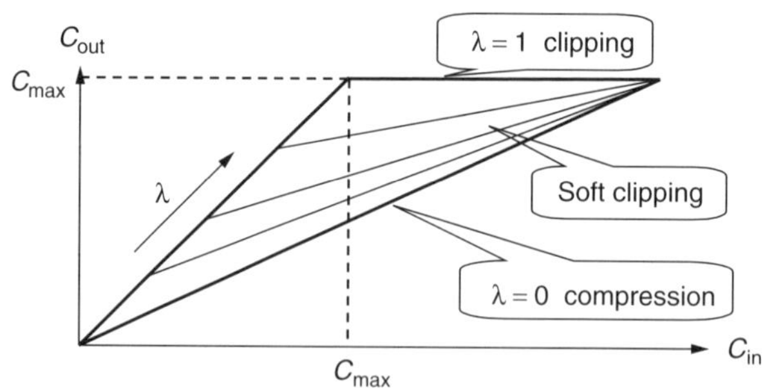

Figure 16.5 Knee function soft clipping.

and μ. The latter is the derivative of the compression part, i.e. the local contrast gradient (Figure 16.1). Here the meaning of C_{in} and C_{out} depends on the chosen coordinate system:

- For focal mapping, C is the spherical radius
- For RLC mapping, C is the cylindrical radius (chroma)

16.4 EXPERIMENTS

In order to make real monitor-to-print comparisons, four images were taken from the Kodak PhotoCD sampler (Figure 16.6): Creek, Girl, Windows and Parrots. A dye sublimation printer served as the reproduction device, with its gamut scaled by 50% reduction to show the differences among the gamut mapping algorithms more clearly.

The images were mapped to the printer device space (RGB) in three steps:

1. The smooth soft-clip lightness scaling was applied with parameters set to $\mu = 0.5$ and $L_{\text{min}} = 14$, corresponding to the real black point of the dye sublimation printer.
2. The images were mapped with the given mapping type and direction. This was done the same way as in our previous experiments.
3. The resulting images were converted using Apple ColorSync and an ICC printer profile. The profile was generated with GretagMacbeth ProfileMaker software.

Finally, the images were printed at a resolution of 150 dpi, since images with a lower resolution were expected to be rejected by observers because of inadequate sharpness.

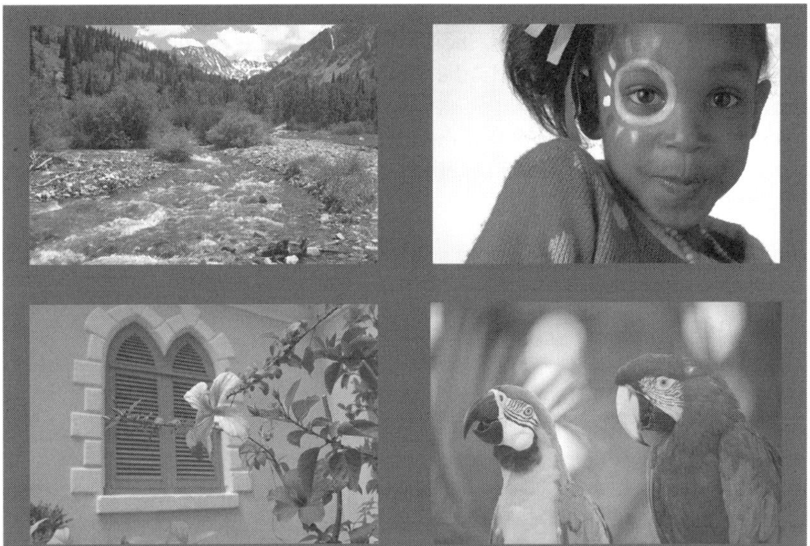

Figure 16.6 Images used in the experiments (Photographs by Don Cochran, Norm Kelly and Steve Kerr from the Kodak PhotoCD sampler, reproduced by courtesy of Eastman Kodak Company).

On the other hand, higher resolution would lead to more detail which cannot be observed in the original image being displayed on the monitor. This could affect the results of the study.

The prints were viewed as pairs using a daylight simulator. The originals were displayed on a Barco CRT, calibrated to the white point of the illuminated dye sublimation paper. Dark surround was used, thus the monitor's lightness ranged from 0 to 100.

The observers had to judge, in paired comparison experiments, which of the two reproductions was more similar to the original. If no difference was noticeable, a 'don't know' decision was allowed. The observer had to turn his or her head and thus was not able to see both the original and the reproductions at the same time. The reproductions were presented in random order. Based on the responses of the observers, psychophysical scales were calculated using Thurstone's law of comparative judgement, case V [6–8].

16.4.1 Experiment 1: Clipping in various directions

In the first experiment, clipping was chosen as the mapping type. Only the out-of-gamut colours were modified and clipped along the chosen mapping direction onto the gamut boundary. The investigated directions were as follows (Section 16.3.2):

- Focal mapping F_{CF} with CF being the (negative) chroma of the focal point: -100, -50, -20, 0
- Relative lightness change mapping with 0% (constant lightness dL0), 25%, 50% and 100%

With 100% lightness change, the colours with the highest possible chroma are mapped onto the cusp of the gamut. Eight observers took part in the experiment. Figure 16.7 shows the calculated overall scale values together with the 95% confidence intervals.

As found in previous experiments, the focal mapping direction performed worse when the focal point was moved towards the lightness axis. In particular, gamut mapping towards a focal point on the lightness axis is judged to be significantly the worst of all methods tested. Figure 16.7 shows that the methods making only slight lightness changes performed best and that the RLC50 method was judged to be significantly worse than keeping lightness constant (dL0).

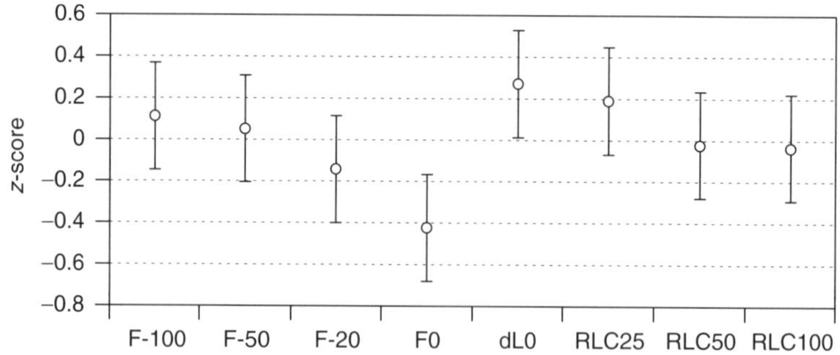

Figure 16.7 Overall results for various mapping directions, shown as a psychophysical scale.

16.4.2 Experiment 2: Soft clipping

The second experiment aimed to determine the best mapping type for two mapping directions, F0 and RLC50. The two mapping types investigated were linear compression and clipping. The images were judged by six observers and again a psychophysical scale was computed. Some results of applying the algorithms to the image Window are shown in Figure 16.8.

The calculated overall scale values of the experimental results, together with the 95% confidence intervals, are shown in Figure 16.9. The mapping type which performed

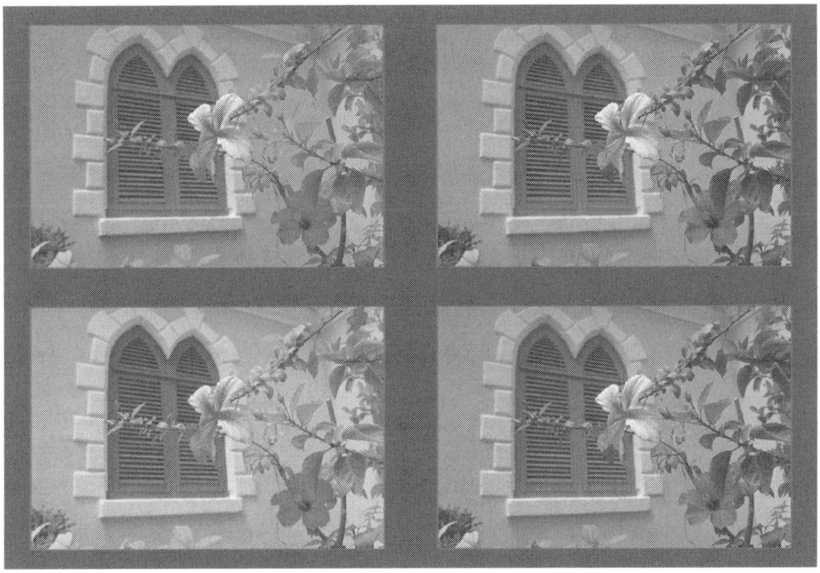

Figure 16.8 Some mapping results for Window: (left) focal mapping F0, (right) RLC50; (top) clipping, (bottom) linear compression. See also Colour Plate 9.

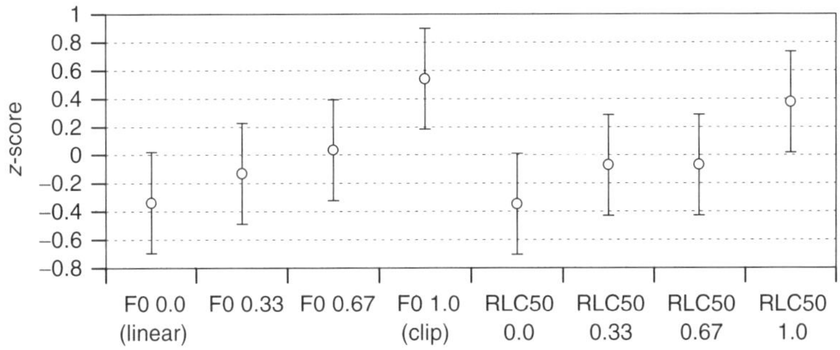

Figure 16.9 Overall results for various mapping types, shown as a psychophysical scale.

best was clipping. The worst type was linear compression, irrespective of the mapping direction.

16.5 DISCUSSION

Since $L^*a^*b^*$ images can be processed by a wide variety of software, the colour space chosen for gamut mapping was CIELAB, although its weakness in perceived hue is recognised [9–12]. From previous studies it was known that clipping is the best mapping type when lightness is kept constant, regardless of the mapping direction as long as the lightness ranges are equal.

In this study, lightness compression had to be applied since the latter condition was no longer true. In order to get comparable results, the same mapping directions and types were applied. In the first experiment, clipping was chosen as the mapping type, and again the focal mapping direction yielded the worst results. Obviously, this kind of direction changes lightness to such a large extent that details get lost, resulting in colourful images with poor rendering of detail.

The relative lightness change method certainly preserves more of the image lightness, but it was not judged to be significantly better than the method of constant lightness. Here are some possible reasons:

- Some colour appearance model should have been applied to minimise cross-media effects.
- Simulation of printer gamut was not equivalent to real cross-media experiments.
- The chosen lightness scaling influenced the optimal chroma mapping.
- Observers had more difficulty in spotting differences, which resulted in higher variances.
- In the reproduction path, there were uncertainties in the printer profile and the printer itself.

16.6 CONCLUSIONS

In this study the same gamut mapping algorithms as in our previous study were applied with a initial smooth soft-clip lightness scaling. Among the algorithms were the well-known focal mapping as well as the recently developed relative lightness change (RLC) method, which enabled the use of cylindrical coordinates without the need for iteration. The mapping was carried out along curved lines.

The study confirmed the results of the previous study, where simulations of prints on a monitor were investigated. One difference lay in the higher variances when judging real prints. Another was that the RLC50 method, which performed best in the simulations, was significantly worse than keeping lightness constant. The reasons for these deviations have yet to be determined.

It was shown that the best mapping type was clipping, regardless of the mapping direction. Thus a modified ΔE^* formula as proposed by [13–15] could provide a gamut mapping solution. Furthermore the gamut mapping algorithm showing the worst performance was mapping towards a focal point on the lightness axis, especially in conjunction with linear compression.

ACKNOWLEDGEMENTS

We are indebted to our observers who patiently did their best to make thorough decisions.

REFERENCES

1. P. G. Herzog and H. Büring (1999) Optimizing gamut mapping: lightness and hue adjustments. *Proc. 7th IS&T/SID Color Imaging Conference*, Scottsdale AZ, pp. 160–166.
2. P. G. Herzog and H. Büring (2000) Optimizing gamut mapping: lightness and hue adjustments. *Journal of Imaging Science and Technology*, **44**(4), 334–342.
3. J. Morovic (1998) To develop a universal gamut mapping algorithm. PhD thesis, University of Derby.
4. P. G. Herzog and M. Müller (1997) Gamut mapping using an analytical color gamut representation. *Proc. SPIE*, **3018**, 117–128.
5. G. J. Braun and M. D. Fairchild (1999) Image lightness rescaling using sigmoidal contrast enhancement functions. *Proc. Color Imaging: Device Independent Color, Color Hardcopy, and Graphic Arts IV*, San Jose, pp. 96–105.
6. L. L. Thurstone (1927) A law of comparative judgement. *Psychological Review*, **34**, 273–286.
7. G. A. Gescheider (1976) *Psychophysics: Method and Theory*. Lawrence Erlbaum, Hillsdale NJ.
8. J. C. Baird and E. Noma (1978) *Fundamentals of Scaling and Psychophysics*. John Wiley, New York.
9. G. Marcu (1998) Gamut mapping in Munsell constant hue sections. *Proc. 6th IS&T/SID Color Imaging Conference*, Scottsdale AZ, pp. 159–162.
10. F. Ebner and M. D. Fairchild (1998) Development and testing of a color space (IPT) with improved hue uniformity. *Proc. 6th IS&T/SID Color Imaging Conference*, Scottsdale AZ, pp. 8–13.
11. G. Braun, M. D. Fairchild and F. Ebner (1998) Color gamut mapping in a hue-linearized CIELAB color space. *Proc. 6th IS&T/SID Color Imaging Conference*, Scottsdale AZ, pp. 163–168.
12. J. McCann (1999) Color gamut measurements and mapping: the role of color spaces. *Proc. SPIE*, **3648**, 68–82.
13. N. Katoh and M. Ito (1996) Gamut mapping for computer generated images, part II. *Proc. 4th IS&T/SID Color Imaging Conference*, Scottsdale AZ, pp. 163–168.
14. M. Ito and N. Katoh (1999) Three-dimensional gamut mapping using various color difference formulae and color spaces. *Proc. SPIE*, **3648**, 83–95.
15. R. Y. C. Wei, M. J. Shyu and P. -L. Sun (1997) A new gamut mapping approach involving lightness, chroma and hue adjustment. *TAGA Proc.*, **1997**, 685–702.

PART 5

Image quality

17

Modelling colour appearance, spatial vision, and image quality

Mark Fairchild

17.1 INTRODUCTION

The prediction of image quality using mathematical models has long been a holy grail of imaging science. This is well illustrated by recent works, e.g. [1–4]. The description of image quality can be thought of as a specialised case of colour difference specification in which the spatial distribution of colour differences (e.g. noise, sharpness, artefacts) is paramount. Unfortunately, research in colour difference and colour appearance measurement has largely neglected the spatial properties of human vision to focus on difficult colour issues with spatially simple stimuli (i.e. simple uniform patches on uniform grey backgrounds). Conversely research on spatial vision models for image quality measurement has largely neglected issues of colour appearance such as chromatic adaptation and focused on colorimetrically simple stimuli (e.g. threshold measurements of monochromatic spatial patterns). There are a few notable exceptions that will be described in more detail below [5–8].

While it is somewhat surprising that these two domains, both addressing issues of image quality, have not had a more synergistic research relationship, it is not entirely unexpected given the complexity of each. It seems that both fields have evolved to the

Colour Image Science, edited by L.W. MacDonald and M.R. Luo.

point where they can no longer pretend the other is unimportant. At this point, it seems likely that significant strides might be made in both areas by combining their strengths in a more unified approach to measurement of image differences. Such an approach is described in this chapter, along with some of the first few steps in a long-term endeavour to advance toward this elusive goal.

The state of the art in colour difference specification is represented by the CIE94 colour difference equation [9] based on the CIELAB colour space. The data on which the CIE94 equation was formulated are for simple stimuli in static, well-defined viewing conditions. Despite this, the CIE94 colour difference equation is often successfully used to specify the colour accuracy of imaging systems and characterisations of such systems. Normally this is accomplished by examining the mean (and histogram) of a collection of uniform colour samples. The CIE94 colour difference equation will soon be supplanted by the improved CIEDE2000 colour difference equation; however, the new formulae are still based on simple, static stimuli. When the viewing conditions are more complex, colour appearance models are required. The state of the art in colour appearance modelling is represented by the CIECAM97s model [10, 11].

CIECAM97s and other similar models have been used successfully in cross-media colour reproduction when it is necessary to reproduce images across significant changes in viewing conditions and mode of viewing. However, these models are applied to images on a pixel-by-pixel basis with the assumption that each pixel can be treated as spatially homogeneous colour stimulus. This approach is successful only because the most common application is one in which the colours in an image are reproduced in a one-to-one spatial correspondence with the original (and on a similar spatial scale). When it is desired to extract the colour appearance of a stimulus within an image or scene and reproduce it in a different context, more complex spatial modelling is required. It is clear that these approaches to colour reproduction quality are neglecting important spatial properties of the images. An excellent example is to consider the average colour difference between a continuous-tone grey patch and a halftone reproduction.

Spatial vision models typically divide images into a pyramidal representation of various spatial frequency components in an attempt to simulate the processing of spatial information in the human visual system. These models can then be used to predict the probability of detection of differences within each of the spatial frequency (and orientation) channels and then (normally via probability summation) the overall probability of detection of a difference between spatially complex stimuli. Examples of recent models of this sort include Lubin's Sarnoff model [12] and Daly's visible differences predictor [13]. These models make impressive predictions of detection thresholds in monochrome images. However, their treatment of colour (and in particular colour appearance issues) is minimal at best. Also, they do not deal with issues of image quality, or image difference scales, which are at least as important as threshold predictions.

There have been a few attempts to combine the strengths of colour difference and colour appearance research with those of spatial modelling. For example, the S-CIELAB image difference metric of Zhang and Wandell [7] incorporates spatial filtering of colour signals with the CIELAB colour difference equation. Jin *et al.* [8] extended the S-CIELAB approach to a multichannel spatial model by combining the CIELAB colour difference equation with Daly's model to produce the colour visual difference model (CVDM).

Lastly, Pattanaik *et al.* [5, 6] formulated a multiscale model of spatial and colour vision that is capable of predicting a wide variety of spatial threshold and colour appearance data and incorporates an intrinsic model of light and chromatic adaptation. All three of these models will be explored and further refined as part of the ongoing research programme described in this chapter.

17.2 A UNIFIED APPROACH TO IMAGE QUALITY

The approach to overall image quality specification proposed in this chapter can be summarised in one rather simple hypothesis: An image quality metric can be derived as a measure of the perceived difference from an ideal image.

The fundamental assumption is that any reduction in quality is caused by some perceived colour difference. If no colour differences can be perceived, then the reproduced image is indistinguishable from the original and the image quality is at its maximum. Questions of image preference or image naturalness can also be addressed in this framework by simply making the reference image the ideal image rather than some arbitrary original. This concept is illustrated in an iconic form in Figure 17.1, where reproductions of an original image with a variety of degradations in image quality are placed along an interval scale of decreasing image quality; image quality decreases to the left. The goal that remains is to derive a model that can place the images at the same locations along the quality scale as those given by human observers. Also note that it is not necessary to actually embody the ideal reference image in order to create a legitimate interval scale of quality, preference or naturalness.

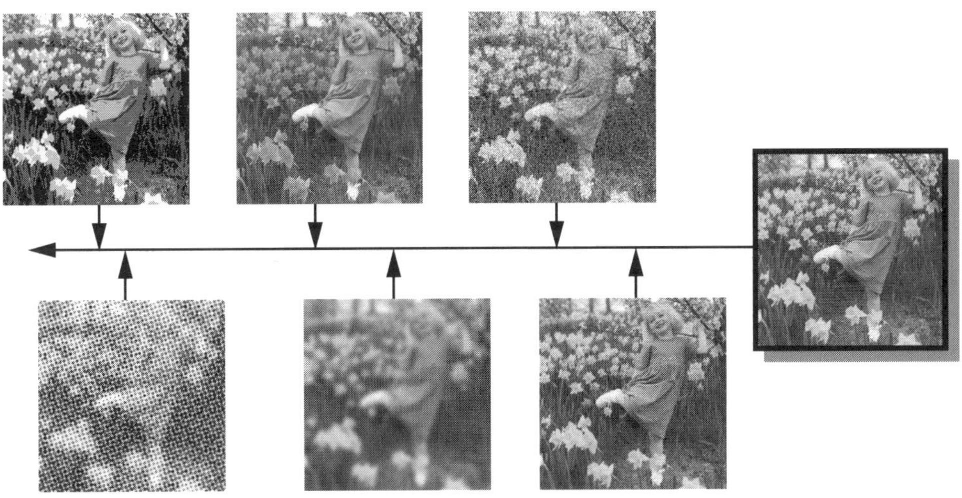

Figure 17.1 Conceptual representation of an interval scale of overall image quality based on metrics of perceived image differences. The extreme right image is the reference image and image quality decreases to the left. See also Colour Plate 9.

Given this fundamental premise, the process of deriving an image quality metric can be formulated into four main steps:

1. Psychophysics to create interval scales of image quality.
2. Formulating a vision model to build a difference metric.
3. Deriving the relationship between the difference metric and image quality scales.
4. Establishing an anchor image for the interval scale.

With these steps in mind, the task becomes finding solutions for each of them. Some potential solutions for each step and proposals for refining these solutions are described in the rest of this chapter. The vision model of Pattanaik *et al.* [5, 6] will be the main focus and is described in Section 17.3. The S-CIELAB [7] and CVDM [8] models will also be examined and potentially refined. Based on image rendering techniques, one approach for obtaining degradation-free images to anchor interval scales and visual experiments is described in Section 17.4. Lastly, some existing psychophysical image quality data and preliminary results from ongoing experiments are described in Section 17.5.

17.3 VISION MODEL

Figure 17.2 is a flow chart of the fundamental structure of the multiscale model of colour and spatial vision proposed by Pattanaik *et al.* [5, 6] The model begins with spectral image data, degrades the image by the optical characteristics of the eye, then spectrally samples through the four photoreceptor responses (rod and three cones). These receptor images are then decomposed into six bandpass spatial frequency channels using appropriate models of light and chromatic adaptation to establish the contrast signals in each channel. These signals are then subjected to non-linear transduction and combined into opponent signals (achromatic, red-green, and yellow-blue). The opponent signals can be transformed to make various predictions of colour appearance or the model can be inverted for a specified set of display viewing conditions in order to implement a visually guided tone and colour reproduction (i.e. gamut mapping) process.

In this model, chromatic adaptation is treated in the step that converts the bandpass pyramids for each receptor type into contrast pyramids. The gain control is based on lower frequency channels and its magnitude is derived to simulate incomplete light adaptation and chromatic adaptation transforms typically found in colour appearance models such as CIECAM97s. Colour appearance correlates are obtained at the last stage of the model through appropriate combinations of the post-adaptational opponent responses, which mimics the approach of typical colour appearance models. Colour difference metrics could be obtained at several stages in the model. For example, one could calculate differences between any, or all, of the appearance correlates or one could simply examine Euclidean distances between the opponent images, A, C_1, and C_2.

This model is capable of performing tone mapping for high dynamic range images [5] and making a wide variety of spatial colour appearance predictions [6]. Some examples of the output of the model include the visual mapping of high dynamic range images into

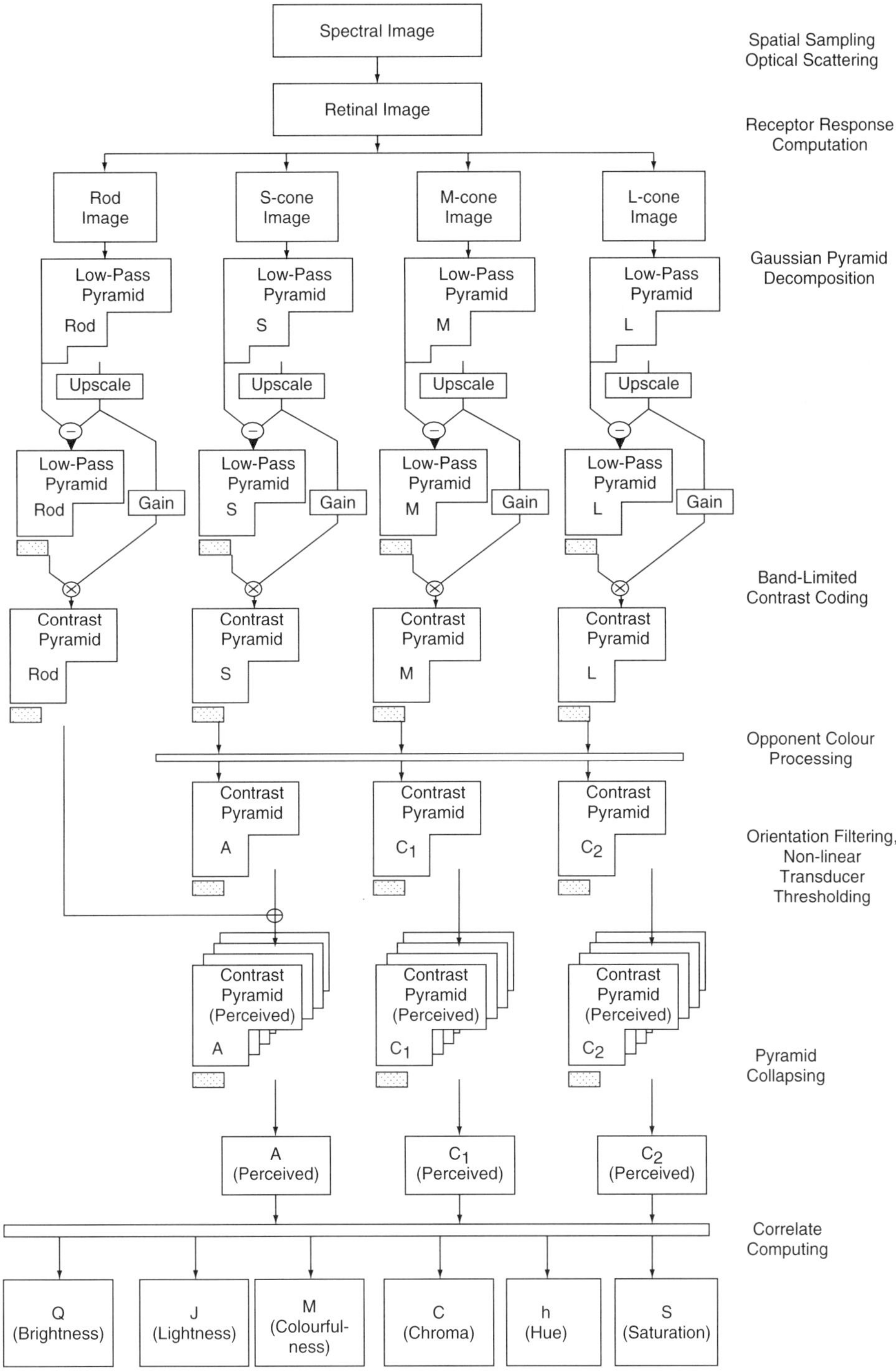

Figure 17.2 Flow chart of the Pattanaik *et al.* [5, 6] multiscale vision model.

the limited dynamic range of display devices (Figure 17.3); the appropriate prediction of colour appearance and visual acuity across a large absolute range of luminance levels (Figure 17.4); and the prediction of incomplete chromatic adaptation (Figure 17.5).

While the Pattanaik *et al.* model shows great promise as the basis for a colour image difference metric, it needs to be extended. Specifically, orientation-sensitive mechanisms must be added to the model to allow proper prediction of thresholds for various spatial orientations and masking effects [14] and a precise formulation of a difference metric in

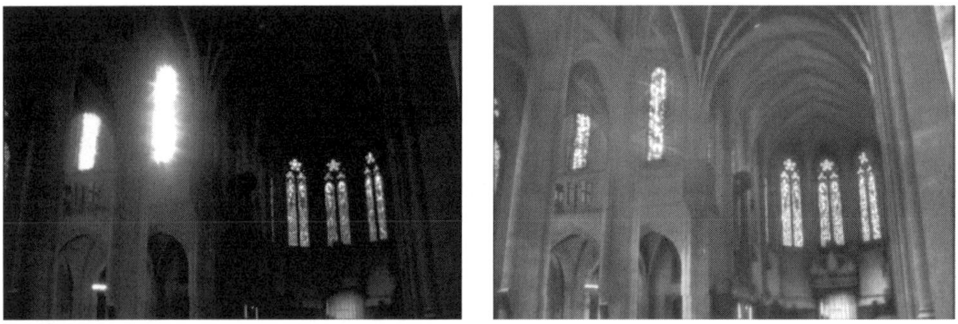

(a) (b)

Figure 17.3 (a) Linear mapping of a high dynamic range image and (b) the visual mapping produced by the Pattanaik *et al.* model (Courtesy of P. Debevec).

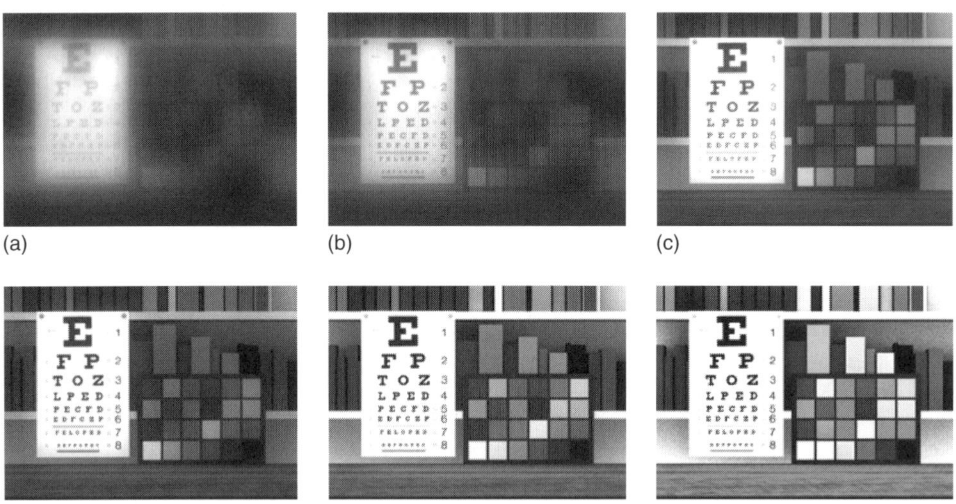

(a) (b) (c) (d) (e) (f)

Figure 17.4 Predictions of the Pattanaik *et al.* model over a large absolute range of luminance (cd m^{-2}): (a) 0.1, (b) 1.0, (c) 10, (d) 100, (e) 1000, (f) 10 000. Note the changes in colourfulness and acuity with luminance level. See also Colour Plate 10.

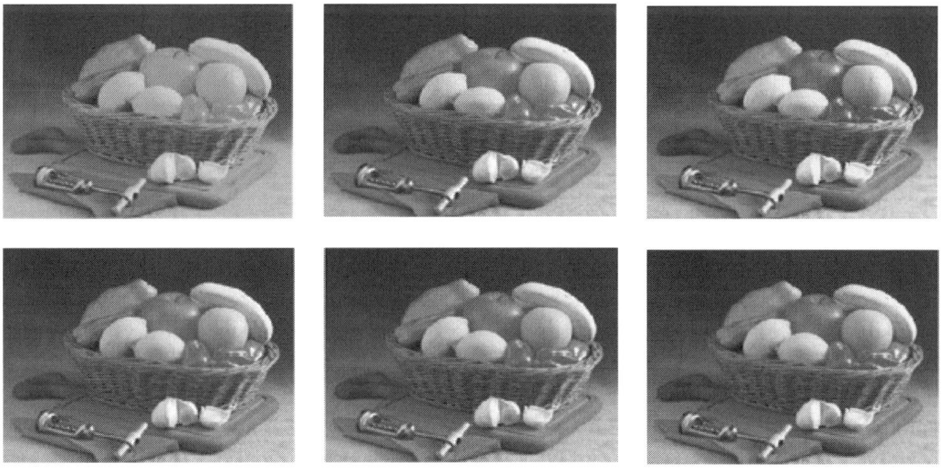

Figure 17.5 The top row shows raw radiance images (no adaptation model) for images simulating yellowish, neutral and bluish illumination. Compare them with images based on the chromatic adaptation model intrinsic to the Pattanaik *et al.* model (bottom row). Note the prediction of incomplete chromatic adaptation. See also Colour Plate 10.

the appearance dimensions must be created. It is hoped that these enhancements will be forthcoming in future publications.

Given the complexity of the Pattanaik *et al.* model, it might be more than is required to predict image quality interval scales (visual assessments with a high degree of variability). To explore this possibility, the S-CIELAB [7] and CVDM [8] models will also be evaluated as potential bases for a general-purpose metric of overall image quality. The simplest of these models that is capable of reasonably predicting previously published and forthcoming data will be focused upon for further refinement. Watson and Ramirez [15] have suggested that fairly simple spatial models should be capable of predicting threshold data. Their results indicate that simply including a contrast sensitivity function with some form of energy model can predict many of the experimentally observed results. They suggest that adding the oblique effect and spatial frequency channels contribute little to the predictive power of a model. It is feasible that the Watson and Ramirez results might guide the level of complexity required for an image quality metric as described in this chapter. Their results would suggest that a model slightly more complex than S-CIELAB, but simpler than CVDM (and thus much simpler than the multiscale model) might be sufficient. It is hoped that such a model can be derived.

17.4 DEGRADATION-FREE IMAGES

Psychophysical and mathematical studies of image quality can easily be confounded by the choice of the original images since these images have already been subjected to the image quality degradations characteristic of the imaging systems used in their acquisition.

To address this potential problem, research was undertaken to develop techniques for producing degradation-free images that could be used as the basis of image quality scales and as input to image simulation systems (thus producing the subject images for image quality psychophysics). The goal was to produce images of three-dimensional objects with texture and shading that could be used to evaluate subtle characteristics of image reproduction that are not well illustrated with simple colour patches (e.g. tone reproduction, sharpness, noise). The approach taken was to extend the OpenGL graphics library [16] to allow rendering of images with arbitrary spectral, spatial and photometric resolution with bump mapping for texture simulation [17, 18]. A typical image might have 16-bit radiometric resolution, 2000 × 2000 pixels, and 31 wavelengths in 10 nm increments through the visible spectrum. Such images could be tiled together to produce arbitrary image sizes and resolutions.

In addition to the enhanced colour accuracy, this spectral rendering system allows the synthesis of images that could not possibly be produced with traditional RGB computer graphics. For example, the system is capable of properly rendering metameric objects (Figures 17.6 and 17.7) and fluorescent objects (Figure 17.8). An object with a bump-mapped towel-like texture is shown in Figure 17.9.

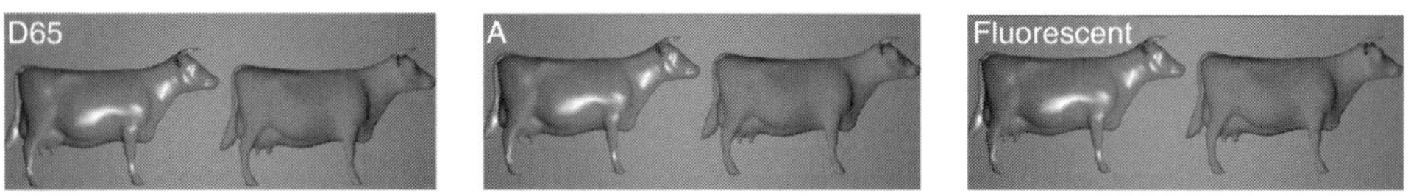

Figure 17.6 Spectrally rendered illuminant metamerism. The two cows have the same reflectance properties under each of the three light sources.

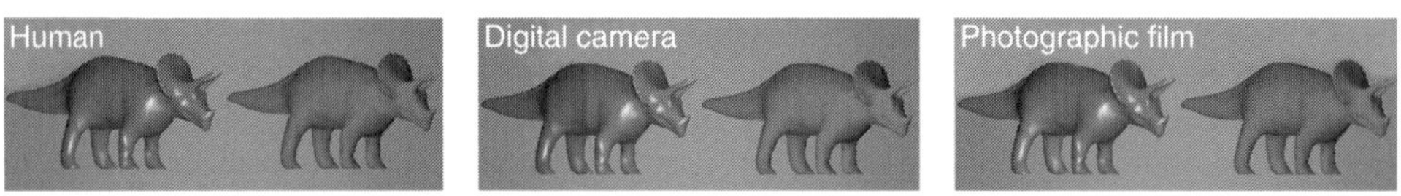

Figure 17.7 Spectrally rendered observer metamerism. The two dinosaurs have the same reflectance properties and illumination for each of the three spectral responsivities.

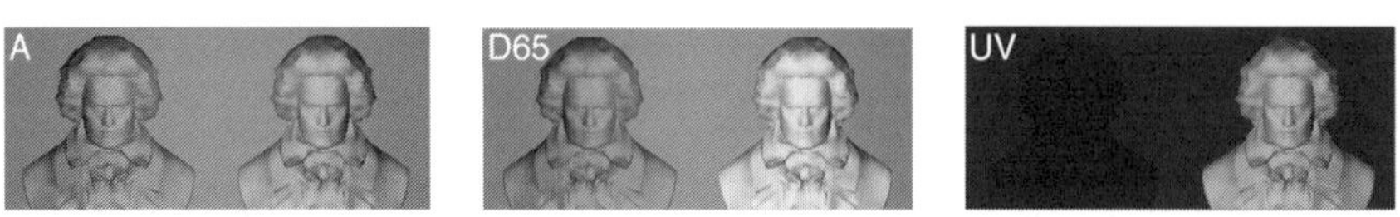

Figure 17.8 Spectrally rendered fluorescence. The left object is not fluorescent. Absorption, emission and reflection properties are identical for each of the three light sources.

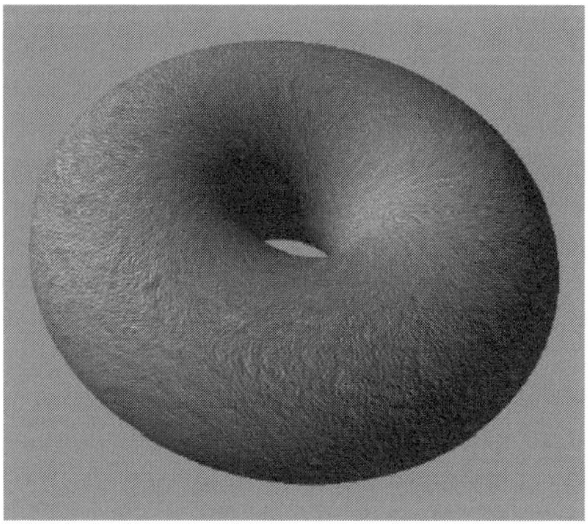

Figure 17.9 Simulation of a towel-like texture in a spectrally rendered image using bump mapping.

Although the OpenGL system can produce a variety of useful images, its fundamental restriction to Gouraud shading limits the possible realism of the produced test targets. To address some of these issues, a similar system is currently being constructed as an extension to a commercially available computer graphics ray tracing and radiosity renderer. A second research project is underway to use image-based rendering techniques to create accurate and pleasing spectral images of human portraiture.

Such degradation-free images represent one of several possible sources of 'ideal reference' images that could be used in image quality studies. They are most appropriate for studies in which the main objective is to examine the visibility of degradations introduced by an imaging system. Thus, it is important to start with an image with no such degradation. In studies where image preference or naturalness is of interest, such synthetic images would be inappropriate because there might well be no intrinsic concept of naturalness and preference judgements might be more widely varying than with natural images. Any generalisable study of image quality should include several types of image, both natural scenes and synthetic scenes.

17.5 VISUAL QUALITY SCALES

Given potential visual models and degradation-free images as starting points, it remains to establish interval scales of perceived image quality. Two approaches are being taken in this respect. The first is to examine previously published data. For example, Vaysman and Fairchild [19] have published interval scales of printed colour image quality as a function of pixels per inch and bits per pixel. Farrell [3] has published similar data for greyscale printed images. Such results can be used to test and refine the various models. Other available data are image colour tolerances from studies such as those by Stokes *et al.* [20] and ongoing work by Gibson *et al.* [21] Combined models of spatial and colour vision should be able to predict these results as well, since the data indicate levels of identical perceptual colour difference for a variety of spatial configurations and colour manipulations. Thus the output of an image colour difference model should also be equal for all the threshold images.

In addition, psychophysical experiments are currently under way specifically to derive image quality interval scales for the formulation and testing of image quality metrics. The first of these is an experiment on perceived sharpness [22], in a paired comparison experiment where observers judge which of two images is sharper. Again, the only possible way to see a sharpness difference is if there are perceptible colour differences between the images. The physical variables in the images are spatial resolution (3 levels of dpi), noise (4 levels of introduced independent Gaussian noise), tone reproduction (3 levels of contrast adjustment), and sharpening (2 levels of spatial filtering). All combinations of these variables are being examined, resulting in 72 images for each scene ($3 \times 4 \times 3 \times 2$). In a paired comparison paradigm, these 72 images result in 2556 pairs ($72 \times 71/2$) to be evaluated visually. Four different image contents (three natural photographic scenes and one synthetic scene) are included, thus producing a total of 10 224 image pairs to be judged for relative sharpness. Assuming 5 s per judgement, this experiment requires

Table 17.1 Image attributes for the 20 images with the highest perceived sharpness

Sharpness rank	DPI	Noise	Contrast	Sharpening
1	300	10	1.2	Y
2	300	20	1.2	Y
3	300	0	1.2	Y
4	300	0	1.1	Y
5	300	10	1.1	Y
6	300	30	1.2	Y
7	300	10	1.0	Y
8	300	20	1.1	Y
9	300	0	1.2	N
10	300	10	1.2	N
11	300	10	1.1	N
12	300	0	1.1	N
13	300	20	1.0	Y
14	300	20	1.2	N
15	300	30	1.0	Y
16	300	20	1.1	N
17	300	0	1.0	N
18	300	30	1.1	Y
19	300	30	1.1	N
20	300	20	1.0	N

Note that the sharpness differences between each adjacent image are not necessarily statistically significant. Results are averaged across four scenes. The image at sharpness rank 17 is the original.

approximately 15 h of observing time to complete. Fortunately, the required judgements are very simple. Observers need only report which image in the pair appears sharper. To date, 50 observers have taken part in random subsamples of the experiments, resulting in complete pairwise experimental data for the equivalent of 15 observers (in addition 5 individuals completed the entire experiment).

Interval scales of perceived image sharpness were derived using Thurstone's law of comparative judgements. The results include verification of some typical expectations (e.g. spatial resolution is most important, a sharpening filter usually increases sharpness) and some surprising trends and trade-offs (e.g. addition of some noise to the image increases sharpness, contrast has a strong effect on sharpness). For example, preliminary observations suggest that sharpness is enhanced by the introduction of appropriate levels of noise and luminance contrast. In some cases these enhancements override changes in spatial resolution. Table 17.1 lists the top 20 images in order of perceived sharpness.

Additionally, the three models discussed above and simple pixel-wise CIE94 colour differences were used to try to predict the sharpness results. The linear correlation

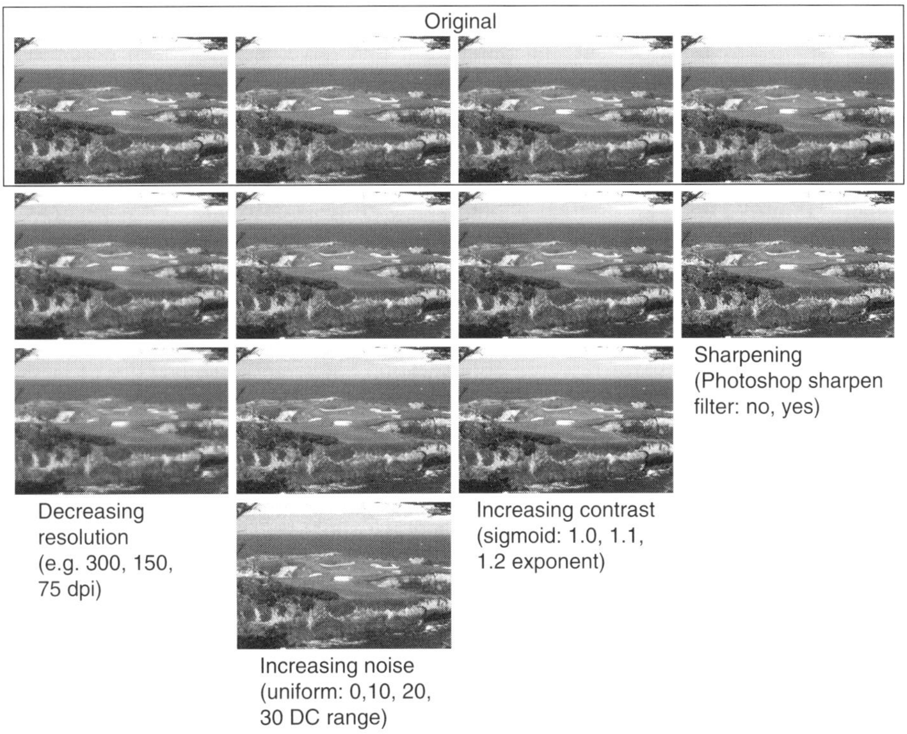

Figure 17.10 Portion of a test image for a sharpness perception experiment. This array illustrates the various levels of the four physical variables being examined (noise, resolution, tone reproduction, sharpening) but it omits all of the 'interaction' images to preserve space.

coefficients (R^2) between the observed predicted image differences were 0.032 for CIE94 alone, 0.004 for S-CIELAB/CIE94, 0.012 for CVDM/CIE94, and 0.505 for the Pattanaik *et al.* multiscale model. Only the multiscale model made reasonable predictions of the experimental results. This is both surprising and disappointing as it was expected that a simpler model should be able to perform as well. Further data analysis and model refinement is under way to try to understand the cause for these predictions and perhaps formulate a more appropriate visual model. Further details can be found in the literature [22] and these data, along with further analyses, will be made publicly available and might represent one of the largest available data sets systematically examining sharpness perception in images. Figure 17.10 illustrates a portion of one of the test images with the various levels of the physical variables. It does not illustrate the images with combinations of the four variables changing.

17.6 FUTURE DIRECTIONS

The synergistic combination of colour vision and spatial vision models for application in image quality assessment seems to be generating significant interest. For example, the visual modelling and psychophysical data described above are complementary to concepts of image sharpness management and perception that have recently been described by MacDonald [23, 24]. Another natural extension of this work is the examination of image preferences or naturalness. It is possible that a similar approach can be taken for the derivation of image preference scales. However, it is likely that the anchor points would be different and that the scales would have to be bidirectional. For example, it is often possible to improve upon an original photograph with respect to preference whereas it is impossible to improve upon a degradation-free image with respect to image degradations.

It is expected that over the coming years there will be natural evolutionary enhancements in all three of the key areas described above (vision model, degradation-free images, and visual quality scales). One exciting recent development in this field is the establishment of formal agreements for research collaboration between the University of Derby in the UK, the University of Chiba in Japan, and the Rochester Institute of Technology in the US; they create a colour image science triangle with the potential to accomplish research objectives on an international scale that could not be considered by any of the three institutions functioning independently. Such collaborations could be particularly fruitful in the area of image preferences, where a multicontinent psychophysical study is currently being implemented.

17.7 CONCLUSION

The framework and collection of research results outlined above suggest that there is some hope that a metric of overall perceived image quality can be derived. A successful result is not assured [2], but it is certain that the attempt is worthwhile and that there is a tremendous amount to be learned along the way.

ACKNOWLEDGEMENTS

This research is directly supported by Fuji Photo Film in collaboration with Kazuhiko Takemura (modelling and psychophysics) and Eastman Kodak Company in collaboration with Paula Alessi (spectral image rendering). Related research is also being supported by the National Science Foundation (NSF), the New York State Office of Science, Technology, and Academic Research (NYSTAR), Pixel Physics, Xerox and IBM. Thanks are also due to the graduate students working on these projects, Garrett Johnson and Qun Sun.

REFERENCES

1. P. Engeldrum (1995) A framework for image quality models. *Journal of Image Science and Technology*, **39**, 312–318.
2. P. Engeldrum (1999) Image quality models: where are we? *Proc. IS&T PICS Conference*, pp. 251–257.
3. J. E. Farrell (1999) Image quality evaluation. In *Colour Imaging: Vision and Technology*, L. W. MacDonald and M. R. Luo (eds), pp. 285–314. John Wiley, Chichester.
4. A. M. Ford (1999) Determination of compressed image quality. In *Colour Imaging: Vision and Technology*, L. W. MacDonald and M. R. Luo (eds), pp. 315–338. John Wiley, Chichester.
5. S. N. Pattanaik, J. A. Ferwerda, M. D. Fairchild and D. P. Greenberg (1998) A multiscale model of adaptation and spatial vision for image display. *Proc. SIGGRAPH '98*, pp. 287–298.
6. S. N. Pattanaik, M. D. Fairchild, J. A. Ferwerda and D. P. Greenberg (1998) Multiscale model of adaptation, spatial vision, and color appearance. *Proc. 6th IS&T/SID Color Imaging Conference*, Scottsdale AZ, pp. 2–7.
7. X. Zhang and B. A. Wandell (1996) A spatial extension of CIELAB for digital color image reproduction. *SID Digest*, **27**, 731–734.
8. E. W. Jin, X.-F. Feng and J. Newell (1998) The development of a color visual difference model (CVDM). *Proc. IS&T PICS Conference*, pp. 154–158.
9. CIE (1995) Industrial colour-difference evaluation. CIE Technical Report **116**. CIE, Vienna.
10. CIE (1997) The CIE 1997 interim colour appearance model (simple version), CIECAM97s. CIE Publication 131. CIE, Vienna.
11. M. D. Fairchild (1998) *Color Appearance Models*. Addison Wesley, Reading MA.
12. J. Lubin (1993) The use of psychophysical data and models in the analysis of display system performance. In *Digital Images and Human Vision*, A. B. Watson (ed.), Ch. 12. MIT Press, Cambridge MA.
13. S. Daly (1993) The visible differences predictor: an algorithm for the assessment of image fidelity. In *Digital Images and Human Vision*, A. B. Watson (ed.), Ch. 13. MIT Press, Cambridge MA.
14. J. A. Ferwerda, S. N. Pattanaik, P. Shirley and D. P. Greenberg (1997) A model of visual masking for computer graphics. *Proc. SIGGRAPH '97*, pp. 143–152.
15. A. B. Watson and C. V. Ramirez (2000) A standard observer for spatial vision. *Investigative Ophthalmology and Visual Science*, **41**(4), S713.
16. www.opengl.org..
17. G. M. Johnson and M. D. Fairchild (1998) Computer synthesis of spectroradiometric images for color imaging systems analysis. *Proc. 6th IS&T/SID Color Imaging Conference*, Scottsdale AZ, pp. 150–153.
18. G. M. Johnson and M. D. Fairchild (1999) Full-spectral color calculations in realistic image synthesis. *IEEE Computer Graphics and Applications*, **19**(4), 47–53.
19. A. Vaysman and M. D. Fairchild (1998) Degree of quantization and spatial addressability tradeoffs in perceived quality of color images. *Proc. SPIE*, **3300**, 250–261.

20. M. D. Stokes, M. D. Fairchild and R. S. Berns (1992) Precision requirements for digital color reproduction. *ACM Transanctions on Graphics*, **11**, 406–422.
21. J. E. Gibson, M. D. Fairchild and S. L. Wright (2000) Colorimetric tolerances of various digital image displays. *Proc. 8th IS&T/SID Color Imaging Conference*, Scottsdale AZ, pp. 295–300.
22. G. Johnson and M. D. Fairchild (2000) Sharpness rules. *Proc. 8th IS&T/SID Color Imaging Conference*, Scottsdale AZ, pp. 24–30.
23. L. MacDonald (1999) Framework for an image sharpness management system, *Proc. 7th IS&T/SID Color Imaging Conference*, Scottsdale AZ, pp. 75–79.
24. L. MacDonald, S. Yendrikhovskij, S. Bech and K. Jensen (2000) Toward optimal colour image quality of television display. *Proc. SPIE*, **3963**, 260–270.

18

Metric approaches to image quality

Ralph Jacobson and Sophie Triantaphillidou

18.1 INTRODUCTION

Metrics have been used for more than 40 years as a means of quantifying image quality, and hundreds of metrics have been proposed to deal with both general and specific aspects of image quality. The basic need for their application in determining image quality comes mainly from designers of imaging chains and their components and those who apply imaging systems in medical, forensic and many other scientific applications [1].

At the end of an imaging chain is the human observer who makes judgements on the quality of the output images and has to be satisfied that the quality is acceptable and appropriate for their intended applications [2]. However, for those devising systems it would be a very laborious process if every modification to the system required extensive numbers of observations by large numbers of observers.

Quantified measures of quality are needed for these purposes that comprise physical measures (Table 18.1) in combination with psychophysical attributes of the human eye and have become known as *image quality metrics* (IQMs). These reduce many complex measures to single numbers that relate to perceptions of image quality. Also they make it possible to model changes in the imaging chain and how they affect the output image. The wide variety of IQMs differ in the number and type of physical measures that are used and the way in which they are combined with parameters of the human eye. A

Colour Image Science, edited by L.W. MacDonald and M.R. Luo.

Table 18.1 Physical measures of image quality

Attribute	Physical measures and data
Colour	Spectral data, chromaticity diagrams, colour spaces
Tone (contrast)	Density, pixel value, characteristic curve, tone reproduction curve, gamma, histogram
Resolution (detail)	Resolving power, l/mm, dpi, ppi
Sharpness (edges)	Acutance, PSF, OTF, LSF, MTF
Noise	Granularity, noise power (Wiener) spectra, autocorrelation function
Information	Entropy, information capacity, DQE

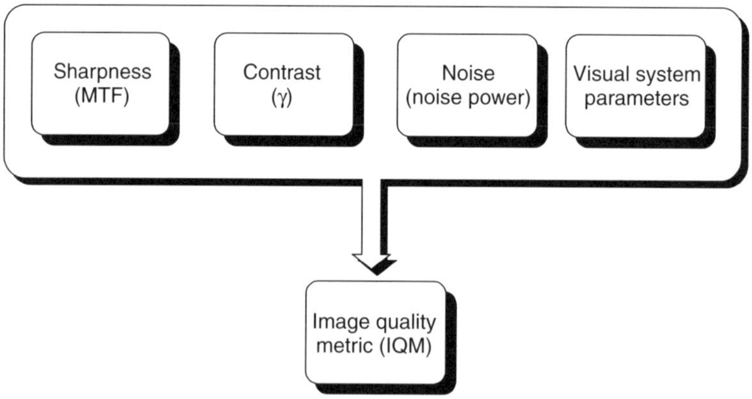

Figure 18.1 Image quality metrics.

simplified diagram is shown in Figure 18.1. Generally they are tested by correlations between the metric values for a series of images and their subjective evaluation by panels of observers.

Unfortunately, IQMs are beset with a number of problems and questions that tend to lower their credibility among many researchers involved in quantifying image quality. Here are a few of the most significant questions:

- Is the single-number approach to image quality valid?
- Which IQM should be used?
- What functions should be used for a standard observer?
- How are non-linearities and thresholds accommodated?
- What types of scene should be used to test any given IQM?
- How do IQMs deal with different scenes?

Although these questions are daunting, IQMs have been used successfully over a number of years in many laboratories and have helped to produce improvements in the quality of images provided by commercial products. However, they lack transferability and they are generally used only in the laboratories where they were devised. Although they may not be quite as fundamental as is often assumed, their application to problems in quantifying image quality is leading to improvements in commercial systems, an increased understanding of imaging systems and how images are judged by the human visual system (HVS).

The physical attributes listed in Table 18.1 arose originally from considerations concerning analogue systems and then translated into the digital environment [3]. In digital systems a number of known artefacts exist which cannot be adequately quantified by the measures listed in Table 18.1. These include aliasing, blocking or Gibbs effects, contouring, jaggies and ringing artefacts. The anisotropic and the non-stationary nature of digital images and non-linearities, inherent in digital imaging chains, also have to be taken in to account, otherwise measures such as modulation transfer function (MTF) and noise power spectra are invalid. It has been suggested [1] that anisotropy can be accommodated by averaging the one-dimensional metric in four directions: 0°, 90°, $+45^\circ$, -45°. All these factors place additional challenges for IQMs that were originally applied to analogue systems.

18.2 IMAGE QUALITY

Perceived image quality has no precise definition and is difficult to quantify [4, 5]. This is not surprising in view of the multiplicity of visual parameters processed in non-linear combinations by observers [5, 6]. A good working definition of image quality has been provided by Engeldrum [7]: the integrated set of perceptions of the overall degree of excellence of an image.

Furthermore, it has been emphasised that there is much confusion between the terms *image fidelity* and *image quality* [5, 6, 8]. Elegant explanations of the distinction between these two related terms have been provided by Klein [9] and by Farrell [5]. Klein [9] distinguishes between *image fidelity* and *image quality* as the difference between the visibility of a factor and the degree to which that factor is bothersome. Farrell [5] defines *image fidelity* as the ability to discriminate between two images and *image quality* as the preference of one image over another. Figure 18.2 illustrates the differences and also includes a third metric, image distortion, which is the numerical difference between two images, e.g. the root mean square error (RMSE).

Figure 18.2 introduces the acronym IQC for ‘image quality consciousness’; this is intended to include all additional factors that observers may or may not consider when asked to judge overall image quality. To produce reliable measures, it is necessary to take into account all the factors influencing the assessment of image quality. More specifically, the subjective assessment of image quality is a function of the HVS, the performance of which is highly dependent on the viewing conditions and the physical properties and characteristics of the stimuli, the context within which the image is to be used, and finally but very importantly the ‘quality consciousness’ of the observer. The quality consciousness itself is based on the observer’s experience in viewing images and various other cognitive factors such as memory, emotions, influences, expectations and many more, and it results in a variation of the assessments between individuals and over time for the

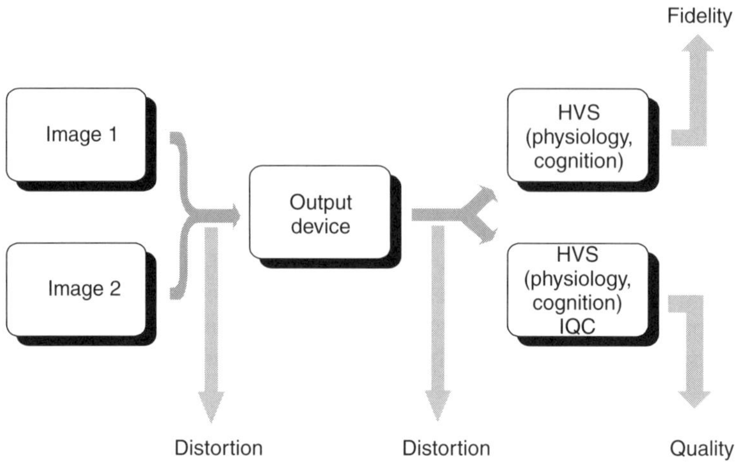

Figure 18.2 Basic types of metric relating to image quality: IQC is the image quality consciousness (Based on diagrams of Ford [10] modified by Triantaphillidou [11]).

same individual. These factors make it difficult to evaluate the quality of images showing natural scenes. Examples of these include prior experience and conditioning, memory of scenes and similar images, points of interest in the images, and indeed the mood and state of awareness of the observer.

The closest approach that attempts to take some aspects of IQC into account is the concept and evaluation of a 'naturalness index' applied to considerations of colour [12]. This approach involved observers responding to a question on their rating of 'the degree of correspondence of displayed images of natural scenes with reality'. Another group was asked for their ratings on 'the degree to which they liked the reproduction of colours in the images'. The naturalness index, arising out of these considerations, is a novel way of providing a colour metric that deals with image quality. It remains to be seen if this approach can sensibly be applied to spatial and other attributes of images of natural scene, ultimately to provide a true image quality metric.

Engeldrum [13] has summarised a unifying approach to the assessment of image quality in the form of an image quality circle (Figure 18.3). The rectangles for customer perceptions and customer quality preferences require subjective judgements, as do the ellipses for image quality models and visual algorithms. The rectangle for physical image parameters is concerned with the parameters listed in Table 18.1 and the rectangle for technology variables covers a substantial number of variables that are either fixed by the system being used or that we can control; examples might include resolution, contrast and screen luminance. In the image quality circle, the connecting links are represented by ellipses: system models, visual algorithms and image quality models. System models are defined as formulae, physical models or algorithms that predict physical image parameters from the technology variables, or vice versa. Visual algorithms are procedures for predicting customer predictions of image quality from physical image parameters, an example is CIE lightness. Image quality models link customer perceptions with customer quality

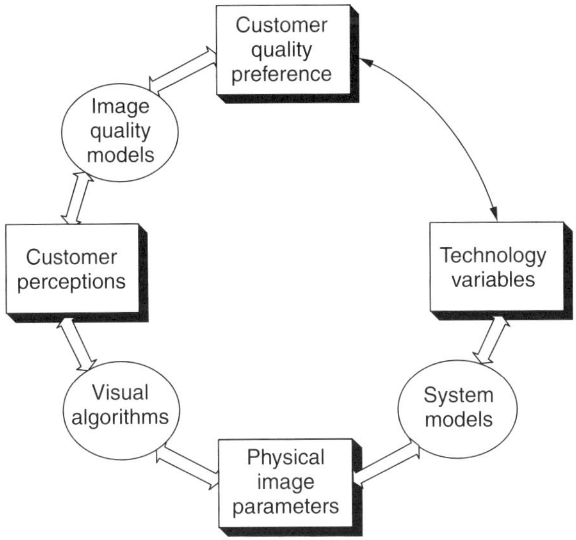

Figure 18.3 The image quality circle [13] (Reprinted with permission of Imcotek Press).

preference which takes in to account the IQC aspects we described earlier. Image quality metrics can be considered rigorous means of embodying most of the features of the image quality circle but they exclude customer quality preference, depending on the judgement being asked of the observers during the application of the metric. For example, is the observer being asked to assess sharpness or to assess quality, which includes sharpness and every other aspect of image quality?

18.3 PHYSICAL PARAMETERS OF THE HVS

One problem concerning the determination of any metric is the choice of the eye's optical transfer function (OT) or contrast sensitivity function (CSF). Those involved in applying colour measurement to imaging systems have had a standard observer defined for 70 years. However, it is less than a decade ago [14] that a physical model for determining the CSF of the eye has been provided which enables a standard CSF to be calculated for varying viewing conditions. Before then, either a function determined in the laboratory by Watanabe *et al.* [15] or a functional distribution was used to represent the spatial response of the human eye. The measurements by Watanabe were determined for one luminance level (34 cd m^{-2}), using only one observer, at an average viewing angle of 16.4°, which may not relate to other viewing conditions. The procedure adopted by Barten [14] for determining the contrast sensitivity of the human eye from a physical modelling approach has been reviewed earlier [16]. It predicts the contrast sensitivity under a variety of viewing conditions relevant to its application in image quality metrics according to the following equation [14]:

$$\frac{1}{M_t(u)} = \frac{M_{opt}(u)}{k}\left[\frac{2}{T}\left(\frac{1}{X_0^2}+\frac{1}{X_e^2}+\frac{u^2}{N_e^2}\right)\left(\frac{1}{\eta\rho E}+\frac{\phi_o}{1-\exp[-(u/u_o)^2]}\right)\right]^{-1/2} \quad (18.1)$$

where M_{opt} is the optical MTF of the eye defined as a Gaussian distribution, k is the signal-to-noise ratio ($k = 3.4$), u is the spatial frequency in cycles per degree, T is the integration time ($T = 0.1$ s), X_o is the image size (degrees), X_e is the maximum size over which the eye integrates information ($X_e = 12°$), N_e is the estimated maximum number of cycles over which the eye integrates ($N_e = 15$), η is the quantum efficiency ($\eta = 2.1\%$), ρ is a photon conversion factor of light units ($\rho = 1.285 \times 10^6$ photons per second per degree^2 per troland), E is the retinal illuminance (trolands), ϕ_0 is the spectral density of the neural noise ($\phi_0 = 1.5 \times 10^{-8}$ s deg^2), and u_0 is the frequency above which lateral inhibition ceases ($u_0 = 11$ cpd).

A comparison between the values predicted by Barten's physical model and those measured by Watanabe is shown in Figure 18.4. This model is also in good agreement with other measurements [14]. For the first time, this approach has provided a standard observer for application in image quality metrics. It is a relatively simple matter to determine the appropriate contrast sensitivity for the viewing conditions employed in the particular image quality investigation. For example, Figure 18.5 shows the calculated contrast sensitivity for varying angles of view, and Figure 18.6 shows the contrast sensitivities predicted by Barten's physical model for different luminance levels at a constant viewing angle.

Farrell [17] has drawn our attention, however, to the limitations of single-channel metrics that are based on functions of the type shown in Figure 18.4. When these functions are used to filter images, they weight the image according to the spatial frequency response of the HVS. Farrell describes the contributions of at least five independent visual channels that contribute to the sensitivity of the HVS to spatial information, which has led researchers to seek multichannel metrics for image quality evaluations. Single-channel

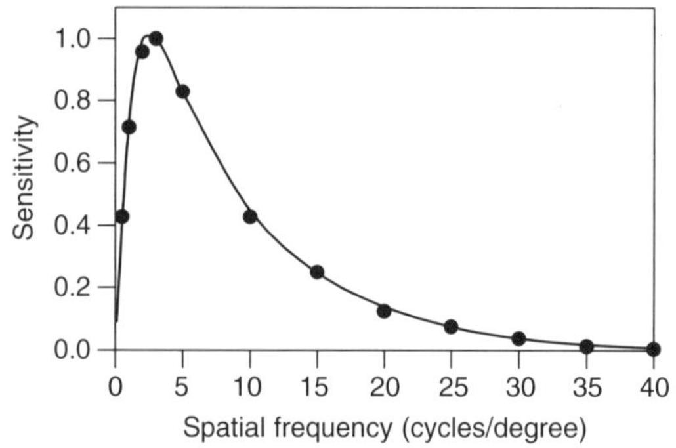

Figure 18.4 Contrast sensitivity function of the human eye (16.4°, 34 cd m^{-2}): the solid line plots values calculated using Barten's equation [14] and the filled circles plot measured values.

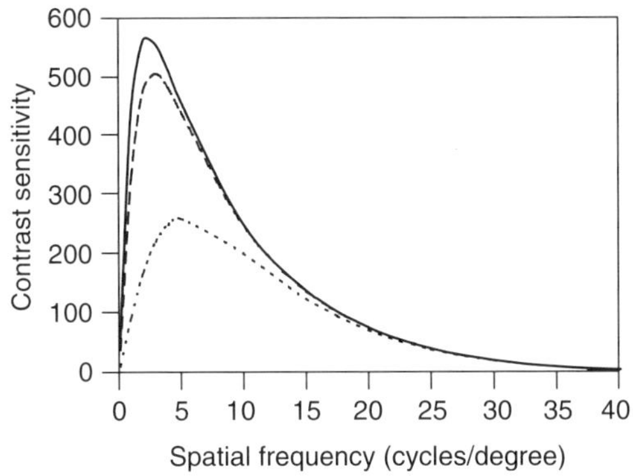

Figure 18.5 Contrast sensitivities determined from Barten's physical model [14] for different viewing angles at D65 and 70 cd m^{-2}: (dotted curve) 2°, (dashed curve) 10°, (solid curve) 60°.

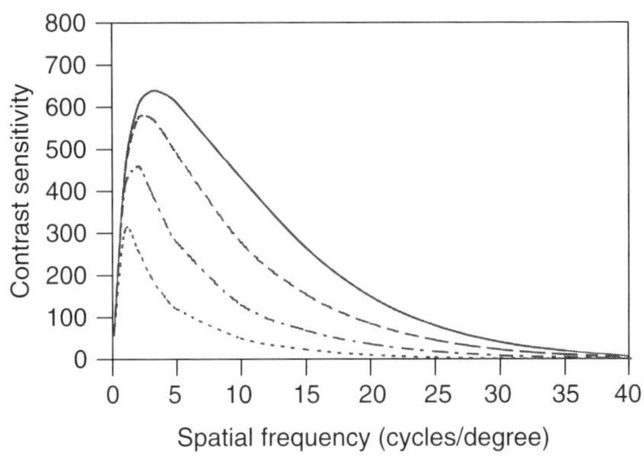

Figure 18.6 Contrast sensitivities determined from Barten's physical model [14] for different levels of luminance at a viewing angle of 60°: (dotted curve) 1 cd m^{-2}, (chain-dotted curve) 10 cd m^{-2}, (dashed curve) 100 cd m^{-2}, (solid curve) 1000 cd m^{-2}.

metrics have nevertheless been successful in predicting aspects of image quality in analogue systems such as sharpness or noise, but are not yet able to deal adequately with many combinations of the attributes in Table 18.1.

18.4 IMAGE QUALITY METRICS

Many different image quality metrics have been proposed but very few have found application in laboratories beyond those in which they were devised. Despite the basic questions raised earlier, metrics are valuable for assessing the visual effects of output images from imaging systems. Individual metrics work well when dealing with single image quality attributes such as sharpness. This applies to an early series of modulation transfer acutance (MTA) metrics, SMTA, CMTA and AMTA [16]. These metrics were effectively applied in their laboratories of origin but they were not used widely elsewhere, although CMTA does find some current use [18].

The image quality metric MTFA (modulation transfer function area) achieved wider acceptability as a standard in the USA for displays [19], although it has been shown to be a very poor predictor of quality when applied to digital systems involving compression [20]. Furthermore, MTFA can be criticised on the grounds that it does not conform to basic rules of cascading, because it takes differences between MTFs when theoretically it should take products:

$$\mathrm{MTFA} = \int_0^{u_{\max}} [M_{system}(u) - M_t(u)]\,\mathrm{d}u \tag{18.2}$$

M_{system} is the cascaded MTF for the imaging chain and M_t is the detection threshold for the observer.

These classical image quality metrics evolved into forms which considered noise as well as sharpness, such as the signal-to-noise metric of Nelson, later fully explained by Higgins [21]. This has proved to be useful for analogue images [21, 22] and more recently for single compressed digital images [20]. The signal-to-noise metric may be defined as follows:

$$\mathrm{SNR} = 10\log_{10}\left(\frac{\sigma^2}{\sigma_d^2}\right) \tag{18.3}$$

where σ^2 is the mean square error (MSE) and σ_d is the standard deviation for the difference image between the original and the modified image.

The mean square error (MSE, σ^2) is a distortion metric, for digital images which is defined as follows:

$$\mathrm{MSE} = \frac{1}{XY}\sum_{x=0}^{X-1}\sum_{y=0}^{Y-1}|f(x,y) - g(x,y)|^2 \tag{18.4}$$

where X is the number of horizontal pixels in the image and Y is the number of vertical pixels, $f(x, y)$ is the original image and $g(x, y)$ is the modified image.

The limitations of the MTFA metric led to the evolution of the square root integral (SQRI) metric of Barten [23] and its further modification to include noise ($\mathrm{SQRI_n}$) [24]. The following equation gives the $\mathrm{SQRI_n}$ metric as reformulated by Töpfer and Jacobson [22] to provide values in just noticeable differences (JNDs):

$$\mathrm{SQRI_n} = \frac{k_1}{\ln 2}\int_0^{u_{\max}}\left[\frac{S(u)M_{eye}^2(u)}{k^2N(u)M_{eye}^2(u) + N_{eye}(u)}\right]^{0.25}\frac{\mathrm{d}u}{u} + k_2 \tag{18.5}$$

The signal spectrum, $S(u)$ in (18.5), is obtained by cascading the original spectrum with the square of the MTFs of the components of the imaging chain [22]. This metric was shown to give excellent agreement with values of the single-channel sharpness (Figure 18.7) when applied to photographic print materials. It has also shown good

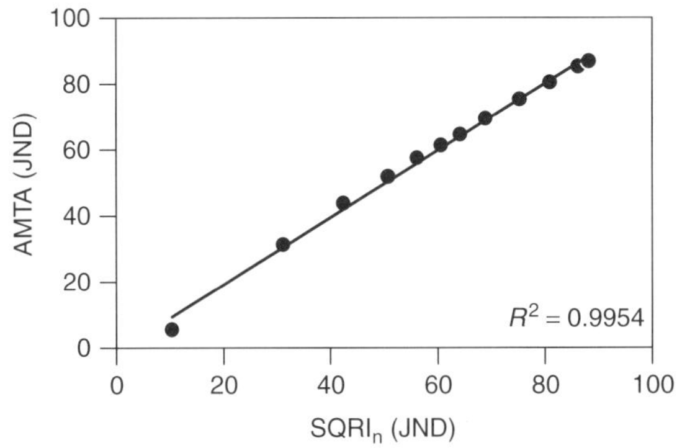

Figure 18.7 Relationship between the SQRI$_n$ metric and sharpness calculated as AMTA in units of just noticeable difference (JNDs) [22].

agreement (correlation coefficients r^2 greater than 0.94) with data from the literature for both photographic and television images [24].

In the application of the SQRI$_n$ metric to compressed digital images of a number of scenes, Ford [10, 25] showed that correlations between perceived quality and the metric gave less good correlations (r^2) which ranged from 0.6925 to 0.9718. But when Gerfelder [20] applied the earlier SQRI metric to digital images, he found negative correlations for some images. Also Ford [10, 25] showed that the results differed markedly from image to image, which indicates the scene dependency in evaluations of IQMs (Figure 18.8). When all the images were combined the correlation coefficient was reduced significantly (Figure 18.9).

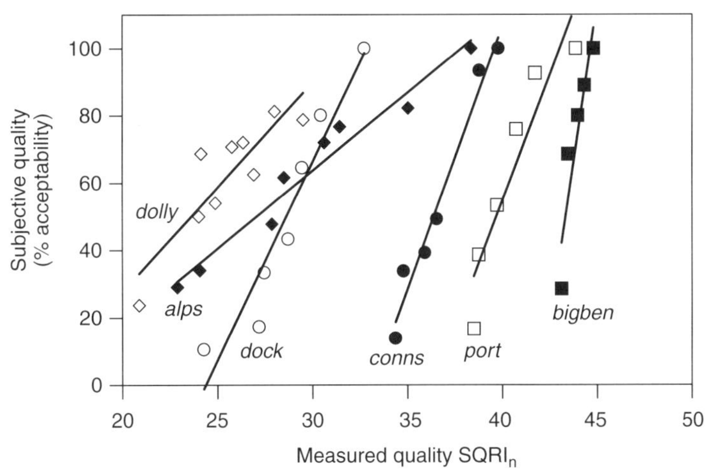

Figure 18.8 Relationship between SQRI$_n$ and subjective quality values above 10% for different images subjected to JPEG compression [25].

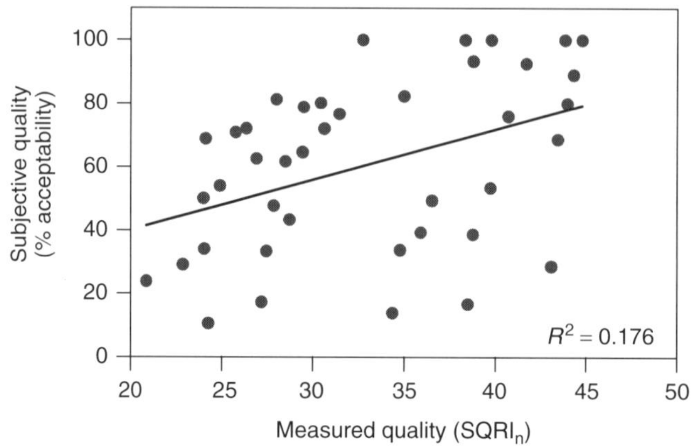

Figure 18.9 Correlation between $SQRI_n$ and subjective quality for all images in Figure 18.8.

Distortion metrics such as the mean square error (MSE), root mean square error (RMSE), normalised mean square error (NMSE) and many other similar metrics [16, 26] also gave very poor correlations with observer responses [26]. This is to be expected when distortion metrics are computed from image data that ignores the output device, the imaging chain and the observer. Better correlations are generally obtained when these distortion metrics are visually weighted by filtering the difference image with the appropriate human CSF of Figures 18.4 and 18.5 [17].

The above IQMs have been concerned exclusively with luminance but other metrics have been devised for determining colour distortions and sharpness. These include the colour reproduction index (CRI) of Pointer, which deals exclusively with colour, and Zhang and Wandell's s-CIELAB, a spatial extension of CIELAB. For simplicity we consider here only spatial and luminance aspects of image quality; details of colour metrics can be found elsewhere [16, 17].

18.5 EVALUATION OF IMAGE QUALITY METRICS

IQMs are generally evaluated by adopting one of the psychometric scales originally proposed by Stevens more than 50 years ago [27]. These four scales are nominal, ordinal, interval and ratio. Nominal scales place items according to named categories, classifying scenes as portraits, landscapes, outdoor, indoor, etc. Ordinal scales place images in ascending or descending order according to some defined attribute such as sharpness or quality. Ordinal scales suffer from the disadvantage that they contain no information about the significance or meaning of distances along the scale and have no defined zero point. Interval scales have equal intervals but no zero. However, if two images are separated by one unit in some attribute at one point on the scale and two other images are also separated by one unit at a different point on the scale, the differences between the two pairs of images will appear the same. Ratio scales embody all the attributes of the previous three scales but also have a zero point. As one moves along the sequence of Stevens' scales from ordinal to ratio, the information provided increases but so does the complexity of the judgements being asked of the observers. Although ratio scales are a rigorous means of quantifying many aspects of image quality, having a zero point provides philosophical and experimental difficulties. For example, what are the meanings of zero image quality or zero sharpness?

The testing of IQMs generally involves the evaluation of image quality metric values for a series of images, or a single image, with one or more attributes being varied. These values are compared with the psychometrically scaled values using one of the scales in the previous paragraph and their correlations are investigated. Figures 18.7 to 18.9 are examples of this procedure. Several texts give more complete information on the variety of experimental approaches to psychometric scaling [28–32].

In most evaluations of image quality metrics, the observer judgements are suprathreshold, but both threshold and suprathreshold issues lend themselves to being determined in an objective way. For example, in the determination of JNDs, a useful approach is to present the observers with combinations of two images (stimuli) differing in some attribute and ask them to select one of the images (two-alternative forced choice approach) based on a defined criterion. A 75% response level corresponds to a JND or a 50% probability of perceiving a difference between the two images. This 50% probability is used for the detection threshold. The forced choice, paired comparison approach is a relatively easy one for observers and their numerical evaluation is also a simple procedure. It involves presenting observers with all possible pairs of images, $n(n-1)/2$, where n is the number of images. Furthermore, it is a very convenient way of evaluating image quality for images on displays and can accommodate inhomogeneity of luminance by randomising the left/right position on the display [10, 11]. The paired comparison technique enables data to be transformed into interval scales and ratio scales by the application of *Z deviates* [28, 32].

The rank order method in which observers place images in sequence according to an aspect of their perceived quality is easily employed, especially when printed images are being evaluated. It is a relatively simple task for observers to place images in order but in practice it is limited to a small number of images, up to 16 [32]. It can provide an ordinal scale, itself of limited value, but it can also be transformed to more useful interval scales, provided it is assumed that the stimuli are distributed uniformly along the attribute being scaled [32]. An additional limitation is that it is a rather impractical method for assessing displayed images because most displays are not large enough to present the required number of images simultaneously at a reasonable size and also may be subject to errors due to spatial non-uniformity.

The rating scale method involves observers estimating a proportion or ratio of two distances of the attribute between the bottom and the top of the scale. There are several forms of rating scale, such as numerical, adjectival and graphical. Experimental data can be transformed into interval and ratio scales [32]. These are rarely used in psychophysical evaluations because of a number of problems [33]. Many workers have argued that it is not legitimate to use numbers assigned to stimuli as direct measures of sensation strength and also because human observers are generally good comparators but relatively bad estimators of absolute magnitude.

Categorical judgements require observers to define the relative position of stimuli with respect to category boundaries. Generally observers are asked to place images into specific defined categories. The minimum number of categories is 5 and the maximum is 9 [34]. Here are some typical category names: excellent, good, acceptable, poor, unacceptable. The advantages of this technique are that data collection is easy for experimenter and observers, and the method lends itself to gathering data for a large number of images and observations. Disadvantages are that transforms to interval scales are complex and laborious and they involve assumptions about the normal distribution of the data. The categories may not be equal and there may be a reluctance for observers to use extreme categories.

Magnitude estimation or direct ratio scaling requires observers to assign numbers to represent the intensity of sensory experiences. A reference image may be presented first to the observer, who assigns a number to it and judges the other stimuli in terms of the remembered reference image. If a reference has not been used in the first place, the images are assessed in the context of the entire series of images that are seen. This technique is somewhat laborious for the observers and is best used for situations in which each observer can estimate a reasonably large number of images in a short time of up to 15 minutes [32]. Unlike the previous method, it does not require any assumptions to be made about the distribution of the attribute being scaled but it does require a relatively large number of observers because of the large variance in the estimates.

Note that in IQM evaluations it is often difficult to correlate results from different research laboratories for subjective assessments from particular metrics. This is due to the widely differing numbers and contents of the images being used, and often a lack of explanation of the viewing conditions and the precise questions being asked of the observers.

18.6 EFFECT OF SCENES

In some investigations the perceived image quality was scene dependent, although in other investigations it was scene independent; this has been reviewed by Corey *et al.* [35]. For example, portraits have been judged differently from landscapes [36]. This could influence the testing of any metric and is superimposed on any scene dependency in the imaging chain, particularly where image compression is involved [20, 25]. Many of the results given in Section 18.4 were shown to vary with the nature and types of the images used in the investigations. One of the many puzzling features of classical image quality metrics is that, in their original applications, scenes were not used in the determination of their numerical values. Barten [1] describes image quality metrics as being generic measures and independent of scene picture content. This means that metrics should be insensitive to different scenes yet there is a strong scene dependency on perceived image quality. This might explain why metrics tend to work for some individual scenes but are less effective when overall correlations are sought for a wide variety of scenes (Figures 18.8 and 18.9).

With the introduction of digital imaging, we now have the ability to quantify every aspect of the digitised image, and we can track images through the entire imaging chain. This means we can begin to understand the influences that different scenes may have on metrics and our perceptions of those scenes. One question we are investigating is: Are there any quantifiable physical characteristics of scenes that can be used to differentiate one scene from another in image quality investigations? At present, when evaluating image quality by whatever process, researchers make a selection of images which they consider relevant to their application. The scenes might be selected on the bases of having different tone ranges, dominant lines and edges, high-frequency information, etc. Engeldrum [37] has defined four key issues that should be considered when selecting images:

- What *categories* should the sample represent?
- What range and distribution of *perceptual attributes* (Engeldrum's 'nesses') should the sample set contain?
- What *image size* should be used?
- What *image content* or image elements should the sample contain?

Bartleson [30] has defined five basic *categories* for describing samples of images:

- *Random and independent* in which each image has an equal chance of being selected and the selection of one image has no influence on the selection of another. This is difficult to achieve in practice because there is no single population from which to sample the images.
- *Stratified* includes the above description and a classification according to a relevant distinguishing feature and the number of items that reflect the population of interest. This is a common kind of sample selection; an example is digital images with subclasses of portraits, landscapes, close-ups, etc.
- *Contrast* a stratified sample with additional items of interest to the investigator. This sample may not be typical of the population as a whole. For example, scenes with dominant edges might be selected in an investigation of the sharpness of an imaging device.
- *Purposeful* samples are either representative of the population or independently variable in some attribute. For example, in the investigation of image compression on image quality outlined earlier, purposeful samples of images compressed to differing levels were used to determine the acceptability of the level of compression.
- *Incidental* samples are those that represent a random independent sample of subgroups of interest, or a special collection of unique images that cannot be added to. This last category is very frequently used within organisations and as a standard image set [38].

Table 18.2 summarises a series of scenes depicted in Figure 18.13 that were selected for an investigation on preferred tone reproduction [11, 39] as being stratified and purposeful. We present them here as a case study with a view to investigating whether there are any simple means of numerically classifying images of the scenes, or distinguishing one scene from another. We determined the power spectra, histograms and entropies of these

Table 18.2 Description of scenes used by Triantaphillidou [11, 39]

Name	Description
angel	Indoor portrait of a woman with oriental complexion, lit by natural daylight
house	Image of a room with a person and various objects; half of the frame is lit by bright light, the other half is in shadow
kid	Distant view of children's playground, lit by bright sunlight
mount	Mountain landscape with little snow and trees and a wooden house in the foreground, photographed on a bright sunny day
object	Indoor still life with various objects varying in colours and tones, lit by natural daylight
olive	Indoor portrait of a man with European complexion, lit by natural daylight
park	Benches and tree landscape, sunlit
sun	Close-up of sunflower and brick wall, lit by sun in partial shade
walk	Person walking close by, heavy cloud cover
wood	Misty landscape with trees and a wooden bench in the foreground

images, originally recorded on black and white film and digitised by a Nikon LS-1000 scanner [39].

18.7 NUMERICAL MEASURES

18.7.1 Power spectra

For the one-dimensional case, the measured power spectrum $W'(\omega)$ of a digital image is defined as

$$W'(\omega) = \frac{1}{X}\left|\sum_{x=1}^{X-1} d(x)\mathrm{e}^{-2\pi i\omega x}\delta x\right|^2 \tag{18.6}$$

where ω is the spatial frequency, X is the number of pixels, $d(x)$ is the measured pixel value (PV) at position x. These functions are shown in Figure 18.10 for the scenes of Table 18.2. The five scenes grouped within the ellipse in Figure 18.10 had the most closely related spectra. To attempt to classify scenes according to their total power as a single number, the areas under the power spectra curves were evaluated.

When measuring areas of functions which increase very rapidly at low spatial frequencies, the measurements are subject to high errors. To reduce these potential errors, bandpass values for integration over the region which includes the maximum spatial sensitivity of the human eye (1–12 cpd) were imposed. The resulting values in Table 18.3 were determined from summations of the actual data, not from the smoothed curves of Figure 18.10. From Table 18.3 it can be seen that the scenes could be grouped into three basic categories: low power (*kid*, *park*, *walk*); intermediate power (*angel*, *house*, *object*, *sun*, *wood*); high power (*mount*, *olive*). Note that this measure is subject to a high degree of error due to the rapid rise of the power spectra at low frequencies, despite limiting the range of the measured values.

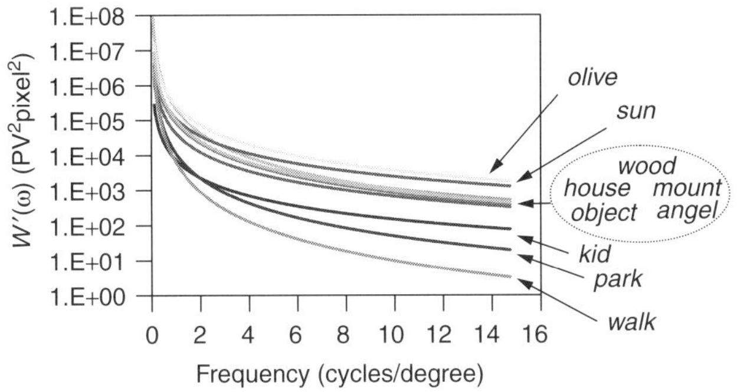

Figure 18.10 Smoothed horizontal power spectra for the scenes described in Table 18.2.

Table 18.3 Numerical characteristics of images

Image	Bandpass power (1–12 cpd)	Mean pixel value	Variance	Skewness	Entropy
angel	3 216	97.9	9 584.4	0.33	7.14
house	3 337	53.1	2 819.6	1.60	6.50
kid	446	160.9	25 888.8	−0.20	7.10
mount	11 112	76.0	5 776.0	1.04	7.48
object	4 749	102.3	10 465.3	0.34	7.70
olive	10 233	107.4	11 534.8	0.10	7.64
park	319	68.1	4 637.6	1.32	6.83
sun	5 029	75.7	5 730.5	0.80	7.44
walk	224	58.0	3 364.0	2.20	6.88
wood	5 879	60.6	3 672.4	1.76	7.12

Note: the corresponding images are shown in Figure 18.13.

18.7.2 Histograms

Histograms of the scenes of Table 18.2 are shown in Figures 18.11 and 18.12, plotted as probability density functions $P(i)$:

$$P(i) = \frac{N(i)}{M} \quad (i = 0, 1, 2, \ldots, k - 1) \tag{18.7}$$

$N(i)$ is the number of pixels with pixel value i; k is the total number of intensity levels; and M is the total number of pixels.

Although histograms do not provide single numbers, they provide the distribution of numbers of pixels of each value. They are indicators of the intensity levels and contrasts of images and they have been used to classify images of scenes into various types [40]. From the probability density functions can be computed measures that quantify their shape and distribution, including the mean, standard deviation and skewness.

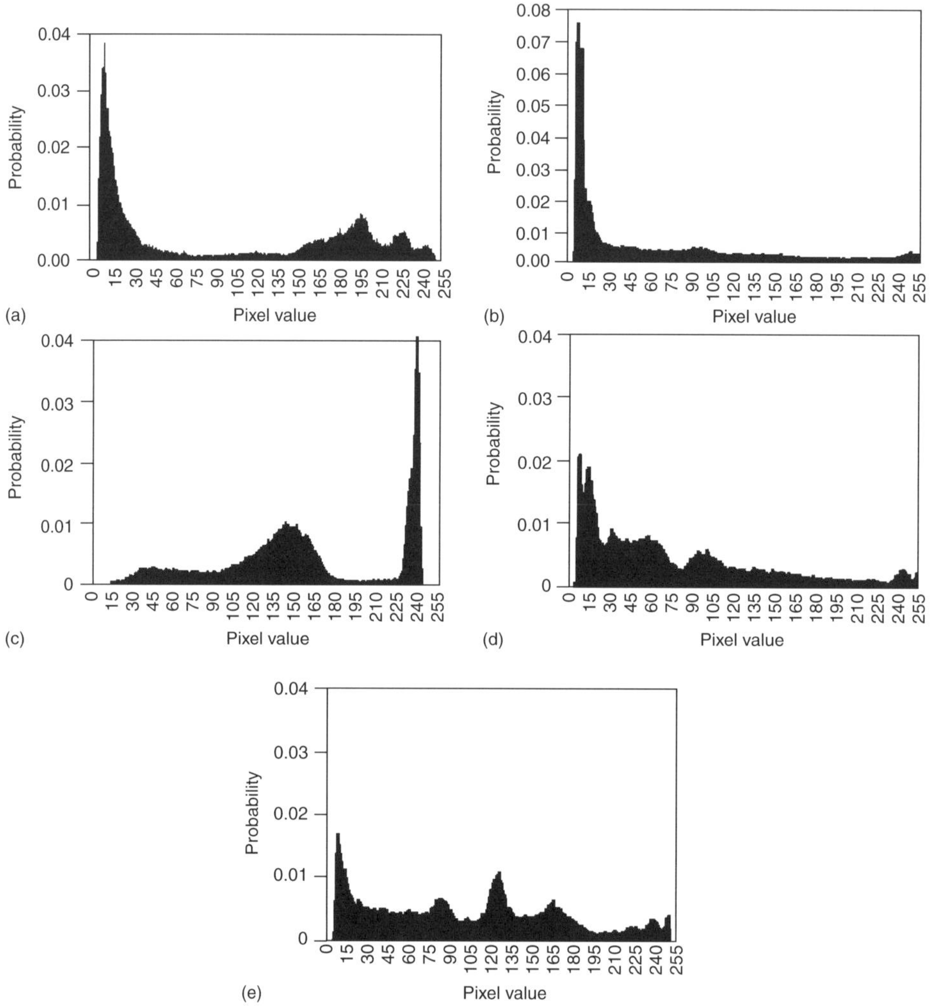

Figure 18.11 Probability density functions for the first five images in Table 18.3: (a) *angel*, (b) *house*, (c) *kid*, (d) *mount*, (e) *object*.

Mean pixel value $\bar{i}$ is given by:

$$\bar{i} = \sum_{i=0}^{k-1} i P(i) \tag{18.8}$$

Variance σ^2 is given by:

$$\sigma^2 = \sum_{i=0}^{k-1} (i - \bar{i})^2 P(i) \tag{18.9}$$

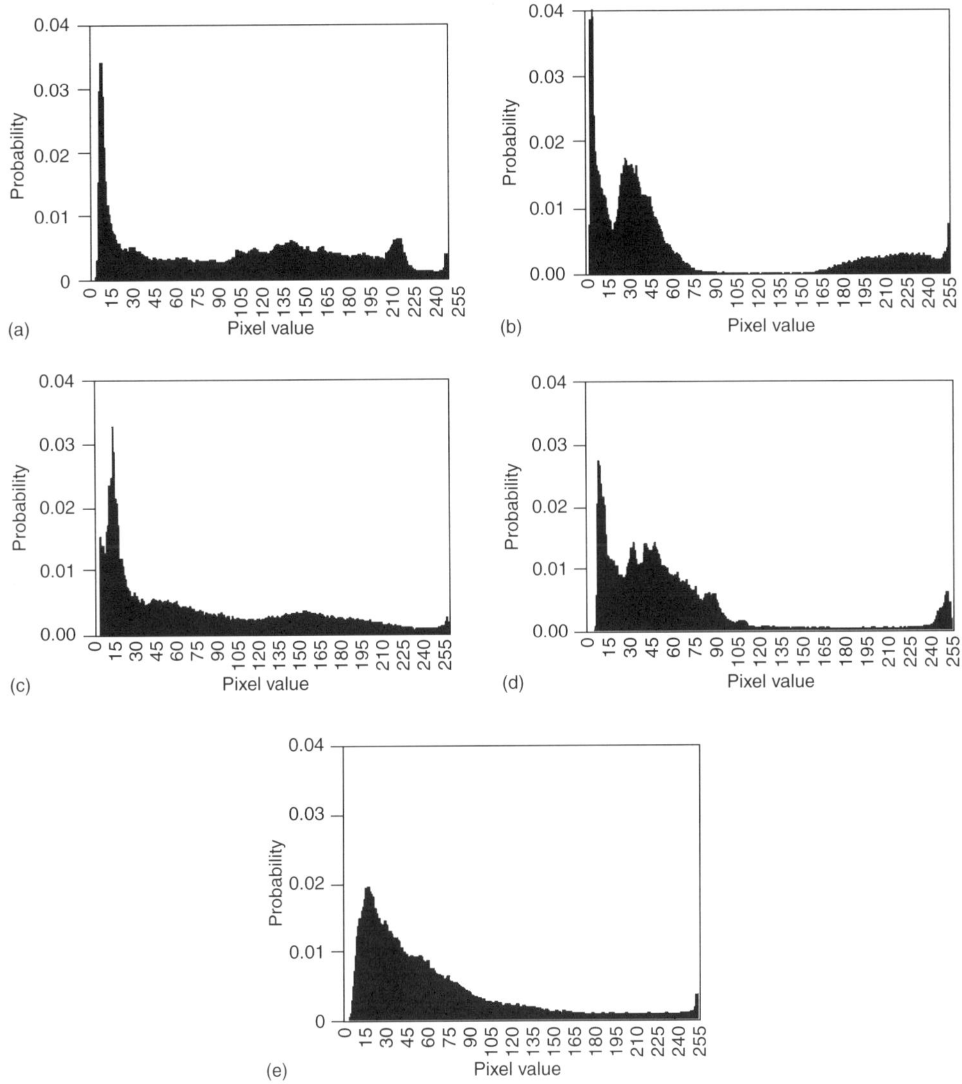

Figure 18.12 Probability density functions for the last five images in Table 18.3: (a) *olive*, (b) *park*, (c) *sun*, (d) *walk*, (e) *wood*.

Skewness S_S is given by:

$$S_S = \frac{1}{\sigma^3} \sum_{i=0}^{k-1} (i - \bar{i})^3 P(i) \tag{18.10}$$

where $P(i)$ is as defined in (18.7).

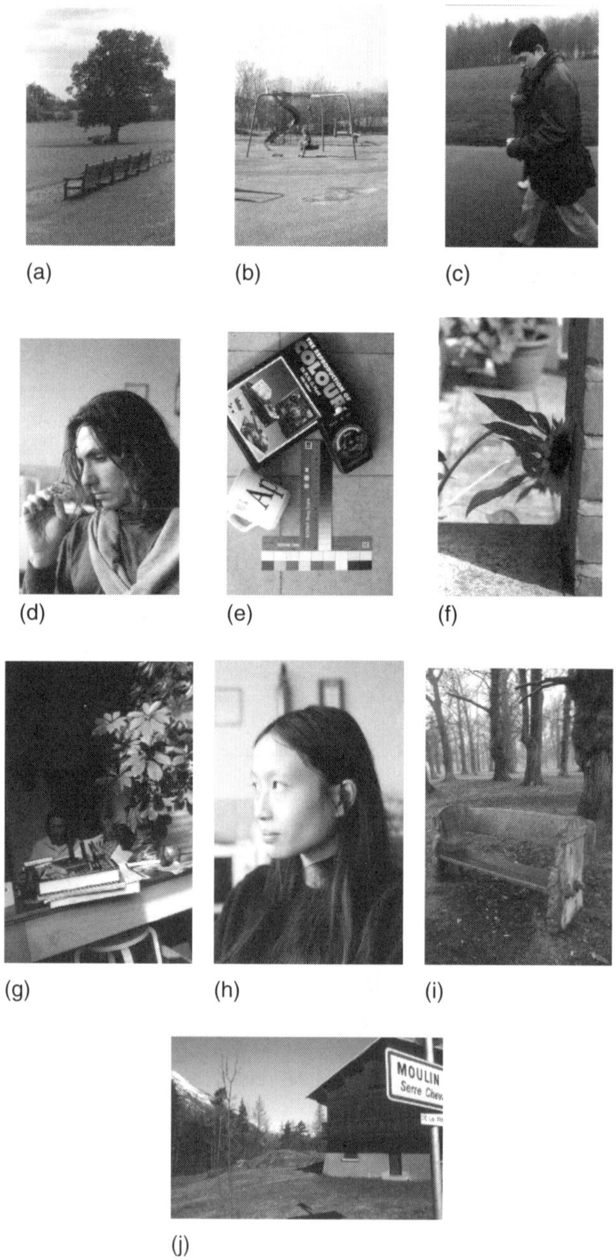

Figure 18.13 The test images of Table 18.3: (a) *park*, (b) *kid*, (c) *walk*, (d) *olive*, (e) *object*, (f) *sun*, (g) *house*, (h) *angel*, (i) *wood*, (j) *mount*.

Table 18.4 Spearman's rank correlation coefficient, r_S, for the ranked data of Table 18.3

	Mean Pixel Value	Variance	Skewness	Entropy
Bandpass power (1–12 cpd)	0.2242	−0.0909	−0.1758	**0.6727**
Mean pixel value		0.5152	**−0.9394**	**0.6485**
Variance			**−0.6364**	0.2727
Skewness				−0.5152

Values of mean, variance and skewness are given in Table 18.3 for the scenes in Figure 18.3. It can be seen that the mean, or average intensity, is large for high-key images such as kid and small for low-key images such as walk and wood. The variance is related to contrast and is high for olive and object but low for park and wood, as expected from their appearance. Unfortunately, it is very high for kid, which appears rather low in contrast, and low for house, which appears quite high in contrast. Therefore variance cannot be regarded as a reliable predictor of scene contrast. Skewness is a measure of the imbalance of the histogram, but its values bear no obvious relationship to the appearance of the images.

18.7.3 Entropy

It is anticipated that images of different scenes should have different information content or entropies [40] and that these values could potentially be used for defining or classifying scenes. The first-order estimate of entropy, S_E, in bits per pixel is given by:

$$S_E = -\sum_{i=0}^{k-1} P(i) \log_2 P(i) \tag{18.11}$$

Values for the entropies of the scenes in Table 18.2 are included in Table 18.3 but there is little variation from one image to another. The numerical characteristics of images in Table 18.3 were subjected to multivariate analysis by successive determinations of Spearman's rank correlation coefficient, r_S, for pairs of data [41], after converting the individual columns of values into ranks. Spearman's rank correlation coefficients for the ranked data are given in Table 18.4.

18.8 DISCUSSION AND CONCLUSIONS

The correlation coefficients in Table 18.4 indicate that in most cases there was no correlation between the measures of Table 18.3 at the 5% probability level, at which values of the correlation coefficients should exceed 0.6319 for correlation to be established [42]. This implies that none of the images of the different scenes could be described by a single set of related numerical values and that scenes are described by a set of unique values. Significant correlation coefficients are shown in bold; they indicate correlations between bandpass power and entropy, mean pixel value and skewness, mean pixel value and entropy, variance and skewness. This implies that relationships exist between these numerical attributes of the images.

Generally it appears that images may best be described by a number of unique numerical attributes. A *scene metric*, combining different values, to characterise different scene types requires further consideration as an aid to rationalising the selection of scenes for evaluation of image quality. For simplicity this investigation has used mainly one-dimensional data, although power and variance have a two-dimensional character. This initial evaluation assumes isotropic scene radiance data which will also have undergone some tone compression in the capturing and subsequent scanning stages. Further work is necessary to evaluate more complete two-dimensional data for a greater number of images, using these and other numerical values in attempting to characterise images of scenes.

Although image quality metrics may work well for individual scenes and test targets, the scene dependency of metrics still poses a problem. Image quality metrics have value in improving the quality of components in imaging chains but the single-number approach should be treated with caution in multichannel applications, and particularly when applied to digital imaging systems.

ACKNOWLEDGEMENT

We gratefully acknowledge the support of the Leverhulme Trust for a fellowship in support of this work.

REFERENCES

1. Barten, P. G. J. (1999) *Contrast Sensitivity of the Human Eye and Its Effects on Image Quality*. SPIE Press, Bellingham, USA.
2. Engeldrum, P. G. (1995) A framework for image quality models. *J. Imaging Sci. Technol.*, **39**, 312–318.
3. Miyake, Y., Inoue, S., Tamota, Y. and Kubo, S. (1984) Evaluation of image quality of digital pictures obtained by drum scanner and photo-printer. In *Photographic and Electronic Image Quality*, H. Graves (ed.), pp. 62–79. Royal Photographic Society, Bath, England.
4. Jacobson, R. E. (1993) Approaches to total quality for the assessment of imaging systems. *Information Services and Use*, **13**, 235–246.
5. Silverstein, D. A. and Farrell, J. E. (1996) The relationship between image fidelity and image quality. *Proc. ICIP–96*, Vol. 1, pp. 881–884.
6. Ahumada, A. J. and Null, C. H. (1993) Image quality: a multidimensional problem. In *Digital Images and Human Vision*, A. B. Watson (ed.), pp. 141–148. MIT Press, Cambridge.
7. Engeldrum, P. G. (2000) *Psychometric Scaling: A Toolkit for Imaging Systems Development*, p. 1. Imcotek Press, Winchester MA.
8. Ford, A. F. (1999) Determination of compressed image quality. In *Colour Imaging: Vision and Technology*, L. MacDonald and M. R. Luo (eds), Ch. 16. John Wiley, Chichester.
9. Klein, S. A. (1993) Image quality and image compression: a psychophysicist's viewpoint. In *Digital Images and Human Vision*, A. B. Watson (ed.), pp. 74–98. MIT Press, Cambridge MA.
10. Ford, A. F. (1997) Relationships between image quality and image compression. PhD thesis, University of Westminster, London.

11. Triantaphillidou, S. (2001) Aspects of image quality in the digitization of photographic collections. PhD thesis, University of Westminster, London.
12. Yendrikhovskij, S., Blommaert, F. J. and de Ridder, H. (1999) Towards perceptually optimal colour reproduction of natural scenes. In *Colour Imaging: Vision and Technology*, L. MacDonald and M. R. Luo (eds), Ch. 18. John Wiley, Chichester.
13. Engeldrum, P. G. (1995). A framework for image quality models, *J. Imaging Sci. Technol.*, **39**, 312–318.
14. Barten, P. G. J. (1992) Physical model for the contrast sensitivity of the human eye. *Proc. SPIE*, **1666**, 57–72.
15. Watanabe, A., Mori, T., Nagata, S. and Hiwatashi, K. (1968) Spatial sine-wave responses of the human visual system. *Vision Research*, **9**, 1245–1263.
16. Jacobson, R. E. (1995) An evaluation of image quality metrics. *J. Photogr. Sci.*, **43**, 7–16.
17. Farrell, J. E. (1999) Image quality evaluation. In *Colour Imaging: Vision and Technology*, L. MacDonald and M. R. Luo (eds), Ch. 15. John Wiley, Chichester.
18. Kriss, M. A. (1998) Trade-off between aliasing artifacts and sharpness in assessing image quality. *Proc. Image Processing, Image Quality, Image Capture Systems Conference 1998*, pp. 247–256.
19. ANSI (1988) American national standard for human factors engineering of visual display of terminal workstations. ANSI/HFS Standard 100-1998. Human Factors Society, Santa Monica CA.
20. Gerfelder, N. and Müller, W. (1999) Objective quality estimation for digital images in multimedia environments. In *Colour Imaging: Vision and Technology*, L. MacDonald and M. R. Luo (eds), Ch. 17. John Wiley, Chichester.
21. Higgins, G. C. (1977) Image quality criteria. *J. Appl. Photogr. Engng*, **3**, 53–60.
22. Töpfer, K. and Jacobson, R. E. (1993) The relationship between objective and subjective image quality criteria. *J. Information Recording Materials*, **21**, 5–27.
23. Barten, P. G. J. (1990) Evaluation of subjective image quality with the square-root integral method. *J. Opt. Soc. Am.*, **7**, 2024–2031.
24. Barten, P. G. J. (1991) Evaluation of the effect of noise on subjective image quality. *Proc. SPIE*, **1453**, 2–15.
25. Jacobson, R. E., Ford, A. M. and Attridge, G. G. (1997) Evaluation of the effects of compression on the quality of images on a soft display. *Proc. SPIE*, **3016**, 114–125.
26. Eskicioglu, A. M. and Fisher, P. S. (1995) Image quality measures and their performance. *IEEE Trans. Commun.*, **43**, 2959–2965.
27. Stevens, S. S. (1946) On the theory of scales of measurement. *Science*, **103**, 677–680.
28. Guilford, J. P. (1954) *Psychometric Methods*. McGraw-Hill, New York.
29. Baird, J. C. and Elliot, N. (1978) *Fundamentals of Scaling and Psychophysics*. John Wiley, New York.
30. Bartleson, C. J. and Grum, F. (eds) (1984) *Optical Radiation Measurements*, Vol. 5, *Visual Measurements*. Academic Press, New York.
31. Engeldrum, P. G. (2000). *Psychometric Scaling: A Toolkit for Imaging Systems Development*. Imcotek Press, Winchester MA.
32. Malone, D. (1973) In *SPSE Handbook of Photographic Science and Engineering*, W. Thomas (ed.), pp. 1113–1132. John Wiley, New York.
33. Boynton, R. M. (1984) In *Optical Radiation Measurements*, Vol. 5, *Visual Measurements*, C. J. Bartleson and F. Grum (eds), p. 360. Academic Press, New York.
34. Zwick, D. M. (1984) Psychometric terms used in category scales of image quality attributes. *Proc. RPS Symposium on Photographic and Electronic Image Quality*, Cambridge, October 1984, pp. 46–55.
35. Corey, G. P., Clayton, M. J. and Cupery, K. N. (1982) Scene dependence on image quality. *Photogr. Sci. Engng*, **27**, 9–13.
36. Frieser, H. and Biedermann, K. (1963) Experiments on image quality in relation to the modulation transfer function and graininess of photographs. *Photogr. Sci. Engng*, **7**, 28–33.

37. Engeldrum, P. G. (2000) *Psychometric Scaling: A Toolkit for Imaging Systems Development*, p. 21. Imcotek Press, Winchester MA.
38. ISO 12 640:1997 Graphic technology – Prepress digital data exchange – CMYK standard colour image data (CMYK/SCID).
39. Triantaphillidou, S. (1998) Preferred tone reproduction of images on soft displays. *Proc. International Congress on Imaging Science, ICPS '98*, Vol. 3, pp. 204–209.
40. Gonzales, R. C. and Woods, R. E. (1993) *Digital Image Processing*. Addison-Wesley, Reading MA.
41. Cohen, S. S. (1988) *Practical Statistics*, pp. 81, 88. Edward Arnold, London.
42. Siegel, A. F. (1988) *Statistics and Data Analysis: An Introduction*, p. 430. John Wiley, New York.

19

Image quality and colour categorisation

Sergej Yendrikhovskij

19.1 THE SCIENCE OF IMAGE QUALITY

The first part of this chapter explores some of the methodological and theoretical aspects of image quality (IQ). The term 'image quality' will be understood here as the subjective impression of how well image content is rendered and/or reproduced. The next sections analyse the subjective phenomenon of IQ in relation to the objective methodology of science. Science can be broadly defined as the body of knowledge that provides through observation, experiment and induction a reliable explanation of phenomena with reference to physical world [1]. Furthermore, science usually includes a set of auxiliary theories, empirical conditions describing the experimental context of the research, and the main substantive theory [2].

19.1.1 Theories of image quality

It would not be an exaggeration to say that the present progress of IQ research would be difficult to achieve without the progress of psychophysics and psychometrics [3]. The ability to measure, i.e. to quantify in a consistent and meaningful way, the attribute

Colour Image Science, edited by L.W. MacDonald and M.R. Luo.

under investigation is a necessary condition for any scientific research. For an observer, presumably, there is not much difference between the two judgements: 'image of a high quality' and 'image of a quality that equals 9 on the scale from 0 to 10'. However, from a scientific standpoint there is an important distinction because the latter judgement includes an origin and a unit that can be related to another origin and a unit of a physical scale. This relationship can be analysed for consistency or correlation.

Early studies on IQ investigated what type of scale (ordinal, interval or ratio) provided more stable results, and whether intervals of these scales were subjectively invariant. For example, Jones and Marks [4] found that judgements on the ratio scale were more consistent than on the ordinal scale and provided more meaningful intervals in the numerical responses.

The focus of recent studies on IQ has shifted towards development of computational metrics that predict IQ in the form of a single number correlating with observer judgements. The IQ metrics are generally derived from physical parameters of images and basic properties of the human visual system (HVS). Therefore, imaging science and visual models are also among the main auxiliary theories of IQ research. Overviews of some modern IQ metrics, image attributes and relevant HVS functions were given, for example, by Jacobson [5] and Farrell *et al.* [6].

Most of the current IQ metrics do not take into account cognitive aspects of IQ. Basically, these metrics provide an answer to the question, "What do people *accept* to see in images?" To answer other important questions, for instance, "What do people *expect* to see in images?" and "What do people *prefer* to see in images?" one has to consider high-level cognitive phenomena such as memory and preference. At present, cognitive models are not yet widely used in IQ research. However, this might be changed in the future. There are few cognitive models that can already be used as auxiliary theories of IQ research.

The phenomena of memory and preference have been studied extensively in colour science. Several experiments revealed a discrepancy between memory colours, preferred colours and actual colours for various objects [7–11] as described in Chapter 2. There was evidence of a significant increase in saturation of memory colours for some object categories (e.g. grass, sky and food items). However, other categories showed no such shift (e.g. sand, skin), or showed it in the opposite direction (e.g. concrete). To explain these results, Newhall *et al.* [8] proposed that the colour shift in memory and preference judgements was caused by the influence of prototypical object colours. Recently, Yendrikhovskij *et al.* [12] developed a computational model of prototypical object colours, which was used to analyse perceived naturalness [13] and quality [14] of colour images.

Prototypes, or the most typical examples of object categories, are presumably developed through the process of generalisation from the population of apparent objects seen in the past. The theory on generalisation proposed by Shepard [15] provides an explanation for generalisation principles that govern the organism's behaviour. The process of generalisation is closely related to another cognitive process, that of categorisation. The general recognition theory [16], which is one of the most advanced categorisation models, demonstrated that the structure of natural categories can be effectively modelled by a multivariate normal (Gaussian) distribution. A comprehensive overview of different categorisation models in perception and cognition can be found in the literature [16].

A computational model of colour categorisation is presented in the second part of this chapter.

19.1.2 Experimental context of image quality

Fifty years ago MacAdam [17] proposed the following programme for IQ research: (1) vary images in a systematic manner; (2) perform visual judgements; (3) analyse the judgements and physical measurements for correlation; (4) find the optima for different conditions; (5) find exceptions; and (6) improve the model of the optima. This is the programme which in general can be found in many current studies of IQ.

There are at least two methodological problems with this programme. The first problem concerns the impact of experimental context on observer response. It was shown that observer's response is determined not only by the presented stimulus, but also by experimental procedure and other stimuli in the experiment [18]. The detailed analysis of the context effect in psychophysical judgements was done by Poulton [19]. The consequences of this effect for IQ research were discussed by De Ridder [20]. Basically, the context effect decreases the internal validity of IQ research: there is no guarantee that the obtained response can be attributed solely to the corresponding image and not to other images in the experiment. In most cases (when an experiment contains more than one stimulus) the context effect cannot be avoided. However, it can be modelled. Several studies have modelled the context effect by including the additional information about the stimulus set (frequency of each stimulus, stimulus sequence, etc.) in psychophysical models [18, 21]. Such an 'integral' psychophysics [21] aims to investigate the whole effect of stimulus and context rather than effect of the stimulus alone.

The second methodological problem, which is especially important for IQ research, concerns individual and cultural differences. There is evidence that magnitude estimation of the same stimulus might vary between individuals [22], between different cultures [23], and (in the case of IQ) between expert and naive observers [24]. The individual differences decrease the external validity of IQ research: there is no guarantee that the response found in a particular experiment can be generalised across the whole population of potential observers. Similar to the context effect, individual differences cannot be avoided but they can be modelled. In general, the overall IQ judgements can be modelled as a weighted sum of essentially the same underlying attributes with the weights varying for different individuals (groups, cultures, etc.). For example, recently [25] it was shown that the overall IQ judgements can be modelled as a weighted sum of the brightness rendering judgements and chromatic rendering judgements. The weights derived by linear regression analysis were observer dependent: some observers associated their quality judgements primarily with optimality of brightness rendering, others with optimality of chromatic rendering.

19.2 SUBSTANTIVE THEORIES OF IMAGE QUALITY

The auxiliary theories of IQ such as psychophysics, psychometrics, visual science, imaging science and cognitive science are not the substantive theory of IQ. Psychometrics, for example, is just a method to relate the psychological impression and the numerical representation, which was initially applied to measure 'attitude towards movies' [26]. Numerical representation is a significant but not sufficient requirement of science. A variable does not have scientific value just because it can be represented on a numerical scale [27]. A good substantive theory should understand the ultimate nature of the phenomenon and determine its underlying dimensions. This can be accomplished from two perspectives: bottom-up and top-down.

The bottom-up approach is largely based on experimental research of physical parameters that underlie IQ. In contrast, the top-down approach focuses on analytical research of the perceptual constraints that determine IQ. Furthermore, even if a piece of research investigates the relationships between overall IQ and underlying perceptual attributes, it still might be bottom-up research when these attributes are reported by subjects and derived *a posteriori* from experimental results. In top-down research, the perceptual attributes are usually derived *a priori* by researchers from a theoretical model of IQ. Both types of research are important and can be combined in a general framework of IQ [25].

19.2.1 Bottom-up perspective

A good example of the bottom-up perspective on IQ is the ADONIS project [28]. The main goal of the project was to develop an integral method for determining the overall perceptual IQ of imaging systems (e.g. displays) and specify the perceptual factors that substantially contribute to IQ. To achieve this goal, a model proposed by Nijenhuis [29] was adopted.

The model starts with consideration of a display plus a viewing environment. The display–environment system can be described by a set of physical parameters: a luminance distribution on the screen, intensity of ambient lighting, etc. These physical parameters are transformed by the visual system into a set of perceptual attributes: brightness, sharpness, colourfulness, etc. The perceptual attributes have a sensory strength depending on the magnitude of the physical attributes and the properties of the HVS. The set of individual sensory strengths with different weighting factors determines a 'total' strength, which forms the basis for the overall assessment of IQ.

One of the important outcomes of the ADONIS project was the development of the RaPID (rapid perceptual image description) method [28]. The method assumes that a high-level sensory attribute, like IQ, is the combination of a number of sub-attributes, which can be described by observers in everyday language. A panel of consumers was asked to list all words that they could think of in terms of IQ. Afterwards they were trained to use these words in scaling judgements of displayed images. The results of these judgements were well correlated with measurements for some physical displays.

The analysis of the experimental results of the ADONIS project showed that the consumers often expressed their judgements in 'negative' rather than 'positive' terms. For example, while judging the displays, they more frequently used the term 'unsharpness' rather than 'sharpness'. This suggests that the quality of a display is more likely judged on the basis of weak points and not on the basis of the strong points. Based on (1) this finding, (2) the close inverse relationship between quality and impairment judgements [29], and (3) the evidence that the impairment terms produce more regular and context-independent scales than the quality terms [4], it is appealing to think about IQ as something opposite to impairment. From this perspective, an ideal image is simply an image without noticeable distortions and its quality can be derived from lack of visibility of annoying artefacts. However, this view raises doubts about the existence of IQ phenomena *per se*. Moreover, from this view it is difficult to explain why some distortions (i.e. deviations from the original) are preferred by observers. For instance, it was shown that subjects have a small but significant preference for more colourful images, even though they realise these images look somewhat unnatural [30, 31, 14]. To explain this finding, one can take a top-down perspective on IQ and try to understand the perceptual constraints imposed on it, and why they are important for an observer.

19.2.2 Top-down perspective

Any top-down model that aims to explicitly describe a phenomenon should consider the ontological aspect (what *is* the phenomenon), the functionality aspect (what is the phenomenon *for*), and the causality aspect (what is the phenomenon *caused by*). These aspects were partly discussed by Janssen and Blommaert [31] in a computational model of IQ. In contrast to the traditional 'signal processing' approach towards IQ, they regard the processing of images as the processing of visual information about the outside world that has to be reconstructed in a visual representation and subsequently matched with memory representations. From this perspective, image quality can be defined as 'the degree to which the image can be successfully exploited by the observer' [31].

Janssen and Blommaert argued that an image with successful exploitation or an image of 'high' quality should satisfy two constraints: usefulness and naturalness. Usefulness was described as the precision of the visual representation. It can be related to the discriminability of items in the image. Naturalness was described as the degree of correspondence between the visual representation and the memory representation. It can be related to recognisability of items in the image. Since the usefulness and naturalness constraints might conflict with each other, the quality of an image can be modelled as a compromise between them. Note that the outcomes of such a compromise may require exaggeration of certain features of the image (e.g. by increasing brightness or colour contrast), resulting in a less natural but more useful appearance of the image. This explains why some people prefer more colourful images, even though they realise these images look somewhat unnatural.

The model of Janssen and Blommaert is a refinement of an earlier model of the colour domain by Yendrikhovskij *et al.* [14], who elaborated on understanding, measuring and optimising the perceived colour quality of natural images. The colour IQ model assumes that when people look at images containing familiar categories of objects, two primary factors shape their subjective impression of how optimal colours are reproduced: colours should be perceived both realistically (naturalness constraint), and distinctly (colourfulness constraint). This hypothesis was tested in a number of experiments with images displayed on a cathode ray tube (CRT). It was shown that quality judgements can be well modelled as a linear combination of the colourfulness and naturalness judgements. Yendrikhovskij *et al.* [14] also specified the naturalness, colourfulness and quality indices on the basis of statistical parameters of the colour point distribution across the images in the CIELUV colour space. The proposed indices were used to optimise the perceived quality of colour reproduction of natural scenes.

19.3 A GENERAL MODEL OF IMAGE QUALITY

The classical (signal processing) approach and the new (information processing) approach have different views on IQ. However, both approaches highlight important requirements that determine IQ. These requirements can be used to develop a general IQ model. An attempt to develop such a model has recently been made [32]. This section describes a slightly modified version. In essence the model assumes existence of the three major dimensions determining IQ: fidelity, usefulness and naturalness (FUN). The overall IQ can be modelled as a weighted sum of the three FUN attributes with their weights ranging from 0 to 1. Different types of image might require different combinations of the weights (Figure 19.1).

19.3.1 Fidelity

Fidelity is the degree of apparent match of the reproduced image with the external reference, i.e. original. This is the constraint related to the classical IQ research on fidelity metrics, visibility of annoying artefacts and perceptual error measure. The original can be a natural scene (landscape, family, etc.), an image from another device (display, printer, etc.) or any unprocessed image (e.g. unsampled, uncoded, uncompressed).

Ideally, an image with the highest degree of fidelity should give an exact impression about the original. An example of the device that produces such images is a perfect mirror. When identical rendering is not possible, the closest corresponding appearance has to be given. For the colour domain, the distinction made by Hunt [33] between the spectral, colorimetric, exact, equivalent, and corresponding levels of colour reproduction is especially important here. The fidelity requirement is crucial for proofs, catalogues, fine art, etc. (Figure 19.1).

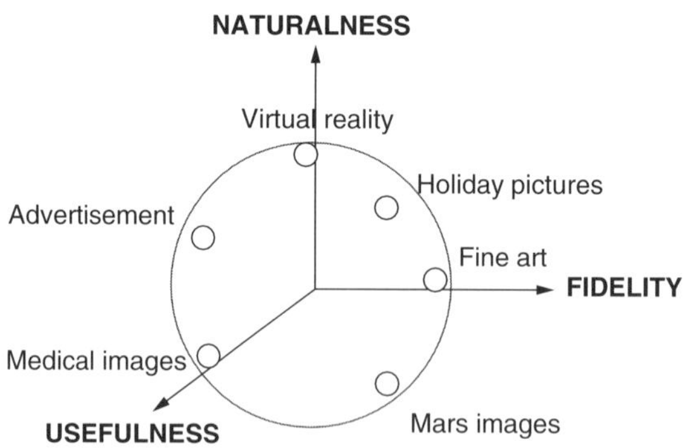

Figure 19.1 The relative importance of the FUN dimensions on the quality of different image types.

19.3.2 Usefulness

Usefulness is the degree of apparent suitability of the reproduced image to satisfy the corresponding task. An exact reproduction of a man in a fog might have a very high degree of fidelity but a very low degree of usefulness if the task is to recognise the person. Details of his facial expression would probably be indistinguishable. The degree of usefulness depends on the needs of the viewer, i.e. 'rendering intents' [34]. An image with red letters on a green background might be very effective for attracting attention in Christmas cards, but not for reading newspapers.

Ideally, an image with the highest degree of usefulness should present the maximum number of distinguishable items for a certain task. Mathematical expressions for an objective measure of usefulness – the maximum discriminability of observed items – have recently been proposed by Janssen and Blommaert [35, 36]. Examples of devices that increase usefulness of an image are microscopes, telescopes and reading glasses. Many contrast enhancement algorithms also increase the usefulness of an image. The usefulness requirement is crucial for medical images, military night-vision images, most remote-sensing images, etc. But for some astrophysical images, such as pictures obtained from the Mars mission, it would probably be desirable to keep the fidelity requirements at least partially valid in order to see the true colour of this planet (Figure 19.1).

For the colour domain, the degree of usefulness can be related to the level of colour contrast and saturation of images [14]. A resemblance between increasing saturation and using cosmetics stimulated a proposal for the so-called flattery index [37], as a special case of the colour rendering index [38]. Illuminants that render object colours with a level of saturation higher than the actual colours were argued to have a high 'flattery index'.

19.3.3 Naturalness

Naturalness is the degree of apparent match between the reproduced image and internal references, e.g. memory prototypes. The influence of this attribute on the quality judgements becomes substantial when a viewer has no immediate access to the original (external reference): when he/she is watching TV, looking at photos, browsing the Internet, etc. The importance of internal references is especially significant when the original does not exist in the real world: when the viewer is watching images from virtual reality, computer games, cartoons, etc. These types of image are usually 'prototypical' and somehow 'idealised' representations of the real/fictitious world.

For the colour domain, naturalness judgements have been systematically studied [13, 14, 31, 35], and attempts made to develop a colour naturalness index (CNI) that evaluates the perceived naturalness of reproduced colours in accordance with observer judgements. CNI gives a measure of the similarity between the colours of objects presented in an image and the prototypical colours of the corresponding object categories. The previous calculations of CNI [13, 14] were based on three internal references only. The next step would be to have 11 references (i.e. red, yellow, green, blue, brown, orange, pink, purple, black, white and grey) using basic colour categories found by Boynton and Olson [39].

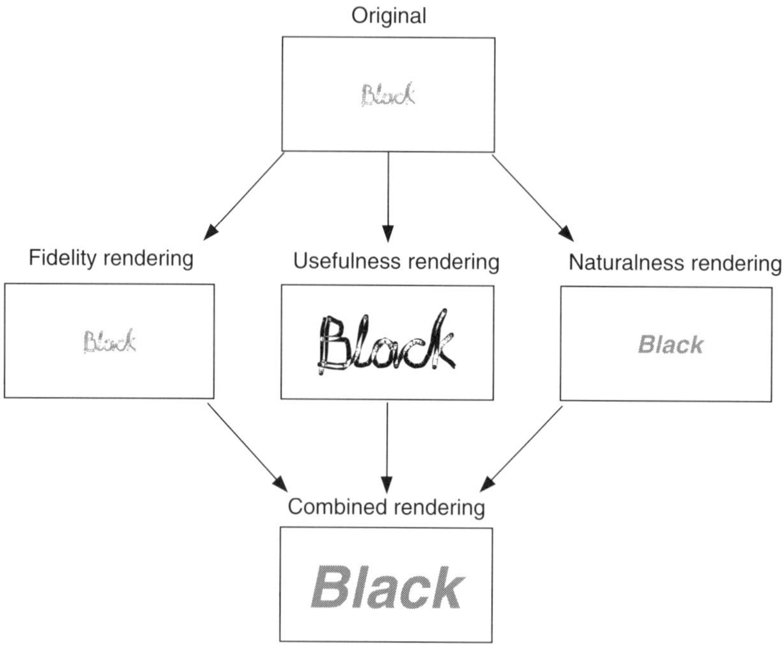

Figure 19.2 Demonstration of the three FUN strategies for rendering an image with a handwritten word 'Black'.

To summarise, let us consider the three FUN strategies for rendering an image with a handwritten word 'Black' (Figure 19.2). A device with a high degree of fidelity would provide a facsimile rendering of this word. A device with a high degree of usefulness would give a magnified and contrast-enhanced ('easy reading') rendering of the word. A device with a high degree of naturalness would provide a prototypical (e.g. italic) rendering of the word. Evidently, a combination of the three strategies is also possible. In this particular example, the combined FUN rendering includes the font colour of the fidelity version, the font size of the usefulness version, and the font style of the prototypical version.

19.4 COLOUR CATEGORISATION

This section describes a cognitive model that might be used as an auxiliary theory of future IQ research. More specifically, the following research goes into detail about the cognitive process of colour categorisation and discusses this process in relation to colour imaging science. What is colour categorisation? How can the process of colour categorisation be modelled? How to compute colour categories? The next sections explore these questions and elaborate on understanding, modelling and computing colour categories based on the colour statistics of natural images.

19.4.1 Understanding colour categories

What is colour categorisation?

Colour categorisation can be defined as the grouping of colour sensations into classes 'by means of which non-identical stimuli can be treated as equivalent' [40]. In general, this grouping has can be performed at different levels of visuo-cognitive processing. A model described in this chapter focuses on the semantic colour categorisation (i.e. colour naming), which takes place between perceptual and semantic levels.

What is colour categorisation for?

The obvious advantage of colour categorisation is the reduction of the immense differences among perceived colour stimuli to cognitively usable proportions. The magnitude of this reduction is enormous: from more than 2 million perceptually distinguishable colours [41] to approximately 30 colours that can be internally represented and identified in cognitive space [42]. One of the useful computational analogies that can be associated with categorisation is vector quantisation in information theory. Vector quantisation is a data compression method where a set of data points is encoded by a reduced set of reference vectors, the code book [43].

What is colour categorisation caused by?

The external (ecological) origin of the particular categorical organisation of colours has been discussed by Shepard [44], who stated that this organisation most likely reflects something about natural groupings of the surface reflection distributions of biologically significant objects or something about the way in which terrestrial illumination has most typically varied during evolutionary history. However, it is important to stress that surface reflectances and illumination spectra are not directly available to observers. As a result, the categorical colour organisation was argued to have an internal (biological) basis and originate from metrical properties of the perceptual colour space [45].

This chapter explicitly assumes that the structure of colour category systems originates from the statistical structure of the perceived colour environment. Note that this assumption combines the ecological and biological factors into one concept, which recognises that colour categorisation is mutually determined by the external properties of the outside world and the internal properties of the sensorial system. From this perspective, the colour categories of a goldfish, for example, should be different from those of a human due to differences in both environment and visual receptors.

19.4.2 Modelling colour categorisation

This section describes a computational model of colour categorisation. The model consists of five major components: physical environment, colour perception, perceived colour environment, colour categorisation, and colour category system (Figure 19.3).

How can the physical environment be modelled?

The physical environment defines any actual state of nature as observed at a particular moment, e.g. a man sitting in a chair, a collection of fruit, a landscape. Since it is nearly

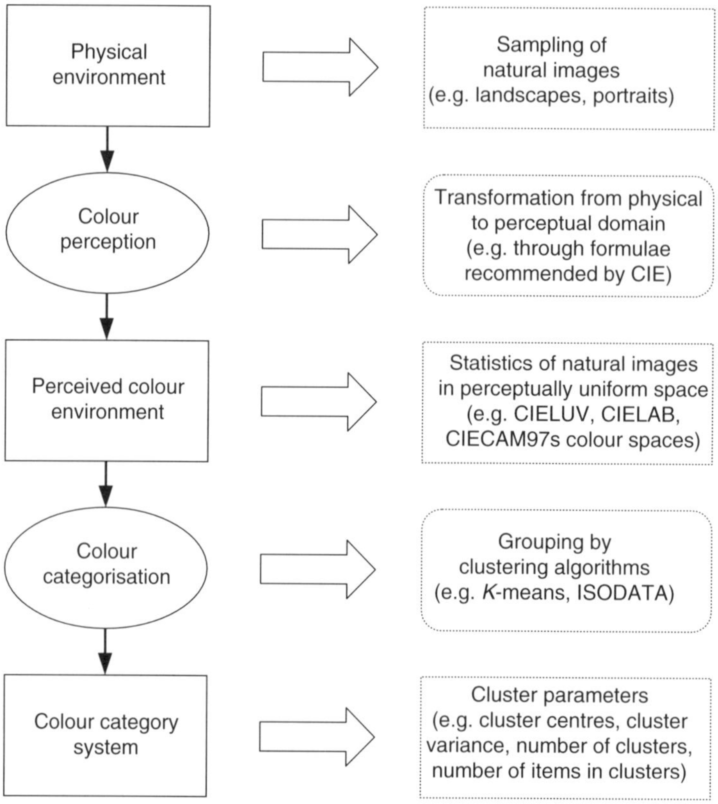

Figure 19.3 Computational model of colour categorisation.

impossible to determine the physical environment directly, one can model it by a large set of natural images. In line with this idea, a set of 630 natural images was collected. The images were taken from photo CDs and TV, and scanned from books about colour in nature. They represented typical categories of scene: portraits, landscapes, natural objects, etc. The whole set of images contained 5 424 000 pixels. These pixels were randomised using a special routine of the CANTATA visual programming environment for the Khoros system [46]. Subsequently, a sampling of 10 000 pixels was chosen for further processing as shown in Figure 19.4.

How can the process of colour perception be modelled?

The process of colour perception can be modelled as a transformation from a physical domain to perceptually uniform colour space. As a suitable approximation one can choose the CIE 1976 $L^*u^*v^*$ colour space (CIELUV for short), because it has an associated perceptually uniform chromaticity diagram. Certainly, other colour spaces (e.g. CIELAB) and appearance models (e.g. CIECAM97s) can be used [47]. The R, G, B signal values

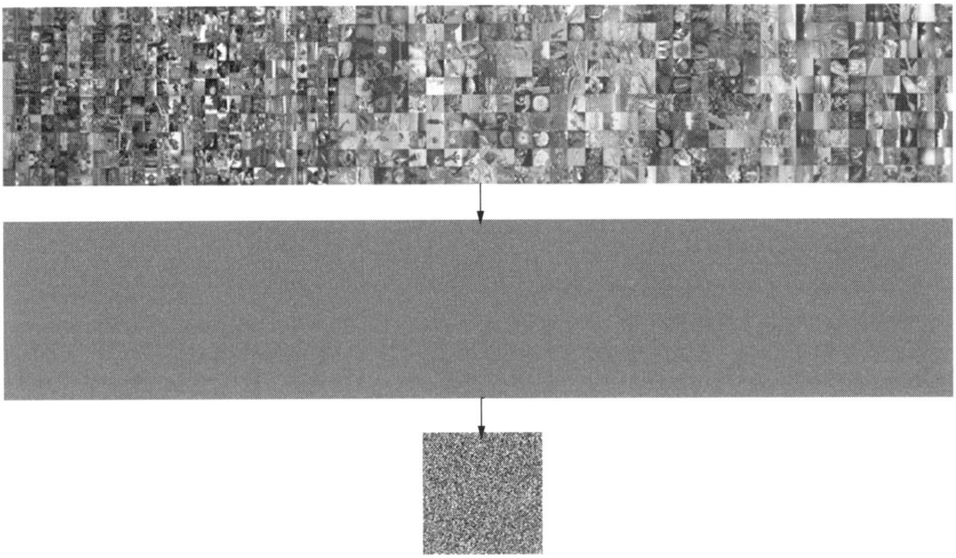

Figure 19.4 (top) The set of natural images collected for the colour categorisation research; (middle) its randomised version; and (bottom) the sampling of 10 000 pixels used to compute colour categories. Reproduced by permission of Eastman Kodak Company. See also Colour Plate 11.

representing the sampling of 10 000 randomly chosen pixels were transformed to r, g, b luminance values, then to the X, Y, Z tristimulus values, and eventually, to the L^*, u^*, v^* colour coordinates. The transformation into the CIELUV colour space was made using standard formulas [38] based on the assumption that the images were to be shown on a CRT display with PAL (European colour television) standard characteristics.

How can the perceived colour environment be modelled?

The perceived colour environment can be modelled as colour point distributions of the set of natural images in perceptual and approximately uniform colour space. The sampling of 10 000 randomly chosen pixels representing the whole set of collected images in the CIELUV colour space is shown in Figure 19.5. The normalised and cumulative histograms of the CIE lightness (L^*), hue (H) and chroma (C^*) values are presented in Figure 19.6. For comparison, Figure 19.6 also shows L^*, H and C^* histograms of 10 000 pixels from an image with uniformly distributed RGB grey values. The uniform (white noise) RGB image was created using the CANTATA visual programming environment for the Khoros system [46].

Apparently, the distribution of the colour statistics from the natural images is not spread uniformly in the CIELUV colour space (Figure 19.5), especially in the hue and chroma dimensions (Figure 19.6). Most of the distribution points are concentrated around the lightness (L^*) axis of the CIELUV colour space. This area represents achromatic colours, i.e. colours of chromaticity close to reference white. Two other areas with a

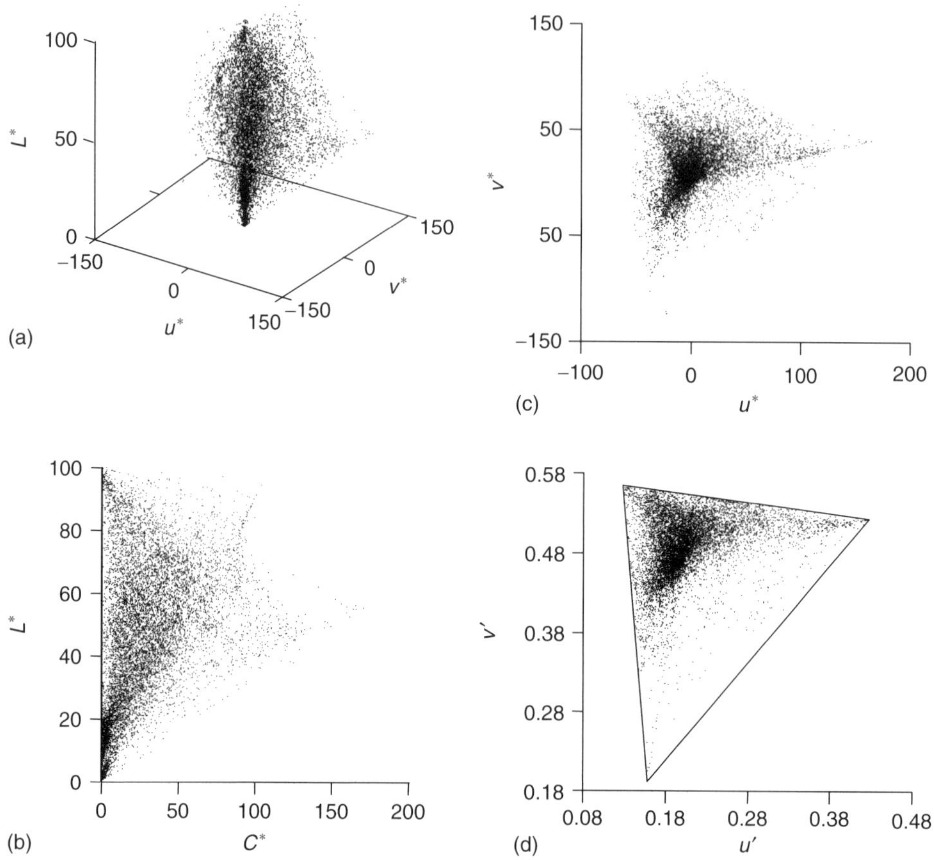

Figure 19.5 Random sampling of the colour statistics of 630 natural images: (a) the CIE $L^*u^*v^*$ colour space, (b) the L^*C^* diagram, (c) the u^*v^* diagram, (d) the $u'v'$ diagram. The solid line indicates the PAL TV colour gamut.

high frequency distribution can be identified in Figures 19.5 and 19.6. These two areas correspond to the red–green and blue regions of the CIELUV colour space. There are very few colours in the green–blue and red–blue regions of the CIELUV colour space.

These data agree well with the measurements reported by Howard and Burnidge [48], Hendley and Hecht [49], Burton and Moorhead [50]. They show that naturally occurring colours are distributed within a restricted area of the chromaticity diagram, and that there are three important groups of colours in nature. Water, sky and distant objects fall within a blue region; green plants fall within a yellow–green region; earth and dried vegetation

Figure 19.6 Normalised (left) and cumulative (right) histograms of the CIE lightness (L^*), hue (H) and chroma (C^*) values; solid curves are for the natural images and dashed curves are for the image with uniformly distributed RGB grey values.

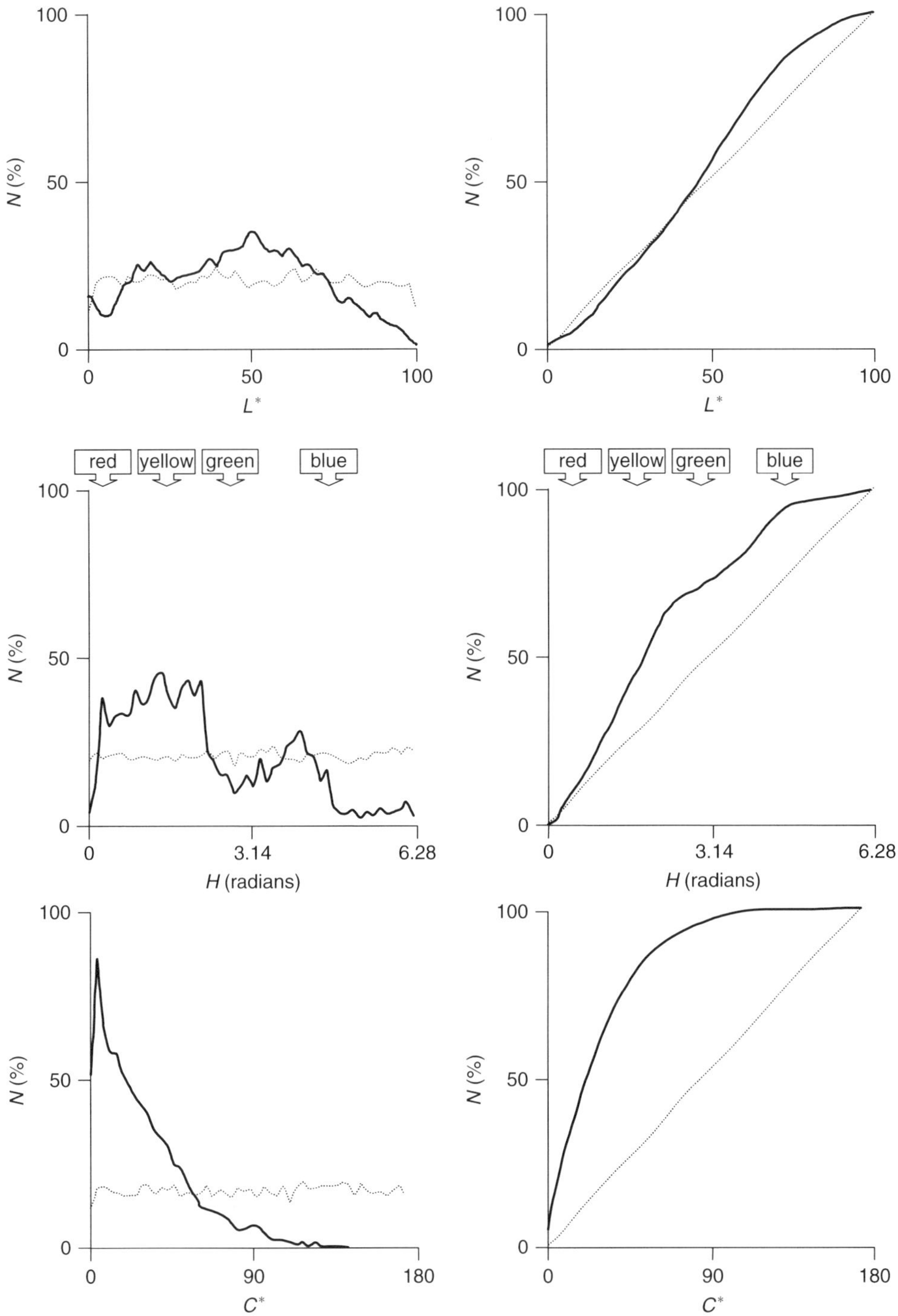
N (%)
L*
red
yellow
green
blue
H (radians)
C*
0
50
100
3.14
6.28
90
180

are yellow to orange-red. The last group also includes the average colour of human complexions, which have a dominant wavelength close to 590 nm [51].

How can the process of colour categorisation be modelled?

The categorisation process can be considered as a grouping of similar items into classes. A relevant computational analogy that can be associated with this process is vector quantisation in information theory. One can assume that the colour categorisation is based on the minimum distance criterion. This implies that points with minimum distance to each other in the colour space are likely to belong to the same colour category. Therefore the process of colour categorisation can be modelled through grouping of the natural image statistics by a clustering technique such as the K-means or ISODATA clustering algorithms.

In general, the K-means algorithm is based on the minimisation of the sum of the squared distances from all points in a cluster to the cluster centre. In the case of image analysis, a K-means routine of the CANTATA visual programming environment for the Khoros system [46] can be used. This routine converts an input image into vectors of equal size and performs the K-means clustering algorithm on the vectors using the K initial cluster centres. After K initial cluster centres are chosen, the image vectors are iteratively distributed among the K cluster domains. New cluster centres are computed from these results, such that the sum of the squared distances from all points in a cluster to the new cluster centre is minimised.

How can the colour category system be modelled?

In general, the colour category system can be modelled by locations, borders, numbers and weights of colour categories. The location of colour categories can be modelled by location of the cluster centres derived by the K-means clustering algorithm from the statistics of the natural images. The borders of colour categories can be modelled by the cluster variances. The numbers of colour categories can be modelled by the numbers of clusters. The weights of colour categories can be modelled by the numbers of items within the clusters.

19.4.3 Computing colour categories

How can the location of colour categories be computed?

The location of colour categories can be computed from coordinates of cluster centres derived by the K-means clustering algorithm from the colour distribution of the natural images in the CIELUV colour space. Figure 19.7 illustrates 11 cluster centres derived by the CANTATA K-means clustering algorithm from the sampling of 10 000 pixels representing the natural images. The cluster centres are plotted in the CIE u^*v^* and $u'v'$ chromaticity diagram together with the 11 focal colours found by Boynton and Olson [39]. The original focal colours were derived by Boynton and Olson on the basis of single-word colour naming of 424 colour samples from the OSA space. The coordinates of focal

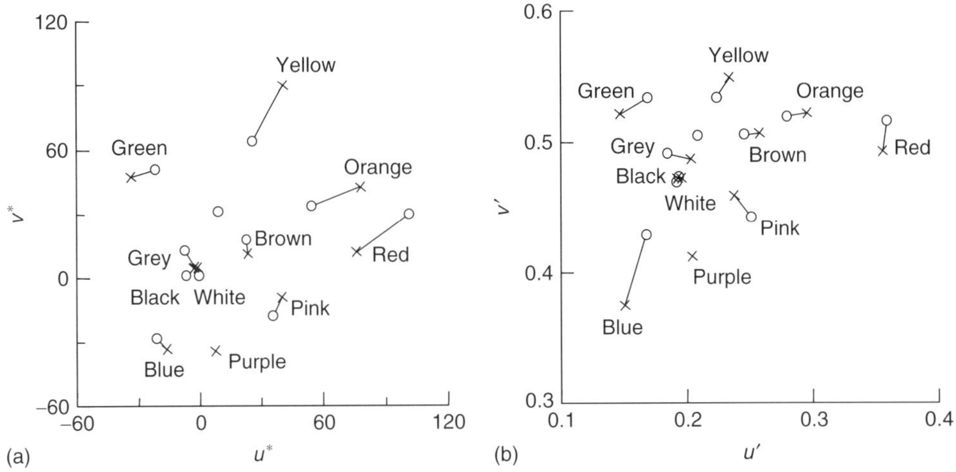

Figure 19.7 Open circles show 11 cluster centres derived from the colour statistics of natural images and the crosses show focal colours found by Boynton and Olson for (a) the CIE u^*v^* diagram and (b) the $u'v'$ chromaticity diagram.

colours shown in Figure 19.7 were obtained through the sequential transformation of the OSA L, j, g values to the CIE Y, x, y values, and eventually to the CIE L^*, u^*, v^* values using standard tables and formulae [38].

The CIE L^*, u^*, v^* coordinates of cluster centres obtained by the K-means clustering algorithm and focal colours found by Boynton and Olson are presented in Table 19.1. Note that the green-yellow cluster obtained by the K-means clustering algorithm does not correspond to the 'purple' focal colour found by Boynton and Olson. A linear regression analysis demonstrates that the coordinates of 10 focal colours and 10 corresponding cluster centres are similar: $r = 0.762$ for lightness (L^*) values, $r = 0.999$ for hue (H) values, $r = 0.876$ for chroma (C^*) values, $r = 0.900$ for saturation (s) values. These results support the idea that the structure of colour categories originates from the statistical structure of the perceived environment.

How can the order of colour categories be computed?

Berlin and Kay [52] have suggested that if languages are ordered according to number of colour category terms, the evolutionary sequence of these terms is generally as follows (in reference to English names): (1) black and white; (2) red; (3) green/yellow; (4) yellow/green; (5) blue; (6) brown; (7) pink, purple, orange, and grey. In other words, if a language has only three colour terms, they are most likely to correspond to English white, black and red, instead of say pink, green and brown. The evolutionary order of colour words shows a remarkable consistency across many languages. The same order was found in the rate of usage of colour words within the English language by McManus [53], who studied the frequency of the colour terms in half a million cases of literature and science databases.

Table 19.1 The *CIE* $L^*u^*v^*$ coordinates for focal colours found by Boynton and Olson and cluster centres obtained by the K-means clustering algorithm from the statistics of the natural images

Name	Colour coordinates	Focal colours found by Boynton and Olson	Cluster centres obtained by the K-means algorithm
	L^*	28.8	15.4
Black	u^*	0.1	−0.8
	v^*	0.5	1.1
	L^*	52.0	43.2
Grey	u^*	0.1	−7.6
	v^*	0.8	12.7
	L^*	83.1	80.0
White	u^*	5.2	−7.2
	v^*	18.8	1.0
	L^*	36.9	48.4
Red	u^*	78.0	101.3
	v^*	12.0	29.9
	L^*	59.0	59.7
Green	u^*	−33.6	−22.0
	v^*	47.4	50.8
	L^*	84.2	75.4
Yellow	u^*	39.9	25.4
	v^*	89.9	64.3
	L^*	26.4	54.2
Blue	u^*	−16.2	−21.2
	v^*	−32.3	−28.0
	L^*	28.7	35.7
Brown	u^*	22.3	22.1
	v^*	14.0	17.7
	L^*	60.1	51.4
Orange	u^*	77.0	54.0
	v^*	41.7	33.9
	L^*	75.3	50.8
Pink	u^*	34.0	35.4
	v^*	−9.5	−17.6
	L^*	38.1	
Purple	u^*	6.9	
	v^*	−34.9	
	L^*		65.2
Green-yellow	u^*		8.4
	v^*		31.3

In general, the order of emergence of the cluster centres resulting from the K-means algorithm is similar to the order of emergence of colour terms described by Berlin and Kay. Figure 19.8 shows a moderately high correlation ($r = 0.710$) between 10 ranks of colour term derived from Berlin and Kay's data and the sum of the two parameters: (1) normalised numbers of items in the clusters and (2) normalised CIELUV distance between the cluster centre and the average centre of all clusters. These results suggest that the development of a colour term across languages might be mutually determined by two constraints: (1) frequency at which colours represented by this term occur in the environment, and (2) perceived remoteness of these colours from colours represented by already existing terms. It is important to emphasise that from this viewpoint, the evolutionary order of colour terms depends on both the external properties of the outside world (frequency of colour occurrence) and the internal properties of the perceptual system (metrics of colour space).

This model might explain the old mysteries of why the colour term 'red' has a particular importance in different cultures and why it evolves before other colour terms in many languages. The possible explanation is simple: the colour term 'red' corresponds to colours that are *both* frequently occurring in the perceived environment of people speaking these languages and substantially distant from other colours in their perceptual spaces. On the one hand, the term 'red' evolves before the term 'purple' because purple colours are relatively rare in nature (Figure 19.5). On the other hand, the term 'red' evolves before the term 'green' because green colours are relatively close to the average centre of all

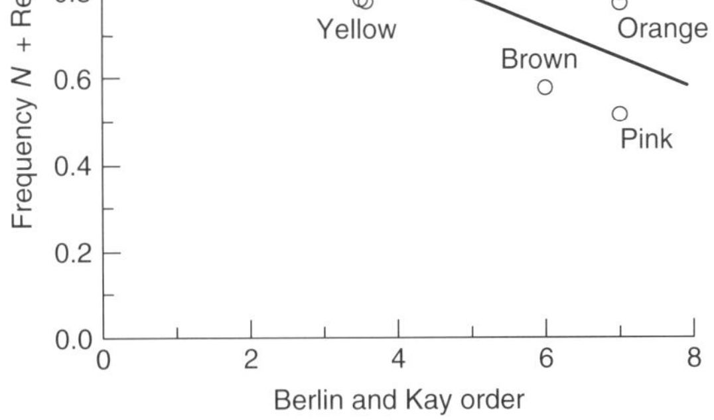

Figure 19.8 Relationship between the colour term ranks found by Berlin and Kay in their psycholinguistic studies and the sum of the normalised frequency N (i.e. numbers of items in the clusters) and normalised remoteness R (i.e. CIELUV distance between the cluster centre and the average centre of all clusters).

colours in the CIELUV colour space and especially in the CIE $u'v'$ chromaticity diagram (Figure 19.5).

How can the number of colour categories be computed?

Rosch [40] has argued that the primary task of category systems is to 'provide maximum information with the least cognitive effort'. This can be achieved if categories represent the perceived world with minimum distortions and minimum complexity. One can assume that the simultaneous minimisation of the distortion and complexity costs (i.e. values) yields an optimal number of colour categories. This is similar to the strategy to optimise jointly distortion errors and a code book complexity function for the design of an optimal vector quantiser proposed by Buhmann and Kuehnel [43]. Considering the colour categorisation process within the framework of optimal vector quantisation is a promising direction for future research. Here is a first step in this direction.

To compute the optimal number of colour categories, we need to specify both a distortion measure and a complexity measure. A widely used distortion measure is the Euclidean distance:

$$D_{i\alpha}(\mathbf{x}_i, \mathbf{y}_\alpha) = |\mathbf{x}_i - \mathbf{y}_\alpha|^2 \tag{19.1}$$

where $D_{i\alpha}(\mathbf{x}_i, \mathbf{y}_\alpha)$ is a difference between a given set of data vectors $\mathbf{x}_i$ and a smaller set of code book vectors $\mathbf{y}_\alpha$. In our case, data vectors $\mathbf{x}_i$ correspond to the CIE L^*, u^*, v^* colour coordinates of 10 000 randomly chosen pixels representing the colour statistics of the natural images before applying the K-means clustering algorithm; code book vectors $\mathbf{y}_\alpha$ correspond to the CIE L^*, u^*, v^* colour coordinates of the cluster centres representing the colour statistics of the natural images after applying the K-means clustering algorithm; $D_{i\alpha}(\mathbf{x}_i, \mathbf{y}_\alpha)$ corresponds to the CIELUV colour difference ΔE^*_{uv} between vectors $\mathbf{x}_i$ and $\mathbf{y}_\alpha$. Figure 19.9(a) shows normalised $D_{i\alpha}(\mathbf{x}_i, \mathbf{y}_\alpha)$ for number of clusters $K = 1, 2, 4, 8, 16$, 32 and 64. Apparently, the bigger the number of clusters, the smaller $D_{i\alpha}(\mathbf{x}_i, \mathbf{y}_\alpha)$.

A detailed analysis of different complexity measures is given by Buhmann and Kuehnel [43]. In general, complexity can be defined by means of entropy from information theory:

$$C(p_\alpha) = -\sum p_\alpha \log p_\alpha \tag{19.2}$$

where $C(p_\alpha)$ is the code book complexity and p_α is the probability of occurrence of the αth value. Figure 19.9(a) shows normalised $C(p_\alpha)$ values, which were calculated by a statistical program of the Khoros system for number of clusters $K = 1, 2, 4, 8, 16, 32$ and 64. Evidently, the bigger the number of clusters, the bigger $C(p_\alpha)$.

To minimise the distortion costs, the number of cluster centres should be increased; to minimise the complexity costs, the number of clusters should be decreased. Since the two constraints conflict with each other, the optimal number of colour categories K can be determined by a compromise between the distortion and complexity costs:

$$K = \min\{\lambda_1 D_{i\alpha}(\mathbf{x}_i, \mathbf{y}_\alpha) + \lambda_2 C(p_\alpha)\} \tag{19.3}$$

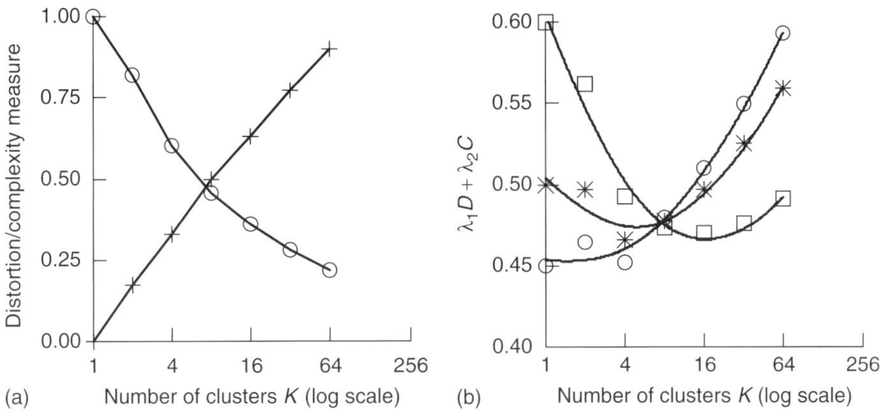

Figure 19.9 (a) Open circles show the normalised distortion D and crosses show the normalised complexity costs C for number of clusters $K = 1, 2, 4, 8, 16, 32, 64$. (b) The sum of the distortion and complexity costs: (circles) $\lambda_1 = 0.4$, $\lambda_2 = 0.6$; (stars) $\lambda_1 = 0.5$, $\lambda_2 = 0.5$; (squares) $\lambda_1 = 0.4$, $\lambda_2 = 0.6$. See text for details.

where λ_1 and λ_2 are weighting parameters. Figure 19.9(b) shows an example of how the weighting parameter might influence the optimal number of clusters representing the colour statistics of the natural images. When the complexity costs have a stronger weight than the distortion costs ($\lambda_1 = 0.4$, $\lambda_2 = 0.6$) the optimal number of clusters is about 2. This situation can be associated with a 'primitive' language distinguishing very few colour terms. When the distortion and complexity costs have equal weights ($\lambda_1 = 0.5$, $\lambda_2 = 0.5$) the optimal number of clusters is about 8. This situation approximately corresponds to the number of colour words used in everyday English. When the distortion costs have a stronger weight than the complexity costs ($\lambda_1 = 0.4$, $\lambda_2 = 0.6$) the optimal number of clusters is about 16. Such a situation relates to an 'advanced' terminology exhibited by professional painters and colour designers, for example.

19.4.4 Possible applications

The result of this research can be applied to different areas of imaging science: colour quantisation, image quality, gamut mapping, etc. For example, the analysis of the colour statistics representing the natural images in the CIELUV colour space revealed that the distribution obtained was rather uniform in the lightness (L^*) dimension, somewhat non-uniform in the hue (H) dimension, and extremely non-uniform in the chroma (C^*) dimension (Figure 19.6). Taking into account a roughly inverse relationship between uniformity and redundancy, one can speculate that the colour distribution of natural images along the chroma dimension is usually more redundant than along the hue dimension, and much more redundant than along the lightness dimension. Speculating even further, one can hypothesise that quantisation along the chroma dimension would probably be less obvious than along the hue and lightness dimensions. Figure 19.10 provides preliminary support of this hypothesis.

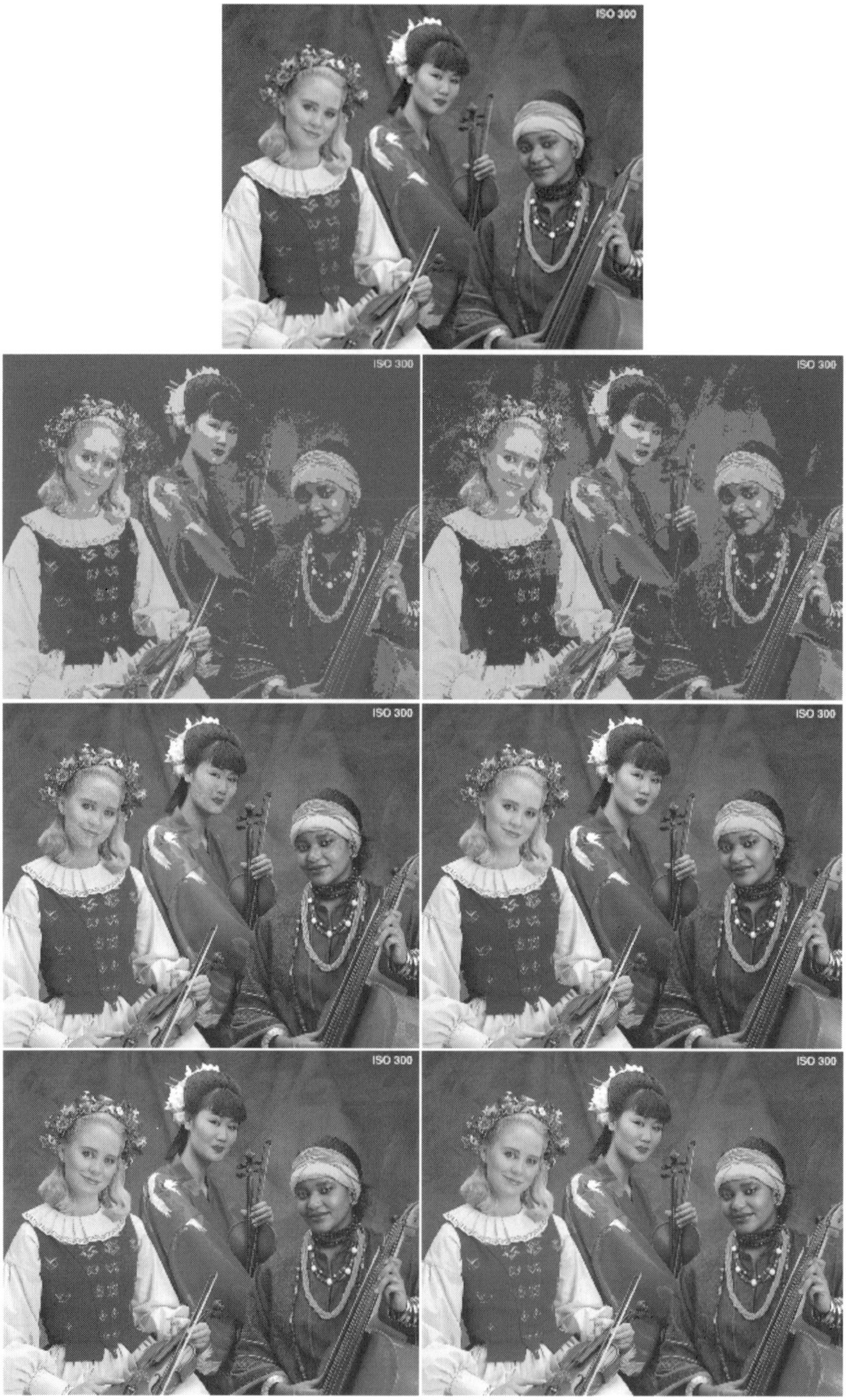
ISO 300
ISO 300
ISO 300
ISO 300
ISO 300
ISO 300
ISO 300

The images shown in the second, third and fourth row of Figure 19.10 have been quantised with four levels of corresponding L^*, H and C^* values of the original Girls image (top) from ISO standard colour image digital data [54]. The right column of Figure 19.10 contains images that were quantised based on the colour statistics of the natural images. The quantisation was done using four cluster centres derived by the CANTATA K-means clustering algorithm independently for the L^*, H and C^* values of 10 000 pixels representing the natural images. The right column of Figure 19.10 contains images that were quantised based on the colour statistics of the uniform (white noise) image. The quantisation was done using four cluster centres derived by the same algorithm for 10 000 pixels representing the image with uniformly distributed R, G, B grey values (Figure 19.6). Schematic illustrations of the colour point distributions of the quantised images in the CIE L^*C^* and u^*v^* diagrams are shown in Figure 19.11.

Two conclusions can be drawn from Figure 19.10. First, it appears that the quantisation of the chroma values is indeed less noticeable than the quantisation of the hue and lightness values. In fact, it is somewhat surprising how well the quantised images (bottom) with only four chroma levels resemble the original image (top) with a wide range of chroma values. Second, it seems that the quantisation based on the colour statistics of the natural images produces a slightly better rendering than the quantisation based on the colour statistics of the uniform (white noise) image. The effect is especially clear if one compares of the girls faces in the two images with hue quantisation (third row).

Colour quantisation can also be performed using the concept of colour categories. A result of such a categorical colour quantisation is shown in Figure 19.13. It shows the original 'Street' image (left) from the ISO standard colour image digital data and the quantised image (right), which was created using L^*, u^* and v^* coordinates of the 11 cluster centres found in this research (Figure 19.7 and Table 19.1). The colour point distributions of the original and quantised images in the CIE u^*v^* diagram are shown in Figure 19.12.

Although there are some visible differences between the original and quantised images in Plate 3, the outcome of the categorical colour quantisation is still remarkably good. The performance of the categorical colour quantisation has to be compared with other quantisation algorithms and tested with a large set of images having different perceptual and cognitive contents. This is a subject of future research. Here our focus is on the role of the categorical colour quantisation within the FUN strategies of image rendering (recall the discussion in relation to Figure 19.3).

The essence of categorical colour quantisation, i.e. the replacement of chromaticity coordinates of all colours in an image by chromaticity coordinates of prototypical colours of corresponding colour categories, is the core of the naturalness rendering strategy for the

---

Figure 19.10 Original Girls image (top) and quantised images with four levels of L^* (upper pair), four levels of H (middle pair) and four levels of C^* (lower pair). Images were quantised using four cluster centres derived from (left) the image with uniformly distributed RGB grey values and (right) the sampling of the natural images. Photos N7 and N7A of ISO Standard 12640:1997, Fig. 1, are reproduced with the permission of the International Organization for Standardization, ISO. This standard can be obtained from any ISO member and from the website of the ISO Central Secretariat at the following address: http://www.iso.org. Copyright remains with ISO. See also Colour Plate 11.

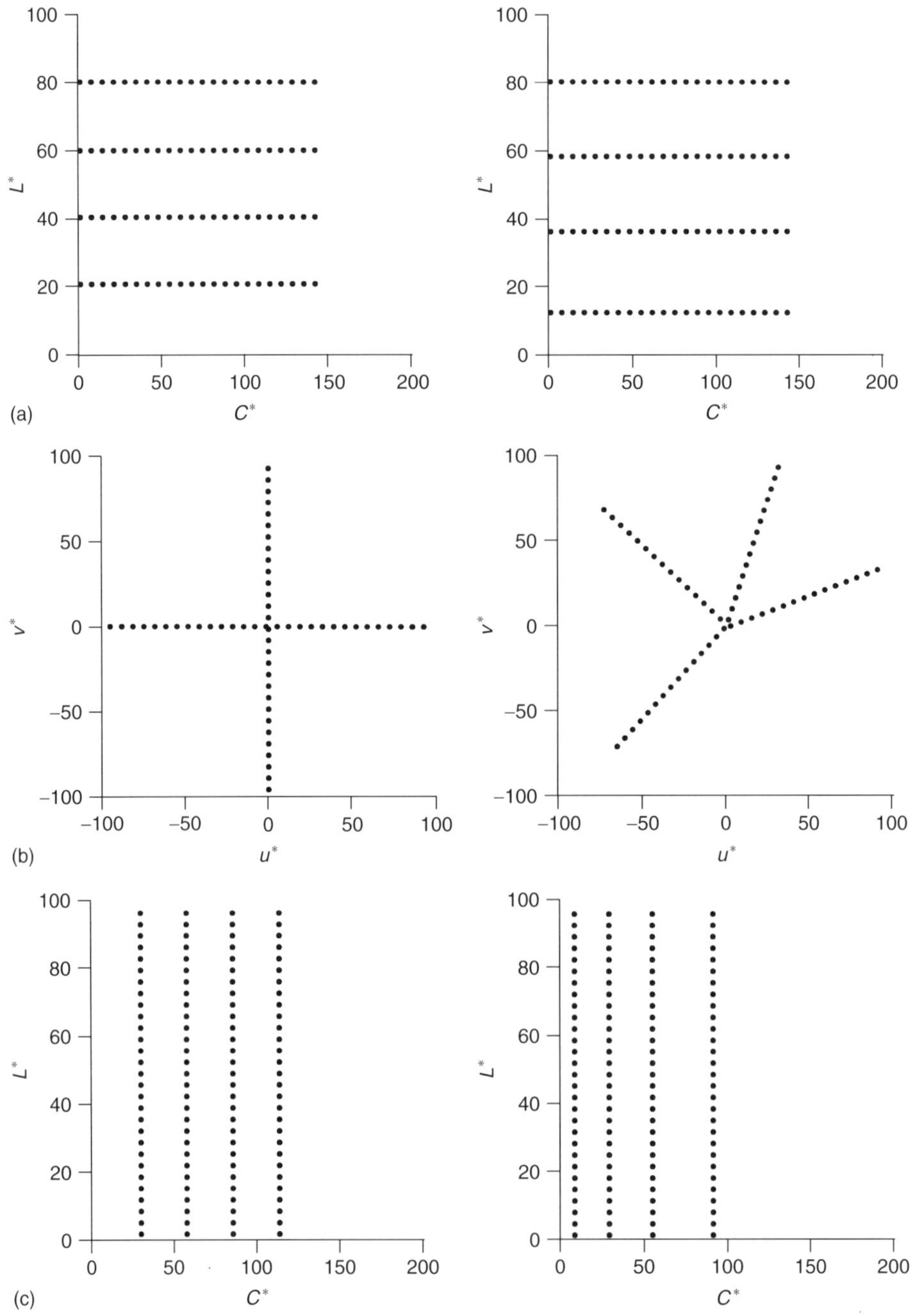

Figure 19.11 Schematic illustration of the colour distribution of the quantised images with (a) four levels of L^*, (b) four levels of H and (c) four levels of C^*. The images were quantised using four cluster centres derived from (left) the statistics of the natural images and (right) the statistics of the image with uniformly distributed RGB grey values.

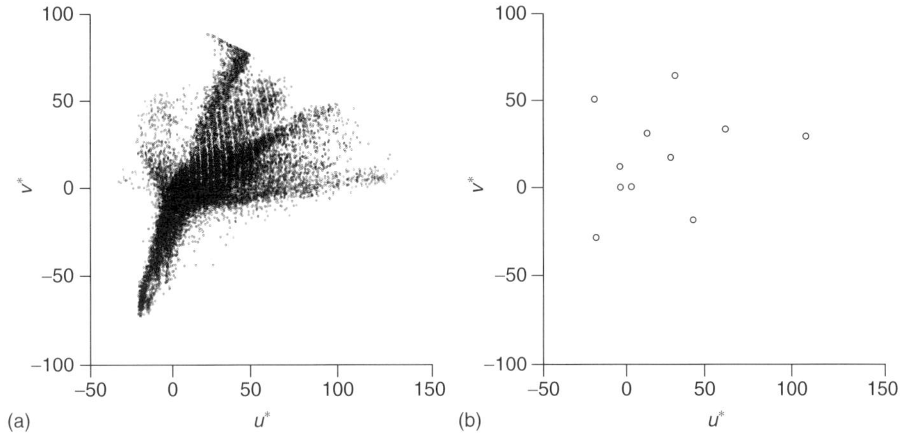

Figure 19.12 The colour point distributions of (a) the original image 'Street' image from the ISO standard colour image digital data and (b) the quantised image created using L^*, u^* and v^* coordinates of the 11 cluster centres found in this research.

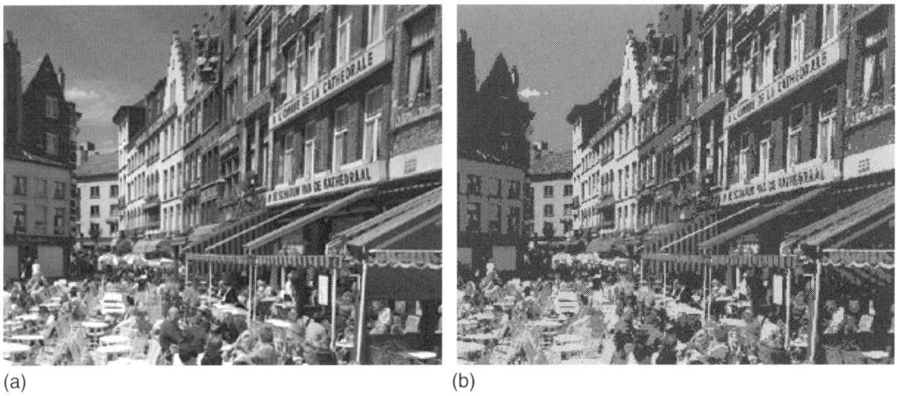

Figure 19.13 Illustration of the categorical colour quantisation: (a) original 'Street' image from the ISO standard colour image data; (b) the quantised image created using L^*, u^* and v^* coordinates of the 11 cluster centres found in this research. These images are N2 and N2A of ISO standard 12640: 1997, reproduced with permission of the International Organization for Standardization, ISO. See also Colour Plate 12.

colour domain. According to the FUN model, an image with a high degree of naturalness should contain only prototypical colours (i.e. centres of colour categories). This is true for the quantised image in Figure 19.13. All yellow colours in this image are equivalent to the prototypical yellow colour; all blue colours are equivalent to the prototypical blue colour; all brown colours are equivalent to the prototypical brown colour; and so on.

The exact position of the prototypical colours still has to be verified in future research, where subjects would judge whether the prototypical colours obtained from the statistics of natural images could be subjectively considered as the prototypical colours. Note that if the process of colour categorisation is determined by the statistical structure of the perceived colour environment, then the prototypical colours might be different for different subjects. For example, prototypical colours of person A might be different from prototypical colours of person B due to differences in their environment (person A lives in rainforest whereas person B lives in desert) and/or visual receptors (person A is a normal trichromat whereas person B is a protanope). Once the exact colour coordinates of the prototypical colours are established, they can be used to create a prototypical colour profile and transform any image into the image with prototypical colours that are specific for an individual and/or for a group of people. This transformation can be complete (i.e. all colours are replaced by the prototypes) or partial (i.e. some colours are replaced or all colours are shifted towards the prototypes).

The idea behind the prototypical colour profile can also be applied to colour gamut mapping. In this case it would be necessary to define a set of prototypical colours produced by a source device (e.g. a CRT monitor) and a set of prototypical colours produced by a destination device (e.g. an inkjet printer). This can be done experimentally by asking observers to estimate the prototypicality of colours produced by both devices. When the prototypical colour profiles of the devices are known, they can be used to convert any image from the source device into the destination device in such a way that the prototypical colours of the source device are mapped into the prototypical colours of the destination device. Interestingly, an algorithm that employs a similar idea and the notion of categorical colours for gamut mapping has been already proposed [55].

The possible applications of the concepts of colour categorisation and colour prototypes for colour quantisation, image quality and gamut mapping might be considered as a first step towards incorporating cognitive aspects of colour in imaging science. One can even hypothesise that some image processing techniques (e.g. colour quantisation, gamut mapping) might be more appropriate to perform in a cognitively uniform colour space than in a perceptually uniform colour space. The equality of distances between centres of colour categories could be the criterion of uniformity for such a space. The development of a cognitively uniform colour space would be an important step not only for colour imaging science but also for colour science in general.

19.5 CONCLUSIONS

The first part of this chapter discussed some of the methodological and theoretical aspects of IQ. Over the past 50 years a lot of experimental results on IQ have been collected. The results were obtained using rigorous measurements of psychometric techniques and systematically varied images. The results can be quantified and related to objective image measurements. The relationship between the objective image measurements and subjective IQ judgements enables us to develop computational IQ metrics. Most of the current IQ metrics are based on visual models but there are a few that incorporate cognitive models in their calculations. The observer's response obtained by psychometric techniques is usually context dependent and may vary significantly from one individual to another. The context effect can be modelled by including the additional information about the stimulus set when analysing the data. The individual differences can be modelled as a weighted sum of essentially the same underlying attributes, with the weights varying for different observers.

At present, there is no generally acceptable IQ theory that provides a complete explanation and description of IQ phenomena. However, over the past several years some significant progress has been made (from top-down and from bottom-up perspectives) towards the development of such a theory. The first part of the chapter contributes to this development by presenting a general IQ model. The model assumes existence of the three major dimensions determining IQ: fidelity, usefulness and naturalness (FUN). The overall IQ can be modelled as a weighted sum of the three FUN attributes with their weights ranging from 0 to 1. Different types of image might require different combinations of the weights.

The second part of this chapter describes a computational model of colour categorisation and discusses it in relation to colour imaging science. The model consists of five major components: physical environment, colour perception, perceived colour environment, colour categorisation, and colour category system. The physical environment has been modelled by a sampling of 10 000 pixels from a set of 630 natural images. The process of colour perception has been modelled by a transformation from R, G, B values of the sampling to the CIE L^*, u^*, v^* colour coordinates. The perceived colour environment has been modelled by a colour point distribution of the sampling in the CIELUV colour space. The process of colour categorisation has been modelled by a grouping of the L^*, u^*, v^* colour coordinates of the sampling by a K-means clustering algorithm. The colour category system has been modelled by locations, numbers and weights of clusters derived by the K-means clustering algorithm. The proposed model of colour categorisation enables us to predict the location, order and number of colour categories. In general, the predictions are in good agreement with phenomenological data obtained from psycholinguistic studies. The concept of colour categories can be applied to various areas of imaging science: colour quantisation, gamut mapping, image quality, etc. The results of this research might also be used to develop a cognitively uniform colour space.

REFERENCES

1. *The Hutchinson Encyclopaedia of Science*. Helicon, Oxford (1998).
2. K. Popper (1959) *The Logic of Scientific Discovery*. Basic Books, New York.
3. R. D. Luce and C. L. Krumhansl (1988) Measurement, scaling, and psychophysics. In *Stevens's Handbook of Experimental Psychology*, 2nd edn, R. Atkinson, R. Herrnstein, G. Lindzey and R. D. Luce (eds), pp. 3–74. New York, John Wiley.
4. B. L. Jones and L. E. Marks (1985) Picture quality assessment: a comparison of ratio and ordinal scale. *SMPTE Journal*, **94**, 1244–1248.
5. R. E. Jacobson (1995) An evaluation of image quality metrics. *Journal of Photographic Science*, **43**, 7–14.
6. J. E. Farrell (1999) Image quality evaluation. In *Colour Imaging: Vision and Technology*, L. W. MacDonald and M. R. Luo (eds), pp. 285–313. John Wiley, Chichester.
7. C. J. Bartleson (1960) Memory colors of familiar objects. *Journal of the Optical Society of America*, **50**, 73–77.
8. S. M. Newhall, R. W. Burnham and J. R. Clark (1957) Comparison of successive with simultaneous color matching. *Journal of the Optical Society of America*, **47**, 43–56.

9. P. Siple and R. M. Springer (1983) Memory and preference for the colors of objects. *Perception and Psychophysics*, **34**, 363–370.
10. S. Sanders (1959) Color preference for natural objects. *Illuminating Engineering*, **54**, 452–456.
11. R. W. G. Hunt, I. T. Pitt and L. M. Winter (1974) The preferred reproduction of blue sky, green grass and Caucasian skin in colour photography. *Journal of Photographic Science*, **22**, 144–150.
12. S. N. Yendrikhovskij, F. J. J. Blommaert and H. de Ridder (1999) Representation of memory prototype for an object colour. *Color Research and Application*, **24**, 393–410.
13. S. N. Yendrikhovskij, F. J. J. Blommaert and H. de Ridder (1999) Colour reproduction and the naturalness constraint. *Color Research and Application*, **24**, 53–65.
14. S. N. Yendrikhovskij, F. J. J. Blommaert and H. de Ridder (1999) Towards perceptually optimal colour reproduction of natural scenes. In *Colour Imaging: Vision and Technology*, L. W. MacDonald and M. R. Luo (eds), pp. 363–382. John Wiley, Chichester.
15. R. N. Shepard (1987) Toward a universal law of generalization for psychological science. *Science*, **273**, 1317–1323.
16. F. Ashby (ed.) (1992) Multidimensional models of categorization. In *Multidimensional Models of Perception and Cognition*, pp. 349–482. Lawrence Erlbaum, Hillsdale NJ.
17. D. L. MacAdam (1951) Quality of color reproduction. *Proceedings of the Institute of Radio Engineers*, **36**, 468–485.
18. A. Parducci and D. H. Wedell (1986) The category effect with rating scales: number of categories, number of stimuli, and method of presentation. *Journal of Experimental Psychology: Human Perception and Performance*, **12**, 496–516.
19. E. Poulton (1989) *Bias in Quantifying Judgements*. Lawrence Erlbaum, London.
20. H. de Ridder (1998) Psychophysical evaluation of image quality. *SPIE Conference Proceedings*, **3299**, 252–263.
21. G. R. Lockhead (1992) Psychophysical scaling: judgements of attributes or objects? *Behavioral and Brain Science*, **15**, 543–558.
22. S. N. Yendrikhovskij, H. de Ridder, E. A. Fedorovskaya and F. J. J. Blommaert (1997) Colourfulness judgements of natural scenes. *Acta Psychologica*, **97**, 73–94.
23. M. Saito (1996) Comparative studies on color preference in Japan and other Asian regions, with special emphasis on the preference for white. *Color Research and Applications*, **21**, 35–49.
24. G. Deffner, M. Yuasa, M. McKeon and D. Arndt (1994) Evaluation of display-image quality: experts vs. non-experts. *SID Digest*, pp. 475–478.
25. S. N. Yendrikhovskij, L. W. MacDonald, S. Bech and K. Jensen (2001) Enhancing colour image quality in television displays. *Image Science Journal*, **47**, 197–211.
26 L. L. Thurstone (1930) A scale for measuring attitude towards the movies. *Journal of Educational Research*, **22**, 89–97.
27. R. M. Dawes (1994) Psychological measurement. *Psychological Review*, **101**, 278–281.
28. S. Bech, R. Hamberg, M. R. M. Nijenhuis, C. Teunissen, H. Looren de Jong, P. Houben and S. K. Pramanik (1996) The rapid perceptual image description method (RaPID). *SPIE Conference Proceedings*, **2657**, 317–328.
29. M. R. M. Nijenhuis and F. J. J. Blommaert (1997) Perceptual error measure for sampled and interpolated images. *Journal of Imaging Science and Technology*, **41**, 249–258.
30. E. A. Fedorovskaya, H. de Ridder and F. J. J. Blommaert (1997) Chroma variations and perceived quality of color images of natural scenes. *Color Research and Applications*, **22**, 96–110.
31. T. J. W. M. Janssen and F. J. J. Blommaert (1997) Image quality semantics. *Journal of Imaging Science and Technology*, **41**(5), 555–560.
32. S. N. Yendrikhovskij (1999) Image quality: between science and fiction. *Proceedings of the PIC Conference*, pp. 173–178.
33. R. W. G. Hunt (1987) *The Reproduction of Color in Photography, Printing and Television*. Tolworth, Fountain.
34. T. Newman (1997) Making color plug and play. *Proceedings of the Fifth Color Imaging Conference*, pp. 284–289.

35. T. J. W. M. Janssen and F. J. J. Blommaert (2000) Predicting the usefulness and naturalness of color reproductions. *Journal of Imaging Science and Technology*, **44**, 93–104.
36. T. J. W. M. Janssen and F. J. J. Blommaert (2000) Visual metrics: discriminative power through flexibility. *Perception*, **29**, 965–980.
37. D. B. Judd (1967) A flattery index for artificial illuminants. *Illuminating Engineering*, **42**, 593–599.
38. G. Wyszecki and W. S. Stiles (1982) *Color Science: Concepts and Methods, Quantitative Data and Formulae*, 2nd edn. John Wiley, New York.
39. R. M. Boynton and C. X. Olson (1987) Locating basic colors in the OSA space. *Color Research and Application*, **12**, 94–105.
40. E. Rosch (1978) Principles of categorization. In *Cognition and Categorization*, E. Rosch and B. B. Lloyd (eds), pp. 27–48. Lawrence Erlbaum, Hillsdale NJ.
41. M. R. Pointer and G. G. Attridge (1998) The number of discernible colours. *Color Research and Application*, **23**, 52–54.
42. G. Derefeldt and T. Swartling (1995) Colour concept retrieval by free colour naming. Identification of up to 30 colours without training. *Displays*, **16**, 69–77.
43. J. Buhmann and H. Kuehnel (1993) Vector quantization with complexity costs. *IEEE Transactions on Information Theory*, **39**, 1133–1145.
44. R. N. Shepard (1992) The perceptual organization of colours: an adaptation to regularities of the terrestrial world? In *Adapted Mind*, J. Barkow, L. Cosmides and J. Tooby (eds), pp. 495–532. Oxford University Press, Oxford.
45. H. S. Smallman and R. M. Boyton (1990) Segregation of basic colors in an information display. *Journal of the Optical Society of America A*, **7**, 1985–1994.
46. http://www.khoral.com.
47. M. D. Fairchild (1997) *Color Appearance Models*. Addison-Wesley, Reading MA.
48. C. M. Howard and J. A. Burnidge (1994) Colors in natural landscapes. *Journal of the Society for Information Display*, **2**, 47–55.
49. C. D. Hendley and S. Hecht (1949) The colors of natural objects and terrains, and their relation to visual color deficiency. *Journal of the Optical Society of America*, **39**, 870–873.
50. G. J. Burton and R. Moorhead (1987) Color and spatial structure in natural scenes. *Applied Optics*, **26**, 157–170.
51. G. B. Buck and H. C. Froelich (1948) Color characteristics of human complexions. *Illuminating Engineering*, **53**, 27–49.
52. B. Berlin and P. Kay (1969) *Basic Color Terms: Their Universality and Evolution*. University of California Press, Berkeley CA.
53. I. C. McManus (1997) Note: half-a-million basic colour words: Berlin and Kay and the usage of colour words in literature and science. *Perception*, **26**, 367–370.
54. ISO Standard 12 640: Standard color image digital data.
55. H. Motomura, O. Yamada and T. Fumoto (1997) Categorical color mapping for gamut mapping, *Proceedings of the Fifth Color Imaging Conference*, pp. 50–55.

20

How to make pictures and please people

Robert Hunt

20.1 INTRODUCTION

The vast majority of pictures are made to be viewed by people. Imaging must therefore be people-dominated. Hence the title, 'How to make pictures and please people', with acknowledgements to Dale Carnegie [1].

20.2 SUBTRACTIVE SYSTEMS

From prehistoric times pictures have been made by painting, but the first colour pictures made by imaging were produced by Jacob Christoph Le Blon around 1720. Le Blon used half-tone images in yellow, red (magenta) and blue (cyan) inks, so his process was the forerunner of modern graphic arts printing by lithography, gravure and letterpress. The first commercially successful subtractive systems of continuous tone colour photography were Technicolor, the first three-colour film being produced in 1932, and Kodachrome, invented by the two professional musicians Mannes and Godowsky (affectionately known to their colleagues as Man and God) and introduced as a 16 mm amateur movie film in 1935, and

Colour Image Science, edited by L.W. MacDonald and M.R. Luo.

as a 35 mm slide film in 1936. Colour films in which the couplers were incorporated in the layers of the film were introduced by Agfa in 1936 and by Kodak in 1942.

In recent years, increasing numbers of colour reflection prints have been made using dye diffusion transfer, electrophotographic and inkjet technologies [2, 3].

In the dye diffusion transfer system, the paper or other support that is to carry the final image is moved by a drum underneath a row of heating elements, usually spaced at between 200 and 300 per inch. A donor web of yellow, magenta, cyan and black dyes moves with the paper between the paper and the heating elements. Signals are sent to the heating elements which raise the temperature to the levels that result in the required amount of dye diffusing to the paper under each element, so that a line of the picture is produced; the movement of the paper on the drum provides the page scan. The paper has to be passed under the line of heating elements once for each of the different coloured dyes. The thermal dye transfer system is capable of giving pictures of very high quality, with excellent tone and colour reproduction, and at 300 elements per inch the sharpness can be very good. The system requires the use of special paper, and the cost of the donor web per picture is quite high because of the large amount of dye in it, most of which is wasted by not being transferred to the paper. The system is also rather slow; it takes about a minute to produce a page of normal size.

In the electrophotographic systems, a positive electric charge is given to a photoconductive drum, and a light beam, usually in the form of a laser, is used to remove the charge in selected areas to produce an image in electric charge. The image is produced by scanning; the line scan is generated using a polygon of mirrors to sweep the light beam rapidly across the width of the drum, and the page scan is generated by rotation of the drum. The positively charged image then attracts a negatively charged toner (in the form of a liquid or a powder) to form a toner image. This image is then transferred to the paper (or other support), and heated to fuse into a stable deposit. Colour images are produced by carrying out the process in succession for each colorant, usually just cyan, magenta and yellow. The process is rather slow, again taking about a minute for a page of normal size. The cost of the materials is quite low, but the equipment can be quite expensive for high-quality output.

The inkjet systems come in two different types. In the drop-on-demand systems, the ink is propelled out of nozzles as required, while the nozzles pass over the support. In the continuous tone systems, the ink is propelled out of the nozzles all the time, and the drops are given an electric charge; when ink is not required, an electrode steers the drops away from the paper into a gutter for later use. The propulsion of the ink out of the nozzles can be by piezoelectric deformation, or by a phase change by melting ink in the form of waxes, or by vaporising the inks by heating. The line scan is usually by mechanical movement to and fro across the paper, and the page scan is by rotation of a drum carrying the paper. Colour images are produced by having nozzles supplying the different coloured inks combined in the same printing head. The nozzles are spaced at about 300–600 per inch, and the number of nozzles in a head can vary from less than 10 to more than 100. The mechanical line scan limits the rate of printing to about a minute for a normal size page, but by having lines of nozzles covering the full page width, the mechanical line scan is eliminated and the speed of printing greatly increased; at 300 nozzles per inch, this requires over 2400 nozzles for each colour an 8 inch width. The cost of the materials is low, and the cost of the drop-on-demand equipment is also low.

20.3 ADDITIVE SYSTEMS

The first additive colour images were demonstrated by James Clerk Maxwell at the Royal Institution in London in 1861, and the system he used was the forerunner of the triple-projection cathode ray tube (CRT) displays widely used in lecture theatres and for in-flight entertainment in airliners.

The inconvenience of triple projection can be avoided by viewing small adjacent red, green and blue areas at a distance such that these areas are not resolved on the retina of the eye; among the earliest commercially successful of these mosaic processes were the Autochrome process introduced by the Lumière brothers in 1904, and the Dufay process in 1908, a more recent example being the system used in the Polavision process for amateur movies introduced in 1976 and in the Polachrome process for slides introduced in 1984. The mosaic system is used in many television display devices: the shadow-mask tube is the most widely used, but liquid crystal, plasma, and light-emitting diode displays are making increasing penetration into the display market.

Liquid crystals can be used to form light valves by placing them in cells bounded by crossed polarising filters having lines etched across their inner surfaces; when the polarising filters are crossed, their sets of lines are at right angles to each other. In the absence of an electric field, the orientation of the liquid crystals changes throughout the depth of the layer from being aligned with the direction of the etched lines, and this results in the direction of the polarisation of the light being rotated through a right angle so as to allow the light to pass; but if an electric charge is placed across the layer of liquid crystals, their molecules stand on end and are no longer rotated, so the light does not pass. By varying the strength of the electric charge, the amount of light passing can be controlled. Liquid crystal displays (LCDs) can be made by having arrays of cells each of which can be separately addressed to produce the required amount of light at its location. Coloured displays are made by covering the array with a mosaic of red, green and blue filters or, in projectors, by using dichroic mirrors to divide a beam of white light into separate beams of red, green and blue, and then putting a separate LCD in each beam. The mosaic type of LCD is very useful for small displays of a few inches diagonal, and for laptop displays. Disadvantages are their high cost, and the difficulty of making displays of size greater than about 20 in diagonal.

The passage of an electric current through a gas can produce radiation; such plasmas are produced in mercury gas in fluorescent tubes and in xenon gas in photographic flash units. In television plasma displays, each pixel is produced by a plasma in a separate cell, the cells being activated in succession as required by the scanning standards. Xenon and neon gases are normally used; the plasmas are extremely brief, as in photographic flash units. However, each cell is covered with one of three different fluorescent powders which convert the radiation (including its ultraviolet content) into either red, green or blue light, and this extends the light emission to a time comparable with one cycle of the picture rate. The contrast of the pictures can be increased by putting red, green and blue filters over the cells; this reduces the light reflected by the cells when they are not activated, and creates much blacker blacks. Plasma displays can be made in large sizes and need only be a few inches deep; they can therefore provide very compact monitors and television displays in the form of pictures that can be hung on a wall. Plasma displays thus have many desirable features, but they cost much more than shadow-mask tubes.

Solid-state diodes can be made that emit light on being energised; these light-emitting diodes (LEDs) can be designed to emit either red, green or blue light. Their size can be small enough for them to be mounted in arrays so that when viewed from a distance their light blends together to form mixture colours from the red, green and blue components. To obtain a white in this way, it may be necessary to have twice as many green units as red or blue. Arrays of such LEDs can provide displays of very high luminances, such as $3000\,cd\,m^{-2}$. The high luminance attainable makes these displays suitable for use out of doors (e.g. at sports events), where sizes as large as about $4\,m \times 5\,m$ are often used.

Another way of adding the red, green and blue lights together is to view them in rapid succession; the first commercially successful example of this field-sequential system was the Kinemacolor process introduced in 1908, and the field-sequential principle is currently used in one version of the digital mirror device (DMD) displays by incorporating a rapidly rotating red, green and blue filter wheel. The DMD uses an array of mirrors, one $16\,\mu m \times 16\,\mu m$ mirror for each pixel. The light is modulated by each mirror being deflected electrostatically to reflect the light into a projection lens, or to discard it completely for different fractions of the picture cycle period.

Yet another way of adding the red, green and blue lights together is by superimposing virtual images of the three records; this was first done in 1895 by F. E. Ives in his Kromscop viewers, and the same principle is currently used in another version of the DMD system by incorporating a dichroic beam-splitting prism block of the type used in high-quality television cameras; the prism block splits the light into red, green and blue components then recombines them after reflection from three DMD arrays.

In yet another version of the DMD system, the filter wheel consists of yellow and magenta sections, so that red light is transmitted all the time, with the blue and green components alternating. A two-way dichroic beam-splitting prism block is then used to separate the red light from the blue and green components, and to recombine them after reflection from two DMD arrays. This configuration is useful because its metal halide mercury lamps emit less red light than green and blue.

20.4 LIMITATIONS OF MAKING PICTURES BY IMAGING

Systems using displays, whether subtractive or additive, all have inherent limitations. These limitations are associated especially with the spectral sensitivities of their acquisition devices, and with the gamut and dynamic range of their reproducible colours; the subtractive displays have additional limitations imposed by the unwanted absorptions of their cyan, magenta and yellow colorants. All systems also have limited resolution, and this can be a particular challenge in digital systems.

20.4.1 Spectral sensitivities

The correct spectral sensitivities to use in an acquisition device are the colour matching functions for the red, green and blue primaries used in the display device. Because the primaries are unable to stimulate the three different cone types of the eye separately, these colour matching functions always have negative lobes. These negative lobes have so far proved impossible to replicate correctly in colour films. In electronic cameras the negative lobes can be introduced by matrixing linear signals, and this is normally done; however, the spectral sensitivities corresponding to the matrixed signals are usually only an approximation to the required colour matching functions (Figure 20.1). These incorrect spectral sensitivities introduce errors into the system at the very outset, errors which can never be corrected later on. The result is that some colours, which are spectrally different but look alike to the eye (metameric colours), may be reproduced as different colours by the system; and other colours, which look different to the eye, may reproduce the same in the system. A further complication in subtractive systems is that the effective primaries change, as different parts of the colour gamut are reproduced, so there is no unique set of associated colour matching functions that is correct to use.

20.4.2 Gamuts

The second limitation, the gamut of reproducible colours, also arises because of the unwanted stimulations of the cones by the primaries. In additive systems the gamut of reproducible colours can be represented on a chromaticity diagram by the triangle formed by the three points at which the three primaries plot, as shown by the triangle labelled

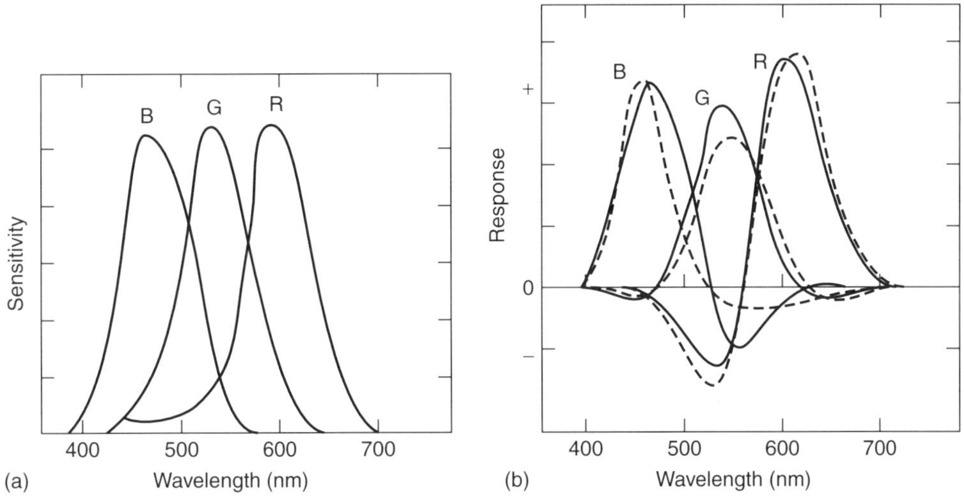

Figure 20.1 (a) Typical spectral sensitivity curves of an electronic camera. (b) The solid curves show typical equivalent spectral sensitivities after matrixing; the dashed curves show colour matching functions corresponding to standard broadcast phosphors (709).

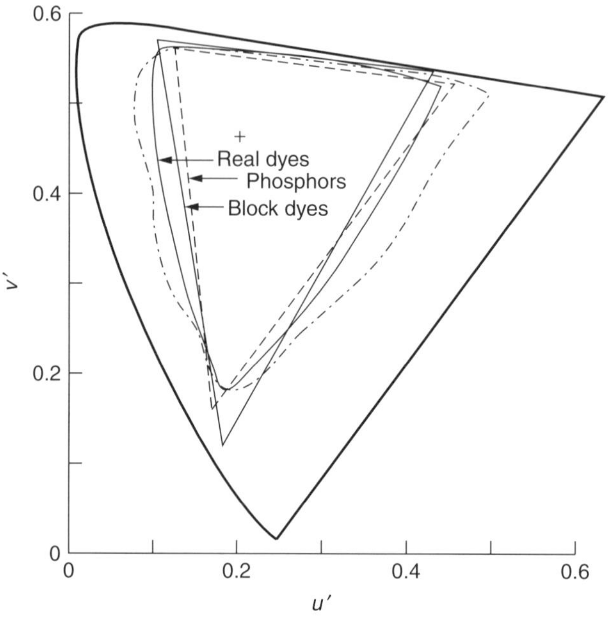

Figure 20.2 Chromaticity gamuts for typical phosphors (broken triangle), subtractive block dyes (solid triangle), typical real dyes (inner solid line), typical real reflecting objects (chain-dotted line), and the spectral locus and purple boundary (outer solid line).

'Phosphors' in Figure 20.2. In subtractive systems, if dyes could be used that absorbed uniformly in each of three blocks of wavelengths, the gamut would be a triangle such as that labelled 'Block dyes'. But the dyes used in subtractive systems do not absorb uniformly in their appropriate blocks of wavelengths, and the gamut is not then a simple triangle, but is usually similar to that labelled 'Real dyes'. The shape and location of subtractive gamuts, although a little larger, are not usually very different from a typical additive triangle. Both the additive and the subtractive gamuts are typically far smaller in size than the maximum gamut of all possible colours (represented by the outermost line in Figure 20.2 [4]), but the gamut of colours commonly occurring in the real world (shown by the chain-dotted line) is also much smaller than the maximum gamut [5], and only slightly larger than the reproduction gamuts; this is what makes it viable to use the reproduction gamuts. The gamut of the real-world colours is restricted because the vast majority of them are produced by dyes and pigments which have broad spectral absorption bands, and which therefore cannot generate colours having only narrow spectral bands; however, colours produced by other means, such as the interference colours in some bird feathers and insect scales or colours produced by lasers, may lie well outside the reproduction gamuts. The use of red, green and blue lasers in additive displays has been tried [6], but although an increase in gamut can be obtained, this advantage has to be weighed against the increased cost, power consumption and inconvenience of these devices.

In graphic arts printing, the use of extra inks, typically an orange, a green and a violet, in addition to the usual cyan, magenta, yellow and black, has sometimes been used for the reproduction of original works of art [7], and in the Hexachrome process additional orange and green inks are used to extend the gamut. Besides extending the gamut, additional inks are useful in making it possible to reduce the degree of metamerism between an original colour and its reproduction, and this can be important in the mail-order catalogue business.

20.4.3 Dynamic range

The dynamic range of reproduction systems is always limited and liable to be exceeded by some types of scene. Reflection prints, when seen in typical room viewing situations, have dynamic ranges that depend heavily on the quality of the printing paper; with the best quality papers, a range of about 1.7 log units may be achieved, but with newsprint it may be only about 1.2 log units. Although densitometers may show that images on paper have densities as high as about 2.2, the viewing flare in typical room situations reduces this to not more than about 1.7, as shown in Figure 20.3.

The dynamic range of self-luminous television displays is usually limited by the ambient light reflected from the front surface of the device; when seen in dim surrounds, ranges of about 1.7 log units are typical, but the dim surround reduces this to an effective range of about 1.7/1.2 or about 1.4 log units of scene luminance (Figure 20.3). The dynamic range of projected images usually depends on the amount of ambient light present, but a typical figure for good projection conditions is about 2.7 log units; however, the effect of the dark surround is to reduce this to an effective range of about 1.8 log units of scene luminance (Figure 20.3).

Some real scenes can have dynamic ranges of 3 or more log units, so it is clear that, for such scenes, some parts of them will lie well outside the tonal gamut of the imaging system. Although flare light in the eye usually reduces the tonal range of the image on

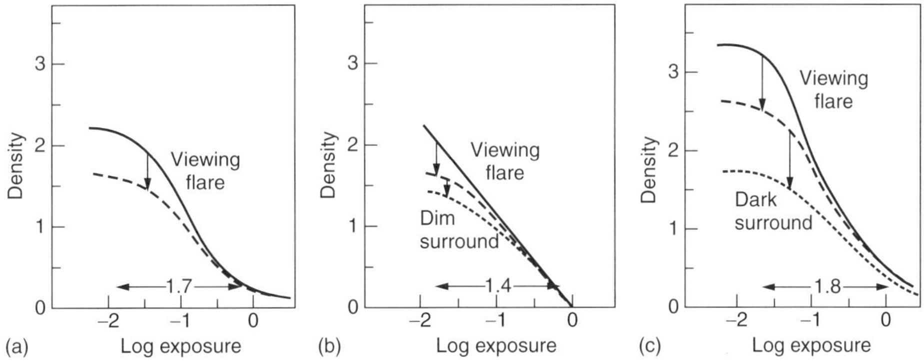

Figure 20.3 Density against log exposure for: (a) a typical reflection print; (b) a typical self-luminous display; and (c) a typical projection darkroom. Solid curves are without viewing flare and dashed curves are with viewing flare. The dotted curve in (b) shows the equivalent densities after allowing for the contrast-reducing effect of a dim surround, and the dotted curve in (c) shows the equivalent densities after allowing for the contrast-reducing effect of a dark surround.

the retina to much less than 3 log units, an additional reduction by the imaging system can be very deleterious; moreover, by scanning the scene with eye movements, the visual system is able to extend its effective range and see into shadows in a way that is not available to most imaging systems.

20.4.4 Unwanted absorptions

Subtractive colorants should ideally absorb each in only one-third of the spectrum. But, as shown in Figure 20.4, they actually absorb in parts of the spectrum where they should be perfectly reflecting or transmitting. These unwanted absorptions make the reproduced colours darker and less colourful than they should be, and correction for their effects is essential. In photography, correction is provided in colour negatives by the use of dye-forming couplers which are themselves coloured; the yellow colour of a magenta-forming coupler corrects for the unwanted blue absorption of the magenta dye, and the pink colour of a cyan-forming coupler corrects for the unwanted green and blue absorptions of the cyan dye.

Unwanted absorptions are also corrected by the use of *inter-image effects* in which the amount of dye in one image is made to depend on the amount of dye in another image;

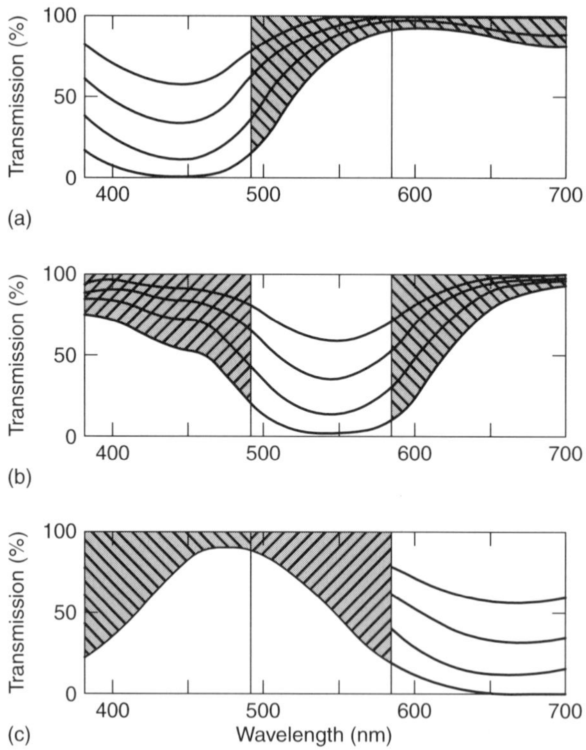

Figure 20.4 Spectral transmittances of a coloured dye at four different concentrations; the shaded areas indicate the unwanted absorptions: (a) yellow, (b) magenta, (c) cyan.

for example, if the amount of magenta dye is made to decrease slightly as the amount of yellow dye increases, then the reduction in the amount of magenta can compensate for the unwanted green absorption of the yellow dye. In graphic arts printing and in desktop publishing, similar adjustments to the amounts of the colorants are usually made electronically by suitable signal algorithms.

Although these means of correction are effective within the gamut of reproducible colours, the medium gamut itself is reduced by the unwanted absorptions of the colorants.

20.4.5 Resolution

Conventional broadcast television has either 483 active lines of 720 pixels (in a 525-line system) or 575 active lines of 860 pixels (in a 625-line system). But if the display device is a shadow-mask tube, its dot structure may consist of only 520 lines of 690 holes (in 525-line systems) or 575 lines of 770 holes (in a 625-line system); furthermore, the electron beam diameter is such that more than one line of holes is irradiated so that the effective definition is restricted even more. High-definition television (HDTV) displays may have 1080 active lines and 1920 pixels per line. Monitors may have up to 2000 or more lines of holes, and these extra lines are useful in reducing the incidence of jagged edges in the displayed images. To reduce the bit requirement in digital images, it is customary to use compression techniques such as the JPEG algorithm.

Because of the limited resolution, fine detail may be lost because of being below the resolution of the system, and aliasing can produce patterns that are not in the original scene at all. The best solution to these problems is to show both general views to give an overall impression, and such close-ups as may be necessary to show detailed parts. This is normal practice in broadcast television, where three cameras are commonly used in studios to provide both general and close-up views; the provision of zoom lenses increases the variety of views very greatly.

Photographic colour films can have resolutions of about 50 cycles, equivalent to 100 pixels per millimetre. In the widely used 35 mm format of 36 mm × 24 mm, this results in ample resolution for most applications, but even more resolution is provided by the 6 cm × 6 cm format (56 mm × 56 mm) often used in professional photography. In cinematography, 16 mm film (7.5 mm × 10 mm) gives adequate resolution for standard television origination, 35 mm film (16 mm × 22 mm) gives good cinema quality, and 70 mm film (22 mm × 48 mm) can be used for very large high resolution images.

Electrophotographic and inkjet systems are basically binary – that is they can only provide two levels of tone, that of the pigment or ink level adopted and that of the paper or other support. The intermediate tones have to be provided by some form of geometrical patterning (half-toning or dithering), with or without the use of the colorant at more than one concentration.

In digital systems the formation of dots of different sizes, to provide the illusion of intermediate tones, can be achieved by using clusters of different numbers of microdots in square arrays. The number of tone levels available has to be large enough to avoid contouring, the appearance of spurious abrupt changes in tone in areas where the gradation should be continuous. In the CIELUV and CIELAB uniform colour spaces, the L^* parameter has values from zero to 100, and each unit on this scale is generally regarded as a just noticeable difference. However, zero is too low a value for a typical black, and it is more realistic to regard an L^* value of 10 as representing a typical good black; if an L^* value of 100 is regarded as the maximum available, it means that, to avoid contouring, the half-toning system need not provide more than 90 levels, provided these levels are uniformly spaced perceptually. If cluster dots are formed in an array of 90 microdots on a non-diffusing support, such as metal, then the 90 tone levels will produce a linear scale of reflectance; but such a scale is perceptually very non-linear and contouring would be evident. Fortunately, the supports most often used are diffusing, such as paper, and this results in what is known as dot gain.

When an array of dots is printed on paper, the light passes through the array of dots on its way into the paper, it is diffused within the paper thickness, and finally emerges by passing through the array of dots a second time. If the diffusion is complete, the effect is to double the optical density of the image; but with typical paper, because the diffusion is incomplete, the increase in density is less than double, although still substantial. This dot gain results in the relationship between the number of microdots used (the size of the cluster dot) and the reflectance being much more nearly perceptually uniform than when there is no diffusion. In Figure 20.5 the reflectance is plotted as reflection density against percentage dot area for the case of no diffusion (curve D), complete diffusion (curve D″), and partial diffusion typical for paper (curve D′). These curves all have a maximum density of 1.52, which has been assumed to be the density when all of the paper is covered with ink. Also shown in the figure is the relationship between L^* and reflection density (dashed curve). Curve D is very different from the L^* curve, but curve D′ is considerably closer to it. This means that, although 90 dot sizes is still not enough

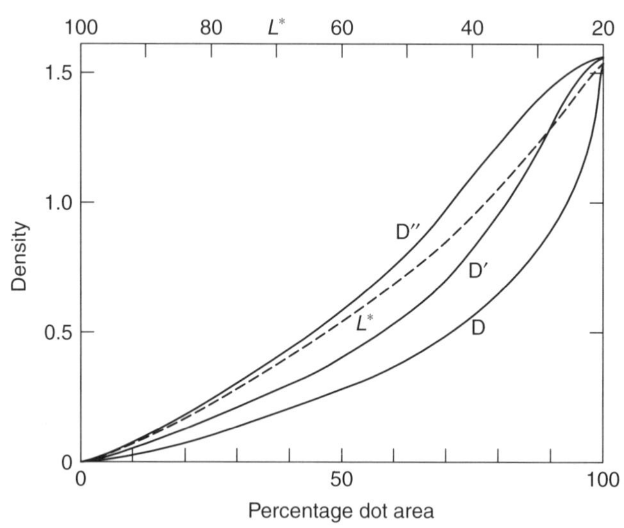

Figure 20.5 Density plotted against percentage dot area for a solid ink of density 1.52. D = no diffusion, D″ = complete diffusion, and D′ = partial diffusion typical for paper. The dashed curve shows the relationship between L^* and density; a uniform scale of L^* is set with $L^* = 100$ at zero dot area and $L^* = 20$ at 100% dot area (L^* has this value for a density of 1.52).

to avoid contouring, it is only necessary to increase this number slightly, and 100 levels is generally regarded as sufficient. This means that a 10 × 10 array of microdots can be used. With such an array, the resulting half-tone dot size is therefore larger than that of the microdots by a factor of 10. If the limit of visual resolution is taken as 10 pixels per millimetre, the microdots should then be 0.01 mm, or 0.004 in, in diameter.

In electrophotography, the requirement for microdots as small as 0.004 in wide has led to the use of lasers to expose the electrostatic image. In drop-on-demand inkjet printers it is not possible to form such small drops; if 300 microdots per inch are used, then to avoid contouring, the half-tone dots have to be at 30 dots per inch (larger by a factor of 10), hence the resolution is very poor. By using a 6 × 6 microdot array the resolution is improved to 50 half-tone dots per inch at the expense of some contouring; the overall performance can then be improved by using a technique known as error diffusion in which the error in any one pixel is distributed among neighbouring pixels. Further improvements can be made by being able to deliver any number from 0 to 4 drops in any pixel, and by using inks at more than one concentration. In continuous inkjet systems, any number from 0 to 32 microdrops of ink can be delivered to any pixel, and when combined with 4 × 4 arrays of pixels in which the average number of drops can be adjusted, excellent resolution and absence of contouring can be achieved.

Dye diffusion transfer systems, being continuous tone, are not limited by any need for half-toning, but sideways diffusion of the dyes does result in loss of resolution. The Technicolor process gives images for 35 mm motion pictures which are acceptable but not as sharp as would be ideal; reflection prints made by dye diffusion transfer can appear to be very sharp indeed when viewed at normal viewing distance without magnification.

20.5 BASIS OF ASSESSING IMAGES

Because of the limitations of colour imaging systems, some errors of colour reproduction are inevitable. The art of making pictures that please people is to confine the errors to those that are least noticeable visually. To know how to do this, it is first necessary to consider how people usually assess colours in pictures.

In a few situations, it is possible to compare a reproduction with its original; this is possible in colour photocopying, and when using a form of ‘instant’ photography when the picture is available for inspection only a few minutes after making the exposure. In the case of electronic cameras, a picture can be available in the viewfinder immediately, but its small size and the fact that it is not a reflection print hinder comparing it with the original. For most pictures, including those made by amateur photographers and those reproduced in books and journals, any comparison with the original is usually impossible, either because the subject is no longer available, or because the viewer was not present when the picture was taken. In these cases, therefore, the basis of assessment is a mental comparison between a reproduced colour and a memory of the usual colour of similar objects. But both the reproduced colour and the input from original colours to the memory are subject to a variety of physical, physiological and psychological effects.

20.5.1 Physical effects

In some objects, variations of hue are quite common. For example, fruit usually varies in hue as it ripens; the hue of foliage changes with the seasons, and is appreciably different on different types of plant; and skin colour changes towards a yellower colour with suntan.

Variations of lightness in objects frequently occur. For instance, the lightness of many plants varies with the degree of moisture in the soil; that of stone and rocks with the weathering effects on their surfaces; and the lightness of clouds is very dependent on the weather conditions. Many surfaces also become partly bleached, hence lightened, by prolonged exposure to bright sunlight. Variations in the geometry of illumination and viewing can also make large differences to the apparent lightness of objects.

Variations in the colourfulness of objects are very widespread indeed. For instance, the colourfulness of objects is reduced in shadow areas; it can also be greatly reduced if objects are viewed through appreciable atmospheric haze; and glossy surfaces have much lower colourfulnesses in those parts where light areas are reflected than where dark areas are reflected. Blue sky has a much lower colourfulness near the horizon than at higher angles, and blue water varies appreciably in colourfulness according to what is reflected by it.

20.5.2 Physiological effects

Although the visual system adjusts its sensitivity to compensate for changes in the level of illumination, the compensation is only partial, and at lower levels both brightness and colourfulness are reduced. Compensation for changes in the colour of the illumination is also only partial, and this results in some residual changes in the appearance of objects seen in lighting of different colours. Their surrounds affect the appearance of colours; dark and dim surrounds lower apparent contrast. The backgrounds to colours also affect their appearance, tending to make them appear more like the complementary colour of the background, especially in lightness.

20.5.3 Psychological effects

Experiments have shown that memory colours of familiar objects are more colourful than the perceptions of the objects themselves [8, 9]. When the area of a colour is reduced, the colourfulness usually decreases [10], so that to evoke the memory colour of a small object in a picture its chroma may have to be increased [11]. It has also been shown experimentally that for distant objects seen through hazy air, the eye partially discounts the visual effects of the air in the light path, and this increases the apparent contrast and colourfulness of such objects [12–14].

20.6 PRIORITIES IN COLOUR REPRODUCTION

A distinction can be made between the perceptibility and the acceptability of errors in colour pictures. If the image is intended to be as accurate a record as possible, then all colour errors should be minimised and the use of a suitable colour difference formula may be justified; examples of this type of imaging would include medical, archaeological and agricultural pictures.

If, on the other hand, the image is intended to be as pleasing as possible, then some errors are likely to be more important than others; examples of this type of imaging would include portraiture, family records and holiday pictures. Many of the physical, physiological and psychological effects described above tend to make the smallest difference in hue, and the greatest difference in colourfulness; this is particularly true of the effects caused by changing the level of illumination, which is a very common occurrence in everyday life. In view of this, the following list of priorities for pleasing colour reproduction can be drawn up:

- Correctness of hues
- Correctness of lightnesses (tone reproduction)
- Colourfulnesses proportional to those in the original
- Colourfulnesses and brightnesses the same as those in the original

Correctness of hues implies that *colour balance* is very important, because any overall bias in an image causes large distortions of hue for pale colours. Correctness of lightnesses emphasises the importance of good tone reproduction, without which an image may look too hazy or too garish. Proportional colourfulnesses will cause them to change in a way similar to what happens when the level of illumination is changed. Having the same colourfulnesses and brightnesses as in the original is usually only possible if the image and original have similar luminance. Following these guidelines can help to balance the inevitable limitations of an imaging system so as to give the most pleasing pictures.

20.7 OBJECTIVES IN COLOUR REPRODUCTION

The objectives of an imaging system depend on the intended use of the pictures. In different circumstances, any one of six different objectives may be appropriate.

- *Spectral* colour reproduction (equality of spectral reflectances or of relative spectral power distributions), although not attainable in most situations, provides a useful basis for determining the degree of metamerism of reproduction systems. This is a relevant objective in the mail-order catalogue business.
- *Colorimetric* colour reproduction (equality of chromaticities and relative luminances) is a useful criterion when the original and reproduction have the same viewing conditions and use illuminants of the same colour; this is usually the case for colour photocopying (although illuminant and observer metamerisms may complicate its realisation).
- *Exact* word space colour reproduction (equality of chromaticities, relative luminances and absolute luminances) ensures equality of appearance for original and reproduction if the viewing conditions are the same for both. This may be a desirable objective in virtual reality displays.
- *Equivalent* colour reproduction (chromaticities, relative luminances and absolute luminances that ensure equality of appearance) can allow for all effects of viewing conditions

(but may be an unrealistic criterion if there is an appreciable difference in luminance level between original and reproduction). This may be a desirable objective for marketing on the web.

- *Corresponding* colour reproduction (chromaticities and relative luminances that ensure equality of appearance when the original and reproduction luminance levels are the same) allows for all effects of viewing conditions except absolute luminance levels, and it provides a realistic criterion for many situations.
- *Preferred* colour reproduction (departures from equality of appearance, whether at equal luminance levels or absolute luminance levels) can be adopted in order to achieve a more pleasing result, and is an appropriate aim for portraiture and for consumer photofinishing. An example of this is the gradual reduction of contrast for very light colours and very dark colours to avoid rendering them outside the dynamic range of the display.

20.7.1 Increasing contrast

Some commercial processes are run at higher contrasts than would be indicated by corresponding colour reproduction; these higher contrasts increase the differences in brightness between light and dark parts of the picture and also increase colourfulness. Here are some possible reasons for this preferred practice of raising the contrast. First, when the original is a scene lit by natural daylight, the reproduction usually has a much lower luminance, and this lower luminance reduces perceived contrast [15], brightnesses and colourfulnesses [16]; hence raising the contrast can produce images which appear more like the original scene. Second, the partial discounting of the effects of haze on distant objects can be mimicked in the imaging system by increasing its contrast. Third, the increase in the colourfulness of memory colours of familiar objects can be mimicked by increasing system contrast; the increased colourfulness acquired by other colours is then desirable to maintain consistency in the picture. Fourth, because colourfulness is reduced in small areas, in reflection prints of postcard size (or smaller) higher contrast can counteract such loss of colourfulness (in larger reflection prints a smaller increase in contrast is usually preferred).

However, there is no doubt that, for some subjects, too much contrast reduces the quality of the reproduction markedly. This is particularly true of pictures of people in sunlight, and in this case good results may only be obtained by using fill-in flash (or other supplementary illumination) to lighten the shadow areas, or by special treatment of these areas by signal processing.

20.7.2 Naturalness

Other reasons for departing from corresponding colour reproduction have been reported in the work on *naturalness* of colour reproduction by Yendrikhovskij, Blommaert, and de Ridder [11]. They have proposed a *naturalness index*; this index represents the likelihood that the perceived colour of an image of an object falls in that part of perceived colour space occupied by the range of memory colours typical for that category of object.

20.7.3 Graphic arts objectives

In graphic arts reproductions, Field has identified three categories of preferred colour reproduction as follows [17]:

- *Corrective colour reproduction*: reproduction from another image which has defects. For example, a colour photograph may have some highlight areas burnt out, or some shadow areas blocked up, because the original scene had a much larger dynamic range than the photographic system used to record it. Corrections are then applied to darken the light areas and lighten the dark areas.
- *Compromise colour reproduction*: reproduction in which emphasis is given to rendering some important areas correctly at the expense of tolerating greater errors in some less important areas.
- *Creative colour reproduction*: reproduction in which changes are made entirely for aesthetic or artistic reasons.

20.8 IMAGE SYSTEM DESIGN

When an image system is being designed, it is essential to define the objective; only then can its performance be properly assessed. If the objective is *spectral*, then departures from the intended result can be assessed by using the CIE metamerism indices for change of illuminant [4, p. 119] and for change of observer [4, p. 120]. If the objective is *colorimetric*, then departures can be assessed by using a CIE colour difference formula; if it is *exact*, then some means for assessing any differences in luminances would be needed in addition; metamerism indices should also be used to test the sensitivities of the systems to change of illuminant and observer. If the objective is *equivalent* or *corresponding*, then the CIE colour appearance model, CIECAM97s [4, p. 230], can be used to allow for differences of illuminant colour and level, and for differences of viewing surround, before using a colour difference formula and metamerism indices. If the objective is *preferred*, then different weightings of different types of error would have to be used in assessing colour differences.

When designing an acquisition device, remember that only if a camera has a set of spectral sensitivities which are a set of colour matching functions will signals be produced that can result in *colorimetric* or *exact* colour reproduction. Such sensitivities are also desirable for *equivalent* and *corresponding* colour reproduction, for only in this way can all colours that look alike in the original be reproduced the same, and all colours that look different in the original be reproduced as different. Some recently designed photographic films have red layers with sensitivities at shorter wavelengths than has been the custom, and this has somewhat reduced the departures of the spectral sensitivities from the colour matching function criterion, but there are still significant differences. Electronic cameras with matrixing circuits provide the opportunity to approximate the colour matching function criterion more closely, and this should be an important consideration when designing these acquisition devices.

When designing an additive display, the choice of the reproduction primaries is an important factor. A balance has to be struck between choosing primaries of high purity, to increase the chromaticity gamut, and high efficacy in light production, to increase colourfulness and brightness and to reduce the effects of ambient light. These conflicting factors have so far constrained the choice of phosphors to those now adopted for broadcast television receivers; other displays, such as monitors and laptop screens, have tended to adopt the same reproduction primaries so as to be compatible with broadcast signals. Displays using lasers can have primaries of higher purity, as may also be the case for other displays yet to be developed, but special signal processing is necessary to make conventional signals suit displays having significantly different primaries.

When designing a subtractive display, the choice of the cyan, magenta and yellow colorants determines the gamut of reproducible colours; it is particularly important to choose colorants that have small unwanted absorptions. If the display is a reflection print then its illuminant metamerism should be checked using the CIE index of metamerism for change of illuminant. With transparent images intended for projection in a defined illuminant, and with those intended for reflection prints, observer metamerism should be checked using the CIE metamerism index for change of observer.

All displays have limited dynamic range, and this factor should be taken into account when choosing a display for a particular application. Remember that the ambient flare light has a marked effect on the dark tones actually presented to the observer, and the nature of the surround requires different aims to be adopted.

The spatial resolution of the system will determine the apparent sharpness of the images and the degree of magnification that can be used; consequently, the choice of camera format in photography needs careful consideration, and the number of pixels in an electronic camera is of major importance.

The signal-to-noise ratio of any system determines the smoothness of areas free of detail. In photographic film, the choice of film speed and camera format are the main factors that determine how grainy the image will appear. In electronic cameras, the light level on the sensor, the inherent sensitivity and area of the individual pixels, and the length of the effective exposure time largely determine how much spurious interference will be present in the image.

20.9 CONCLUSIONS

There are many different ways of making pictures in imaging systems, but they all have inherent limitations. Successful systems confine the inevitable errors to those that are least noticeable visually, and these are likely to be changes which are common in everyday life, such as those caused by changes in the level of illumination. The objective of an imaging system depends on the intended use of the pictures, and six different objectives are possible. Departures from similarity of appearance to that of the original may be preferred because of physiological effects, such as adaptation; because of psychological effects, such as memory, the effect of angular subtense on appearance, and discounting the effects of haze; and because of aesthetic or artistic requirements. This means there are many factors to consider when designing an imaging system to make pictures that please people.

ACKNOWLEDGEMENT

A shorter version of this chapter appeared in the *Proceedings of the Seventh Color Imaging Conference: Color Science, Systems, and Applications*, pp. 9–13, IS&T, Springfield VA (1999).

REFERENCES

1. Carnegie, D. (1981) *How to Win Friends and Influence People*, revised edition. Simon & Schuster, New York.
2. Coote, J. H. (1993) *An Illustrated History of Colour Photography*. Fountain Press, Kingston-upon-Thames, England.
3. Hunt, R. W. G. (1995) *The Reproduction of Colour*, 5th edn. Fountain Press, Kingston-upon-Thames, England.
4. Hunt, R. W. G. (1998) *Measuring Colour*, 3rd edn. Fountain Press, Kingston-upon-Thames, England.
5. Pointer, M. R. (1980) The gamut of real surface colours. *Colour Res. Appl.*, **5**, 145–155.
6. Eymann, W. A (1998) New approach to cinema: an all-in-one screen with laser projection. *Cinema Technol.*, Jan, p. 10.
7. MacDonald, L. W., Deane, J. M. and Rughani, D. N. (1994) Extending the colour gamut of printed images. *J. Photogr. Sci.*, **42**, 97–99.
8. Bartleson, C. J. (1961) Colour in memory in relation to photographic reproduction. *Photogr. Sci. Engng*, **5**, 327–331.
9. P'erez-Carpinell, J., de Fez, M. D., Baldovi, R. and Soriano, J. C. (1998) Familiar objects and memory colour. *Colour Res. Appl.*, **23**, 416–427.
10. Burnham, R. W. (1952) Comparative effects of area and luminance on colour. *Am. J. Psychol.*, **65**, 27–38.
11. Yendrikhovskij, S. N., Blommaert, F. J. J. and de Ridder, H. (1999) Colour reproduction and the naturalness constraint. *Colour Res. Appl.*, **24**, 52–67.
12. Henry, R. C. (1995) Colorimetry in the natural atmosphere. *Proceedings of the First ISCC Pan-Chromatic Conference*, p. 22.
13. Henry. R. C. and Matamala, L. A. (1990) Visual colorimeter for atmospheric research. *Colour Res. Appl.*, **15**, 74–79.
14. Mahadev, S. and Henry, R. C. (1999) Application of a colour-appearance model to vision through atmospheric haze. *Colour Res. Appl.*, **24**, 112–120.
15. Hunt, R. W. G. (1965) Luminance levels in colour transparencies and reflection prints. *J. Photogr. Sci.*, **13**, 108–113.
16. Hunt, R. W. G. (1953) The perception of colour in 1° fields for different states of adaptation. *J. Opt. Soc. Am.*, **43**, 479–484.
17. Field, G. G. (1999) *Colour and Its Reproduction*, 2nd edn. GATF Press, Pittsburgh PA.

Index